Contemporary Security Studies

Contemporary Security Studies

FOURTH EDITION

Edited by

Alan Collins

Great Clarendon Street, Oxford, OX2 6DP,
United Kingdom

Oxford University Press is a department of the University of Oxford. It furthers the University's objective of excellence in research, scholarship, and education by publishing worldwide. Oxford is a registered trade mark of Oxford University Press in the UK and in certain other countries

First edition 2007
Second edition 2010
Third edition 2013

Impression: 1

Published in the United States of America by Oxford University Press
198 Madison Avenue, New York, NY 10016, United States of America

British Library Cataloguing in Publication Data
Data available

Library of Congress Control Number: 2015944362

ISBN 978–0–19–870831–5

Printed in Italy by
L.E.G.O. S.p.A.

Preface

The fourth edition maintains the structure of the previous editions: the Approaches section is followed by the Deepening and Broadening of the subject before we finish by looking at a range of Traditional and Non-Traditional security issues. The significant changes from the previous edition include two new chapters in the Approaches section. The first is an additional chapter on Critical Security Studies, which has enabled the book to maintain the chronological explanation of the divisions within Critical Security Studies that has underpinned the Critical Security Studies chapter from the previous editions, while, in the new chapter, enabling an empirical examination of a number of issues from a Critical Security Studies approach. The second new chapter is on postcolonialism. This edition therefore boasts an increase in the theoretical and conceptual chapters that inform our understanding of contemporary security.

A number of chapters have benefited from having a new author or becoming jointly authored, and others have been substantially reorganized. They have all been updated to take account of contemporary changes in the field of security studies. This includes developments in Syria and Greece, as well as the outbreak of Ebola of 2014. Finally, the international breadth of expertise found in the previous editions with contributors drawn from Europe, the United States, and Asia has been maintained.

Acknowledgements

With all projects there are many people to thank, and this is no exception, for without their support this book could not have been produced. First and foremost thanks must be given to the contributors, first for agreeing to write their chapters and then for diligently submitting them on schedule, complete with pedagogic features. Thanks must also be given to those reviewers who commented in detail on the third edition; the fourth edition has benefited from—and been adjusted in the light of—their useful thoughts. Special thanks also go to Gillian Rollason, who was responsible for preparing and producing the resource centre that supports the book. I am also grateful to Professor John Baylis for originally encouraging me to take on this task. Finally, thanks also go to Sarah Iles and Francesca Mitchell at Oxford University Press for their professionalism and assistance during the preparation of this book.

New to this edition

- Expanded coverage of Critical Security Studies across two complete chapters reflects the growing importance of this approach to the subject.
- A new chapter on postcolonialism demonstrates the global focus of the text.
- Fully updated to take the latest developments in Security Studies into account, including cyber-security, renewed tensions between the West and Russia, and the emergence of non-state actors such as ISIS.

Brief Contents

Detailed Contents

Notes on Contributors

Christine Agius Lecturer in International Relations and Politics at Swinburne University of Technology, Melbourne, Australia. She is the author of *The Social Construction of Swedish Neutrality: Challenges to Swedish Identity and Sovereignty* (Manchester: Manchester University Press, 2006).

Jon Barnett Professor in the School of Geography at the University of Melbourne, Australia, and Australian Research Council Future Fellow. He is the author of *Climate Change in Small Island States* (London: Earthscan, 2010), and *The Meaning of Environmental Security: Ecological Politics and Policy in the New Security Era* (London: Zed Books, 2001). He is a lead author for the Intergovernmental Panel on Climate Change, and co-editor of the journal *Global Environmental Change*.

J. Marshall Beier Associate Professor in the Department of Political Science at McMaster University, Canada. He is the author of *International Relations in Uncommon Places: Indigeneity, Cosmology, and the Limits of International Theory* (Basingstoke: Palgrave Macmillan, 2005, 2009), and editor of *Indigenous Diplomacies* (Basingstoke: Palgrave Macmillan, 2009) and *The Militarization of Childhood: Thinking Beyond the Global South* (Basingstoke: Palgrave Macmillan, 2011, 2014).

Alex J. Bellamy is Professor of Peace and Conflict Studies and Director of the Asia-Pacific Centre for the Responsibility to Protect at The University of Queensland, Australia. He is also Non-Resident Senior Adviser at the International Peace Academy, New York. Recent books include, *Responsibility to Protect: A Defense* (Oxford: Oxford University Press, 2014) and *Massacres and Morality: Mass Killing in an Age of Civilian Immunity* (Oxford: Oxford University Press, 2012).

Barry Buzan Emeritus Professor of International Relations at the London School of Economics, UK. His latest books include *The United States and the Great Powers: World Politics in the Twenty-First Century* (Cambridge: Polity Press, 2004), and, with Lene Hansen, *The Evolution of International Security Studies* (Cambridge: Cambridge University Press, 2009).

Alan Collins Professor of International Relations in the College of Arts and Humanities at Swansea University, UK. He is the author of *Security and Southeast Asia: Domestic, Regional and Global Issues* (Boulder, CO: Lynne Rienner, 2003) and *Building a People-Oriented Security Community the ASEAN Way* (Abingdon: Routledge, 2012).

Sophia Dingli Teaching Fellow at the University of Hull working on Yemeni and Cypriot politics and on issues of silence and marginalization in international relations theory and practice. Her work has been published in the *European Journal of International Relations, Civil Wars, and Politics.*

Myriam Dunn Cavelty Senior Lecturer and Deputy for Research & Teaching at the Center for Security Studies at ETH Zurich, Switzerland. She is the author of *Cyber-Security and Threat Politics: US Efforts to Secure the Information Age* (Abingdon: Routledge, 2008) and many other publications on cyber-insecurity issues.

Stefan Elbe Professor of International Relations and Director of the Centre for Global Health Policy at the University of Sussex, UK. He is the author of *Virus Alert: Security, Governmentality and the AIDS Pandemic* (New York: Columbia University Press, 2009) and *Security and Global Health: Towards the Medicalization of Insecurity* (Cambridge: Polity Press, 2010).

Ralf Emmers Associate Dean and Associate Professor at the S. Rajaratnam School of International Studies (RSIS), Nanyang Technological University (NTU), Singapore. He is the author of *Resource Management and Contested Territories in East Asia* (Basingstoke: Palgrave Macmillan, 2013), *Geopolitics and Maritime Territorial Disputes in East Asia* (Abingdon: Routledge, 2010) and *Cooperative Security and the Balance of Power in ASEAN and the ARF* (London: RoutledgeCurzon, 2003).

Jeanne Giraldo Lecturer in the Department of National Security Affairs at the Naval Postgraduate School, Monterey, USA, and Program Manager of the Defense Institution Reform Initiative for the Office of the Secretary of Defense, USA. She is co-editor of *Terrorism Finance and State Responses: A Comparative Perspective* (Palo Alto, CA: Stanford University Press, 2007).

Charles L. Glaser Professor of Political Science and International Affairs, Elliott School of International Affairs, the George Washington University, USA. He is the author of *Analyzing Strategic Nuclear Policy: The Logic of Competition and Cooperation* (Princeton, NJ: Princeton University Press, 1991) and *Rational Theory of International Politics* (Princeton, NJ: Princeton University Press, 2010).

Suzette R. Grillot Dean of the College of International Studies, Vice Provost for International Programs and William J. Crowe, Jr Chair in Geopolitics at the University of Oklahoma. She is the author (with Rachel Stohl) of *The International Arms Trade* (Cambridge: Polity, 2009), the author (with Rebecca Cruise) of *Protecting Our Ports* (Farnham: Ashgate, 2010), and co-editor (with Zach Messitte) of *Understanding the Global Community* (Norman: University of Oklahoma Press, 2013).

Eric Herring Professor of World Politics in the School of Sociology, Politics and International Studies, University of Bristol, UK. He is co-author with Glen Rangwala of *Iraq in Fragments: The Occupation and its Legacy* (London: Hurst and Cornell University Press, 2006) and co-author with Barry Buzan of *The Arms Dynamic in World Politics* (Boulder, CO: Lynne Rienner, 1998).

Richard Jackson Professor of Peace Studies, University of Otago, New Zealand. He is the author of a research-based popular novel entitled *Confessions of a Terrorist* (London: Zed Books, 2014), and co-editor (with Samuel Justin Sinclair) of *Contemporary Debates on Terrorism* (Abingdon: Routledge, 2012).

Peter Viggo Jakobsen Associate Professor at the Royal Danish Defence College and Professor (part time) at the Center for War Studies, University of Southern Denmark. He has written extensively on coercion and the use of force. His most recent book is *Nordic Approaches to Peace Operations: A New Model in the Making?* (London: Routledge, 2009).

Caroline Kennedy Professor of War Studies at the University of Hull. She is the author of *The Origins of the Cold War* (Basingstsoke: Palgrave Macmillan, 2007) and many articles on contemporary security. She is currently running a project on IEDs, suicide bombers, and women in contemporary conflict.

Mark Laffey Senior Lecturer in International Politics in the Department of Politics and International Studies, School of Oriental and African Studies, University of London. He is the co-editor of *Cultures of Insecurity: States, Communities and the Production of Danger* (Minneapolis: University of Minnesota Press, 1999) and *Democracy, Liberalism and War: Rethinking the Democratic Peace Debates* (Boulder, CO: Lynne Rienner, 2001).

Brenda Lutz Ph.D. Department of Politics, University of Dundee, UK, and Research Associate, Decision Sciences and Theory Institute, Indiana University-Purdue University, USA. She is the co-author of *Terrorism: The Basics* (London: Routledge, 2011), *Global Terrorism* (3rd edn, London: Routledge, 2013), and *Terrorism in America* (New York: Palgrave, 2007).

James Lutz Professor and Head of the Department of Political Science at the Indiana University-Purdue University, USA. He is the co-author of *Terrorism: The Basics* (London: Routledge, 2011), *Global Terrorism* (3rd edn, London: Routledge, 2013) and *Terrorism in America* (New York: Palgrave, 2007).

Patrick Morgan Emeritus Professor of political science and emeritus Tierney Chair in Global Peace and Conflict Studies at the University of California, Irvine. He is the author of *Deterrence Now* (Cambridge: Cambridge University Press, 2003), *International Security: Problems and Solutions* (Washington, DC: CQ / SAGE Press, 2006), and co-editor of *Complex Deterrence: Strategy in the Global Age* (Chicago: University of Chicago Press, 2009).

David Mutimer Professor and Chair in the Department of Political Science at York University, Canada. He is the author of *The Weapons State: Proliferation and the Framing of Security* (Boulder, CO: Lynne Rienner Publishers, 2000) and co-editor (with Neil Cooper) of *Reconceptualising Arms Control* (Oxford: Routledge, 2012). He is also the founding editor of *Critical Studies on Security*.

Suthaharan Nadarajah Lecturer in International Relations in the Centre for International Studies and Diplomacy, School of Oriental and African Studies, University of London. His work has appeared in *Review of International Studies, Security Dialogue*, and *Third World Quarterly*.

Randolph B. Persaud Associate Professor of International Relations at the School of International Service (SIS), American University in Washington, DC. He is also Director of Comparative and Regional Studies at SIS. He is the author of numerous articles on race and International Relations and *Counter-Hegemony and Foreign Policy: The Dialectics of Marginalized and Global Forces in Jamaica* (Albany: State University of New York Press, 2001).

Nana K. Poku Executive Director of the Health Economics and AIDS Research Division (HEARD) and Research Chair in Health Economics at the University of Kwazulu Natal, Durban. Most recently, he is co-author of *Politics in Africa: A New Introduction* (London: Zed Books, 2011) and co-editor of *Third World Quarterly* Special Issue: *The Millennium Development Goals: Challenges, Prospects and Opportunities* (January 2011).

Sam Raphael Senior Lecturer in International Relations at the University of Westminster, London, UK. Co-Director of The Rendition Project (www.therenditionproject.org.uk), publishing comprehensive data and analysis on the CIA's torture programme. His publications include, with Doug Stokes, *Global Energy Security and American Hegemony* (Baltimore, MD: Johns Hopkins University Press, 2010).

Paul Roe Associate Professor in the Department of International Relations and European Studies at the Central European University, Budapest, Hungary. He is the author of *Ethnic Violence and the Societal Security Dilemma* (London: Routledge, 2005).

Paul Rogers Professor of Peace Studies in the Department of Peace Studies at the University of Bradford, UK. He is the author of *Losing Control: Global Security in the 21st Century* (3rd edn, London: Pluto Press, 2010) and *Global Security and the War on Terror: Elite Power and the Illusion of Control* (London and New York: Routledge, 2008).

Michael Sheehan Professor of International Relations in the College of Arts and Humanities at Swansea University, UK. He is the author of *International Security: An Analytical Survey* (Boulder, CO: Lynne Rienner, 2005) and *The International Politics of Space* (London and New York: Routledge, 2007).

Gary M. Shiffman Professor (Adjunct) in the School of Foreign Service, Security Studies Program, Georgetown University, Washington, DC, and President and CEO of Giant Oak, Inc. He is co-author with J. Jochum of *Economic Instruments of Security Policy: Influencing Choices of Leaders* (2nd edn, New York: Palgrave Macmillan, 2011).

Doug Stokes Professor of International Relations at the University of Exeter, UK. He is the co-editor of *US Foreign Policy* (Oxford: Oxford University Press, 2012) and the co-author, with Sam Raphael, of *Global Energy Security and American Hegemony* (Baltimore, MD: Johns Hopkins University Press, 2010).

Jacqueline Therkelsen Senior Research Fellow at the Health Economics and AIDS Research Division (HEARD), University of Kwazulu-Natal, Durban, South Africa.

Harold Trinkunas Charles W. Robinson Chair and Director of the Latin America Initiative in the Foreign Policy program at the Brookings Institution in Washington, DC. He is the co-editor of *Ungoverned Spaces: Alternatives to State Authority in an Era of Softened Sovereignty* (Palo Alto, CA: Stanford University Press, 2010).

Ole Wæver Professor of International Relations in the Department of Political Science at the University of Copenhagen, Denmark, and founder of CAST, Centre for Advanced Security Theory, and director of CRIC, Centre for Resolution of International Conflict. He is the co-author, with Barry Buzan, of *Regions and Powers: The Structure of International Security* (Cambridge: Cambridge University Press, 2003) and co-editor, with Arlene B. Tickner, of *International Relations Scholarship Around the World* (London: Routledge, 2009).

James J. Wirtz Dean of the School of International Studies and Professor in the Department of National Security Affairs at the Naval Postgraduate School, Monterey, USA. He is the author of *The Tet Offensive: Intelligence Failure in War* (Ithaca, NY: Cornell University Press, 1991, 1994) and co-editor of *Over the Horizon Proliferation Threats* (Stanford, CA: Stanford University Press, 2012).

List of Figures

List of Tables

List of Boxes

KEY IDEAS

THINK POINTS

BACKGROUNDS

CASE STUDIES

KEY QUOTES

Guided Tour of Learning Features

This textbook is enriched with a range of learning tools to help you navigate the text and reinforce your knowledge and understanding of Security Studies. This guide shows you how to get the most out of your textbook package.

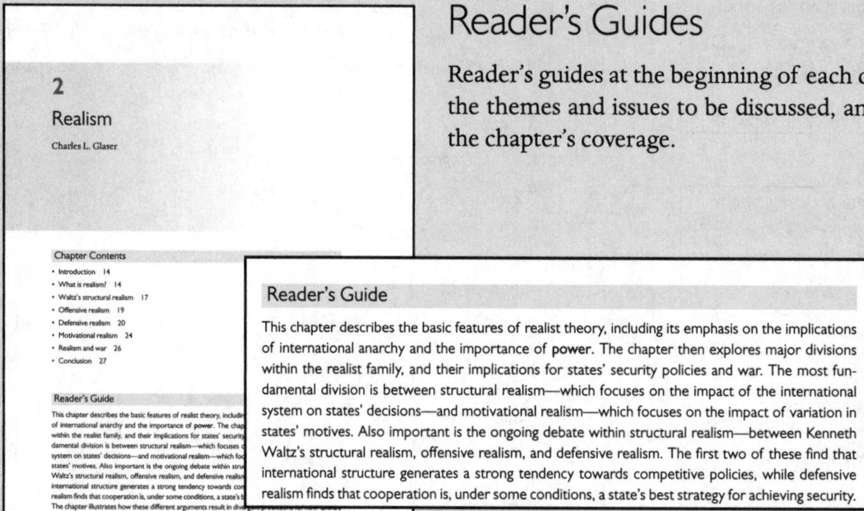

2

Realism

Charles L. Glaser

Chapter Contents

- Introduction 14
- What is realism? 14
- Waltz's structural realism 17
- Offensive realism 19
- Defensive realism 20
- Motivational realism 24
- Realism and war 26
- Conclusion 27

Reader's Guide

This chapter describes the basic features of realist theory, including its emphasis on the implications of international anarchy and the importance of **power**. The chapter then explores major divisions within the realist family, and their implications for states' security policies and war. The most fundamental division is between structural realism—which focuses on the impact of the international system on states' decisions—and motivational realism—which focuses on the impact of variation in states' motives. Also important is the ongoing debate within structural realism—between Kenneth Waltz's structural realism, offensive realism, and defensive realism. The first two of these find that international structure generates a strong tendency towards competitive policies, while defensive realism finds that cooperation is, under some conditions, a state's best strategy for achieving security.

Reader's Guides

Reader's guides at the beginning of each chapter set the scene for the themes and issues to be discussed, and indicate the scope of the chapter's coverage.

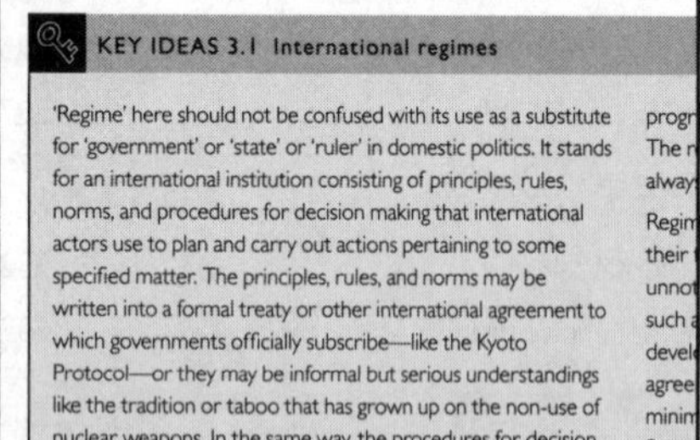

KEY IDEAS 3.1 International regimes

'Regime' here should not be confused with its use as a substitute for 'government' or 'state' or 'ruler' in domestic politics. It stands for an international institution consisting of principles, rules, norms, and procedures for decision making that international actors use to plan and carry out actions pertaining to some specified matter. The principles, rules, and norms may be written into a formal treaty or other international agreement to which governments officially subscribe—like the Kyoto Protocol—or they may be informal but serious understandings like the tradition or taboo that has grown up on the non-use of nuclear weapons. In the same way, the procedures for decision making may involve using a formal international organization with rules of procedure and a clear definition of what it is to

Key Ideas

Throughout the book, 'Key Ideas' boxes outline the thoughts of key political thinkers relevant to the chapter's argument.

THINK POINT 3.1 Liberalism and the Arab Spring

Recent developments have put the liberalist perspective under great strain, developments that emerged in a relatively surprising and rapidly escalating fashion. This is particularly true of the Arab Spring, which has been an enormous disaster from a liberalist perspective. It can be interpreted in various ways:

- as demonstrating that liberalism is unpopular, unacceptable, and unappreciated in much of the world;
- as evidence that liberalism poses a serious threat to many

Think Points

'Think Point' boxes throughout the chapters help you to expand and deepen your understanding of the subject.

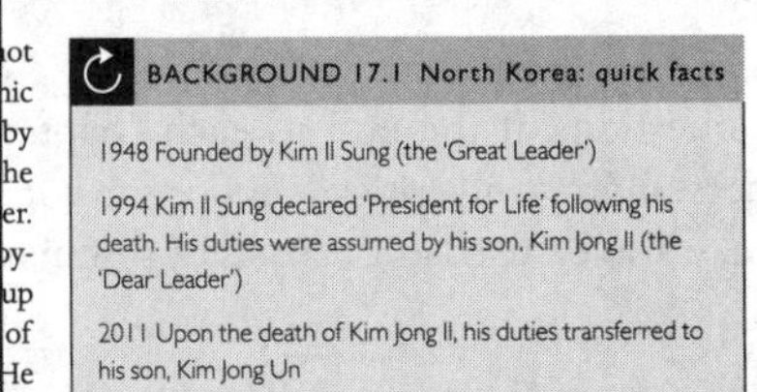

BACKGROUND 17.1 North Korea: quick facts

1948 Founded by Kim Il Sung (the 'Great Leader')

1994 Kim Il Sung declared 'President for Life' following his death. His duties were assumed by his son, Kim Jong Il (the 'Dear Leader')

2011 Upon the death of Kim Jong Il, his duties transferred to his son, Kim Jong Un

According to the CIA World Factbook (Central Intelligence

Background

'Background' boxes provide important information which helps you to understand the context within which events take place and ideas develop.

CASE STUDY 2.1 China's rise

Will China's continuing economic growth lead to international competition and insecurity? For two decades following the end of the Cold War, there was little security competition between the world's major powers. During this period, the United States was clearly the world's dominant economic and military power. Now, however, growth in China's economy and military forces is beginning to pose a potential to challenge America's global dominance. China has recently become a major regional power in Northeast Asia. If it continues to grow successfully, China will

Case Studies

'Case study' boxes in each chapter demonstrate the real world manifestations of political ideas, concepts, and issues, helping you link theory and practice.

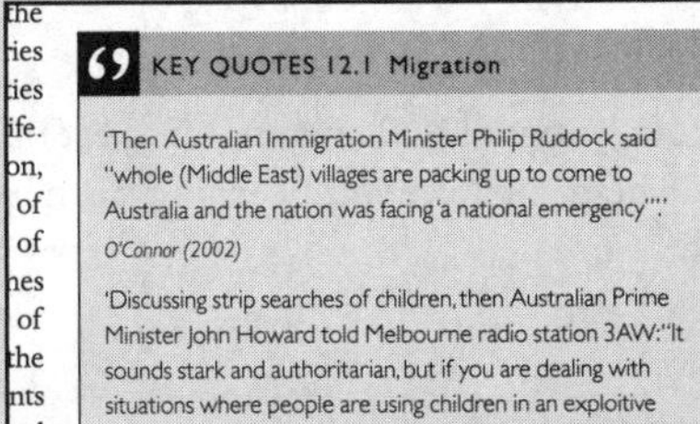

KEY QUOTES 12.1 Migration

'Then Australian Immigration Minister Philip Ruddock said "whole (Middle East) villages are packing up to come to Australia and the nation was facing 'a national emergency"'.'
O'Connor (2002)

'Discussing strip searches of children, then Australian Prime Minister John Howard told Melbourne radio station 3AW: "It sounds stark and authoritarian, but if you are dealing with situations where people are using children in an exploitive

Key Quotes

'Key quotes' boxes contain important and memorable quotes from politicians, scholars, and others, bringing issues and theoretical concepts to life.

Glossary

There is no single correct or agreed-upon definition of any of these terms, as you will no doubt have noticed already. This can be unsettling if you are used to the idea that there is a 'right answer' or the 'right defin-

Glossary Terms

Key terms appear in bold throughout the text, and are defined in a glossary at the end of the book to help you broaden your vocabulary and aid with exam revision.

KEY POINTS

- Realism's basic shared assumptions include that the international system is anarchic, power is a defining feature of the international system, and states are rational, unitary actors.
- A key divide within realism is between theories that focus on the structure of the international system and those that focus on states' motives.
- There is debate within structural realism over whether

Key Points

Each chapter ends with a list of key points that summarize the most important ideas and arguments discussed in the chapter.

QUESTIONS

1. Why is realism better understood as a family of theories than
2. What assumptions are shared by most realist theories?
3. What is the key divide between structural and motivational re
4. Why does Waltz believe that the international system tends t
5. Why does offensive realism believe that states maximize pow
6. Why does defensive realism believe states should attempt to

Questions

A set of carefully devised questions at the end of each chapter help you to check your understanding and critically reflect on core themes and issues. These may also be used as the basis of seminar discussion or coursework.

FURTHER READING

- Copeland, D. (2000), *The Origins of Major War*, Ithaca, NY: Corne of preventive war.
- Glaser, C. (2010), *Rational Theory of International Politics*, Prince rational theory that integrates structural and motivational realis key dimension of their international environment.
- Jervis, R. (1978), 'Cooperation under the Security Dilemma', discussion of how offence–defence variables influence the secur

Further Reading

Each chapter includes a further reading list to guide you towards the key academic literature in the field, and to help you find out more about the issues raised within each chapter.

IMPORTANT WEBSITES

- **http://davidharvey.org** David Harvey is the world's leading Ma website contains many of his writings and videos of many of his
- **https://zcomm.org** Z Communications is a huge online ne languages for HM-influenced activists, journalists, and scholars, i
- **http://www.caat.org.uk** The Campaign Against the Arms Tra arms trade as militarized capitalism.

Important Websites

At the very end of the chapters, you will find an annotated list of important websites which will help you take your learning further and conduct further research.

Guided Tour of the Online Resource Centre

www.oxfordtextbooks.co.uk/orc/collins4e

The Online Resource Centre that accompanies this book provides students and registered instructors with ready-to-use teaching and learning materials, designed to maximize the learning experience.

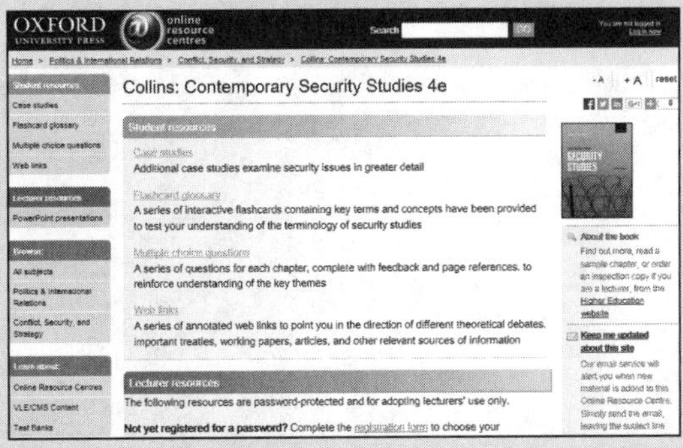

FOR STUDENTS:

devastation caused, the complexity of issues surrounding the condition, and the ability of the pandemic to impact severely and directly on national security.

What is securitization?

Securitization is a concept; it is a model which explains the transition by which an issue, such as influenza, can be moved from the non-political sphere to the political sphere, and ultimately into the realm of security. The Securitization model emerged from the Copenhagen School which is characterised by the writings of Barry Buzan, Ole Waever, Jaap de Wilde and others based at the Conflict and Peace Research Institute in Copenhagen (Chapter 9). Its practical use is as a framework for analysis that defines

Case Studies

Five additional case studies examine pressing real-world security issues in greater detail.

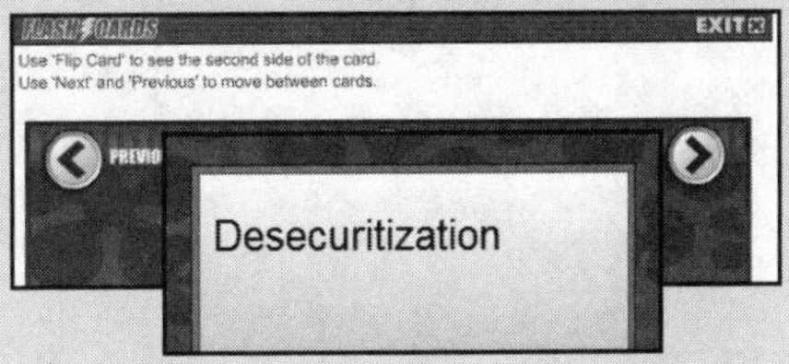

Flashcard Glossary

A series of interactive flashcards containing key terms and concepts has been provided to test your understanding of key terminology, and aid exam revision.

Question 1

How can we best describe liberalism?

a) Liberalism is a fundamentally pessimistic approach that regards the international system as destined to the escalation of conflict. It is the dominant conception in the practice of international politics.

b) Liberalism is the dominant conception in the theory of international politics, whilst realism dominates the conduct of international affairs. It is an optimistic approach that defines the ways in which states should relate to one another, particularly during

Multiple Choice Questions

Self-marking multiple-choice questions have been provided for each chapter of the text to enable you to test your understanding of key themes and act as an aid to revision.

http://www.zmag.org/
Z Communications is a huge online nexus of analysis and discussion in many languages for left-wing activists, journalists, and scholars, including those who combine those roles.

http://www.caat.org.uk/
The Campaign Against the Arms Trade (CAAT) is a non-governmental organization (NGO) that aims to reduce and eventually to end the arms trade and the militarization of arms-producing countries. From an HM perspective, CAAT is significant in that it challenges the arms trade as such rather than particular corrupt or counterproductive aspects of it and frames the arms trade as a militarized capitalism.

Web links

A series of annotated web links points you in the direction of helpful and relevant sources of information, including important treaties, working papers, and articles.

FOR INSTRUCTORS:

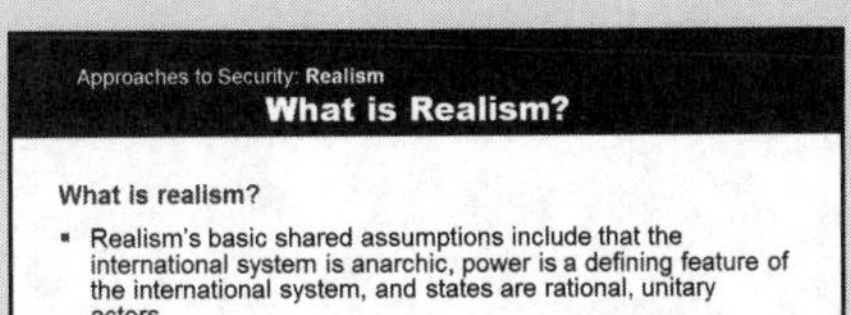

PowerPoint Presentations

Fully customizable PowerPoint slides complement each chapter of the book, providing a useful resource to instructors preparing lectures and in-class handouts.

1

Introduction: What is Security Studies?

Alan Collins

Chapter Contents

Introduction

Welcome to Security Studies: *the* sub-discipline of International Relations. It is the study of security that lies at the heart of International Relations. It was the carnage of the First World War, and the desire to avoid its horrors again, that gave birth to the discipline of International Relations in 1919 at Aberystwyth, United Kingdom. This concern with the origins of war and its conduct enabled International Relations to 'distinguish itself from related disciplines such as history, economics, geography, and international law' (Sheehan 2005: 1). It is the survival of agents, which for much of the discipline has meant sovereign states, that has become accepted as the dominant explanatory tool for understanding their behaviour. Security is a matter of high politics; central to government debates and pivotal to the priorities they establish. Quite simply, 'no other concept in international relations packs the metaphysical punch, nor commands the disciplinary **power** of "security"' (Der Derian 1995: 24–5).

Definition of security

Welcome, then, to a subject of great importance and, since you are about to embark upon the study of this subject, no doubt you would like to start with a definition of security. Or, what it means to be secure. You will see in Key Quotes 1.1 that many scholars have done so. The good news is that a consensus has emerged on what security studies entails—it is to do with threats—and the even better news is that hidden within that simple definition lies the complexity that you are about to delve into. What is most striking about the definitions in Key Quotes 1.1 is that, while war and the threat to use force is part of the security equation, it is not exclusively so. The prevalence of threats is sufficiently far-reaching for Security Studies to encompass dangers that range from pandemics, such as **HIV/AIDS**, and environmental degradation through to the more readily associated security concerns of direct violence, such as terrorism and inter-state armed conflict. The latter, which so dominated the discipline that during the Cold War it became synonymous with Security Studies, is actually a sub-field of Security Studies and is known as Strategic Studies. Oxford University Press publishes a textbook that is concerned with Strategic Studies: it is called *Strategy in the Contemporary World* (Baylis and Wirtz 2012).

With the Cold War over, Security Studies has re-emerged, and core assumptions about what is to be secured, and how, have come to occupy our thoughts. Traditionally the state has been the thing to be secured, what is known as the **referent object**, and it has sought security through military might. In the chapters that follow, you will find alternative approaches to security; approaches that offer different referent objects, different means of achieving security, and that indicate that past practice, far from enhancing security, has been the cause of insecurity. You are, then, about to study a subject that is undergoing great change as it questions its past assumptions, deepens its understanding of what should be secured, and broadens its remit to encompass a diverse range of threats and dangers. Of course, this broadening of the subject matter creates a blurring in the distinction between Security Studies and the study of International Relations more generally. In this sense the broadening of Security Studies mirrors the wider blurring between International Relations and Political Science. The process of globalization has led to internal issues becoming externalized and external issues internalized. The role of domestic agents and policy concerns appear prominently on global agendas, whether it is the future political structure of Syria and the Middle East more generally or deforestation in the Amazon. This blurring of the demarcation between International Relations, Political Science, and Security Studies can be seen in the breadth of topics covered in this book and the centrality of security in theories of international relations (for more on this see Chapter 28). This is to be welcomed. I know it can appear confusing and it would be much easier to categorize topics neatly, but this is to misunderstand the nature of the social sciences. These disciplines are sub-disciplines precisely because they overlap and have 'something to say' about the same topics. Instead of looking for different subject matters, it is better to think about different approaches. Despite the contested nature of security, you know that ultimately we are interested in how referent objects are threatened. With that thought in mind, examining this diverse range of topics might seem rather less daunting.

Structure

The book is not designed to be read from start (Chapter 1) to finish (Chapter 28) because that is not the way to read an academic text. If this seems a peculiar thing for me to write, then let me explain. You are not reading a novel in which the aim is to keep you in suspense until the final pages where you discover who committed the crime or whether the lovers live happily ever after. You want to know the questions and the answers as soon as possible, and then, because—as important as the answers are, they are not the most important thing—you should want to know why these are the answers and how they were reached. Think of it as a complicated maths question in which the mathematician has scribbled furiously on the blackboard (or more likely today the whiteboard) a series of, to a layperson, unintelligible equations that eventually lead to an answer. It is the bit in between the question and the answer (the bit in between is those impenetrable equations) that reveals why the answer was found and found in that particular way. It is like this with your studies too. You should want to know, and your tutor will certainly want to know, why you believe in the answers you have found: to know your thought processes. Knowing why you think about a subject the way that you do, so that these thought processes can be convincingly articulated in oral and written form, is what reading for a degree is all about.

Therefore in this book, when reading the chapters, it is perfectly fine to read the introduction and then the conclusion, but you then have to read the bits in between to know why the answers found in the conclusion were reached. Understanding the author's thought processes will help you develop yours. So, having read what this book contains, which you will find in this chapter, then read the conclusion. Chapter 28 will present you with the state of Security Studies, and the theorizing that has taken place in the discipline. It provides you with the context of why we, students and tutors (scholars of the

KEY QUOTES 1.1 Definitions of security

'Security itself is a relative freedom from war, coupled with a relatively high expectation that defeat will not be a consequence of any war that should occur.'

Bellamy (1981: 102).

'A nation is secure to the extent to which it is not in danger of having to sacrifice core values if it wishes to avoid war, and is able, if challenged, to maintain them by victory in such a war.'

Walter Lippman, cited in Buzan (1991a: 16).

'National security may be defined as the ability to withstand aggression from abroad.'

Luciani (1989: 151).

'A threat to national security is an action or sequence of events that (1) threatens drastically and over a relatively brief span of time to degrade the quality of life for the inhabitants of a state, or (2) threatens significantly to narrow the range of policy choices available to the government of a state or to private, nongovernmental entities (persons, groups, corporations) within the state.'

Ullman (1983: 133).

'Security, in any objective sense, measures the absence of threats to acquired values, in a subjective sense, the absence of fear that such values will be attacked.'

Wolfers (1962: 150).

'Security–insecurity is defined in relation to vulnerabilities—*both internal and external*—that threaten or have the potential to bring down or weaken state structures, both territorial and institutional, and governing regimes.'

Ayoob (1995: 9; emphasis in original).

'Emancipation is the freeing of people (as individuals and groups) from the physical and human constraints which stop them carrying out what they would freely choose to do. . . . Security and emancipation are two sides of the same coin. Emancipation, not power or order, produces true security. Emancipation, theoretically, is security.'

Booth (1991: 319).

'If people, be they government ministers or private individuals, perceive an issue to threaten their lives in some way and respond politically to this, then that issue should be deemed to be a *security* issue.'

Hough (2008: 10) (emphasis in original).

'Security . . . implies both coercive means to check an aggressor and all manner of persuasion, bolstered by the prospect of mutually shared benefits, to transform hostility into cooperation.'

Kolodziej (2005: 25).

'"Security" is not just a social concept or topic to be studied or analyzed; it is also a problem to be managed or otherwise controlled by human communities on a regular basis if they hope to survive.'

Smith (2010: 2).

subject), think about the subject the way that we do. In particular, the chapter reveals the differences between American and European approaches to theorizing about security, as it traces past, present, and possible future trends in how security is studied by today's scholars. For those new to Security Studies and/or International Relations, it will be a testing read, but stick with it, because it will be a chapter that you will want to read more than once as you increase your knowledge of this subject; in each read you will discover something new. Once Chapters 1 and 28 have been read, the book becomes a pick 'n' mix, so if you want to start with weapons of mass destruction (Chapter 20) or terrorism (Chapter 21) then go right ahead. That is not to say that the structure has no meaning, and I would strongly advise that you at least begin with the Approaches section and especially Chapters 2 and 3 in order to appreciate the primary role that states and power have had in the study of security. By beginning with the Approaches section, you will be able to appreciate just how hugely important different approaches are in establishing what constitutes security; a point that will be evident once you have read Chapter 28.

The book is divided into three sections: differing approaches to the study of security; the deepening and broadening of security; and, finally, a range of traditional and non-traditional issues that have emerged on the security agenda. The first section is where you will find the main theories and concepts that underpin our study of international security. This section contains not only the traditional approaches but also a range of new ways of understanding security and critiquing the traditional ones. This section is important because while you may have been drawn to the subject of security because of events in the news, getting behind the headlines to understand what is really at stake, and whether we can ever really know, requires appreciating the theories and concepts that underpin your way of interpreting the world and how far this limits your understanding.

The next section is concerned with the division of security into different sectors and referent objects, which will be instantly recognizable to you from the Security Studies literature. This section is not about identifying particular security issues as this is the function of the final section of the book, although some security issues will appear in case studies within the six chapters that constitute our second section. Here five areas (although it has six chapters, two are devoted to economics) are examined to reveal what form security takes in each sector and indeed whether thinking of it as a matter of security is unproblematic. For example, the chapter on societal security enables us to consider the significance of identity in examining what is threatened and protected in conflicts that are routinely labelled 'ethnic'. The chapter is not concerned with ethnic conflict per se, although it contains case studies of such conflicts, but rather reveals what can be thought of as security once we conceive of identity as the thing being threatened. The environment chapter likewise enables us to query whether this is about how environmental catastrophe represents a threat to people or about how the environment is itself being threatened by human activity. Is thinking of the environment as a security issue, and thus perhaps adopting the notion of defending the status quo, the best way to address environmental concerns which may require drastic and fundamental changes to the way people live? Particular environmental security issues, such as diseases, are examined in the final section. The final section is where you will find a mix or **traditional security** matters, such as the use of force, WMDs, and terrorism, and also new and emerging **non-traditional security** subjects, such as energy, transnational crime, and cyber-security.

The authors come from a range of countries, and their examples are global in scope. Nevertheless, the field of Security Studies, as with International Relations more generally, is dominated by Western thought and approaches. For more on this, see Chapter 9. One of the refreshing changes in post-Cold War Security Studies is that the security problems of the developing world are no longer either ignored or seen through the prism of the East–West conflict. We are therefore examining these security problems and, perhaps, in doing so, we will witness the emergence of specifically African or Asian approaches to the study of security that will force us to rethink core assumptions and gain a greater understanding of the Security Studies field. For more on this, see the final section of Chapter 28. In the meantime the field, while global in scope, remains dominated by Western thought.

Approaches

In the book's first substantive chapter, Chapter 2, Charles Glaser introduces the first of the two dominant explanations of why and how states have sought security: realism. Realism is not one approach but rather a set of approaches, and in this chapter you will be introduced to the divisions within this explanation of why states behave the way they do as they seek security in an anarchic international environment. One such division concerns debates within structural realism, but there is also a more fundamental division within realism: structural realism versus motivational realism. Utilizing the emergence of China as a great power, this chapter explains the key concepts realism brings to the study of security as well as the breadth of approaches that fall within its framework. The second dominant explanation of why and how states have sought security is the focus for Chapter 3. Here, Patrick Morgan will introduce you to liberalism. Whereas realism seeks an explanation for state behaviour in the international system, liberalism looks to the state as the unit of analysis and places importance on domestic actors' power and preferences and the nature of their political systems. Since behaviour is a product of domestic circumstances for liberalists, states are not alike, and this means that international relations are determined by the choices people make; the world can operate in a realist manner, but for liberalists it does not have to. The recognition among state leaders that they have common, shared, values means that they can establish agreements on a range of issues from trade to human rights that will benefit them all and thus create a secure environment. Liberalism, while recognizing that cooperation can be difficult, is nevertheless an optimistic approach that posits lasting security as a possibility.

We can think of these opening chapters as covering traditional approaches to understanding the search for security because they have underpinned much of our thinking during the twentieth century; they remain hugely influential, and just because they are traditional does not mean they have been replaced by more recent thinking. New thinking about security has emerged, especially in the post-Cold War period, and such approaches are explained and examined in the other chapters in the Approaches section. You should think of these new approaches as challenging the dominance of the traditional insights offered by realism and liberalism. It may be that you find the traditional explanations of how security can be conceived of and achieved convincing. This is fine so long as you reach that conclusion with an understanding of the other approaches—in other words, that you find an approach to understanding security convincing based not on ignorance of other approaches but with a full understanding of them.

The first alternative approach has one of the most recent labels to enter the security studies field—historical materialism—but it hails from a tradition on a par with the previous two chapters; in this instance Marxism. Written by Eric Herring, it provides both an explanation of what historical materialism is and how it relates to the other approaches in this book's first section. The exploitative nature of capitalism and the insecurities this generates form the focal point for this approach to understanding what constitutes security, and this is explained with reference to the arms trade industry and international development. Since this book is not intended to be read one chapter after another you might want, after having read this chapter, to look at Chapter 24 (The Weapons Trade) and especially Chapter 18 (Globalization, Development, and Security) to explore what insights an appreciation of historical materialism provides in these particular issue areas. Francis Fukuyama's 'End of History' was, in part, an obituary for Marxism but perhaps in a slightly modified form you will consider it has much to reveal about the insecurities that plague the contemporary world (Fukuyama 1992).

The next alternative approach, and one that shares with realism, liberalism, and Marxism a long tradition, is peace studies, although as a formal field of study its origins are found in the post-1945 period. Here the approach to security is distinctively broad based, both in the nature of threats that the field covers and also in its approaches to finding solutions. Thus, although initially concerned with the arrival of nuclear weapons, peace studies, long before the post-Cold War era, were noting the security implications of environmental degradation and poverty. With its wide agenda, it is not perhaps surprising to learn that academics working in peace studies come not just from politics and international relations but other disciplines in the social sciences, notably anthropology and sociology, as well as the natural sciences, such as physics and mathematics; it is a truly interdisciplinary field. In Chapter 5 a leading authority, Paul Rogers, provides a historical account of how peace studies developed, highlighting its characteristics and revealing its continued relevancy to contemporary security studies.

Our next chapter covers an alternative approach that is relatively new: first coined in 1989, social constructivism has rapidly emerged as an established third explanation (alongside realism and liberalism) for state behaviour. As with realism and liberalism, it is not one approach, and in Chapter 6 Christine Agius introduces us to two broad camps: conventional and critical constructivism. For constructivists, identities matter in explaining the search for security, and identities are constituted through interaction. Since state identities are malleable and can change as a consequence of interaction, this means we create the world in which we live. Conceiving of relations as a product of how we think of them—as opposed to them being something independent from us—enables us to think of threats as socially constructed. This can, as Chapter 6 reveals, provide important insights into topics such as NATO enlargement and the War on Terror.

The following two chapters capture the reflections that took place by some scholars studying security in the immediate post-Cold War period. Labelled Critical Security Studies (CSS), these reflections pre-date the end of the Cold War, but they have flourished since the removal of the nuclear sword of Damocles that hung over the study of security. David Mutimer provides an explanation of the different approaches that have developed since CSS first arrived on the scene in 1994. For those new to critical thinking, it is a demanding read, but thoroughly worthwhile, because, amongst many of the things on which it will give you pause to ponder, it unashamedly forces you to think through your assumptions, and it reconnects security with its normative origins. In Chapter 8, Marshall Beier continues this examination of a Critical perspective on our understanding of what constitutes security. In this chapter, you will be shown how approaching subjects, even traditional ones such as military power, from different perspectives casts a new light on them, thus providing new insights and raising new questions. For example, this chapter explores the importance of motherhood in military recruitment strategies and thus, in turn, the importance of mothers to a state's military power. It explains why it is possible to ask did the 1991 Gulf War really happen? It is also here that an examination of child soldiers, and the extent to which they can be political agents, can be found. The chapter concludes with an examination of indigenous people and their non-existence in traditional approaches to security.

The place of indigenous people, or indeed the lack of a place, in our understanding of international security is in part the concern of Chapter 9: Postcolonialism. In this chapter, Mark Laffey and Suthaharan Nadarajah will introduce you to a postcolonial approach to understanding the field of security studies. This chapter is concerned with how the framing of security in Eurocentric terms infuses an imperial discourse within Security Studies: one in which the West is interpreted as secure and the global south, although increasingly just the rest, are insecure. However, it is imperial because the interaction between the West and the rest is one of domination and hierarchy, thus pointing to the significance of decolonization. It is a chapter that will force you to consider how entwined the fates of the people of the world are and whether the field of security studies, so central to the discipline of International Relations, is part of the problem of global insecurity.

One of the new 'buzz words' in the security literature is **human security**, although as Randolph Persaud explains in Chapter 10, the topics that are covered by human security have a long history. It shares much in common with critical approaches to security, the most notable being its critique of the state-centrism found in the traditional approaches, and, as the name suggests, the referents for security are humans. This change of referent object reveals a close connection between development and security, thus expanding the remit of security studies, but this brings with it the challenge of maintaining analytical rigour. This chapter will challenge you to consider whether adding the label 'human security' to a vast array of threats to peoples' well-being and livelihoods adds anything to responding to these threats. Does thinking of these matters as security matters help or hinder our understanding of the threats that people face in their everyday lives?

A criticism aimed not just at security studies but at the wider field of international relations is the failure to appreciate the important insights that gender provides. In the penultimate chapter in the Approaches section, Caroline Kennedy and Sophia Dingli reveal two elements that gender can provide in our understanding of security: a practical appreciation of the role women have been ascribed in the security field and a discursive element that reveals the implicit link between militarism and masculinity. The latter highlights how the notions of honour, nobleness, and valour are associated with masculinity and war, implicitly therefore leaving femininity devoid of such positive attributes. The former notes how women, if they are mentioned at all, are portrayed in a secondary, supporting role to men, whereas the reality is that in many ways (rape, prostitution, breeders) women are victims and their plight has remained a silence in the study of security.

The final chapter in the Approaches section, Chapter 12, examines a process known as 'securitization', which was introduced to the literature by scholars working at the Conflict and Peace Research Institute (COPRI) in Copenhagen. Known collectively as the Copenhagen School, these scholars place primary importance on determining how an issue becomes a security issue, by how it is articulated. That is, we think of something as a security issue because the elite, such as political leaders, have convinced us that it represents a threat to our very survival. They are, therefore, interested in the 'speech acts' that the elite use in order to convince an audience that, in order to counter a threat, they require emergency powers. It is then a subjective approach to determining what constitutes security. A threat exists because an audience has been convinced it exists by the elite and it has granted the elite the authority to use emergency powers to counter the threat. The threat therefore is not something that simply exists; it has to be articulated as a threat for it to become a matter of security. Ralf Emmers explains this process, notes limitations with the concept of securitization, and uses case studies ranging from Australian reaction to undocumented migration to the invasion of Iraq in 2003.

Deepening and broadening

The middle section of the book examines the deepening and broadening that has taken place in Security Studies. As will have become evident from the

Approaches section, the theoretical approach you take towards examining security will determine the type of subject matter that you consider constitutes security. This part of the book contains six sectors of security; these are the recognizable sectors that you will find in the Security Studies literature. The exception is regime security, which I have included instead of political security, first because political security has a tendency to become a miscellaneous section in which security issues that cannot fit in the other sectors end up, and secondly because, while political security is concerned with external threats (concern with recognition), its greater utility lies in internal threats (concern with legitimacy) to the regime. Labelling the chapter 'regime' therefore clarifies what the referent object is and also highlights the internal dimension of this security sector. Whether these sectors do constitute security is contentious, so, as with all your reading, adopt a critical, enquiring mind, and see if you are persuaded.

We begin with military security because it is the home of our traditional understanding of what constitutes security; the use of or threat to use force. In Chapter 13, Michael Sheehan provides a clear exposition of the issues that are the staple diet of military security: war, deterrence, alliances, arms control, and so on; but, while these can be explained by traditional approaches, this chapter reveals that the alternative approaches have something to say about these issues as well, and, in so doing, shed new light on the subjects. Military security used to be the *sine qua non* of Security Studies, and, while it no longer dominates the discipline as it once did, it remains very much part of the security agenda and remains an indispensable component. What has changed is what constitutes military security, and this chapter reveals the breadth and depth of the subject in a concise and accessible fashion.

Turning our attention to the security concerns within states enables us to appreciate that life in the developed world is far from indicative of that lived by most of the planet's inhabitants. The majority of people living in the developing world face a vast range of insecurities, from half a million people dying each year from the use of light weapons to 40,000 dying each day from hunger. There is, as Richard Jackson writes in Chapter 14 on regime security, 'a profound disjuncture between the kinds of security enjoyed by a small group of developed nations and the kind of security environment inhabited by the majority of the world's population'. In this chapter, you will have the opportunity to understand the underlying causes of the developing world's inherent insecurity and why it is that, far from being the providers of security, governing regimes become the main source of their peoples' insecurity. It is a bleak picture that is portrayed, but after reading the chapter you will appreciate the complexities that make bringing security to these millions of people both urgent and yet extremely difficult. The notion of an insecurity dilemma captures not only the spiralling nature of the violence but also how problematic it is to find a solution.

The broadening of security so that it means more than a preoccupation with the state and military defence should have been appreciated by now. In Chapter 15 on societal security, an alternative to the state, and indeed the individual, is posited. In this instance you will be introduced to the notion of a collective of people becoming the thing to be secured. In recent times the term 'ethnic' has become a popular label for describing conflict between groups within states. In this chapter, Paul Roe introduces you to a means of examining the dynamics behind those ethnic conflicts where identity lies at the conflict's core. Importantly, he does so by focusing on non-military issues that can give rise to insecurity and thereby shows how ambiguity in such seemingly non-threatening issues, such as education, can indeed become matters of great concern. If you have an interest in the nexus between security and identity, this is a must-read chapter.

Although it pre-dates the end of the Cold War, it was in the 1990s, and especially because of concern over ozone depletion and global warming, that environmental change began to be thought of as a 'new' security threat. In Chapter 16, while you will be exposed to the vast array of environmental degradation that is occurring in today's world, the question of interest is what makes environmental change a matter of security. Jon Barnett provides an explanation of why the environment emerged on the security agenda before providing six interpretations of environmental security. You will, therefore, have the opportunity to consider whether the environment really is a security issue and whether labelling it as a matter of security helps or hinders attempts to reverse environmental degradation. For those with a normative interest in studying international security, this is an important chapter to read.

The final two chapters in this section are concerned with economics from two very different perspectives. In Chapter 17, Gary Shiffman utilizes the rational decision making that underpinned Adam Smith's explanation of human nature to indicate how economic instruments of the state can be used to pursue security goals. With an appreciation of what explains human behaviour, it then becomes possible to pursue economic policies, such as sanctions, trade agreements, or aid strategies, to fulfil policy goals. Drawing upon a variety of examples, such as US economic engagement with North Korea and US financial controls on terrorist assets, the chapter reveals the security considerations that underpin economic policy.

The final chapter of the deepening and broadening part of the book, Chapter 18, continues the economy theme, but here the focus is on how the liberal international political economic order provides prosperity for the developed North at the expense of the developing South. Globalization is thus presented as an explanation for those structural conditions that expose people to a range of insecurities. Insecurities that ultimately can drive demands for change and such change might be manifest in rebellion, riots, and regime change. In this chapter, Nana Poku and Jacqueline Therkelsen draw upon the recent events in Egypt and Greece to highlight the insecurities that a globalized world has created.

Traditional and non-traditional

The final section of the book highlights a series of traditional and **non-traditional security** issues that have emerged on the Security Studies agenda. The section begins with **traditional security** concerns and then moves to the non-traditional issues that have emerged as the subject area has expanded. We begin by addressing the traditional security concern of the threat and use of force. This is examined by looking at how Western strategy has evolved post-Cold War away from deterrence to compellence and in particular to the use of coercive diplomacy. This captures the logic behind Western, and in particular US, strategic thinking.

The Bush administration's willingness to talk of 'pre-emptive' use of force, and indeed to implement it, revealed a significant change in strategic thinking in the West. It is no longer simply enough to deter opponents from taking action; it is now necessary to persuade, coerce, and, on occasion, force them to change their behaviour. This, as Peter Viggo Jakobsen writes, has led to the post-Cold War era witnessing the pursuit of coercive diplomacy. Coercive diplomacy is the threat, and if necessary the limited use of force, designed to make an opponent comply with the coercer's wishes. It is action short of brutal force and thus an attempt to achieve a political objective as cheaply as possible. It has been used to respond to acts of aggression, halt weapons of mass destruction (WMD) programmes, and stop terrorism. Chapter 19 provides you with the criteria for what constitutes coercive diplomacy and the obstacles to its success, and concludes that Western efforts have largely failed. If you want to understand the strategy that underpins how great powers are using, or threatening to use, force since the end of the Cold War, this is a chapter for you.

Since the tragic events of **9/11**, the acronym WMD has been catapulted into everyday usage. Weapons of mass destruction, and the fear that rogue states or terrorists will target the USA or Europe with such weapons, has become a central concern for Western states. The belief that Iraq had an undisclosed arsenal of WMD provided the justification for the USA's decision to remove Saddam Hussein's regime, and it was the nuclear programmes of both North Korea and Iran (the former a declared weapons programme; the latter a potential and feared possibility) that earned them membership of Bush's 'Axis of Evil'. What, though, are WMD, why are they considered so different from conventional weapons, how easy are they to use, and what has been their impact on international relations? These are the questions that James Wirtz addresses in Chapter 20.

Terrorism, perhaps even more than WMD, has come to occupy a top spot on the security agendas of states. In Chapter 21, Brenda and Jim Lutz provide a definition of terrorism and explain the various types (religious, ethnic, ideological) and causes of terrorism. Using a typology that sees terrorism as either a form of war, or crime, or disease, they are able to explain why certain countermeasures are adopted by states and their implications for civil liberties. The chapter will provide you with information relating to terrorists ranging from the Ku Klux Klan to **Al-Qaeda** and reveal the incidence of terrorism that has occurred throughout the world in recent times.

After the end of the Cold War but prior to 9/11, the subject that came to prominence in the field of international security concerned the use of (primarily Western) military force to intervene in cases of severe human suffering; it has not gone away, and in Chapter 22, Alex Bellamy charts the arguments for and against humanitarian intervention. The atrocities committed in Bosnia and the genocide of Rwanda heralded the arrival of the **responsibility to protect (R2P).** What R2P means, what it means for coercive state intervention, and what future R2P has in a world where mass atrocities continue—as witnessed in Libya in 2011 and ongoing in Syria at the time of writing—are the subjects the chapter examines.

We then turn our attention to the increasing demands for energy coupled to the declining pool of available resources; in the light of this, it is not surprising that energy security has become a critical issue for states (and people). Chapter 23 on energy security provides both a detailed coverage of the topic, specifically related to oil demand, and a link to previous chapters in the Approaches and the Deepening and Broadening sections. You will, for example, have an opportunity to look at what historical materialism argues about the state of energy security, and at the connections that energy security has to economic and regime security, as well as thinking about energy security as an issue not just for states but for human security as well. The USA figures prominently, and reading this chapter will enable you to appreciate that energy security involves a complex nexus of geopolitical, economic, and strategic concerns, which link together distant regions of the globe, and disparate security concerns.

Chapter 24 examines the last of the traditional security issues in this book: the arms or defence trade. In this chapter, Suzette Grillot provides an historical overview of how the trade in arms has evolved, including recent trends, as well as the connections between the legal and illicit arms trade. It concludes by examining the methods implemented to control the defence trade. The chapter reveals the defence trade to be multifaceted and complex with a variety of actors engaged in the production and procurement of weapons. Case studies include the procurement of weapon systems by terrorists as well as efforts to limit the trade in particular weapon systems, such as landmines.

In Chapter 25, we turn to our first non-traditional security issue, health, and here Stefan Elbe examines how diseases such as AIDS, SARS, and Ebola are a threat to both human and national security. AIDS is a pandemic; of the 35 million people living with HIV in the world, 19 million do not know their HIV-positive status. In 2013, there were 2.1 million people newly infected and 22 million people who were not accessing life-saving treatment. This chapter shows how diseases can be thought of as a security issue for individuals, ranging from their economic impact to specific effects on food security for instance, to national security matters, such as the prevalence of HIV amongst soldiers. While diseases represent an exacerbating factor for national security, they are a direct threat when individuals are the referent object. This chapter concludes by noting that terrorists have deliberately used a biological agent to spread terror, and the potential for further attacks has enhanced the salience of bio-security on states' security agendas.

Our next chapter focuses on another non-traditional security matter that has become increasingly prominent on national security agendas; transnational crime. In 1999, Thailand identified the narcotics trade as the country's number one threat to national security. Drug trafficking, along with, among others, human trafficking and money laundering across national frontiers, are all forms of transnational crime, and, as the Thai experience reveals, this non-traditional security issue has risen rapidly up the national security agendas of states in the post-Cold War era. In Chapter 26, Jeanne Giraldo and Harold Trinkunas reveal the multiple ways in which transnational crime impacts directly, and indirectly, on human and national security. They explain why it has become more prevalent since the 1990s, the links between organized crime and terrorism, and the various responses that states have taken to curb its operation. If you want to appreciate a 'dark side' of globalization and how transnational criminal activity has impacted on international security, this is a must-read chapter.

The examination of what non-traditional issues constitute Security Studies today concludes by examining one of the most current topics to appear in the field of security studies; cyber-security. Whether in the fields of security, diplomacy, or indeed any aspect of international relations, information and its generation, management, and manipulation has always been considered paramount. The ability to control knowledge, beliefs and ideas are as central to achieving security as tangible resources, such as military forces and raw materials. It is the realm of cyberspace, connoting a fusion of communication networks, databases, and sources of information, that is the environment for this chapter's examination of information control. Utilizing three different discourses (technical, cybercrime and cyber-espionage, cyber-war) Myriam Dunn Cavelty explains the inherent insecurity of information infrastructure, although she does conclude that the level of cyber-risk is often overrated.

Conclusion

You are, as I am sure you appreciate, about to embark upon a whirlwind tour of a fascinating subject—a subject that has undergone, and continues to undergo, a thorough introspection of its core assumptions. It is a wonderful time to be a scholar of the discipline—and by scholar I mean students and tutors—because there is so much new and innovative thinking taking place that it is impossible for it not to open your mind. Listen to the ideas contained in the chapters that follow and if, by the end of it, you are more confused than you are now, then it has been a worthwhile enterprise. A caveat should, though, be added: that your confusion is not a reflection of ignorance but an appreciation of how complicated and complex the subject is and how challenging it is therefore to be a scholar of Security Studies. The chapter began with the question: what is Security Studies? It is all of this and more. Happy reading.

Visit the Online Resource Centre that accompanies this book for lots of interesting additional material: www.oxfordtextbooks.co.uk/orc/collins4e/

PART I
Approaches to Security

2

Realism

Charles L. Glaser

Chapter Contents

Reader's Guide

This chapter describes the basic features of realist theory, including its emphasis on the implications of international anarchy and the importance of **power**. The chapter then explores major divisions within the realist family, and their implications for states' security policies and war. The most fundamental division is between structural realism—which focuses on the impact of the international system on states' decisions—and motivational realism—which focuses on the impact of variation in states' motives. Also important is the ongoing debate within structural realism—between Kenneth Waltz's structural realism, offensive realism, and defensive realism. The first two of these find that international structure generates a strong tendency towards competitive policies, while defensive realism finds that cooperation is, under some conditions, a state's best strategy for achieving security. The chapter illustrates how these different arguments result in divergent predictions for how China's continuing economic growth is likely to influence international security.

Introduction

Realism is widely accepted as the dominant theory of international politics. Its roots reach back to Thucydides, the Greek historian who explained the war between Athens and Sparta as a result of Athens' growing power. Realism's philosophical foundations can be found in the work of Machiavelli, Hobbes, and Rousseau (Doyle 1997). Although it has a long historical lineage, realism has not lost its relevance. Realist arguments continue to play a central role in contemporary debates over states' national security and foreign policies. In popular and elite discourse, realism is most frequently used to refer to arguments that give priority to states' national interests and their military and economic power. In comparison, these arguments give less weight to the role of international norms and institutions in influencing states' policies and international outcomes.

As one would expect, while sharing many of these lines of popular argument, scholarly treatments of realism offer a clearer and more precise analysis. Realism is a theory of international relations that addresses how states achieve security and possibly other goals. Virtually all states place great value on maintaining their international security—remaining free from attack and coercion by other states. Realism attempts to explain the security strategy a state should choose. In the broadest terms, realism asks whether a state should choose a competitive or a cooperative strategy. Competitive approaches for achieving security include building up arms, searching for allies, and using military force. In contrast, cooperative approaches include negotiating arms control agreements and exercising unilateral restraint in the acquisition and use of force. Closely related, realism attempts to explain a variety of international outcomes—arms races and arms control agreements, alliances and their dissolution, and war and peace.

Realist theories attempt to understand states' choices and international outcomes by employing a general framework that abstracts away from the details of specific states and the international system. Realism is therefore considered a high-level or grand theory of international relations. States are typically characterized in terms of their basic motives and interests, most prominently security. The international system is characterized in terms of states' potential to achieve their objectives, most prominently their power. Realism gives little or no weight to individual states' political systems, their leaders, and other specific attributes of their domestic political systems.

While many scholars reject at least some of its arguments, most acknowledge the importance of key elements of realist theory. Realism's central place in international relations theory should hardly be surprising. Its enquiry is driven by the most consequential international issues—states' security, war, and peace. And realism focuses on the elements of the international system—states, power, and international anarchy—that are clearly essential for understanding international security.

What is realism?

Given its central place in debates over international relations theory and states' security strategies, it may be unexpected that realism is not a single, well-defined theory, but instead a broad family of theories and arguments. Within the realist family we find disagreements about such key issues as the factors that drive international politics; the implications of key assumptions; and the possibilities for international cooperation and for peace between states. This section begins with a description of the elements that are shared by most realist theories; it then describes the key divides within the realist family.

Basic shared elements

There are a few basic features that characterize the realist family. First, realism emphasizes that the international system is anarchic—there is not an international authority that can enforce agreements and prevent the use of force. In this context, anarchy does not refer to state behaviour; it does not mean that international relations are chaotic. Instead, anarchy simply describes the lack of authority in the international system.

Second, realism views power as a defining feature of the international environment that states face. In fact, for most realists power is *the* defining feature. Although a more complicated concept than it might initially appear, for our purposes power is adequately understood as the resources available to a state for building military forces. Key elements of power include a state's wealth, population, and technological sophistication. More powerful states can build larger and more sophisticated military forces.

The importance of power and military capabilities follows closely from the anarchic nature of the international system. Without an international authority to protect them, states need to rely on their own capabilities to achieve their international goals. Power plays a central role in enabling states to acquire these capabilities.

Third, realism envisions states as essentially unitary actors. This is clearly not an accurate assumption—states are made up of leaders, governing institutions, interest groups, and populations. Realist theories make this assumption because it is analytically productive—helpful for understanding the key features of the choices states face and, closely related, for understanding their strategic interactions.

Fourth, realism sees states as rational actors: states make decisions that are well matched to the achievement of their interests, given the constraints imposed by their capabilities and the uncertainties they face about other states' capabilities and motives. States are strategic when making these decisions—that is, they take into consideration how other states will react to their policies. Although there are realists who do not adopt this rational actor assumption and question its importance, and others who are not clear about the rationality of states, the rationality assumption is employed sufficiently widely for it to provide a reasonable characterization of this overall body of theory.

Fifth, and related to the unitary-actor assumption, realist analysis 'black-boxes' opposing states: states assess each other in terms of their power and capabilities, not in terms of the variation that exists within states, including such domestic characteristics as regime type, the nature of leadership, ideology, and so on. Some realists do use the information provided by opposing states' observable international actions to help assess their motives, but others do not.

Sixth, realists tend to see states as the key actors in the international system. The primary alternative is international institutions. Realists argue that international institutions play a less important role than states; many argue that they play a relatively unimportant role. Some realists take the key role of states as an assumption; others argue that the limited role for institutions follows deductively from the theory's basic assumptions. Either way, the dominant importance of states is a common strand that runs across the realist family and places it in sharp contrast to institutional theories and strands of liberalism that place much greater importance on international institutions and organizations.

Finally, realism is maybe most frequently associated with its bottom line—states exist in an international system that is characterized by the possibility of war, which drives into military and economic competition, and sometimes into war itself. Although the following section makes clear that this characterization is no longer fully deserved, being aware that realism is commonly characterized this way is helpful for appreciating its role both in the debate over international relations theory and in debates over foreign and national security policy.

Map of the realist family

Beyond these important similarities, to get a fuller understanding of the realist family requires distinguishing between its key members.

International structure versus states' motives

The most fundamental divide within realism is between the strand that emphasizes the impact of the international system and the strand that emphasizes the impact of states' motives and fundamental goals. The former, which is termed **structural realism** or **neorealism**, argues that the constraints and opportunities created by a state's international environment are the key to understanding its behaviour. States that are interested only in maintaining sovereign control of their territory can end up in arms races and war because of the pressures created by the anarchic international system. These states—which I term 'security seekers'—want only to be secure in the status quo. Nevertheless, competition and conflict can occur between rational security seekers because the international system generates insecurity and drives them into competition.

In contrast, the latter strand of realism, which I term 'motivational realism' (and which includes some of classical realism and neo-classical realism) emphasizes the importance of states that have an inherent desire to expand for explaining international competition and conflict. These states—which I term 'greedy states'—are interested in territorial expansion even when they are secure in the status quo. From this perspective, the international environment is not unimportant—it will constrain these states and provide opportunities for them to expand. But, in contrast to the structural-realist argument, for motivational realism the international environment is not the source of these states' desire to take territory and, in turn, of conflict between states.

Classifying states according to their motives often turns out to be more difficult than might be suggested by the analytically neat categories of security-seeker and greedy. In practice, there is often serious debate over states' motives. There are, however, some relatively clear historical examples. Hitler's Germany is widely considered to have been a greedy state—motivated to expand primarily by a toxic mix of racial and ideological beliefs that called for territorial expansion. In contrast, pre-First World War Germany is commonly characterized as a state motivated by insecurity, which reflected Germany's belief that it was surrounded by hostile major powers and that it was becoming weaker relative to Russia.

Divides within structural realism: Waltz versus offensive versus defensive realism

There are a number of competing theories within structural realism. While less fundamental than the state versus structure divide, understanding the divides within structural realism is important for two reasons. First, structural realism has been extremely influential since the 1970s, which makes the intra-structural-realist debate important. Second, the divergent strands focus attention on different logics of interaction and result in quite different assessments of the likelihood of international competition and the prospects for cooperation. Consequently, whether structural realism's standard bottom line is correct—that is, whether the international system consistently generates competition between states—depends on which version of the theory is most compelling.

Kenneth Waltz (1979), who established the foundation of structural realism, finds that international structure generates a general tendency towards competition between security-seeking states. The pressures and incentives created by the international system greatly limit the potential benefits of cooperation. Waltz does, however, also argue that states recognize the importance of limiting their pursuit of power. Power is a means to achieving security. A state's acquisition of excessive power convinces other states to align against it, thereby undermining this strategy. Recognition of this dynamic moderates the competitive nature of the international system.

By comparison, offensive realism sees a still more competitive world. John Mearsheimer (2001), whose formulation defines offensive realism, agrees that states pursue power as a means, not an end, but finds that states try to maximize their power and pursue hegemony when possible. Consequently, offensive realism understands international politics to be still more competitive than does Waltz's neorealism.

In contrast to both Waltz and offensive realism, defensive realism finds that international structure does not create a general tendency towards competition. Under a range of conditions, states can best achieve security by cooperating. The **security dilemma** lies at the core of the defensive realist argument—competitive policies that a state pursues to increase its own security can reduce its adversary's security. Decreasing the adversary's security is a potential danger, because the adversary may react to this insecurity by pursuing policies that then reduce the state's own security. As a result, under some conditions a state's best option can be cooperation or restraint, not competition. And, under some conditions, even though the international system is anarchic, states can be highly secure.

The following sections explore these versions of structural realism, laying out their basic arguments and assessing how they reach their divergent conclusions.

Realism and suboptimality

Before turning to that task, it is important to make one further distinction. Starting in the 1980s, a number of theories that address states that are pursuing suboptimal policies—that is, states that are not acting rationally—have been classified as realist. Some theories commonly considered to be defensive realist have this feature. For example, one set of arguments focuses on states that misevaluate the international environment they face because their militaries have a biased view of the feasibility of offensive military missions, believing that they are easier than is actually the case. According to this strand of analysis, prior to the First World War, Germany exaggerated both its insecurity and the prospects that war could solve its security problems because a 'cult of the offensive' led Germany's leaders to exaggerate the feasibility of strategic offensive missions. Combining this theory of military organizations with a defensive-realist foundation leads to the conclusion that competition and war have been more frequent than required by international structure alone (Van Evera 1999). Another theory of this broad type that is built on a rational defensive-realist foundation makes a related argument, holding that certain types of domestic regimes are likely to be captured by narrow interest groups, including militaries, which leads these states to pursue overly competitive

Figure 2.1 Types of realist theories and multi-level theories built on realist foundations

		Theory emphasizes	
		States' motives	**International structure**
States act rationally/ optimally	**Yes**	**Motivational realism**	**Structural realism, including offensive and defensive realism**
	No	**Neo-classical realism = motivational realism + unit-level misperception of complexity, limits on state's extraction capability, etc.**	**Defensive realism + unit-level theories of military bias, flawed state decision making, etc.**

and expansionist policies. Jack Snyder (1991: 113) identifies Japan as a prime example, arguing that 'the overexpansion of the late 1930s was due to logrolling between the army and navy elites and to blowback from their self-serving imperial ideologies'.

Another grouping of theories that addresses states that make suboptimal choices is termed neo-classical realism. These theories are built on a motivational realist foundation, which emphasizes the importance of greedy motives, and, like other realist theories, sees power having a large impact on states' interactions. However, these theories also stress that the international environment that states face is quite complex, and, as a result, their assessments of power are influenced by domestic variables. Moreover, states' abilities to extract resources and convert them into military capabilities also vary and, therefore certain states build smaller military forces than they could and should. As a result, power does not translate as directly into outcomes as is suggested by structural and motivational realism, and states' policies may be flawed when judged against these theories.

Although these arguments contain major elements that are included in realist theories, classifying them as realist is potentially misleading, because the states they explore are not acting rationally, or at least are constrained domestically in ways that significantly influence their behaviour. We need to draw a sharp line between theories of states that pursue rational policies and those that adopt suboptimal ones. At the risk of rejecting widely used terminology, it might not be going too far to exclude these theories from the realist family. At a minimum, we need to highlight that these are multi-level theories that combine a rational realist foundation with a theory of suboptimal state behaviour. Figure 2.1 captures some of the key distinctions already made.

KEY POINTS

- Realism's basic shared assumptions include that the international system is anarchic, power is a defining feature of the international system, and states are rational, unitary actors.
- A key divide within realism is between theories that focus on the structure of the international system and those that focus on states' motives.
- There is debate within structural realism over whether the international system creates a general tendency towards competition or whether instead cooperation is under some conditions a state's best strategy.

Waltz's structural realism

Kenneth Waltz's *Theory of International Politics* (1979) transformed realist theory, shifting the focus of explanation towards the international environment that states face and away from states themselves, which played a central role in classical realist theories that preceded it. Waltz begins with the simple, minimal assumption that all states give priority to ensuring their own survival; although states may have other goals, we can understand their interactions by focusing on the survival motive alone.

Survival is a benign motive—the goal is not to take what other states have, but simply to protect what one already has. Maybe the most striking finding of Waltz's structural realism, therefore, is the seemingly counter-intuitive conclusion that international politics will have a strong tendency towards competition. The international system will drive states into competition, even though they lack fundamental conflicts of interest. Waltz (1989: 43) argues that, 'their individual intentions aside, collectively their actions will yield arms races and alliances'.[1]

Competition

What explains the competitive nature of the international system? Waltz explains that international anarchy puts states into a condition of 'self-help'—without an international authority capable of protecting them, major powers must look out for themselves. Self-help is usually understood to mean that states will pursue unilateral competitive policies to protect their own interests. Waltz (1979: 111) argues that a 'self-help situation is one of high risk—of bankruptcy in the economic realm and of war in the world of free states'.

Facing these dire possibilities, states have a strong inclination to pursue policies that will increase their ability to defend themselves and are especially reluctant to adopt policies that could result in reductions of this capability. 'The possibility that force may be used by some states to weaken or destroy others does, however, make it difficult for them to break out of the competitive system' (Waltz 1979: 118–19). The possibility that an adversary will cheat on an agreement is also a major barrier. Even an agreement that would initially increase a state's ability to defend itself could be too risky if the adversary might cheat on the agreement, leaving the state more vulnerable to attack.

[1] There is an ongoing debate about whether structural realism is a theory of states' foreign policies or instead only a theory of international politics that captures the tendencies created by the international system; see Elman (1996) and Waltz (1996).

This inclination towards competition is reinforced by uncertainty about states' future motives and intentions. Even if confident today that other states have benign intentions, a state cannot be confident about others' future intentions. Uncertainty about others' intentions makes cooperation difficult. When uncertain about the opposing state's intentions, a state must worry not only about whether cooperation will make it better off—increasing its security or prosperity—but also about which state will gain more. Even if cooperation would make the state better off—that is, provide absolute gains—the state might reject cooperation because its adversary would gain more. This is because allowing its adversary to achieve these *relative* gains could leave the state worse off, because in the future its adversary might use its increased capability to attack or coerce the state.

Balancing

How do states go about achieving security? The key to security is for the state to possess the ability to protect itself from attack. States value power—manifested in some combination of territory, population, economic resources, and military capabilities—because it enables them to protect themselves against attack. Power is, therefore, the essential means for achieving security. Economic resources provide the state with the option of building military capabilities and can deter attack by indicating a state's potential to win a long war. Military capabilities provide the state with the immediate ability to fight and defend, and therefore play an essential role in protecting the state against the possibility that its adversary will attack with the expectation of being able to win a war quickly and decisively.

Waltz argues that states have two basic options for acquiring power and the capability to defend. The first is external **balancing**—forming **alliances** with other states, thereby enabling the state to draw on other states' resources. The second is internal balancing—increasing the state's own economic capability and building larger and/or better military forces. Although balancing behaviour is commonly envisioned as possible only in a system of three or more major powers, in fact balancing is possible when there are only two major powers. In this bipolar case, major power alliances are not an option, leaving internal balancing as the key form of balancing. States' efforts to offset others' advantages (and possibly to acquire their own) generate arms races, instead of alliances. According to this argument, although NATO and the Warsaw Pact were important alliances during the Cold War, internal balancing and the arms race that resulted were the key means by which two superpowers—the United States and the Soviet Union—pursued security. Although the major West European states contributed significantly to NATO's overall power, these states were disproportionately dependent on the United States; they had little prospect of providing for their own security against the Soviet Union, whereas the United States had reasonable prospects of defending itself without its alliance partners. The relative importance of the United States was reflected in its ability largely to determine the contours of NATO's military policy.

When there are three or more major powers, states have a choice between searching for allies and building up arms. Major powers will tend to do some of both. Alliances have the advantage of reducing the resources the state needs to devote to security, because the state gets to rely on its allies' resources. But alliances also bring risks—a state's allies might fail to meet their commitment to defend the state, leaving it vulnerable to attack; and the state's alliance commitments might draw it into wars that it would otherwise have been able to avoid (Snyder 1997).

The key alternative to a balancing alliance is a **bandwagoning** alliance. In a balancing alliance a state joins the weaker side to offset the power advantage of the stronger side. In contrast, in a bandwagoning alliance a state joins the stronger side. Why does structural realism see states balancing instead of bandwagoning? It is not immediately obvious—would not the state be more secure on the stronger side? The problem with bandwagoning is that on the stronger side there is the danger that the state will be attacked by one of its allies, because on the stronger side the state is not essential to the alliance's security. By comparison, on the weaker side the state is more secure because its allies need its contribution to offset the power of the stronger side.

If, on the other hand, a state were trying to maximize its power to satisfy its greedy motives, bandwagoning could be more attractive than balancing. The more powerful alliance would have better prospects for conquering territory, which it could then divide among its members. Unlike structural realism, motivational realism explores states that have greedy motives and develops this argument about bandwagoning; a following section examines motivational realism. The Soviet Union's decision to ally with Hitler's Germany provides an example of this type of behaviour—although Stalin was motivated partly by security concerns, he also desired the territory that the alliance would yield, because it satisfied his non-security expansionist goals (Schweller 1998: 137–9). In contrast to a greedy state, a state that values only its security would be less willing to run the risks of being vulnerable within the alliance.

Waltz emphasizes that balances of power tend to form not because states necessarily desire balance, but rather because states try to offset others' power advantages and to gain advantages of their own to protect themselves. With states acting and reacting to offset advantages in power, balances of power tend to form.

KEY POINTS

- Power is a means for achieving survival, not an end in itself.
- Structural incentives—the necessity of self-help, the importance of preventing adversaries from acquiring military advantages, and concern about relative gains—lead states to adopt competitive policies.
- States can enhance their ability to defend via internal and external balancing.
- States tend to balance instead of bandwagon.

Offensive realism

Power maximization

A still more competitive version of structural realism is offered by offensive realism. John Mearsheimer (2001) argues not only that states face uncertainty about others' intentions, but in addition that states should assume the worst about these intentions. Consequently, states focus solely on other states' capabilities; they compete for power, attempting to increase it whenever feasible.

According to offensive realists, therefore, states attempt to maximize their power. The reason is straightforward—the more powerful a state is, the better its prospects for defending itself if attacked. A state would be most secure if it were the dominant, hegemonic power; states will pursue competitive policies to achieve this position, if they have a reasonable probability of success.

It is important to emphasize that for offensive realism power maximization is a means, not an end. As with Waltz, survival is the end that all states give priority to achieving. According to offensive realism, the best way for states to ensure their survival is to maximize their power.

This offensive-realist position runs counter to Waltz, who argues that states do not maximize power. This is a key disagreement, so it is worthwhile considering how it arises. From Waltz's perspective, the most obvious reason a state should not try to maximize its power is that these efforts are likely to fail: balancing coalitions will form to offset advantages in power and to defeat states that go to war to take territory and increase their power. Recognizing the likelihood of effective opposition, states work to protect the power they have, but tend to forgo major efforts to acquire more. Waltz's point here is not that more power would be undesirable, but rather that other states' reactions make acquiring it infeasible.

Inefficient balancing and buckpassing

In contrast, offensive realism holds that balancing is often insufficiently effective to make clear to states that territorial expansion is infeasible. Potential allies are sometimes geographically separated, which reduces their ability to come to each other's aid, thereby reducing the value of balancing. In addition, states may be slow to balance, because they disagree about how to coordinate their efforts and how to share the costs of fighting. Moreover, states may choose not to balance against an expansionist state, hoping that the state that is immediately threatened will be able to defend itself and/or that other allies will come to its aid. In other words, a state may *buckpass* instead of balance. Major powers that have been slow to balance are not hard to find—for example, both the United States and the UK were slow to throw their full weight into opposing Germany during the Second World War. The possibility that balancing will be ineffective, and may not even occur at all, increases the probability that a state's efforts to increase its power will succeed, thereby opening the door to rational power-maximizing behaviour.

This discussion points to another difference between Waltz and offensive realism. Waltz emphasizes the constraining implications of the tendency of states to balance, although he recognizes that states have incentives not to balance. In contrast, offensive realism argues that states prefer to buckpass than to balance and holds that buckpassing is the more common behaviour. As previously explained, the result is that the international system fuels behaviour that is more competitive (see Case Study 2.1).

It is worth noting, however, that the gap between Waltz and offensive realism may be smaller than it first appears: both see a world in which the anarchic international system consistently produces competition between states; both provide arguments that lead to important qualifications regarding power maximization; and the more competitive world explained by offensive realism seems to be quite possible for Waltz. Waltz (1979: 125, 164–5, 170–2) acknowledges that balances are sometimes slow to form, that states have incentives to pass the buck, and that states sometimes make mistakes that could lead them not to balance when they should. Given the benefits of gaining power, a state that recognizes these possibilities will be more inclined to maximize its power as a means of maximizing its prospects for survival. On the other hand, Mearsheimer (2001: 37) argues that, although major powers always desire more power, they recognize the constraints imposed by the international system and therefore do not always pursue it: 'before great powers take offensive actions, they think carefully about the **balance of power** and how other states will react to their moves. . . . If the benefits do not outweigh the risks, they sit tight and wait for a more propitious moment.'

KEY POINTS

- In the face of uncertainty, states should assume the worst about others' intentions.
- Although power is a means, not an end, states try to maximize their power, because this is the best way to ensure their survival.
- There are many reasons that effective balances may not occur, which create the possibility for successful power maximization.

Defensive realism

Although it starts with essentially the same assumptions as Waltz and offensive realism, defensive realism finds that cooperation and restraint will be a state's best options under a range of conditions. In sharp contrast to the other structural realist theories, defensive realism argues that the international system does not generate a general tendency towards competitive behaviour; under some conditions states can be highly secure (Glaser 1994–5) (see Case Study 2.1).

The **security dilemma** plays a central role in defensive realism. A security dilemma can exist when the military forces that a state deploys to increase its security are also useful for attacking a potential adversary. In such a case, the state's efforts will reduce the adversary's ability to defend itself, which can make the adversary less secure.

Before we look at why the adversary's insecurity is a problem, two features of the security dilemma deserve to be highlighted. First, uncertainty about the adversary's type—whether it is a security-seeking state or a greedy state—is an essential element of the security dilemma. If a state were confident that other states were security-seekers (and were also confident that they would remain so), then other states' capabilities to attack would not make it insecure. In contrast, a state will be insecure when it is uncertain about its adversary's motives and the adversary possesses capabilities for attacking it. Second, the security dilemma is the key to explaining competition between states that are security-seekers. If states could build forces that provided the capability to defend, but not to attack, then security-seekers could increase their security without making other states more insecure. In this case, contrary to Waltz's structural realism and offensive realism, the international system would not produce insecurity or competition.

CASE STUDY 2.1 China's rise

Will China's continuing economic growth lead to international competition and insecurity? For two decades following the end of the Cold War, there was little security competition between the world's major powers. During this period, the United States was clearly the world's dominant economic and military power. Now, however, growth in China's economy and military forces is beginning to pose a potential to challenge America's global dominance. China has recently become a major regional power in Northeast Asia. If it continues to grow successfully, China will become as powerful, or more powerful, than the United States.

The different realist theories provide a range of views on the implications of this change in the balance of power. Offensive realism sees China striving to become the hegemonic power in its region. Regional hegemony would require China to build military forces capable of defeating its neighbours, thereby gaining tremendous political influence. In addition, China would attempt to push the United States out of Northeast Asia, because, if America remains active in its region, China would fail to acquire the influence and security provided by hegemony. The United States, however, would be threatened by Chinese hegemony and would therefore respond. One option would be to form a balancing coalition—including Japan, India, Russia, and South Korea—to contain China.

Competition would intensify as China tried to split the American-centred alliance and the United States worked to hold it together. Both sides would build up their arms to offset, if not overwhelm, the other, and both sides would be insecure because they would lack confidence in the adequacy of their forces.

Defensive realism sees greater potential for a relatively calm region. China need not pursue regional hegemony, because its security does not require large military advantages. China's power—its size, large population, and wealth—would provide the resources necessary for effective defence. In addition, China's separation by water from Japan makes defence easier. Maybe most important, nuclear weapons would provide China with an excellent deterrent capability. These defensive capabilities would not threaten the United States. China's nuclear deterrent could be designed to avoid threatening America's nuclear deterrent. Moreover, even if China does pursue a more threatening nuclear force, the United States would have little difficulty reacting and preserving its deterrent capabilities. The United States would not be directly threatened by China's conventional military capabilities because the two countries are separated by a vast ocean. Finally, because it can be secure with the United States still actively involved in its region, China would probably not press the United States to leave; and the United States would probably stay, providing Japan and other allies with insurance via security guarantees.

Motivational realism focuses on whether China turns out to be a greedy state, determined to expand even though it is secure. If it does, then the region will be competitive and dangerous. China has pursued a more assertive policy since 2010, adopting a harder line on its maritime disputes in the South China Sea and the East China Sea, including insisting that the United States not try to play a role in resolving these disputes. Many observers have interpreted China's policy shift as an indication of its greedy motives.

(continued)

CASE STUDY 2.1 China's rise (continued)

Power will play a central role in determining China's success. If it becomes as powerful as the United States, China will have significant military advantages within its region. If China is a very greedy state—willing to run large risks to expand—then the prospects for deterrence will be poor. A less expansionist China might be deterred, especially given the risks of conventional war in a nuclear world. Even in this case, however, China and the United States and its allies will all engage in intense military competition.

KEY POINTS

- In contrast to Waltz and offensive realism, defensive realism finds that the risks of competition can make cooperation a state's best strategy.
- Cooperation can under some conditions increase a state's prospects for avoiding military disadvantages and enable it to signal its benign motives, thereby increasing its security.
- Variation in the security dilemma influences the pressures for competition, and the feasibility and risks of cooperation.
- States balance against threats, not power.

Risks of competition

The adversary's insecurity is a potential problem, not because the state places inherent value on its adversary's security, but instead because the adversary's insecurity may in turn reduce the state's own security. This interaction can proceed through three key mechanisms. First, in response to the state's acquisition of new military capabilities, the adversary could respond by building up its own forces to increase its security. The adversary's build-up could leave the state less secure than it was before its own build-up because the adversary's build-up might more than offset the state's build-up. These build-ups could also leave both states less secure because their new forces add more to their ability to attack than to defend, leaving both states more vulnerable to attack.

Second, the adversary's insecurity can lead it to pursue policies that increase the probability of crises and war. Under some conditions, expansion would increase the adversary's security—for example, by increasing its power, or by reducing the state's power, or by providing strategically valuable territory that improves its prospects for defence. Because it is now more insecure, the adversary is more willing to pursue

Figure 2.2 Implications of offence–defence variables

Offence and defence can be distinguished	Advantage: Offence	Advantage: Defence
No	Arms races are intense Expansion is easy War is frequent	Arms races are mild Expansion is difficult War is infrequent
Yes	Qualitative arms control is feasible and valuable, but risky Signalling is feasible and valuable, but risky	Qualitative arms control is feasible, but less valuable, because security is high Signalling is feasible, but less valuable

these dangerous, risky policies to regain its security. Consequently, the state is also more insecure.

Third, the adversary's build-up can convince the state that it is more likely that it faces a greedy state—one that values taking territory for reasons other than increasing its security. Because a greedy state is willing to pay greater costs to expand and is therefore harder to deter, the state concludes that it is more insecure, which, as described already, can call for more competitive policies. Moreover, as a state increases its assessment that its adversary is greedy, cooperation becomes more risky, making competitive policies still more attractive. These interactions can lead to a continuing deterioration of political relations, fuelling a negative political spiral (Jervis 1976; Glaser 1997; Kydd 2005).

Benefits of cooperation

Because competitive policies can generate these negative effects, a state needs to consider the risks and benefits of cooperative policies. In terms of military forces, cooperative policies could include arms control and unilateral restraint. An arms control agreement that limits the size of deployed forces can provide protection against losing an arms race. An arms control agreement that limits forces that are especially effective for attacking can enhance both states' abilities to defend and deter, leaving both more secure than if they had competed in that type of offensive weaponry.

In addition to enhancing states' military capabilities, cooperative policies can improve their political relations, and in turn increase their security. By cooperating, a state may be able to communicate information about its motives, leading the adversary to conclude that the state is more likely to be a security-seeker. Cooperative policies have the potential to generate a positive political spiral—as a state finds its adversary more likely to be a security-seeker, cooperation become less risky, which leads states to adopt cooperative policies that make cooperation still more attractive.

Sending this information requires the state to send a 'costly signal'—an action that is less costly for a security-seeker than for a greedy state. Communicating information requires a costly signal because a greedy state has incentives to mislead its adversaries into believing that it is a security-seeker, because its adversaries would then be more likely to adopt policies that leave them vulnerable, which would improve the greedy state's prospects for achieving its expansionist objectives. An arms control agreement can serve as a costly signal because forgoing the possibility of winning an arms race is more costly for a greedy state than a security-seeker. Similarly, an agreement that limits both sides' offensive capabilities is more costly for a greedy state, because offence is more valuable for it than for a security-seeker. A state can also send a costly signal by unilaterally limiting the size or type of forces it deploys. However, unilateral restraint will often be more risky than arms control, because the adversary may continue its military build-up, thereby undermining the state's defensive capabilities. Consequently, unilateral restraint is less likely to increase the state's security.

Cooperating, however, is not without risks of its own. Most obvious, an adversary may cheat on an agreement, increasing the state's vulnerability to attack. The challenge, therefore, is for states to design and agree to monitoring arrangements that provide timely information of violations. If effective, the risks posed by the adversary's cheating can be smaller than the risks of losing an arms race. Another danger lies in the possibility that the adversary is a greedy state and that cooperation will lead it to question the state's resolve. If facing a greedy adversary, the state should worry less about the adversary's insecurity and more about whether cooperating would lead the adversary to question the state's determination to protect its interests. Thus cooperation under uncertainty about motives is risky.

Defensive realism does not find that states should in general cooperate or compete. Instead, the benefits and risks of both types of policies need to be compared. There is not a general answer because the benefits and risks will vary, depending on the international situation a state faces. Much of the relevant variation is in the magnitude and nature of the security dilemma.

Variation in the security dilemma

Unlike versions of structural realism that define the international situation entirely in terms of the distribution of power, defensive realism includes an additional variable—the security dilemma (see Figure 2.2). When the security dilemma is severe, security will be harder to achieve, states will find competition more attractive, and war will be likely. When the security dilemma is mild, the opposite will result.

The intensity of the security dilemma depends on two material variables (Jervis 1978). The offence–defence balance reflects the relative difficulty of offensive and defensive missions. The more an adversary needs to invest in military forces to defeat a state's defence, the larger the advantages of defence. In other words, the larger the advantage of defence, the easier it is to defend.

When defence has the advantage, the security dilemma is less severe, because a state can increase its ability to defend while posing a relatively small additional threat to its adversary's ability to defend. Thus, arms races should not be intense. Moreover, arms control agreements will be less risky, because cheating on an agreement will pose a smaller danger, so cooperation should be still safer. War will be less likely for a variety of reasons. Negative political spirals will be less likely and less intense. Defence advantage not only makes expansion more difficult, but also makes it less valuable, because states can be secure without acquiring more territory and greater wealth.

In contrast, offence advantage has the opposite effects. Arms races are more intense; arms control agreements are harder to achieve because cheating has greater potential to leave a state vulnerable to attack. Territorial expansion is more valuable, which fuels insecurity, and in turn competition and efforts to expand.

The offence–defence balance can be influenced by a variety of factors, maybe most importantly by technology and geography. Distance makes attacking more difficult and therefore tends to favour defence. The same is true for terrain and water that are difficult to cross because they slow or expose attackers. Nuclear weapons favour defence because survivable retaliatory capabilities, which are the key to deterrence, are much easier to maintain than are the forces required to deny nuclear retaliation.

The security dilemma also depends on whether the forces that are useful for defensive missions are also useful for offensive missions. If offence and defence can be distinguished, then states can choose to build only defence and can negotiate qualitative arms control agreements that limit forces that support offensive missions. This distinguishability of offence and defence reduces the severity of the security dilemma.

Offensive realists have challenged defensive realism over the importance of these offence–defence variables. Common criticisms hold that the concept of the offence–defence balance is not well defined and that states are incapable of measuring it. If correct, then states would focus on power, not on the combined effect of the offence–defence balance and power, and the cooperative possibilities identified by defensive realism would be reduced or even eliminated.

Threats and balancing

Defensive realism also offers a different analysis of the conditions under which states form balancing alliances. Instead of focusing entirely on power, defensive realism focuses on the danger (or threat) posed by potential adversaries (Walt 1987). Threat reflects the combination of the adversary's offensive capabilities and its motives. Threat increases with increases in the adversary's offensive capabilities, in the probability that the adversary is greedy, and in the extent of its greed. An opposing state's offensive capabilities reflect its power and the offence–defence balance: greater power and greater offence advantage make greater offensive capability possible.

This different assessment of balancing flows from key differences between defensive realism and the other structural realisms. Defensive realism emphasizes states' abilities to perform military missions, not power alone. This follows directly from the theory's core logic because a state's security depends on its ability to acquire defensive capabilities. We see this distinction reflected in the emphasis that the theory places on variation in the security dilemma and in offence–defence variables.

Defensive realism also places much greater weight on states' assessments of others' motives and, closely related, their political relationships. Instead of assuming the worst about others' motives, or essentially neglecting them altogether, defensive realism argues that states that ignore the information they have about others' motives are failing to make rational decisions. While there are risks in cooperating with a state that might be greedy, there are also costs in competing with a state that might be a security-seeker. States need to consider both types of dangers in choosing between competitive and cooperative policies.

Motivational realism

In contrast to structural realism, which essentially assumes that states are security-seekers, what I am terming 'motivational realism' emphasizes the importance of variation in states' motives and goals. More specifically, motivational realism argues that the key to understanding competitive and conflictual international behaviour lies in the nature of individual states—specifically their greedy motives—not in international structure. On the one hand, in a world in which all major powers are security-seekers, cooperation and peace are likely; on the other hand, in a world in which one or more major powers are greedy states, competition and war are likely (see Case Study 2.1).

The motivational realist argument is not that international structure does not matter, but rather that structure is not itself a cause of competitive behaviour. Instead, structure influences the ability of states to expand, but does not cause their desire to expand. This argument stands in stark contrast to structural realism—including the Waltzian, offensive, and defensive varieties—which focuses on whether and how international structure causes security-seeking states to pursue competitive policies.

In fact, in significant ways the theoretical importance of motivational realism depends on one's conclusions about the divide within structural realism. If Waltz is correct that the international system consistently produces competition, then variation in states' motives would matter relatively little. Across the full range of international conditions, pure security-seekers and greedy states would adopt competitive policies, forgoing opportunities for cooperation and unilateral restraint. As a result, explanations that focus on differences in states' motives would be less important. The more purely structural theory would be preferable, offering much greater parsimony at little cost in explanatory power. In contrast, by explaining that security-seekers should sometimes pursue cooperative policies, defensive realism gives motivational realism something to explain. Under those international conditions that defensive realism finds should lead states to cooperate, motivational realism would be required to explain why rational states pursued competitive policies.

Motivational realism need not provide an explanation for states' greedy motives. Instead, it can simply posit greedy states and ask what strategies they should choose, given the international situation they face. This said, some well-established realist theories that are at least partially consistent with motivational realism do provide such explanations. Maybe best known is Han Morgenthau's classical-realist argument that states' pursuit of power is rooted in human nature, which is characterized by 'an essential and universal lust for power as an end in itself that knows no limits' (Smith 1986: 136). According to his argument, all states have greedy motives. State greed could, however, reflect a wide range of other sources, including a state's desire to increase its wealth and prosperity, and to spread its political ideology or religion. According to these explanations, some states could have greedy motives, while others might not. In fact, some prominent motivational realists have emphasized this variation in greedy motives (Schweller 1998).

There are conditions under which a greedy state should choose competitive policies, but security seekers would choose cooperation. Recall that this is why defensive realism is insufficient on its own to explain or prescribe strategy for all types of states. Unlike in the case of security-seekers, there is no puzzle in understanding why greedy states choose competitive policies: their basic motives cannot be satisfied without competition, requiring threats or the actual use of force to take territory. Consequently, whereas a security-seeker could prefer to cooperate when it had an even chance of winning (and losing) an arms race, a greedy state would be more likely to prefer to compete. The greedy state would see greater value in the military advantages provided by winning the race, because these advantages would be necessary to achieve its expansionist objectives. In addition, the greedy state might also see smaller costs in the negative political impact of arms racing, because it understands that its goals are necessarily incompatible with good political relations. Similarly, a greedy state might start a war when a security-seeker would not. Assuming it places greater value on territory than does the security seeker, the greedy state will be prepared to pay higher costs in fighting the war and therefore will be harder to deter. Closely related, the greedy state will bargain with more determination to acquire the territory, increasing the probability that coercion would lead to a crisis that would escalate to war.

This said, it is important to note that greedy states will not always pursue competitive policies. A greedy state will be deterred from expanding if it anticipates that the costs of acquiring territory are too high and/or the probability of success is too low. Put another way, under some conditions balancing against a greedy state can succeed. Similarly, the less likely a greedy state is to win an arms race, the lower the probability that it will initiate one. As these comparisons suggest, the power of opposing states should play an important role in a greedy state's choice of strategy.

Greedy states may also make different alliance choices than security-seekers (Schweller 1998). They have a greater incentive to bandwagon, because they place greater value on gaining power. A key factor pushing security-seekers away from bandwagoning is the danger presented by other states on the more powerful side. Greedy states are more willing to run this risk because they place greater value on the potential gains that the stronger side may be able to provide. A prevalence of bandwagoning creates the possibility of a still more competitive and dangerous world. Instead of states balancing to offset advantages in power, or buckpassing and thereby neglecting potential imbalances of power, in a bandwagoning world states actively join together to create imbalances of power in their favour. Possibilities for war and for hegemony therefore increase.

In response to these motivational realist arguments, structural realists argue that at a minimum the motivational realist argument underestimates the potential impact of international structure. Specifically, anarchy and the security dilemma can combine to drive states into competition. Essentially, structure can by itself drive states into competition. However, structural realism can (and, as I argue in the Conclusion, should) concede that greedy motives can also matter for whether states decide to engage in military competition and war, and therefore need to be factored into assessments of states' security policies.

KEY POINTS

- Greedy states, not international structure, are the driving force behind competitive international policies.
- Greedy states can be deterred, so the balance of power plays an important role in determining whether they will attempt to expand.
- Greedy states will be inclined to bandwagon instead of balance.

Realism and war

The preceding discussion has been cast in the broad categories of competition and cooperation, with the most immediate logic applying to arms competition and alliance choices. Realism also offers a more specific set of arguments about the causes of war. Because of space limitations, only a brief review of these arguments, all of which are contested, is possible here.

An unresolved debate is over whether war is more likely in **bipolar** or **multipolar** systems. Bipolar systems have two major powers; multipolar systems contain three or more major powers. Some realists argue that war is less likely in bipolar systems. In a multipolar system, states have incentives to buckpass, which can undermine effective balancing and create opportunities for expansion. Relatedly, in multipolar systems there is greater uncertainty about the size and commitment of opposing coalitions. Even if opposing states are going to balance, a potential attacker can underestimate the true likelihood of balancing, which makes war appear more attractive. In addition, war can be more likely in multipolar systems simply because there are more major power dyads across which war could occur.

The standard counterargument is that balancing in multipolar systems can provide large power advantages to states joining together to defend the status quo. In contrast, in bipolarity, the balance of power between the major powers is roughly equal, making war more attractive than in multipolarity, in which states balance effectively. Moreover, in multipolarity, even if balancing fails to occur, a major power attacking an equal major power has prospects that are no better than in bipolarity.

A second important argument about war focuses on the impact of changes in states' power. A state that is declining can have incentives to start a war before it becomes significantly more vulnerable to attack and coercion (Copeland 2000). This type of war is commonly termed preventive war. A state that prefers peace to war could nevertheless prefer war sooner (while it is stronger) both to war later (when it is weaker) and to the political concessions it would have to make to avoid war once it is weaker.

In deciding whether to launch a preventive war, a state needs to consider not only shifts in power, but also the probability that the rising power would attack or coerce it. Uncertainty about the rising state's future motives makes this a complicated calculation and may tend to lead states towards war. The inability of a state to promise credibly that it will not use its increased power against the declining state is an unavoidable result of international anarchy and contributes to the incentives for preventive war.

A third set of arguments, already touched on above, focuses on the offence–defence balance and the security dilemma, in addition to power. As described there, when offence has the advantage, competition will be more intense and political relations will be worse, which will increase the probability of crises. Offence advantage also increases the instrumental value of territory, because it increases the prospects for successful expansion, which makes war more attractive. Offence advantage also increases incentives to strike first in a crisis, thereby increasing the probability of pre-emptive war (Van Evera 1999). Defence advantage has the opposite effects, making peace more likely.

A fourth set of arguments, collectively termed the 'bargaining model of war' provides a more complete foundation for the above realist causes of war. Game theorists have demonstrated that war between rational states—whether deliberate escalation from a crisis, pre-emptive or preventive—requires either that a state does not have a full understanding of the opposing state's military capabilities or resolve, or that a state cannot credibly promise to agree by the terms of an agreement (Powell 1999). If states had a full understanding, they would reach a negotiated agreement instead of going to war. If states could make credible promises, they could make lasting deals that would avoid preventive wars and defuse arms races.

KEY POINTS

- Debate over whether war is more likely in bipolar or multipolar systems remains unresolved.
- A state whose power is declining will have incentives to launch a preventive war.
- War is more likely when the offence–defence balance favours offence.

Conclusion

The preceding discussion makes clear that realism, while sharing a number of key assumptions, is a broad family of arguments that diverges on some important issues. Some of this divergence reflects disagreement over the deductive logic of the structural-realist arguments. A sign of progress will be the eventual resolution of these disputes.

Other disagreements are more reconcilable and suggest the possibility of a more general realist or rational theory (Glaser 2010). There are two reasons for merging structural realism and motivational realism. First, their assumptions are compatible and complementary. Both see an important role for international structure, although the theories do emphasize quite different implications. The theories focus on different types of state motives—with structural realism focusing on security-seekers and motivational realism focusing on greedy states—but there is nothing inconsistent about considering the interactions of both types of states fully.

Second, we lack a strong theoretical rationale for giving special weight to one theory over the other. Defensive realism shows that international structure does not consistently and intensely drive competition; greedy states could matter. It also shows that structure can by itself drive competition and, therefore, cannot be reduced to a factor that simply constrains states' choices.

This more general theory has the advantage of spanning both basic types of states. As a result, it eliminates a key debate within the realist family and refocuses attention on a range of empirical issues, including the types of states that are interacting, and the severity of the security dilemma they face. The more general theory makes clear that a state's choice of security policy should depend both on its motives and goals, and on the international situation it faces; neither is generally sufficient on its own for explaining or prescribing a state's strategy.

As important, this more general theory (Glaser 2010) establishes a central role for information about opposing states' motives. Defensive realism points in this direction, showing how threats depend on an adversary's intentions, as well as its military capabilities; and identifying the value of sending costly signals that enable a state to communicate information about its own motives. The full rational theory adds information about adversaries' motives as a key variable defining the international environment and explains that the magnitude of the security dilemma depends on this information variable, as well as the more traditional offense–defence variables. The security dilemma is less severe when a state believes its adversary is likely to be a security seeker. The overall result is a theory that some will argue is no longer realism, because contrary to realism, which focuses on power, it places roughly equal importance on material and information variables. Nevertheless, whatever label is applied, the rational theory provides a general framework that builds on Waltz's structural realism, clarifies and extends the role that information about motives plays in states' choices of international policies, and integrates the central variable—a state's own motives—from motivational (and classical) realism. The more general theory also helps to close the gap with important theories that are typically understood as alternatives to structural realism. Neoinstitutionalists argue that institutions, and the information they provide, are essential to making international cooperation possible; the general theory highlights the role of information, but concludes that institutions do not play a fundamental role in cooperation. The theory also closes the gap with key elements of social constructivism, by making clear that a state's beliefs about an opposing state's type—an information variable, not a material variable—should influence the state's behaviour. Whether this more general theory will advance or simply fuel debate remains to be seen.

QUESTIONS

1. Why is realism better understood as a family of theories than a single theory?
2. What assumptions are shared by most realist theories?
3. What is the key divide between structural and motivational realism?
4. Why does Waltz believe that the international system tends to generate competition?
5. Why does offensive realism believe that states maximize power?
6. Why does defensive realism believe states should attempt to signal their benign motives?
7. What variables influence the severity of the security dilemma and how do they matter?
8. How can a state's declining power create incentives for preventive war?
9. How does defence advantage reduce incentives for war?

FURTHER READING

- Copeland, D. (2000), *The Origins of Major War*, Ithaca, NY: Cornell University Press. Provides a nuanced realist theory of preventive war.
- Glaser, C. (2010), *Rational Theory of International Politics*, Princeton: Princeton University Press. Presents a general rational theory that integrates structural and motivational realism, and adds states' information about motives as a key dimension of their international environment.
- Jervis, R. (1978), 'Cooperation under the Security Dilemma', *World Politics*, 30/1: 167–214. Provides the classic discussion of how offence–defence variables influence the security dilemma.
- Mearsheimer, J. (2001), *The Tragedy of Great Power Politics*, New York: Norton. The definitive statement of offensive realism.
- Schweller, R. (1998), *Deadly Imbalances: Tripolarity and Hitler's Strategy of World Conquest*, New York: Columbia University Press. A motivational realist analysis that emphasizes the importance of greedy states and variations in the balance of power.
- Smith, M. (1986), *Realist Thought from Weber to Kissinger*, Baton Rouge, LA: Louisiana State University Press. Provides an analysis and comparison of key classical realists.
- Snyder, J. (1991), *Myths of Empire: Domestic Politics and International Ambition*, Ithaca, NY: Cornell University Press. Combines realist and domestic-politics arguments to explain why states over-expand.

- Van Evera, S. (1999), *Causes of War: Power and the Roots of Conflict*, Ithaca, NY: Cornell University Press. Explores the many ways in which military opportunities and pressures can lead to war, and how military biases can exacerbate these causes.
- Walt, S. (1987), *The Origin of Alliances*, Ithaca, NY: Cornell University Press. Analyses alliance formation, moving beyond power by bringing in intentions and offence–defence variables.
- Waltz, K. N. (1979), *Theory of International Politics*, New York: McGraw Hill. The seminal statement of structural realism.

Visit the Online Resource Centre that accompanies this book for lots of interesting additional material: www.oxfordtextbooks.co.uk/orc/collins4e/

3

Liberalism

Patrick Morgan

Chapter Contents

Reader's Guide

This chapter presents the liberalist approach to the theory and practice of international politics. As one of the two classic conceptions, along with realism, of international politics, its chief characteristics are identified and the major liberalist schools of thought are described and briefly examined, particularly with reference to how they overlap with, yet depart in significant ways from, the realist perspective. There is a brief discussion of how this perspective dominates contemporary international politics, the ways critics attack it for its alleged intellectual weaknesses and its adverse effects in practice.

Introduction

The liberalist tradition is usually traced back to the Enlightenment, particularly to the philosophers John Locke and, on certain matters, Immanuel Kant. In the field of international politics it is considered to have reached an initial high point in the years just after the First World War, particularly under the intellectual and political leadership of President Woodrow Wilson, who sought to make it the basis for radically transforming international politics so as to do away with major warfare. In his efforts, Wilson highlighted all the main themes that have been displayed in the liberalist approach ever since (Kegley 1995; Cooper 2009). It was then somewhat eclipsed, particularly in academic studies of international politics, by the rise of Fascism and the Second World War followed by the Cold War, but it played an important role in the development of international relations among the Western countries throughout the Cold War. It blossomed when the Cold War ended, the East–West conflict dissolved, and the Soviet Union disappeared.

Characteristic features of the liberalist approach

Several characteristics, taken together, are associated with liberalism and define its distinctive approach to international politics. Perhaps the most obvious is that it is fundamentally optimistic. It is optimistic about politics, economics, and the broad prospects for international politics, including cooperation among international actors and chances for a peaceful world. It holds that international politics is not inherently conflict ridden and violent, that peace and security are plausibly attainable and getting more so. Cooperation among states and societies need not be limited and difficult. There is no inherent **security dilemma** in international politics. In short, it need not be as doleful as much of its history has been, and therefore the study of it is not a modern-day **dismal science**.

A second notable characteristic is that, while the liberalist approach offers elements of a theory, it is not one. It is a broad analytical approach with a family of related ideas and preferred practices. While it offers guidelines, advice, conclusions, and orientations for the better conduct of international affairs, it is short on well-developed theoretical explanations of those things. Analysts cite similar deficiencies in other theoretical approaches, but liberalism seems to display this more than most. Nevertheless, it has a strong appeal and robust vigour. It is the dominant conception in the *practice* of international politics today and influential in the *study* of international politics as well. However, some analysts fear international politics is rapidly becoming more conflictual and dangerous now.

Next, it is old enough to be a classical approach and overlaps a good deal with the other great classical perspective, realism, while discarding central realist contentions. It identifies nation states as the most important actors, the ones whose behaviour we most care about and most wish to explain, but gives considerable attention to other actors as well: international governmental organizations (**IGOs**), **international regimes**, non-governmental international organizations (**NGOs**), multinational corporations, and domestic actors such as interest groups, elites, political parties, and government bureaucracies. In the same way, liberalism accepts the idea that the international system, its nature and its structure, can have important effects on the behaviour of the actors, yet rests on the contrary view that the system is ultimately not as important in determining states' behaviour as (1) domestic actors' **power** and preferences; and (2) the nature of states' domestic political systems.

Pulling this together, the liberalist approach insists that nation states are not basically alike, and that how international politics operates tends to reflect their differences in character. With the 'right' sorts of (liberal) political systems and domestic (liberalist-oriented) groups running them, states can arrange to have international cooperation flourish and can tolerate the vigorous participation of international organizations and numerous sorts of non-state actors, with the resulting constraints on state behaviour those actors impose. Thus international politics is not the same everywhere; it is 'realist' only in some places and at certain times. Its nature is not always dictated by how anarchy and the resulting international system shape the members' behaviour. Instead, it is also shaped by the political, economic, and social choices people in states make, choices not necessarily driven by the international system. Liberalists agree with realists that international politics can be highly realist in character, but not on whether it *must* be.

This is an 'inside-out' approach to describing and explaining why governments do what they do, in contrast to a realist approach in which the external environment is crucial. States make important choices in conducting their interactions, and, like domestic policies and actions, their foreign policies and actions are significantly shaped by domestic factors, particularly the *political* elements that determine who rules, who crafts decisions, whose perspectives and preferences are in charge. For example, domestic political struggles and competing bureaucratic interests and perspectives are important, plus the pressures from elites, interest groups, and others in the society, not just the pulling and hauling between states. Domestic politics is itself a competition among perspectives and interests, with elites, groups, and leaders vying for power, office, and influence. The shifting results eventually determine foreign policy. External pressures and opportunities, especially threats, are certainly important but seldom decisive. Hence it is sometimes suggested, especially for very powerful states, that foreign policy is an effort by domestic political elements to pursue their domestic preferences and policies abroad—foreign policy is domestic preferences projected outwards. Whether this is the case or not, the state's national interests and its policies on pursuing them are not semi-automatic or predetermined; somebody has to decide what they are.

This makes the state as an entity, apart from its society, an important component of foreign policy making but, in comparison with realism, less as a semi-autonomous actor and more often as an agent of the dominant domestic interests and coalitions. While states have interests and concerns of their own, the controlling factor is often who rules, which involves a constant struggle inside the government and major elites and among important interest groups. Hence states are not unitary actors, and domestic forces, values, interests, and perspectives are significant factors in international politics. For instance, in seeking to maintain state security, what influential domestic elements think is good for *their* concerns and interests can be quite different from what the state's military officials would like, and the policies preferred by those domestic groups might well be adopted.

KEY POINTS

- Liberalism is basically optimistic about improving international politics and making it safer.
- It describes international politics as evolving, becoming more imbued with interdependence, cooperation, peace, and security.
- While seeing states as the most important actors it also highlights other kinds of actors—IGOs, NGOs, major private economic entities, and international regimes.
- It depicts states' behaviour as mainly the result of the perceptions, preferences, and decisions of elites and officials, which are often related to the nature of each state's political system.
- Thus the character of international politics can change depending on the nature of its members, their objectives, and their decisions on what to do, how to interact.

Central elements in liberalist thinking; commercial liberalism

Politically, liberalism prefers certain perceptions, values, and interests, and favours related policies. While there is controversy on details, liberalism is associated with: strong support for democracy which is considered vital for the legitimacy of a government; strong support for private property and free enterprise—a market economy—at home and abroad; a belief in open relationships among societies—not only in trade and investment but in flows of information and ideas, people, and culture; strong support for international cooperation such as in international organizations; and a strong commitment to human rights based on the importance of the individual.

Adherents differ a good deal about which of these deserve the most attention or how to rank them in priority, leading to a somewhat confusing array of analytical claims and policies. Analysts sort all this out by classifying liberalist views into the following categories: *commercial* or *economic* liberalism, *human rights* liberalism, *international organization* or institutions liberalism, and *democratic* liberalism.

The oldest may well be *commercial* or *economic* liberalism. It descends from the free-trade ideas that emerged and grew steadily more influential in the eighteenth and early nineteenth centuries, particularly in Great Britain. The term 'free trade' encompassed flows not just of goods but also of capital, and proponents had both domestic and international economic activities in mind. The general idea is that the production and accumulation of wealth are most rapid and efficient if economic activities are largely conducted by private owners/actors who interact mainly in accordance with the dictates of markets. This is in contrast to having economic activities operated, organized, or tightly regulated by governments, as owners or through laws, regulations, and other restraints. Restrictions on transnational flows are therefore discouraged. After 1945, the United States became the main proponent of this kind of economic system, at home and abroad, and it continues in this role today. The contemporary global economic system, basically constructed among non-communist countries just before and during the Cold War, is characterized by vast flows of capital (well over a trillion dollars daily), constantly expanding trade, considerable transfers of technology, and notable movement of workers across national boundaries, legally and illegally. In degree of interdependence, it is roughly equivalent to the international economic system that existed before 1914, which was disrupted by the two world wars, but on a much larger scale and subject to elaborate governmental and international institutions and regulations.

A regular contention about such domestic economies and this kind of international economic system is that rising economic interdependence ultimately brings about peace and security. Prior to the First World War some said that wars would decline because they were bad for business—too costly, disruptive, and expensive for societies to tolerate. After the Second World War, this view was an important influence in the creation of the European Common Market, forerunner of the European Union (EU), with economic integration undertaken not just for greater well-being but to promote better political relations among the members so that warfare among them would disappear.

A current version of the benefits of an open international economy contends that when the main governments in a region are controlled by liberalism-oriented elites strongly interested in economic growth plus greater freedom and mobility, they will promote export-led national development, often seeking foreign investment to develop productive capacities for exporting. To maintain the right environment for this, they reduce their conflicts and expand their economic contacts while expanding cooperation to better manage their rising interactions. As a result, chances of war among them decline, as does the likelihood they will develop nuclear weapons, while prospects for successful arms control rise (Solingen 1998, 2007).

Thus one reason for liberalism's optimism is the continuing expansion of capitalism in the belief that this brings wealth and higher living standards in such a way that war is typically irrelevant or counterproductive, curbing the influence of elites historically devoted to war, conquest, and the national power and glory associated with them. Instead there is a rising *common* interest in international cooperation to facilitate these developments and manage their complex effects.

Interest in the potentially pacifying results of rising economic interdependence gained greater prominence after the Cold War as most former members of the communist world joined the liberal international economic system (Russia being the most recent) and **globalization** surged. Globalization is a powerful contemporary expression of the liberalist view, especially in economic activities. Proponents see it further eroding national boundaries, knitting the world together in a global community.

KEY POINTS

- Liberalism strongly supports democracy, private property, and free enterprise, widespread international interactions and cooperation, and human rights.
- Commercial or economic liberalism stresses the benefits of open-market economies and widespread international trade and investment.
- Expected benefits include greater cooperation plus less conflict and war, an important motivation behind European integration.
- In other regions, governments with open economic systems relying on exports for national development have been highly likely to pursue conflict reduction and greater cooperation with neighbours.
- A reason for optimism is that the world has been developing along these lines for decades, including rising globalization today.

The pursuit of human rights

A second, and very striking, school of liberalist thought and action today is preoccupied with *human rights*. In a sense its roots lie in concerns, from early in the **Westphalian** international system, states have often had about how religious and ethnic groups of great interest to them were treated by their neighbours, concerns expressed in diplomatic pressures, military interventions, and peace agreements (Krasner 1999). Initially this was due not to liberalist sentiments but to deep attachments to members of ethnic and religious groups abroad. This began changing in the nineteenth century, especially with the movement in Britain and elsewhere to end the slave trade by espousing not a specific national concern but a universal human right. Such thinking eventually extended to support for national self-determination, targeting colonial empires in particular. An intensely debated topic at the peace negotiations after the First World War and a source of bitter recrimination by nationalities not favoured in the peace agreements, it was of even greater importance after the Second World War.

Modern human-rights-oriented liberalism is still concerned with self-determination. It does not widely support separatism because most countries are multi-ethnic and supporting separatism would invite chaotic dissolutions, but will endorse it when separation looks unavoidable and serious fighting and other bloodshed seem certain without it. This was illustrated in the 1990s in the slow evolution of the Kosovo problem towards an independent Kosovo, or the way a liberalist view holds that former Soviet republics are entitled to reject membership in a Russian sphere of influence and are not to be subjected to a forcible Russian takeover. Religious persecution also remains a broad liberalist concern. In all these matters the goal is protecting an inherent human right, not advancing underlying national interests of a different sort.

Liberalism's adherents, private and governmental, support a broad list of human rights pertaining to economic, medical, political, sexual, and other forms of deprivation and discrimination. The democracies regularly pressure other kinds of governments, and each other, to be more supportive of and sensitive to human rights concerns. They take actions in support of political prisoners, rights and opportunities for women, religious freedom, civil rights, victims of famine, and so on. Those efforts are influenced by domestic groups devoted to human rights concerns, and groups that reinforce the relevant policies internationally through a huge network of private organizations (NGOs), often referred to as **international civil society**, another aspect of globalization. They campaign for human rights, actively promoting them in **peace building** efforts and other activities abroad, drawing on extensive private resources plus funding from governments and international organizations.

KEY POINTS

- Liberalism's interest in human rights in the nineteenth century is notable for the focus on slavery and national self-determination, including anticolonialism.
- Added in the twentieth century, particularly since the Cold War, were campaigns on behalf of persons subject to economic, sexual, gender, religious, and political persecution, discrimination, or deprivation.
- Much of the impetus on these matters now comes from potent private organizations operating both inside their societies and internationally.

Liberalism and international organizations

Adherents of liberalism have long sought to enhance international cooperation and bolster national and international security via international organizations. Early in the twentieth century, interest was high in forming a league or alliance of governments to prevent wars. Woodrow Wilson put great emphasis on inserting this into the agreements signed at the peace conference after the First World War and in his campaign after that to get the USA to join the new League of Nations, reasoning that, once it was in place and operating, many other improvements in international politics would become possible.

Of course, the USA did not join, and the League failed to prevent wars in the 1930s and the Second World War. However, the idea was revived after the Second World War with the creation of the United Nations, and (in the **Bretton Woods system**) the World Bank, the International Monetary Fund, and other institutions for managing international economic affairs. In the ensuing decades, many additional organizations have been created. This contributed to a continued emphasis on cooperation as desirable and possible.

This has been reinforced by two additional developments. One, mentioned already, is the surge in NGOs and their activities, adding an impressive additional dimension to the concept of international cooperation. The other is the concept of '**international regimes**', which further expanded notions of international cooperation (see Key Ideas 3.1). Cooperation often takes the form of **norms** and understandings as to appropriate behaviour on important, often sensitive matters (such as non-proliferation or the continuing non-use of nuclear weapons). **Regimes** can exist not only in connection with international treaties and formal international organizations but even without them. This made it apparent that there was a good deal more cooperation, more management, in international politics than previously understood. Today all the forms it takes are referred to as international 'institutions'.

The liberalist view of international institutions runs along three different lines. One is *neoliberal institutionalism*—sometimes called rational-choice liberalism. It accepts the realist view that anarchy makes cooperation very difficult—the temptation to cheat is too great and fear of being cheated is pervasive. Then,

KEY IDEAS 3.1 International regimes

'Regime' here should not be confused with its use as a substitute for 'government' or 'state' or 'ruler' in domestic politics. It stands for an international institution consisting of principles, rules, norms, and procedures for decision making that international actors use to plan and carry out actions pertaining to some specified matter. The principles, rules, and norms may be written into a formal treaty or other international agreement to which governments officially subscribe—like the Kyoto Protocol—or they may be informal but serious understandings like the tradition or taboo that has grown up on the non-use of nuclear weapons. In the same way, the procedures for decision making may involve using a formal international organization with rules of procedure and a clear definition of what it is to decide. Or the decisions might be made by governments independently. For instance, under the non-proliferation regime, non-nuclear powers promise not to try to develop nuclear weapons, but actual decisions to not do so are made when opportunities arise to start or continue a nuclear weapons programme, decisions made by each government on its own. The regime includes the expectation that those decisions will always be negative.

Regimes are attractive not only for what they do but because of their flexibility. For instance, they can emerge gradually, even go unnoticed for quite a while. The **democratic peace** is, in fact, such a regime. Thus a regime can emerge partially and then develop over time, something harder to do with a formal agreement, because such an agreement normally requires a minimum number of signatories to go into operation. Sometimes, regimes emerge even when the formal agreement does not go into effect, because those who signed decide to adhere to it anyway—which can put pressure on non-signatories to join after all, especially if the regime is having a noticeable effect without them. Sometimes states join unofficially by living up to a regime's requirements but not formally signing it. This kind of flexibility is often useful, such as when officially signing would be politically awkward or impossible.

using an analytical approach developed by economists, it explains how regimes and international organizations can nevertheless facilitate it (Oye 1986). For instance, the cooperation needed for agreements can be inhibited if governments have too little information about the problem cooperation is designed to solve and about its likely effects; international organizations may be able to generate that information. Cooperation often requires extensive interaction and bargaining; international organization can provide forums for this along with expert advice. Governments will fear that, if they follow agreements, others will **free ride**—gaining the benefits without doing their share—or simply cheat; international organizations can monitor compliance to discourage free riding and cheating and reassure governments it is not taking place, or provide procedures to resolve disagreements on compliance. They can also administer agreements and report on their effectiveness. In other words, international organizations and regimes are *practical* in that they reduce **transaction costs**. Being useful makes them valuable, thus hard to do without once they are up and running, which is why cooperation in international politics is often durable. This analysis has been influential, in part because it bridges realist and liberalist thinking.

Another view is that international institutions are 'natural', an obvious recourse for an increasingly interdependent world. As cooperation grows, so does everyone's stake in it, giving rise to increased support for organizations, rules, and even laws. Like demand for a traffic light at a busy intersection, the magnitude of the interaction incites coordination arrangements. This is a *functionalist* view—rising interactions generate important functions that need to be performed; international organizations are either created to meet them or flourish because they turn out to meet them. The Law of the Sea Treaty is an example of the former, and the World Health Organization's growing role in dealing with threats of global epidemics embodies the latter.

The third approach says that governments can be induced to accept less sovereignty to create governing international institutions. They may want more efficient decision making, or less domination by the most powerful or wealthiest members, or greater legitimacy for a norm, or some other compelling need. Examples include the development of the EU and, more recently, the European Central Bank, or the recent emergence of international criminal courts. The permanent members' veto power in the UN Security Council is often cited to illustrate how devoted to sovereignty nations are, but the Council's power to order military action to deal with threats to peace and security is quite impressive and shows how far international governance can be carried. The World Trade

Organization settles major issues as a potent actor, not just as an agent of the members.

Still, parting with elements of sovereignty and autonomy is a drastic step. Is something else needed to induce governments to accept it? One argument is that it takes a **hegemon**—a dominant state that provides leadership, organizes the cooperative effort, provides necessary enforcement, and so on. The establishment of the Bretton Woods system after the Second World War, largely by the USA, for the international economy is often considered the supreme example. Another argument is that, if cooperation is important enough, nations redefine national interests to embrace the necessary shrinking of national **autonomy**—the national interest then transcends **sovereignty** and autonomy.

Finally, one liberalist conception of international cooperation is shared with constructivism. This is the idea that international politics develops elements of community, one indication being the emergence of international institutions with a network of norms and rules to which leaders, governments, and societies are expected to adhere. Liberalism has consistently promoted 'higher-order' norms and principles, sometimes advocating forcible steps to enforce them. Examples include avoiding advocacy of secession, non-use of nuclear weapons, and, inside society, avoidance of genocide. An example of a slowly emerging norm is the idea that sovereignty is not simply a right to national autonomy; it is also an obligation of a government to treat its society with reasonable decency, and that failure to do so can be rectified by international intervention. (This was on display during the Arab Spring revolts in 2011–12.) It is not that international politics must eventually embrace and inculcate these particular norms, but that, as an elaborate social activity, international politics needs elements of community, including a structure of norms. Liberalists are busy pushing their preferred norms with this in mind.

From a liberalist perspective, therefore, states are not necessarily rigid about sovereignty and autonomy, and not averse to cooperation. A final aspect of this is that liberalism adherents see cooperation as encouraged and reinforced when participants expect it—and its benefits—to be reiterated, which is technically referred to as the influence of the '**shadow of the future**'. Under these conditions it is easier to get cooperation, trust others, and make agreements in the present.

KEY POINTS

- Liberalism has been interested for at least a century in building international organizations. To this it has more recently added advocacy of the use of NGOs and international regimes, enlarging the arsenal of cooperative arrangements.
- Explanations of the contributions of organizations, norms, and the like range from neoliberalism's elucidation of their facilitative contributions, to functional analyses, to claims that organizations can meet certain political needs.
- Elaborate cooperation is apt to require something else: perhaps a hegemon, or an innovative redefinition of the national interest.
- International cooperation represents, and benefits from, the development of community, and is enhanced by a significant likelihood that it will be recurring.

Liberalism and democracy

Not surprisingly, liberalism rejects the idea that warfare is all but inevitable, and has a strong preference for non-violent methods in pursuing national objectives. The main evidence cited on this now is the 'democratic-peace' thesis, which brings us to *democratic liberalism*. The thesis treats a notable statistical pattern in relations among modern liberal democracies as a virtual law: modern liberal democracies never go to war with each other. In fact, they spend no effort preparing even for possible wars with each other. Despite often being amply armed—frequently with significant *offensive* military forces that might be expected to produce great insecurity in others—democracies display no signs of a security dilemma in their relations, and coexist peacefully even when they have serious disagreements. Technically, they constitute a **pluralistic security community**: even with no superior ruling authority, these states have no fear of being attacked by each other.

Liberalism champions the spread of democracy to achieve security—'if you want peace promote democracy', so to speak. The goal is a universal pluralistic security community. This is not a new idea (Kant suggested it; Woodrow Wilson endorsed it), but it is the democratic peace thesis that makes it so prominent now. It is an extension of liberalism's inside-out approach and the belief that the nature of an international system is significantly shaped by the character of its members. It contends that a system composed of democracies will be a sharp departure from much of the history of international politics.

Sceptics cite the fact that democracies that are new and not deeply rooted often display aggressive, expansionist behaviour and national pugnacity (Mansfield and Snyder 1989; Snyder 1998). Moreover, analysts agree that democracies may readily go to war with non-democracies, so it is not pacifism that creates the democratic peace. Critics also note that liberalist analysts lack a consensus as to what generates the democratic peace—they have no accepted theory to explain it (see Key Ideas 3.2).

This has not slowed the promotion of democracy. It is now integral to the liberal democracies' foreign policies. In response to the 9/11 attacks, President Bush proposed a war to end terrorism by, in large part, promoting democracy in the Middle East. Many commentators concluded that this called liberal internationalism into ill repute and that vigorously, even forcefully, promoting democracy is dying out, but that is not the case. Western countries have vigorously encouraged democracy throughout the former Soviet empire in Eastern Europe to help ensure the area will be peaceful. The Western approach to peace building in societies torn by civil war is intervening to, in part, promote the rule of law, political parties, elections, an active media, and civil rights as the proper recipe for creating stable societies and responsible governments.

As noted earlier, a related aspect of this is the rise of 'international civil society'. A pervasive element in liberalism is respect for the private sector, not just in economic activities but in intellectual, cultural, social, and political spheres. Individuals and groups are expected to make important contributions to society on their own, apart from (as well as in cooperation with) the government. This is viewed as an essential component of democracy. International civil society is reproducing the activism and non-governmental character of domestic activities characteristic of civil societies in liberal democracies, for the purpose of containing threats to peace and security. These activities reflect a profound belief in both the existence of a global community and the need to expand it.

KEY IDEAS 3.2 Explaining the democratic peace

Here are examples of how varied the explanations for the democratic peace are, drawn from the suggested readings or sources cited in the chapter. One explanation is that democracies have a unique ability to get along without fighting because they see democracy as legitimizing a government and therefore treat other democracies as deserving of respect and trust—limiting how far conflicts among them are carried. A related argument is that democracies are devoted to resolving political issues through compromise, so they trust and respect each other to use that to avoid a war.

Another is that democracies make leaders accountable to many groups, some of which oppose wars, and this makes it hard to secure the broad support leaders want in a war, or will want in the next election—so leaders are reluctant to have to build that support. A related explanation is that democracies put restraints on their governments—constitutions, legal restrictions, public opinion, separation of powers, opposition parties, and so on—making it difficult for a democratic government to go to war. Or the restraints make it hard to get into a war quickly, allowing more time for negotiations or other approaches to work. A classic view is that republics are particularly sensitive about concentrating too much power in the government's hands and wars have that effect, so republics are wary about taking on wars.

It is possible that, since democracies are more transparent than other kinds of political systems, they more readily interact with confidence and with less concern about hidden motives. It is also the case that democracies are more open to opinions, pressures, and so on from outside, particularly from other democracies, and this makes them more responsive to each other's points of view in conflicts. The oldest argument is that citizens hate the costs of war and that makes it harder for democratic governments to get into one.

Finally, it is argued that democracies more readily develop a wide range of interactions and a higher level of interdependence with each other, and more readily set up international institutions as a result. This allows analysts to argue that liberalism's emphasis on those things as good for reducing warfare applies particularly strongly to democracies, making the various facets of liberalism interactive and reinforcing in keeping democracies from fighting each other.

Naturally, there are many ways to disparage these arguments. And, while there are ways to test many of them, there are strenuous debates about whether those tests are properly done. There is not even agreement on just when a government is a democracy, or is enough of a democracy, for inclusion in a list of democracies over time as a sample for the testing.

KEY POINTS

- Democratic liberalism has long promoted democracy to change international politics. Now that is reinforced by the democratic peace thesis: democracies do not go to war with each other—they constitute a pluralistic security community.
- However, adherents of this view lack consensus on why democracy has this effect, especially since democracies are quite capable of making war on non-democracies.
- Spreading democracy is now a major part of the foreign policies of democracies.
- This is reinforced by the pro-democracy orientation and activities of much of international civil society.

Conclusion—and a critique

Liberalism has been optimistic since the Cold War and with good reason. For the first time in history, the world's richest, most economically potent nations were in the liberalist camp or (as in the cases of Russia, China, and India) significantly interacted with it. Wars between governments virtually disappeared, and internal wars posing threats to international peace and security began to decline also and many have been targets of moderate to vigorous international efforts to end them and discourage their return. The number of democracies rose significantly. Efforts to expand international cooperation grew, especially on environmental management, economic matters, crime, terrorism, and non-proliferation of weapons of mass destruction.

Opposition to the liberalist vision was somewhat fragmented. Fukuyama's declaration of the **'end of history'** after the Cold War, asserting that the challenges to democracy have been defeated so contention over the best form of social and political organization was at an end, has been premature in view of the Islamic world's opposition to the West through terrorism, but that could be treated as a frantic response to the liberalist vision, not another great challenge like Fascism and Communism.

Certainly there were critics of liberalism. Some have been analytical, lamenting aspects of liberalism in theory. Some treated the correlation of democracy and the absence of war as spurious, suggesting a third factor was responsible for the democratic peace (Rosato 2003). Since all kinds of wars had declined, maybe the democratic peace just reflected the growing obsolescence of war (Mueller 1989). Maybe the democracies just had identical or overlapping national interests, making them natural allies with problems not worth fighting about, a criticism hard to refute because the liberal democracies do indeed have important interests in common, and this has been true for a long time.

Constructivist and postmodernist approaches, which have rejected some or all of liberalism's methodologies and theoretical explanations, have found liberalism out of touch, failing to appreciate the inherent limitations of trying to develop a somewhat 'scientific' theory of international politics, not appreciating how liberalist impulses were, in much of the world, part of the problem of international politics instead of being the solution.

Consider the possibility that liberalist influence merely reflects Western dominance. What if, as many analysts have predicted, that dominance is finally coming to an end with the rapid development of non-Western states and societies that encompass well over half the world? If the sun sets on the West's pre-eminence, will it also set on the liberalist perspective? This could mean an end to the spreading of democracy (Boix 2011), a clash of civilizations, perhaps the return of a very realist world. After all, in the international economic system, the global recession stimulated efforts to reorganize world economic governance but also provoked steps away from cooperation and openness: sovereign wealth funds that nationalize major economic assets and investments in giant state-owned firms in key industrial sectors (like Petrobras in Brazil); the growing use of state-sponsored and funded forms of development in designated sectors (in Brazil, India, Russia, China, etc.). Analysts have cited illiberal practices spreading on cyberspace as governments limited web access from inside and outside to screen out politically unacceptable materials and curb cyberattacks.

The developments of the Arab Spring have thus proved to be a complication for the liberalist school, but there have also been other, equally unexpected developments elsewhere in the world which pose a challenge to liberalist theory. For example, the sudden emergence of Western conflict with Russia over the Ukraine, leading to Russia's seizure of the Crimea and its efforts to semi-detach another part of the country that it could also dominate, called into question the liberalist confidence that the threat of great-power warfare was now minimal. The prospect of increasing NATO forces and raising the alert status contradicted liberal ideas of how the world had seemed to be going.

At the same time, relations between liberalist states and China have deteriorated, with Beijing steadily increasing military, economic, and other pressures on Vietnam, as well as on several Asian democracies that are also American allies. Rising alienation between China and the USA, Japan, and the Philippines has been very clear. Disagreements over who owns various portions of the seas around China, about China's air space, and about Chinese assertions that democracy is a serious threat to the stability of the nation have all been occurring against the backdrop of China continuing the largest national military expansion and modernization effort in the world today.

The liberalist approach has also consistently failed to make major progress in Africa, despite a modicum of economic development on the continent below the Sahara. Weak and/or corrupt regimes remain common in many parts of Africa, as does the lack of democracy and security, a widespread disregard for human rights, and considerable terrorism or outright civil war.

However, perhaps the most telling development is the emergence in the democracies, particularly in the West, of profound malaise about these developments, especially in the form of a widespread reluctance to take on serious military, financial, and other burdens to promote liberalism around the world. This is apparent in the rather limited, contained, Western approach to the Arab Spring since the ousting of the Libyan government. This malaise is obvious in public opinion about sending forces to suppress serious violence, maintain peace and security, prevent serious human rights violations—the opposition to trying to militarily suppress even terribly illiberal situations (such as over four million refugees pouring out of Syria) is very substantial, and Western governments have largely reacted accordingly. At work is the combination of continuing unhappiness about the terrific impact of the recession, the lamentable results of the Afghan and Iraq Wars, and a rising Western sense that peoples elsewhere are 'not ready for' and will not fully accept the liberalist perspective.

This perspective clearly lacks a theoretical and political grip on just when and how liberalism in world affairs is to spread. It is therefore also lacking on when or why its adherents should be optimistic about the future development of international politics, and thus when and how to intensify acting effectively to promote that development. This is now close to becoming a crisis for liberalism in terms of efforts to permanently enhance global peace and security, and—until the recession is undoubtedly behind us—of efforts to return to steadily rising global economic development and prosperity.

Liberalism in practice, then, has annoying limitations as a guide because it is often internally inconsistent (see Think Point 3.1) and ineffective. For peace and security, is it best to cooperate with autocratic governments, such as on arms control agreements, or sanction and isolate them because they reject democracy and violate human rights? In approaching a difficult government like that of North Korea, is engagement such as aid, normal relations, and even foreign investment the best approach, or is it better to sustain an effort to undermine the regime via sanctions, isolation, and military threats? Which should come first in peace building: a stable, reasonably democratic government, or effective economic policies (a good tax system, slashing graft)? This was Egypt's conundrum in the Arab Spring—the USA sided with an armed forces coup as it was more likely to bring economic stability. Which should come first: democracy or decent human rights improvements (like equal treatment for women)? Why, one might consider, should citizens elsewhere approve better treatment of women if that is disparaged in their religion and culture? How will economic, human rights, and other reforms take hold without a reasonably strong democracy to legitimize them? What if no such democracy seems possible?

The oldest such inconsistency is the tension between self-determination and the need for a viable state. Creating a state for a disaffected minority often alarms other minorities within its boundaries, and such fears may be well founded, as was the case in Georgia when it became independent from Russia, and is the case in Ukraine now. Liberalism offers no ready way to resolve these situations, and little help to governments on making the relevant decisions.

There is also great difficulty for liberalist governments in deciding when to use force. Governments frequently disagree about when force is justified or how to determine the will of the international community–that is how to 'legitimize' using force. This

THINK POINT 3.1 Liberalism and the Arab Spring

Recent developments have put the liberalist perspective under great strain, developments that emerged in a relatively surprising and rapidly escalating fashion. This is particularly true of the Arab Spring, which has been an enormous disaster from a liberalist perspective. It can be interpreted in various ways:

- as demonstrating that liberalism is unpopular, unacceptable, and unappreciated in much of the world;
- as evidence that liberalism poses a serious threat to many rulers, elites, societies, and cultures—especially those who benefit from illiberal beliefs and practices—thus generating substantial but eventually futile resistance to it, or instead generating (even in liberalist societies) the loss of significant support for this way of dealing with international politics;
- as evidence that the 'natural' realist propensities of international politics are reasserting themselves and will soon displace liberalism.

Thus the Arab Spring has, almost simultaneously, displayed the impact, plus the complications, and the deficiencies of the liberalist perspective. It has demonstrated the appeal and power of liberalist values and operations among citizens. Initially, mass demonstrations displayed broad support for major elements of democracy, human rights, and economic liberalism, with outbreaks in one country provoking similar efforts in others. Clearly liberalism remains very influential in international politics, and an existential threat to non-democratic regimes.

The Arab Spring also epitomized the impact domestic political developments can have in foreign affairs, reflecting the liberalist inside-out character. Domestic upheavals have sharply altered international politics in the Middle East, with reverberations making Russia, China, Iran, and other non-democracies uneasy about possibly having to face similar developments. The Arab Spring has reflected the tremendous power of contemporary social networks and mass communications at the individual level, somewhat curbing the power of states to shape information flows and political perceptions (such as through propaganda or news management), and reflecting the power as well of elite-directed mass movements on nationalism, ethnic identity, religious solidarity, etc.

The demonstrations were initially leaderless and unorganized, lacking elaborate programmes for action or well-defined objectives, but were certainly not aimless mobs. In Libya and Syria, demonstrations coalesced into actual (though crude) fighting units that, unplanned and only partly organized, turned uprisings into ad hoc violent revolutions.

The Arab Spring also displayed the initial impact of liberal democracies in these crises. They put heavy pressure on the targeted autocratic regimes, and provided political, financial, and finally some military support for the insurgents. Liberalist norms were invoked to, in effect, declare the outlawing of violent resistance by autocratic regimes and eventually call for their ousting for doing so, typically in response to heavy pressure from the democracies' citizens. Particularly striking was how the Western military efforts in Libya were primarily led and operated by Europeans rather than Americans, displaying the broad scope of the liberalist sector of the world.

However, the Arab Spring has also showcased some of liberalism's contradictions and adverse effects. The chief difficulty has been that the liberalist perspective is heavily based on Western conceptions of democracy, free enterprise, civil rights, and human rights to which many Arab and other Middle Eastern societies either do not, or do not fully, subscribe—for instance, societies where human rights often do not include equal rights for women or homosexuals, and democracy does not mean freedom to promote any religious belief. This has been demonstrated twice in the Egyptian regimes that have emerged, in Turkey to a growing extent, as well as in Iraq, in Syria, and in Libya—in initial democratic elections all the way to extremist participation in insurrections. The Western democracies have often found themselves having to use highly complicated efforts to try to supply assistance to various governments and other parties without thereby fortifying actors hostile to liberalist practices and objectives. The Arab Spring has demonstrated the relative irrelevance of some liberalist ideas, practices, and governance, not only in the Middle East but in similar developments in Afghanistan and Pakistan.

Thus intervention to promote liberalist objectives has led not to reduction or suppression of conflict but often to its expansion—particularly domestic conflicts, which have been terribly costly and damaging not only directly but also via the resulting refugee flows and even terrorism in other countries. The activities of terrorist elements have been expanded all over the region and at least partially to Europe, Australia, the United States, and Canada. Thus far, intervention has expanded not democracy but authoritarian rule, generated greater stress on existing democracies, and frequently produced considerable anarchy. Liberalism has found it difficult to offer guidance on how to deal with these situations. The complexities have been nightmarish. For example, the USA sympathized with people in Bahrain pressing for democracy, but gave in to fear that ousting the monarchy would undermine the headquarters of the American forces there. These forces are important because they offset Iran's power and influence in the Persian Gulf. They thus help to uphold Saudi Arabia's national interests, which are deemed crucial due to the country's oil reserves. If pro-democracy elements threatened to cause instability that could disrupt the international oil situation, Western and global recovery from the 'great recession would be damaged'. It may thus seem little wonder that some analysts see the Arab Spring as less a product of liberalist ideals, norms, and practices than of Islamic fundamentalist perspectives on how to reinvigorate the Arab and Islamic World, making the Arab Spring more a danger to liberalist practices than an extension of them.

was the issue between the USA and others over the invasion of Iraq in 2003. Should taking action always be suspended when there is serious disagreement? What if there is unhappiness with a particular situation and a willingness to see force used to deal with it—but widespread reluctance to bear the costs—as is typical in serious security situations in Africa? The moral and analytical justifications for using force often conflict with political, financial, and other considerations.

Criticism poured forth when the USA, unable to gain Security Council approval for invading Iraq in 2003, did it anyway, seemingly confirming realist assertions that power and a state's interests still regularly trump international norms and the general welfare. The Bush administration was lacerated by contrasting criticisms. On the one hand, it was open to the charge that it was abandoning many central liberalist tenants: showing disdain for various multilateral agreements and international organizations, ignoring many human rights in the war on terrorism, and often putting American 'interests' ahead of international cooperation. On the other, it was also depicted as **'Wilsonian internationalism** [liberalism] on steroids' in wanting to bring democracy and a respect for human rights to Iraq (and perhaps other rogue states) at the point of a gun.

As noted earlier, a weightier criticism is that liberalism, particularly in its more forceful version, often deteriorates into an updated expression of Western imperialism, rationalizing what is really a hegemonic effort to promote actions that make the global environment more congenial for the West. Subscribers to this view see Western practices as provocative and subversive, undermining many established ways of life, and reject claims that the West is promoting universal values (Johnson 2006).

This is certainly debatable. After all, liberalism helped undermine Western colonialism and now promotes enhanced development and improved living standards around the world. Future historians may see international politics in our time as still being uplifted by a continued unfolding of the eighteenth century's democratic revolution and its attendant values. On the other hand, this means that liberalism is revolutionary: advocates of the democratic peace, for instance, are hardly status quo oriented and this is not comfortable in much of the world. Western governments and peoples are always ready, even eager, to see numerous political systems toppled and many social and economic systems radically altered. No wonder many see the liberalist effort as imperialistic (see Think Point 3.2).

! THINK POINT 3.2 Liberalism as revolutionary and a threat

In 1989, student activists, moved by the death of a former national leader who had sought reforms in China's political system and been removed from high office as a result, began demonstrating for democracy in the leading public square in Beijing, Tiananmen Square. The demonstration quickly grew and took over the square, with thousands of students sleeping/sitting in, and similar demonstrations appeared in other cities. The demonstration remained peaceful but the government eventually suppressed it violently.

The important aspects of liberalism in action were these. The demonstration attracted enormous Western media coverage almost totally in support of the students. The Communist Party leadership feared the regime would begin losing support and dissolve, and that chaos would ensue. The Western response was to condemn the suppression and institute significant sanctions, despite China having recently been practising close cooperative relations with Western countries, moving to participate more normally in international institutions and introducing capitalism and a wide open relationship (by Chinese standards) with the international economic system. Western governments were supporting an effort to alter China's political system anyway, with hostility towards the regime because it was still at variance with Western liberalism—on democracy, on human rights—and therefore treating it as somewhat illegitimate.

The incident has since made the Chinese ruling elite extremely wary of introducing Western political practices and ideals, treating them as threats to its survival, and seeing Western attitudes as imperialist and revolutionary, as interference in China's internal affairs. This spilled over into other issues. It has encouraged Chinese leaders to see the US position on Taiwan as yet another way of trying to disrupt or weaken China. It inhibits China's leaders from taking the West's liberalism seriously on its own terms. The key to the American position on Taiwan is that it is a vigorous democracy; an effort by China to invade would therefore be opposed by the USA and condemned by democracies around the world. Instead, Chinese leaders are prone, in good realist fashion, to view all this as the West trying to contain China's power and prevent its rapid rise in the international system. Each side insufficiently understands what the other's perspective is and why.

This is reinforced when globalization produces short-, or long-range, effects at odds with liberalist values, like environmental degradation from rampant economic growth, whole ways of life rudely uprooted by land seizures and other economically driven dislocations, or the rapid erosion of sovereignty and national autonomy for many countries, on many levels. For example, this contributes to the reaction against global free-trade efforts in favour of **regional trade arrangements** and **free-trade agreements** limited to only a few countries. Global negotiations to further liberalist economic agendas therefore have often been dismal failures.

There is plenty of evidence that nationalism and states remain powerfully attractive. They continue to be vehicles for evoking and conveying the most intense human feelings now in play in international politics, yet liberalism often seems to suggest that all this should be dying out. Maybe reports of their demise are greatly exaggerated.

Also disturbing is that the leading states in the North Atlantic region have actively promoted democracy, capitalism, an open international economy, and rising interdependence several times in the past. After the first such era, the military savagery of the First World War ensued. The second attempt, after that war and the arrival of Wilsonian internationalism, did not prevent the Great Depression, the rise of Fascism, and the Second World War. The third effort, in the first decades of the Cold War, was part of Western efforts to woo developing countries by offering rapid progress towards modernization. Broadly speaking, that effort also failed despite the immense efforts and resources applied. What seemed to work for a while after the Second World War was the close linkage of Western Europe, the United States, Japan, Australia, and a few other states to promote liberalism's goals in warding off the threat from the Soviet bloc. For other states things went better when governments and societies worked out for themselves why and how to start to introduce Western values and methods. Then in the years after the end of the Cold War the United States led the way in aggressively promoting liberalist elements, ultimately setting off the developments that Western societies are now uneasy about. For example, the United States plunged into a post-war campaign to rapidly Westernize Russia. It was so unsuccessful it created a political backlash; Russians condemned the campaign, based on its effects, as an American plot to ruin the country. We have been down this road before. What if elements of the Western world cannot be readily transferred but must be absorbed by others only when they wish and only at their own pace?

The best conclusion for now is to settle for ambiguity. It is too soon to say that liberalism in international politics, in theory and practice, has run its course and is on the decline. It is also too soon to say with confidence that liberalism is not headed that way but will instead survive and thrive.

KEY POINTS

- There are good reasons for optimism by adherents of liberalism—many developments are going in their preferred direction.
- However, liberalism faces challenges intellectually, with critics complaining that it is theoretically thin and out of date.
- There are annoying internal inconsistencies in liberalism that limit its utility.
- Liberalism is also criticized as just Western imperialism, or the latest attempt to remake societies from the outside, something that has failed too often.
- The future of liberalism is therefore unclear.

? QUESTIONS

1. What are the main characteristics of the liberalist orientation?
2. What are the main categories or types of liberalism in the study and conduct of international politics?
3. In what sense can liberalism be considered the dominant perspective in international politics today?
4. How do NGOs now play a role in international politics in the pursuit of liberalist objectives and values?
5. Why is liberalism relatively optimistic about the possibilities for cooperation, and for cooperation leading to significant improvements in international politics?
6. What are the main components of commercial or economic liberalism?

7. What is the democratic peace thesis and what are its implications for understanding and trying to improve international politics?
8. In what ways is liberalism often inconsistent in dealing with important issues in international politics?
9. Why do some critics see liberalism as a form of Western imperialism?
10. In what sense is liberalism revolutionary in international politics and, as such, a serious threat?

FURTHER READING

- Adler, Emanual and Barnett, Michael (1998), *Security Communities*, Cambridge: Cambridge University Press. Valuable on pluralistic security communities and other cooperative arrangements in international politics.
- Doyle, Michael (1997), *Ways of War and Peace*, London: Norton. Contains an excellent review of the foundations of democratic peace theory.
- Brown, M. E., Lynn-Jones, S. M., and Miller, S.E. (eds) (1996), *Debating the Democratic Peace*, Cambridge, MA: MIT Press. Good coverage of many elements of democratic peace theory and its alleged deficiencies.
- Ikenberry, John, G. (2000), *After Victory*, Princeton, NJ: Princeton University Press. How the USA led the way in constructing the Western community along liberalist lines during the Cold War.
- Keohane, Robert O. (1984), *After Hegemony: Cooperation and Discord in the World Political Economy*, Princeton, NJ: Princeton University Press. A good introduction to theory on hegemony in international politics, and the foundation volume on neoliberal institutionalism on cooperation in international politics.
- Kissinger, Henry (2014), *World Order*, New York: Penguin Press. Puts the future of the management of world order in a broad historical context.
- Kupchan, Charles A. (2014), 'The Normative Foundations of Hegemony and the Coming Challenge to Pax Americana', *Security Studies*, 23/2: 219–57. A striking and plausible explanation of how liberalism will eventually not dominate the management of international politics.
- Moravcsik, A. (1997), 'Taking Preferences Seriously: A Liberal Theory of International Politics', *International Organization*, 51/4: 513–53. One of the most interesting efforts to develop a theory of liberalism for international politics.
- Smith, Tony (1994), *America's Mission: The United States and the Worldwide Struggle for Democracy in the Twentieth Century*, Princeton, NJ: Princeton University Press. The US effort to promote democracy traced in detail. A strong case offered for liberal internationalism.
- Zacher, Mark W. and Matthew, Richard A. (1995), 'Liberal International Theory: Common Threads, Divergent Strands', in Charles Kegley, Jr (ed.), *Controversies in International Relations Theory*, New York: St Martins Press 107–50. Pulls together many aspects of the liberalist perspective.

IMPORTANT WEBSITE

- **http:nobelprize.org/nobel_prizes/peace/articles/doyle/index.html** This is a link to Michael Doyle's essay on 'Liberal Internationalism: Peace, War and Democracy'.

Visit the Online Resource Centre that accompanies this book for lots of interesting additional material: www.oxfordtextbooks.co.uk/orc/collins4e/

4

Historical Materialism

Eric Herring

Chapter Contents

Reader's Guide

This chapter begins with an overview of the social scientific, philosophical, and political dimensions of historical materialism (HM). This overview is followed by an elaboration of what HM involves, including its diversity, value, and potential but avoidable pitfalls. Key HM concepts are set out and used to show how capitalism generally and in its recent neoliberal form aim to generate insecurity for labour and security for capital. Rather than being a narrow approach to security that focuses on economics, at its best HM is a holistic approach that provides a way of putting into perspective and relating the many components of security. It goes on to explore the relationships between HM and approaches to security in a wider context (realism, liberalism, social constructivism, and gender) and then to various perspectives on security (securitization and the sectoral approach, peace studies, Critical Security Studies, and human security). Accompanying the text are Think Point 4.1 on using HM to understand arms production and the arms trade, and Think Point 4.2 on using HM to understand the connections between development and security. The conclusion provides an overall assessment of the contribution of HM to the scholarship and politics of security and insecurity.

An overview of historical materialism

Historical materialism (HM) is rightly seen as one of the key paradigms (systems of thought) of the social in its broadest sense alongside **realism** and **liberalism**. This chapter treats HM as a particular version of **Marxism** (the system of thought based on the ideas of Karl Marx and Friedrich Engels in the mid- to late nineteenth century) that also tends to draw on other theories, and that takes into account subsequent historical changes that require consideration of how they relate to Marxist ideas as initially conceived. HM has three dimensions—the social scientific, the philosophical, and the political (Therborn 2008: ch. 3)—which will be considered in turn.

First, some scholars approach HM as **social science**, meaning that they assume that fact and value (judgements of worth such as right and wrong) can be separated sufficiently to generate theoretically grounded claims that can be tested against evidence. In other words, description (what is), explanation (why it is), and prescription (what should be) are treated as separable. As social science, HM offers analyses of how particular forms of the ownership and control of the production of goods and services shape the emergence of classes, how related forms of politics, the social, and the individual develop, and how conflicts between classes generate change. At its most useful, HM is not only about economics: it does not assume that the economic drives everything else, and considers how this all operates at all levels from the individual to the global. The 'historical' part of HM refers to the indispensability of the **empirical**, both in terms of the facts of particular phenomena, such as wage levels, but just as importantly in terms of the character of entire phases of world history. The generalizations of HM are intended to be specific to those particular phases rather than universal (applying to all historical eras). To put it another way, HM argues that 'every mode of production has a specific systemic logic of its own' (Wood 1995: 4). The 'material' part of HM refers mainly to its focus on the **class** and productive basis of societies, which entail entire ways of living and being. In this context, material does not refer merely to objects or money as it usually does in everyday speech. The material in HM also refers to the social reality that constrains and enables what people think, say, and do, and it contains potential new social realities. From this perspective, **discourse** is not just spoken or written language: it is also physical actions, including the creation and use of objects such as tools. Hence discourse and matter (the natural world such as oil) combine to produce social meaning, and the social meaning that results combines structurally and relationally to constitute the material. Where the discursive does not structure social reality in any substantial way, it remains in the realm of the ideal, such as when ideas are advocated but fail to be adopted or acted upon more widely. HM contrasts with approaches that focus more narrowly on discourse as language.

Second, as philosophy, HM involves a commitment to the systematic use of reason in order to grasp the nature of social reality, for example, that the development of **capitalism** (defined in some detail later) required the development of ideas of the rightness and naturalness of private property. HM is interested in how changes in particular productive systems and the inequalities of **power** associated with them are intimately connected to the rise and fall of discourses. HM is particularly well suited to being grounded in the philosophical approach known as **critical realism**. This is not the same as the realism depicted in Chapter 2 of this book, because that realism is a specific social scientific theory of world politics that HM rejects. Critical realism 'relates epistemological relativism (we can know the social only indirectly through our interpretation of it) to ontological realism (there is a powerfully influential social reality that includes but is much more than our knowledge claims about it) via judgemental **rationalism** (knowledge claims can be tested against social reality, though always in an indirect, interpreted, and fallible way)' (Herring and Stokes 2011a: 10–11). The critical realist notion that any existing social structure contains within it potential for change has particular resonance with HM, as HM analyses how tensions and contradictions in existing class relations are motors for social change. This lends itself to a view of the world as inherently dynamic and changing.

This philosophical interest in the potential for change links to the third dimension of HM—namely, the political. For many, HM is irredeemably tainted by having been the official ideology of the **Cold War** communist states and in particular the extremely repressive regimes of the Soviet Union under Joseph Stalin and China under Mao Zedong. Both regimes were directly responsible for the deaths of millions of their citizens. It still is the official ideology of China and its ruling communist party. However, HM analysis can be connected to a completely different politics that rejects such repression. Furthermore, HM provides a unique perspective on the exploitation and alienation that are inherent to capitalism. The politics of HM can involve serious commitment to the human rights espoused by liberals but with much more understanding of the role of class relations in generating human rights violations and resistance to them. Such thinking has been an important part of what has been called the global justice, anti-capitalist, anti-globalization, or alter-globalization (alternative globalization) movement (Wall 2005; Barker et al. 2013). Since 2001, this movement has held the World Social Forum, which defines itself as a space 'of groups and movements of civil society opposed to neoliberalism and to domination of the world by capital and any form of imperialism' (World Social Forum 2002). The global justice movement is diverse and decentralized. Many in that movement see hope for the practical expression of their ideas in the rise since the early 1990s of Latin American left-wing social movements, political parties, and elected governments committed to redistributing wealth to the poor and resisting US domination and the subordination of their economies to foreign corporations (Rodríguez-Garavito et al. 2008). It has developed new momentum in the form of the Occupy protests in response to the crisis in the global financial system since 2007. Talk and some action regarding the nationalization of banks, shutting down tax havens, and introducing stricter financial regulation by states went from being wild radicalism to mainstream common sense in 2008, although the reversal of **neoliberalism** (defined in the next section of this chapter) is limited thus far. If anything, neoliberals have made headway in arguing that the only way out of this crisis is even more neoliberalism (even though, as critics argue, neoliberalism was central to causing the crisis). Without a clear alternative to capitalism or route to getting there, the global justice movement, while working on those issues, is also concerned with how some of capitalism's more extreme manifestations can be reined in. HM thinking is generally impressed by capitalism's ability to mobilize human productive capacities as well as being critical of its production of insecurity in the forms of poverty, inequality, and environmental degradation, and such thinking can contribute to the work of the global justice movement.

KEY POINTS

- Historical materialism (HM) has social scientific, philosophical, and political dimensions. HM argues that particular forms of the ownership and control of the production of goods and services result in related class conflicts at many levels from the local to the global.
- HM sees underlying systems for producing goods and services and the class relations that go with them as playing a powerful role in the emergence of ideas and in generating social change. HM is usually but not necessarily associated with the political goal of transcending capitalism.
- The framework offered by HM provides a way of putting security issues in context and analysing them holistically: it provides a way of understanding their meaning and significance.

Capitalism and neoliberalism: insecurity for labour, security for capital

Up to this point, this chapter has been using a very simplified version of HM which only hints at its content, value, diversity, and potential pitfalls. This section of the chapter takes a closer look, so that the ground is prepared for Think Point 4.1 on HM, arms production, and the arms trade. It does so by setting out some key HM concepts and using them to explain how capitalism and neoliberalism seek to promote security for capital and insecurity for labour. Even this closer look is a mere glimpse of what HM has to offer: the guide to further reading and the suggested web links at the end of this chapter offer routes towards deepening your understanding.

HM as it is defined in this chapter seeks to understand the world not via static abstractions and timeless generalizations but in specific historical epochs (currently the capitalist epoch) with a focus on how change occurs. For HM, the contemporary context is one of **imperialism** (relations of domination and subordination across societies), which connects the global order to particular forms of state–society relations in class terms (Rupert and Smith 2002). In the realist and liberal paradigms, capitalism is seen as involving private property, the profit motive, competition, and freedom of contract, with this system guaranteed by the state and international organizations. HM agrees with this at one level but disputes the notion that this is a free, just, mutually beneficial, and timeless system in tune with human nature. The representation of aspects of economics by realists and liberals as private (and hence somehow non-political) is regarded by HM as serving the interests of capitalists by allowing them to retain unelected, and for the most part unaccountable, control. Similarly, **exploitation** in the sense HM uses it refers to the fact that workers are paid less than the value that results from their labour and do not retain control of the remainder of that value: this surplus value, as it is called in HM, goes to the capitalist, who accumulates it as capital to spend or reinvest. Hence the concept of exploitation is used here both to describe something and also to make a negative value judgement on it. As for the notion that workers are free to work, HM points out that workers do not own the means of production and so are forced to sell their labour to capitalists who have the 'right' to buy it at less than the full value that results from it or even not at all. This produces extremes of inequality, with vast numbers of people suffering and potentially going to an early grave because they are unable to sell their labour for much. This is a profound kind of insecurity, and the concepts HM offers can deepen our understanding of this structural violence and human (in)security. This is because it does not depoliticize explanations of why these phenomena exist or treat them merely as a product of individual failure, and it is linked to a politics of trying to find alternative social orders that would overcome them. This lack of control by most people of their labour, in a context in which this is represented as natural and inevitable, is defined as **alienation**, and people often feel this alienation emotionally, as they spend most of their lives doing work they do not believe in just to survive. This connects with the human security notion of freedom to live life in dignity (see Chapter 10).

Capitalism was for Marx in these respects—imperialism, exploitation, alienation with enormous amounts of inequality, and human suffering in the midst of enough for all—a repulsive way of running a society, even though he was also impressed by its unleashing of human productive capabilities. He thought that a just alternative would be a communist system—that is, one in which workers collectively owned and controlled the economy. In 1875, he set out as a principle of communism: 'From each according to his ability, to each according to his needs' (Marx 1875: ch 1, n.p.). He thought that, in a communist society, people would want to work at whatever they could contribute to the collective good rather than doing what work they had to do in order to be paid, and that what one received would vary depending on what one needed. These ideas go against most of the 'common sense' of our current system of individualism, alienated labour, and private reward for 'competing' successfully (on the basis of what is in reality unequal ability and unequal opportunity—see Cohen 2009). However, Marx (1859) argued that the common sense of any age is to a great extent a product of its productive material circumstances:

> The mode of production in material life conditions the general character of the social, political, and spiritual processes of life. It is not the consciousness of men that determines their existence, but on the contrary, it is their social existence which determines their consciousness.
>
> Marx (1859: preface, n.p.)

This could be interpreted as a rigid separation of the productive material and ideational with the former straightforwardly determining the latter. However, this would not be representative of Marx's work overall or of contemporary HM. Instead, HM explores the ways in which they are mutually constitutive (that is, not separate from each other and then shaping each other but fundamentally bound up with what they are). The point of continuing relevance is that willing socially valuable work, from this point of view, which in a capitalist era might seem absurdly unrealistic, would, Marx thought, seem natural in a communist one. Even in the capitalist era there are numerous examples of willing work without material reward in the voluntary sector that might suggest such possibilities on a wider scale, and also of cooperatives (businesses owned and controlled by workers). In a market relationship, the rational thing to do is to give as little as possible in return for as much as possible. From the point of view of community, this is a rather obnoxious way to behave—in a community, you give (whatever it may be—time, money, skill) because giving feels right and because you have a general expectation that others in the community, and not necessarily the person to whom you have given, will give not only to you but to others. Furthermore, the idea of to each according to their needs has significant purchase even in the present world order, as indicated by the existence of some, if variable, welfare rights.

In a capitalist system, corporations prioritize control and then profit. For HM, arms production and arms trading are basically a militarized manifestation of this

! THINK POINT 4.1 Historical materialism, arms production, and the arms trade

Some HM research argues that taxpayer subsidies to arms companies mean that the arms trade is not nearly as profitable for the taxpayer (as opposed to the arms companies) as it is usually made out to be, that there are more effective ways to create jobs, that arms sales are a weak instrument of influence, and that the increasing tendency for the parts of weapons to be produced in different countries means that there is no independent military-industrial base anyway, especially for countries other than the United States (Mayhew 2005). Realists tend to neglect these points and see the arms trade as a rational instrument of the state to advance the national interest strategically and economically: it is about profit and jobs, strengthening friendly states, gaining influence over other states, or maintaining an independent military-industrial base.

Liberals usually favour voluntary or legal codes of conduct as a way of discouraging sales of weapons that are likely to be used for external aggression or internal repression, or that waste the money of poorer countries. It is often pointed out that these codes of conduct have been violated by liberal democratic states and are both vague and weakly monitored (Saferworld 2007). HM scholars accept this but point out that there would be a deeper problem even if codes of conduct were operating effectively by the criteria of those who created them. Specifically, codes of conduct promote the idea that there is a legitimate arms trade that is beneficial in relation to security, the economy, and society. In contrast, HM scholars argue that the so-called legitimate arms trade has a range of pernicious effects. For example, they argue that it encourages **militarism**, which is the belief that **militarization** is a good thing in itself and preferable to alternative means of achieving goals, even when those alternative means are more effective (Bacevich 2006; Stavrianakis et al. 2012). Militarism therefore can also involve turning to military means without serious consideration of non-military alternatives.

In his farewell address in 1961, US President Dwight D. Eisenhower warned of the dangers posed by the US 'military-industrial complex', by which he meant coalitions of military and industrial interests that promoted their own sectional interests in government policy-making at the expense of national interests. Instead, HM treats the arms trade as a much bigger problem of militarized capitalism in which there is a revolving door between, and overlap of, elites within government, the military, arms industries, and academia who conduct the arms trade in their class interest. Furthermore, this militarized capitalism operates at a global level as part of a hierarchical and imperial capitalist order, with the arms industries not separate from the state but deeply integrated into it as part of national and transnational capitalist elites who profit from arms sales despite their costs through subsidies, war, and diversion of resources from other purposes (Melman 2003; CAAT 2005; Stavrianakis 2010).

(see Think Point 4.1). The logical function of humanity and the physical environment in such a system is to be mobilized to generate profit for capitalists in ways that do not challenge their control. This may involve pressuring people to work harder and for longer hours for the lowest wages possible and inducing them to use their non-working hours spending those wages and borrowing when the money runs out. When people have the things they need, wants are created through advertising and wants must not be satisfied through purchasing: more wants must be created all the time, and relations of all kinds must be monetized as far as possible. Capitalism has an inherent drive towards turning previously non-monetary social relations into monetary relations (**commodification**) and the actual functioning of items has, for capitalism, no inherent value: the purpose of goods is to generate profit. Capitalism involves many contradictions (social relations that pull in opposite directions at the same time) (Harvey 2014). For example, on the one hand, the state has a vital role in preserving freedom for capitalists, but the needs of the state may require it to reduce that freedom to protect its own interests. Another is that capitalism involves pressure to push down wages (thus increasing the surplus value from production) but also to increase wages (thus increasing demand for what is produced and hence profit from sales).

Among HM scholars, there is considerable disagreement about the likelihood or desirability of revolution (fundamental, possibly rapid, transformation of capitalism into another system) or how revolution relates to reform (incremental modification of class relations that leaves their fundamental elements intact). There is also disagreement about the extent to which conscious political efforts can bring about revolution or whether it would occur mainly through the objective working out of class conflict. In its determinist form, HM claims to have discovered the **objective** laws of history that are unfolding towards the inevitable transition from capitalism to communism. In its more sophisticated and open form focused on class conflicts and contradictions within capitalism, HM argues that conscious human agency and social structures interact in ways that leave open many possible directions. See Think Point 4.2 for an overview

THINK POINT 4.2 Using historical materialism to understand the development–security nexus

In all the criticism of capitalism that HM involves, it is easy to forget that HM scholars see capitalism as having progressive as well as reactionary dimensions in relation to development. For example, capitalism, especially in its phase where territories across the world were subjected to direct imperial rule, has involved enormous brutality in terms of physical violence and the shattering of indigenous societies. From Marx's perspective, this was negative in terms of its human cost but also positive in terms of being necessary to take those societies from their pre-capitalist feudal systems (with ordinary people bound through custom to be subservient to tribal and other leaders) through capitalism as a process that might lead to socialism (state control of the means of production) and possibly then to communism (popular control of the means of production). Even if one does not take a determinist or teleological line, one can still see respects in which capitalism has been progressive in terms of releasing human creative potential and producing goods and services that are life enhancing.

The focal point of debate in much of contemporary HM analysis is whether realist and liberal approaches to the development–security nexus legitimize an unequal world in which low levels of material welfare in the South is the norm for the long term and in which the North can use violence if necessary to enforce that inequality. Older realist thinking considers how insecurity can trigger development through the mobilization of resources to deal with threats. Similarly, current neoliberal thinking is that insecurity, at least for labour, is vital for development. However, in most contemporary realist and liberal analysis, insecurity prevents development and lack of development generates insecurity. This has led to the mantra 'You can't have development without security and you can't have security without development'. The questions that then arise are whether it is possible to promote development that leads to security, whether you need security first, or whether you can and must promote both at the same time. Realists look for ways rationally to promote the national interest in this situation, while, for liberals, states, international organizations, and non-governmental organizations need to find ways to promote their common values in relation to these issues. HM's major contribution to thinking on the development–security nexus is to go beyond this narrow analysis of the interaction of two policy sectors into a global and historical perspective. HM scholars argue for a fundamental change in the frame of reference from an imperial one serving the interests of the global North to a postcolonial one (Barkawi and Laffey 2006). In such a frame of reference, Security Studies is not based on the question of what the global North should do to deal with the problems posed by the global South; the problem of development is not assumed to be the global South's lack of the global North's qualities; the role of the South in the development of the North is recognized; and opposition (including armed opposition) to the global North by actors in the global South is not automatically assumed to be illegitimate (for more on postcolonialism, see Chapter 9).

of how HM scholars have responded to the evolving connections between development and security.

It may even be that capitalism will for the indefinite future find a way to reform and indeed change so dramatically that its positive dimensions overwhelmingly eclipse its negative ones. Capitalism may turn out to be manageable in a way that is environmentally sustainable and able to deliver high living standards and work perceived as fulfilling for virtually all. Or it may turn out catastrophically in environmental and human terms. Ruling out either of these outcomes and insisting on the inevitable triumph of communism is dogmatism (over-confidently sticking to a claim, interpreting facts to fit, and not taking alternatives seriously).

Other pitfalls to be avoided are reductionism (insisting that all phenomena are really about one thing, such as claiming that all aspects of security can be explained as forms of class conflict) or left functionalism (insisting that everything that the capitalist ruling class does is in its interests—such as economic sanctions on Iraq up to 2003, the invasion of Iraq in 2003, the way the occupation was conducted, and then the agreement made in 2008 that US forces should withdraw). These weaknesses are not inherently part of HM; careful scholarship can avoid them.

In sum, capitalism can be defined as a historically specific, class-based system of market competition in which people are coerced economically into being exploited as wage labourers by capitalists, with this system being underpinned by, yet in some ways operating as a sphere distinct from, politics, the law, and armed coercion (Wood 1995, 2005).

Since the 1970s, capitalism has moved towards **neoliberalism**, that is, the idea that the highest principle of rational and just social organization is individuals pursuing their own interests in global competitive capitalist free markets. At the heart of this process of neoliberalization has been a shift in power and wealth from labour to capital, as the power of organized labour was seen by leading Western capitalists to be the main restriction on the ability of capital to make profit (Harvey 2007). Labour had to be made insecure to force it to accept lower wages and more flexible working conditions. The global financial crisis since 2008 has been of a different kind; with the power of labour much reduced since the 1980s, consumption of goods and services from which capitalists could profit was fuelled by unsustainable debt. The continuing crisis reflects a different problem for capital: the power of finance capital now far outweighs the power of industrial capital (Harvey 2014), which is why we hear so much talk even from capitalists of the need to re-balance Western economies towards industry. The process of neoliberalization is: inherently incomplete, because there can be no fully free self-correcting markets (in practice, all markets must be managed and regulated); hybrid and diverse, because neoliberalism must interact with different social contexts; contradictory, because regulation both underpins and limits markets; and unstable, because it produces crises of commodification and regulation (Brenner et al. 2010; Herring 2011). Capitalism in general and neoliberalism in particular revels in the idea of insecurity as a positive force and seeks to create it—insecurity produces competition, and competition produces efficiency and sorts out the successes from the failures. In practice, capitalists, especially the bigger ones, tend to be very successful at securing themselves from competition by relying on state subsidy and protection and tax avoidance on a massive scale. Precarious lives of insecurity are reserved as far as possible for labour.

KEY POINTS

- Central concepts within HM include imperialism, surplus value, exploitation, commodification, and contradictions, as well as class.
- These concepts help HM to develop its argument that lack of ownership and control of the means of production is a fundamental cause of life-threatening insecurity for huge numbers of people, even as capital makes itself more secure.
- HM goes beyond superficial explanations of the global financial crisis since 2008 by showing that the fundamental dynamic is one in which power has shifted from industrial capital towards finance capital, as consumer demand was propped up by debt compensating for low wages. It shows that this continuing crisis flowed from the success of neoliberal moves to transfer power and wealth from labour to capital since the 1980s.

This brief outline already indicates many connections with security defined broadly to include all threats to the survival of lives, livelihoods, and valued ways of life. Even if security is defined only narrowly as actual or perceived freedom from violence and threats of violence for political purposes, HM has as much to say about why such threats arise, whose interests they serve, the legitimacy of the threats and violence used to try to secure those interests, and how change might come about to close down the space for threats and violence. In terms of scholarship, the field of Security Studies in the West is seen in HM terms to have been created to service dominant Western capitalist class interests in the Cold War (there was almost no academic Security Studies in the communist countries or in the less industrialized world). Hence HM was on the opposite side of the class divide from HM scholars in the West. It meant that, during the Cold War, the concept of security was seen by HM scholars as politically suspect. HM scholars were divided over their attitude to the Cold War communist states but were seen by some realists and liberals to be on the side of those states. In this atmosphere, HM was unlikely to be central to Security Studies even as it managed to be one of the three key paradigms of **international relations** (IR) scholarship. Furthermore, HM scholars have considered the concept of security to be inferior as a focal point of research in comparison with HM's own already well-developed concepts, which they see as necessary for understanding the issues that are supposedly the preserve of Security Studies. However, in the post-Cold War period, Security Studies has become more diverse, with more HM security analysis being published. The next section of this chapter elaborates on the relationship between HM, (in)security, and Security Studies.

Historical materialism, (in)security, and Security Studies: an alternative, not just a critique

This section examines how HM relates to perspectives that put (in)security in a wider context (realism, liberalism, **constructivism**, and gender) and then relates it to key approaches to security (securitization and the sectoral approach, peace studies, Critical Security Studies, and **human security**). All of these subjects have their own chapters in this book. The discussion below illustrates the point that HM is not simply a critique of existing approaches. Instead, it provides an alternative analytical framework of its own.

(In)security in wider context

Realism

HM has something in common with realism in relation to the notion that there are discernible regularities in human society. HM sees these regularities as historically specific to each mode of production, whereas realists are more likely to represent them as essentially timeless, even if they change in specific content. Realists are also concerned with the operation of these contextual regularities in relation to the power of nation states and with how to ensure its effective exercise by them. For example, realists such as John Mearsheimer (2005) argued that the US-led invasion of Iraq was against US interests and motivated by the ideological wishful thinking of neo-conservatives (those who wished to use US military and other power resources to overthrow dictatorships and to establish liberal democracies and less regulated capitalist economies open to global capital). HM accepts that states are important but argues that states represent not national interests—something that it treats as a ruling-class ideological myth—but class interests, with the nature of classes and their interests being peculiar to each epoch. As it happens, E. H. Carr, one of the founding figures of realism, accepted aspects of this critique, a point missed by realists generally. Carr (1981) wrote of the notion of there being a harmony of interests between classes:

> It is the natural assumption of a prosperous and privileged class, whose members have a dominant voice in the community and are therefore naturally prone to identify its interest with their own. . . . The doctrine of the harmony of interests thus serves as an ingenious moral device invoked, in perfect sincerity, by privileged groups in order to justify and maintain their dominant position.
>
> Carr (1981: 80)

Carr was using the term 'class' in the more general sense of social class (the hierarchical stratification of society), in comparison with HM's more specific use of **class** as process and relationship which animates any specific **mode of production** (way of producing, distributing, and exchanging goods and services, including the wider social relations associated with that, such as ideas about the meaning of freedom, individuality, and so on) (see Wood 1995: ch. 3). Advocates of HM want to assist the effective exercise of a particular state's power only if they see that state as representing working-class interests, a situation that does not usually exist in the capitalist world. HM scholars do understand that social class is important (including for feelings of dignity to which human beings attach a great deal of value), and that class is a great deal more complex than a simple capitalist ruling class–working class distinction (for example, when the pension fund investments of workers mean that they are to a limited extent **capitalists** themselves). What they reject is the idea that the only form of class that matters is social class, and they focus predominantly on class in relation to the process of exploitation and capital accumulation.

Liberalism

Liberalism involves a belief, shared with HM, in progress and reason. Liberalism is grounded in a commitment to the idea of individuals with freedoms (including the right to private property enforced by states), with restrictions on their liberties only to the extent necessary to protect other individuals. These freedoms are nowadays couched in universal terms (applying to everyone). Liberals relate this to security in terms of the creation, defence, and extension of an international society, defined as the existence of shared **norms** and practices around the survival of diversity within universal values and also complex interdependence (mutual dependence and a high level of connectedness) that encourages peace by making war less valuable as a means of achieving political goals. The most prominent activist HM scholar since the 1960s, Noam Chomsky (1973), argues that liberal ideals are actually anti-capitalist in origin:

> With the development of industrial capitalism, a new and unanticipated system of injustice, it is libertarian socialism that has preserved and extended the radical humanist message of the Enlightenment and the classical liberal ideals that were perverted into an ideology to sustain the emerging social order. In fact, on the very same assumptions that led classical liberalism to oppose the intervention of the state in social life, capitalist social relations are also intolerable.
>
> Chomsky (1973: 156)

HM points out that the international society that contemporary liberals value rests on a capitalist system in which most people do not control or own the means of production. This means that they are usually free in terms of not being slaves (owned by their employers) but are forced to sell their labour if they are not to starve or live in poverty: this lack of freedom is not named as such in contemporary liberalism. In its most sophisticated forms, HM rejects **teleology** (the notion that history inevitably involves overall progress in a single direction) while arguing that there is the possibility of progress towards a more humane world in various ways and that action can be taken to try to bring it about (Wood 1995: ch. 5).

Social constructivism

Social constructivism is not actually a theory of security. It is more a general approach to understanding social meaning. Its central premise is that meaning is created inter-subjectively—that is, as a collective human product of interpretation of words and actions. Hence, instead of taking social reality for granted (such as a particular way of thinking about terrorism), it looks at how social reality is produced through human interaction, so that it appears commonsensical rather than a specific interpretation that could be replaced by others. Social constructivists are particularly interested in challenging the idea that security is about actors with settled identities acting to secure their existence (such as Pakistan building nuclear weapons to deter attack by India). Instead, they are interested in how identity is produced by actions in the name of security (such as Pakistan's building of nuclear weapons and the claims to justify them as being a bid to establish a particular identity for Pakistan by acting out that identity and getting others to act as if that identity is natural). HM accepts that meaning is socially constructed, but it also offers a particular substantive theory of each mode of production (in the current era, capitalism) as a structured process in which objective conditions and subjective meanings are mutually constitutive.

Gender

Gender is also not a theory of security or indeed a theory of anything. It is an issue that may be approached from numerous different theoretical standpoints. HM goes beyond treating class and gender as two separate categories that interact to an exploration of how particular modes of production can result in constructions of gender identities and relations that are functional for those modes of production. HM analysis shows that, while capitalism can profit from gendered oppression, such oppression is not necessary to capitalism and conflicts with capitalism's ideology of legally equal individuals. The implication of this is that capitalism is compatible with gender equality. However, women will continue to suffer class exploitation, an exploitation for the most part concealed by the process of women selling their labour for a wage because the appropriation by capitalists of the surplus value that results from women's wage labour is not usually perceived to be exploitation. The same general arguments apply to other forms of identity-based oppression and their relationships to capitalism (racial, ethnic, religious, and so on) (Wood 1995: ch. 9). Hence, far from focusing on the politics of class to the exclusion of the politics of identity, HM offers unique insights into identity, oppression, and **emancipation**.

Perspectives on Security Studies

The sectoral approach and securitization

The sectoral and securitization approaches have been developed together. Barry Buzan, Ole Wæver, and Jaap de Wilde (1998) represented security as having military, economic, environmental, societal, and political sectors, and this is reflected in the organization of the middle section of this book. HM's claim to be a better way of thinking about security lies in its holistic approach. In other words, instead of treating them as if they are five separate sectors, HM treats the supposedly separate sectors as making most sense when examined together. Buzan and colleagues also see Security Studies as having global, non-regional subsystemic, regional, and local levels, and they argue that the referent object (that which is being secured) of military security is usually the state. These claims mean that their work is much more compatible within the realist and to a lesser extent the liberal paradigms than the HM paradigm: the focus is on states, the political and economic are treated as distinct from each other, and class (whether national or transnational) as a referent is not part of the picture. The same can be said of their proposal of the categories of non-political, political, and security issues. Buzan et al. have also developed the concepts of securitization and desecuritization: instead of taking at face value whatever is currently labelled a security issue, they examine how issues become labelled that way (**securitized**) and how they cease to be labelled that way (desecuritized). Furthermore, they recommend that, for something to be categorized as a security issue, it should threaten survival and require urgent and exceptional political action, and so they see security as a label that is overused. These (de)securitization ideas could be adapted for use within HM. Putting it more strongly, (de)securitization could be understood much better if the sectoral approach were replaced by HM's holistic framework.

Peace studies

The well-established field of peace studies is geared towards the promotion of positive peace (harmonious, fulfilling social relations) as well as negative peace (absence of violence). It seeks to expose what Johan Galtung (1969) called **'structural violence'** (deaths and suffering caused by the way society is organized so that huge numbers of people lack the means necessary to avoid starvation, preventable illness, and so on). Its methods are social scientific and lean towards the empirical more than the theoretical, and it has an impressive track record of involvement in developing and implementing practical solutions to security problems, often at local level. HM shares with peace studies this opposition to structural violence, and provides a theoretically grounded argument as to why capitalism and related class relations are inherently structurally violent. Furthermore, many left-wing political activists whose thinking is grounded in HM engage in the kind of practical peace building that is central to peace studies. HM has some more theoretical and more revolutionary elements within it, while peace studies has more atheoretical, liberal, and reformist elements. That said, there is also extensive overlap between the two. Where HM has an important advantage is in its understanding of how the civil society actors on which peace studies to a great extent depends for progressive action can be implicated in the structural violence of capitalism. They do so when they function to subordinate people to the capitalist market by propagating and obscuring market-oriented values and subjectivity. Civil society can be a valuable counterweight to oppression. However, this is despite its origins in the privatization and depoliticization of capitalist market discipline (Wood 1995: ch. 8). This can be seen when civil society actors focus on particular cases of irresponsible or insufficiently regulated arms trading and thus implicitly legitimize the supposedly responsible capitalist market in arms dominated by the USA, Russia, Germany, France, and the UK, as well as China (see Think Point 4.1).

Critical Security Studies

HM is much less prominent in Critical Security Studies (CSS) than would be expected from the fact that HM is central to the origins of the critical theory on which much of CSS draws. It is difficult to find a piece of CSS scholarship that does not refer to Robert Cox's classic essay 'Social Forces, States and World Orders: Beyond International Relations Theory' published in *Millennium* in 1981 and republished with a postscript in 1985 in Robert O. Keohane (ed.), *Neorealism and its Critics*. However, what is generally missed is that the critical theory Cox proposes in this essay is explicitly an HM one, an argument he sets out at length. A focus on discourse as language to the exclusion of historically located assessment of class conflict is not what he sees as critical theory. He concludes his postscript as follows (Cox 1985: 248–9; see also Cammack 2007):

> There is a structuralist Marxism which . . . has analogies to structural realism, not in the use to which theory is put but in its conception of the nature of knowledge. There is a determinist tradition . . . which purports to reveal the laws of motion of history. And there is a historicist Marxism that rejects the notion of objective laws of history and focuses upon class struggle as the heuristic model for the understanding of structural change. It is obviously in the last of these Marxist currents that this writer feels most comfortable. . . . [A]s things stand in the complex world of Marxism, he prefers to be identified simply as a historical materialist.
>
> Cox (1985: 248–9)

Despite occasional positive references to Marxism, CSS is at the very least predominantly **post-Marxist** (a perspective which claims to draw on but also to have transcended Marxism). Indeed, most of CSS is so post-Marxist as to be non-Marxist: what lingers are commitments to change and emancipation (freeing people from the constraints that prevent them from living full lives) but with little understanding of how capitalism shuts down or opens up spaces for emancipation. For example, Karin Fierke's survey study Critical Approaches to International Security (2007) has no entry in the index for class or capital or neoliberalism and few mentions of Marx. It is structured around the concepts of change, identity, production of danger, trauma, human insecurity, immanent critique, and emancipation. Scholarship that approaches CSS from a social constructivist and linguistic discursive perspective is valuable, but CSS imposes a severe limitation on itself by mostly failing to consider the implications of capitalism and its neoliberal variant for security and emancipation. Furthermore, in focusing on individuals, CSS underplays the potential for collective emancipatory agency (Blakeley 2013).

Human security

Interest in the notion of human security has grown rapidly in the post-Cold War period. Its focus on ensuring freedom from fear, want, and indignity for individuals, social groups, and humanity as a whole gives it some appeal to peace studies and CSS scholars, whereas securitization scholars tend to argue for the retention of a focus on states (Buzan 2004a). The human security agenda looks very much like peace studies in its focus on structural as well as physical violence (although some proponents of this sub-field focus only on the latter), on its empirical rather than theoretical methods, and on practical reforms. People are often insecure because of repression by their own state, neglect by a functioning state, or the state being willing but unable to provide security. These are all powerful reasons for not focusing on the security of states and for not assuming that, if the state is secure, so are the people who live within its borders.

From an HM point of view, the idea of human security can be used in a progressive way to challenge repression, structural violence, and the prioritization of states over people. But HM also alerts the observer to the possibility that the idea of human security can be an ideological weapon of dominant capitalist actors (Bilgin and Morton 2002; Gruffydd Jones 2008). Specifically, human security can be used to frame poverty and violence in states of the **global South** (the part of the world that consumes minimally and in which many of the people are marginalized, uninsured, policed, and repressed) as having purely internal causes with no blame attached to the **global North** (the part of the world that has high consumption levels, is deeply integrated into capitalism, and securitizes the global South). It can then be used to justify imperial intervention by the North in Southern 'weak' or **'failed' states** (states that cannot or will not meet the basic needs of most of their population). In other words, this intervention is supposedly for the benefit of the people of the South but can turn out to be mainly for the benefit of the capitalist ruling class of the North and South. The concept of human security and the related one of human development can be used as part of the resistance to capitalist class domination rather than being an instrument of it: which role it plays will depend on the contingencies of particular struggles (Herring 2011).

KEY POINTS

- HM has some aspects in common with realism, liberalism, and social constructivism but offers something distinctive in having as its central focus analysis of class conflict within capitalism as a historically specific phenomenon.
- The notion that there are separate sectors of security that shape each other is challenged by HM's holistic approach, which regards these 'sectors' as fundamentally part of each other.
- HM sees capitalism itself as involving structural violence and sees the idea of human security as potentially being employed either by dominant capitalist actors to justify policies which reinforce that structural violence, or by those opposing that structural violence.
- Capitalism and its neoliberal variant are based on insecurity for workers in relation to their access to the means of production, and on the exploitation of workers when they do have access to them. Workers must try to sell their labour competitively to survive or not live in poverty. All of this is obscured by liberalism as the freedom to work.
- While CSS tends to neglect its HM roots, some scholars within CSS are drawing on HM to analyse major contemporary security issues such as state terrorism, the arms trade, and energy security.
- During the Cold War, Security Studies and HM scholars mostly viewed each other with suspicion politically. However, in the post-Cold War period, the diversification of Security Studies is resulting in an increased role for HM ideas.

KEY POINTS

- Some versions of HM suffer from a variety of weaknesses such as claiming to have uncovered the objective laws of history with communist revolution as the inevitable outcome, explaining everything as being about class struggle, or interpreting everything that capitalists do as serving the interests of capitalism.
- These weaknesses are not necessarily part of HM: they are avoidable.
- The contribution of HM to understanding the various connections between security and development illustrates the argument that HM is a crucial resource.

Conclusion

The key figure in the founding of CSS, Ken Booth (2007: 197), has stated with regard to class: 'in what is supposed to be a post-Marxist age this is a much-ignored referent, despite massive life-threatening and life-determining insecurity being the direct result of poverty' (see also Booth 2007: 49–56). As Booth (2005a: 261) has also commented: 'The Marxian tradition offers a deep mine of ideas that are especially useful for thinking about ideology, class, and structural power.' In understanding the modern world, HM is a major resource for making sense of state and non-state terrorism in the service of (and for explaining why terrorism is antithetical to effective resistance to) the system of capitalist exploitation (Blakeley 2009; Herring and Stokes 2011a: 16–18; Joseph 2011: 34–6). Indeed, the entire agenda of Security Studies—including central issues such as energy security (see Chapter 23)—could be tackled productively using the analytical tools of HM. The critical power of HM is maximized when capitalism is treated as an entire social order rather than just a kind of economy, when subjectivity (what people think and feel) is engaged with as a force for action and change rather than as merely a product of material forces, and when analysis is developed in relation to concrete historical circumstances rather than simply in the abstract.

QUESTIONS

1. What are the social scientific, philosophical, and political dimensions of historical materialism?
2. Historical materialism is a key paradigm of International Relations thought and yet it is absent from most of Security Studies: why has this been the case and why might it be changing?
3. What does historical materialism share with realism and liberalism? What does it offer that is distinctive in comparison with realist and liberal thinking about security?
4. Why do historical materialists reject a sectoral approach to thinking about security in favour of a holistic one?
5. Historical materialists accept that states are important for security but see states as reflecting class interests rather than national interests: what are the implications of this approach?
6. What are the links between historical materialism and Critical Security Studies?
7. How can historical materialism improve our understanding of structural violence and human security?
8. What do historical materialists mean when they argue that arms production and the arms trade are forms of militarized capitalism?
9. What are the potential pitfalls of a historical materialist approach to understanding security and how might they be avoided?
10. What can historical materialism tell us about the relationships between development and security?

FURTHER READING

- Barker, Colin, Laurence Cox, John Krinsky, and Alf Gunvald Nilsen (eds) (2013), *Marxism and Social Movements*, Leiden: Brill. This important work integrates social movement theory with Marxism.
- Blakeley, Ruth (2009), *State Terrorism and Neoliberalism: The North in the South*, London: Routledge. Wearing its HM perspective lightly and applying it effectively, this significant scholarly contribution shows that Northern liberal democracies have been involved in state and non-state terrorism in the South as part of their efforts to integrate it into a neoliberalized global political economy.

- Harvey, David (2007), *A Brief History of Neoliberalism*, Oxford: Oxford University Press. A superb, wide-ranging HM analysis of the nature and implications of neoliberalism.
- Harvey, David (2014), *Seventeen Contradictions and the End of Capitalism*, London: Profile Books. Characteristically brilliant analysis that considers which contradictions sustain capitalism and which put it at risk, with implications for the (in)security of all.
- Herring, Eric and Stokes, Doug (eds) (2011), 'Special Issue: Bringing Critical Realism and Historical Materialism into Critical Terrorism Studies', *Critical Studies on Terrorism*, 4:1. This set of articles demonstrates the value of critical realism and HM for understanding the roles of terrorism within capitalism.
- Rupert, Mark and Solomon, Scott (2006), *Globalization and International Political Economy*, Lanham, MD: Rowman & Littlefield. HM ideas are used by Rupert and Solomon to critique globalizing capitalism and show how it is being contested through violent and non-violent means. Those ideas enable them to integrate the themes of gender, class, imperialism, resistance, and terror into a coherent whole.
- Stavrianakis, Anna (2010), *Taking Aim at the Arms Trade: NGOs, Global Civil Society and the World Military Order*, London: Zed. This insightful HM study shows how civil society organizations can either legitimize or challenge the capitalist global arms trade.
- Stokes, Doug and Raphael, Sam (2010), *Global Energy Security and American Hegemony* Baltimore, MD: Johns Hopkins University Press. This valuable book, grounded in HM theory, explains the connections between US counter-insurgency warfare to stabilize oil-rich states across much of the world and increased rivalry for diminishing energy supplies.
- Wall, Derek (2005), *Babylon and Beyond: The Economics of Anti-Capitalist, Anti-Globalist and Radical Green Movements*, London: Pluto Press. Wall explores central themes in the thinking of the heterogeneous global citizen movement seeking progressive ways of addressing the insecurities facing humanity and the global ecosystem.
- Wood, Ellen Meiksins (1995), *Democracy Against Capitalism: Renewing Historical Materialism*, Cambridge: Cambridge University Press. The value of HM theory for understanding capitalism and its implications for humanity is explained in this incisive study.
- Wood, Ellen Meiksins (2005), *Empire of Capital*, London: Verso. The central argument of this book is that militarism is an inherent feature of contemporary capitalism rather than being peculiar to the administration of any particular US president. The journal *Historical Materialism* (2007), 15:3 contains a symposium on this fascinating book and includes a reply by the author.

IMPORTANT WEBSITES

- **http://davidharvey.org** David Harvey is the world's leading Marxist scholar. He has influenced many disciplines. This website contains many of his writings and videos of many of his lectures.
- **https://zcomm.org** Z Communications is a huge online nexus of analysis, discussion, and resources in many languages for HM-influenced activists, journalists, and scholars, including those who combine those roles.
- **http://www.caat.org.uk** The Campaign Against the Arms Trade (CAAT) adopts an HM approach in opposing the arms trade as militarized capitalism.
- **http://www.marxists.org** The Marxists' Internet Archive is a vast resource in dozens of languages containing the writings of numerous selected Marxists, a thematic archive, a historical archive, and a searchable encyclopaedia.

- **http://www.newleftproject.org** New Left Project. Its resources include free download of the e-book by Robin Hahnel and Erik Olin Wright *Alternatives to Capitalism: Proposals for a Democratic Economy* published in 2014.
- **http://www.plutobooks.com/** Pluto Press is among the world's leading publishers of progressive scholarship, with books on numerous HM-related themes such as digital technology and class power, economic democracy as an alternative to the crises, unmet needs, and inequality that characterize capitalism.

Visit the Online Resource Centre that accompanies this book for lots of interesting additional material: www.oxfordtextbooks.co.uk/orc/collins4e/

5

Peace Studies

Paul Rogers

Chapter Contents

Reader's Guide

This chapter examines the origins and development of the field of peace studies after the Second World War, initially in relation to the East–West confrontation and the nuclear arms race. It analyses how peace studies responded to the issues of socio-economic disparities and environmental constraints as they became apparent in the 1970s, and explores its development as an interdisciplinary and problem-oriented field of study, often in the midst of controversy. The chapter then assesses the state of peace studies now, before concluding by examining how it is relevant to the new security challenges facing the world.

Introduction

Peace studies is a field of study that developed after the Second World War, largely because of the failure of a range of social and internationalist movements to prevent the outbreak of two world wars within twenty-five years. Its early development in the 1950s was hugely conditioned by the East–West nuclear arms race and the very real threat of a catastrophic nuclear war, but peace studies was also quick to embrace major issues of the North–South wealth/poverty divide and the potential effects of global environmental constraints. It is a field that has had more than its share of controversies—peace studies was frequently labelled 'appeasement studies' at the height of the Cold War—but has survived and thrived, especially in recent years, with a marked increase in interest in issues of peacekeeping, conflict resolution, and post-conflict peace building. There has been a particular interest in many parts of Latin America, Africa, the Middle East, and much of Asia, and the concern of the peace studies community to rise above the Western ethnocentric attitudes that still dominate much of international relations (IR) has been greatly aided by this global context.

The early years

Peace studies only became established as a formal field of study, with its own institutions and journals, in the post-1945 period, although earlier pioneers included Pitrim Sorokin, Quincy Wright, and the British meteorologist Lewis Fry Richardson (Sorokin 1937; Wright 1942; Richardson 1960). A more sustained interest in peace studies developed after the Second World War (Galtung 1969) as the combination of the early years of the nuclear arms race, the proxy wars of the Cold War era such as Korea, and the violence in a number of colonies, all contributed to a perception of a world of profound instability, even more shocking given that this was barely a decade after the world's worst ever conflict. It was in this pessimistic environment that the origins of peace studies are to be found.

The universities get involved

In these early years, peace studies developed primarily in North America and Western Europe, with some of the developments even preceding the tense years of the 1950s. Theodore Lenz's Peace Research Laboratory was founded in St Louis in 1945 and in Europe the Institut Français de Polémologie was established in the same year. One of the main European contributors to the new field of peace research was the Dutch jurist Bert Rolling. He had been a judge at the Japanese war-crimes tribunal and went on to establish peace studies, or polemology, in the Netherlands.

Another key feature of peace studies was established in the early post-war era—the entry into the field of mathematicians and natural scientists into what was otherwise a social sciences area of study. This was later prominent both in the contribution of the **Pugwash** movement and in the publication of the *Bulletin of the Atomic Scientists.* It has been an enduring feature of peace studies since the mid-twentieth century that its interdisciplinary nature stretches well beyond the range of social science disciplines to embrace the physical and natural sciences and mathematics.

One of the earliest initiatives in the United States was the publication in the *American Psychologist* in April 1951 of a letter from two social scientists, Kelman and Gladstone, arguing for a serious and systematic study of pacifist approaches to foreign policy. Coming at a time of heightened tensions, and with anti-communism rampant in the United States, this was a courageous suggestion and it resulted in the establishment of the *Bulletin of the Research Exchange on the Prevention of War* the following year.

The middle 1950s were to see major developments on both sides of the Atlantic. In the United States, a key research group came together at Stanford University's Center for Advanced Studies in the Behavioral Sciences. As well as Herb Kelman, this included Kenneth and Elise Boulding and Anatol Rapoport. Joining them was Stephen Richardson, the son of Lewis Fry Richardson, who brought with him his father's copious but largely unpublished material on microfilm. This combination produced a highly active and innovative group that was to develop the *Bulletin* into the *Journal of Conflict Resolution*, based at the newly established Center for Conflict Resolution at the University of Michigan. In the first issue of the *Journal,* the editors gave two reasons for establishing it, and these give the flavour of those early years:

> The first is that by far the most important practical problem facing the human race today is that of international relations—more specifically the prevention of global war. The second is that if intellectual progress is to be made in this area, the study of international relations must be made an interdisciplinary enterprise, drawing its discourse from all the social sciences, and even further.
>
> *Journal of Conflict Resolution*, 1/1 (1957), 3.

In parallel with these developments in the United States, peace studies developed apace in Europe and Japan, with the establishment of more departments, research centres, and journals (see Background 5.1).

BACKGROUND 5.1 Peace centres and journals

Away from the United States, Bert Rolling founded the Polemological Institute at the University of Groningen in the Netherlands, and the Norwegian peace researcher Johan Galtung founded the forerunner of what became the Peace Research Institute of Oslo (PRIO), which publishes two key journals, *Security Dialogue* and the *Journal of Peace Research*.

Two of the largest peace studies centres were to be established in Sweden and the United Kingdom. To celebrate 150 years of peace, the Stockholm International Peace Research Institute (SIPRI) was set up in 1966 and went on to establish a worldwide reputation for its work on arms races and arms control. Its yearbook, *Arms and Disarmament*, has long been seen as an essential source of data. Seven years after the founding of SIPRI, members of the Society of Friends (Quakers) in Britain sought to establish a British equivalent and were able to aid the University of Bradford in setting up a Department of Peace Studies. One of the most striking developments of recent years has been the large number of peace studies centres established in the global South, especially sub-Saharan Africa and Latin America.

Elsewhere, the Japanese Peace Research group was founded in 1964, the Canadian Peace Research and Education Association was established two years later, and the Tampere Peace Research Institute was founded in Finland. One of the other key journals, *Peace and Change*, was started by the US Conference on Peace Research and History, which had itself been formed in 1963. Given the global spread of this new field, the final development was the formation of the International Peace Research Association, which holds biennial conferences.

Some were essentially started at the instigation of governments and obtained most of their money from central government sources, continuing to do so successfully over many years. As such, they had a degree of financial support that was welcome, but such centres could also be subject to sudden political change. The Peace Research Centre at the Australian National University in Canberra failed to survive a change of government, and the Copenhagen Peace Research Institute was to lose its independence in a centrally directed amalgamation of institutes.

KEY POINTS

- Peace studies developed as a response to the carnage of the First and Second World Wars, with the Cold War providing a further impetus in the 1950s.
- Most early work on peace studies was carried out in North America and Scandinavia.
- By 1970, there were established centres and journals.

Evolution amidst controversy

In the early 1960s, there were sharp divides between the outlooks of peace researchers and those of the 'realist' school in international relations. Realist IR scholars saw the failure of the League of Nations and the intensity of the ideological division between Western liberal democracies and the totalitarian systems of the Soviet bloc as providing an urgent need to undertake research that would essentially favour the survival of the former. The standpoint was very much that of an Atlanticist outlook.

Many peace researchers, on the other hand, considered this a narrow Western ethnocentric outlook that failed properly to analyse what they saw as the reality of two competing systems locked into a single dynamic of military confrontation and escalation. They had much in common with 'idealist' outlooks in international relations, and their work attracted particular attention at a time when the nuclear arms race was accelerating.

In late 1962, the United States and the Soviet Union came very close to an all-out nuclear confrontation over the latter's plans to deploy medium-range nuclear missiles in Cuba, close to the United States. The crisis was resolved, with difficulty, and one consequence was a new-found determination by the United States and the Soviet Union to seek progress in arms control, leading to a period of relative détente in the mid-1960s.

A new agenda: environment and poverty

Given that peace studies had developed partly in response to Cold War tensions and the risk of global nuclear war, it might have been expected that it would have gone into decline in the wake of these improvements in East–West relations. In practice this did not happen, as three other major international issues were coming to the fore that were to become central to the developing field.

One was the widely held view that former colonies had successfully achieved political independence in the

1950s and 1960s but had certainly not achieved economic independence—the anticipated progress from the much-vaunted Development Decade of the 1960s has simply not materialized. Such a view, common in the newly developing field of development studies as well as within peace research, was regarded as a radical analysis by most mainstream economists. As far as the discipline of International Relations was concerned, North–South relations were simply not important and received scant attention from most scholars, an aspect that to this day tends to differentiate peace researchers from most of the international relations community.

A second issue, surfacing initially in the late 1960s, was the state of the global environment. The first **UN Conference on the Human Environment**, in 1972, placed an emphasis on the possible limits to economic growth if the global ecosystem was to prove to be unable to cope with rapidly increasing human impacts. This suggested that such growth alone could not meet the needs of the majority of humankind in the South. Environmental security therefore had to be linked to development aspirations, and prospects for international development were necessarily linked to the asymmetric environmental impact of industrialized states. Otherwise, a world beset with deep socio-economic divisions that also had finite limits on its economic growth potential set by environmental constraints would be a world of much potential violence, fragility, and insecurity. This debate of the early 1970s is being revisited with even greater urgency as the impact of climate change becomes rapidly more apparent, and the Persian Gulf, with its massive fossil-fuel resources, becomes a locus not just of economic competition but of open warfare (see Case Study 5.1).

CASE STUDY 5.1 Conflicts to come: energy wars and climate change

Whether or not the termination of the Saddam Hussein regime in Iraq had much to do with the control of Iraq's oil reserves, these are one part of a regional concentration that is quite remarkable. Just five Gulf States—Saudi Arabia, Iran, Iraq, Kuwait, and the United Arab Emirates—control well over 60 per cent of known oil reserves. During the latter part of the Cold War, the United States became particularly concerned about a possible Soviet threat to Gulf oil resources, and this resulted in the establishment of the Rapid Deployment Force at the end of the 1970s. Following the Iranian Revolution of 1979–80 and the start of the 1980–88 Iran–Iraq War, the Rapid Deployment Force was elevated into a full unified military command, Central Command (CENTCOM). It was this organization that fought the 1991 Iraq War and has been responsible for operations in Afghanistan and Iraq in recent years.

The key reason for potential conflict in the region is that most of the world's major industrial regions, including Western Europe and East Asia, are becoming increasingly dependent on Gulf oil reserves as their own production decreases and demand rises. Thus, one of the core security issues for the next twenty years or so is whether there can be sustained international cooperation over the utilization of Gulf oil reserves, or whether the region will be a focus for conflict. Moreover, this is part of the wider problem of whether the global community can continue to rely on fossil fuels or whether the security implications of climate change will make that mode of living redundant.

Although climate change was seen as an important issue by the early 1990s, it was expected that the major effects would be felt by the richer countries of the North and South temperate latitudes, which might best be able to cope. By the mid-1990s, though, some of the climate modelling was showing a disturbing picture of much greater effects on tropical climates than had previously been thought likely. In particular, there was a growing likelihood that climate change would have a major impact on rainfall distribution across the tropics and subtropics, the main effect being a tendency for rainfall to decrease substantially over these land masses and increase over the world's oceans and over the Polar regions (Rind 1995).

If this does happen, and the timescale is over thirty years, then the effects will be profound. The majority of the world's population, well over four billion people, live in the tropical and subtropical land masses, with almost all of them dependent on locally grown food. If the tropical regions 'dry out', then there will be a substantial decrease in the 'ecological carrying capacity' of some of the world's richest croplands. The effects will be massive, not just in terms of increases in famine and malnutrition, but in increased migratory pressures as many millions of people seek to move to countries where they can survive.

The phenomenon of climate change and its impact on the tropical land masses is likely to become one of the key international security issues. Countering the likely effects over the next decade or so, and moving more insistently towards low carbon-sustainable economies, may well be one of the greatest single contributions to ensuring a more peaceful and stable world, and it could also markedly reduce the risk of conflict over energy resources.

The 'maximalist' agenda and structural violence

Finally, one specific conflict, the **Vietnam War**, was to cause deep controversy as some radical peace researchers argued that the injustices were such that there could be occasions when violence could be justified in the pursuit of justice. That brief controversy was in the context of the development of a 'maximalist' agenda emerging in European peace research, especially with Johan Galtung's conception (1969) of **structural violence**. This proposed that the condition of peace required the absence not just of overt violence but also of structural violence—the persistence of economic and social exploitation in societies that might otherwise be said to be at peace. In similar vein, Herman Schmid (1968) argued that much of peace research was not critically engaged with defining peaceful societies as entities in which justice genuinely prevailed. An absence of war could obscure deep injustices that made a mockery of notions of peace. Others engaged in peace research saw this as a constant expansion of the peace research agenda 'acquiring the qualities of an intellectual black hole wherein something vital, a praxeological edge or purpose, is lost' (Lawler 1995: 237).

This dispute, sometimes described as between maximalists and minimalists, has never been fully resolved, but most peace researchers came to accept that, in addition to the original aim of seeking to prevent nuclear war, other themes were of legitimate concern for those working in the field. The primary issues were initially those of global North–South disparities and the risk of an environmental crisis, but, significantly, a concern for gender inequalities also came to prominence rather earlier than in the fields of development studies or international relations.

New goals: equality, justice, and dignity

By 1973, and as a result of such changes, the editors of the *Journal of Conflict Resolution* sought to broaden its original remit beyond its previous concentration on inter-state conflict and the nuclear issue:

> The threat of nuclear holocaust remains with us and may well continue to do so for centuries, but other problems are competing with deterrence and disarmament studies for our attention. This journal must also attend to international conflict over justice, equality, and human dignity; problems of conflict resolution for ecological balance and control are within our proper scope and especially suited for interdisciplinary attention.
>
> *Journal of Conflict Resolution*, 17/1 (1973), 5.

By the end of the 1970s, this much broader focus was embedded in peace studies but was then overtaken by the development of the final and perhaps most dangerous phase of the Cold War. The Soviet invasion of Afghanistan, the Iranian Revolution and hostage crisis, the election of the Reagan and Thatcher governments, and the deployment of new generations of strategic nuclear weapons all combined to give a renewed urgency to those very issues that peace researchers had largely eschewed. For the best part of a decade, many researchers returned to issues of deterrence and disarmament, contrasting their analysis markedly with that of international relations realists and, on occasions, earning the enmity of their own governments.

Even so, issues of environment and development continued to be addressed, and there was a substantial increase in research on techniques of mediation and other forms of conflict resolution, on peacekeeping and post-conflict peace building (see Think Point 5.1). Partly because of this, a number of peace studies centres not only survived the sudden ending of the Cold War in 1989–90 but were able to adjust to the post-Cold War world much more easily than many of the international relations centres, which were, to an extent, floundering in the face of such unexpected change.

KEY POINTS

- Peace studies sought to provide a non-state-centric and more global view of major issues of conflict.
- By the 1970s, it was responding to issues of socio-economic divisions and environmental constraints.
- In the 1980s, in the final period of the Cold War, there was bitter opposition to what was sometimes seen as 'appeasement studies'.
- Within peace studies, one of the later developments was a major interest in conflict prevention, conflict resolution, and peacekeeping.

THINK POINT 5.1 Conflict resolution

The area of study and practice usually grouped under the term 'conflict resolution' has been one of the fastest-growing aspects of peace studies since the 1990s, but has not been without its controversies. Involving such processes as mediation, conflict transformation, and post-conflict peace building, it has been an active field of academic study as well as burgeoning into an 'industry' involving non-government organizations and international agencies.

Two problems have emerged, one theoretical and one practical. First, at the theoretical level, some critical theorists have argued that conflict resolution is palliative rather than transformative—being concerned with a 'sticking-plaster' approach that may appear to promote peace but does not address underlying reasons for conflict. In a sense this is a replay of the 'maximalist' controversy of the 1970s. They further argue that much of the practice of peace building carries the risk of exporting western ideas of a 'liberal peace' which may retain an element of exploitative inequality, thus hindering effective progress in emancipation.

Second, at the practical level, many of the organizations attempting to resolve conflicts, at whatever level, need to demonstrate success, not least to ensure their continuing sources of funding. There can, therefore, be a tendency to overstate their claims of progress. In practice, the best forms of mediatory intervention are those with very modest expectations of success and an ability to remain unpublicized. Some of the 'peace churches' such as the Quakers have a good record in this respect.

As to the wider criticism, many peace researchers would argue that conflict resolution should properly be seen as a specific and integral part of the peace studies tradition. As Ramsbotham et al. (2011) argue:

> 'We suggest that peace and conflict research is part of an emancipatory discourse and practice which is making a valuable and defining contribution to emerging norms of democratic, just and equitable systems of global governance. We argue that conflict resolution has a role to play in the radical negotiation of these norms, so that international conflict management is grounded in the needs of those who are the victims of conflict and who are frequently marginalized from conventional power structures.'
>
> *Ramsbotham et al. (2011)*

What is peace studies now?

Peace studies in the early twenty-first century is an established and thriving field with a range of journals, a number of research institutes such as the Peace Research Institute of Oslo (PRIO) and the Stockholm International Peace Research Institute (SIPRI), many centres in universities and colleges, and an international body, the International Peace Research Association (IPRA). In countries of the South there has been a real increase in interest in peace studies since 2000, with a particular concern with what peace studies can offer in countering violence and open conflict. Furthermore, since the effects of wars can be so much more long-lasting in poorer regions, there is an added impetus to work towards war termination, conflict resolution, and peace building.

What are the main characteristics and key concepts of peace studies? Ramsbotham (Rogers and Ramsbotham 1999) suggests a number of features that mark it out as a defined field of study:

1. *Underlying causes.* A concern to address the root causes of direct violence and to explore ways of overcoming structural inequalities and of promoting equitable and cooperative relations between and within human communities. This means that peace studies goes well beyond the absence of war to work towards societies that are intrinsically more peaceful. This means addressing a wide range of inequalities whether rooted in class, race, or gender divisions, with these analysed at a range of levels from the individual and community through to the international.
2. *Interdisciplinary approaches.* A realization that an interdisciplinary response is essential, given the multifaceted nature of violent conflict. The larger peace studies centres will have among their staff people drawn from political science, international relations, psychology, anthropology, economics, history, sociology, and other disciplines. They may well have people trained originally in mathematics, physics, or the biological sciences. This leads to conceptual enrichment, but can also cause disputes about appropriate methodologies and theoretical frameworks.
3. *Non-violent transformations.* A search for peaceful ways to settle disputes and for non-violent transformation of potentially or actually violent situations. This does not mean endorsing the status quo, since unjust and oppressive systems are seen as some of the chief causes of violence

and war. It does mean the comparative study of peaceful and non-peaceful processes of social and political change; and of ways to prevent the outbreak of violence, or, if it does break out, of ways to mitigate it, bring it to an end, and prevent its recurrence thereafter. Within these parameters there is continuing debate about the efficacy and legitimacy of the use of force in certain circumstances. This is especially true in the case of humanitarian intervention in internal conflicts.

4. *Multi-level analysis.* The embracing of a multi-level analysis at individual, group, state, and inter-state levels in an attempt to overcome the institutionalized dichotomy between studies of 'internal' and 'external' dimensions that are seen to be inadequate for the prevailing patterns of conflict. This is seen as particularly significant given the relative decline of inter-state conflict and the rise of sub-state conflict. It is also seen as relevant in analysing the tendency towards 'trans-state' conflict. This may include detention without trial, across state borders, of individuals who have status neither as conventional criminals nor as **prisoners of war** under the terms of the **Geneva Conventions**. This has become a feature of the **Global War on Terror**, as has the 'rendition' of individuals—their transfer to countries likely to use torture in extracting information.
5. *Global outlook.* The adoption of a global and multicultural approach, which locates sources of violence globally and regionally as well as locally, and draws on conceptions of peace and non-violent social transformations from all cultures. Such an approach has become even more relevant as peace studies centres have increased in East and South Asia, Africa, and Latin America.
6. *Analytical and normative.* An understanding that peace studies is both an analytic and a normative enterprise. While there has been a tendency to ground peace studies in quantitative research and comparative empirical study, the reality is that most scholars have been drawn to the field by ethical concerns and commitments. Deterministic ideas have been largely rejected, whether in realist or Marxist guises, with large-scale violence and war seen not as inevitable features of the international system, but as consequences of human actions and choices.

With ethical commitments among the core motivations of peace researchers, it can be argued that such an environment can result in the sloppy pursuit of causes with little concern for academic rigour. This was a particular issue in several countries in the 1980s (see Think Point 5.2), but the level of critical analysis of peace studies programmes actually helped ensure that unusually high standards had to be, and were, set.

7. *Theory and practice.* Linked to this is the close relationship between theory and practice in peace studies. While a clear distinction is persistently made between peace studies and peace activism, peace researchers very frequently engage systematically

! THINK POINT 5.2 The war on peace studies

In the early years of the 1980s, Cold War tensions were particularly high, and there was a strong perception of renewed danger, with a palpable risk of all-out nuclear war. This fed into a burgeoning anti-nuclear movement across Western Europe, together with a renewed interest in peace studies, especially in schools, but also in universities. In Britain, political polarization was particularly evident and conservative opponents of peace studies viewed it as unpatriotic appeasement studies.

The opposition was focused very largely on politicians and rarely stretched to the armed forces—indeed the defence colleges were keen to debate the issues openly and frequently asked peace researchers to lecture to their students. The 'war on peace studies' lasted from around 1981 to 1987, but died away as the Cold War came to an end. Indeed, peace studies attracted much greater attention over the following few years, as many other areas of peace research, such as the theory and practice of peacekeeping and issues of environmental security, came to the fore.

Some of the academics involved in peace research at that time now reflect that the 'war on peace studies' was very good for the emerging discipline. As well as attracting some particularly able students into the area, the constant critical scrutiny of research output, especially on areas such as armaments and arms control, meant that standards of work had to be particularly high. Peace researchers became subject to far tougher scrutiny of their work than most other scholars in international relations and many of them now think that they became better academics as a result.

with non-government organizations (NGOs), government departments, and intergovernmental agencies. They frequently see this as part of a process of empirical testing of theoretical insights, regarding it also as a two-way process.

Many people working in the field regard the policy implications of their work as more significant than its reception among fellow academics. Given the modern era of 'research assessment' in some Western countries that is primarily geared to academic output in the conventional literature, this can be a disadvantage for the discipline. Furthermore, this 'engagement' with the policy process does not fit in with the prevailing academic culture in most Western countries, even if it is more commonly found in academic centres in the majority of the world.

KEY POINTS

- Core elements of modern peace studies include a concern with underlying causes of conflict and the search for non-violent approaches to conflict transformation.
- It remains an interdisciplinary field that embraces multi-level analysis from the individual to the international.
- It is both analytical and normative, frequently involving ethical motivations on the part of students and researchers.
- Peace studies engages persistently with opinion formers and policy makers.

Responding to the new security challenges

Given these characteristics, how relevant is the peace studies agenda in the early twenty-first century and how valuable might it be in responding to the major issues of conflict and insecurity that might face us in the coming decades? To answer these questions, we need to analyse the main security challenges likely to face us and then look at the main attributes of peace studies in terms of its possible contribution.

Global security during the forty-five years of the Cold War was dominated by the East–West confrontation but was also a period of major conflicts in many parts of the world, with over 100 wars leading directly to more than twenty million deaths and well over fifty million injuries, as well as much more suffering in post-war environments, especially in impoverished communities. The ending of the Cold War, while leading to the settlement of some long-standing disputes, also increased instability, not least in the Caucasus and the Balkans, and there were also continuing tensions in the Israeli/Palestinian confrontation, the 1991 Iraq War, and the devastating conflicts of the Great Lakes region of Central Africa.

By the end of the 1990s, a number of these conflicts had been transformed into an uneasy peace, and others such as Northern Ireland also showed some prospects of settlement (see Think Point 5.3). Against this, the terrorist attacks in New York and Washington in September 2001 were to herald a vigorous military reaction from the United States, leading to the termination of regimes in Afghanistan and Iraq and the beginnings of potentially long-drawn-out conflicts in both countries.

While these were immediate issues of conflict in the early twenty-first century, they were evolving in an international context in which two much broader issues are becoming salient. The first is the deep and enduring inequalities in the global distribution of wealth and economic **power**, likely to ensure that, within thirty years, one-seventh of the world's population will control three-quarters of the wealth, largely but not entirely on a geographical basis. While there have been immense efforts at development, almost entirely from within the poorer countries themselves, the global picture is one of enduring disempowerment and increasing socio-economic polarization. This is not just the case at the global level, but is particularly marked in countries such as China and India, where despite the experience of rapid economic growth, most of the increases in wealth are concentrated among a minority of the population.

Furthermore, environmental constraints are likely to exacerbate the effects of human activity on the global ecosystem, making it increasingly difficult for human well-being to be improved by conventional economic growth. The combination of wealth–poverty disparities and limits to growth is likely to lead to a crisis of unsatisfied expectations within an increasingly informed global majority of the disempowered.

On the basis of these issues, three broad conflict trends are probable. The first arises from a greater likelihood of increased human migration through economic, social, and environmental motives. Focusing on regions of relative wealth, this is already leading to shifts in the political spectrum in recipient regions, including increased nationalist tendencies and cultural conflict, not least in Western Europe and Australasia.

THINK POINT 5.3 A more peaceful world?

In the years since the 9/11 attacks, most people in Western countries would probably say that the world has become distinctly more dangerous. It is not just the memory of the planes crashing into the World Trade Center followed by the collapse of the towers; it is also the impact of the subsequent wars in Afghanistan and Iraq. This may actually be an illusion, as some research suggests that the world has actually become more peaceful since the end of the Cold War. The 2005 *Human Security Report*, published at the height of the Iraq War, for example, cited a 40 per cent decrease in armed conflicts overall since the early 1990s and an 80 per cent decrease in major conflicts. The study was undertaken at the Liu Institute for Global Issues at the University of British Columbia in Vancouver, and the resulting report was a powerful antidote to many common assumptions.

As well as an overall decrease in conflicts, the report pointed to a decline in the number of autocratic regimes, with their penchant for human rights abuses, and also claimed that an expansion in UN peacekeeping operations, as well as a much greater emphasis on conflict prevention, have combined to good effect. The results may seem surprising but were supported by a number of similar studies from the Center for International Development and Conflict Management at the University of Maryland.

In addition to the impact of conflict prevention and peacekeeping operations, other factors may be at work. The Cold War era was characterized by numerous 'proxy wars' fought on an East–West axis but rarely involving the two superpowers in direct conflict. These included Korea, Vietnam, Afghanistan, and the Horn of Africa. Furthermore, the early part of the Cold War period coincided with numerous wars of decolonization, including French Indo-China, Malaya, Kenya, Cyprus, and Algeria. Almost all the colonial conflicts had ended by the 1970s.

There were also particular conflicts associated with the ending of the Cold War, especially in the Caucasus, as well as the break-up of Yugoslavia. These had reduced, if not ended, by the turn of the century, and even the enduring conflicts in Northern Ireland and the Basque region of Spain were winding down. When all these factors are put together, it is easier to understand the results from the *Human Security Report*. The question remains as to whether this is a long-term trend or a welcome but potentially short-lived period of relative calm before new conflicts kick in, especially over issues such as energy resources and climate change.

Such tendencies are often most pronounced in the most vulnerable and disempowered populations within the recipient regions. If, as seems probable, climate changes induce a partial 'drying-out' of the tropical land masses (see Case Study 5.1) then the migratory pressures will be greatly accelerated.

Second, it is probable that environmental and resource conflict will escalate. This may be local or regional on issues such as food, land, fresh water, or marine resources, and global on issues such as fossil fuel and mineral resources. The Persian Gulf, as the repository of much of the world's remaining reserves of fossil fuels, is likely to be a particular focus for competition and conflict (see Case Study 5.1).

Finally, and probably most importantly, competitive and violent responses of the disempowered should be expected within and between states and also in the form of transnational movements. The Zapatista revolt in southern Mexico, the earlier Shining Path guerrilla movement in Peru, the neo-Maoist rebellion in Nepal, the Naxalite movement in India, social unrest in China, and disempowerment responses in North Africa and the Middle East may all be early examples of a developing trend, not infrequently exacerbated by political, religious, and nationalist fundamentalisms. This is linked to underlying historically conditioned weaknesses in many postcolonial states, struggling as they are to accommodate the twin pressures of globalization and fragmentation, and a prey to sectarian and factional exploitation. Increased internal political tensions, not least secessionist movements, in populous states such as China, India, and Indonesia, would have very wide repercussions, the Uighur issue in western China being one example.

The key development that links with socio-economic divisions and environmental constraints is the marked improvement in education, literacy, and communications across much of the world since the 1960s. Achieved largely through indigenous efforts, primary-level education is now much more prevalent than at the end of the colonial period, and this has been accompanied by substantial improvements in levels of literacy. While male literacy levels increased first, levels of female literacy are at last starting to catch up.

Coupled with these changes, there has been an explosion of technological change in relation to radio, television, and the print media. For much of the world's 'data-poor' majority, the impact of the web, e-mail, and even DVDs are still to come, but the changes that have already taken place mean that there is a much greater awareness of world developments. The implications of this are fundamental, in that there is a much greater recognition among the disempowered majority of the world's population of that very disempowerment. The end result is not so much a revolution of rising expectations, a feature of consumerism in the 1970s, as a revolution of frustrated expectations as the levels of exclusion become more readily apparent.

Moreover, the development of non-Western satellite news channels such as Al-Jazeera means that reporting of events in Iraq and other countries of the Middle East is no longer under the influence of local elites and therefore subject to censorship. Nor is it more widely dominated by transnational broadcasting organizations that may provide minimal coverage to their international audiences except in instances of major violence.

The consequences of the effects of marginalization are legion, from the high levels of urban crime in many Southern cities, the need for heavily protected gated communities for the elite rich, elements of the Arab Awakening that focus on anger at the power of the rich elites, through to some of the radical and extreme social movements in Nepal, India, Pakistan, and elsewhere. Although the Al-Qaeda movement may be rooted in South West Asia and is specific to extreme interpretations of one religious tradition, its evolution into a transnational phenomenon owes much to the persistent publicizing of the human consequences of the war on terror, not least in Iraq.

A choice of responses

Responses to socio-economic divisions and environmental constraints might best take the form of consistent cooperation for sustainable development, including debt relief, trade reform, and development assistance at a level much higher than that of recent years, coupled with a multiplicity of programmes for conflict prevention and resolution as embodied in the UN **Agenda for Peace**.

They might, on the other hand, take the form of a vigorous programme of maintaining the status quo, ensuring that the wealthy sectors of humankind maintain their privileged position by appropriate trading and financial measures, backed up by military force where necessary. Described as 'liddism', or keeping the lid on a potentially fractured international system, this would appear to be the current trend, and the consequence of this might well be Brooks's fear, expressed over forty years ago, of 'a crowded glowering planet of massive inequalities of wealth buttressed by stark force and endlessly threatened by desperate people in the global ghettoes . . .' (Brooks 1974).

For twelve years after the 9/11 attacks, the prevailing security paradigm was very much dominated by the United States and buttressed by stark force. Two regimes were terminated, well over 200,000 civilians killed in the process, 120,000 people were detained without trial, torture and prisoner abuse were widespread, and there were over seven million refugees. Even by 2015, extreme Islamist groups were not just active but were expanding their operations, most notably Islamic State in Iraq and Syria and Boko Haram in Nigeria. US troops returned to Iraq in 2014 and the drawdown from Afghanistan was partial at most. Furthermore, other forms of control, most notably armed drones, Special Forces, and privatized military forces were coming to the fore.

Whether the 'control paradigm' will collapse under the weight of its own inadequacies or whether it will survive and prosper may depend on the degree of critical analysis of its underlying assumptions, coupled with the promotion of viable alternatives that might be undertaken by a vigorous academic community.

This is a challenge for the international relations community as a whole, and the peace studies community in particular. The short-term responses include the principal *Agenda for Peace* peace-support elements, themselves in part drawn from peace-research terminology, such as crisis prevention, peacekeeping, peacemaking, and the shorter-term elements in post-settlement peace building. This also involves ethically involved intervention and regional and global arms control and demilitarization. They are required of an international community of states that shows little evidence of wisdom or leadership and consequently places most responsibility on an under-resourced UN system. While improvements in efficiency and capability must come from within the UN, the NGO role is substantial, especially in the more powerful states of the UN, with improved links between NGOs and the academic community an essential part of the process.

There are longer-term processes involved in conflict resolution and conflict transformation (see Think Point 5.1). This is a wide agenda, but now quite well understood and reasonably clearly focused, involving contextual, structural, relational, and cultural elements in the analysis of protracted social conflict with, beyond this, an increasing need for fundamental responses at the global level.

KEY POINTS

- Major issues for the future centre on the effects of a combination of socio-economic divisions and environmental constraints.
- The 9/11 attacks and the subsequent war on terror have yet to address the underlying reasons for current perceptions of insecurity.
- Responding to a potentially fragile and insecure international system will require sustained analysis combined with persistent efforts to suggest viable alternatives to the current security paradigm.

Conclusion

If the analysis offered in this chapter of a polarized, constrained, and potentially fragile and unstable world is correct, then the issue of rich–poor confrontation is likely to acquire a far greater saliency in future. This will demand a comprehensive rethinking of concepts of security, incorporating unprecedented cooperation for sustainable international economic development and environmental management. This needs to be paralleled by progressive demilitarization linked to the establishment of regional and global conflict prevention processes. For peace researchers there is now an even greater imperative for them to deepen their understanding of the interconnected problems of international economic relations, the possibilities of sustainable development, and their relationship to security.

Peace studies has developed over the past half-century and has seen the rigidities and dangers of the Cold War evolve into a more uncertain and unpredictable world. In its own development it has embraced a strong interdisciplinary outlook, a consciously global orientation, and a determined linkage between theory and practice. While it has sought to respond to the problems of conflict in the past sixty years, in all probability its greatest challenges are yet to come, though its evolution and current approaches may make it particularly well suited to the task of embracing that challenge.

QUESTIONS

1. What was the impetus for the development of peace studies in the 1950s and was it specific to that decade?
2. Why was there bitter opposition to peace studies in the 1980s and does this provide general lessons for innovative areas of research?
3. Is it possible for peace studies to be both analytical and normative or does this produce irresolvable tensions?
4. Should peace researchers engage with policy makers or should they concentrate on academic discourse?
5. Should peace studies explore underlying causes of conflict or should its main emphasis be on more immediate responses to more specific conflict situations?
6. Was the post-9/11 security paradigm of rigorous control of threats the appropriate response?
7. How can peace research contribute to assessing whether climate change is a threat to international security?
8. How have 24-hour news reporting and the development of new social media influenced the coverage of conflict?
9. How do conflicts in the Middle East since 1990 relate to the control of oil and gas reserves?

FURTHER READING

- Black, Jeremy (2005), *Why Wars Happen*, London and New York, Routledge. A quarter of a century covered with skill and detachment.
- Booth, Ken (2007), *Theory of World Security*, Cambridge, Cambridge University Press. A thoughtful and forward-looking analysis of international security.

- Carter, April, Clark, Howard, and Randle, Michael (2013), *A Guide to Civil Resistance*, London: Green Print, Merlin Press. A succinct survey of a major if neglected area of human progress.
- Graham, G. (1997), *Ethics and International Relations*, Oxford: Blackwell. A stimulating text raising many issues significant in peace studies.
- Jackson, Tim (2009), *Prosperity Without Growth: Economics for a Finite Planet*, London and Sterling VA: Earthscan. An innovative and influential analysis of the potential for low-impact economics.
- Kegley, Charles W. and Blanton, Shannon L. (2009), *World Politics: Trends and Transformations, 2009–2010 Update Edition*, New York: St Martin's Press. One of the few international relations textbooks that avoids an excessively Western ethnocentric style.
- Myrdal, Alva (1980), *The Game of Disarmament: How the United States and Russia Run the Arms Race*, Nottingham: Spokesman Books. A definitive and well-informed account of the Cold War arms race and of processes of international militarisation.
- Pogge, Thomas (2010), *Politics as Usual*, Cambridge and Malden: Polity Press. A well-argued critique of pro-poor rhetoric.
- Ramsbotham, Oliver, Woodhouse, Tom and Miall, Hugh (2011), *Contemporary Conflict Resolution*, 3rd edn, Cambridge and Malden: Polity Press. The third edition of what has become the standard work on conflict resolution.

IMPORTANT WEBSITES

- **http://www.sipri.org/** The Stockholm International Peace Research Institute (SIPRI) is one of the world's main centres for the analysis of arms and disarmament.
- **http://prio.no/** The Peace Research Institute of Oslo (PRIO) is noted, in particular, for its work on civil wars.
- **http://brad.ac.uk/acad/peace/** Currently the world's largest university centre for peace studies.
- **http://www.incore.ulst.ac.uk/** INCORE (International Conflict research) is a joint project of the University of Ulster and the UN University.
- **http://humansecurityreport.info/** The site for the Human Security Report Project.
- **http://opendemocracy.net** One of the liveliest open source sites, especially on international issues.
- **http://fpif.org** Foreign Policy in Focus is a US site providing wide-ranging analysis on international security and foreign policy themes.
- **http://oxfordresearchgroup.org.uk** Oxford Research Group is a UK-based think tank working on innovative approaches to international security, especially the concept of sustainable security.
- **http://remotecontrolproject.org** Examines the transition to armed drones, Special Forces, privatized security, rendition, and cyberwar as newer means of maintaining security.
- **http://nef.org** The New Economics Foundation's *Great Transition* project focuses on the transition to low-carbon equitable economic systems.

Visit the Online Resource Centre that accompanies this book for lots of interesting additional material: www.oxfordtextbooks.co.uk/orc/collins4e/

6

Social Constructivism

Christine Agius

Chapter Contents

Reader's Guide

Since the late 1980s, social constructivism has emerged as an influential approach in international relations theory and international politics. This chapter examines its impact on security studies and how it calls into question the assumed orthodoxy of rationalist approaches to security and the international system by asking how security and security threats are 'socially constructed'. It focuses on the importance of social relations and why identity, **norms**, and culture matter. Whereas rationalist approaches focus on material forces to understand and theorize security, social constructivism argues that ideational as well as material factors construct the world around us and the meanings we give to it. Therefore, its significance for security studies is crucial in terms not only of conceptualizing security but of providing alternative readings of security. However, constructivism is not a uniform approach. As this chapter demonstrates, it is broadly divided into two camps, which differ on questions of methodology and particular aspects of how knowledge and identity are interrogated. Throughout this chapter case studies of constructivist approaches to security questions will be discussed, and the chapter concludes with a consideration of the critiques of constructivism.

Introduction

Social constructivism (henceforth shortened to 'constructivism') brings to the fore the importance of ideas, identity, and interaction in the international system, revealing how 'the human world is not simply given and/or natural but that, on the contrary, the human world is one of artifice; that it is "constructed" through the actions of the actors themselves' (Kratochwil 2001: 17). Since Nicholas Onuf coined the term in 1989, constructivism has risen rapidly, reshaping debates in International Relations (IR) and challenging the dominance of rationalist theories such as neorealism and neoliberalism.[1] Many of its core concepts have been inspired by sociological theory (see Key Ideas 6.1). With the emergence of Critical Security Studies (see Chapter 7), the constructivist approach[2] forms part of the post-Cold War transformation in security studies, and argues that 'security' can be socially constructed. It therefore offers the possibility of alternative readings of security that go beyond rationalist theorizing which tends to neglect ideational forces in favour of material ones. The world is social, and not purely material. This has implications for thinking about security and security relations internationally. Constructivism puts into context the actions, beliefs, and interests of actors and understands that the world they inhabit has been created by them and impacts on them.

Constructivism has three basic ontological positions. First, normative or ideational structures are important and matter as much as, if not more than, material structures. This means that ideas are centre stage and are privileged. This presents a different picture compared to dominant theories such as neorealism and neoliberalism. For neorealists, the key to understanding state behaviour has been the anarchic international system and the importance of the distribution of material capabilities in the international system; for neoliberals, even though cooperation and international institutions are the focus, state interests are also defined in material terms.

The second ontological claim of constructivism is that identities matter. Identities give actors interests and those interests tell us something about how actors act/behave and the goals they pursue. Quite simply, actors cannot act without an identity. Since neorealists see all units (states) as similar, it is difficult to make sense of why a state such as the USA may have conflictual relations with one state (for instance, Iran), and friendly relations with another (say, Australia). Identity is therefore crucial to constructivists—as Alexander Wendt (1996: 50) puts it: 'A gun in the hands of a friend is a different thing from one in the hands of an enemy, and enmity is a social, not material, relation.' For neorealists and neoliberals, actors such as states are rational, unitary actors, pursuing their interests in the international arena. However, we understand only the material interests of such actors in these two accounts. Material forces, which Wendt (1999: 371) defines as 'power and interest', do not readily tell us where ideas, values, beliefs, and norms come from; the task is to examine how their content and meaning are made up by ideas and culture. By focusing on how interests are obtained and developed, constructivists argue that we get a better picture of identity and relations as social. Identity is not given but is constituted through interaction.

Third, agents and structures are mutually constituted. This attention to how actors shape the world and how the world shapes actors means that human relations are inherently social and we create the world that we live in and it influences us as well. International politics is not something that is independent from us; if the world 'out there' is a *World of our Making* (as the title of Onuf's (1989) book suggests), it means that different understandings of security may be possible. As part of the **agency–structure debate**, constructivism's appreciation of the mutual constitution of both agents and structures is important. When Alexander Wendt (1992) states that 'anarchy is what states make of it', he means precisely this. If we exist in a world of **anarchy** (the absence of an authority above the state),

[1] For some, its impact has been so great that constructivism is seen to form the 'fourth debate' in IR theorizing (constructivists versus rationalists), usurping older debates between realists and liberals (Fierke and Jørgensen 2001: 3).

[2] Debate still exists over whether constructivism is a theory or an approach. Wendt's *Social Theory of International Politics* (1999) is widely regarded as an attempt to elevate constructivism as a theory, or a form of systemic theorizing. However, constructivists themselves have maintained that it is not a substantive theory of politics but rather 'a social theory that makes claims about the nature of social life and social change' (Finnemore and Sikkink 2001: 393). Ruggie (1998: 879) also contends that it is not an IR theory in the same manner that the balance-of-power theory is; rather it should be seen as 'a theoretically informed approach to the study of international relations'.

KEY IDEAS 6.1 Origins of constructivist thought

Constructivism owes its origins to earlier philosophical and sociological modes of thought. From Kant, constructivists gain an appreciation that our knowledge about the world may never be objective because we process that knowledge through our own structures of understanding. Social facts, such as 'money', rely on common agreement about their meaning. Money in itself has no intrinsic meaning apart from our common understanding of it. We use it to buy things, it has a function in the market, and we may associate it with our own security. Sovereignty is a social fact because states and citizens understand its principles of non-interference and recognition in the international system. From Searle, constructivists understand that social facts differ from 'brute' facts such as a lake or a mountain; they are common understandings not only about the object but also about its broader meaning. This implies that the world 'out there' is not given but constructed by those who inhabit it. Giddens's structuration theory has been influential here with regard to how structure has a dual nature, constraining human actions but also altered by it (Ruggie 1998: 875). Weber regarded humans as 'cultural beings', 'endowed with the capacity and the will to take a deliberate attitude towards the world and to lend it significance' (Weber cited in Ruggie 1998: 856). His concept of *verstehen* ('understanding' the meaning that someone intends or expresses) relates to analysing individualized experiences in a broader collective framework (Ruggie 1998: 860; Fierke 2001: 117). Social ideas and beliefs frame our understanding of the world. Durkheim proposed that different relations in a particular social order could influence social outcomes. In explaining why suicide was less likely to be prevalent in Catholic societies than in Protestant, he looked to the social bonds and belief systems that constructed Catholic society and the belief that suicide was a 'sin' as an explanation (Ruggie 1998: 856–8). Berger and Luckmann (1991), by developing a sociology of knowledge, sought to understand how everyday life and practice relate to ideas about reality—the 'social construction of reality'. Through our actions and shared beliefs, our reality becomes 'institutionalized', sedimented, and habitual.

The more critical form of constructivism draws its influences from ideas about the power of language and speech. Wittgenstein's notion that language is a form of action that is constitutive of the world and Habermas's theory of communicative action add insights into how language games, argumentation, speech acts, and the social nature of language construct our reality. The idea that speech is a form of action is crucial in this regard, and constructivists working along these lines draw inspiration from Searle, Austin (who distinguished between different types of speech acts), Foucault on discourse and its relationship to **power** and knowledge, and Derrida's deconstruction and the idea that text matters (Fierke and Jørgensen 2001: 4–5).

it is because we have come to believe that is how the world is, and our actions correspond to that reading of an 'anarchic world'. Thus, if we find ourselves in an anarchic system, it is because we believe it is anarchic. Anarchy is not a given feature of the international system; it is an idea that states buy into, and, because they buy into it and understand the world as 'anarchic', they act accordingly. Therefore, anarchy is not a natural part of the international system; actors who believe it to be so construct it as such.

Social constructivism has contributed to understanding 'security' by focusing on this agenda. It has lent new insights to topics such as European integration, NATO's persistence and enlargement since the end of the Cold War, national security policy, the social construction of threat (such as Islamic fundamentalism and the 'war on terror'—see Think Point 6.1—and immigration), the impact of norms and values in the international system (such as respect for human rights), and, also, the possibility for change in the international system. An important part of the constructivist agenda is to show how identity and interests are not fixed over time and space and are open to change and revision. This has important implications for security studies, offering the possibility of moving beyond the logic of anarchy and the ahistoric, 'timeless wisdom' of realist theorizing. The identity and interests of states (or any other kind of actors) differs over time and place. States also have more than one identity—the UK is a member of the European Union (EU), but it also has a history and relationship with other states (such as the USA or the Commonwealth and former colonies) and international organizations (such as NATO, the UN, and the Organization for Security and Cooperation in Europe (OSCE)). Constructivism also brings identity, beliefs, and norms together in understanding security: 'Global security arrangements include beliefs about the world (e.g. the nature of security), norms about social relationships (e.g. the appropriateness of the use of force), and identities about self and other (e.g. enemy, rival, citizen, or friend)' (Frederking 2003: 365).

THINK POINT 6.1 Security as 'socially constructed': the war on terror

The terrorist attacks of 9/11 were defined by former US President George W. Bush as an attack on freedom and democracy on a global scale, requiring a new response to a new kind of war. When framing the attacks, Bush drew on shared values and collective meanings in both the international and the domestic context. For the international community, the attacks represented a threat to freedom, security, and modern ways of life. Equating the ideologies and methods of Al-Qaeda and fundamentalist terrorism with 'Fascism, Nazism and totalitarianism', Bush (2001) claimed that this is 'the world's fight . . . civilization's fight. This is the fight of all who believe in progress and pluralism, tolerance and freedom.' Fierke (2002: 342) observed that the initial characterization of the attacks as a 'clash' or 'crusade' (which could alienate Muslim populations and states) shifted to an emphasis on bringing together a global coalition of states to 'fight terrorism'. Domestically, Bush drew comparisons with the attack on Pearl Harbor in 1941, which remains a significant event in the American collective memory, where America was caught by surprise, leading to massive losses. Bush argued that the attacks represented a new kind of war that requires new strategies, resources, and tools, such as deploying intelligence, diplomacy, force, cutting off the financial resources and support of terrorist groups, and other methods. The Office of Homeland Security, established in 2002, coordinates security responses to threats to US security. It brings together a number of government agencies, such as immigration and emergency planning. In its first five years, the Office of Homeland Security claimed to have increased border security, screened millions of travellers, increased the number of agents in the field, enforced immigration laws, and protected vital infrastructure. The impact of the war on terror has affected not only international relations but also everyday life. At the international level, states coordinate information and policy more closely in order to combat terrorism. Notions of pre-emptive action and the treatment of 'enemy combatants' at sites such as Guantanamo Bay, where normal legal codes did not apply, are also some of the ways in which the regular norms of security have changed. In terms of our daily practices, the war on terror is deemed to affect us in numerous ways, such as identity fraud, heightened surveillance, and conditions on our free movement (airports use technology to scan us, its personnel frisk us and tell us what we cannot take on board a flight, and so on). In the USA, threat levels are monitored daily, ranging from green ('low') to red ('severe').

But this is one dominant 'story' about the war on terror. Constructivism's task is to show how security is a socially constructed idea. The meaning that actors give to such constructions of security differs. For the hijackers, the suicide mission was a 'rational act' within their own structures of meaning (perhaps self-sacrifice for the greater good of Allah). For those outside this structure of meaning—and even within—this act was seen as 'irrational' (Fierke 2002: 342). More recently, Western discourses about the Islamic State have drawn on labels of barbarism and depravity and threats to human rights and Western modernity. Richard Jackson (2005: 50–1) claims that the events of 9/11 could have been interpreted in a number of different ways (such as the North–South divide or movements against the state and revolutionary actors), but the story that dominated was that of the threat of barbarism versus civility, conceptualizing terrorism as a 'threat and response' problem. Both Jackson (2005) and Hülsse (2008) suggest that terrorism needs to be interrogated more critically and that we need to understand how it is socially constructed by discourses and categories that are broadly accepted (see Chapter 21 for further discussion of terrorism).

KEY POINTS

- Constructivism has become a major approach in IR and security studies, drawing attention to the importance of ideas, identity, and interaction.
- It offers alternative ways of thinking about security, such as how 'anarchy' itself is socially constructed.
- It gives attention to ideational factors, in contrast to rationalist approaches such as neorealism and neoliberalism, which rely on material factors in their analysis.

Definitions and key concepts

In order to delve a bit deeper into constructivist understandings of phenomena and security, some of its key concepts require elaboration. By focusing on identity and interests, and how they inform each other, constructivists pay more attention to a dynamic that goes beyond causation. Considering how things are 'put together' or socially constructed implies interpretation, and seeing how certain types of political behaviour and outcomes are possible (Finnemore and Sikkink 2001: 394). This also applies to understanding identity change. The introduction gives a snapshot of the ideas that animate constructivists, and, in order to help you grasp the meaning of identity, collective or shared knowledge and culture, and norms, this section explores them further and contrasts them with rationalist positions on the questions constructivists pursue.

Identity

Identity is central to constructivist research for a basic reason: identity tells us who actors are, what their preferences and interests are, and how those preferences might inform their actions. Quite simply, interests cannot be pursued without a particular identity, and 'the identities, interests and behaviour of political agents are socially constructed by collective meaning, interpretations and assumptions about the world' (Adler 1997: 324). Shared ideas construct identity and interests and are not given by nature. Why does the USA consider five North Korean nuclear weapons to be more of a threat to its security and interests compared to five hundred British nuclear weapons? Wendt (1999: 1, 255) argues that it is because of 'shared understandings'. The UK is an ally of the USA, but, furthermore, it shares similar ideas, beliefs, and a liberal democratic identity. It also has a historical 'special relationship' with the USA, one that former Prime Minister Tony Blair (2000) claimed was 'about bonds of kinship and history. It is about a shared language and most of all it is about shared values.' **Intersubjective** meanings are ideas and concepts that are shared and held in common, and from these we can understand action and behaviour (Hopf 1998: 173). This differs from rationalist thinking, which relies on **causality** (that one thing impacts on another in a straight line of 'action–reaction'). Intersubjective meanings involve a different type of relationship, where practices and meanings come from interaction (Fierke and Jørgensen 2001: 117).

For rationalists, identity is either given (assumed to already exist and therefore unchangeable) or negligible as a factor in relation to security. For neorealists, states are 'like units', all seeking security in an anarchic world. The anarchic system 'tells' states what they want and what they should do to get it. Variants of liberalism generally agree on this aspect—states have certain goals to secure in the international realm. They may try and secure those goals via cooperation, but the same assumption is the rule—states have material interests. If states cooperate in the international system, they do so for their own (pre-given and assumed) interests, and do not cooperate on the basis of how they interact with other states. Interaction for rationalists is largely for strategic reasons. If neoliberalists look to identity and interests, they may examine the domestic realm or ignore interest formation, assuming it to be **exogenous** (relating to or caused by external factors) rather than **endogenous** (having internal cause or origin) (Wendt 1994: 384; Ruggie 1998: 879). Constructivists, however, think more deeply about identity and argue that the process of acquiring identity is *interaction*; actors form their identity when they meet and interact with others, and this can set up friendly, conflictual, or other types of relations. Constructivists owe this idea of identity formation to earlier social theories. Berger and Luckmann (1991: 194) provided the notion that 'identity is formed by social processes'. The behaviour of states is not simply the result of exogenous forces. Germany and France have historically been enemies, but, through their cooperation in the context of European integration, their relationship has evolved into a different one. War between the two is now considered impossible, because their relationship has evolved through interaction and the development of shared understandings to one of friendship. Interests and therefore identities have altered due to interaction and processes of socialization. In another example of how security is not determined solely by the structure of the international system, some have examined the social construction of **neutrality**, explaining its persistence after the Cold War and the meanings it contains for domestic identity (see Case Study 6.1).

Wendt distinguishes between different types of identity. In an early work he contrasted corporate and social identity. Corporate identity refers to the intrinsic, self-realized identity of an actor. The interests of a corporate actor exist before interaction with others, and an actor can have only one corporate identity, which is the basis for developing other identities. Social identity refers to 'sets of meanings that an actor attributes to itself while taking the perspective of others'. Actors can have multiple social identities that vary in importance (Wendt 1994: 385). He later adds 'type', 'role', and 'collective' identity to this. Type identities are multiple, intrinsic to actors, and self-organizing, and, in the international system, capitalist states and monarchical states are examples of type identities (in that we can classify them according to their 'type'). Wendt (1999: 226) claims that these

CASE STUDY 6.1 Neutrality

Realists on the whole argue that neutral states' security policies are conditioned by the international system and exogenously given—if a state is neutral it is because it is weak, geographically unfortunate, or isolationist. However, the end of the Cold War saw this logic challenged. With the end of bipolarity, rationalists expected neutrality to be consigned to the dustbin of history—after all, there was nothing to be neutral between. Neutral states were expected to 'get with the programme' and join NATO. However, that logic did not readily translate into reality. In Western Europe, neutrals such as Sweden, Austria, Finland, and Ireland did not rush to join NATO, and, even if political leaders wanted to ditch neutrality and sign up to European security initiatives, such a move was on the whole unpopular with the public, which came to associate neutrality with the identity of that state. A constructivist reading of neutrality examines the norms and values attached to neutrality over time. Constructivists argue that 'neutrality is what states make of it'—neutrality need not be interpreted in one way (isolationist and self-interested states not dirtying their hands in the ugly business of war) but can also contain other meanings (neutral states can promote change and peaceful initiatives in the international arena and are not part of power politics). Sweden is a case in point here. Its neutrality has existed for over 200 years and it has influenced the way in which Sweden sees security and itself. The hegemonic Social Democratic Party also saw neutrality as part of Sweden's domestic and international profile—concepts of solidarity, which had meaning domestically, were associated with Sweden's foreign policy. Sweden practised an 'active neutrality policy' and bucked the assumption that neutral states were isolationist and self-interested. It promoted peaceful initiatives such as dialogue and cooperation, disarmament, mediation, and peacekeeping, and took a deeper view of security in terms of inequalities in the international system in the North–South divide. It was also a vocal critic of superpower politics, defying the idea that neutral states are isolationist, keeping their heads down to protect their own interests (Agius 2006).

When Sweden joined the EU, it, along with Finland, 'exported' the core ideals associated with neutrality to the Amsterdam Treaty of the EU via the 'Petersberg Tasks', suggesting a less militaristic approach to the EU's security profile. These tasks included the areas where active neutral states had great experience: crisis management, peacekeeping, humanitarian and rescue tasks, and peacemaking. This is an example of small states being norm entrepreneurs. However, identities are malleable and subject to change. As Sweden interacts with the EU, it takes on its norms and values too. Sweden now defines its security in the context of European security. Although militarily non-aligned, Sweden contributes to European security cooperation. Laurent Goetschel (1999) has also applied constructivist ideas and themes to the relationship between EU security policy and neutral member states of the EU. Other works that adopt constructivist rather than rationalist readings of neutrality include Mlada Bukovansky's work on the importance of domestic and international processes with regard to identity and US neutrality in the early nineteenth century. She argues that, rather than isolationism, US neutrality was connected to a specific reading of US identity, Jeffersonian ideals, and republicanism (Bukovansky 1997). Karen Devine's work on Irish neutrality (2006) takes a critical constructivist position, deconstructing the 'Unneutral Ireland' discourse that drives the idea that Irish neutrality is a 'myth' (a device used by those who advocate dropping neutrality). Agius and Devine (2011) show that competing meanings attached to neutrality are mired in a political struggle over its meaning and status.

do not rely on other states for their existence. Role identities exist only in relation to others. The example Wendt provides is that of professor and student—this is an institutionalized role, part of our 'stocks of collective knowledge'. The role of 'student' cannot exist without that of 'professor' or 'teacher', and vice versa. Collective identity 'takes the relationship between Self and Other to its logical conclusion, identification'. This is where self and other becomes blurred. It is a mix of role and type identities (Wendt 1999: 226–9). As we will see later, many scholars are critical of this categorization of identity, but this provides some basis for thinking about how identity differs and how it is formed in terms of process and interaction.

Beliefs, collective ideas, and culture

Identity does not simply emerge but is part of a historical process of interaction, made up of beliefs, which, according to Frederking (2003: 364–5), are 'social rules that primarily make truth claims about the world . . . . Beliefs are shared understandings of the world.' Shared knowledge is important in identity formation, as it sets up shared understandings between individuals, communities, states, and the system of states. Collective meanings and shared knowledge constitute how we understand the world and respond to it. When humans and Martians encounter each other for the first time in Tim Burton's film *Mars Attacks!*, the gesture of releasing a dove is interpreted by the Martians in a completely different way from how we, as humans, might ordinarily understand it. We know that releasing a dove is a gesture of peace and goodwill. The Martians, however, interpret this as hostile and obliterate it with their ray guns. Ignoring for the moment that the Martians had intended all along to destroy Earth—and happily get down to the business of completing this task for most of the film—how would they have known the symbolic significance of the act of 'releasing a dove'? We, as humans, are aware of the significance and meaning of this act (because it forms part of our collective knowledge), but its construction and associations may be unknown to the aliens.

In this respect, constructivism gives more attention to culture (see Key Quotes 6.1). Most constructivists regard culture as a set of practices that give some sort of meaning to shared experiences and actions. Katzenstein's edited volume *The Culture of National Security* (1996b) contains chapters linking national culture to security beliefs and practices. Berger's study of German and Japanese post-war anti-militarism makes the argument that, instead of considering explanations of international structure, we can further understand both states' defence policies by examining the domestic cultural–institutional context. Berger argues that the impact of their defeat in the Second World War affected domestic societal and political actors. Their reluctance to use military force became institutionalized, changing their approach to national security in ways that other states may not contemplate (Berger 1996: 318). These studies of strategic culture examine the impact that the culture of a nation may have on grand strategy, military organization, security and defence policy, and political and societal actors. Wendt (1996: 49) described the Cold War as a 'cultural rather than material structure', and Huntington's (much criticized) idea of 'cultural clashes' or 'civilizational clashes' demonstrates growing attention to this category. Culture can have an impact on how states see security, but it is also crucial in terms of constructing the values and rules that inform identity. Whether it be fear of immigrants and refugees as a 'threat' to security, or fear of the cultures of others that are drastically different from our own, culture can be an important underlying reason when defining security problems that affect the state and other agents. That human rights are considered an important issue to individual and societal security also has cultural influences, because culture refers to standards that we set as acceptable to us.

> **KEY QUOTES 6.1 Culture**
>
> 'Culture refers to both a set of evaluative standards (such as norms and values) and a set of cognitive standards (such as rules and models) that define what social actors exist in a system, how they operate, and how they relate to one another.'
>
> *Katzenstein* (1996a: 6).
>
> Clifford Geertz (1973: 89) defined culture as 'an historically transmitted pattern of meanings embodied in symbols, a system of inherited conceptions expressed in symbolic form by means of which men communicate, perpetuate, and develop their knowledge about and attitudes towards life'.

Norms

Shared knowledge and practices produce norms, which are the 'collective expectations about proper behaviour for a given identity' (Katzenstein 1996a: 5). Norms are vital to identity formation; the norms that we adhere to (or choose not to adhere to) are part of how we define ourselves. Norms can be seen as good or bad, but they contain specific meanings for actors and provide a social guide to behaviour. Norms do not appear out of nowhere but are constructed by actors who have strong ideas about appropriate or desirable behaviour (see Key Quotes 6.2). Finnemore and Sikkink (1998) examine the cycle of norms, which start when cognitive frames are set, normally against existing norms. They illustrate this in their work on women's suffrage, and how this confronted traditional ideas about women and the appropriate role for women. New ideas about appropriate behaviour compete with existing norms, then cascade (or spill over) and become institutionalized. Berger and Luckmann (1991: 70–2) see institutionalization as habitualized human activity, from the individual to the collective.

Constructivists distinguish between *constitutive* and *regulatory* norms. Constitutive norms define the

KEY QUOTES 6.2 Norms

'Norms are the intersubjective beliefs about the social and natural world that define actors, their situations, and the possibilities of action. Norms are intersubjective in that they are beliefs rooted in and reproduced through social practice. . . . Norms constitute actors and meaningful action by situating both in social roles.'

Farrell (2002: 49).

'Norms do not determine outcomes, they shape realms of possibility. They influence (increase or decrease) the probability of occurrence of certain courses of action.' Norms are 'a shared expectation about behavior, a standard of right or wrong. Norms are prescriptions or proscriptions for behavior.'

Tannenwald (1999: 435–6).

'Norms are social rules that primarily make appropriateness claims about relationships.'

Frederking (2003: 364).

identity of an actor, constituting their behaviour and interests. Regulatory norms tell us what to do; they are the standards that tell a given identity how to act. A common illustration is that of sovereignty. The regulative norm of sovereignty is that it tells actors how to behave in order to be identified as 'sovereign' and sets out the rules of the game. The constitutive effect is that, as 'sovereign states' behave according to these precepts, they 'become' sovereign—their interests and preferences are shaped by sovereignty and others recognize *this actor as sovereign* (Katzenstein 1996a: 5; Hopf 1998; Ruggie 1998: 71). Nina Tannenwald's work (1999) has examined the norm of the nuclear 'taboo', arguing that it represents both a regulative and a constitutive norm. She argues that realism's reliance on deterrence to explain the non-use of nuclear weapons since 1945 is incorrect and lacking in empirical evidence. She asks the following questions:

- When the threat of retaliation was absent, why have nuclear weapons not been used? The USA had the opportunity to attack its enemies when its nuclear programme was in the ascendancy.
- Why have nuclear weapons not failed to deter attacks by non-nuclear states against states that possess nuclear weapons?
- If deterrence matters, then why have many states chosen not to develop nuclear weapons, particularly if they have not been included under the 'nuclear umbrella' of a larger nuclear state? And, if the 'nuclear **security dilemma**' exists, then why do non-nuclear states fail to conform to its logic?

Tannenwald argues that the nuclear taboo delegitimatizes nuclear weapons as weapons that can be used in war. The norms (both regulative and constitutive) surrounding nuclear weapons both stabilize and restrain states from acting in a self-help manner on this issue. Furthermore, the taboo is international and systemic. Public opinion, international organizations, and other types of multilateral fora all reinforce the taboo, the notion that this weapon should not be used. International agreements and regimes exist (such as the Nuclear **Non-Proliferation Treaty** (NNPT), arms-control agreements, and nuclear weapon-free zones, as well as general laws of armed conflict) to control and restrict the use of nuclear weapons. Taking US policy as a case study, she examines how norms surrounding the use of nuclear weapons shifted in decisive contexts. When the USA used nuclear weapons against Japan in 1945, there was no nuclear 'taboo', even though some forms of constraint, such as **just war theory**, codes of military conduct, ethical issues, and international law, were well established. It was during the **Korean War** when the norm against non-use emerged, growing in strength by the time of the Vietnam War. By the time of the Gulf War in 1991, the norm against use was taken for granted and institutionalized. Central to the taboo were ideas of 'civilized states', which set the boundaries for identity and behaviour. States that possessed nuclear weapons were judged by their restraint in using them. Restraint was associated with 'being civilized'. The taboo was both a regulative and a constitutive norm. It proscribed behaviour (non-use, thus *regulative*), but it also had constitutive effects (relating its non-use to civilizational associations of the Self and Others).

Norms have been central to the work of many constructivists. Finnemore (1996) shows that humanitarian norms have influenced patterns of humanitarian military intervention since the mid-nineteenth century. Decolonization and the abolition of slavery are amongst her examples and she demonstrates that unilateral and multilateral interventions on the basis of humanitarianism, whilst not entirely new, are important and are related to what is considered appropriate

CASE STUDY 6.2 The International Criminal Court

Caroline Fehl combines a rationalist and constructivist examination of the establishment of the International Criminal Court (ICC), which came into existence in 2002 despite US opposition to it. The US government did not wish for its own troops to be held accountable and tried outside US jurisdiction with respect to war crimes. However, the ICC came into being without the USA, largely because the norms of human rights and the need for international criminal justice were held not only by the states that signed up to the ICC but by international NGOs actively lobbying for its creation. Even though some regarded the influence of NGOs as problematic, signalling a 'new diplomacy' where non-state actors have greater power, there were those who would have preferred an effective ICC rather than one that would be watered down if the USA signed up to it. These 'norm entrepreneurs' argued that problems of legitimacy existed when it came to effective criminal justice in national and international courts (such as the UN international criminal tribunals for Rwanda and the former Yugoslavia). Fehl is interested in the constitutive effects of norms, how human rights norms and the problem of effective international justice were of increasing concern. Since the 1970s, more human rights conventions were adopted and ratified by more and more states, resulting in an almost universal acceptance of this norm (Fehl 2004: 371). Furthermore, human rights norms are more than just 'institutional rules'; they also define the identity of the members who are part of it. Even though some states might not comply, the norm has a constitutive effect in that it represents a *standard* for states.

over time. Newman (2001) also looks at humanitarian intervention as part of norm change, where the individual is the referent object of security. Intervention to protect against human rights abuses is emerging as a stable norm in the international arena. Constructivism posits that collective meanings can change over time and affect norms. Audie Klotz (1995) argued that transnational anti-apartheid activists influenced the USA to instigate sanctions against South Africa. The norm operating here was a normative view of racial equality, and the activist groups linked the issue of civil rights in the USA with apartheid. To discriminate on racial grounds was considered by these activists to be a 'bad thing', even though the USA had material strategic and economic interests in South Africa, and the norm of sovereignty (non-interference in domestic affairs) was strong. Rationalist approaches relying on explanations of material interest, Klotz argues, do not fit this change in US policy. Fehl (2004) also suggests that non-state actors had an important role to play in the establishment of the International Criminal Court (see Case Study 6.2).

Constructivists also examine 'epistemic communities' and 'norm entrepreneurs'. The former refers to groups with specialized expert knowledge, who share norms and create new norms informed by their expertise. Constructivists see epistemic communities playing an important role, transmitting shared ideas and causal belief with respect to policy problems. This form of 'evolutionary epistemology' (inspired by Habermas's notion of communicative action) sees actors alter how they deal with problems and their notions of problem solving. Rather than adapting to the constraints of the international system (Ruggie 1998: 868), the 'learning' that takes place in epistemic communities has implications for security, as Adler (1992) demonstrates in relation to international arms control. He argues that the high level of socialization and shared ideas amongst those forming this epistemic community (made up of individuals from the RAND corporation, Harvard, and MIT) imparted essential norms about the necessity of arms control via their scientific expertise. The diffusion of American arms-control ideas to the USSR was important with regard to creating the Anti-Ballistic Missile (ABM) regime.

Mutual constitution

For Alexander Wendt—one of constructivism's leading figures and the one who generates most debates about constructivism (more on this later)—'anarchy is what states make of it'. He argued that neorealism has given anarchy a privileged position in explaining international relations. For neorealists, anarchy produces a self-help world. The lack of a power above the state means that the 'logic' of self-help produces competition in the international system, creating security dilemmas and problematizing the possibilities for collective action. Interaction never affects this process, and interests and identities are ignored. Wendt argues that self-help and power politics are not a logical or causal aspect of anarchy. Anarchy contains no logic in itself. Instead, practices matter: 'Self-help and power politics are institutions, not essential features of anarchy. *Anarchy is what states make of it'* (Wendt 1992: 394–5). Wendt defines institutions as 'a relatively stable set or "structure" of identities and interests'. These structures can take the form of rules and norms but are dependent on collective knowledge. Institutions might be conflictual or cooperative. Wendt (1992: 399–401) sees self-help as just one kind of anarchy, an institution.

By thinking about anarchy in this way, Wendt highlights two important critiques of the rationalist dependency on anarchy as structuring the world. Wendt suggests that the structure is not given but rather constituted by the actions and practices of actors, whose identities and interests have a role to play. This relates to the agency–structure debate in IR theorizing, and here Wendt is influenced by Anthony Giddens's structuration theory, which stresses the duality of structures. His ideas about identity are informed by the symbolic interactionism of Herbert Blumer and George Herbert Mead, who examine how the self is constituted by and reflects processes of socialization (Wendt 1992). The actions of states and how they interact with each other constitutes international relations, and this can produce cooperation or mistrust. Once again this reinforces the idea that the world is made up of social relations and is not simply *given*.

When it comes to security, many constructivists refer back to Karl Deutsch's idea (1957: 36) of a security community, the idea that integrated interests produce a 'we-feeling'. Security communities represent common interests and a preference for peaceful conflict resolution. Deutsch suggested that two forms of security communities existed: amalgamated, which refers to a unified security community where government is shared, and a pluralistic one, where integration is deep but states retain their political independence. The Nordic region was seen as a pluralistic security community, where a shared sense of culture, history, and economic links strengthened consensus and cooperation (Deutsch 1957: 6). Adler and Barnett (1998) have developed Deutsch's ideas along constructivist lines, placing an emphasis on shared values, identities, and meanings when they consider how security communities emerge. They identify how conditions, process, structure, trust, and collective identity are important for the emergence and development of security communities, from 'nascent' to 'ascendant' to 'mature'.

If the world is not given, then this provides some scope for thinking about its dynamism and the potential for change. This is the distinction between rationalist and constructivist approaches (Hopf 1998: 172). Neorealist theorizing pays little attention to the possibility of change in the international system. It seeks to identify 'regularities' and patterns of behaviour, but moreover neorealism tends to argue that its account of international relations provides a 'timeless wisdom'—its rules and regularities can be observed and are repeated across space and time. As Wendt points out, for neorealists, the 'logic of anarchy is constant'. Although neorealism acknowledges structural change, it accounts for change only with regard to the shift from one distribution of power to another. Social change—for instance, moving from feudalism to a system of sovereign states—is not considered to be structural, because anarchy still exists and the distribution of power remains unchanged (Wendt 1999: 17). The following section examines Wendt's consideration of the types of anarchy that characterize the international system, and then explores the critiques directed at his conceptualizations.

KEY POINTS

- Relations are social, not material, and identity determines interest. Identity is formed via interaction and shared meanings.
- The norms that actors hold guide their choices in the international arena, and norms are both regulative and constitutive.
- Actors and the social world they inhabit are mutually constitutive. Therefore, if we live in an anarchic international system, it is because we make it so.
- However, there is possibility for change. Norms and ideas can change, pushing actors to alter their relationships and understandings, potentially from antagonistic to cooperative. Norm entrepreneurs, epistemic communities, and other forms of shared ideas can create security communities or more cooperative forms of security collaboration.

Wendt's three cultures of anarchy

If 'anarchy is what states make of it', then this opens up the possibility to explore different types of international security worlds that go beyond neorealist configurations. Wendt develops this idea further in *Social Theory of International Politics* (1999), where he proposes three cultures of anarchy: Hobbesian, Lockean, and

Kantian. Neorealists are limited to viewing anarchy as producing one type of system based on war, military competition, and the **balance of power** (Wendt 1999: 247). Wendt does not stray far from Waltz's idea of anarchy—he simply suggests that there can be more than one culture of anarchy, and anarchy does not have to lead to a self-help system.

Wendt suggests that at the centre of each type of anarchy there exists a particular posture: in Hobbesian cultures, the relationship between states is that of 'enemies'. The logic of Hobbesian anarchy is that of a 'true' self-help system, where no self-restraint exists and actors cannot rely on each other for help. Survival relies on military power, security dilemmas abound, and security is a zero-sum game. Wendt (1999: 265) argues that a Hobbesian culture has characterized the international system over time, but not all the time. A Lockean culture is characterized by rivalry, and Wendt sees this culture dominating since the Treaty of Westphalia and the beginning of the modern system of states. In a Lockean culture, actors regard each other as rivals but exercise some restraint in violence; warfare is accepted but at the same time contained (Wendt 1999: 283). A Kantian culture is characterized by friendship, where force and violence are eschewed in favour of cooperation in matters of security. Here, friendship is a 'role structure' where states resolve disputes in a non-violent manner and protect each other (collective security). There exist three levels or degrees of cultural internalization: coercion, interest, and legitimacy. When an actor is forced to comply with a norm (because non-compliance would result in some form of punishment), this is first-degree internalization. Second-degree internalization is different, in that states will comply with a norm because of self-interest. When states comply with and internalize a norm as legitimate, this represents third-degree internalization. Why does this matter? It matters because Wendt suggests that shared ideas may not lead to cooperation. It is possible to have a Hobbesian culture that is deeply underlined by shared ideas (that war is good) or a weak Kantian culture where ideas about security cooperation are only weakly shared by actors (Wendt 1999: 254). Wendt is adamant that there is no such thing as a 'logic of anarchy': 'What gives anarchy meaning are the kinds of people who live there and the structure of their relationships' (Wendt 1999: 308–9). Structural change occurs when actors redefine who they are and what they want. The shift from one culture to another and structural change is propelled by four 'master variables'—interdependence, common fate, homogenization, and self-restraint—which affect collective identity formation. The first three are active causes, and the more actors engage in these 'pro-social' forms of behaviour the further the egotistic Self erodes, bringing in Others. However, identifying with Others might pose a threat to the Self or survival; Wendt (1999: 336–6) suggests that the problem of being 'engulfed' by Others we identify with can be managed through self-restraint. Wendt's view (1999: 314) is that in the West structural change signifies the move from a Lockean to a Kantian culture in the late twentieth century, compared to most of international history resembling a Hobbesian culture, 'where the logic of anarchy was kill or be killed'.

Wendt's constructivism has generated much debate, largely because he accepts a number of neorealist tenets, such as states being the main actors in the international system and a commitment to a particular scientific understanding of phenomena, which jars with many of his critics. In this sense he is a 'conventional' constructivist because he sees similarities between constructivism and **rationalism**. Critical constructivists are more sceptical of this link, and the following section explores the differences between these two brands before moving on to the critiques of rationalists and post-structuralists.

KEY POINTS

- There is not one type of anarchy that is understood only in terms of self-help, and Wendt suggests three cultures of anarchy: Hobbesian (where actors see each other as enemies), Lockean (as rivals), and Kantian (as friends).
- Each 'culture' does not produce a definitive structure of anarchy; this depends on how deeply certain shared ideas are internalized.
- The possibility for change in the international system exists, and Wendt believes we are moving towards a Kantian culture.

Conventional and critical constructivism

Wendtian constructivism tends to generate the most debate, but it is important to note that constructivism is not a uniform approach; rather it houses a number of different ways of thinking about identity and social relations. United as they may be about the point that the *ideational* matters, constructivists have been broadly divided into two camps: conventional and critical.[3] What separates the two tends to revolve around questions of methodology and how identity is interrogated. Conventional constructivists tend to accept key aspects of neorealist systemic theorizing, such as the centrality of the state and the importance of a scientific or positivist approach to comprehend phenomena. Constructivists such as Wendt, Katzenstein, and Adler see constructivism as a bridge between rationalist and reflectivist approaches, enabling both to benefit from the insights of the other. In *Social Theory of International Politics*, Wendt (1999: 39–40) declares he is a positivist, because he thinks what really matters is what there is to know (ontology) rather than how we know it (epistemology) and that science should be question-driven, not method-driven.

Critical constructivists find this reliance on positivism problematic and argue that the distinction between the ideational and the material world simply reproduces the binary distinctions that characterize positivist methodology (such as strong/weak, man/woman, and, in this case, ideational/material) (Fierke 2001: 116). Inspired by Foucault, Derrida, and Lyotard, critical constructivists query the power of discourse, language, reality, and meaning, adopting a more cautious approach to truth claims and power relations (Fierke and Jørgensen 2001: 5). Critical explorations of identity can also be found in the work of Doty (1996: 2), who explores civilizing discourses in North–South relations and how they established 'regimes of truth and knowledge'. Weldes's work (1999a) on the **Cuban missile crisis** presents an image of social construction in terms of US identity and its claims to being a global power. Works such as these are important because they remind us that 'many of the categories we treat as natural are in fact products of past social construction processes, processes in which power is often deeply implicated' (Finnemore and Sikkink 2001: 398). In this respect, critical constructivists problematize identity more so than their conventional counterparts do, preferring to see identity as more complex than stable, less solid and given, and more reliant on power and representation (see Case Study 6.3). For instance, when we think of American or Australian identity, we see only the dominant interpretations, not voices that have been silenced. These omissions are dangerous, because we privilege one construction of identity over possible others, such as sub-national groups. There is also the assumption that domestic politics is consistent at all times (McSweeney 1999: 126–9).

Critical constructivists also pay deeper attention to language and point to its role in constructing reality. The works of Onuf, Kratochwil, and Fierke focus on how language is crucial in terms of comprehending meaning and interpreting the relationship between word and world. Onuf relates rules to language, taking Wittgenstein's notion of language as similar to the rules of a game. Speech acts, which relate language to action, and rules, constitute actors. Onuf (1998: 66–8) identifies three types of speech acts: assertions, directives, and commitments. Assertions relate to knowledge about the world (for instance, 'democracies do not fight each other'). Directives give us instructions: what to do, what will happen if we fail to do something (we may be threatened with a punishment for failing to comply). Commitments entail promises (such as signing up to a treaty). By examining the meanings that speech acts invoke, we gain a stronger sense of how language structures our world and relations, and a more complex sense of communication between actors. Language is constitutive and does not simply represent the world as it is: 'By speaking, we make the world what it is.' Speech *produces* (for instance, rules and policies) and *expresses* our goals and intentions (Onuf 2002: 126–7; see also Fierke 2002). Fierke's focus on 'games' also highlights a different way of seeing security (see Case Study 6.4). Language and speech acts have enormous importance because they can 'securitize', as Huysmans (2002: 44–5) observes: 'Language is not just a communicative instrument used to talk about a real world outside of language; it is a defining force, integrating social relations.' Security language can create a different picture about a social problem or a source of insecurity, and Huysmans draws attention to the role of language in constituting a link between migration and security problems (such as drug trafficking, terrorism, and fundamentalism, as a threat to the economy or the welfare state, to name some). The

[3] In the literature on constructivism, different authors label these distinctions in different ways, such as 'modern' and 'postmodern' (Reus-Smit 1996: 187–8), 'conventional' and 'radical' (Fierke and Jørgensen 2001: 5), or 'thick' and 'thin'. For the sake of simplicity I label these divisions in the same way as Hopf (1998: 171), into 'conventional' and 'critical'.

CASE STUDY 6.3 NATO's persistence after the Cold War and its expansion

A number of constructivist explanations have emerged over NATO's persistence since the end of the Cold War (despite realist predictions that it would fold) and its enlargement to include new members. Adler (2008) claims that NATO recognized the shifting nature of security in the post-Cold War where borders between East and West blurred, and new security threats emerged, adjusting its rationale to include NATO's Strategic Concept of 1999 repositioned it from a Cold War defence pact to a 'security community' based on the common values of democracy, human rights, and the rule of law. It created the institutions (such as Partnerships for Peace) to prepare applicant countries for membership through 'social learning' (that is, 'teaching' newcomers to adapt to NATO norms and practices, such as training and assistance). Gheciu (2005a) also notes that 'teaching and persuasion' were crucial for NATO in terms of projecting liberal democratic norms to the former Eastern bloc states. NATO was able to shape ideas about appropriate action (peaceful dispute settlement, multilateralism, and the promotion of human rights). This in turn impacted on the national identities of the former Soviet states. Many of these states were seeking a new 'home' in the international system, a 'return to Europe'. The Czech Republic, Poland, and Hungary were the first to join, because they made significant advances in internalizing Western democratic norms and values (Schimmelfennig 1998). Networks emerged to promote cooperation in both military and civilian circles, focusing on self-restraint and security cooperation, which in turn provided NATO with a new purpose—transforming it into a different security community.

However, others see this change in more complex terms. Fierke and Wiener (1999) argue that speech acts and language are important in understanding the enlargement process, and that we cannot assume that socialization happens unproblematically. For instance, what of Russia's problems with NATO expansion? How did these discourses affect the applicant countries and NATO itself? Williams and Neumann (2000) also point to the importance of narratives and recognizing different discourses that exist in this context, arguing that NATO represented a symbolically powerful civilizational entity that had cultural commonalities. NATO's enlargement also had implications for Russia, framing its options in specific ways.

'security knowledge' produced by police agencies and the military, the media and other official bodies, are powerful in that they can articulate threat or danger; speaking and writing can construct security problems. Those who deploy language when examining the construction of threat, danger, and identities claim that we gain a better understanding of the complexity and construction itself.

At the core of the distinctions between conventional and critical variants of constructivism is the degree to which there is an acceptance on what is 'fixed'. Critical constructivists aim to denaturalize identity and the logic through which we comprehend the world, focusing instead on the context of interaction and intersubjective meanings. As Fierke points out, these things matter. Uttering an apology or describing a conflict as **'genocide'** has implications for meaning and action, constituting what is possible and what is not. The reluctance of the USA to describe the conflict in Rwanda as 'genocide' existed for a reason—to do so would have compelled intervention. Understanding the conflict as one of 'local tribal warfare' would not imply intervention because of the different moves and understandings invoked by sovereignty (Fierke 2002: 348).

CASE STUDY 6.4 Cold War endings

Understanding how the Cold War ended is crucial with regard to thinking about dominating ideas of how the demise of bipolarity was evidence of a 'triumph of the West' and liberal capitalist democracy. However, constructivists and others read this change in different ways, and saw it as linked to Soviet foreign and domestic policies of the mid-1980s–early 1990s. Rather than the Soviet Union 'losing' the Cold War, it was Gorbachev's programme of *perestroika* and *glasnost* that set a new framework for Soviet foreign and domestic relations. For Risse-Kappen (1994: 185), structural or functional explanations for the end of the Cold War (whether realist or liberal) could not account for the change in Soviet foreign policy and the Western response to it. For Fierke (2001: 131–3), the end of the Cold War was not about a victory or the end of a game; it was about the conflict between two different games of security. One game was defined by deterrence, the threat or use of force and the balance of power. The other was about the possibility of change via dialogue promoted by human rights and peace initiatives in both the East and the West, which was eventually adopted by the superpower leaders, Gorbachev and Reagan, which resulted in the breakdown of the Cold War structure.

> **KEY POINTS**
>
> - Conventional constructivism puts forward the idea that there can be a *via media* (a synergy or 'bridge') between rationalist and reflectivist approaches. Critical constructivists argue that this goal is contradictory and problematic.
> - Both differ in their treatment of identity. Critical constructivists argue that identity is more complex and multiple than conventional constructivists present it. The latter tend to see identity as uniform and solid, ignoring questions of power and representation.
> - Critical constructivists argue that language structures our reality and has a constitutive role, something that conventional constructivists tend to ignore or downplay. This has resulted in a positivist (conventional) and post-positivist (critical) divide between the two camps.

Critiques of constructivism

Critical constructivism's problems with its conventional sibling hints at a broader set of critiques that have emerged around this approach. Despite its stellar rise, constructivism faces a number of attacks and this section explores the rationalist and poststructuralist complaints. Let's start with rationalism. On a general level, rationalists claim that constructivism cannot test its claims empirically and fails to recognize that alternative theories may say essentially the same thing. When constructivists try to explain how ideas have been crucial in shaping the interests and actions of states—for instance, on what basis and for what reason would a country join the EU?—Moravcsik (2001: 177–84) argues that other theories such as liberal intergovernmentalism draw upon similar explanations (see also Kowert 2001: 165). So the questions that Moravcsik asks are: what makes constructivism different and what sort of contribution does it make to how we understand the world?

Kowert (2001: 161–5) is sceptical about the value of identity and Wendt's lack of a theory of identity formation. Wendt's three cultures of anarchy also appear to be separate worlds of their own and limited to these three images of enemy, rival, and friend. Dale C. Copeland (2006) also critiques Wendt for failing to account for an important realist category: uncertainty. Wendt does not consider that actors might deceive each other and his theory of systemic constructivism does not comment on the present and future intentions of other actors. Copeland suggests that we cannot know if another actor is acting cooperatively—they may be acting so in order to mask aggressive goals. Both Copeland and Krasner argue that there is little empirical evidence about cooperation. Krasner is also doubtful about the power of norms, particularly when interests are at stake. A norm of sovereignty is the principle of non-interference but this norm can be violated (Krasner 2000). How can we 'prove' norms exist and affect behaviour? Furthermore, how do we know which norms are at play in a given situation (Farrell 2002: 60–1)? Another common criticism is that constructivism takes the state as given and assumes it to be the most important actor, neglecting internationalization in a globalized world (Keohane 2000). Constructivist research tends to focus on the state and 'good norms'. The centrality of the state is a point of contention for poststructuralist critiques, which argue that the reification of the state is a key problem of constructivism.

David Campbell also sees the constructivist treatment of identity as problematic. He argues that identity is always constructed as difference and we must be aware of how this creates 'insides and outsides' and the need to confront these divides when examining the construction of danger from 'evil others' outside the state. Identity has been the basis of problematic interventions by states into the outside world, defining others as inferior and relations as hierarchical. Furthermore, Campbell sees the turn to culture, norms, and ideas as troublesome. 'Culture' can become a variable that is given causal qualities. These categories can be constructed as a threat, ignoring larger ethical-political issues at stake. Additionally the notion that ideas have a causal power is problematic. Campbell argues that, by privileging the ideational as causal, conventional constructivists simply replace material causality with ideas. This contradicts one of the central claims of constructivism: inter-subjectivity, which is a **dialogical** (relating to or in the form of dialogue) relationship where meanings and practices stem from interaction. What is more interesting is the possibility of deconstructing and denaturalizing identity, to consider alternative readings of identity (Campbell 1998a: 218–23; Fierke 2001: 116–17). Ronen Palan (2000: 598) also argues that the potential to explore the relationship between practice, theory, and institutional behaviour has been lost through an inaccurate employment of social theory, which results in a problematic form of 'idealism'. Both Cynthia Weber and Maja Zehfuss

! THINK POINT 6.2 Contestable identities and the limits of Wendtian identity

Wendt's treatment of the state is problematic because he sees states as the most important actors and takes their identity as given. Zehfuss argues that we fail to get a sense of more complex readings of identity from Wendt's formulation of it—how do we know how it came about, what shaped it, and if it is in fact 'whole'? Zehfuss (2002: 61) also criticizes the lack of attention to the domestic level. In Wendt's reading of identity and change, we only get a sense of change coming from outside forces or influences. Zehfuss reveals the level of complexity that can be gained from a more critical reading of identity. In her examination of Germany's decision to undertake military intervention in the 1990s, she argues that the discourses of the past ('never again war', 'never again dictatorship') made German identity contestable. The power of these discourses (never again to become an aggressive military force) competed with new challenges (what to do about ethnic cleansing in Europe's backyard). Its military participation in these efforts also had implications for understanding Germany's future identity and its place in Europe. Hence, by failing to pay attention to language and power relations, Wendt's identity lacks these depths. Wendt relies only on gestures and signals where interaction is concerned, meaning we only get a sense of how states communicate through their behaviour rather than through language (Zehfuss 2002: 48–9).

KEY POINTS

- Rationalists criticize constructivism because its claims cannot be tested or observed empirically. Norms, values, and identities are something we cannot 'see'. Furthermore, intentionality is difficult to discern and rationalists argue that we cannot say for sure which norms are operating in a given situation.
- Wendt is limited in his three cultures of anarchy and cannot tell us much about domestic identity formation because his focus is the states system.
- Poststructuralist critiques point to a reification of the state and a singular or essentialized identity. Placing culture at the centre may be dangerous in itself and privilege dominant power relations.
- Furthermore, constructivism results in an uncritical and apolitical explanation of politics and security problems.

put deeper concerns about the implications of constructivism forward. For Weber (1999: 439–40), constructivism is an 'evacuation' of politics, 'replumbing' neorealism through identity construction; it privileges state-centrism and resurrects the anarchy myth. Zehfuss (2002: 262) also claims that constructivism is apolitical and limits the space for critical thinking, because it takes 'reality' as given, closing off alternatives (see Think Point 6.2) and Charlotte Epstein (2011) levels a strong critique of the constructivist understanding of 'self' and the use of the concept of 'identity' via a Lacanian approach to the 'speaking subject'.

Conclusion

This chapter has explored some of the central themes of constructivism and how it relates to security. By making the claim that identity matters, constructivism presents a challenge to rationalist theorizing. Neorealist theories contend that states are bound to do the same thing in the international system—seek security and power—because the anarchic international system provides the logic that this is what a state must do to survive. Wendt's suggestion that 'anarchy is what states make of it' brought the debate back to agency, arguing that it is states who make the system anarchic, not that anarchy is a natural feature of the international system. This opened up the possibility of change. New norms can enter collective understandings and recreate the international system of states. Interaction means that states do not just bump against each other as in the billiard-ball model, but through interaction states can alter their identities and establish new frameworks for cooperation and shared understandings. Social learning and communication are important in interaction, and actors learn from each other. France and Germany are now allies, not enemies, via their interaction in European integration, and, although the USA treated Iraq as an ally in the 1980s, how do we explain its shift to viewing Iraq and Saddam Hussein's regime as an enemy in the 1990s? Shared norms, values, and beliefs, constructivists argue, can explain much more than rationalist theorizing. The central point is that we construct the world according to the meanings we give it.

Constructivism has lent insights into a number of security issues such as NATO's survival and enlargement, why neutral states have not yet joined NATO, and why human rights have become a central concern in the security policies of states and international organizations such as the UN, the OSCE, and others. But the way in which we can undertake a constructivist analysis differs. Conventional forms of constructivism tend to accept that there exists some compatibility between rationalist and constructivist approaches. By highlighting identity, norms, and values, some constructivists believe that they can fill in the gaps of rationalist theories. Others remain sceptical about this possibility, arguing that we must pay attention to power, the importance of discourse, and language, and interrogate them critically. Conventional constructivists such as Wendt accept that the state is the most important actor in the international system and that the identity of a state is given. Many critical constructivists find this to be lacking and argue that we must investigate identity more rigorously in order to uncover its meaning and construction.

Constructivism now forms one of the dominant modes of analysis in international relations and security studies. Its attention to identity, norms, values, culture, and interaction have produced some alternative readings of security problems, how we frame and define them, and how our shared ideas impact on security issues. The idea that we construct the world around us and what it means suggests an escape clause from realism's 'timeless wisdom'.

QUESTIONS

1. Why does identity matter to constructivists?
2. What are norms and how do they affect security?
3. What is the difference between conventional and critical constructivism? Does it matter? If so, why?
4. How do constructivists think about agents and structures?
5. What is problematic about Wendtian constructivism?
6. How do constructivist accounts of security questions, such as the persistence and expansion of NATO after the Cold War, differ from rationalist accounts?
7. Is security always about identity?
8. Do any of Wendt's three cultures of anarchy accurately reflect the international system today?
9. What is beneficial and problematic about conventional constructivism's claim to build bridges between rationalist and reflectivist approaches?
10. To what extent is culture important in terms of security?

FURTHER READING

- Biersteker, T. J. and Weber, C. (eds) (1996), *State Sovereignty as Social Construct*, Cambridge: Cambridge University Press. An excellent edited volume that contains numerous essays exploring the social construction of sovereignty in relation to a number of topics and themes, such as colonial imperialism and national identity.
- Fierke, K. M. and Jørgensen, K. E. (eds) (2001), *Constructing International Relations: The Next Generation*, New York: M. E. Sharpe. A very good introduction to constructivism, particularly critical constructivism, with contributions from key poststructuralist scholars.

- Guzzini, S. and Leander, A. (eds) (2006), *Constructivism and International Relations. Alexander Wendt and his Critics*, Abingdon and New York: Routledge. Contains some rather advanced essays on constructivism, all directed at Wendt's *Social Theory of International Politics*, with a reply by Wendt in the final section.
- Katzenstein, P. J. (ed.) (1996), *The Culture of National Security. Norms and Identity in World Politics*, New York: Columbia University Press. Excellent for getting to grips with conventional constructivism, strategic culture, and security questions. This edited volume contains contributions from Wendt, Finnemore, Barnett, and many other names associated with security and constructivist analysis. Focuses more on norms.
- Kubálková, V. (ed.) (2001), *Foreign Policy in a Constructed World*, New York: M. E. Sharpe. This edited collection contains essays outlining constructivism and applications of constructivism to foreign policy and security case studies.
- Weldes, J. , Laffey, M. , Gusterson, H. , and Duvall, R. (eds) (1999), *Cultures of Insecurity: States, Communities, and the Production of Danger*, Minneapolis: University of Minnesota Press. An extremely useful and relevant edited volume, this brings together security and culture with a great range of chapters covering various topics related to security.

IMPORTANT WEBSITES

- **http://www.fernuni-hagen.de/ecpr-identity/** The European Consortium for Political Research (ECPR) has a Standing Group on Identity. Here you can find publication details of work in this area, including its Young Scholars School section that has a focus on European identity.
- **http://www.e-ir.info/** e-International Relations. A great website for students of international relations and security studies, containing contributions from students and scholars on current affairs as well as theoretical debates. There are a number of good engagements with constructivist theorizing or approaches here.
- **http://www.iamanamericanproject.com** Cynthia Weber's project 'I am an American' explores different interpretations of American identity in response to the United States' Ad Council campaign to unite the nation after the 9/11 attacks. Weber's documentary problematizes these idealized images of American unity represented by the Ad Council with representations of Americans who fall outside of this ideal.

Visit the Online Resource Centre that accompanies this book for lots of interesting additional material: www.oxfordtextbooks.co.uk/orc/collins4e/

7

Critical Security Studies: A Schismatic History

David Mutimer

Chapter Contents

Reader's Guide

This chapter provides a partial history of a label. It is partial both in that it is not, and cannot be, complete, and in that I am both the author of, and participant in, the history. It is therefore partial in the way all other history is partial. The label is 'Critical Security Studies'. The chapter tells a story of the origin of the label and the way it has developed and fragmented since the early 1990s. It sets out the primary claims of the major divisions that have emerged within the literatures to which the label has been applied: constructivism, critical theory, and **poststructuralism**. Ultimately, the chapter suggests that Critical Security Studies needs to foster an 'ethos of critique' in either the study or refusal of security, and that the chapter is an instance of that ethos directed at Critical Security Studies itself.

Introduction: 'Follow the sign of the gourd'

Very soon after being identified as the Messiah in *Monty Python's Life of Brian*, Brian is chased by a growing crowd of would-be followers. In his haste to get away, Brian drops the gourd he has just bought and loses one of his sandals. Several of the followers remove one of their shoes and hop about on one foot, convinced this is what their newly found Messiah has told them to do. One follower picks up the shoe and shouts 'Follow the sign of the shoe.' Another picks up the gourd, shouting Follow the sign of the gourd.' Perhaps predictably, within seconds, those hopping are fighting those who are following the shoe who are fighting those who are following the gourd. Brian's 'ministry' has splintered into sects before it has even had the chance to establish itself as a ministry. The Python gang were, of course, satirizing the tendency of religious movements to fragment, as they had at the outset of the film satirized the similar tendency of political movements: 'Are you the Judean People's Front?' 'Fuck off! We're the People's Front of Judea . . . Judean People's Front . . . SPLITTERS!'

Sadly, perhaps, this all too human tendency to fragment into ever-smaller and more exclusive and exclusionary clubs affects academic movements every bit as much as it does religious and political. Any society of ideas is, in addition, a potential source and expression of **power**. It provides the intellectual resources around which to mobilize people and resources of other kinds: whether these are tithes/alms, ballots/arms, or even tenure/articles. None of this should be in any way surprising to those who work within the area covered by this chapter. While the chapter will show the divisions into which **Critical Security Studies** has rapidly fallen, one of the shared commitments of the work it will discuss is to the political potency of ideas. The social world is produced in and through the ideas that make it meaningful, which are themselves necessarily social. A consequence of this observation is that study of the social world is inextricably bound up with the world it studies; it is part of the productive set of ideas that make the world.

This chapter provides a partial history of a label. It is partial both in that it is not, and cannot be, complete, and in that I am both the author of and a participant in the history. It is therefore partial in the way all other history is partial. The label is 'Critical Security Studies'.[1] It is a label that has (one of) its origins in a conference held at York University in Canada in 1994. As a label it has been fought over rather more than it has been applied. It does not denote a coherent set of views, an 'approach' to security; rather it indicates a desire. It is a desire to move beyond the strictures of security as it was studied and practised in the Cold War, and in particular a desire to make that move in terms of some form of critique. It is a desire articulated in the first line of the first book bearing the title 'Critical Security Studies': 'This book emerged out of a desire to contribute to the development of a self-consciously critical perspective within security studies' (Williams and Krause 1997: vii).

The form of security studies against which Critical Security Studies was directed has been neatly captured by one of the proponents of the traditional approach:

> Security studies may be defined as the study of the threat, use, and control of military force. It explores the conditions that make the use of force more likely, the ways that the use of force affects individuals, states, and societies, and the specific policies that states adopt in order to prepare for, prevent, or engage in war.
>
> Walt (1991: 212)

The focus on the threat, use, and control of military force imposed a series of important strictures on the study of security in this period. Military forces are generally the preserve of states, and, what is more, there is a normative assumption that they *should* be the preserve of states, even when they are not. Indeed, our common definition of the state is that institution which has a monopoly on the legitimate means of violence. Therefore, by studying the threat, use, and control of military force, security studies privileges the position of the state. Furthermore, such an approach implies that the state is the primary object that is to be secured—that is, the state is the **referent object** of security. Finally, and most obviously, thinking of security as the threat, use, and control of military force reduces security to *military* security, and renders other forms of security as something else.

[1] When I refer to the label or to the 'field' of enquiry that is increasingly gathered under that label, I will capitalize Critical Security Studies. Otherwise, I leave the terms in the lower case.

The various scholars who followed the desire towards a critical security study were troubled by all three of these major assumptions underlying the conventional study of security. They wondered, first of all, whether our concern needed to be only on the state and its security. What of the security of people living within states? The standard assumption of security studies is that the people are secure if the state is secure, but those drawn towards Critical Security Studies wondered about those times when this was not the case: when states ignored the security of some of their people, when they actively oppressed some of their people, or when the state lacked the capacity to provide security for its people. They were therefore led to wonder whether we should be thinking about referent objects other than the state.

Questioning the referent object of security leads inexorably to questioning the exclusive focus on the threat, use, and control of military force. Large, powerful, stable states such as those in which 'security studies' tended to be practised—the United States, the United Kingdom, or Canada—may be seriously threatened only by war. On the other hand, other potential referent objects, particularly people and their collectives, can be threatened in all sorts of ways. Therefore, once you question the referent object of security, you must also question the *nature and scope* of security, and thus of security studies.

Not everyone who questioned the referent object and the nature and scope of security would be drawn to a desire for a critical security study, however. That desire was driven by a recognition of the power of ideas, and thus a discomfort with the way **traditional security** studies focused on the state. The concern was not that there were other objects to be secured in other ways, but rather that the *effect* of studying security as the threat, use, and control of military force tended *in and of itself* to support and legitimate the power of the state. While other scholars sought to broaden and deepen security studies to consider other referents and other threats, those whose desire ran to a 'self-consciously critical perspective' were centrally concerned with the politics of knowledge. Security studies as it had been practised provided intellectual and, ultimately, moral support to the most powerful institution in contemporary politics: the state. Those drawn to a critical security study sought a different security politics as well as a different security scholarship.

The remainder of the chapter traces what happened as scholars acted on this desire for a self-consciously critical security study. In doing so, it sets out the major fault lines that have emerged among those initially animated by this shared desire. The signs that have driven these fault lines are not simply Monty Python's signs of the shoe and the gourd, but rather represent disagreements about the nature of critique and thus of different forms of critical security study. Thus, while the chapter outlines the sects into which critical desire has fractured, it also sets out a range of answers to the question of what Critical Security Studies might be. My history of these splits begins in 1994.

Toronto desire: *Critical Security Studies*

In May 1994, a small conference was held at York University in Toronto entitled *Strategies in Conflict: Critical Approaches to Security Studies*. It brought together from around the world a variety of scholars, both junior and senior, with interests in security and with a concern about the direction of security studies in the early post-Cold War era. It was in the course of the discussions at and around that conference that the label 'Critical Security Studies' started to be applied to the intellectual project that drew the participants to the conference, and it was used as the title of the book, edited by Keith Krause and Michael C. Williams, that the conference produced: *Critical Security Studies: Concepts and Cases* (1997b).

The conference and book were an expression of the desire for self-consciously critical perspectives on security, but they both worked extremely hard to avoid articulating a single perspective in response to that desire: 'Our appending of the term *critical* to *security studies* is meant to imply more an orientation toward the discipline than a precise theoretical label . . .' (Williams and Krause 1997b: x–xi). The book therefore served to launch the label Critical Security Studies, but not to fill it with precise content (see Key Quotes 7.1 for some of the ways in which Critical Security Studies *has* come to be defined). Metaphorically, it threw open the doors of the church of critical security and tried to welcome the followers of the shoe *and* the gourd, and even those hopping around on one foot.

KEY QUOTES 7.1 Definitions: Critical Security Studies

Critical Security Studies has proven reasonably resistant to clear definition. This has been largely intentional, as the provision of a definition is limiting in a way that those behind the *Critical Security Studies* text wished to avoid. Nevertheless, there are some definitions in the literature:

'Our appending of the term *critical* to *security studies* is meant to imply more an orientation toward the discipline than a precise theoretical label, and we adopt a small-c definition of *critical* . . . Perhaps the most straightforward way to convey our sense of how *critical* should be understood in this volume is Robert Cox's distinction between problem-solving and critical theory: the former takes "prevailing social and power relationships and the institutions into which they are organized . . . as the given framework for action, while the latter calls them into question by concerning itself with their origins and how they might be in the process of changing". Our approach to security studies . . . thus begins from an analysis of the claims that make the discipline possible—not just its claims about the world but also its underlying epistemology and ontology, which prescribe what it means to *make* sensible claims about the world.'

Williams and Krause (1997: x–xi).

'An emerging school of "critical security studies" (CSS) wants to challenge conventional security studies by applying postpositivist perspectives, such as critical theory and poststructuralism. Much of this work . . . deals with the social construction of security, but CSS mostly has the intent (known from poststructuralism as well as from constructivism in international relations) of showing that change is possible because things are socially constituted.'

Buzan, Wæver, and de Wilde (1998: 34–5).

'Critical security studies deal with the social construction of security. The rhetorical nature of "threat discourses" is examined and criticized. . . . Critical security studies consider not only threats as a construction, but the objects of security as well. . . . Critical security studies . . . have an emancipatory goal.'

Eriksson (1999: 318).

'Critical security studies is a sub-field within the academic discipline of international politics concerned with the pursuit of critical knowledge about security. Critical knowledge implies understandings that attempt to stand outside prevailing structures, processes, ideologies, and orthodoxies while recognising that all conceptualisations of security derive from particular political/theoretical/historical perspectives. Critical theorising does not make a claim to objectivity but rather seeks to provide deeper understandings of oppressive attitudes and behaviour with a view to developing promising ideas by which human society might overcome structural and contingent human wrongs. Security is conceived comprehensively, embracing theories and practices relating to multiple referents, multiple types of threat, and multiple levels of analysis.'

Booth (2007: 30).

'There is no singular definition of what it means to be critical in security studies—and any rigid definition of the term critical security studies will tell you more about the position from which that definition is attempted than anything else.'

Peoples and Vaughan-Williams (2010: 3).

In their contribution to that volume, Krause and Williams aimed to set out the scope of a critical security study, and it has served as a touchstone in the further development of Critical Security Studies. They began their case for Critical Security Studies from the concerns with the traditional conception of security I have recounted. In particular, Krause and Williams began by questioning the referent object of security: who or what is to be secured. The traditional answer to this question is that the referent object is the state: security refers to protecting the state from external threats, and the people living within the territory of the state are considered secure to the degree that the state is secure. As Krause and Williams put it, such a view largely reduces security for the individual to citizenship: 'Yet, while to be a people without a state often remains one of the most insecure conditions of modern life (witness the **Kurds** or the Palestinians), this move obscures the ways in which citizenship is also at the heart of many structures of insecurity and how security in the contemporary world may be threatened by dynamics far beyond these parameters' (Krause and Williams 1997a: 43). If the focus on state as a referent object is insufficient, what if we adjust our focus to the individual human being, or perhaps to the community in which humans live? What, indeed, if we ask about the security of humanity as a whole, beyond rather than within the states in which most of us now find ourselves? These are the questions Krause and Williams pose as the foundation of Critical Security Studies. They argue that posing such questions opens a broad and complex agenda for security studies, an agenda that is largely hidden by the traditional focus on the state and the military. Suddenly we can ask about the ways states pose threats to their own people, as well as asking about the responsibility for providing security when the state does not. This question of the responsibility of an international community for the security of those inside a state cannot be seriously posed within traditional security studies, and yet only a few years after the Toronto conference, an International Commission on Intervention and State Sovereignty proclaimed a 'responsibility to protect' those subject to radical insecurity within their own states (see Background 7.1 and see also Chapter 22).

While the broadening of the security agenda was an important feature of the foundations that Krause and Williams were attempting to lay, rather more significant were the **epistemological** implications they drew from the challenges to the traditional conception of security. They argue that by looking at individuals, and particularly the communities in which they live, a critical security study has to take seriously the ideas, **norms**, and values that constitute the communities that are to be secured. Traditional security studies treats its referent object as just that: an object. The state is a 'thing' that is found, out there in the world, and subject to objective study by security analysts. By contrast, Krause and Williams argue that thinking of the varied communities in which people live requires an interpretative shift, a recognition that ideas (at least in part) constitute communities and that therefore the ideas of analysts are not entirely separable from the objects studied.

Having opened the doors of what they hoped would be a broad church, Krause and Williams set out the agenda of what would attract scholars to the service. Critical Security Studies would:

- question the referent object of security: while states were clearly important, human beings were both secured and rendered insecure in ways other than by states and military force; Critical Security Studies would engage in research that recognized this and explored its implications;
- consider security as more than just military security: once the referent object was opened up, so too were the questions of what rendered referents insecure, and how security was to be achieved, both for the state and for any other referent objects; and
- change the way security was studied, as the objectivity assumed by traditional approaches to security is untenable; indeed, once you consider the way human communities are constituted by ideas, norms, and values, it becomes clear that this applies even to the state, and so Critical Security Studies becomes a **post-positivist** form of scholarship. With the *Critical Security Studies* text, a range of scholars responded to this invitation in a variety of different ways, laying the foundations for the variation in Critical Security Studies we continue to see.

BACKGROUND 7.1 The responsibility to protect

In 1999 and 2000 the UN Secretary-General challenged the members of the UN to address the questions raised by recent incidents of genocide and ethnic cleansing: Somalia, Rwanda, Bosnia, and Kosovo. In particular, in a world of sovereign states, what could and should the international community do when those inside the state were subject to extreme abuses of their human rights? In response, funded largely by the Government of Canada, the International Commission on Intervention and State Sovereignty (ICISS) was formed, and in 2001 the Commission released its report, *The Responsibility to Protect.*

Synopsis of *The Responsibility to Protect*

Basic Principles

A. *State sovereignty implies responsibility*, and the primary responsibility for the protection of its people lies with the state itself.

B. Where a population is suffering serious harm, as a result of internal war, insurgency, repression, or state failure, and the state in question is unwilling or unable to halt or avert it, the principle of non-intervention yields to the international responsibility to protect.

Elements

The responsibility to protect embraces three specific responsibilities:

A. *The responsibility to prevent:* to address both the root causes and direct causes of internal conflict and other man-made crises putting populations at risk.

B. *The responsibility to react:* to respond to situations of compelling human need with appropriate measures, which may include coercive measures like sanctions and international prosecution, and in extreme cases military intervention.

C. *The responsibility to rebuild:* to provide, particularly after a military intervention, full assistance with recovery, reconstruction, and reconciliation, addressing the causes of the harm the intervention was designed to halt or avert.

ICISS (2001: xi).

When students and scholars discuss the breadth of the initial desire of *Critical Security Studies*, they will often make almost immediate reference to Mohammed Ayoob's contribution: 'Defining Security: A Subaltern Realist Perspective' (Ayoob 1997). Ayoob focuses on the first of Krause and Williams' challenges, and questions the assumed nature of the state in traditional security studies. He argues that the state in traditional security studies is the state of the advanced, industrial north. He seeks to expand that notion of security to account for the security concerns of the majority of the world's states, concerns that 'mirror the major security concerns evinced by most Western European state makers during the sixteenth to the nineteenth centuries' (Ayoob 1997: 121–2). Thus, while Ayoob questions the nature of the referent object of traditional security studies, he does not introduce alternative possibilities, nor does he enquire very far into other means of providing security, and he certainly does not contest the epistemological nature of security study.

R. B. J. Walker's contribution to the volume is exemplary of a much more radical break with the traditions of security studies understood as the threat, use, and control of military force. Walker seeks to understand the conditions that make possible certain ways of thinking and speaking about security, and in doing so explores the intimate connections between security and the history of the modern state. Ultimately, he argues that to think seriously about security in the present is to think about the reformulation of politics broadly: 'If the subject of security is the *subject* of security, it is necessary to ask, first and foremost, how the modern subject is being reconstituted and then to ask what security could possibly mean in relation to it' (Walker 1997: 78). This is a profound challenge, but one that has been taken up by a range of scholars who assemble around the label of Critical Security Studies, as we shall see later.

In between the avowed realism of Mohammed Ayoob and the radical political philosophy of R. B. J. Walker, the *Critical Security Studies* text showcased a number of responses to Krause and Williams's challenges (see Key Ideas 7.1 for one of the more intriguing), which drew on a range of theoretical traditions and explored concrete problems of contemporary security. Several chapters drew on the constructivism that was making an important mark more broadly in international relations. Others were more inclined to draw theoretical inspiration from the heterogeneous products of twentieth-century continental philosophy that are often lumped together as 'poststructuralism'. In addition, Ken Booth and Peter Vale, in considering critical security in the southern African context, began a journey that would lead ultimately to the post-Marxist Frankfurt School (see the section 'Aberystwyth exclusions').

Krause and Williams expressed the desire that led first to Toronto and then to the *Critical Security Studies* volume as seeking a 'critical perspective' on security. They worked hard to ensure that this critical perspective was not monopolized by a single theoretical approach, and so opened the conference and the volume to a range of theoretical positions. Nevertheless, the desire for a (single) perspective somehow remained as scholars responded to the challenges they laid down in creating their foundation for Critical Security Studies. Thus, despite their claims to catholicism, Krause and

KEY IDEAS 7.1 Security and Ken Booth

One of the most interesting and unusual contributions to *Critical Security Studies* is Ken Booth's chapter 'Security and Self: Reflections of a fallen realist' (Booth 1997). Booth came to Critical Security Studies as a well-established practitioner of traditional strategic studies—in his own words, a realist. That tradition trains you to keep yourself out of your research and writing, because its epistemology instructs the strict separation between the object of analysis and the analyst. Critical Security Studies emerged from a tradition that rejected that separation, and in 'Security and Self' Booth explores the consequences of that change through what he describes as 'an experiment in autosociology'. He examines the way in which the field has functioned as a discipline, to produce students and teachers of a particular type and to create a field of questions and limit the types of answer that can be given to those questions. The conclusion he reaches is 'that there is a critical relationship between the me/I as a theorist of security and what it means to study security. The argument has been that the meaning of studying security is not simply or necessarily created by the changes out there in the world, but by the changes—or lack of them—in here (who we think we are, and what we think we are doing)'.

Booth (1997: 112).

KEY POINTS

- The Critical Security Studies label emerges from a 1994 conference in Toronto, and is then used as the title for the book that conference produced.
- The initial agenda of Critical Security Studies was set by a series of challenges to the traditional conception of security: the state was not a sufficient referent object for security; thinking more broadly about referent objects required thinking more broadly about the sources of both insecurity and security; these forms of rethinking required an epistemological move beyond the empiricist, positivist traditions of security studies.
- Critical Security Studies tried to create a broad church for the critical study of security, seeing 'critical' as an orientation rather than a unique theoretical perspective.
- The desire for a critical security study initially drew scholars from a range of theoretical perspectives, including constructivism, poststructuralism, and post-Marxism.

Williams create the conditions for schism—the schism I continue to trace. In doing so, one of the key questions I consider is: 'If Critical Security Studies is not a perspective, not a position, what is it?' The first answer to this question was given by those of the so-called Copenhagen School.

Copenhagen distinctions

The year after *Critical Security Studies* had appeared, Barry Buzan, Ole Wæver, and Jaap de Wilde published *Security: A New Framework for Analysis* (1998). This book was intended to serve as a relatively comprehensive statement of what has come to be known as 'securitization studies', or the Copenhagen School.[2] I will not discuss Copenhagen in detail, as it is treated elsewhere in this volume (see Chapter 15), but it warrants a short sideline, for it has made two important contributions to the history I am tracing.

Security: A New Framework for Analysis is built around two important conceptual developments in the study of security: Buzan's notion of sectoral analysis of security and Wæver's concept of 'securitization'(see Chapter 12). Both of these ideas have helped to inform the broad church of Critical Security Studies, but it is the notion of 'securitization' that has been the more theoretically important. 'Securitization' is perhaps the most significant conceptual development that has emerged specifically within security studies in response to the epistemological challenge Krause and Williams note. Essentially, Wæver suggests that we treat security as a **speech act**: that is, a concrete action that is performed by virtue of its being said. 'Securitization' raises a number of very interesting questions that have informed critical security study since Wæver introduced the concept.

Despite this influence on Critical Security Studies, the Copenhagen School has sought to distance itself from Critical Security Studies. In part this is a function of an incoherence inherent in the approach between the sectoral analysis of security and the concept of securitization. While securitization opens the possibility of the radical openness of social life, the sectoral approach, as it had developed before merging into the Copenhagen School, draws on a largely objectivist epistemology. In other words, the epistemological underpinnings of the concept of securitization do not cohere with those of the sectoral analysis of security. It is the epistemology of securitization, however, that does cohere with that called for by the desire to a critical security study. In *Security: A New Framework for Analysis*, the authors argue that Critical Security Studies is informed by poststructuralism and constructivism, and thus is open to the possibility of social change. By contrast, they suggest that the Copenhagen approach recognizes the social construction of social life, but contends that construction in the security realm is sufficiently stable over the long run that it can be *treated as* objective. In other words, they resolve the incoherence by assuming long-term stability and so enabling a largely positivist epistemology (Buzan et al. 1998: 34–5).

The explicit separation of the Copenhagen School from Critical Security Studies did more than simply

[2] Bill McSweeny (1996) is generally credited with coining the label 'Copenhagen School' to refer to the work of Buzan, Wæver, and a series of collaborators.

announce that Copenhagen is *sui generis*. One function of the text has been to create 'Critical Security Studies' as something more concrete and less heterogeneous than the original desire. The Copenhagen authors talk of Critical Security Studies an 'an emerging school', and they shorten it to CSS. What is more, they ascribe to this emerging school two specific theoretical positions, poststructuralism and constructivism. This text, then, marks an important moment in the creation of Critical Security Studies as something other than an orientation towards the discipline, and also effects conceptual exclusions that are the subject of contestation, not least by scholars at Aberystwyth University, who have considerable institutional claim to the Critical Security Studies label.

KEY POINTS

- *Security: A New Framework for Analysis* (Buzan, Wæver, and de Wilde 1998) sets out a distinctive position on security studies, often known as 'the Copenhagen School', blending Buzan's 'security sectors' with Wæver's 'securitization'.
- There is an epistemological incoherence at the heart of the Copenhagen School between the epistemology of sectoral analysis and that of securitization.
- The Copenhagen School resolves its incoherence by arguing that the social production of security is sufficiently stable to be treated objectively.
- *Security: A New Framework for Analysis* seeks to distinguish between its approach and Critical Security Studies, and in doing so tends to produce Critical Security Studies as an emerging 'school'.

Aberystwyth exclusions

Rather ironically, the most aggressive attempt to produce a coherent approach for Critical Security Studies—to marshal all adherents to the sign of the shoe or the gourd, but not both—has been made from a position largely excluded by the Copenhagen School's characterization of Critical Security Studies as being informed by constructivism and poststructuralism. The attempt has been focused around scholars based in Aberystwyth (indeed, Steve Smith (2005) calls it the Welsh School), and has found its most complete expression to date in two volumes: *Critical Security Studies and World Politics* (2005) and *Theory of World Security* (Booth 2007). Central to both of these books is the work of Ken Booth, who edited the first and wrote the second. Indeed, *Theory of World Security* is intended to be a fairly definitive statement of Booth's thirty-year research programme leading to a critical theory of security (Booth 2007: xvii–xviii).

In both these texts, Booth is explicit in arguing that not everyone who would consider themselves working within Critical Security Studies will accept his orientation to a critical security theory. In other words, he is making a clear case for a restrictive understanding of critical security theory—he is saying to us, follow the sign of the gourd, and means it. He argues, in fact, that the formulation of a singular 'critical security theory' is the second stage of Critical Security Studies work. Booth's intervention, therefore, is an unapologetic desire for fragmentation. As he says: 'There are times when definite lines have to be drawn' (Booth 2005a: 260). He distances himself sharply from the Krause and Williams of *Critical Security Studies*, rejecting the broad church in favour of a single tradition aimed at giving rise to a coherent critical theory of security.

In his first cut at elaborating a critical theory of security in 2005, Booth followed his Aberystwyth colleague Richard Wyn Jones, who had drawn on the Frankfurt School tradition to think about security theory in his 1999 book *Security, Strategy, and Critical Theory*. Both see the Frankfurt School tradition as centrally important to the development of a critical theory for security studies (see Think Point 7.1 for an example of the sort of security analysis this tradition can produce). In *Critical Security Studies and World Politics*, Booth throws his net slightly wider than Frankfurt in identifying the tradition, adding Gramscian, Marxist, and Critical International Relations to the Frankfurt School. In other words, Booth drew on the range of post-Marxist social theory, particularly as it has been drawn into International Relations, with pride of place to the work of the Frankfurt School in general and Jürgen Habermas in particular.

The theoretical net of Booth's critical theory of security was expanded still further with his 2007 *Theory of World Security*. Here he took an explicitly eclectic approach to theory building, engaging in what he terms *Perlenfischerie* (pearl fishing), following Hannah Arendt, picking theoretical pearls from a range of schools and perspectives. His first set of pearls is the same set he drew from the post-Marxist oyster bed

THINK POINT 7.1 The persistent puzzle of national missile defence

The approach to security which starts with Frankfurt School Critical Theory has, as yet at least, not produced a great deal of scholarship which seeks to analyse contemporary issues or practices of security. One notable recent exception is Columba Peoples' *Justifying Ballistic Missile Defence* (2010), which began life as a PhD dissertation at Aberystwyth University under the supervision of Richard Wyn Jones. Peoples' book explores the (remarkably) long debates in the United States over ballistic missile defence, asking how supporters maintained their justification of successive missile defence programmes in the face of both scientific and strategic critiques. He argues that the supporters are able to draw on a cultural 'common sense' to maintain that justification. The idea of 'common sense' as hegemonic discourse he draws from Gramsci, while he uses the Frankfurt School's ideas on technology to analyse the content of the American common sense. The result is one of the only detailed discussions of a central issue of military, or indeed other form of, security from an avowedly post-Marxist Critical Security Studies perspective.

People's book is worth reading in conjunction with another volume that appeared shortly before it, Natalie Bormann's *National Missile Defence and the Politics of US Identity (2008)*. In this text, Bormann also takes up the (puzzling) persistence of ballistic missile defence in US political discourse, despite, as she puts it, a case that does not add up. Bormann provides, in the words of her subtitle, a 'post-structural crititque', drawing in particular on the work of Michel Foucault and her supervisor, David Campbell. The two texts make interesting companion pieces, tackling very similar problems while working out of the two leading theoretical traditions which have informed critical scholarship in security studies, and beyond: German post-Marxism and French post-structuralism.

in 2005, and still with the Frankfurt School the first among them. To this he adds a second, lesser, set of ideas: world order, peace studies, feminism, historical sociology, and social idealism. He calls the whole of the string of pearls that his fishing produced *emancipatory realism*.

What would such a critical security theory look like? Booth argues that there are eight themes that can be drawn from the collection of post-Marxist theory useful to a critical security theory (the eight are summarized in Key Ideas 7.2). He begins with the central claim of the Frankfurt School, that all knowledge is a social process—that is, knowledge is not simply 'there', but rather is produced socially, and thus politically, and there are 'interests of knowledge'. Knowledge benefits some and disadvantages others; it is, in the noted words of Robert Cox in International Relations, 'always for someone and for some purpose'. A critical security theory, therefore, must reveal the politics behind seeming neutral knowledge. Such a conception of knowledge implies a critique of traditional theory, including traditional security theory, which, by not recognizing its political origins and content, tends to a naturalism, assuming the ability to maintain a rigid division between the analyst and the social world she is analysing. If Critical Theory, therefore, reveals the false naturalism of traditional theory and the political content of all knowledge, it provides the basis for social change—indeed for progress. This third theme, of the possibility of progress, leads to a fourth: that the test of a social theory is its capacity for fostering **emancipation**. Change is possible, and progressive change is emancipatory.

KEY IDEAS 7.2 Themes of post-Marxist Critical Theory

- All knowledge is a social process.
- Traditional theory promotes the flaws of naturalism and reductionism.
- Critical theory offers a basis for political and social progress.
- The test of theory is emancipation.
- Human society is its own invention.
- Regressive theories have dominated politics among nations.
- The state and other institutions must be denaturalized.
- Progressive world order values should inform the means and ends of an international politics committed to enhancing world security.

Booth (2005a: 268).

The first four themes Booth derives from the broad Critical Theory tradition in social theory. To these four he adds four gathered from the specific, emergent critical tradition in International Relations. The first is that human society is its own invention. Indeed, this is a necessary condition for the operation of his earlier themes, for only if society is a social invention can knowledge serve as the basis for social change and open the possibility of emancipation. The second theme that Booth derives from critical IR is a particular claim about contemporary world politics: that regressive theories have dominated the field. If all knowledge is *for* someone and *for* some purpose, regressive theories are the ones that are *for* those presently in power with the purpose of maintaining their dominance. Critical IR theory has shown how the mainstream theories, including security studies, serve just this purpose. If this is true, then, the final two themes Booth develops are aimed at overcoming the regressive nature of world politics. The first is that the state and other international institutions must be *denaturalized*, so as to open the possibility of change, and finally that, in effecting that change to global (security) practices, politics must be governed by emancipatory values.

These themes enable Booth to argue that a critical security theory can serve as the basis for answering three sets of crucial questions in relation to security:

- First, what is real? If we reject naturalism, which assumes that the social world can be treated as objective in the same fashion as the natural world, then we cannot assume that the social world we investigate is 'real' in the same sense as the physical. Critical Theory's focus on knowledge provides a way into understanding social **ontology**, and thus the creation of social facts.
- Second, Critical Theory of this kind provides a means of thinking about knowledge, or the epistemology of social life. It directs our attention to the interests that underlie knowledge claims, and leads us to ask whom particular forms of knowledge are for, and what function they serve in supporting the interests of those people or groups.
- Finally, it suggests asking the old Leninist question, what is to be done? Critical Theory is a theory of praxis, a step in a process of political engagement designed to transform the world. As Marx put it: the point is not to understand the world; the point is to change it.

These reflections provide the basis for a specific critical theory of security (see Key Quotes 7.2 for Booth's definition of this theory). It draws on a relatively coherent body of social theory and its application to International Relations, and aims to inform scholarship and political practice in the future. While developed largely in parallel to the critical tradition in International Relations, Booth's critical security theory is quite clearly designed to provide a specific theory of security within critical IR. What this means is that Booth and his colleagues in the Welsh School have provided a clear answer to the question posed at the end of the discussion of *Critical Security Studies*: critical security study *should* be guided by a single, specific theory, and that theory should be informed by Critical Theory, with capital letters.

> **KEY QUOTES 7.2 Critical security theory**
>
> In his recent work, Booth (2007) has argued for the development of a distinctive critical theory of security, and proposed the following definition of such a theory, beginning from the Frankfurt School of Critical Theory:
>
> 'Critical security theory is both a theoretical commitment and a political orientation concerned with the construction of world security. As a theoretical commitment it is a framework of ideas deriving from a tradition of critical global theorising made up of two main strands: critical social theory and radical international relations theory . . . As a political orientation it is informed by the aim of enhancing world security through emancipatory politics and networks of communities at all levels, including the potential community of all communities—common humanity.'
>
> *Booth* (2007: 30–1).

In order to make the case for exclusion as forcefully as possible, once he has set out the elements of a critical security theory, Booth (2005a: 269–71; 2007: 160–81) distinguishes it from other possible sources of critical security study. He explains, in other words, what is wrong with following the sign of the shoe or with taking off our shoes and hopping around on one foot. In particular he distinguishes critical security theory from four pretenders: feminism, the Copenhagen School, constructivism, and poststructuralism.

The exclusion of feminism is the most troubling to Booth's position in some ways, but in others the easiest to achieve. As most feminist writing will freely admit, there are various feminisms that draw in their turn from a wide variety of social theory traditions in developing analyses of gender. These traditions include the Critical Theory tradition from which Booth proceeds. Therefore, gender analysis can be considered already to be within Critical Theory, and thus within a critical security theory; however, other forms of feminist theorizing are as antithetical to critical security theory as their theoretical traditions are to Critical Theory more broadly. The Copenhagen School is similarly dismissed with relative ease. The near-naturalism of the Copenhagen approach to society—so stable it can be treated as objective—leaves it 'only marginally "critical"', and in Booth's eyes (2005a: 271) suffers the same forms of incoherence I have already noted in this chapter.

There remain two challengers to the critical security theory Booth champions, the same two that the Copenhagen School identified in *Security: A New Framework for Analysis*. The first is constructivism, which Booth (2007: 152–3) argues is not a theory at all, but rather an orientation to world politics that serves as a basis on which to reject traditional theories. While Booth's argument may be true, it ignores the possibility, which I will explore later, that there are within that orientation various constructivist theories that do have something to say about security—just as other orientations, including Booth's, contain a number of specific theories within them. For Booth (2005a: 270) that leaves only poststructuralism, which is just too dangerous with its toxic mix of 'obscurantism, relativism, and faux radicalism'. In other words, Booth (2007: 177–8) argues, poststructuralism provides no basis for political action.

As might be imagined, and as Booth freely admits, the dismissal of constructivism and poststructuralism as elements of Critical Security Studies is not shared by all. These two theoretical positions represent, in fact, the conceptual underpinning of most of what might be drawn under the label, understood as the broad church. But even among them the sign of the shoe is defended against those hopping around on one foot.

KEY POINTS

- Ken Booth, Richard Wyn Jones, and their Welsh School colleagues argue for a specific critical security theory.
- The tradition within which they develop this theory is the post-Marxist tradition identified with Gramscian and other Marxist International Relations and, particularly, with Frankfurt School Critical Theory.
- The elaboration of the Critical Theory tradition gives rise to eight themes and a definition of critical security theory.
- Critical security theory provides the possibility of answering three key questions: what is real, what is knowledge, and what is to be done?
- Critical Security Studies should be organized around this critical security theory, and should not include feminism, the Copenhagen School, constructivism, and particularly poststructuralism.

Constructing security

If we exclude the Copenhagen School and feminist writings on security,[3] and further if we watch those committed to a critical theory of security build a hard-and-fast line between themselves and the rest of what might be considered Critical Security Studies, what are we left with? Keith Krause provided an answer in a review of the research programme of Critical Security Studies in 1998, and it is the same answer to which Booth came: constructivism and poststructuralism. Indeed, as with *Critical Security Studies*, Krause's (1998) review largely elides any difference between these two positions—the church is still broad, and so you can follow the sign of the shoe or take off your shoe and hop around on one foot if you like.

In an attempt to impose some order on the studies that compose Critical Security Studies, without resorting to the definitional strictures employed by both Booth and the Copenhagen School, Krause organizes a range of literature into a broad research programme. The effect of this move is to provide a characterization of Critical Security Studies, which, while still inclusive, clearly privileges constructivism. He organizes the scholarship of Critical Security Studies under three headings: the construction of threats and responses; the construction of the objects of security;

[3] The exclusion of feminism in the production of the Critical Security Studies label is a truly fascinating issue, worthy of complete treatment on its own. As we have seen, Ken Booth effects this exclusion through arguing that feminism is a broad church in its own right and that certain feminist analyses of gender form an important element of Critical Theory. Keith Krause (1998: 324 n.4) effects a similar exclusion in his review of the scholarship of Critical Security Studies: 'I have not treated the principal themes of feminist or gender scholarship on security as a separate category. These are dealt with in detail by [others].' Lene Hansen (2000) has reflected on this same exclusion in the case of the Copenhagen School.

possibilities for transforming the **security dilemma**. Krause explicitly does not intend these headings to capture the full range of critical security scholarship, nor does he suggest that scholars will tend to treat these issues separately. Nevertheless, the effect, particularly appearing at a time in which the Critical Security Studies label was being established, and coming from one of the editors of the *Critical Security Studies* volume, was to mark the character of Critical Security Studies as concerned with 'the social construction of security' (Eriksson 1999: 318).

There are two important features of Krause's review in the story of the creation of the Critical Security Studies label. The first is that it demonstrates the impressive array of research that is being conducted and published to which this label could be attached, countering, as Krause (1998: 316) notes, 'the oft-heard charge that critical scholarship is inevitably sloppy or unsystematic'. Second, he is able to derive from the review a characterization of Critical Security Studies that is far more specific than that provided by *Critical Security Studies*, and is clearly distinct from Booth's critical security theory. Krause suggests that there are six claims that tie Critical (Security) Studies together:

1. Principal actors (states and others) are social constructs.
2. These actors are constituted through political practices.
3. The structures of world politics are neither unchanging nor determining because they too are socially constructed.
4. Knowledge of the social world is not objective, as there is no divide between the social world and knowledge of that world.
5. Natural-science methodology is not appropriate for social science, which requires an interpretative method.
6. The purpose of theory is not explanation in terms of generalizable causal claims, but contextual understanding and practical knowledge.

A pair of books by Alexandra Gheciu illustrate the approach Krause sets out and demonstrate the sort of rigorous scholarship that is possible within the research programme. In *NATO in the New Europe* (2005b) Gheciu explores the socialization of former Eastern Bloc states by NATO in the years after the end of the Cold War. Socialization is an important idea in social construction, because it is the means by which actors are constructed to become members of a particular social system or community. Gheciu provides a detailed account of the way in which NATO socialized the Czech Republic and Romania to become 'Europeans' in a sense that allied with the liberal democratic notions of what it meant to be European in the 1990s. Furthermore, she shows how this socialization was an explicit security strategy, which she terms a Kantian or 'inside' approach to security—the formation of the state as a particular kind of state and thereby productive of security (Gheciu 2005b: 7–9). In *Securing Civilization* (2008), Gheciu explores the 'inside' approach to security further, by looking at the ways in which three key European security institutions—the EU, NATO, and the Organization for Security and Cooperation in Europe (OSCE)—respond to the post-9/11 threat of international terrorism. At the heart of these responses is the constitution of members as civilized/secure and those outside as barbaric/threatening (Gheciu 2008: 5).

The focus on the social construction of agents and structures, together with a commitment to interpretative method, contextual understanding, and practical knowledge, marks Krause's account of Critical Security Studies as largely rooted within the tradition of constructivism in International Relations, a tradition Gheciu (2005b), for example, then explicitly claims. Constructivism clearly shares homologies with both post-Marxist Critical Theory and post-structuralism, but it is not the same as either. Those following the sign of the gourd are welcome, as are those hopping around on one foot, but they may feel that they are then expected to join in following the sign of the shoe.

KEY POINTS

- Social constructivism forms an important strand within Critical Security Studies.
- Constructivism takes agents and structures as constituted in and through political practices.
- Constructivism denies the division between the social world and the analyst, and thus seeks an interpretative rather than a naturalist methodology.
- While attempting to maintain the broad church, the constructive account of Critical Security Studies privileges social constructivism.

Everyone's other: poststructuralism and security

Ken Booth's antipathy to poststructural approaches to International Relations in general and security studies in particular reflects a common, and commonly virulent, reaction. In addition to obscurantist, relativist, and faux radical, approaches labelled post-structural have been called prolix and self-indulgent (Walt 1991), and accused of having no research programme (Keohane 1988). For examples of the kind of research that is actually conducted by scholars labelled post-structural, see Think Point 7.2. The virulence of the rejection of poststructural work reflects, I would suggest, its radical promise. It shares with the rest of the work discussed in this chapter a pair of key commitments: a rejection of positivist epistemology and hence methodology, and commitment to social critique. However, unlike any of the other forms of critical scholarships I have thus far discussed, it does not stop short of the radical implications of these commitments. Indeed, a crucial commitment shared by poststructural scholarship but not by other forms of critical theory is a rejection of overarching grand narratives, and thus an acceptance that knowledge claims are always unstable and contingent. As a fairly sympathetic critic has put it: 'it is for this reason that most social constructivists and critical security studies writers are at such pains to establish the difference between their work and that of poststructuralists. Put simply, poststructuralists deny the form of foundations for knowledge claims that dominate the security studies debate. As can be imagined, this has led to much hostility toward post-structuralism . . .' (S. Smith 2005: 49)

The work that is generally labelled poststructural—and, as with the other labels we are discussing, is more commonly applied by others than by a scholar to her own work—draws on a series of intellectual traditions largely having their roots in French philosophy (as opposed to the German philosophy that animates the Welsh School, for example). While the work draws on an eclectic collection of writing, the most common points of departure are the work of Jacques Derrida

! THINK POINT 7.2 Traditional subjects in a poststructural gaze

Poststructural writing can take on subjects that on the surface appear to be the same as those found in traditional security studies. What the poststructural traditions provide, however, is often a radically different way of asking questions and providing answers. Here are two examples: the first, 'about' nuclear weapons; and the second, Canadian policy towards missile defence.

Hugh Gusterson, *Nuclear Rites* (1998)

Gusterson is a social anthropologist whose discipline privileges a particular kind of fieldwork leading to ethnographic writing. Traditionally such ethnographies are written about others' cultures, often the cultures of indigenous populations that have been (largely) untouched by European expansion. (Fortunately for the anthropologists, such cultures are often found on south Pacific islands!) Gusterson is part of a movement in anthropology turning the ethnographic gaze on his own society. In *Nuclear Rites*, he engages in an ethnographic study of the scientists at one of the US nuclear weapons laboratories. Making use of both ethnographic method and Foucault's notions of discipline, he investigates the ways in which the laboratories function to create the conditions of possibility for the building, testing, and deployment of nuclear weapons. As the title suggests, some of what he finds is that the design, building, testing, and deployment of nuclear weapons have evolved into a ritualized culture among the scientists that has little or nothing to do with the stories we tell ourselves about the needs of deterrence and defence.

Marshall Beier, 'Postcards from the Outskirts of Security' (2001)

In his study, Beier reflects on a study trip he took with a number of other Canadian scholars to visit the North American Aerospace Defense (NORAD) headquarters. NORAD is located in the middle of a mountain, usually identified as being on the outskirts of Colorado Springs. It is actually closer to the small town of 'Security' Colorado, and Beier uses this observation as the starting point for a reflection on the ways in which semiotic markers can affect group dynamics and contribute to the disciplining of dissent. He examines the ways in which opposition to missile defence was silenced within the tour, and considers the implications for the decision the Canadian government had to take on whether and how to participate in the US missile defence programme.

and Michel Foucault.[4] The rejection of grand narratives—such as those of 'progress' and 'emancipation' that inform the Welsh School—together with the varied and eclectic theoretical inspirations for poststructural work, means that there are no simple summaries or sets of bullet points that can be adduced, as with the other approaches. Ultimately, to borrow an expression, the only way in is through, and many of the texts called poststructural demand close and careful reading.[5] Therefore, rather than providing such a summary, I will consider a number of important authors and texts that are routinely cited, and thus form an important part of the story of the production of the Critical Security Studies label—even though few, if any, of these authors would slap the label on their own work.

One of the first of these works is Bradley Klein's 1994 book *Strategic Studies and World Order*. In terms of the history of Critical Security Studies, the importance of the text is that it took on one of the central problems that motivate the later development of the label: what are the political consequences of traditional security studies—that is, strategic studies. Klein considered strategic studies as a discourse constitutive of the global state and military system it purports to study. His approach to that discourse is informed by Foucault's work, which Foucault discusses as a history of the present, or a genealogy. Genealogical work seeks to reveal the historical trajectory that gave meaning to particular discourses and how they then function in the present. Famously, Foucault provided such genealogies—for example, of criminal punishment and Western sexuality. Klein turns this form of investigation on strategic studies, and in the process makes a compelling case for one of the founding assumptions of Critical Security Studies: that theories about the world constitute that world, and thus that theory, including security theory, has political effects. What Klein shows is that strategic studies is productive of the very system that makes contemporary global violence possible.

Simon Dalby's first book, *Creating the Second Cold War* (1990), similarly turns the poststructural gaze on a central problem of conventional security studies: in his case, the renewed Cold War confrontation under the Reagan administration in the United States. Dalby explores the intellectual underpinnings of US security policy, or, as he puts it in his subtitle, the discourse of politics. As a geographer, Dalby (1990) is particularly concerned with the ways in which geopolitics serves as a discourse underpinning the militarism of Reagan's international policy, and it is a concern with geopolitics as discourse which has then animated much of the rest of his work. In 1998 he teamed with Gearóid Ó Tuathail to edit *Rethinking Geopolitics*, which sought 'to radicalize conventional notions of geopolitics through a series of studies of its proliferating, yet often unacknowledged and under-theorized, operation in world politics past, present and future' (Dalby and Ó Tuathail 1998: 2). More recently Dalby turned his attention to security studies more explicitly, and explored the effects of geopolitical discourse in relation to attempts to 'securitize' the environment, and the environmental effects of this discourse when it largely ignored the environment (Dalby 2002).

Perhaps the most widely cited of the scholars working within these traditions is David Campbell, and for good reason. As Steve Smith (2005: 50) notes, 'David Campbell has written some of the best empirical work in poststructuralist security studies.' The first of these works is *Writing Security* (1998a), in which Campbell

[4] In his attack on poststructural IR, Booth suggests that most of those in IR who work from Foucault use his work on psychiatry, and then goes on to dismiss the IR work through criticisms of this early work of Foucault. To my knowledge, few working in poststructural security studies draw extensively on *Madness and Civilization*, an early work Foucault called 'archaeology', but rather on the later genealogical work, particularly *Discipline and Punish*, *The History of Sexuality*, and two incomplete elements of a larger programme on politics and war, *Society must be Defended* and 'Governmentality'. See, among others, Campbell (1998a), Gusterson (1998), Edkins (2003), Duffield (2007), Dillon and Lobo-Guerrero (2008), and Grayson (2008).

[5] One of the concerns with much of the criticism directed at poststructural work in IR generally is that it is not always founded on such a reading of the texts it purports to criticize. As David Campbell (1998a: 210) notes: 'What is most interesting about the conventional critics of "postmodernism" is the unvarnished vehemence that adorns their attacks. Accused of "self-righteousness", lambasted as "evil", castigated for being "bad IR" and "meta-babble", and considered congenitally irrational, "postmodernists" are regarded as little better than unwelcome asylum seekers from a distant war zone. Of course, had the critics reached their conclusions via a considered reading of what is now a considerable literature in International Relations, one would repay the thought with a careful engagement of their own arguments. Sadly there is not much thought to repay.'

explores the manner in which the United States has been produced in and through discourses of danger. He asks of US Foreign Policy some of the same questions, inspired by Foucault, that Klein used to think about Strategic Studies. In the book, he shows how Foreign Policy discourse is inseparable from what he terms foreign policy (the capitalization is the key)—that is, the production of an American self and a (dangerous) other, or a (secure) domestic and a (threatening) foreign. As with Klein's work, the contribution to Critical Security Studies thinking is clear. In the case of Campbell's work, both what Critical Security Studies will call the *referent object* and the *agent* of security (the state in both instances) is shown to be produced in its own practices.

The principal objection Ken Booth (2005a: 270) raised to poststructuralism as part of a broad Critical Security Studies church was its supposed inability to inspire a politics, and in particular its inability to '"shape up" to the test of Fascism as a serious political challenge'. This is, of course, a serious criticism of any form of critical theory that sees itself in any sense part of a politics of change, as it is difficult to imagine a politics more in need of change than Fascism. It is also an argument repeatedly raised by critics of poststructural scholarship, regardless of how many times it is answered. In Campbell's case, his most extended answer came in his 1998 book *National Deconstruction: Violence, Identity, and Justice in Bosnia* (1998b). The Yugoslav wars of the 1990s posed exactly the sort of challenge alluded to by Booth, as it appeared to mark the return to Europe of the kind of violent Fascism to which all had said 'never again' in 1945. (For a number of responses to Bosnia, see Think Point 7.3.) In a sophisticated and compelling text, Campbell engages directly with the question Booth demands to be answered: 'What is to be done?'

! THINK POINT 7.3 Researching Bosnia

The challenge of the wars in the former Yugoslavia, particularly the war in Bosnia, attracted the attention of a number of scholars in the poststructural tradition. The ethical and political challenge of the violence is central to these works, but what also emerges is a concern with the place of Western scholarship, and the nature of the research enterprise. In order to establish his argument about the political potential of deconstruction, Campbell (1998b) first provides a deconstructive reading of the violence in Bosnia. He explores the production of identities in Bosnia that enabled the violence of the wars and their attendant 'ethnic cleansing'. Making use of Derrida's notion of 'ontopology', he explores the production of identities tied to place in such a way that the other could not be allowed even to inhabit certain spaces without undermining the self. He then turns to the responses, particularly the international responses, to the violence, and shows how various Western discourses (including security studies) created the conditions that made the genocidal violence in Bosnia possible.

While critical of some of the intellectual moves Campbell makes, Elizabeth Dauphinée takes up similar themes in her book, *The Ethics of Researching War: Looking for Bosnia* (2008). Dauphinée too is concerned with the place of Western discourses in the violence of Bosnia, but she does not limit herself to an impersonal account of scholarly influence. Rather, she turns the scholarly gaze on her own place as researcher, asking what it means that, in the words with which she opens the text, 'I am building my career on the loss of a man named Stojan Sokolovic (and on the loss of many millions of others who may or may not resemble him)' (Dauphinée 2008: 1). Her answer takes seriously the poststructural recognition that the observer is never, and can never be, detached from what she observes, and in doing so provides a telling account of the limits of our ethics, and our research.

Questions of research are also central to Lene Hansen in her *Security as Practice: Discourse Analysis and the Bosnian War* (2006). The book also picks up the themes Campbell developed in both *Writing Security* (1992) and *National Deconstruction* (1998b), as Hansen develops a poststructural account of identity and foreign policy, and then uses that account to inform an analysis of Western policy in response to the Bosnian War. Where Campbell analyses Bosnia in part to answer the critics' challenge that poststructuralism provides no politics, Hansen analyses the same war in part to answer the challenge that poststructuralism does not engage in rigorous research. Hansen sets out a detailed method of analysis, drawing on, among others, Foucault and Derrida, which she then applies to Bosnia. Indeed, she concludes by comparing her analysis to Campbell's in an attempt to open an 'intra-poststructuralist debate', but holds true to her starting point by doing so not to determine who is right and wrong, but rather to explore the analytical effects of methodological choices (Hansen 2006: 217–20).

Campbell's answer (1998b: 196) to the question of politics demands to be read, and read closely, but centres around fostering the ethos of democracy: 'Democracy is not a substance, a fixed set of values, a particular kind of community, or a strict institutional form . . . what makes democracy democratic, and what marks democracy as a singular political form, is a particular attitude or spirit, an ethos, that constantly has to be fostered.' This is not an answer that many find comfortable, because it provides no simple blueprint, no single strategy. Fostering the ethos of democracy does not mean that when you hold a competitive election and anoint a 'democratic' government your work is done, and so the politics that is demanded by Campbell's accounts of responsibility and democracy are profoundly more difficult and challenging than those found in most areas of security studies, even Critical Security Studies. The difficulty has led, in fact, to a concerted effort among a number of scholars working in a poststructural tradition to consider issues of ethics and responsibility in relation to 'the worst'. Much of their work draws its philosophical inspiration, in part, from the work of Emmanuel Levinas, as did Campbell in developing his arguments about a politics in response to Bosnia.

The idea of fostering an ethos is also central to the notion of critique in much of the writing labelled poststructural. Both Welsh School critical security theory and constructivist Critical Security Studies provide an answer to one of the questions I posed at the outset: what is meant by 'critical'. For the Welsh School, it involves revealing the interests behind knowledge claims, with a goal of social change. Similarly for the constructivists, it is reaching a contextual and practical understanding to know whom knowledge claims serve. Both of these are relatively static conceptions of critique: they can be done in a finite sense. Just as Campbell argues democracy is never reached, but rather is an ethos ever to be fostered, so too is critique. Poststructural writing sees its critical purposes as fostering an ethos of critique, always working to destabilize 'truths', revealing their contingency and the nature of their production. It is not a finite project, however, but rather a process in which to be constantly engaged. As with its politics, the poststructural conception of critique is difficult for many to accept, because again it is not easy. It does not allow for finite claims and finished projects, and, as students of society, we are trained to provide 'findings' and test them in a settled fashion.

Neither Bradley Klein nor David Campbell—nor indeed a number of others often also included in a poststructural security studies list, such as James Der Derian, R. B. J. Walker, Cynthia Weber, or even Michael Dillon—applies the label 'Critical Security Studies' to his work. They are surely and avowedly engaged in critical scholarship—that is the fostering of an ethos of critique—and much of their work is centrally concerned with security. Michael Dillon (1996), for example, has written an extended political philosophy of security out of the tradition of French social theory, and his more recent work explores Foucault's notions of **biopolitics** in relation to the post-9/11 security strategies of the United States and other western powers (Dillon 2006; Dillon and Lobo-Guerrero 2008; Dillon and Neal 2008). Similarly, R. B. J. Walker is one of the leaders of a large research programme on 'Liberty and Security', in relation to the contemporary practices of the war on terrorism.

While most of these scholars have not entered the broad church of Critical Security Studies, their work has inspired some within it to take off a shoe and jump around on one foot. In doing so, some have hopped right back outside again, wondering what applying the label Critical Security Studies to their work adds to the project in which they are engaged. Indeed, the ethos of critique that work of this kind aims to foster demands that we turn our critical gaze on the very scholarly practices in which we are engaged. It demands that we ask about the politics of our own labelling, including the Critical Security Studies label, one of whose stories I am telling.

KEY POINTS

- 'Poststructuralism' is a marker for a diverse set of writing inspired by a number of, generally French, philosophers including Michel Foucault and Jacques Derrida.
- A number of works in this tradition within International Relations are claimed by Critical Security Studies, most notably those of Bradley Klein, David Campbell, R. B. J. Walker, and Michael Dillon.
- Despite criticism to the contrary, poststructural work does provide answers to questions of political action, just not the kind of comfortable answers many are seeking.
- Central to the political and critical nature of poststructural writing is the idea of fostering an ethos of democracy and an ethos of critique. These are never finite, never reached, but something for which we must constantly strive.

Beyond divisions? CASEing the joint or returning the gift?

As we approach a quarter of a century since the Toronto conference, what can we say of the state of the Critical Security Studies label, and the divisions into which it has been broken? It certainly seems well established within the global security studies community, with courses and even whole degrees offered, as well as finding mention in most collections on the range of approaches to security, and even having a growing number of books dedicated to its introduction (see Fierke 2007; Peoples and Vaughan-Williams 2010). There have also been moves to transcend the label, the first by healing the schisms which have riven the broad church of Krause and Williams; the second by recommending that we jettison not only Critical Security Studies, but security itself!

In 2006, a group of scholars attempted to reconstruct the broad church of Critical Security Studies that had been central to the original Toronto desire. These scholars met first in Paris, and gathered together students of security from across Europe who shared a commitment to some form of critical scholarship about security, broadly conceived. Out of this meeting was produced an article later published in *Security Dialogue* as 'Critical Approaches to Security in Europe: A Networked Manifesto', with the author given as 'The CASE Collective'. The goal of the collective was explicit in aiming to overcome precisely the sorts of divisions I have outlined in this chapter: 'the aim of working and writing as a collective, a network of scholars who do not agree on everything yet share a common perspective, is based on a desire to break with the competitive dynamic of individualist research agendas and to establish a network that not only facilitates dialogue but is also able to speak with a collective voice' (CASE Collective 2006: 444). Specifically, they sought to bridge the gaps they saw between the 'Copenhagen', 'Welsh', and 'Paris' schools (with the latter a largely poststructural position centred around Didier Bigo at *Science Po* in Paris).

The near impossibility of constructing a broad church is clearly demonstrated in the responses the CASE Collective generated. In a series of rejoinders published by the journal, Andreas Behnke, Mark Salter, and Christine Sylvester took the Collective to task for a series of exclusions they effected even in their attempts to forge an inclusive network (Behnke 2007; Salter 2007; Sylvester 2007). Behnke and Salter take the Collective to task for its 'European' focus, asking both what is meant by 'Europe' (Behnke 2007: 106), and what about the critical scholars who are clearly not European in any sense, but still involved in the critical security project (Salter 2007: 114). Behnke (2007: 108) also wonders about the exclusion of theoretical positions from this reformed church, as there seems no room for his interest in Carl Schmitt, for example. Sylvester makes a similar, and even more damning critique, in asking where the feminists are in this network—even a poststructural feminist security scholar such as Lene Hansen, who actually works in Copenhagen, but whose work is missing from this broad network (Sylvester 2007). Salter and Miguel de Larrinaga then went further to build on the critique of the narrow European focus of CASE in 'Cold CASE: A Manifesto for Canadian Critical Security Studies', which appeared as the lead article in a special issue of *Critical Studies on Security* exploring Canadian critical approaches to security (Salter and de Larrinaga 2014: 1–19).

Despite the criticisms, the goal of the CASE collective is clearly to draw at least some of the fractious followers of different signs together in a common critical security effort. A more recent intervention which might reach a similar end through a very different means was published in *Critical Studies on Security* in 2013. Anthony Burke notes that 'Comopolitanism' has a long history of thinking and practice in international politics, '[y]et it has rarely been applied to questions or practice of security' (Burke 2013: 13). From this starting point, Burke attempts to refound the ontological and ethical framework within which we can think and act security in cosmopolitan terms. Starting as it does from an ethical rather than analytical assumption, security cosmopolitanism holds out the possibility of an ecumenical joining across some, though by no means all, of the divisions I have sketched. Burke's proposed framework has proven controversial, generating significant criticism and debate. At one end, Mary Kaldor commends the attempt to move beyond 'human security' while recognizing the transnational human subject (Kaldor 2013: 42–5). Significantly less sympathetic are Neil Cooper and Mandy Turner, who see Burke's framework as a critical-sounding gloss to put on the violence of liberal interventionism (Cooper and Turner 2013: 35–41)!

The attempt to overcome divisions within critical studies of security is certainly not the project underpinning Mark Neocleous' book, despite its title: *Critique of Security* (2008). Neocleous comes to his critique not from security studies, critical or otherwise, but from the study of the state in general and then 'police' in particular. Indeed, his question is 'What if security is little more than a semantic and semiotic black hole allowing authority to inscribe itself deeply in human experience?' (Neocleous 2008: 4). The answer is suggested by the very form of the question, and in a relentless and powerful text, Neocloeus shows how security functions as 'a political technology . . . through which the state shapes our lives and imaginations' (Neocleous 2008: 4–5). He begins by showing how security, not liberty, is at the heart of liberalism, and so, *contra* Booth, emancipation is not the flip side of security, but rather it is oppression. From there he traces this technology of government through the practices of the twentieth century, concluding with a sustained critique of the role played by the 'security Fuckers' (Kelman, quoted in Neocleous 2008: 1), the professionals who make their living from security, including the academics who lay claim to the Critical Security Studies label. His conclusion is that we must 'eschew the logic of security altogether', something that 'could never even begin to be imagined by the security intellectual' (Neocleous 2008: 185). He calls on us to go far further than any of the adherents of any of the signs I have discussed to this point, to 'return the gift' of security, and not to seek to put anything in its place (which would simply be the far easier, and common, task of 'rethinking' security). The church can be as broad as it likes, but it must still be dismantled, for as with any other institutionalized religion, it holds only oppression.

Conclusion

This chapter has been unlike many in a textbook of this kind. I have not provided clear and unproblematic answers to questions such as 'What is Critical Security Studies?', 'What is meant by "critical" and "security"?', 'How do you "do" Critical Security Studies?' Rather, I have tried to turn the ethos of critique that should animate a critical study of security on the very label I was asked to discuss. I have told a story of the short history of the label and its politics, a story that attempts to reveal how Critical Security Studies came to be what it is, and what the effects are of that coming. Questions of history and politics are the questions—though by no means the only questions—that an ethos of critique leads us to ask, and the kind of story told here is one of the ways—though, again, by no means the only way—that they can be answered.

Since the conference in 1994 with which I began this story, the issue of 'security' has taken on a greatly renewed significance. During the Cold War, the Soviet–American rivalry and the ever-present possibility of nuclear war lent an urgency to questions of security that seemed to have been lost with the fall of the Berlin Wall. Such a decline in urgency was surely to be welcomed, and led, indeed, to the possibility of an idea like Critical Security Studies taking hold. Many of the concerns that animated the conference and the book had been articulated before the end of the Cold War, but that historical context made it impossible to follow them through. Critical Security Studies was a label ripe for reception at the moment it was spoken. With the events of 9/11, security regained its urgency.

In the context of a war on terrorism, wars in Iraq and Syria against a self-styled 'Islamic State', annual updates of 'anti-terror' legislation, the reorganization of government to provide 'homeland security', and the growing recognition that supposedly civilized states are resorting to torture in the name of security, security studies has never had it better (this thought alone should give us pause, as it bolsters Neocleous' case about the close connection of security studies to such extravagant violence). What is the state of the label Critical Security Studies in this present context? It seems the broad church is edging toward institutionalization, and the dangers that entails. There are now courses taught in universities on Critical Security Studies, and departments advertise for specialists under this label. As you know from reading this chapter, textbooks include Critical Security Studies in their lists of approaches. Journals have refocused their scope, and even been created, in order to house critical security work together. Perhaps because of this, the followers of the sign of the gourd are still squabbling with those following the sign of the shoe and particularly with those holding their shoes and hopping around on one foot. The stakes in this contest over the label are now higher: jobs are at stake, as are authorships of chapters.

Nevertheless, in an age in which security is so important, and some of the practices of security so troubling to those committed to liberty and justice—to the ethos of democracy—security study demands an ethos of critique. The question that remains, and the one with which I will end, is whether such an ethos demands Critical Security Studies or, rather, the refusal of security altogether.

QUESTIONS

1. If you were to become a critical security scholar, which sign would you follow and why?
2. Why did Krause and Williams aim to create a 'broad church' of Critical Security Studies? What are the advantages and disadvantages of such a conception? Who does it favour, and who does it marginalize?
3. What are the various understandings of the term 'critical' that are found in the literature on Critical Security Studies? Which one do you find the most convincing?
4. Should the Critical Security Studies label apply to the Copenhagen School?
5. Do you think that the 'war on terrorism' makes the claims of Critical Security Studies more or less convincing?
6. The Welsh School suggests that Critical Security Studies should be guided by Critical Theory, which is the theory developed by the Frankfurt School. This suggestion makes intuitive sense; do you agree with it?
7. What is the difference between 'constructivism' and 'poststructuralism' in security studies? Does it make a difference?
8. Do an ethos of critique and an ethos of democracy provide sufficient guidance for a progressive politics of security in the contemporary world?
9. Should we 'return the gift' of security, and if so what would that mean?
10. How does the rendition of a 'partial history of a label' differ from other ways of presenting approaches to security studies? What difference does it make?

FURTHER READING

Constructing Security

- Krause, Keith (1998), 'Critical Theory and Security Studies: The Research Programme of "Critical Security Studies"', *Cooperation and Conflict*, 33 / 3: 298–L 333. In this article, Krause provides a useful overview of the broad church of Critical Security Studies and the literature to which the label may be applied.
- Krause, Keith and Williams, Michael C. (1997), *Critical Security Studies: Concepts and Cases*, Minneapolis: University of Minnesota Press. This edited volume launched the label 'critical security studies' and continues to be a standard reference.

There are a number of good texts that apply explicitly constructivist theory to important contemporary questions of security: Alexandra Gheciu (2005b), *NATO in the New Europe: The Politics of Socialization after the Cold War*, Stanford, CA: Stanford University Press (a constructivist account of NATO enlargement); Alexandra Gheciu (2008), *Securing Civilization: The EU, NATO, and the OSCE in the Post-9/11 World*, Oxford: Oxford University Press (the re-configuration of European security to confront the 'threat' of terrorism); Jennifer Milliken (2001) *The Social Construction of the Korean War: Conflict and its Possibilities*, Manchester: Manchester University Press (an account of the decision making around the Korean conflict); Jutta Weldes (1999b), *Constructing National Interests: The United States and the Cuban Missile Crisis* (an account of the decision making around the Cuban Missile Crisis).

The Copenhagen School

- Balzacq, Thierry (ed.) (2011), *Securitization Theory: How Security Problems Emerge and Dissolve*, London: Routledge. Balzacq is one of the leading scholars of securitization scholarship that has grown from the early Copenhagen School work, and this book provides a useful overview of both current theoretical thinking and its use as an analytic approach to contemporary security problems.
- Buzan, B., Wæver, O., and de Wilde, J. (1998), *Security: A New Framework for Analysis*, Boulder, CO: Lynne Rienner. This work is the most elaborate statement of the Copenhagen School approach, and clearly distinguishes it from CSS.

The Welsh School

- Booth, Ken (2005a), *Critical Security Studies and World Politics*, Boulder, CO: Lynne Rienner; and Booth, Ken (2007), *Theory of World Security*, Cambridge: Cambridge University Press. These are the most explicit statements of a Welsh School of Critical Security Studies, with Booth's own contributions arguing for a specific critical security theory, rather than the broad church.
- Wyn Jones, Richard (1999), *Security, Strategy and Critical Theory*, Boulder, CO: Lynne Rienner. Wyn Jones's book is the most philosophically elaborated statement of the Welsh School approach.

For one of the few avowedly Welsh School treatments of an issue in contemporary security, see Columba Peoples (2010) *Justifying Ballistic Missile Defence: Technology, Security and Culture*, Cambridge: Cambridge University Press.

Poststructuralism and Security

- Dalby, Simon (1990), *Creating the Second Cold War*, New York: Guilford Press; and Klein, Bradley (1994), *Strategic Studies and World Order*, Cambridge: Cambridge University Press. These two books are among the first to draw on poststructural philosophy to think about the areas of conventional security studies, and in particular the politics of the study of security itself.
- Campbell, David (1998a), *Writing Security: United States Foreign Policy and the Politics of Identity*, rev. edn, Minneapolis: University of Minnesota Press. Campbell's first book is a touchstone for virtually all poststructural security studies literature. The epilogue to the second edition provides a very useful account of the distinction between poststructural IR and constructivism.
- Campbell, David (1998b), *National Deconstruction: Violence, Identity, and Justice in Bosnia*, Minneapolis: University of Minnesota Press. In *National Deconstruction* Campbell responds to the standard criticism of poststructuralism that it cannot stand up to Fascism.

There are a number of books that use poststructural theory to consider questions of contemporary security: Simon Dalby (2002), *Environmental Security*, Cambridge: Cambridge University Press (looks at the relationship between the environment and security and shows how thinking about geopolitics has shaped this discussion); Elizabeth Dauphinée (2008), *The Ethics of Researching War: Looking for Bosnia*, Manchester: University of Manchester Press (considers the place of the academic and West more generally in violent conflict); Kyle Grayson (2008) *Chasing Dragons: Security, Identity, and Illicit Drugs in Canada*, Toronto: University of Toronto Press (explores the relationship of drugs and security in the making of Canadian identity); Benjamin Muller (2010) *Security, Risk and the Biometric State: Governing Borders and Bodies*, London: Routledge (examines the instantiation of security in 'virtual borders' through the institution of biometric technologies).

IMPORTANT WEBSITES

- **http://www.libertysecurity.org** The Liberty & Security Project is a site at the focus of a wide-ranging project looking at the intersection of security and liberty in a world characterized by a global war on terror.

- **http://www.infopeace.org/index2.cfm** The Information Technology, War and Peace Project is an online portal for a project exploring the relations among information technology, contemporary media, and global security.
- **http://www.criticalsecurity.ca** The Canadian Critical Security Studies Network is a community of scholars who identify with the Critical Security Studies label.

Visit the Online Resource Centre that accompanies this book for lots of interesting additional material: www.oxfordtextbooks.co.uk/orc/collins4e/

8

Critical Interventions: Subjects, Objects, and Security

J. Marshall Beier

Chapter Contents

Reader's Guide

Taking its main cues from poststructuralists' approaches to Critical Security Studies, this chapter asks some unconventional questions about somewhat unconventional subjects for a field that has traditionally been more inclined to centre states in its investigations. In so doing, it brings to light the concealed political commitments that are a part of any attempt to theorize security and which fix arbitrary limits on whom and what gets foregrounded in the security stories we tell. Placing particular emphasis on recovering agency and political subjecthood, we are able to see the crucial part played by other actors both in the everyday practices of security and in how we have come to define it. We are also led to better appreciate both the problems and promise of our own roles in producing security—and insecurity—in the ways we approach it as students and scholars.

Introduction

What could **Indigenous people**, children, and **smart bombs** possibly have in common, and what on Earth could the surprising intersections that can be traced between them possibly have to do with Security Studies? The beginnings of an answer to this question actually reside in the very sense of a need to ask it. That the significance of these and other things to a more fulsome understanding of security is not immediately apparent already tells us something about traditional Security Studies and how its agenda has, in many respects, been set for us in advance of our beginning to ask questions. Though not always appealing readily to our common senses about what we should be asking, where we should be looking, and whom we ought to be listening to if we want to make sense of security, there is much outside of our received traditions and habits of thought that has important things to tell us. Scholars working under the broad (and still broadening) umbrella of Critical Security Studies urge us to consider what lies beyond the well-worn paths. Peering through conceptual openings created by critical contributions of the last two decades, this chapter inquires into what might seem quite disparate points of intervention: Indigenous peoples, childhood, and weapons technology. My aim here is not to suggest that these somehow delineate the terrain of Critical Security Studies—in fact, I might be inclined to argue that they are due more attention than they have received even from critical scholars—but simply to sketch something of the sorts of things that have been held invisible in traditional Security Studies.

One of the first things critical approaches draw to our attention is that Security Studies is not merely an area of inquiry. Even more fundamentally, Security Studies can be understood as practice—or, more accurately, as a set of practices. As David Mutimer points out in Chapter 7, treating knowledge as though it is value neutral tends to naturalize it and, thus, to obscure the political commitments behind opting to see the world on status quo terms, which favour those whose interests are best served by those terms. The same can be said of Security Studies itself. As a field of study, it is not something that is just objectively 'there'. Like other academic fields and disciplines, it is made or performed into being by the ways we choose to approach it. If we do not imagine that there might be important senses in which it is about childhood, for example, we will leave childhood unexplored and the work we produce is unlikely to take note of children as political actors. The field of study we perform into being through exclusions such as this will, through the sum of the ways in which we go about doing our work in it, make the exclusions seem natural—Security Studies will seem not to be about childhood because the Security Studies we keep performing back into being does not take notice of it. The boundaries we imagine, then, will always reflect a politics of inside and outside and of who is on which side of the boundary.

Equally applicable to those things we study and to the ways we render Security Studies itself, is an important question posed by Jef Huysmans (1998a: 242): 'How does a security story order social relations?' For Huysmans, 'security' is not a concept but, rather, a 'thick signifier' that entails particular claims about social relations; see Key Ideas 8.1. Encoded in every iteration of 'security' are political commitments about the contours of the social world, its privileged sites, and its margins, all performed into being in ways that recommend approaching Security Studies as a potent social force in its own right. It is in this context, where the pretence to a neutral field analysing an objective world has been caught out, that its exclusions are suddenly revealed as indispensable to understanding any account of security—they are both conditions of possibility and products of all such accounts. Recognizing that Security Studies, however we might choose to draw its boundaries or to define what is apposite to inquiry within those boundaries, is always also a story about who and what matters, orients us to reflect on the inherently political nature of all claims as to security's subject (who or what acts in the name of security), object (that which is to be secured), and content (what counts as security or insecurity). All of these have drawn the attention of Critical Security Studies, although subjecthood somewhat less so.

The traditional fixation on the state as both the **referent object** and the acting subject of security has had much to do with the close connection between Security Studies and disciplinary International Relations (Beier and Arnold 2005) and, to a lesser extent, the field of Diplomatic History. Critical Security Studies recommends considering what might speak to questions of security in other fields of scholarly inquiry: Political Sociology, Indigenous Studies, Childhood Studies, among others. Here too are exclusions that have a great deal to tell us about the subsumed political commitments of dominant stories about security. Although sometimes seemingly quite remote in their foci from the usual

KEY IDEAS 8.1 Security as a 'thick signifier'

Approaching security as a thick signifier is a way of resisting the disappearance of the politics behind definitions and conceptual analyses. It involves denaturalizing and contextualizing claims about 'security' to reveal their indebtedness to and validation of particular forms of social relations wherein those who define security simultaneously define its winners and losers. Every account of security depends on embedded accounts of whom and what it is for, who may act and who may not, and what will count as a legitimate security practice or stand as a condition of being secure. Uncovering the political work that produces these things entails critically interrogating the stories about the world encoded in, implied by, and relied upon by dominant understandings of security. According to Jef Huysmans,

> 'In a thick signifier analysis, one tries to understand how security language implies a specific metaphysics of life. The interpretation does not just explain how a security story requires the definition of threats, a referent object, etc. but also how it defines our relations to nature, to other human beings and to the self. In other words, interpreting security as a thick signifier brings us to an understanding of how the category 'security' articulates a particular way of organizing forms of life.'
>
> *Huysmans (1998a: 231)*

preoccupations of traditional Security Studies, work undertaken in these other fields enables thinking not only about different referent objects but also different articulations of political subjecthood and, through them, different ways of understanding and engaging the nature and content of security as a thick signifier. It is with all of this in mind that I turn now to some less likely security stories. In doing so, I will focus primarily on the still underinterrogated constructions of political subjecthood in relation to security and thereby hope to make a contribution in that regard at the same time.

KEY POINTS

- 'Acting subject(s)' concerns who or what is acting to produce security or insecurity. 'Agency' refers to the capacity to act, while 'subjecthood' bespeaks mastery of one's own agency or the idea that actions are products of one's autonomous choices. Does my visible agency express my will as a political being or am I merely an instrument of someone else's?
- Referent object(s) are whom or what we seek to make secure. For realists, the referent object is the state, but other possibilities include individuals, groups, forms of political community other than the state, or even nonhuman referents as vast as the biosphere.
- Substantive content concerns what we refer to in terms of what being secure looks like and what conditions must exist for us to be able to say we are secure. For some, security is about protection from physical violence. Others suggest this is not enough and that security should be understood to entail freedom from deprivations that compromise well-being and which might even threaten survival.

Secret agents and power bases

Breaking with the traditional centring of states in Security Studies disturbs much in the way of what had previously been relatively stable conceptual ground. On the one hand, it might seem a bit unsettling to let go of a reassuring sense of certainty about the subjects and referent objects of security. It can be disconcerting to contemplate the prospect of a field devoid of consensus on such fundamental commitments, even amongst the critical scholars themselves—a portion of the larger field marked by the apparent disorder of divisions between the sign of the shoe, the sign of the gourd, and those hopping around on one foot, as Mutimer cleverly describes the fragmentation of Critical Security Studies in Chapter 7. But it might also turn out to be the case that the price of comfortingly clear and familiar subject and object assignments is that we miss seeing important circuits of action and bases of power. Some of these might even bear on our understanding of the state itself, making them relevant also to traditional approaches that continue to centre states in their accounts of security. Clearly, there is much at stake in this, making it well worth the effort to consider agents whose roles in the production of security practices have been a 'secret' to us only by dint of our homage to definitional convention and disciplinary habits of thought. It is instructive, then, to take seriously other sites of political subjecthood and what they tell us about things we might have been taking too much for granted as 'common sense'. Thinking in terms of what Mutimer describes as the poststructuralists' ethos of critique is especially helpful here as we make it our task to denaturalize ideas and assumptions so deeply held in many cases that they may be allowed to pass without critical scrutiny.

We can begin with the idea of power itself. Traditionally, Security Studies has been very concerned with military wherewithal as the basis of state power. Not surprisingly, this led to a focus on the use or threat of force and, accordingly, an interest in the relative balance of military capabilities that back it up. Given the important part played by states in our world, it is difficult to dispute the need to understand the basis of this kind of power. But if our inquiry is too concerned with the characteristics of new weapons technologies, for instance, we run the risk of losing sight of the acting subjects behind their development and use. That is, we might miss seeing the political 'work' done by different kinds of actors that gives meaning and effect to the weapons. It might even start to seem as if the weapons themselves are somehow 'doing' things in the world—indeed, it is increasingly easy to slip into this from the ways we have come to talk about 'smart' bombs, drones, and 'autonomous' weapons as if they were agents. The fact, though, is that weapons—even 'smart' weapons—do not choose or decide to do anything in the world. Rather, they are purposefully made and employed by other actors, and those actors represent the real sites of political subjecthood. They may include weapons designers, builders, operators, and the political elites whose policy choices underwrite all of this. But they may include others too, some of whom could seem quite remote from the kinds of acting subjects that have traditionally preoccupied security scholars, but who might nonetheless be requisite even to the wielding of military might.

Exemplary on this point, Cynthia Enloe (2010) reveals how mothers become indispensible to the exercise of military power; see Key Ideas 8.2. This manifests in different ways, but a key one concerns the role of mothers in promoting enlistment of their children for military service. Enloe shows how military recruitment strategies are crafted with mothers specifically in mind. Different in kind from those targeting fathers and even would-be recruits themselves, they are designed to foster a view of military service, even in time of war, as a positive developmental experience for young adults and one connecting them to a proud tradition of service. Tapping into the aspirations and loyalties of mothers as complex political subjects, active in their children's lives and in the lives of their communities, militaries hold out the promise of positive experience-building, skills development, and longer-run opportunities for those who join their ranks. For some parents—and, indeed, for many young people—this might activate resistance, but in the balance of crosscutting concerns for their children's ultimate well-being, enlistment can also come to seem a positive choice and an answer to other developmental concerns as well as a chance to 'make something' of oneself by following in a respected tradition. The role of the 'military mom', a visible and often vocal—informally, through associations, and via social media—focal point of a community's vicarious experience of military service, is no less important an agent of recruiters' fortunes.

KEY IDEAS 8.2 'Emma and the Recruiters'

Through the case of a Texas mother, Emma Bedoy-Pina, and her two sons (one already in the military and one courted by recruiters), Cynthia Enloe (2010) shows how employing a feminist curiosity to inquire into everyday life finds women's lives not only impacted by war but very much a part of it. Enloe reveals how US military power comes to depend upon mothers' belief that enlistment will be good for their children. This does not just happen naturally but, rather, is something in which military recruiters and recruitment strategies play a complex and purposeful part. In 2005, with the US-led war in Iraq becoming increasingly unpopular with Americans and as the job of Army recruiters consequently grew more difficult, Emma, as the mother of a teenage son in his senior year of high school and as a Latina, was a key demographic target of Defense Department recruitment planners. While both mothers and fathers have to be factored into recruitment strategies in light of the influence they can be expected to have in their children's lives, the prevailing standards by which mothers' parenting is judged in their communities typically differ from those applied to fathers. Recruitment strategies tailored to mothers take account of this, both presuming and playing to mothers as nurturers and as concerned primarily for their sons' and daughters' well-being. With the Latino proportion of overall US population projected to rise steadily, Emma became doubly important to the recruiters as someone with the potential to exert influence in support of the Army's present and future recruitment needs. Through Emma's case and those of other women, Enloe exposes the dependence of the military on a great deal of gendered and raced work not visible in traditional Security Studies and how acting subjects like Emma, although not traditionally considered in Security Studies, are indispensably at work in this also.

Enlistment in the military, even in peacetime, entails not only a professional obligation with a fixed term but also commitment to a demanding way of life. This compounds the challenge non-conscript militaries face in maintaining required personnel levels. Writing several years into the Iraq War, Enloe (2010: 130) asks us to 'think like a recruiter' and thereby to catch a glimpse of 'how much gendered strategizing it took to raise and sustain an American military force—even one stretched thin—capable of waging a prolonged war'. The subjecthood of the military recruiter comes sharply into relief when the basis of military power is examined from this perspective, but so does that of military mothers. These mothers are not merely passive objects of the recruiters' strategies. Rather, those strategies recognize mothers as acting subjects, and very important ones at that. The aim of the recruiters goes beyond seeking the acquiescence of mothers to their children's enlistment. Far more than this, it presumes their active role in their children's lives and in their communities more broadly and looks to harness that engaged subjecthood to the promotion of military service.

Looking for different subjects means finding different bases of power: in this case, mothers and motherhood, respectively. Although it might seem somewhat counter-intuitive to traditional understandings and still-prevailing commonsense about the constitution of military power and its expression in the material capabilities of weapons systems, Enloe gives us the important insight that mothers are essential acting subjects in the production and maintenance of the military capabilities of the most powerful state in the world. The fact is that a technologically sophisticated military requires a very high degree of professionalization and, as such, cannot rely on conscription as a means by which to meet its personnel requirements. Volunteer enlistment on a grand scale is vital and it turns out that mothers play a crucial part in actively promoting recruitment and retention. Absent this, the weapons systems, just part of an integrated system that also requires layers of highly trained professional personnel, would be rendered less effectual. Coming to understand the workings of political subjecthoods left out of traditional discourses on security thus allows us to see how motherhood may be made manifest as a base of power that is actually prior to whatever might be quantified in terms of the material capabilities of even the most technologically advanced military in the world.

KEY POINTS

- Limiting our focus to agents already familiar to traditional Security Studies, such as the state, might bring order and clarity to the field but it does so at the cost of our understanding of the crucial role played by other, seemingly unlikely agents.
- Employing the poststructuralists' ethos of critique helps us to denaturalize ideas and assumptions about who and what counts in the production of security.
- Looking for different acting subjects does more than just populate Security Studies with a wider range of actors: it also reveals different bases of power and gives us a fuller understanding of what enables the security practices of states as well.

The subject of 'smart' bombs

As indispensible as motherhood is as a site of political subjecthood sustaining military power, it does not produce that power by itself. Another aspect of its production inheres in something more readily recognizable to traditional Security Studies: precision-guided munitions (PGMs). These are the 'smart' bombs and other advanced weapons of the so-called Revolution in Military Affairs (RMA) that moved into popular consciousness beginning with the 1991 Gulf War. On the eve of that war, there was considerable trepidation at the prospect of a major engagement with the Iraqi military, which was assessed to be among the most powerful in the world. Less than two decades after the end of the **Vietnam War**, in which the United States had been unable to achieve its aims even after years of fighting and despite horrific losses, many feared that a war in Iraq could end up being the same or worse. When the fighting began in January 1991, however, Iraqi defences crumbled with astounding rapidity in the face of what turned out to be the overwhelming technological superiority of, chiefly, US forces. Over the days and weeks that followed, global publics became acquainted with the ideas and material expressions of 'smart bombs', 'surgical strikes', and 'costless war' waged from afar. We were introduced to the reality that aircraft, even large bomber aircraft, could be made 'stealthy' in the sense that they were virtually invisible to radar. And we saw the devastating effect of a profound imbalance in access to these new capabilities, many of which seemed at the time as though they had been lifted straight from the pages of a science fiction novel.

Few, including in the field of Security Studies, foresaw the extent of what has since come to be regarded as a transformative change in the nature of warfare, at least as practised by the most technologically advanced militaries. Dubbing it an 'RMA' claims no less. Previous RMAs include those associated with the advent of firearms and artillery, the internal combustion engine and wireless communications that introduced mobility, and, of course, nuclear weapons. In each case, the watershed was expressed not only in terms of some exceptional advance in the instruments of warfare but in its most fundamental logics and characteristics, with implications for the organization of social life writ large as well. Artillery, for example, has been linked with the demise of the fortified town as the main unit of sociopolitical organization in Europe once stone curtain walls could no longer be relied upon as a defence in the face of cannon that could reduce them to rubble. The mobility revolution of the early twentieth century unlocked the emergent potential for total war—that is, war involving whole societies—by freeing it from the relative confines and stasis of the battlefield that had been exemplified in the fixed trench warfare standoff of the First World War. The nuclear era brought with it the logic of strategic deterrence wherein the point in having the weapons was to ensure their non-use, although at the cost of holding all of humanity in constant peril.

The latest RMA, associated with 'smart' bombs, with unprecedented information handling capabilities, and with other advanced military technologies that we increasingly take very much for granted, has wrought its own transformations. In the main, it has come to mean that the US military (and, to a much lesser extent, a few others) is so utterly without peer that a traditional military counter by any of its likely adversaries has become all but unthinkable. The central lesson of the 1991 war between Iraq and the US-led Coalition has been well learned: conventional military opposition to the USA is doomed to failure. In the short span of a few days, cable news coverage of the opening of hostilities in the Gulf War acquainted us with the new reality of PGMs' devastating accuracy, even when dispatched from hundreds of kilometres away against Iraqi forces that never even knew they had been singled out for destruction. US and Coalition casualties were consequently a tiny fraction of the total number on the Iraqi side. It is probably no accident, then, that those who have sought to resist US military power in the decades since have mostly opted instead for the forms of unconventional warfare we know as insurgency or terrorism. This is one sense in which PGMs have led to broader sociopolitical transformation, and it is relatively uncontroversial to identify it as such. But it is also just one possible version of the story.

Approaching the same developments from a more critical perspective, one that takes seriously questions of political subjecthood, allows us to see what might be even more profound kinds of change. The first thing to notice here is that the ways in which we have grown used to talking about PGMs mystifies the location of political subjecthood. Again, this increasingly makes it sound as though the weapons themselves are the subjects—that they have agency and are out there in the battle spaces of our new wars, *doing* something. However, it is also important to ask about those targeted by the weapons and what might become of their subjecthood. Considering how hopelessly outclassed Iraqi forces were in 1991, unable even to see those who targeted and destroyed them with relative impunity, it would seem that their subject position in warfare was, quite literally, obliterated. Powerless to act in any practical sense, they were reduced to objects of annihilation brought by 'smart' bombs that seemed never to err.

It is in this context that we are better able to understand the sources and implications of unconventional forms of 'insurgent' warfare as an approach by which some actors have sought to recover and assert a viable subject position in war. Lacking access to the advanced technologies of the RMA, they have resorted to means that are much less sophisticated and which tend to be regarded as illegitimate because they do not meaningfully discriminate between combatants and noncombatants. For critical scholars, and poststructuralists in particular, this draws attention to the as yet underinterrogated rhetorical dimension of the RMA because the fact is that PGMs *also* kill noncombatants, all rhetoric to the contrary notwithstanding. This once again challenges us to look beyond the material attributes and capabilities claimed for the weapons and to consider how those claims might themselves turn out to be key to the exercise of military power. It also reminds us that stories about security entail claims about social relations which favour some subjects while marginalizing others and that Security Studies is implicated in the production of sites of margin and privilege by its endorsement of particular stories.

Stories are told in different ways. Much in the way of the dominant story of legitimacy in contemporary warfare has been told visually. Images of PGMs apparently living up to the claims made for them have become commonplace in popular culture since the Gulf War. What once astonished audiences to the point that news reports about the extraordinary capabilities of this or that weapons system eclipsed coverage of the war itself has since receded into the everyday through the ad nauseam repetition of images in media forms ranging from print journalism, to cinema, to video games. We have come to expect that the technology enables reliable discrimination between combatants and noncombatants, in part because we have seen the capability rehearsed before our eyes and in part because those who wield the weapons have insisted that this has become their contemporary practice of war. Of course, both the explicit rhetoric and the images are products of the careful management of perception—the video evidence of PGMs missing their targets (and they do so more frequently than is generally imagined) is not so eagerly shared with us and the carefully cultivated popular faith in the weapons' ability to preserve noncombatants from harm is thus insulated from the dissonance such images might otherwise inspire. Recognizing how this came to define the popular perception of the 1991 war, Jean Baudrillard (1995) provocatively proclaimed that 'the Gulf War did not take place', by which he meant that the war we thought we saw was actually a constructed account (see Key Ideas 8.3). The images that have become so familiar, although seeming to report objectively on an objective reality, are products of framing and composition both in what was left out of the camera's view and in the choice of which images have been made available for our viewing. In sum, they are the telling of a very particular and very political story.

Where the political implications of this story really come into relief is with the accompanying rhetoric about those whom the RMA has left behind and, specifically, in the characterization of their practices of warfare as inherently indiscriminate. This is significant because before the advent of PGMs any popular expectation of meaningful discrimination between combatants and noncombatants had long since perished in the rise of total war. The rapid shift in expectations driven by the RMA turned on the idea that 'smart' bombs could be used to carry out 'surgical strikes'. This was closely tied to claims of a more just practice of warfare, one leaving civilians and critical civilian infrastructure unharmed, and quickly came to define a new standard of legitimacy in war. The truly transformative effect of this is that it denies the possibility of a practical and legitimate subject position in opposition to the USA. None can hope to survive meeting the US military in conventional combat, nor can they match the widely presumed ability of US forces to discriminate between combatants and noncombatants—a presumption on which legitimacy in the exercise of violence has come to depend. These developments reached their logical fulfilment in popularization of the idea of the 'unlawful combatant': a truly revolutionary development in which the acting subject's very subjecthood is rhetorically precluded for want of legitimacy.

States invest considerable resources in building and sustaining popular consent for the use of force. The failure to do so can idle even the most advanced military if the political support for its deployment cannot be raised. The discursive contortions around subjecthood in contemporary warfare are thus reflective of struggles about who is able to make legitimate recourse to political violence and who is not. The critical

KEY IDEAS 8.3 The Gulf War did not take place

The familiar imagery of the RMA can be understood as what Jean Baudrillard (1994) calls 'simulacra'. For Baudrillard, the simulacrum is something taken to be a copy of an original but for which the original has never really existed. Still, because it is accepted as an authentic representation of the (in reality, nonexistent) thing that it is understood to signify, the 'copy', in effect, is that 'truth'. As the sum of these representations comes to be widely accepted as real and authentic, they produce a hyperreality: the simulation of a reality that has never existed but which, analogous to the virtual worlds of video gaming, comes to be experienced as though it does. Applying this idea, Baudrillard (1995) argues that 'the Gulf War did not take place'. The point, of course, is not that the war literally did not occur but, rather, that what did take place was not at all as we (thought we) saw it. Through careful management and selection of imagery (simulacra) the hyperreality of a war made 'costless' by 'smart bombs' and 'surgical strikes'—a war that did not, in fact, take place—became the accepted account.

insight that the management of a visual economy of war imagery and its attendant rhetorics have become key to enabling organized violence reveals different bases of state power than those habitually assumed in traditional Realist-inspired accounts. As in the case of motherhood, asking critical questions about the broader politics of subjecthood points to sites and practices which, it turns out, may be even more fundamental and no less necessary to state power than the material capabilities of any arsenal. Looking for acting subjects other than those we may be more used to thinking about in traditional Security Studies also yields insights into political circulations of power that give a different account of what might really be most revolutionary about the Revolution in Military Affairs. Once again, whom and what we write into or leave out of our stories about security determines the sorts of things we will be able to find as well as what remains concealed from us when the questions we ask about security are defined by those stories.

KEY POINTS

- RMAs involve not only changes in the practice of warfare but the transformation of the relationship between war itself and the broader social worlds in which we live.
- While the most recent and ongoing RMA, associated with 'smart bombs' and 'surgical strikes', appears to be chiefly about exotic weapons technologies, a critical lens finds its greatest significance to reside in an extremely potent set of rhetorical practices.
- Critically inquiring into how the portrayal of precision-guided munitions has worked to mystify political subjecthood reveals truly revolutionary changes in the way in which legitimacy in the exercise of political violence is conferred or withheld.

Complicated subjects: children

Something similar comes to light when we look for children in dominant stories about security. Children are not easily found in these stories, and even Critical Security Studies has only recently begun to ask why. That does not mean, however, that stories about security are not *about* children in important ways also. Indeed, a critical interest in the politics of subjecthood is revealing of ways in which children, though not present in Security Studies' dominant stories, are actually indispensible to them. But the ways in which they are relied upon conceptually also insist on their objectification, with the result that they do not appear as acting subjects. As in the cases of military mothers or 'unlawful combatants', this reminds us that, as a thick signifier, traditional Security Studies' account of security also entails an account of social relations that implicates it in particular political commitments and allies it with status quo interests. As in those other cases, it conceals much that could contribute to a fuller understanding of the bases of power and the circuits through which power operates.

That children's subjecthood poses something of a problem for traditional Security Studies is apparent in how the issue of child soldiers is approached. On first gloss, child soldiers appear quite unmistakably to be acting subjects. They are, after all, conspicuous agents of violence. We see this embodied in what have become almost formulaic images of gun-toting, typically African, pre-adolescent boys that figure in human rights and developmental aid campaign literature, media reports, and popular cinema. A critical reading, however, finds that this evident agency is not actually expressed as child soldiers' own political subjecthood. Very much to the contrary, accompanying discourses and narratives thoroughly objectify the young people we are confronted with in the images. We can see this in each of two seemingly contradictory predispositions about child soldiers, one of which casts them as terrifyingly dangerous while the other sees them as victims in need of protection. That these outwardly opposed renderings easily coexist, even in the same breath, points once again to the necessity of critically engaging the politics of subjecthood.

Taking the first predisposition, child soldiers are made to seem all the more frightening by the common view of children's agency as very much in need of regulation. This fits with the 'commonsense' understanding of childhood as a period of 'becoming' and, ideally, of innocence. As sound as this view may seem, however, it has neither always nor everywhere been so. Rather, it is a perspective with distinctly modern, Western lineage, traceable most famously to the eighteenth-century French philosopher, Jean Jacques Rousseau, whose ideas on childhood have exerted a powerful influence over prevailing approaches to education and its social purposes, and which continue to cast a long shadow in terms of dominant ideas about children's relationship to the adult world. Central to Rousseauian thinking is the claim that children lack rationality and require an adult-imposed curb on their presumed inclination to immoderate behaviour and general excess. Clearly, this is not the basis for a view of children as meaningful and authentic political subjects.

Dominant ideas about childhood do help to make sense of the construction of child soldiers as simultaneously dangerous and vulnerable once we take account of how those ideas work to locate political subjecthood in other (adult) actors. That is to say, although their actions may be taken in a very visible political purpose, it is not typically imagined that children can truly be the authors of those actions. Instead, as famously articulated by way of the controversial 'Kony 2012' campaign that went viral on social media in March 2012, the actions of child soldiers are usually understood to have been coerced, attributable to some martinet figure from the adult world—a warlord, perhaps—but not to the autonomous choices of children themselves. To be sure, there are many historical and contemporary examples of just this sort of forced 'recruitment' and the egregious abuses that go with it. The trope of childhood innocence in these instances at once underscores victimization and raises the unsettling spectre of instruments of violence in the hands of those thought not yet to be possessed of fully formed moral and rational faculties and thus characterized by incapacity to navigate the contradictions and ambiguities of the adult world of political life—an anxiety with broad cultural purchase also, as seen in William Golding's 1954 novel, *Lord of the Flies* in which a marooned group of pre-adolescent boys descend into savagery.

But all of this tells only a part of the story. We might pause to consider, for example, that young people under the age of eighteen—the threshold definition of children under the UN Convention on the Rights of the Child—are routinely recruited into military reserve and cadet programmes in numerous countries, including Canada, the United Kingdom, and the United States. Military service may even be held up in such contexts as a corrective to youth delinquency (Basham 2011). Still absent from the story, however, are those child soldiers who, even in conflict zones, may have chosen that role for themselves as a consciously conceived survival strategy. Importantly, this also leaves off the agenda other sources of insecurity which are dire enough to move children to see child soldiering as a form of respite and a means by which to hopefully improve their circumstances (see Key Ideas 8.4).

KEY IDEAS 8.4 Rethinking child soldiers

The dominant conception of child soldiers, founded largely on a universalized image of heavily armed pre-adolescent African boys, erases the heterogeneity of the actual experiences of child soldiers. For instance, although they do account for the majority, not all child soldiers are boys. Most are not pre-adolescent, although they are, by definition, below the age of eighteen. Not all are directly engaged in combat—indeed, in many contexts they are more likely to be relegated to 'support' roles ranging from portering to food preparation to sexual slavery. Moreover, they are not identifiable only with conflict in the global South—countries of the North have relied on child soldiers even in combat roles at various times and a number consistently maintain cadet or junior reserve programmes made up of young people of high school age or younger. Recovering the subjecthood of child soldiers demands an openness to the full range of their experiences. Doing so reveals myriad expressions of subjecthood, expressed as voluntary participation in some cases and as resistance to forced recruitment in others.

Mary-Jane Fox (2004) draws attention to the gendered construction of the universal figure of the child soldier. Addressing the dearth of attention to girl soldiers and their experiences, she reveals a manifest failure not only of state-centric security thinking but also of human security discourse that fails to challenge the dominant image of child soldiers.

Chris Gilligan (2009) reveals how the reduction of child soldiers to a presumed condition of abject victimhood—an ascription which mystifies their subjecthood—is enabled by the Western conception of childhood innocence which makes it difficult to imagine them otherwise.

Lorraine Macmillan (2009) finds that the dominant discourse on child soldiers derives from and imposes hegemonic convictions about childhood to the exclusion of the child soldiers' own expressions of their needs and concerns, losing sight of their subjecthood in the process.

For critically inclined scholars, a Security Studies that cannot see these other forms of often profound insecurity is left with an unduly circumscribed sense of the substantive content of what it has long held as its core concept, but which Huysmans urges us to view as a thick signifier. The question of child soldiers brings into relief the ways in which what we understand 'security' to mean in substantive terms is bound up also with how political subjecthood is variously produced, claimed, ascribed, and denied. Denying children's capacity for autonomous political action reduces them to objects of the security practices of others whom we do invest with political subjecthood. Withholding recognition of young people's roles in the realm of political life raises again one of the first vital questions posed by Critical Security Studies: security for whom? It also prompts us to ask, security *according* to whom? And it reveals too that choosing whether to engage children as subjects or objects involves taking an inherently political stance.

Unpacking the politics at work here is instructive. How status quo interests are invested in the objectification of children might not be immediately apparent, and traditional Security Studies is not well equipped to help us make sense of this since doing so requires that we look to sites, actors, and power circulations beyond its usual ambit. The historic relegation of women and children to the private sphere, for instance, is key to understanding the sorts of security projects facilitated by their construction outside of political life and, thus, as objects of protection by others (Peterson 1992). This is reflected in the social construction of combatant and noncombatant identities, with men and older boys more likely to be marked as legitimate targets of violence (Carpenter 2006). As the quintessential innocent civilians, children occupy a crucial place in the rhetorical claims that have accompanied the visual economy of the RMA. Accordingly, the degree of their protection from harm is an important and compelling arbiter of the legitimacy of contemporary practices of organized political violence.

Discovering children as bona fide political subjects in their own right destabilizes this and, with it, the status quo interests it serves. This suggests indeterminacy in the construction of victimhood which, in turn, exposes its inherently political nature. Making of children what dominant discourses and narratives need them to be requires their objectification and denial or recapture of their subjecthood—as, for example, by attributing its 'real' sources elsewhere. That this turns out to be key to understanding the new bases of legitimacy in warfare discussed above alerts us to the unacknowledged political commitments concealed by the traditional view of Security Studies as value neutral. In fact, traditional Security Studies encodes a politics that, in the case of childhood, not only writes some actors out of the story of security but, in so doing, also works to enable and sustain ideas necessary to the contemporary practice of warfare by the most technologically advanced states, the United States foremost among them.

KEY POINTS

- Asking critical questions about children allows us to see how, although they might not be visible in Security Studies' dominant stories that does not mean those stories are not about children in very important ways—in fact, they turn out to be indispensable to many of them.
- Seeking to recover children's political subjecthood and coming to an understanding of the vital roles they play not only in security discourse but in actual security practices draws our focus to some of the ways in which Security Studies becomes deeply implicated in the reproduction of unequal social relationships of power.
- Finding children in Security Studies suggests other ways of thinking about the substantive content of security, as well as whom it is for and who may define it.

Indigenous peoples and a cautionary tale

Alerted to the politics of political subjecthood, we may feel we are now well equipped to take seriously other subjects. Certainly, this is something that most self-consciously critical approaches to Security Studies would urge us toward. Here again, though, the advice of the poststructuralists is well worth heeding. In particular, the ethos of critique they advocate has a significant part to play in keeping us attentive to new and ongoing practices that objectify, silence, and consign others to the margins. This means that our critical interventions do not operate as if from a toolkit on which we draw to resolve a problem in order that we may then move on. Rather, as Mutimer explains, critique is something that must be sustained and brought to bear as well on our own roles in the practices of knowledge production. We see something of the importance of this by turning a critical eye to how we make critical engagements of the very sort I have been advocating in this chapter. In fact, this might turn out to be the most vital critical move of all, since the failure to make it can undo so much of the rest of a Critical Security Studies project.

An illustrative example is found in the case of scholarly work inquiring into the absence of Indigenous peoples from Security Studies and International Relations more broadly (see Background 8.1). Once called into question, this is an absence that is really quite puzzling given the long and well-documented history of Indigenous peoples' various and important roles in global politics and, no less, for their rich *sui generis* traditions of conceiving and practising security, sovereignty, and much more that is central to our fields' preoccupations. Indigenous peoples have evinced meaningful and sustained autonomous subjecthood in global politics since the earliest days of contact with the European states system. On that system's own most fundamental terms, this has been expressed in such things as the centuries-long and ongoing practice of making treaties—international legal instruments otherwise reserved to the management of relationships between states and empires—with Indigenous peoples. No less important are the many and diverse traditions of diplomatic interaction between Indigenous peoples themselves that long predate contact with Europeans and which functioned to regulate complex systems of contact and exchange whilst tending to issues of security and the resolution of disputes (see, for example, de Costa 2009; Parisi and Corntassel 2009). Engaging with these histories, the ongoing expression of non-state forms of political community arising from them, and their distinct approaches to the substantive content of security, positions us to bring our critical sensibilities to Security Studies' inattention to Indigenous peoples as authentic global political subjects.

One important project along these lines addresses The Great Law of Peace of the Haudenosaunee (Iroquois) Confederacy. The Great Law is remarkable for having regulated and sustained two centuries of peaceful interaction among previously warring peoples who came together as the Five (and, later, Six) Nations Confederacy. That Security Studies has seemed uninterested in this is curious considering that much

BACKGROUND 8.1 Sustaining critique

At roughly the same time that Critical Security Studies was emerging, a few very important scholarly contributions challenged the absence of Indigenous peoples from dominant stories about global politics and security.

Franke Wilmer's (1993) book-length investigation of historic and ongoing Indigenous peoples' subject positions in world politics sought, among other things, to account for the increasingly effectual Indigenous diplomacies of the late twentieth century, which included important gains at the United Nations. In Wilmer's analysis, normative changes in the international system away from *realpolitik* and toward a rights-based norm of self-determination are key to understanding the increasing audibility of Indigenous peoples' claims.

Neta Crawford (1994) brought the focus directly to the provision of security and also gave a very powerful and persuasive defence of oral histories as legitimate and well-regulated documentary sources—something very helpful to affirmation of the need for scholars to acknowledge and engage Indigenous peoples' subjecthood. Crawford argued that the Haudenosaunee Great Law of Peace is understandable and should be taken seriously in terms already familiar to traditional Security Studies, as a security regime.

David Bedford and Thom Workman (1997), responding to Crawford, argued that casting the Great Law as a security regime loses much of what is unique about its account of the substantive content of security. The Great Law must instead be approached on its own terms. The obvious implication with regard to Indigenous political subjecthood is that it is pushed to the margins once more if the ideas and practices it expresses are remade into what an academic discipline's own assumptions and commitments need them to be.

Karena Shaw (2002), although very much in sympathy with these interventions, is even more explicitly concerned with the disappearance of Indigenous subjecthood in the process. She argues, for example, that Wilmer's emphasis on norms of the international system removes Indigenous peoples from the account of their own diplomatic ascendancy by explaining it in terms of the evolution of the dominant approach to sovereignty. And, bringing it back to our roles in the production of knowledge, she expresses concern that Bedford and Workman's call for scholars to learn from the Great Law, even on its own terms, is ultimately about our scholarship and its needs, thus objectifying Indigenous peoples as bearers of memory rather than acting subjects engaged in present political struggles.

attention has been devoted to Europe's Congress of Vienna and the nineteenth-century balance of power system—a system which endured half as long and which, far from preventing war, institutionalized it as the means by which to maintain equilibrium. Appealing to conceptual terrain familiar to traditional Security Studies, Neta Crawford (1994) offers a reading of the Haudenosaunee Confederacy as a well-functioning security regime. She finds it exemplary in this regard, having successfully established norms of conduct and resolved uncertainty under conditions of anarchy, with the result that it was able to produce stable collective security over an extended period of time.

This seems to hold great promise and opportunity for recognition of an Indigenous political subjecthood, articulated through a functioning non-state form of political community. Two significant problems arise, however. First, in making appeal to a Western derived concept such as the security regime, there is the danger that it becomes the standard according to which the significance of the Haudenosaunee Confederacy is assessed—that is, according to the degree of its arguable conformity to what security scholars have deemed important. Proceeding from a careful reading of The Great Law, David Bedford and Thom Workman (1997) raise concern also about what is lost in the attempt to force it into a conceptual space that is unable to anticipate and which therefore cannot accommodate much in the way of its important nuance. Pointing out that the Great Law tends to social life in depth—including in-group rights and responsibilities, the role of clans in social life, funerary observances, and more—and that it conceives all these things as related and integral to a particular understanding of 'living well' upon which peace is founded, they argue that it is irreconcilable with the state-centric rendering of security regimes.

What we are confronted with here is the troubling circumstance that even critical efforts to recover political subjecthood could unwittingly mask new ways of enforcing the absence of other subjects from Security Studies. In the limits of our ability to faithfully represent them—and those limits likely are always inescapable—we might be doing no more than speaking simulacra of other subjects into security discourse. Within Security Studies itself, in its practices of knowledge production, the subjects remain unchanged: they are the security scholars. It is therefore imperative that critique be sustained beyond their efforts to recover other subject positions and that it be brought to bear just as trenchantly on those very projects themselves, lest we do no more in the end than replace old absences and erasures with new ones that might actually be more difficult to detect.

KEY POINTS

- A Critical Security Studies project is always in danger of being undone by the failure to sustain critique and, importantly, to bring it to bear also on our own practices of research and knowledge production.
- The Great Law of Peace of the Haudenosaunee Confederacy presents something of a challenge for traditional Security Studies inasmuch as it represents a significant and proven non-state approach to the problem of security and political order which Security Studies is ill equipped to engage on its own terms.
- The case of the Great Law alerts us to the problem of failing to sustain an awareness of the political subjecthood that we, as students and scholars of Security Studies, embody and how we might unwittingly re-objectify others even in projects that aim to do precisely the opposite.

Conclusion

Returning to the questions with which this chapter opened, what draws together a coherent discussion around Indigenous peoples, children, and smart bombs is a critical interest in the ways in which subjecthood is claimed, constructed, withheld, and denied in security narratives and discourses. The stories we tell in Security Studies, as we have seen, are about much more than they might appear on the surface. A story about state power that omits motherhood is a story we can examine for the political commitments that choose to locate power elsewhere. But, in a sense, it is still a story about motherhood to the extent that it implicitly says that motherhood is not something that should activate our curiosity. Critically interrogating such things offers insights into how Security Studies is, in this way, actually about all sorts of acting subjects that it does not seem to be about at all. In so doing, we may catch a glimpse of the complexity of children as autonomous political subjects or of how the denial of their subjecthood may be linked to an unprecedented ability to persuasively claim a monopoly on recourse to war whilst delegitimizing even defensive measures that might be undertaken by others. Asking critical questions about the absence of Indigenous peoples leads us to see subjects left out in state-centric projects, expressing forms of political community other than the state and different ways of thinking about the substantive content of security, such as being about a comprehensive understanding of living well that extends to the most mundane aspects of everyday life. And we are also confronted with the danger that we will remake these things if we do not take care to foster an ethos of critique that reaches not only traditional approaches but all that identifies itself as Critical Security Studies as well.

This project is not just about looking in different places or learning about different kinds of security. That is to say, it is not simply a matter of more terrain being mapped out, pushing out the margins from a stable centre of 'core' Security Studies that continues to do what it has always done well in the ways it has always done it. Rather, what we discover in the new realms of inquiry opened up to us by Critical Security Studies is of relevance to and speaks back to that centre as well. Making visible other political subjects, for example, enables us to take seriously things that, for example, Enloe reveals about motherhood underwriting and being indispensible to the military wherewithal of the global hegemon itself. It is also revealing of the concealed political commitments subsumed within all approaches, critical and traditional alike, and alerts us to fact that, as Robert Cox (1981: 128) famously said of theory, claims about security are always for someone and for some purpose.

QUESTIONS

1. Whom or what should we count as a subject in Security Studies and why?
2. In what sense can we say that Security Studies is an important social force in its own right? If true, what is the significance of this?
3. How might motherhood be identifiable as necessary to the production of military power? What are the implications of this?
4. What does it mean to say 'the Gulf War did not take place'?
5. In what ways does talk about 'smart' bombs affect how and where we see political subjecthood?
6. What is at stake and for whom in the ways child soldiers tend to be portrayed?
7. What is behind the apparent paradox of saying that dominant stories about security are actually about children, despite children's absence from those stories?
8. How would you support the claim that traditional Security Studies is itself implicated in children's insecurity? What assumptions does this make about subjecthood, referent objects, and the substantive content of security?
9. How do Indigenous peoples present a challenge to traditional Security Studies?
10. To what extent is Critical Security Studies equipped to take the Great Law of Peace on its own terms? What are the limits of attempting to do so? Are there implications to be weighed in the choice not to?

FURTHER READING

Subjects and bases of military power

- Basham, Victoria (2013), *War, Identity and the Liberal State: Everyday Experiences of the Geopolitical in the Armed Forces*, Abingdon: Routledge. This book inquires into how gender, race, and sexuality are deeply intertwined with the geopolitics of war.

- Enloe, Cynthia (2007), *Globalization and Militarism: Feminists Make the Link*, Lanham: Rowman & Littlefield. Enloe shows how dominant ideas about gender and the subject roles and positions they underwrite are key to understanding militarism.
- Enloe, Cynthia (2015), 'The Recruiter and the Sceptic: A Critical Feminist Approach to Military Studies', *Critical Military Studies*, 1/1: 3–10. Explores the complex play of gender, race, class, and more and the ways in which they are mobilized in support of military recruitment.

'Smart' bombs and (il)legitimate war

- Gregory, Derek (2010), 'War and Peace', *Transactions of the Institute of British Geographers*, 35/2: 154–85. This article disturbs the distinction between 'discriminating' and 'indiscriminate' forms of warfare, foregrounding the horror of all war and demystifying the politics of its seeming disappearance.
- Gregory, Derek (2011), 'From a View to a Kill: Drones and Late Modern War', *Theory, Culture & Society*, 28/7–8: 188–215. This piece considers senses of proximity and remoteness as they pertain to drone warfare.
- Zehfuss, Maja (2011), 'Targeting: Precision and the Production of Ethics', *European Journal of International Relations*, 17/3: 543–66. This work interrogates the idea of precision in warfare and its relationship to the production of the idea of more ethical exercises of organized violence.

Childhood and security

- Brocklehurst, Helen (2006), *Who's Afraid of Children? Children, Conflict and International Relations*, Aldershot: Ashgate. Brocklehurst shows how children have been and continue to be indispensable to International Relations and security despite their construction as outside of politics.
- Jacob, Cecilia (2015), '"Children and Armed Conflict" and the Field of Security Studies', *Critical Studies on Security*, 3/1: 14–28. Generating new insights into how Critical Security Studies might productively theorize children and childhood, Jacob investigates their centrality to armed conflict in Syria.
- Wagnsson, Charlotte, Maria Hellman, and Arita Holmberg (2010), 'The Centrality of Non-Traditional Groups for Security in the Globalized Era: The Case of Children', *International Political Sociology*, 4/1: 1–14. The authors of this article offer a framework for engaging children's agency in globalized security.

Indigenous peoples

- Bedford, David and Thom Workman (1997), 'The Great Law of Peace: Alternative Inter-Nation(al) Practices and the Iroquoian Confederacy', *Alternatives*, 22/1: 87–111. A response to Crawford that reveals how the substantive content of security might also be understood differently from traditional approaches.
- Crawford, Neta (1994), 'A Security Regime Among Democracies: Cooperation Among Iroquois Nations', *International Organization*, 48/3: 345–85. Crawford exposes the limitations of traditional framings of the possibilities for provision of security and of political order.
- Shaw, Karena (2002), 'Indigeneity and the International', *Millennium: Journal of International Studies*, 31/1: 55–81. This article cautions that efforts to engage Indigenous peoples' political subjecthood according to security studies' needs and assumptions can be diminutive of that subjecthood.

ACKNOWLEDGEMENT

Research for this chapter was supported by an Insight Grant from the Social Sciences and Humanities Research Council of Canada.

Visit the Online Resource Centre that accompanies this book for lots of interesting additional material: www.oxfordtextbooks.co.uk/orc/collins4e/

9

Postcolonialism

Mark Laffey and Suthaharan Nadarajah

Chapter Contents

Reader's Guide

In this chapter, we introduce postcolonialism as a recent and increasingly influential set of positions and perspectives within the wider discipline of International Relations, and sketch its implications for security studies. We begin with postcolonialism's genealogies, tracing its emergence in a set of transnational debates about the mutually constitutive relations between knowledge and imperialism. The chapter then lays out the standard account of world history as organized around Westphalian sovereignty which informs security studies and shows how postcolonialism puts it in question, forcing us to reconceive of the international as the context within which security is defined, practised, and studied. Third, we put postcolonialism to work and discuss what it might mean to decolonize security studies. In a short conclusion, we return to the question of the tense and contested relations between security studies and postcolonialism itself.

Introduction

For most of its history, security studies, in common with International Relations (IR) more generally, largely ignored or marginalized the colonial and imperial character of world politics, past and present (Barkawi 2010). Instead, IR and security studies took an imperial view of the world for granted, as in the persistent assumption of European 'great power' relations—more often than not inter-imperial relations—as definitive of the international and central to understandings of security. In recent years a growing number of scholars have adopted postcolonial approaches to the study of security. Postcolonialism stresses the past and continuing role of colonial and imperial relations and practices in the constitution and production of our world and our knowledge about it. Postcolonial analysis exposes the embedded **Eurocentrism** (see Key Idea 9.1) which structures both IR and security studies—conceptually, empirically, and normatively. It proceeds by locating security studies as a field and security as a practice in relation to European imperialism and the world it helped to make. In particular, it prompts us to ask how—if at all—security studies registers these hierarchical relations, from whose point of view, and with what effects. However, in common with other critical perspectives such as feminism and historical materialism, postcolonialism is not a theory of security. In that sense, it is not competing directly with realism or liberalism to provide an alternative paradigm. Nor is it trying to do security 'better' in any simple sense. From a postcolonial perspective, conventional understandings of security, even critical ones, are problematic insofar as they express a set of Eurocentric knowledge practices and assumptions (Beier 2005). Security is routinely treated as a universal category, invented or discovered in Europe but applicable to any human society. In this sense, the very concept is expressive of a Eurocentric view of the world that appears in the guise of a rational and objective policy science: security studies. Repositioning security studies in relation to this imperial and colonial history enables us to identify its characteristic biases and blind spots, and to re-imagine what security might be, who it is for, and how we should study it, as part of a wider project to decolonize the discipline and produce an anti-imperial world.

From its formal inception in the years immediately after the Second World War, security studies was defined as providing practical advice to the great powers that dominated world politics, in particular the USA and Great Britain; like IR more generally, it is an Anglo-American field of study (Hoffmann 1977). This meant taking for granted the policy problems and strategic concerns of the USA and to a lesser extent Britain in the production of useful knowledge, an orientation cemented by patterns of institutionalization and funding (Buzan and Hansen 2009). Seen in this light, security studies is an imperial field of knowledge, in at least two senses. First, it emerges and is defined in relation to the interests and power of the USA and Britain during a period in which they actively

KEY IDEA 9.1 Eurocentrism

'Eurocentrism refers to the presumption of the centrality both empirically and normatively of Europe in analysis of world history. On this view, Europe is conceived as separate and distinct from the rest of the world, as self-contained and self-generating. Analysis of the past, present, and future of world politics is then carried out in terms—conceptual and empirical, theoretical and normative—which take this centrality for granted. Europe becomes central to accounts of how the world has developed over time, as well as the key site for the production of the epistemologies and methodologies through which analysis takes place. The conception of Europe which informs and structures Eurocentrism is best understood as an ideological category rather than a geopolitical one, both because it serves to homogenize and obscure differences within "Europe"—between those states which have been empires and those which have not, for instance, as well as imperial and hierarchical relations within Europe—and also because the meaning, content, and location of Europe shifts over time. Eurocentrism is about both a real and an imagined Europe. Over time the location of "Europe" shifts, expands, and contracts, eventually crossing the Atlantic and the Pacific and becoming synonymous with the "West", which is also best understood in ideological rather than geographical terms. One of the signature features of Eurocentrism is the assumption that the end-point of development and modernization is defined by the contemporary "West". Thus understood, Eurocentrism is not simply a form of prejudice or an ideology, however, but is rather both constitutive and reflective of European domination in world politics over the past five centuries.'

(Barkawi and Laffey 2006).

pursued or defended colonial and imperial relations with the global south, whether in US policies towards Latin America and Southeast Asia, for example, or British policies towards its (soon to be) former possessions in Africa and the Middle East. These relations persist into the present, as in the theory and practice of counter-insurgency (Khalili 2013), drone warfare (Chamayou 2015), and humanitarian intervention (Campbell 2013). Second, and more fundamentally, security studies is an imperial field of knowledge because it adopts a perspective which postcolonial scholars refer to as 'the colonizer's view of the world' (Blaut 1993). This entails both a set of Eurocentric empirical claims about world politics and epistemological and normative assumptions about how we come to know world politics and its defining features (Jones 2006). In postcolonial perspective, security studies is not merely shaped by power but is itself a form of imperial power/knowledge: through its categories and the practices to which it gives licence, security studies participates in the production of a hierarchical world it purports only to describe (Weldes et al. 1999: 16–17).

As a form of critical theory, postcolonialism relates to security studies in at least three ways (cf. Grovogui 2002; Seth 2011). First, in highlighting the consequences for analysis of Eurocentrism in all its forms, postcolonialism promises, minimally, better social scientific explanations of world politics by reconceiving taken-for-granted conceptual and theoretical frameworks, including excluded variables or taking seriously formerly excluded or marginalized points of view (Niva 1999). Second, in identifying the multiple ways in which security studies expresses, both implicitly and explicitly, the point of view of the colonizers and the imperialists, postcolonialism raises important normative questions about how security is defined, for whom, and to what effects (Muppidi 2012). Third, and more profoundly, as a critique of the social science enterprise, itself understood as yet another manifestation of Eurocentric practices of knowledge production, postcolonialism also holds out the possibility of more plural, enabling, and transformative understandings of our world (Mignolo and Escobar 2010). Postcolonialism thus represents a politically engaged intervention in the practices through which knowledge of the international is produced, siding both implicitly and explicitly with the **subaltern**, with those who have been excluded, marginalized, or silenced in world politics. As such, its implications extend far beyond the field of security studies narrowly defined.

A view from elsewhere: genealogies of the postcolonial

Postcolonialism arrived relatively late in IR, first appearing in the discipline in the early 1990s (Krishna 1993). By that time, it was already a contested concept, sitting at the heart of a discursive field defined by historical materialist and poststructuralist positions, as well as growing engagement with non-European forms of knowledge, including Indigenous or Fourth-World peoples. Unsurprisingly, rather than expressing a singular or settled position, postcolonialism is the site of vigorous and lively ongoing debate. There is no such thing as *the* postcolonial theory of international politics and there is no postcolonial theory of security—nor is there likely to be. Instead, as a politically engaged intervention in security studies it is better understood as opening a space for **postcolonial critique**. Postcolonialism interrogates security and world politics more generally from a specific empirical, political, and ethical position; a position which interprets European imperialism and its consequences across the past five centuries from the point of view of those who were subject to it. Neither imperialism nor colonialism are unknown in world history prior to 1492, the date at which Christopher Columbus 'discovered' the Americas, thus inaugurating the hierarchical imperial practices and relations emphasized in postcolonial analyses. But European imperialism is distinctive owing to its sheer scale as well as the wide-ranging and continuing consequences for how the world has been produced and known. The key insight is the *mutual constitution* of the imperial metropole and the colony: 'what we now call Europe, Africa, the Americas and Asia were constructed *together* in the midst of a relationship, at once economic and cultural, military and political' (Drayton 2002: 103; emphasis added). Postcolonialism brings to the fore the past and continuing consequences of European imperialism and asks how dominant forms of security practice and knowledge relate to them.

As both an orientation to the world and also as theory, postcolonialism is distinguished from other perspectives on security in at least two ways. First, postcolonial critique is distinctive because of the central role it accords to violence in world politics. Indeed, it takes violence more seriously than does either realism or security studies itself, despite their shared focus on war, particularly great power war (Barkawi and Laffey 2006). Postcolonialism takes account of such conflicts but is also attentive to so-called 'small wars', 'asymmetric conflicts', and other interventions routinely carried out by imperial powers. These are conceived of not as marginal or peripheral to world politics but rather as central, particularly from the point of view of those in the global south where they typically take place. It is also attentive to the often considerable violence structuring everyday life, particularly in colonial and settler societies. In this respect, it has similarities with feminism and historical materialism, which are also attentive to the impact of both large- and small-scale violence on, respectively, gender and class relations. But in another sense, for postcolonialism violence is more fundamental: violence is constitutive of the imperial encounter itself and plays a continuing and defining role within colonial relations. As Achille Mbembe (2001) observes, with many others, colonial rule was a rule of force, not of consent or of hegemony. Postcolonial analysis identifies three analytically distinct moments or forms of violence which are usually found in combination. First, postcolonialism highlights the sheer scale of the **material violence** unleashed by European colonialism against populations in the Americas, in Africa, and in Asia, something typically not focused on by security studies. Second, postcolonialism also focuses on **epistemic violence**, understood as the imposition of European knowledge systems onto other people and places, whether in terms of simple naming, for example, or in the active denial, discrediting, and destruction of local knowledge systems. Finally, **structural violence** refers to the systematic relations of exploitation and domination which define daily life and its reproduction in colonial spaces. Colonialism and imperialism were never only about force or culture, broadly understood, but also the role of institutions such as property rights and 'free trade' in the quite deliberate destruction or transformation of existing social relations, often with deadly consequences (Wolf 1997; Davis 2001). These relations of violence continue into the present, as in practices of so-called humanitarian intervention or the functioning of a global capitalist economy—one historically organized and dominated by former colonial powers. Postcolonialism is concerned with both the differences but also the similarities across time and space in terms of how different forms of violence serve to constitute people and places in the context of hierarchical international relations of diverse kind.

Third, unlike other perspectives on security, postcolonialism is not predominantly or exclusively a European form of knowledge, even if some of its most prominent expressions emerge, like security studies before it, within the global Anglo-American academy. On the contrary, the sources of postcolonial thought are in principle global, grounded in the long and entangled histories of imperial relations and the resistance to them, both in the colonies themselves but also in the metropole. In this sense, postcolonialism engages and reflects the world in its diversity, both in terms of the different sites of imperial encounter and experience, but also in terms of the diverse traditions, cosmologies, and histories which were confronted by and linked together through colonialism. By its nature, imperialism was not singular but diverse, taking different forms in different places. For instance, colonization could be relatively informal, established or carried out through diverse relations with local authorities, perhaps confined to a few cities and ports, or it could be a deep settler colonialism, carried out through the violent destruction of indigenous institutions, practices, and peoples. Similarly, decolonization also took different forms, in some places the product of armed revolutionary struggle, while in others the colonizer negotiated a more peaceful withdrawal. Nevertheless, the impact of colonialism continues in the form of institutions, identity categories, socio-economic hierarchies, and, most visibly, colonial-era borders. Thus, as Siba Grovogui observes, 'the legacies of colonialism manifest themselves today according to the different colonial trajectories, their modes of administration, and the extent of participation of subject populations in the political economy and the production of knowledge' (2002: 36). Just as colonialism was not a singular phenomenon so there is no such thing as *the* postcolonial condition. Part of the reason for the contested nature of postcolonialism is precisely the diverse set of relations and experiences to which it refers, draws on, and reworks in contemporary context, and the traditions of thought thereby implicated.

Situated in this way, postcolonialism can be understood in two broad senses: as a *periodizing* concept and, in its dominant form, as an *ideological* or *struggle* concept. We trace these different meanings to their diverse contexts below. As it emerged after the Second World War, 'postcolonial' was initially understood as a periodizing term, an historical or geopolitical category deployed mostly by historical materialist scholars to refer to states in Latin America, Africa, and Asia that previously had been colonized (Alavi 1972). In this sense, postcolonial meant literally 'after colonialism' and was linked to the Third World project which emerged out of the meeting of newly independent African and Asian leaders in Bandung, Indonesia in 1955 (Prashad 2012). This was a project of Third-World nationalism reflecting the intellectual and political dynamics of the nineteenth- and twentieth-century anti-colonial struggles, with their emphasis on achievement of political sovereignty and the national-popular project of development. Given its role in liberation struggles from early in the century, historical materialism was prominent in efforts to legitimate and to explain the postcolonial state and its international context. In the late 1970s, however, political sentiment in the USA and Western Europe turned sharply against efforts to reform international institutions such as the United Nations and the world economy in ways that reflected the interests of newly independent states. By the middle of the 1980s, confronted with the debt crisis, structural adjustment policies that prefigured neoliberalism, and the reassertion of Western and in particular US dominance in international institutions, the Third World project was in crisis. It was in this new global context that postcolonialism emerged in its contemporary form, as an ideological or struggle concept. In this sense, postcolonialism means after the (defeat of the) Third World project. It was thus defined in opposition to key elements of that project, in particular the state, the nation, development, and historical materialism, all of which were regarded as manifestations of Eurocentrism (Escobar 1995). So understood, postcolonialism intervenes in theoretical debates by pointing us towards the ways in which modes of subjectivity, social forms and global relations are bound up with—if not reducible to—the 500-year world history marked by European forms of colonialism and imperialism. To say 'postcolonial' is to invoke this history and its contemporary manifestations, and to position oneself on the side of those in 'most of the world', Partha Chatterjee's (2004: 8) evocative term for what used to be called the Third World or the global south. By way of elaborating this second meaning of postcolonialism, we focus on two key moments in its development: the publication in 1978 of Edward Said's seminal text *Orientalism*, and the formation in the early 1980s of the influential Subaltern Studies research project.

Edward Said and *Orientalism*

Orientalism (Said: 1978) is a study of the relations between Western 'knowledge' of the Orient, in particular the Middle East and Islam, and the colonization and exploitation of those societies by Western states, especially Britain and France. Said highlighted the close relations between imperialism and culture, defined as the production of knowledge—including academic knowledge—and specifically the forms of representation through which the Orient is produced as an object of knowledge. These representations are hierarchically ordered, operating through a set of stereotyped contrasts between the Orient and the Occident or West. The 'Orient' was defined in opposition to 'the Occident' in raced and gendered terms as mysterious, unchanging, emotional, violent, barbaric, and ultimately inferior. In contrast, 'the Occident' was defined as known, progressive, rational, peaceful, civilized, and superior. Said argued that it was through these discursive practices that the Orient was made available as an object of conquest and exploitation by the West. *Orientalism* became a foundational text in postcolonial analysis, although such arguments were not new, having been made, for example, by anticolonial critics such as Frantz Fanon ([1952] 2008) and Anwar Abdel Malek (1963). Writing at the dawn of the twentieth century, Tang Tiaoding, a Chinese scholar observing the US suppression of anti-imperialist revolt in the Philippines, denounced what he called 'white people's histories', which he said 'provide plenty of indisputable evidence on the extent of native peoples' primitive customs and ignorance, as proof for why those people deserve to be conquered' (quoted in Karl 2002: 107). More significantly, Said's text was interpreted in poststructural terms, and this rapidly became the dominant understanding of how postcolonial analysis was to be conducted, as a form of discourse analysis (Milliken 1999). Such an interpretation, however, was at best only a partially accurate understanding of Said's position. While he had drawn on the work of Michel Foucault in framing the text, Said also positioned *Orientalism* in the longer tradition of anticolonial writings to which historical materialism (see Chapter 4) had been an integral part, citing the work of Abdel Malek, Samir Amin, and C. L. R. James, all distinguished Marxist thinkers, as 'the earliest studies of the post-colonial' (Said 1995: 5). Said was himself critical of Foucault, in particular his tendency to overstate the significance of discourse in relation to other forms of power (Said 2004). At the time *Orientalism* was published Said was Professor of English and Comparative Literature at Columbia University in New York and the initial impact of the book was felt overwhelmingly in English and Literature departments, reinforcing both the poststructural interpretation of Said's work and the emphasis on culture. But Said was also perhaps the most prominent Palestinian intellectual in the USA, and from 1977 to 1991 a member of the Palestinian National Council. As someone actively engaged in the Palestinian liberation struggle, he was well aware that Israel's settler colonialism was not simply a matter of discourse but also entailed institutional, structural, and material power (Collins 2011). It is thus unsurprising that in his subsequent work, most notably *Culture and Imperialism* (1993), Said engaged directly with contemporary forms of imperialism after formal decolonization, in particular that of the USA, and addressed more closely the relations between representation and other forms of imperial power.

Subaltern Studies

One of the criticisms of *Orientalism* was its relative lack of attention to the Oriental subject itself and the question of resistance to imperial power. The Subaltern Studies Collective, emerging in the field of Indian history in the early 1980s, addressed itself directly to this question through its engagement with the subaltern and their role in the making of postcolonial India (Chaturvedi 2000). The historiography of Indian independence focused on elite actors or elite-led class struggle and marginalized or ignored subaltern actors, in particular the Indian peasantry. Where Said had found conceptual resources in poststructuralism, Subaltern Studies, at least in its earliest incarnation, drew inspiration from historical materialism and in particular the Italian Antonio Gramsci who had first proposed the concept of the subaltern to refer to the lowest classes in Italian society. Ranajit Guha, the Indian historian primarily responsible for establishing the Subaltern Studies project, defined subaltern to mean 'the general attribute of subordination in South Asian society whether this is expressed in terms of class, caste, age, gender and office or in any other way' (1988: 35). Defined in this way, it became possible to apply the idea of the subaltern to a wide range of different subjects, both in India and in world politics more generally. Using this expanded notion of the subaltern, the collective produced a series of studies which in effect rewrote Indian history to incorporate the agency and cultures of subjects hitherto ignored, many of whom were illiterate. The Subaltern Studies project was hugely influential, for example, spurring similar projects in Africa and Latin America (e.g. Beverley 1999). This led not only to closer engagement with forms of thought and ways of life such as those of peasants and Indigenous or Fourth-World peoples, which had been largely ignored in the national histories of places such as India or Brazil, but also to the questioning of social science categories derived from the European experience through which those histories had been produced. For instance, the Indian Subaltern Studies group gradually evolved away from its original historical materialist commitments because, in part, historical materialism seemed not to provide a set of categories for making sense of the peasantry that did not imply that they were either necessarily backward or in the process of being transformed into workers. Neither of these categories made space for engaging the peasantry on their own terms. For this reason, over time, the group shifted to a more poststructural position focused on the critique of European forms of colonial power/knowledge and the promotion of various forms of indigenous community as a positive contrast. This led Sumit Sarkar, one of the earliest members of the group, to complain that it had substituted cultural determination for political economy, while also embracing a form of reactionary nativism in its uncritical validation of indigenous cultures, which, he argued, were often deeply hierarchical—in caste and gender terms, for instance—long before the British arrived. 'The decisive shift in critical registers from capitalist and colonial exploitation to Enlightenment rationality, from multinationals to Macaulay, has opened the way for a vague nostalgia that identifies the authentic with the indigenous . . .' (Sarkar 2002: 422). Vigorous debate over these and related issues continues to animate the diverse Subaltern Studies projects.

Thus, although the predominant tendency in postcolonial analysis is to define itself against the older traditions and institutions associated with the moment of the Third World project in favour of a set of poststructural commitments (Krishna 2009), as this brief discussion of Said and the Subaltern Studies project makes clear, postcolonialism emerges from and continues to be defined by a set of complex relations between and among at least three sets of ideas: poststructuralism, historical materialism, and various forms of non-European thought. Feminist scholarship had also become increasingly prominent and influential, reflecting the evident role of gender categories in colonial and imperial relations. Taken together, these provide a powerful set of diverse resources with which to challenge what remains of the shared problematic of Eurocentrism in thought and practice.

KEY POINTS

- Postcolonial critique foregrounds the past and continuing consequences of European imperialism for world politics and how these are constitutive of dominant forms of security practice and knowledge.
- Postcolonialism focuses on the role of violence in world politics, in particular material, epistemic, and structural violence, and their joint role in imperialism's shaping of people, places, and relations.
- The sources of postcolonial thought are in principle global, grounded in the long and entangled histories of imperial relations and resistance to them both in the colonies and the metropole.
- Postcolonialism can be understood in two ways: as a periodizing geopolitical concept or as an ideological struggle concept.
- Postcolonialism stresses the close relations between imperialism and culture defined as the production of knowledge, including academic knowledge.

Security and the colonizer's view of the world

As a critical intervention in the production of knowledge, postcolonialism prompts a rethinking of the relations between security studies and our accounts of world politics, between the theories and models we build and the imagined histories and geographies those theories take for granted. As a field, security studies rests on a Eurocentric narrative of world politics, expressive of the 'Westphalian commonsense' of IR as a discipline (Grovogui 2002; Laffey and Weldes 2004). This narrative begins with a world of sovereign entities called states which are the primary subjects of world politics. These subjects emerge in Europe with the Treaties of Westphalia in 1648 and progressively diffuse across the globe. Within its territory, the state is assumed to have a monopoly on the legitimate use of force, to have pacified the population, and to be the sole source of binding decisions. Externally, sovereignty means mutual recognition within an anarchic system of states and independence from outside interference. World politics is then defined in terms of the relations between and among sovereign states. Substantively, this means accounts of world politics organized primarily in terms of the rise and fall of European great powers (Barkawi and Laffey 2006). The assumptions structuring the sovereignty narrative are in turn fundamental for how security is understood. Security and security studies are defined in terms of the state, understood as the protector of its population and territory against the anarchic international system. The sovereign state is both the subject and the object of security: the state is the agent responsible for producing security and security is ultimately the security of the state.

Security in this sense is treated as a universal category invented or discovered in Europe and applicable to all peoples and places. These assumptions thus serve to define world politics as fundamentally European and from a European point of view. Imperial and colonial relations and perspectives are taken as normal and unexceptional but at the same time as marginal or secondary to the production of modernity in Europe and its spread across the world's surface. Developments elsewhere, to the extent they are considered at all, are seen as a function of European factors or as marginal to them. Alternatively, they are located on a hierarchy of social development in which Europe is at the top and other places are either in the process of becoming more European or represent past or residual forms to be transcended: geography is thus transformed into history (Fabian 2002). Resistance to European institutions and practices—where it is acknowledged at all—is treated as a problem to be overcome, as aberrant or, as in decolonization struggles in the nineteenth and twentieth centuries, as reaffirming the essential centrality to world politics of sovereignty itself. This Eurocentric perspective is evident, for example, in descriptions of local conflicts on the margins of imperial power as 'small wars'. From the point of view of an imperial power such as Great Britain or France, they are small in contrast to an inter-imperial war, but for those on the other end of the guns the consequences are often devastating; for them, such conflicts are anything but small (Lindqvist 1998). Similarly, descriptions of the Cold War as 'the long peace' express a moral perspective which places peaceful great power relations between the USA and the Soviet Union in Europe above the millions who died elsewhere as a result of this conflict (Gaddis 1986; cf. Young 1991). Security studies is thus conceptually, empirically, and normatively Eurocentric.

The Westphalian commonsense expressed in the sovereignty narrative is exemplary of what J. M. Blaut (1993) calls 'the colonizer's view of the world'. Specifically,

> the economic and social modernization of Europe is fundamentally a result of Europe's *internal* qualities,

not of interaction with the societies of Africa, Asia and America after 1492. Therefore: the main building blocks of modernity must be European. Therefore: colonialism cannot have been really important for Europe's modernization. Therefore: colonialism must mean, for the Africans, Asians and Americans, not spoliation and cultural destruction but, rather, the receipt-by-diffusion of European civilization: modernization.

(Blaut 1993: 2)

This is an explicitly hierarchical conception of world history, one which sees Europe, in particular its institutional forms and cultural practices, as discrete, self-generated, and normatively superior, with only contingent and relatively unimportant connections to other places. This model is evident, for example, in the Cold War framing of world politics—the putative context in which security studies emerges—in terms of the Three Worlds problematic (Pletsch 1981). A Europe-centred modernity—the First World—becomes the model of the normal: the most advanced, the most developed, and the most enlightened part of humanity, as well as the most secure. The Second World, which corresponds to the Soviet and Communist bloc, is seen in relation to the First, as modern in various ways, most notably its industrialization and its military, but as deficient in terms of its political and economic systems. The Third World, encompassing what today we would call the global South, is defined as a residual category in terms of its lack of the markers of modernity such as functioning states, which means a lack of security (Doty 1996). During the Cold War and since, it is understood as the location and object of great power competition, a source of threats, or as a site of intervention, as in state building for example. As a field, security studies in its dominant forms takes this hierarchical conception of the world for granted, as defining the meaning of security and the context of security practices.

There are a number of problems with the sovereignty narrative, both as an empirical account of the world and also as a frame for thinking about security (Paul 1999). Perhaps most important is a failure to take account of the myriad ways in which Europe and its outside are mutually constituted through imperial and colonial relations. Throughout the period since 1648, the symbolic starting date of the sovereignty narrative, Europe has been dominated by a succession of imperial powers, dating back at least to 1492 and the arrival of Christopher Columbus in the 'New World'. In rendering colonialism and imperialism invisible or marginal, the colonizer's view of the world obscures their role in the production of Europe, and indeed of the modern international system itself. Ironically, security studies' core categories of sovereignty and anarchy make it harder to see the hierarchical relations through which world politics is constituted and produced. For example, both as an institution and a set of practices, sovereignty did not emerge in Europe and then diffuse to the rest of the world, but was produced in and through the violent European encounter with the 'New World' (Anghie 2005; Branch 2014). For security studies, its basic categories such as the state of nature and anarchy also derive from the colonial encounter and reflect a deeply racist view of world politics (Jahn 2000; Richardson 2013). Making sense of sovereignty and security, bound tightly together in the sovereignty narrative, thus requires they be resituated within what Walter Mignolo (2000) terms the modern/colonial world system. Events seemingly outside Europe such as the colonization of the Americas and the Atlantic slave trade for example, were neither an aberration from, nor marginal to, Europe's modernity but rather integral to it.

At the same time, one of the great achievements of European imperialism, observes Said (1993: xxi–xxii), was 'to bring the world closer together', to connect and interweave peoples, places, and cultures, even as it also constructed hierarchical relations between them. Out of this came what he refers to as 'overlapping territories and intertwined histories'. This did not mean the reduction of diverse social worlds to a single unified history, however; as Mignolo (2010: 2) observes, 'there are several histories, all simultaneous histories, interconnected by imperial and colonial powers, by imperial and colonial differences'. Through these hierarchical and unequal relations were produced *connected histories* (Bhambra 2007), such that plantations and slavery in the Caribbean were integrally linked to landed estates and consumption patterns in England, for example. The postcolonial point is that neither end of these relations can be understood in isolation from the other. Such relations enabled the extraction of immense wealth from colonial territories, a point made repeatedly by anticolonial thinkers such as Fanon (1990: 81): 'in a very concrete way Europe has stuffed herself inordinately with the gold and raw materials of the colonial countries: Latin America, China and Africa'. Racial categories and relations produced out of these connected histories were in turn integral to the constitution of Europe and its cultural and political forms, as in the violent reaction in France and elsewhere to the Haitian Revolution, the first successful slave revolt in the history of Atlantic slavery, which revealed clearly the racism underpinning liberal understandings of human rights (Grovogui 2006). Violence was a persistent feature of these relations. This was in part a corollary of the securitized development imperialism implies, particularly in settler colonies faced with the need to separate the natives from their land and possessions (Elkins and Pederson 2005). Such violence was consequential for colonizer and colonized. As Aimé Césaire, another anti-colonial thinker observed in 1955,

> colonial activity, colonial enterprise, colonial conquest, which is based on contempt for the native and justified by that contempt, inevitably tends to change him who undertakes it . . . the colonizer, who in order to ease his conscience gets into the habit of seeing the other man as *an animal*, accustoms himself to treating him like an animal, and tends objectively to transform *himself* into an animal. (Césaire 2000: 41)

Violent colonial practices were not disconnected from Europe but rather moved back and forth between the colony and metropole, as in the case of policing practices, for example (McCoy 2009). During the Second World War, like the First World War an inter-imperial war, Adolf Hitler's plans for Eastern Europe and the Soviet Union were modelled on his admiration for what the British had achieved in North America in terms of the extermination of the native population, thus producing empty spaces for colonization. The territories in the East were to be the 'German Indies' and the war with the 'natives' of Eastern Europe was equated with the 'war against the Indians' (Losurdo 2015: 185–9). From this viewpoint, argued Césaire and others, the Holocaust itself was not exceptional or an aberration but simply the return to the metropole of practices which were a commonplace in the colonies. Writing in the 1920s, W. E. B. Dubois (1925: 423) said modern imperialism wore a 'democratic face' in the metropole and a 'stern and unyielding autocracy' in the colonies. Four decades later, in 1961, Fanon (1990: 76, 81) was more blunt: '[t]he well-being and the progress of Europe has been built up with the sweat and the dead bodies of Negroes, Arabs, Indians and the yellow races. . . . Europe is literally the creation of the Third World.' In contrast to the sovereignty narrative, which leads to an image of the international as a spare anarchic space, a postcolonial perspective reveals the international as a hierarchically ordered 'thick space', comprised of a dense set of political, economic, social, military, and cultural relations, generated out of colonial and imperial practices and through which the sovereign entities focused on in IR's 'Westphalian commonsense' have been constituted and produced (Barkawi and Laffey 2002).

The sovereignty narrative continues, however, to exert a powerful grip on the imagination of security studies. How can we explain this? Postcolonial scholars point to a set of discursive mechanisms deployed in representations of the relations between European and non-European subjects, between a Western 'self' and its 'others'. As in Said's work, they emphasize the ways in which these hierarchical forms of representation enable relations of conquest and domination. At the same time, they also focus on the ways in which these representations serve to produce a Western 'self'. Complementing Said's analysis, Fernando Coronil introduced the concept of Occidentalism to refer to the implicit conception of the West or Europe which animates representations of non-Western subjects. So defined, Occidentalism is not the reverse of Orientalism but its condition of possibility. As Coronil (1997: 14) describes this relationship, 'Occidentalism . . . entails the mobilization of stereotypical representations of non-Western societies as part of the West's self-fashioning as an imperial power. . . . Occidentalism is thus the expression of a constitutive relationship between Western representations of cultural difference and worldwide Western dominance.' This process is effected through a specific set of discursive operations: 'separating the world's components into bounded units; disaggregating their relational histories; turning difference into hierarchy; naturalizing these representations; and thereby intervening, however unwittingly, in the reproduction of asymmetrical power relations' (Coronil 1997: 15). These bounded units may be states, as in the sovereignty narrative, but they could also be regional or global categories such as Middle East, Third World, global South, the West, and so forth. Through these operations, people and places connected and coevally produced through colonial and imperial relations—often over centuries and long before 'globalization' and 'interdependence' (Wolf 1997)—are treated as separate, distinct, and hierarchically ordered. Occidentalism thus underpins the colonizer's view of the world. Seen in postcolonial perspective, the sovereignty narrative emerges as part of European self-fashioning, as a means by which a particular understanding of the West and its role in the world is culturally produced. In turn, this hierarchical understanding provides a warrant for the continuing deployment of power in all its forms against non-Europeans. To the extent it reflects and reinforces these hierarchical representations of world politics, security studies can be understood as an imperial form of power/knowledge, to which postcolonialism presents itself as a direct challenge, both conceptually and empirically, politically and normatively.

KEY POINTS

- Security studies in its dominant form rests on a Eurocentric sovereignty narrative of world politics which reflects the colonizer's view of the world.
- Security is usually understood as a universal category invented or discovered in Europe and applicable to all people, places, and times.
- Postcolonialism stresses the mutual constitution of Europe and its outside through colonial and imperial relations, leading to a 'thick' view of world politics in contrast to the 'thin' view of the sovereignty narrative.
- Occidentalism is the condition of possibility of Orientalism and helps to explain why the sovereignty narrative persists as part of Western self-fashioning as a subject of world politics.

Decolonizing security: strategies

If postcolonialism is not a theory of security, what is its main contribution to security studies? The primary implication of postcolonialism is straightforward: to decolonize security. Decolonization is itself a complex concept: as postcolonial scholars show, decolonization was never simply a matter of forcing the colonizer to leave, but also entailed challenging a variety of institutional and cultural forms through which colonial relations had been made possible. Decolonizing security has similar implications: first, challenging conventional understandings of security; second, challenging security studies as a field; and third, challenging the practice of security in the world. As this suggests, the explicit aim is to contest or transform imperial or colonial fields of knowledge and the wider relations of domination—social, economic, cultural, and political—of which they are a part. Postcolonialism thus constitutes a self-consciously political intervention to make space for other ways of being, to resist the continuing colonization of the world through 'security', and to contribute to transforming what remains of an international system defined by colonial and imperial relations.

How does postcolonialism set out to achieve these goals? An important first step is to engage subaltern knowledge and experience in its diversity and on its own terms. Notable by their absence in security studies are the voices of those who have been the targets of colonial and imperial relations. Indeed, Pinar Bilgin (2010) argues the erasure of non-Western or subaltern subjects is not accidental but rather constitutive of the field of security studies. The coherence of security as a policy science of and for the great powers is undermined if it takes seriously the competing historical, political, and ethical claims of those on the receiving end of colonial and imperial violence. As discussed above, part of the problem here is the tendency of security studies to implicitly and sometimes explicitly adopt the point of view of the imperialists and the colonizers, leading to analyses which ignore or marginalize subaltern perspectives—often framed in Orientalist terms—and the connected histories produced by colonial and imperial relations. An example is how the problem of 'failed states' is attributed to the contemporary internal dynamics of the states and peoples in question, rather than the legacy of colonization, decolonization, and repeated post-independence interventions by former colonizers, either directly or indirectly, for example, through restructuring of the global economy (Duffield 2001). To counter this, postcolonial scholars engage in *contrapuntal analyses*, to put colonizer and colonized, dominant and subordinate, in the same analytical frame. As defined by Said (1993: 51), a contrapuntal analysis entails 'a simultaneous awareness both of the metropolitan history that is narrated and of those other histories against which (and together with which) the dominating discourse acts'. The approach can be illustrated through analysis of nuclear strategy. The 1950s is routinely described as a 'golden age' for security studies, defined by a focus on nuclear strategy, literally planning for the possibility of global atomic war (Walt 1991; Buzan and Hansen 2009). Much of this took the form of highly abstract, mathematical models of rational deterrence between the USA and the Soviet Union. While abstraction in analysis is unavoidable, what matters is the form it takes: what is included as relevant and what is excluded as extraneous. As Sankaran Krishna (2001) argues, abstraction is one of the key ways in which IR and security studies—as in realist and liberal analyses, for example—sanitizes and obscures the role of colonial and imperial violence in world politics.

A contrapuntal analysis of the 'golden age' might begin by tracing the possibility of nuclear strategy to the development of the bomb itself in the southwestern USA. Indeed, Los Alamos National Laboratory, where the bomb was designed and built, sits on land claimed since 1967 by San Ildefonso Pueblo, in US law a sovereign Native American 'domestic, dependent nation'. Joseph Masco (1999: 205) describes the southwest as 'among the most politically contested regions in North America', bringing together not only the US nuclear military establishment but also the competing claims and aspirations of Native American and Nuevomexicano communities. Post-Second World War testing by the USA in the Pacific was conducted on territories conquered during the war, part of an island empire dating to the acquisition of Hawaii in 1898. Similarly, French testing initially occurred in Algeria, colonized in 1847, until the Algerian War of Independence forced its relocation in 1962 to Moruroa and Fangataufa in the Pacific, French colonial possessions in Polynesia (Danielsson and Danielsson 1986). Similar patterns are evident in British testing in Australia, Soviet testing in Kazakhstan, and Chinese testing in Xinjiang. In each case, the development of nuclear weapons is enabled by hierarchical relations linked to patterns of past and present imperial power. Indigenous peoples, who are in no doubt that they remain colonized, are a persistent victim of these practices but their voices and concerns, such as increased cancer rates or the defence of traditional lands and cosmologies, are completely absent from discussion of the 'golden age' (cf., Masco 2006). There is no space in the study of nuclear strategy for the different worlds of the subaltern subjects whose histories become intersected with global nuclear competition, even as nuclear security produces acute insecurity for them. Unsurprisingly, internal diversity within these subaltern subjects—whether in terms of class, gender, or some other form of difference—is also ignored. From a postcolonial perspective, security studies thus effects a 'strategy of containment' (Krishna 2001): colonial and imperial violence linked directly to the development and testing of nuclear weapons, and hence to the very possibility of a 'golden age', is simply erased, highlighting the partial, contestable, and dangerous—at least for some—conception of security it defends.

Following Meera Sabaratnam (2013), we can identify a number of decolonizing strategies pursued by postcolonial scholars and then trace their implications for how we might think differently about security. These strategies all take for granted the necessity of putting dominant and subaltern subjects into a single frame of analysis. The strategies are: challenging Orientalist representations of world politics; deconstructing historical myths of Europe as the central subject of world history; questioning the primacy of European categories in the analysis of world politics; engaging subaltern voices as a challenge to dominant ones; and diversifying the legitimate subjects of security and their forms. These strategies, some of which we have already encountered in outline above, focus on questions of representation and voice. Taken together, they enable a progressive dismantling and reworking of how we think about security.

The first strategy identified by Sabaratnam focuses on the dominant representations of world politics taken for granted in analysis of security. This strategy seeks to expose the ways in which the conceptual framings of both security issues or problems and world politics more generally express and reinforce hierarchical relations between the different subjects of world politics. The aim is to show how these representations work and to challenge them as self-evident or objective descriptions. Picking up on our discussion of nuclear strategy, a good example is nuclear proliferation. As Hugh Gusterson (1999) shows, much recent discussion of nuclear proliferation turns on what he refers to as 'nuclear Orientalism'. This entails a sharp distinction between the West and the non-West. On one side, the West is represented as a responsible and rational agent able to possess nuclear weapons safely; indeed, in the West's hands, they contribute to global security. On the other side is 'an infantilized third world given to impulse, passion, and fanaticism as untrustworthy custodians of nuclear weapons' (Biswas 2014: 101); nuclear weapons in these hands lead to global insecurity. In this context the Nuclear Nonproliferation Treaty 'has become the legal anchor for a global nuclear regime that is increasingly legitimated in Western public discourse in racialised terms' (Gusterson 1999: 11). Such representations lead directly to the view that it is the responsibility of the nuclear-armed West to police the unarmed Rest and criticism from the Indian government, for example, as a form of nuclear apartheid (see Key Quote 9.1)

A second, closely related, strategy focuses more narrowly on the position of Europe or the West in these accounts. Typically, as in the nuclear proliferation example, the West is presented as both central to world politics and in some sense an exemplary subject: it is the model for how to handle nuclear weapons in a safe and responsible way, for instance. Gusterson demonstrates that this latter claim is at best contentious, if not simply wrong, by showing how the same arguments typically put forward to justify why Third-World states cannot have nuclear weapons apply with equal force to Western ones, in particular the USA

KEY QUOTE 9.1 Nuclear apartheid and the Nuclear Non-Proliferation Treaty (NPT)

'[I]t is hard to dispute the fact that the inequity inscribed within the treaty—recognizing and legitimizing the nuclear weapons of the five states that had exploded a nuclear device prior to 1967 practically in perpetuity (given the indefinite extension in 1995), while prohibiting all other states from acquiring any nuclear weapons—has become a political weapon wielded by some states to point to the hypocrisy of the nuclear five (coincidentally also the Permanent Five of the Security Council) and occasionally to pursue their own weapons programs. Thus India was able to wield the charge of "nuclear apartheid" as it declared itself a nuclear power in 1998, followed shortly by Pakistan. India state leaders framed 'the US-led non-proliferation regime as a racist, colonial project' meant to deny India's hard-won achievements (Perkovich 1999: 7). Indian external affairs minister during those nuclear tests Jaswent Singh stated quite explicitly that the division between nuclear haves and nuclear have-nots within a discriminatory and flawed nonproliferation regime that sets "differentiated standards of national security" creates 'a sort of international nuclear apartheid" (Singh 1998: 48). To use the word *apartheid* is clearly to use a racial signifier, and one that carries with it a certain contemporary political resonance, given the very recent shameful history of the complicity of many first-world states with the racist regime in South Africa. Under very different circumstances no doubt, the nuclear apartheid argument is in one sense an attempt to point to the continuing exclusions and marginalizations faced by people of colour in third-world countries in a global order dominated and controlled by privileged whites in first-world countries. Now it is clear that this black–white distinction is problematic. Not only can China, as one of the nuclear five, clearly not be categorized in the latter category, but it is also problematic to conflate state boundaries with racial boundaries, despite the racial implications of all boundary-making exercises. However, the articulation of "whiteness" with power is deep and compelling for many and draws on a particular postcolonial logic.'

(Biswas, 2014: 102–103)

CASE STUDY 9.1 Orientalism and the right to bear nuclear arms

In his study of nuclear Orientalism, Hugh Gusterson (1999) identifies a set of claims routinely made about the differences between those states which can be trusted to have nuclear weapons and those which can't. Those claims are: (1) Third-World states are too poor to afford nuclear weapons; (2) deterrence will be unstable in the Third World; (3) Third-World governments lack the technical maturity to handle nuclear weapons; and (4) Third-World regimes lack the political maturity to be trusted with nuclear weapons. In order to begin to decolonize the discourse around nuclear proliferation, he takes those claims and applies them also to nuclear states—those granted legitimate possession of nuclear weapons in the **NPT**, in particular the USA. These claims, as he shows, rest on an Orientalist view of the world, as divided into different types of states and societies within a hierarchical international order; hence his term nuclear Orientalism. But the distinction breaks down when it can be shown that precisely the same criticisms often made of non-nuclear states apply also to existing nuclear ones. For instance, in relation to the affordability argument, Gusterson points out that nuclear weapons are routinely justified as comparatively cheaper than other weapons ('more bang for your buck') and as stimulating economic development ('military Keynesianism'). If these arguments work for the USA, then if anything they apply with even greater force in a comparatively poorer state such as India. While Third-World states often have high levels of poverty, it is not the case that the USA or any other nuclear state has solved poverty in their own societies, so arguments that resources might be better spent on non-nuclear issues apply with similar force to them also. Likewise, arguments about technical maturity overlook the considerable problems within the US arsenal itself in terms of guaranteeing the safety of these weapons. As Gusterson and also Eric Schlosser (2014) show, given the history of accidents and near-disasters, the assumption that nuclear weapons are a safe technology in the hands of the USA is deeply problematic. Finally, the claim that existing nuclear states are more politically mature than non-nuclear states also does not hold up well under inspection: not only have US leaders repeatedly treated nuclear weapons as a legitimate means of threatening other (non-nuclear weapon) states, elements of the US military have acted against the chain of command or expressed millennial religious beliefs which undermine the standard image of rational command and control. What Gusterson achieves, then, is a critical re-working of the usual claims made about why 'we' can be trusted with nuclear weapons—and 'they' cannot—by questioning the taken-for-granted representations of the nuclear states on which analysis of nuclear proliferation relies.

(see Case Study 9.1). At stake here is the self-image of Europe or the West and the ways in which this positions it in relation to other places. As Sandra Halperin (2006: 43) notes, even critical scholars attuned to the Orientalism in European representations of non-Europeans 'tend to reproduce Europe's profoundly erroneous highly ideological representation of its own history'. Against claims that European development was internally generated, for instance, often presented as evidence of European intellectual superiority, John Hobson (2004) demonstrates the dependence of what he calls the 'oriental West' on a long history of assimilation of Eastern inventions and technologies. Other versions of this de-centring strategy challenge the assumed moral superiority of the West, key to much discussion of its role in security. An example is Mike Davis's (2001) account of the role of a London-centred liberal world economy in the production of the famines responsible for the deaths of millions in India, China, and Brazil and integral to the production of what came to be known as the Third World (see Think Point 9.1).

Such strategies are an important first step inasmuch as they seek to denaturalize what are often taken-for-granted, commonsense and widely circulated claims—as in popular culture, for instance—about security and danger in world politics. A third strategy cuts more deeply into the conceptual underpinnings of dominant representations, by challenging the subjects and categories on the basis of which they are constructed. Typically these categories—such as the state, society, the nation, the economy, democracy, class or emancipation—derive from and reflect European historical experience. Applying them elsewhere represents a form of what Susanne Hoeber Rudolph (2005) refers to as 'the imperialism of categories'. A good example would be how some complex and multifaceted crises in the global south are understood and studied as essentially 'state failure' or 'weakness'. Thus, the building blocks of social science are, in this strategy, put in question. A thoroughgoing example of such work is the Latin American coloniality / decoloniality research project (Mignolo and Escobar 2010). Its main driving force, as summarized by Arturo Escobar, is 'a continued reflection on Latin American reality, including the subaltern knowledge of exploited and oppressed social groups' (2010: 34). Drawing creatively on a range of different traditions of

! THINK POINT 9.1 Mike Davis on the 'making of the Third World'

European institutions and practices such as free trade and capitalism are typically presented as diffusing to the rest of the world, engendering development and modernization. In contrast, the Third World is presented as undeveloped and impoverished. The Orientalism of the framing is evident in the assumption that this hierarchical relationship is long-standing and definitive of the relative development of the different parts of the world. But as Mike Davis points out in his provocative account of the relations between climate change, social institutions, and the making of the 'Third World', by the beginning of the nineteenth century the sharp vertical class differences within particular societies were not duplicated in differences of wealth between them. The relative living standards of French and Chinese peasants were comparable, whereas the differences between the peasants and rulers of France and China, respectively were huge. By the beginning of the twentieth century, however, 'the inequality of nations was as profound as the inequality of classes' (Davis 2001: 16). What changed? Adopting what he terms a political ecology approach—combining environmental history with historical materialism—Davis traces the impact that incorporation into the London-centred liberal world economy had on the social vulnerability of peasant farmers in north China, south Asia, northeast Brazil, and southern Africa to extreme weather events after 1870. In particular, Davis was concerned with famine. Famines are not simply about a lack of food but rather the failure of particular political and economic systems. During the eighteenth century, for example, social systems in places like India and China were comparatively robust, minimizing the effects of famine on the local population. However, as these and other areas were incorporated into the world economy, these institutional arrangements were weakened. 'Forcibly imposed trade deficits, export drives that diminished food security, over-taxation and predatory merchant capital, foreign control of key revenues and developmental resources, chronic imperial and civil warfare, a Gold Standard that picked the pockets of Asian peasants . . . ': these were the mechanisms by which the social vulnerability of peasant farmers to severe climate change was increased (Davis 2001: 306). During the latter part of the nineteenth century, the world went through a period of such change as a result of the El Niño-Southern Oscillation (ENSO), which induces changes in weather and in particular rainfall across a large part of the tropics. As a result of the ENSO, there occurred a series of huge famines across China, south Asia, Brazil, and Africa. In Davis's (2001) words,

'The great Victorian famines were forcing houses and accelerators of the very socio-economic forces that ensured their occurrence in the first place. . . . What we today call the "third world" (a Cold War term) is the outgrowth of income and wealth inequalities—the famous "development gap"—that were shaped most decisively in the last quarter of the nineteenth century, when the great non-European peasantries were initially integrated into the world economy. . . . By the end of Victoria's reign . . . the inequality of nations was as profound as the inequality of classes. Humanity had been irrevocably divided.' (Davis 2001: 15–16) thought, including dependency theory, liberation theology and participatory action research—all of which derive from Latin American critical thought in the twentieth century—as well as Subaltern Studies, it sets itself against the Christian, liberal, and Marxist narratives which provide much of the conceptual and theoretical materials on which social science rests. In so doing, the project reframes contemporary social science as itself part of 'the colonial matrix of power' established in the Atlantic in the sixteenth and seventeenth centuries.

A fourth strategy shifts from criticizing dominant strategies and categories to a more positive reconstructive effort to pluralize the subjects of international politics and undertake analysis of security from subaltern points of view. For instance, Mohammad Ayoob (1995) has argued forcefully that security studies has a mistaken conception of the security problematic of the Third-World state. Whereas in Europe, processes of internal pacification and nation building are mostly complete, for the Third-World state this is not the case. The Third-World state thus faces not only an external security dilemma but also an enduring internal one. In taking seriously the concerns of Third-World states, Ayoob's work pluralizes the subjects of security. However, it does so on a terrain that remains largely defined by the sovereignty narrative, despite taking account of the different circumstances of the state in the global south. A different approach is evident in analysis of the *Cuban* role in the Cuban Missile Crisis, until recently mostly overlooked in Anglo-American scholarship. Contrary to the usual Cold War framing of the crisis—as a dangerous moment in superpower nuclear rivalry—Laffey and Weldes (2008) show how engagement with Cuban points of view in their diversity opens up a perspective on the crisis which sees it as a peak moment in a longer history of imperialism out of which Cuba and Latin America have been produced. As these examples suggest, the implications of engaging with other subjects are shaped by the conceptual and theoretical context in which they are placed: adding Cubans' perspectives to an unchanged great power account of the crisis turns them into a kind of native informant and reinforces existing relations of international hierarchy, thus draining the engagement of its postcolonial potential (see Case Study 9.2).

Finally, a fifth strategy takes this reconstructive project one step further by seeking to recover what Sabaratnam (2013) calls alternative forms of political subject, both in the past and the present. For example, security studies treats contexts labelled 'ethnic conflict' or

CASE STUDY 9.2 The *Cuban* role in the Cuban Missile Crisis

The Cuban Missile Crisis (1962) is perhaps the most well-known and the most-studied security crisis in history. Its interpretation is central to debates about decision making, nuclear proliferation, deterrence, and crisis management, amongst others. Yet for most of the half-century since it took place, and despite a vast literature, the role of Cuba in the crisis has been marginalized or ignored. Instead, the crisis has been treated as having only two participants: the United States and the Soviet Union. The great power bias in security studies is evident in the invisibility of Cuba in the crisis, or its treatment as merely the place where it happened (Laffey and Weldes 2008). Aside from anything else, ignoring the Cubans means analysis of the causes and dynamics of the crisis is rendered unreliable. Against accounts of the crisis as lasting thirteen days, for instance, which is the standard great power chronology, Cuban state actors pointed to a much longer history of US aggression against Latin American states going back at least to 1898. Indeed, the year before the crisis Cuba had defeated a US-backed invasion at the Bay of Pigs by Cuban exiles aimed at overthrowing the government. For Cuba, the presence of Soviet missiles would deter such—and more direct—US interventions which were taking place in many parts of the Third World. Moreover, from a Cuban point of view, the crisis did not end: not only was Cuba not party to the negotiations between the USA and the Soviet Union—as Fidel Castro said, 'We had to endure the humiliation'—key Cuban demands such as the removal of US troops from the Guantanamo Base and an end to the US economic embargo of the island were ignored. Against accounts which ignore the Cubans or see them as merely a puppet of the Soviet Union, engaging the subaltern also reveals a far more complex and conflictual relationship between Cuba and the Soviets, who in fact complained of not being able to get the Cubans to do what they wanted. Against analyses which see the lessons of the crisis primarily in great power terms, as about crisis decision making and deterrence or about how to manage nuclear crises better, the lessons of the crisis from a Cuban perspective pointed to the devastating effects of intervention in small Third-World states and called for greater recognition of the sovereign interests of these states and the importance of obeying international law. Attending to the diverse Cuban reactions to the crisis also raises significant issues for the decolonization of the dominant account: the crisis looks different if attention is paid to popular experience, for example, whether of the crowds in Havana's Tropicana nightclub at the height of the crisis or of the fear induced by low-level flights by US aircraft over the island.

'civil war' as, at base, 'internal' conflicts between ethnic 'groups' or between the state and armed non-state actors. In this way, the state is naturalized as the basis for restoring 'peace' and repairing a 'fractured' society, and thus as the object and subject of security. However, those involved in struggle and conflict often have different conceptions of themselves and the histories, including colonial histories, by which they came to be entangled within the territorial state. In Sri Lanka, for example, Tamils and Sinhalese understand themselves as nations, albeit with competing historically constituted claims to the island's northeastern territories (e.g. Krishna 1999). Thus inherent to conflict are competing perspectives on the 'naturalness' of the state itself. Indeed, unification of the island's various pre-colonial entities under a single territorial administration was an act of British colonial convenience in 1832. Consequently from a Tamil perspective, colonialism incorporated their nation and its historic homeland (in the northeast) into what became after independence a Sinhala majoritarian state and social order. However, from a Sinhala perspective, the island is the historic homeland of the Sinhala nation, and claims to a Tamil homeland are a legacy of successive colonialisms—occupation by South Indian empires followed by the Dutch, the Portuguese, and finally the British. Security studies typically treats such subjectivities as transient ideological effects of elite manipulation, a reading that patronizes and infantilizes those in conflict while at the same time rationalizing interventions on their behalf. By contrast, postcolonialism emphasizes not only how such identities and struggles are shaped by local and global colonial legacies—borders, institutions, categories, and so on—but, just as importantly, how they are reproduced through the lived experiences and practices of ordinary people, and in that sense, how they are also interwoven with and intervene in diverse social hierarchies and political contestations along gender, caste, class, regional, and other elite/subaltern and 'intra-group' cleavages (Nadarajah and Rampton 2015).

Such decolonizing strategies, pursued in an academic setting, operate primarily in epistemological terms, as challenging forms of knowledge and knowledge production. Decolonization in this sense amounts to reworking the scholarly imagination of security and security studies. But as Julian Saurin (2006) has argued, pointing to the grounding of postcolonialism in the long, transnational history of anti-colonial struggle, the problem to which it is addressed extends beyond forms of knowledge and their effects, important as those might be, to the form and content of contemporary world politics itself. It is not just that our accounts of security forget or ignore colonialism and imperialism but rather that we live in a world in which relations of domination and hierarchy—often justified and carried forward in the name of 'security'—continue to shape and determine how millions of people live and die. The point, to paraphrase Marx, is not simply to reinterpret the world in postcolonial ways, but to change it. Such a perspective shifts attention to the role played by postcolonialism in concrete anti-imperialist projects, both in the past and the present. Decolonizing security, if it is to be meaningful, thus requires going beyond epistemological critique to practices of social transformation.

KEY POINTS

- Decolonizing strategies work through contrapuntal analysis which puts the dominant and the subordinate subjects of world politics in a single analytic frame, enabling alternative understandings from a subaltern point of view.
- Sabaratnam identifies five such strategies: challenging Orientalist representations of world politics; deconstructing historical myths of Europe as the central subject of world politics; questioning the primacy of European categories in analysis; engaging subaltern voices; and diversifying the legitimate subjects of security.
- Decolonizing security entails both an epistemological challenge and practices of social transformation.

Conclusion: should we 'forget security studies'?

Part of the impulse behind the emergence of postcolonialism was to enable the previously silenced subaltern to speak, thus to challenge prevailing representations and practices of world politics (Sabaratnam 2016). As it entered the field of security studies, however, it became apparent that postcolonialism was also rapidly becoming a new academic commodity, available for appropriation in unexpected and problematic ways. Some, such as the so-called 'imperial turn' in security studies, amount to little more than 'rediscovery' of imperialism within a largely unchanged field (Bayley 2014). Something similar is apparent in comparative studies of empires and imperial formations (Abernethy 2000; cf. Burbank and Cooper 2010). Other juxtapositions are more problematic, such as the suggestion 'Brown' Britain should exploit its colonial legacy of multiculturalism to adopt a 'postcolonial grand strategy' (Barkawi and Brighton 2013). This is postcolonialism as policy science: in adopting the point of view of the post-imperial British state, the proposal ignores the question of what a 'successful' postcolonial grand strategy conducted by a prototypical neoliberal state would mean for diverse communities within Britain and elsewhere. As these examples suggest, much of this scholarship is not postcolonial in any rich sense: postcolonial critique is reduced to a problem-solving tool for a more sophisticated security studies. The authority of the disciplinary subfield is powerfully reaffirmed. There is a considerable distance between work of this kind and that which treats IR, and security studies in particular, as an imperial ideology (Krishna 2001; Saurin 2006), precisely as a preliminary step towards overturning it.

Viewed in postcolonial perspective, security studies is and remains an imperial field of knowledge, even or especially after it has been 'broadened and deepened'. Indeed, it might be argued that the continuing extension of security and its logics to ever more social domains reflects a discernibly colonial or imperial logic. To paraphrase Krishna's (2001) reflections on the character of IR more generally, the idea of a postcolonial security studies is an oxymoron. The implications of postcolonialism for security studies are to put the field itself in question. Krishna goes on to argue, in common with Roland Bleiker (1997) and others, that in light of its complicity with the past and continuing imperial character of our world we should 'forget IR'. Should we 'forget security studies' too? In at least one sense, we cannot: security studies is not simply a set of scholars and academic texts but also, as postcolonial and other critical scholars remind us, a force in the world, closely bound up with and partially constitutive of a hierarchical international system. Put another way, security studies is dangerous. Postcolonial engagement implies not 'broadening and deepening' security in order to do it better, but rather 'broadening and deepening' our critical understanding of the field as we try to get beyond it, in order to make a world that is more equitable and so less dangerous.

? QUESTIONS

1. What is Eurocentrism and why is it a problem?
2. What does it mean to say that from a postcolonial point of view international relations is a 'thick space'?
3. What is the colonizer's view of the world and what are its implications?
4. What is the relationship between culture and imperialism according to postcolonialism?
5. What is the subaltern and why is it significant to postcolonialism?
6. What is Orientalism?
7. What is Occidentalism and how does it relate to a postcolonial analysis of world politics?
8. What is a contrapuntal analysis and how does it enable a postcolonial critique of security studies?
9. What does it mean to decolonize security studies?
10. Can there be a postcolonial security studies?

FURTHER READING

- Anievas, A., Manchanda, N., and Shilliam, R. (eds) (2015), *Race and Racism in International Relations: Confronting the Global Colour Line*, London: Routledge. In contrast to the historical inattention to race in the discipline, this collection of essays puts race and racism at the centre of world politics.

- Barkawi, T. (2006), *Globalization and War*, Lanham: Rowman and Littlefield. Short but brilliant and accessible effort to rethink the place of war in world politics from a postcolonial point of view.
- Biswas, S. (2014), *Nuclear Desire: Power and the Postcolonial Nuclear Order*, Minneapolis: University of Minnesota Press. To date this is the most compelling effort to combine poststructural and historical materialist insights in analysis of a key security issue.
- Doty, R. (1996), *Imperial Encounters: The Politics of Representation in North–South Relations*, Minneapolis: University of Minnesota Press. Seminal poststructural analysis of the role of representation in the reproduction of hierarchical relations between north and south.
- Inayatullah, N. and Blainey, D. (2004), *International Relations and the Problem of Difference*, London: Routledge. Challenging study of a key theme in postcolonial thought combining both international relations theory and international political economy.
- Jones, B. G. (ed.) (2006), *Decolonizing International Relations*, Lanham: Rowman & Littlefield. Stimulating collection of essays providing an excellent introduction to the range of questions and issues raised by the effort to decolonize IR.
- Krishna, S. (2009), *Globalization and Postcolonialism: Hegemony and Resistance in the Twenty-First Century*, Lanham: Rowman & Littlefield. To date the most sustained and comprehensive overview of postcolonialism as it relates to international relations, viewed through the prism of globalization.
- Muppidi, H. (2012), *The Colonial Signs of International Relations*, London: C. Hurst and Co. Brilliant series of very accessible essays arguing for the importance of an anti-colonial IR.
- Seth, S. (ed.) (2011), *Postcolonial Theory and International Relations: A Critical Introduction*, London: Routledge. Strong collection of essays offering both a postcolonial critique of core areas within international relations as well as a series of alternative postcolonial readings.

IMPORTANT WEBSITES

- **http://thedisorderofthings.com/** The Disorder of Things, probably the leading postcolonial website in IR. Wide range of contributions on topics relevant to the postcolonial analysis of world politics from a dynamic group of mostly junior scholars.
- **http://globalsocialtheory.org/** Global Social Theory is devoted to the development of non-Eurocentric social theory. Provides good introduction to key thinkers and concepts relevant to postcolonialism.
- **http://africasacountry.com** Africa is a Country provides a wide range to contributions with the common theme of challenging Orientalist and other stereotypical representations of Africa. Also contains Latin America is a Country, which works to challenge similar stereotypes of that region.

Visit the Online Resource Centre that accompanies this book for lots of interesting additional material: www.oxfordtextbooks.co.uk/orc/collins4e/

10

Human Security

Randolph B. Persaud

Chapter Contents

Reader's Guide

This chapter examines the concept of human security. It does so in descriptive, analytical, and empirical terms, drawing on both the scholarly and policy relevant literatures. The chapter describes the development of human security, with references to the academic literature where necessary. Accordingly, the emergence, contribution, and impact of the most important drivers of human security, especially in institutional terms, are examined. These include the 1994 UNDP *Human Development Report* (HDR), the Commission for Human Security, the International Commission on Intervention and State Sovereignty, the **Millennium Development Goals**, and the International Criminal Court. The chapter takes up a recurring question about the newness of human security by looking at its intellectual and institutional genealogy. The chapter provides a detailed overview of the most trenchant critiques of human security. These critiques are placed into the following categories—too broad to be useful; national interest and co-optation; reformist tool of global capitalism; and neo-colonialism.

Introduction

Since its first systematic articulation in the United Nations 1994 *Human Development Report* (HDR), the idea of human security has gained considerable ascendency in academe, among policy makers, INGOs, NGOs, and activists. In that report, the UNDP suggested that the dominant notion of security, that is national/international security, should be broadened and deepened (Tadjbakhsh and Chenoy 2009). This should happen because a restricted notion of security does not allow for analysis of, and action on, a whole host of threats to millions of individuals, and the communities and societies in which they live.

Consistent with a more inclusive approach to security, the UNDP suggested seven critical areas that warrant sustained attention. These areas are economic, health, food, environmental, community, personal, and political security. Human dignity was later added as a key value to be defended. The expansiveness of human security is neatly captured in the UNDP's definition of the concept which includes chronic physical and economic threats and also threats that are more sudden due to natural disasters or political crisis.

Proponents of the human security approach argue that there is a plethora of destructive effects that are *already* ravaging individuals and communities throughout the world (Sommaruga 2004; Soeya 2005). The basic argument is that if security threats ultimately result in instability, destruction, and even death, as the national security problematic is concerned with, then these consequences are already widespread in the world. The only difference from mainstream security is that the death, destruction, and instability are not *directly* caused by interstate war or the war on terror. It is, as Bellamy and McDonald (2002) call it, death by economics rather than by politics. Millions die, for instance, from preventable or treatable diseases such as **HIV/AIDS**, malaria, diarrhoea, and measles. In 2014, thousands died, and tens of thousands were infected from an Ebola outbreak in West Africa, especially concentrated in Liberia, Guinea, and Sierra Leone (for more on this, see Chapter 25). Approximately 18,000 children die from poverty-related causes every day. Entire regions and even nation states are regularly subjected to the ravages of hurricanes, earthquakes, floods, tsunamis, epidemics, and other natural disasters (Owen 2004). These events often drive thousands or even hundreds of thousands from their homes and villages, causing large-scale displacements accompanied by widespread suffering. Environmental destruction, as detailed in Chapter 16, exerts both demand and supply pressures on resources and results in a range of deleterious consequences including destruction of cropland, food scarcity, and insecure livelihoods. In many parts of the world identity-based conflicts, and especially politically motivated ethnic confrontations, have led to brutal violence. The genocides in Rwanda, Srebrenica, and Darfur are only the most notable instances of such macabre violence. In other places, such as the DRC and Sudan, ethnic violence is tearing apart entire societies with the effects of destabilizing whole regions. The deadly conflict in Syria that came late in what has been called the Arab Spring has already resulted in over 200,000 deaths, and four million refugees. The enormous casualties from non-state causes are easily seen in Table 10.1.

There can, therefore, be little doubt that there is massive insecurity and equally massive death and destruction outside of those caused by inter-state violence. The proponents of human security acknowledge that it is precisely because of these pervasive assaults on human welfare, physical security, and human dignity, that the concept of security must be broadened.

As is the case with most concepts in international relations, however, human security has become highly contested (Oberleitner 2005). While the specific critiques cover a range of theoretical, methodological, and substantive matters, it is important to note that most of these critiques of human security are about its analytical capacity or usefulness. Put differently, most scholars and policy makers accept the developmental and human rights aspects of the new theorization. What they do not accept, however, is the insertion of these issues into the core of traditional security analysis.

The main objections come from scholars who insist that too much broadening and deepening of the concept of security would overstretch it so much that it would no longer be of any analytical use (Liotta 2002; Ewan 2007). Neorealist scholars, for instance, argue that states are still the most important actors, and that issues such as human rights and economic problems are in part the results of the general structure of global power as expressed in the inter-state system where survival through self-help is the basic value. It is well to remember that realist and neorealists are either apprehensive or openly hostile to international institutions and practices that are not calculated on the basis of national interest. Keep in mind that unlike classical liberals, neoliberal institutionalists also privilege the state, which they see as a rational actor bent on maximizing power.

Human security has unquestionably generated passionate and productive debates that span academic,

Table 10.1 Recent casualties from disasters

Year	Location	Event	Killed/missing/injured	Displaced or affected
2014, May	Bosnia	Flooding	45	1 million
2013, November	Philippines	Typhoon	6,300	1,473 families; 9 million individuals
2013	Niger	Weather-related food shortage	10,000 (min.)	1,000,000
2011	Somalia	Famine	260,000	10 million
2011, March	Japan	Tsunami	18,000; 15,000	Millions due to nuclear meltdown
2010, January	Haiti	Earthquake	230,000; NA; 300,000	Millions
2008, May	Yangon, Myanmar	Cyclone Nargis	133,000 (ASEAN)	2.4 million
2005, August	Louisiana/Mississippi United States	Hurricane Katrina	1,833	250,000 displaced (New Orleans alone)
2005, October	Kashmir Pakistan/India border area	Earthquake	87,350	3 million homeless
2004, December	South East Asia 14 countries	Tsunami	230,000–250,000	Millions

policy-making, and activist communities, and in that sense, it has now become an integral dimension of international relations scholarship and practice.

Arguments for human security

The 1994 *Human Development Report* (HDR) was, and remains, the clearest statement and most comprehensive conceptualization of human security. Three quotations from the report (see Key Quotes 10.1) clearly illustrate its intent, scope, and purpose. A number of key ideas in the reports have since become mainstreamed in the human security literature. First is the idea that security is a contestable concept, rather than a practice or condition that is self-evident or natural. Second, the focus only on violent conflicts among states is too restrictive both in terms of theory and policy. Third, security as territorial protection through force of arms is an unnecessarily limited understanding of both sovereignty and protection. Instead of the narrowly conceived security as state security, the 1994 HDR called for socio-economic variables to be brought into the picture, without abandoning the usual demands consistent with national security.

KEY QUOTES 10.1 Quotes from the 1994 *Human Development Report*

'For too long, the concept of security has been shaped by the potential for conflict between states. For too long, security has been equated with threats to a country's borders. For too long, nations have sought *arms to protect* their security.' (p. 3).

'The battle of peace has to be fought on two fronts. The first is the security where victory spells freedom from fear. The second is the economic and social front where victory means freedom from want. Only victory on both fronts can assure the world of an enduring peace.... No provisions that can be written into the Charter will enable the Security Council to make the world secure from war if men and women have no security in their homes and their jobs.' (p. 3).

'A new development *paradigm* is needed that puts people at the centre of development, regards economic growth as a means and not an end, protects the life opportunities of future generations as well as the present generations and respects the natural systems on which all life depends. Such a paradigm of development enables all individuals to enlarge their human capabilities to the full and to put those capabilities to their best use in all fields economic, social, cultural and political.' (p. 4).

The 1994 HDR is a clear statement that security is human-centred, meaning that it is inextricably linked to human development and, further, that there are major limitations with the prevailing development approaches needed to address the freedom from want. Thus the HDR formulation goes beyond *want*, and speaks about human capabilities.

Four main features of human security were detailed in the 1994 HDR. First, human security is universal, meaning that it is based on principles that have trans-cultural, and trans-systemic value, and global applicability. Second, the different aspects or components of human security are *interdependent*, a point that is consistent with the maximalist or holistic approaches to human security (Stoett 1999). Third, the focus should be on *prevention* in all areas of freedom from fear and freedom from want. One specific implication of the focus on prevention is the need to have more productive than destructive resources. It is important to keep in mind that the HDR arguments for a re-direction of resources were made in the context of the end of the Cold War and the expected benefits of a peace dividend. Prevention must also be multi-level, participatory, and reproducible. Fourth, human security must be *people-centred*, that is to say human beings must become the referent objective of security. Individuals, however, do not live solipsistic lives. Rather they live in communities, including national communities. Table 10.2 shows the sharp differences between the national and human security approaches.

Commission on Human Security

In 2001, the Commission on Human Security (CHS) was launched to undertake a broad study of conditions of insecurity and actionable recommendations to enhance human security. The CHS received broad support from *inter alia*, the governments of Japan and Sweden, the Rockefeller Foundation, the World Bank, the Greentree Foundation, UNDP, and the Kennedy School of Government at Harvard University. The objectives of the CHS were stated as follows:

- to promote public understanding, engagement, and support of human security and its underlying imperatives;
- to develop the concept of human security as an operational tool for policy formulation and implementation; and
- to propose a concrete programme of action to address critical and pervasive threats to human security.

Importantly, the CHS basically reinforced the key ideas of the 1994 HDR. The most important of these were the stress on the people-centredness of security and the interdependent nature of security provision. The report was important because between the HDR of 1994 and early 2001 when CHS began its work, human security, although of great interest to academics, state leaders,

Table 10.2 National versus human security

Type	National security	Human security
Threat location	External/international system	Internal; international; global
Source of threat	Other states; terrorists	Own state; climate change; hate groups; corporations, traffickers; failed state; terrorists; foreign intervention
What is to be protected	National sovereignty; state institutions; state territory; core economic, political, and cultural values	Human life; individuals; communities; vulnerable groups; minorities; refugees; democratic institutions
Forms of security provision	Defensive or offensive war; counterterrorism, counter-insurgency, intelligence, sanctions	Humanitarian intervention; climate change measures; some economic redistribution; corporate reform; reduction of poverty and inequality; gender equality; empowerment
Security actor	State; coalition of states; UN Security Council, state-sponsored private security firms	States; NGOs; INGOs; UN Security Council; civic groups
Philosophical roots	Realism, neorealism, neoliberal institutionalism	Liberal multilateralism; international law; human rights scholarship; critical theory; critical feminism

NGOs, and activists, was severely criticized. The CHS report, therefore, played a key role in strengthening the intellectual and policy credentials of the concept and its associated policies. Of great interest was the explicit effort to link human security to state security as a sort of complementary plank rather than as a replacement. Accordingly, the report noted that in addition to focusing on individuals and communities, human security adds to state security because (a) it includes menaces to peoples' security not normally given consideration; (b) expands the range of actors; and (c) expands the empowerment of people as an important dimension of self-sustenance.

Two further points must be made about the CHS report. The first is that the Commission introduced what may be considered 'conservative' elements into the analysis. The concept of empowerment, for instance, is consistent with neoliberal ideas of personal responsibility in economic affairs and well-being. The effort to show ways in which human security complements state security may also be interpreted as an acknowledgement of the limits of security too broadly defined, or in other words, over-securitization (see Chapter 12). On the other hand, the CHS also strongly insisted on the connection among security, development, and human rights. It did so through a call for shared sovereignty and a critique of unilateralism. The dust had barely settled on the work of the CHS when another major effort of human security began in earnest through the International Commission on Intervention and Sate Sovereignty.

International Commission on Intervention and State Sovereignty (ICISS) and the Responsibility to Protect

While the work of the CHS contributed to a consolidation of the broadening of security, the ICISS did exactly the opposite by focusing on intervention in crisis situations where mass atrocity crimes such as genocide, crimes against humanity, war crimes, and ethnic cleansing is happening or likely to happen. ICISS was sponsored by the Canadian government, in part due to the impact of the Rwandan genocide (1994) and mass killings in Srebrenica (1995), and also reflective of its narrower approach to human security (Acharya 2001). The commission submitted its report under the title *The Responsibility to Protect* on 30 September 2001 (see Chapter 22).

Few things in human security, human rights, and for that matter international security are more complex than the contradictory demands of protecting human life in the face of mass killings, and the imperative of preserving and respecting state sovereignty. Both of these values are of paramount importance, the first to human life itself, the second to the central ordering principle of the Westphalian state system and world order more generally. Mass atrocities immediately after the end of the Cold War in Somalia, Bosnia, Kosovo, and Rwanda saw the rise of a new form of international relations that came to be known as humanitarian intervention (see Chapter 22). While on the surface foreign intervention, and especially those with the approval of United Nations Security Council, would appear to be beyond reproach, there are multiple factors that have given cause for suspicion, mistrust, and at times downright denunciation. It was these contradictions that led UN Secretary-General Kofi Annan in 2000 to pose the question that ultimately led to the formation of the ICISS. In his Millennium Report to the General Assembly, Anan asked:

> if humanitarian intervention is, indeed, an acceptable assault on sovereignty, how should we respond to a Rwanda, to a Srebrenica—to gross and systematic violations of human rights that offend every precept of our humanity?
>
> ICISS (2001: 2)

The ICISS took note of several contentious issues in carrying out its undertaking. These included but are not restricted to considerations of national interest, issues of legitimacy, (in)consistency in intervention, new security threats, rising civilian deaths in the post-Cold War period, the strict construction of national sovereignty versus 'sovereignty as a responsibility', root causes of conflicts, limited resources in mounting an adequate response, proportional force, 'right intention', command and control matters in terms of operational actions, threshold criteria, and linkages with the new and evolving concept of people-centred human security. Perhaps the most important recommendations in the ICISS report revolve around the conditions of intervention referred to as the 'just case threshold'. The threshold is met if and when there is actual or imminent harm to human beings as a result of state action or neglect. The threshold is certainly met in cases where there is a failed state, and/or in instances of forced expulsion, ethnic cleansing, genocide, terror, or rape (R2P, XII).

The threshold specifications themselves are underpinned by three core 'elements', namely, the responsibility to prevent, the responsibility to react, and the responsibility to rebuild. Notably, the ICISS left intact the UN Security Council as the authoritative source of military intervention, a position that left it open to charges of preserving the status quo albeit in the form of the international community which critics find too ambiguous and thus prone to exploitation for the purposes of national interest.

Millennium Development Goals (MDGs)

On 18 September 2000 the General Assembly of the United Nations adopted Resolution 55/2, in effect the United Nations Millennium Declaration (UNMD). The declaration reaffirmed the necessity of establishing a lasting peace through continued support for the principles of the UN Charter, which the resolution called 'timeless and universal'. At the same time, the resolution also inserted a set of principles entirely consistent with the concept of human security. The UNMD insisted that a shared responsibility is required to deal with the externalities of globalization. Freedom, equality, solidarity, tolerance, and respect for nature, were advanced as the core principles of shared responsibility.

The UNMD set eight goals (hence MDGs), these being to eradicate poverty and hunger, achieve universal primary education, promote gender equality and empower women, reduce child mortality, improve maternal health, combat HIV/AIDS, **malaria**, and other diseases, ensure environmental sustainability, and develop a global partnership for development. It is evident that these goals are entirely consistent, if not a replication of the long-term objectives of human security stated in the 1994 HDR. Those objectives include providing universal primary education for boys and girls, primary health care with a stress on the immunization of children, cutting by half adult illiteracy rates and achieving parity between men and women in literacy, eliminating severe malnutrition and halving moderate malnutrition rates. Universal safe drinking water and sanitation and greater distribution of credit were also targeted (UNDP 1994: 7). See Table 10.3.

Table 10.3 Selected results in Millennium Development Goals

MDG Goals	Result (July 2014)	Challenge
(MDG 1) Cut extreme poverty rate by half (from 1990)	Met 5 years before 2015 deadline (173 million less)	1.2 billion still live in extreme poverty
(MDG 2) Achieve universal primary education	90 per cent met	58 million still out of school
(MDG 3) Promote gender equality and empower women	Equality between boys and girls in primary education met	Women still face discrimination in many countries in education, work, and decision making
(MDG 4) Reduce child mortality	17,000 less die per day compared to 1990	6 million die before fifth birthday
(MDG 5) Improve maternal health	45 per cent decline in MMR from 1990	Only half of women in G-South get recommended health care
(MDG 6) Combat HIV/AIDS, malaria, other diseases	9.7 million receiving medicines for HIV in 2012; 173 million less malaria infection; 3.3 million malaria deaths prevented in little over a decade	Every hour, 50 young women infected with HIV; 627,000 killed by malaria in 2012; rise of new challenges such as Ebola
(MDG 7) Ensure environmental sustainability	2.3 billion people gained access to clean drinking water since 1990	2.5 billion lack basic sanitation—toilets or latrines
(MDG 8) Establish global partnership for development	Record high aid money in 2013—$134.8 billion; notable decline in debt service	Aid shifted away from poorest countries

Source: http://www.endpoverty2015.org/en/2014/07/07/the-millennium-development-goals-report-2014/.

The International Criminal Court

The **International Criminal Court** (ICC), which came into effect on 1 July 2002, is a major component of human security, however defined. The ICC is an independent international organization that is governed by the Rome Statute, which was adopted on 17 July 1998. It is a permanent court, and its principal function is to hold accountable and bring to justice those that are known to have committed, or are accused of committing, genocide, crimes against humanity, and war crimes. The ICC follows in the tradition of the Nuremberg and Tokyo trials which prosecuted war criminals immediately after the Second World War, and the International Criminal Tribunal for the former Yugoslavia and Rwanda. Although the Rome Statute was adopted before the ICISS, there is clear correspondence between the two in several areas, including their core principles built around universal concepts and practices of justice. The ICC works with the guidance that the court is a last resort and that the court will only take up a case if there are good reasons to believe that an investigation at a state level is compromised. Investigations of crimes can originate from any State Party (countries that have signed and ratified the Rome Statute), or from the UN Security Council. The Office of the Prosecutor can also initiate an investigation through *proprio motu* authority (meaning prosecutorial discretion usually in extraordinary or exceptional situations). To date, twenty-one cases and nine situations have been before the court.

Laudable though the ICC is for many, it has its critics. While the criticisms range from hostile to reformist, perhaps the most telling one is to be found in the record of the court itself. Specifically, to date, all cases brought before the ICC have been from Africa. Not much has actually changed over the past twelve years, as the current dossier remains the same. Currently there are nine 'Situations' before the Court, all of them from Africa, and eight 'preliminary examinations' for Afghanistan, Colombia, Nigeria, Georgia, Guinea, Honduras, Iraq, and Ukraine.

BACKGROUND 10.1 Key developments in the emergence of human security

- 1994—UNDP Human Development Report. Credited with introducing the concept in a systematic way and linking it to human rights, human development, and personal security, and protection of the environment.
- 1995—UN Commission on Global Governance
- July 1998—120 states adopted the Rome Statute which formed the legal basis for the International Criminal Court (ICC).
- March 1999—United Nations Trust Fund for Human Security launched by Government of Japan and UN Secretariat.
- September 2000—UN Millennium Declaration launched (MDGs).
- 30 September 2001—Commission on Human Security.
- December 2001—ICISS Report—The Responsibility to Protect.
- 10 July 2002—Sixty states ratified the Statute of Rome thereby entering it into force in the institutional form of the ICC.

KEY POINTS

- The concept of national security is too narrow and too static to be useful in analysing the broad threats that currently exists. Conceptual change is thus warranted.
- Most of the cases of large-scale instability, destruction, and deaths do not result from state to state conflicts but from intra-state causes and 'natural' disasters.
- Human dignity and human rights are core values of any secure society.
- For the national security approach, real threats are to states, by other states, and military in form. For human security, threats are to human beings and their communities, emanating from multiple sources, and can take various forms.

The genealogy of human security: what's new?

The genealogy of human security

Although the 1994 HDR is widely and deservedly credited with introducing the concept of human security, a number of writers trace its origins to earlier developments in the literature and practices of human rights, international law, and various forms of institutionalized cooperation (MacFarlane and Khong 2006). Sadako Ogata and Johan Cels, for instance, note that the notion of vital freedoms contained in the definition of human security by The Commission on Human Security already existed in the various international declarations and certainly in the Universal Declaration of Human Rights (Ogata and Cels 2003: 74). The connection here is so strong that it is often argued that human security is actually a subset of human rights, the latter having a history that goes back to the nineteenth century, and certainly back to the Geneva Convention (Oberleitner 2005). See Background 10.1 for key moments in the historical evolution of human security.

Three commissioned reports also contributed to the emergence of a broader understanding of security. In 1977, the president of the World Bank, Robert McNamara, commissioned a study of North–South economic relations with a view to addressing questions of global poverty. The commission was led by Willy Brandt, former Chancellor of West Germany, and it authored *North–South: A Program For Survival* (1980). Much like the 1994 HDR 1994, *A Program for Survival* drew attention to the great disparities in the quality of life between the North and the South and offered a perspective consistent with subsequent multilateral efforts at reducing the amalgam of measurable material deprivations evident in the global South.

The Palme Commission also questioned the narrowly constructed national security framework, even if only in the context of European security in the Cold War. The Commission advanced the notion of *common security* outlined in its report, *Common Security: A Blueprint for Survival* (1982). While *A Blueprint for Survival* stayed within the ambit of physical/military security, it did move away from a tight understanding of national security. For instance, it insisted that security is a *right* rather than only a product of strength. More pointedly, the concept of common security questioned the purely military basis of achieving security.

The World Commission on Environment and Development (chaired by Gro Brundtland), which produced its report *Our Common Future* in 1987, specifically made a connection between environmental degradation, economic underdevelopment and violent conflict (see Key Quotes 10.2). The report specifically took the position that national security, narrowly constructed, is inadequate to the task of mapping out the full spectrum of threats to peoples, nations, and the planet as a whole. It went beyond establishing the links among the seemingly disparate threats or issuing warnings and called for a reprioritization of resources, away from spending and towards environmental protection and human welfare. This was a reiteration of a call made by the Brandt Report, and later by HDR of 1994. The Brundtland report insisted that there are no military solutions to environmental insecurity.

> **KEY QUOTES 10.2 Human security**
>
> The deepening and widening environmental crisis presents a threat to national security—and even survival—that may be greater than well-armed, ill-disposed neighbours and unfriendly alliances. Already in parts of Latin America, Asia, the Middle East, and Africa, environmental decline is becoming a source of political unrest and international tension. The recent destruction of much of Africa's dryland agricultural production was more severe than if an invading army had pursued a scorched-earth policy. Yet most of the affected governments still spend far more to protect their people from invading armies than from the invading desert.
>
> *World Commission on Environment and Development (1987)*

It is also well to remember that apart from these rather specific instances of security broadening prior to the 'official inauguration' of human security in 1994, there had been a consistent effort by countries of the global South, both individually and through collective efforts, to address the sources of insecurity now attached to the 'freedom from want' and 'freedom from fear' dimensions of the current discourses of security. Evidence of this can be found, for instance, in the Final Communiqué of the Asian-African Conference of Bandung (1955) which addressed problems of physical, political, and economic security framed in terms of a global duty to all humanity. Analogous to today's language of human security, the Communiqué underlined the interdependent relationship between freedom and peace. Similar calls for economic justice, political security, and freedom from subversion of various sorts were consistently demanded by the Group of 77 as evident in the call for a New International Economic Order.

Human security also has a scholarly genealogy grounded in various schools of thought. Some scholars hold the view that the English School and the Copenhagen School have been so associated (Makinda 2005). In a reply to the work of Alex J. Bellamy and Matt McDonald (two noted contributors to the human security literature) Makinda argues that these authors incorrectly attribute the concept of human security to the 1994 HDR. He claims that many of the critical strands of the broadening of security contained in that report had been around for much longer, albeit without that *label*. What is a little baffling is that while he rejects the label human security, he at the same time notes that the latter is a 'manifestation' of the English School.

If the connection between human security and the English School is one of 'manifestation', then the connection between Human Security and the Copenhagen School is rather more decisive. This argument has been most systematically made by Šárka Waisová, who observes that the focus on the individual significantly predates the 1990s focus on human security (Waisová 2003: 58). In the 1980s, the Copenhagen Peace Research Institute, (hence the **Copenhagen School**) critiqued the limitation of the traditional security approach and called for new issues to be given consideration. This new, broader approach, offered five categories of security based on the sources of threat. These were military, political, economic, environmental, and societal. It is important to note, however, that in *Security: A New Framework for Analysis* Barry Buzan, Ole Wæver, and Jaap de Wilde, three major Copenhagen School scholars, insist that the sectors are not exclusive of each other, but more importantly, that the division is mostly for analytical purposes (Buzan et al. 1998: 168). For Waisová, the move away from the 'national security paradigm' began in the 1970s, perhaps best exemplified by the work of Robert Keohane and Joseph Nye, who wrote about the decline of military power which had been at the apex of the international agenda. Their work on interdependence, and especially on denser global economic relationships, was a shot fired against the 'hegemony' of security narrowly constructed around military power.

Another tradition leading up to the unfolding of human security in its full-fledged form, comes from non-Western sources through a combination of security theorization, general international theory, and especially via critical political economy, development studies, and also through government policies. Third-World scholars have, for a long time, been engaged in what for all practical purposes are some of the central concerns, claims, and propositions of human security both at the theoretical and practical/policy levels.

Mohammed Ayoob is perhaps the most well known for providing a perspective on security that is uniquely aimed at the Third World. Ayoob paid attention to the dynamic of colonization and decolonization with added emphasis on the institutional structures, the internal geopolitics of ethno-nationalist irredentism, and the consequences of economic path dependency. In his 1995 book, *The Third World Security Predicament: State Making, Regional Conflict, and the International System*, he specifically identified '. . . national liberation from colonial rule, state creation, and regime legitimacy' as major sources of conflict and violence in the Third World (Ayoob 1995: 49). The relevance to human security is most clearly associated with Ayoob's determination that the core security problem of the Third World hinges on what he astutely called *adequate stateness*. Drawing heavily on Charles Tilly's work on state formation in Europe, Ayoob theorized that the quintessential security dynamic of the Third World is the process of state formation, much of it still in the making even in the twenty-first century. It should be clear that in contradistinction to the national security problematic which takes the state as an *already made* unit/actor and referent object, this Third-World perspective focuses on the historicity of these processes.

Many scholars from the Third World, or writing about the Third World from a critical political economy position, had for decades preceding the 1990s addressed issues of poverty, global inequality, malnutrition, clean water, maternal and infant mortality rates, famine, refugees and other forms of displacement, poor housing, and an amalgam of deprivations linked to practices of race, ethnicity, gender, class, and environmental degradation (George 1976; Wilber 1979). Notions of sustainable development, sustainable livelihoods, basic needs, and other frameworks of economic and social reform aimed at bettering the lives of the millions of the insecure were standard fare. Books such as *How the Other Half Dies* by Susan George were widely read. *The Political Economy of Development and Underdevelopment* edited by Charles K. Wilber which came out in several editions, carried more than a dozen essays dealing with what is now known as the freedom-from-want aspects of human security. In fact, in the 1979 edition of that volume, Mahbub ul Haq, who is widely credited with authoring the concept of human security in the HDR, wrote a powerful essay in which he addressed the international dimensions of what in 1994 he would call human security. Most importantly, ul Haq also insisted that the problems now labelled human security have strong internal dimensions. Interestingly, in addition to ul Haq, two other scholars with articles in the Wilber edited volume, Keith Griffin and Paul Streeten, also contributed to the 1994 HDR.

Mahbub ul Haq himself called for the systematic study of global inequality and practically chastized the West for essentially explaining away global poverty and inequality with default references to the Cold War. Radical scholars (from the left) had also done detailed historical studies and theoretical critiques of a slew of socio-economic maladies. In 1981, L. S. Stavrianos made what has turned out to be an almost miraculous prediction when he noted that even if the Soviet Union were to disappear global instability would continue unabated due to the inequalities that exist (Stavrianos 1981: 796). He also linked poverty-driven instability to challenges of hegemonic maintenance of order.

Finally, we should take cognizance of the ways in which state policies have contributed to the rise of human security. The most notable case here is Japan which had, since the 1970s, effectively extended the definition of security beyond national security narrowly defined. Thus, the Japanese idea of *comprehensive security* had broadened the definition of security to include the attainment of energy and food security, and also of catastrophic natural events such as earthquakes and tsunamis. The Japanese broadening, however, is actually controversial and perhaps it is better to talk about comprehensive *national* security (Acharya 2001; Evans 2004).

KEY POINTS

- Human security is intimately related to human rights and human development.
- While HDR 1994 is acknowledged as the original articulation of human security, many of the key ideas in it have a longer history.
- The following were major precursors leading up to the concept of human security: Universal Declaration of Human Rights (1948); Final Communiqué of the Asian-African Conference of Bandung (1955); *North–South: A Program For Survival* (1980); *Common Security: A Blueprint for Survival* (1982); *Our Common Future* (1987). They contributed to a more global understanding as well as the institutionalization of human rights, economic and social justice, environmental awareness, and improved North–South relations.

Critiques of human security

Too broad to be useful

Human security, both as a concept and as practice/policy has been widely criticized. The most notable concern expressed is that the concept is too broad to be analytically useful. Scholars complain about its conceptual boundaries especially with regards to threats, actors, issue areas; vagueness as to priorities; and even the definition of the key referent object: the individual (Thomas and Tow 2002). Roland Paris's famously sardonic construction of human security in its then extant form as 'hot air' was so resonant that it is one of the most cited articles on the subject (Paris 2001). Others think that the label human security is actually a step backwards or that it is too taxing of resources, thus causing donor fatigue. Still others express concern with weaknesses in measuring both threats and outcomes (King and Murray 2001–02). Still at the conceptual level, there are claims that human security is not really critical, or not critical enough, not least because in the drive to be policy relevant it is trapped in the dominant, non-transformative epistemology and ontology of liberal international relations (Newman 2010). Finally, it goes without saying that realist and neorealist theories have had no room for human security. John Mearsheimer's 1994 dismissal of international institutions and multilateralism is still symbolic of the inflexibility of traditional security.

National interest and co-optation

Critics of human security argue that foreign policies based on human security, or within the ambit of human security, are actually driven by narrower considerations of national interest, rather than global altruism (Soeya 2005). In fact, even Japan's comprehensive security policies have been explained in terms of self-interest. Some scholars have convincingly shown that there were specific Japanese national interest considerations that led to the emergence of comprehensive *national* security, rather than the supposedly more enlightened comprehensive form (Akaha 1991; Sakai 2003). Although Canada and Norway have played major roles in the emergence of human security theory and practice, their foreign policies linked to the enlightened approach are said to have been an equal reflection of their middle power status. Astri Suhrke, for instance, argues that Canada used its position on the United Nations Security Council to advance human security and to enhance its middle power status. In an even broader critique, Suhrke argues that there was an Oslo–Ottawa axis intended to promote a progressive global agenda in which the two countries saw themselves as representatives of the Third World (Suhrke 1999: 266).

The word co-optation has also been inserted into the national interest-inspired critique, and there are some basic grounds for this claim as the following case highlights. In April 2014 the US Navy's Annual Naval Academy Foreign Affairs Conference was built around the theme of *Human Security in the Information Age*. The conference specifically called for thinking beyond traditional security by focusing on the individual. It also made reference to human security as a paradigm shift. The use of human security as the conference theme was, therefore, not a residual consideration. Rather, it was given paradigmatic status, language consistent with a real acknowledgement of the importance of human security. As expected, most of the participants were from the military, with others from the diplomatic community, business, and a sprinkling from philanthropy. The main speaker was Bill Clinton, former president of the United States. A review of the issues addressed at the round tables, however, reveals a clear focus on a national security approach. The following topics were included: the role of intelligence agencies; military reconnaissance; corporate surveillance; media; Bitcoin and other crypto-currencies; the relationship among cyber-space and authoritarian and totalitarian states; People's Republic of China; pro-government Syria hackers; cyber criminals; terrorist financing; the role of **non-state actors** in cyber warfare; rogue citizens; psychological warfare; artificial intelligence and the dynamic of war; and so on. While there were topics such as humanitarian intervention, human trafficking, slavery, and even a panel on Africa, the conference was basically built on the ways in which information technology might present threats to state security, or be used as a resource to combat those same threats. See Think Point 10.1 and also Case Study 10.1 which provide the basis for a discussion on co-optation.

CASE STUDY 10.1 Can the ICC be co-opted to serve 'national interest'?

On 1 January 2015, Palestine applied to join the ICC under article 12(3). The previous day, the United Nations Security Council had voted down an effort by Palestine to compel Israel to withdraw from occupied Palestinian lands by 2017. One of the publicly disclosed intents of the Palestinian acceptance of the ICC jurisdiction is that it would be able to bring cases against Israel (no individuals named). Israel and the United States immediately threatened to punish Palestine for accepting the ICC jurisdiction. The US State Department issued a statement saying that it is deeply troubled by the Palestinian Authority's ICC gambit, and that the effort was an 'escalation' of the situation.

(www.politico.com/story/2014/12/palestinian-authority-international-criminal-court-state-department-113909.html).

US Ambassador to the United Nations Samantha Power not only criticized the Palestinian Authority but also the ICC. She stated that the ICC is actually a threat to Israel. It took only three days (3 January 2015) for Israel to announce that it would cut tax revenue ($125 million per month) and will, itself, seek to bring war crimes prosecution against Palestinian leaders.

(www.america.aljezeera.com/articles/2015/1/3/Israel-palestineicc.html).

THINK POINT 10.1 Precision wars and human security

The ways to fight a war have gone through major changes over the past two decades. One of the most important developments has been the emergence of precision wars due to step-level advances in military technology, especially in the form of Precision Guided Munitions (PGMs). These new capabilities have led to what some specialists claim to be a new way of fighting wars, including terrorism. It is built on a Revolution in Military Affairs (RMA). This new way of war, as it has been called, is underpinned by reliance on air power. Proponents claim that the key advantage of the new American way of war is a drastic reduction in American casualties, as well as of the enemy civilian population. Based on these technological developments, there has been a call for war transformation, meaning wars that are more information and technology based, including the use of drones.

In May 2003 Chairman of the Joints Chiefs of Staff (United States), Richard B. Meyers delivered an address to the US Air Force Academy in which he essentially made the case for the new American way of war. The crux of the General Meyers text is that wars of annihilation or attrition are no longer needed because the new strategy can strike at the pillars of the enemy, with precision. Wars could be won though a preponderance of air power and because of that there is a gradual obsolescence of ground wars. Critics of these types of war argue that the results of smart wars have been exaggerated and that the human cost has been demonstrably high, especially with the use of drones in the prosecution of the war on terror (Ahmed 2013). The question is—are smart wars consistent with human security based on the claims of quick intervention and fewer civilian casualties?

Liberal reformist tool of global capitalism

Some of the most systematic critiques of human security concern economic questions, or more broadly, the matters that pertain to the freedom from want. This is partly true, and ironically so, because it is exactly here that there is the most consensus about the *obligation to intervene*, if we may coin yet another expression. There are, however, diverging perspectives on what are the main causes for the conditions of poverty that afflict millions in the Third World, and also what needs to be done, and by whom, or through what mechanism. These were the precise ambiguities that led Alex J. Bellamy and Matt McDonald to famously pose the questions—'Which humans? What security?' (Bellamy and McDonald 2002).

Another popular strand of objections comes from supporters of human security, but supporters who are concerned about '. . . the growth of a global market and the dominance of a fundamentalist belief in deregulation and privatization' (Kaldor 2011: 444). Concomitantly, many scholars see the language and accompanying economic policies aimed at alleviating economic and social vulnerabilities as a Trojan Horse for neoliberal reform, if not liberal imperialism (Luckham and Kirk 2013). Evidence for this charge may be found in the Millennium Challenge Corporation information, much of it stressing private business. Threshold Programs have stated goals such as reducing the cost and time of a business. Others object to the security development complex and prefer to delink the two (Wilkin 2002). That said, many of these critics of neoliberal capitalism and associated forms of governance are ambivalent about specific policies to address the problems related to human insecurity (Thomas 2000; Wilkin 2002).

Neo-colonial

Many critics argue that human security is a form of neo-colonial domination or at least a set of practices that legitimize the violation of sovereignty of Third-World countries (Bain 2001; Owens 2012). Writers such as Ikechi Mgbeoji, in fact, hold the view that the structures of violence, economic exploitation, and cultural domination during colonialism are still in place, and that no progress in human security can be made until these are torn down. Moreover, the historical relationships that played major roles in the production of human insecurity in the Third World *and* prosperity elsewhere tend to be played down, resulting in massive de-historicization (Mittelman 2010). When this happens, the explanation for violence and economic deprivation are laid at the doorstep of the sufferers. Instead, more effort should be placed on understanding the historical roots of insecurity (Mgbeoji 2006: 864).

A more specific criticism concerns the problem of humanitarian intervention. The first major issue here, as Mohammed Ayoob has argued, concerns who decides when rights have been violated. The concern about human rights violation has tremendous elasticity. Sometimes it is stretched to absolve friends and allies; at other times it is expanded to incriminate political or strategic enemies. On still other occasions there is simply abandonment, such as happened in Rwanda, Darfur, and now Syria. Ayoob argues that since the early 1990s humanitarian intervention has been a new form of interventionism, undertaken for strategic or political purposes and legitimized by framing the action on behalf of the international community (Ayoob 2002: 83).

The charge of neo-coloniality also has economic dimensions, mostly based on new forms of exploitation in the age of globalization. An example of this can be found in the terms and conditions of a compact signed between the US government through The Millennium Challenge Corporation (MCC) and Tanzania. The agreement (in the amount of 698 million dollars) prohibits Tanzania from pursuing policies that would result in job losses and other problems in the United States. A further condition is that none of that disbursement can be used, either directly or indirectly, for the performance of abortions or family planning programmes that might lead to an abortion. Those with a flair for semiotics would no doubt notice that the MCC uses the peculiar language of a student–teacher relationship, referring as it does to states that *graduate* from one level of development to another. A radical, postcolonial interpretation of this construction might very well view graduation as infantalization, backed up by hegemonic resources.

KEY POINTS

- The concept of human security is criticized for being too broad, too imprecise, and too elastic, and thus not analytically useful.
- Most of the issues dealt with in human security, such as human rights, environmental degradation, economic development, and poverty—are already receiving substantial attention in other sub-fields. Critics argue that there is no need to *securitize* them.
- It is interest-based, and should be. While the issues of human security are real they do not, cannot, or should not displace the centrality of the state as the main actor, or the states' system as one that is driven by the logic of survival.
- Critics argue that human security is too reformist, not critical enough, and also promotes global capitalism.
- Human security is also critiqued as neo-colonial, in that it is compromises sovereignty and is biased.

Conclusion

Few recent topics in international relations have received as much attention as human security. There are several reasons for this and they need some elaboration. First, there was great enthusiasm at the end of the Cold War about a peace dividend, and more broadly, about a more democratic and prosperous world. For many, the deepening of globalization meant the possibility of greater economic prosperity due to freer movement of goods, services, and capital. Developments in communication technologies and especially increasing access to the Internet led to feelings of a world more in touch. People travelled more internationally, and talked more much on the phone due to significant reductions in costs. Sovereignty it seemed, although intact in the old territorial sense, was seen more as a resource, rather than a Maginot Line against the outside world where threats traditionally come from.

Second, on the security front, one of the greatest confrontations of all time came to an end, a fact all the more scintillating because of the dramatic tensions that existed right up to the collapse of the Berlin Wall. This double movement of history, that is, simultaneous progress in global economics and security led to the language of a New World Order.

Third, the demise of the bipolar period of world security and political order also opened up room for contesting the theories that were most attached to the power politics of the Cold War. Realism and neorealism in particular began to be seen as inadequate. There was a gradual shift from the hegemony of strategic studies to more open ended and interdisciplinary security studies. Barry Buzan's (1983) *People, States & Fear: An Agenda For International Security Studies in the Post-Cold War Era* was at once a careful but dramatic rupture with the old ways of thinking about security. The **state-centricity** and military orientation of realism and neorealism were under constant attack from a range of perspectives, including but not limited to, constructivism, gender studies, and forms of liberalism such as the democratic peace. On the economic side, neo-Gramscian political economy made a huge impact, and so did a more progressive kind of market liberalism in the form of cosmopolitan multilateralism advocated by writers such as David Held.

Fourth, events on the ground, many of them bloody and chaotic, pushed not only scholars and international organizations but also politicians to look for alternative ways of coming to grips with these challenges. Multiple atrocities in the Balkans, genocide in Rwanda and Darfur, state failure in Somalia, combined with increasing criticism of the relationship between globalization and inequality (prosperity for whom?) gave succour to the ideas that were articulated in the 1994 HDR and the subsequent campaign for a more nuanced and possibly transformative approach to security.

Context matters a great deal, and these were the circumstances that, in part, made human security come to fruition. There was, so to speak a perfect storm, that *enabled* the decidedly liberal character of human security to not only emerge, but to simultaneously command attention from governments, scholars (including graduate students), international organizations, NGOs, and activists. As noted above, there was already an intellectual tradition consistent with the broad aims and objectives of what came to be called human security, and what is now, unquestionably anything but hot air.

QUESTIONS

1. What is human security? How is it different from traditional forms of security analysis?
2. What are the main intellectual and institutional sources of human security?
3. What is the relationship among human security, human rights, and international law? Illustrate your answer with a case study.
4. Human security is now so entrenched in international institutions, the foreign policy of governments, in the work of NGOs, in academic scholarship, and among activists, that it can no longer be 'dismissed'. Discuss.
5. What are the human security grounds for and against humanitarian intervention? Write your answer with reference to two specific cases since the end of the Cold War.
6. How does critical theory help you understand the emergence of human security as an 'intellectual project'?
7. What, if any, are the limits to addressing the 'freedom-from-want' components of human security within the current structure of global capitalism?
8. Great power politics are the main impediment to meeting the demands associated with the freedom from fear and freedom from want. Discuss.

FURTHER READING

- MacFarlane, Neil S. and Khong, Yuen Foong (2006), *Human Security and the UN: A Critical History*, Bloomington: Indiana University Press. Students will find this book especially useful in trying to understand the role of the UN in the emergence and implementation of human security. The strength of this work is that it historicizes ideas about security by linking various analytical approaches to different world orders.
- Martin, Mary and Owen, Taylor (eds) (2013), *Routledge Handbook of Human Security*, New York: Routledge. This is an excellent reference book on human security with contributions from many of the most notable scholars on the subject. There are twenty-five chapters that deal with conceptual as well as policy issues. Both the narrow and broad views of security are represented and there is good geographical diversity.
- Peou, Sorpong (2014), *Human Security Studies: Theories, Methods and Themes*, London: World Scientific Publishing. This book is useful on many levels, one of them being that it is written with great clarity. It also does a fine job of describing human security from different theoretical perspectives, broadly situated into 'sceptical' and 'optimistic' sets. Key issue areas such as small arms and light weapons, sanctions, military intervention, and democracy are deftly engaged in their relationship to human security. There are many useful methodological reflections in the work.
- Rice, Susan E., Graff, C., and Pascual, C. (eds) (2010), *Confronting Poverty: Weak States and U.S. National Security*, Washington, DC: Brookings Institution Press. Although the book does not explicitly use the concept of human security per se, it systematically engages the relationship among poverty, weak states, and security threats linked to climate change, infectious diseases, and violent extremism. The book also provides a unique American perspective on human security and American foreign policy.
- Tadjbakhsh, Shahrbanou and Chenoy, Anuradha M. (2009), *Human Security: Concepts and Implications*, New York: Routledge. This is probably the best textbook on human security. Considerable attention is paid to the relationship between human security and human rights, human development, the domestic state, and the role of the international community. There is also a chapter on the relationship between *underdevelopment* and human security. Students will find many useful tables and diagrams throughout the book. The authors also make their own contributions to a broader view of human security.

IMPORTANT WEBSITES

- **http://www.hsrgroup.org/** This is the site for the Human Security Report Project at Simon Fraser University in Canada. It provides access to several official Human Security Reports which can be downloaded.
- **http://hdr.undp.org/en** UNDP Human Security Development Office Library has different country reports which can be accessed in multiple languages. It is very good for methodological considerations on data collection and analysis.
- **http://www.un.org/humansecurity/** This is the website for the United Nations Trust Fund for Human Security. It has a wealth of up-to-date information including human security events, conferences, as well as an interactive panel for discussions.
- **http://www.hpcrresearch.org/research/human-security-network** This website is associated with the Harvard University Humanitarian Initiative. It has a wealth of technical information, as well as a library of journal articles. It is very good for materials on the communication of human security issues.
- **http://www.twn.my/** The Third World Network site has voluminous materials on North–South economic relations, multilateral governance, and significant resources in issues areas such as food, biotechnology, global finance, and gender among others.

Visit the Online Resource Centre that accompanies this book for lots of interesting additional material: www.oxfordtextbooks.co.uk/orc/collins4e/

11

Gender and Security

Caroline Kennedy and Sophia Dingli

Chapter Contents

Reader's Guide

This chapter examines issues of gender and security. It begins with an explanation of what we mean by gender and explains why issues of gender are central to understanding security. International Relations specialists have over the last three decades explored and interpreted the ways in which men and women have responded to the national and international policies which have governed conflict, terrorism, and war. The chapter demonstrates that through understanding and placing notions of gender at the centre of any debate on security we can unleash a series of interlocking understandings of the way men and women relate to insecurity, violence, and war.

Introduction

Gender and **security** are both concepts that invite endless categorization and clarification. Security has been conceived in many different ways (Krause and Williams 1997b; Buzan et al. 1998). Much of this difference can be understood and illuminated in terms of gender. But gender too has multiple meanings and applications, as its different deployments within contemporary scholarship and politics indicate (Tickner 1992).

This chapter outlines the significance of considering gender and security together by examining two angles of vision. We distinguish between 'practical' and 'discursive' aspects of the relationship between gender and security. Practical aspects are exemplified by the concrete role of women in militaries, or as victims, bystanders, or helpers of military conflict or of militarization in general. Discursive aspects are exemplified by the traditional connections made between **militarism** and **masculinity** and between nurturing, peace, and **femininity**.

This distinction is wedded to two further developments that reinforce the central relationship between gender and security. The first involves the acceptance of a broader concept of security than was traditional. A number of terms have been used to describe this process, '**human security**' (see Chapter 10) or '**soft security**' being the most common. Up until the events of 9/11, this involved a relative downgrading of the traditional focus on military matters within security, with implications both from and for the practical and the representative aspects of the gender–security relationship. A second process was one that allegedly meant that from the 1990s, technological innovation allowed for a remote control of a 'virtual' war, such as in Kosovo, removing the need for 'men' (or rather, men drawn from Western states) in battle. Arguably war and battle had been rendered gender neutral. Within this rubric, technology meant military intervention could 'save strangers' in danger without human cost. However, as we will go on to see, it was not that simple. Kosovo may have been just such a specific example of risk free warfare but the ferocious fighting experienced by Western forces in Iraq and Kosovo meant a return to visceral and costly warfare. Indeed, recent American drone strikes—surely a clear example of technological superiority—demonstrate that some traditional gendered roles remain intact for those on the receiving end of such military intervention. Men may be killed in fighting but the women then remain as widows, mothers, and often in some difficulties as bread winners in traditional societies.

So, interest in the gender/security nexus if anything deepened after the terrorist attacks of 9/11. Specifically the subsequent wars in Iraq and Afghanistan and the chronic instability in Pakistan caused in part, but not wholly, by the struggle with the Taliban and Al-Qaeda highlighted how gender and issues of gender affect security locally, nationally, and globally. The advent of female suicide bombers in the Middle East, in Afghanistan and now in Africa as well as the activities of terrorist groups such as The Black Widows in Russia have combined to sustain both an academic and public curiosity in women and violent political activity (Bloom 2007). The scholarship and public commentaries examining the place of women in violence continues to be endlessly fascinating and exposes the complexity of the nexus between men, women, and the propensity to violence rather than peace.

Representations

Perhaps one of the most general trends in recent international relations theory in the 1990s was the growing recognition of the role of what we might loosely call 'ideas' or, perhaps more accurately, discursive contexts in international political life (Onuf 1989; Kratochwil 1991; Walker 1993; Rengger 1999; Wendt 1999). The most popular image of the international system—that states perceive themselves as inhabiting a zero-sum and therefore dangerous international environment of self-help—was taken as evidence of that; in Alexander Wendt's (1992) famous phrase 'anarchy is what states make of it'. The discursive construction of gender was and remains a prime example of how systems of knowledge (discourses) possess power which influences every facet of social life and determines the limits of the possible for a variety of actors. This section therefore focuses on the effect of gender on the constructions of security and insecurity for different actors in the international arena.

Gender, at its simplest, refers to an identification of masculinity with characteristics of strength and militarism and of femininity with vulnerability, the idea of nurturing and peace. Here we note that we should bear in mind that sex and gender are not necessarily one and the same. Indeed, identifying men with masculinity, militarism, and a propensity for violence and women with femininity, vulnerability, and victimhood, only reproduces the gender dichotomies feminist theorists have sought to undo. Doing so also obscures the fact that one may identify or be identified with masculinity or femininity irrespective of actual sex and may also divert us from investigating the important links between race, class, sexuality, and gender. The identification of sex and gender may also ignore the gender-specific vulnerabilities men suffer. Here we may think of the manner in which young men, for example in Iraq, were identified as 'insurgents', rounded up and incarcerated and then tortured, sometimes in a sexual manner, always it seems on the basis of both their gender and ethnicity.

That said, in disentangling the web of gendered discourses and their effect on security, we should start from the beginning, namely with the discourses of patriarchy. Cynthia Enloe (2004: 4) helpfully defined this term as 'the structural and ideological system that perpetuates the privileging of masculinity'. It would be difficult to argue that the world of international politics is not one which privileges certain notions of masculinity. It is a world seemingly run by men. What Enloe (1989) pointed out in her seminal book *Bananas, Beaches and Bases* is that this world is neither a natural nor a neutral one. It is one created and sustained through the use of a certain type of power. Throughout her career, Enloe has invariably urged that to understand these power structures it is necessary to unpack what patriarchy means. Enloe has highlighted that it is precisely the labour of women, whether it be domestic or public, which is the necessary ingredient which permits men at both the highest level (diplomats) and the lowest (say the ordinary conscript) to go about their business, waging wars, forging alliances, or conducting the business of the state.

Women have typically been excluded from the public practice of such endeavours. So taking part in combat, at least officially, was in the past closed to the female. This very construction of war as a domain of the masculine had wider implications. Jean Elshtain (1987) explains just how in her book *Women and War*. Elshtain claims that a distinction between 'beautiful souls' (women) and 'just warriors' (men) has been at the core of much of the theorizing about the respective role of women and men in both war and also society. These narratives of war, she argues, have played a crucial role in reinforcing traditional gender roles within a domestic/social context. This is because of an ongoing connection between war, maleness, and the essence of the modern state. The modern state was born in war and consolidated through war: as Charles Tilly (1990) famously phrased it, 'war made the state and the state made war'. This is important because in some, one might say in many, cultures, masculine attributes have traditionally been rewarded with social advancement or the holding of political office.

Elshtain's argument is supported by much of the historical archive which illustrates the relations between patriarchy, war, and the state and specifically how militaries serve and are constructed to reinforce certain norms. Historically, war and combat have represented the highest aspirations of the male members of political, social, and cultural elites, across time and culture. In ancient Greece, some form of military training was regarded as a prerequisite to manhood. Shakespeare famously has Henry V declare to his troops before Agincourt that 'Gentlemen in England now abed will think themselves accursed to be not here.' Theodore Zeldin (1998: 214) has explained that men fight to 'kill dissatisfaction with themselves more than their foe . . . but that adventure and honour have been their goals'. The idea of combat as serving a purpose of maleness resonates from Shakespeare's 'Band of Brothers' to that of Stephen Ambrose's more contemporary and like-named TV series. So, military service for one's country has long been regarded as a badge of honour.

War and combat are associated with masculine values such as physical strength and courage. In certain societies, those men who would not or could not fight might be classified as 'women': vilified as lacking male attributes. Military training was always (and is still is) designed to reinforce certain notions of masculinity. The use of boot camps, a degree of violence, and bullying associated with basic training are all designed to cultivate and construct certain notions of what it is to be a 'man' (Steans 1998) and as a result reinforces what it is to be a 'woman'—man's lesser other. **Misogyny** can be a useful component: males can be goaded into grinding down whatever might be regarded as womanly or feminine and thus an attribute unfit for a soldier. Norman Dixon, for example, has argued that various British military conventions were in certain periods designed to subordinate female characteristics: hence piano playing was denounced (Dixon 1976). To sacrifice one's life for one's country in war has been regarded as the highest form of patriotism, but a failure to fight is the act of a coward or evidence of some physical or mental weakness that renders the male less than he should be. For example, homosexuality in the British Army could have led to punishment by death. The recent film based on the autobiographical novel by Vera Brittain entitled *Testament of Youth* has highlighted the shame and the punishment meted out to those soldiers found 'guilty' of homosexuality. Furthermore, one may argue that any sanitized interpretation of what it is to be a man and a soldier is somewhat at odds with real accounts of the sexual abuse of both female and male soldiers. In the last few years several accounts that confirm this argument have been made, especially in regard to the US Armed Services. These accounts have been given wide exposure in *The Invisible War*, a recent documentary by director Kirby Dick, which illustrates the violent culture of the American military, in which it appears that sexual assault is seen as a 'normal' part of what it means to be a soldier within. Reports show, that though sexual violence is not solely directed against women, a higher proportion of women are assaulted. Namely, in the Air Force one in five women are assaulted as opposed to one in fifteen men in the same service. These numbers are based on reported cases, although the real numbers are likely to be much higher (Ellison 2011). Nevertheless, they allow us to confidently argue that the disproportionate scale of female soldiers' victimization is likely the result of army training, with its deification of the male and the demotion of the female, facilitated through the operationalization of misogyny.

Women, in contrast to men, have long been regarded as the carers and the nurturers of the young. In many narratives of war, women have inhabited only the private sphere tasked with the defence of that ubiquitous feature of national life—the home front, implying that women, even in war, never really left the home (Sherry 1995). This polarization between the sexes has been described in the following terms: 'Women are excluded from war talk and men excluded from baby talk' (Elsthain 1987: 222). Yet women, although depicted historically as 'carers', such as the nurse figure embodied in Florence Nightingale, have also had other connections with war. Frequently they have been represented as the 'spoils of war'. This perception of women as 'spoils of war' was consistent historically with the legal status of women: they were regarded as the property of the male. **Rape** (see Think Point 11.1) was perceived as an injury to the male estate, and not to the woman herself.

The rape of women during and after war is now well documented, as are examples when rape appears to have been used as a 'tactic' of war to humiliate or demoralize the enemy. We now know, thanks to the work of historians such as Anthony Beevor, of the routine use of rape by soldiers of the Red Army as it advanced on and occupied German cities in the spring of 1945. Members of the NKVD encouraged the use of rape, not just as a tool of revenge but as a way of dispiriting the male population left in the city. Scholars have also examined the use of rape as a supposed tactic of war by Serbian and Croatian soldiers in the wars in the Balkans.

Recent research in the Democratic Republic of Congo (DRC) reveals that rape is not simply a tactic used in wartime. In the DRC, the cases of rape seem to have increased since the 2003 peace agreement between the government and rebel groups. This has prompted Maria Eriksson Baaz and Maria Stern (2009) to conduct interviews with former soldiers in the DRC. Their conclusions are both interesting and provocative. In this case, rape seems inexorably connected with what they call hegemonic masculinity (Baaz and Stern 2009: 514). Baaz and Stern (2009: 496) reject the common explanation that the acts of rape committed in the DRC are actually a result 'of the supposed animal-like bestiality of the rapist'. They do so since they recognize that such a line of argument has obvious racial connotations and has its roots in colonial discourses which presented the masculinity, and in extent the femininity, of colonial subjects as pathological (Said 1978). These discourses which link race, gender, and in many cases sexuality arguably seem persistent features of contemporary conflict. Instead they argue that in the DRC, rape is connected to

! THINK POINT 11.1 Rape

Although we are now familiar with historical cases of rape in war, the phenomenon remains with us. Rape remains a weapon that can be used in times of conflict against enemy populations or indeed as an instrument of the state in times of peace to stifle debate and dissent. It has also emerged as a striking feature of contemporary conflicts in Africa and the Middle East. Throughout 2014, the plight of Yazidi women abducted by the so-called Islamic State (IS) in Iraq and allegedly raped and/or sold as sex slaves to IS fighters featured prominently in the headlines. During that same year, Boko Haram abducted over 200 Christian school girls from Chibok, Northern Nigeria. These girls, according to reports, were then either sold or forced into marriages with fighters. Boko Haram had over a five-year period seized many women; some were young girls and others as elderly as 65. Human Rights Watch reports that in captivity these girls and women are forced to convert to the Islamic faith but utilized as forced labour or as accessories to raids and assaults on villages. Rape is a common and distressing feature. The on-going plight of women in the Congo has evoked international concern with the UN estimating that in 2006, some 27,000 sexual assaults took place in one region alone (see Diken and Laustsen 2005; Gettleman 2007; and also www.warchild.org.uk).

ideal hyper-masculine identities. Men who joined the army with the promise that as soldiers they would be respected by their communities and exalted, found themselves after the war unable to find work or support their communities and disrespected by their women. As a result, 'the soldiers locate the impetus for their resorting to violence in the mismatch between their embodied experiences and their aspirations to inhabit these impossible subject positions' (Baaz and Stern 2009: 514). In other words, rape serves to reaffirm these soldiers' masculinity and their identities as men and soldiers.

Although yet to be fully developed or embedded in international relations theory, the idea of hegemonic masculinity derives from work originally carried out by, amongst others, the sociologist, R. W. Connell. His research was concerned with the practices that promote the dominant social position of men and the subordinate social position of women. His work, which investigated the dominant role of white middle-class men, asked why this group maintained dominant social roles over women and other gender groups. His findings were that hegemonic masculinity represented a culturally idealized form of manhood that was brutal, pseudo natural, and tough. It was characterized by violence, aggression, and stoicism. These characteristics were valued above those of so-called feminine values. Transferring his findings away from the behaviour of white heterosexual males, it seems that that idea may go some way to explain the behaviour not just of certain groups in the Congo but some groups within the US military. It is worth noting that quite often the operation of hegemonic masculinities includes the subordination not just of women but of homosexual men or certain ethnic groups (Connell and Messerschmidt 2005). We should note though that Connell has issued a series of warnings as to the complexity of gender hierarchies, emphasizing the importance of the geography of masculinity and the importance of the agency of women in any given setting.

As Baaz and Stern argue, the discourse of gender is linked in complex ways with the discourse of class and race in many cases, not just in the DRC. The results of such interlinkages are both discursive and practical. For example, the wars in Iraq and Afghanistan were at least in part constructed as campaigns which would allow good Western men (and actually women) to save the victimized Afghan and Iraqi women from the patriarchal structures which had enslaved them over many decades. These discourses should not be ignored since they have been embraced not only by British and American politicians but also by liberal feminists. These two wars were supposed to deliver Iraqi and Afghan women to a form of Western enlightenment and more importantly 'emancipation'.

The importance of women, both Afghan and non-Afghan, to all aspects of that war was striking. Not only was the woman issue highlighted by politicians but gender affected the very conduct of the Counter-Insurgency. There is something very interesting here. Laleh Khalili (2011: 1471) argues that the gendered character of the counter-insurgencies (COIN) in Iraq and Afghanistan was especially obvious when soldiers actually came into contact with the local population. In these interactions, it became obvious that women were typically coded as civilians while men—all men over the age of 14—were coded as combatants. As a result, men were targeted as the enemy whether by combat units or drones. This may seem rather obvious—men fight and women are passive victims of an ongoing conflict; but is it? As early as during the 1966 Algerian conflict, insurgents wise to the racist and gendered beliefs of the French army would dress in Burqas and easily cross through checkpoints which were closed to men but open to women (Evangelista 2011: 39–57).

During the 9/11 wars, racially informed gender stereotypes did not only inform border policy but COIN in general. In Iraq, US forces had largely ignored the female population, in part because of the sensitivities of engaging with women in a traditional society. Insurgents in turn took advantage of these cultural sensitivities by disguising themselves in the all-enveloping female clothing to avoid detection whilst perhaps plotting or perpetrating attacks. This in turn forced Western forces to deploy women soldiers at checkpoints precisely to be able to search females without causing offence. On the other hand in Afghanistan by 2011, female soldiers were perceived as in some ways central to waging COIN, with female units utilized precisely to make contact with the female population. Of course this engagement also provided intelligence-gathering opportunities (Katt 2014). Despite some controversy over the intelligence role, this embedding of all female cultural teams alongside special operations forces has widely been regarded as successful in enabling access to the 50 per cent of the population usually sidelined in the business of war.

Another part of the story of the women of Afghanistan is that while Western women were quite literally on the frontline, the emergence of an Afghan National Army has also seen indigenous women co-opted into the armed services. Indeed the Afghan theatre is fascinating precisely because in all aspects women are fulfilling functions associated with men but also associated with Western practices and the evolution of Western societies.

Even though we may applaud these developments, we should always remember how stereotypes inform our understandings and practices in Afghanistan and beyond. As Hirschkind and Mahmood (2002) have highlighted, the twin figures of the Islamic fundamentalist and female rape victims have helped consolidate and popularize the view that hardship and sacrifice were in the end for Afghanistan's own good. The argument is that the ends of emancipation justify the means. In other words, invasion, bombing, war, and occupation should be endured to secure a greater good. Sadly the evidence, as produced by public bodies and journalists, is that conditions for women remain pretty grim in Afghanistan and they are subject to rape, beatings, and kidnappings and at the prey of the warlords (*The Guardian* 2014). The experiences of women in the conflict have been represented in the oral tradition of Landays, traditional short verses which reflect the impact of drones strikes, military occupation, and war experiences. These verses might speak of the glory of war but also provide telling accounts of what it means to be female. Violent images abound, hence one such rhyme:

Embrace me in a Suicide Vest
but don't say I won't give you a kiss
(Poetry Foundation 2013)

In this complex theatre women are, unusually for this traditional society, also resorting to violence. Nowhere is this perhaps more obvious and controversial than in the role of suicide bombers.

In Afghanistan there was, at least initially, a prohibition against the use of female 'martyrs'. However, for a multiplicity of reasons, we have witnessed an increase in female suicide bombers since 2009. This followed an open letter issued by Umayama al-Zawahiri (the wife of Al-Qaeda leader Ayman al-Zawahiri) urging her sisters to assist the terrorist groups through suicide missions. The use of females created the conditions for surprise attacks but had the added 'bonus' of creating an additional pool of resources. Martin Van Crevald, a military historian, has argued that women are only ever used in battle/conflict when men are not available, or reluctant to take part (Van Crevald 2001). It appears that his thesis may also be applicable in terms of improvized explosive devices (IEDs) borne by women. A greater use of the suicide IED requires more recruits, whether they are women or children. Or it may be that the female IED has an especially shocking resonance in societies where women have traditionally inhabited a 'private', not 'public', role.

This is challenging because gender cannot be reduced to any simple equation of men with masculinity and women with femininity. There are a number of reasons for this: first, because of the self-identification of actors, and second, because to do so would cast men as the perpetrators of violence and women only as perennial victims. Insecurity in the era of the so-called war on terror still depends on gendered discourses but does not necessarily follow the logic of men and violence and women and peace. Increasing numbers of women suicide bombers, prison guards, or women in gangs, like the infamous Lynndie England, perpetuate violence. So we need to further interrogate the traditional links made between men and violence and women and peace. The 'War on Terror' underpinned a series of activities including extraordinary rendition and the widespread use of torture at detention facilities in both Iraq and the Guantanamo Bay Detention Centre in Cuba. These initial wars of the twenty-first century in Iraq and in Afghanistan rendered permissible a range of activities which were technically prohibited after 1945—but certainly in Latin America some had been part and parcel of covert American activities for many decades (Stokes 2005). But what concerned some scholars was what appeared to be an institutionalization of the practices of 'torture'. As Nancy Sherman has argued, torture is rarely solo work. She defines it as a systematic practice, institutionalized by nations and states, supported hierarchically, and requiring the participation of professionals of many stripes (Sherman 2010: 147). This includes women. In Abu Ghraib female interrogators, like Lynddie England, were used to humiliate and intimidate the prisoners. Imprisoned men were forced to wear women's garments, perform or simulate homosexual acts, and endure a variety of physical and emotional acts.

Finally, we need to re-examine the further practical implications of gendered discourses on security practices and on the construction of gender-specific insecurities.

KEY POINTS

- Patriarchy has defined the roles of women and men in international politics, leaving women on the sidelines performing practices which make possible men's involvement in international politics.
- War and military service have historically been crucial for the construction of the state. As a result, the exclusion of women from taking part in combat perpetuates patriarchal structures although in the West, the combat exclusion clause is slowly being removed.
- Gendered discourses produce gender-specific insecurities not only for women but also for men.
- We need to look at the intersection of racial and gender discourses.

Practical context I: war

According to some female scholars, even in the contemporary era, experience in combat can still be a way of earning high office or, in a state such as America, of securing political election (Steans 1998). Just as ancient and medieval civilizations gave special respect to citizens who had proved themselves in war; it can still be a special mark of respect to be a war **veteran**. This is an honour that historically is denied to women. Women have traditionally been thought unfit or unsuited for the holding of high offices associated with the military or issues of national security. If women were rarely warriors, they were equally unlikely to be heads of the CIA or Strategic Air Command. If in olden times it was men who headed armies, it is predominantly men who still act as the heads of militaries, intelligence services, and nuclear industries. In the United States, there may be greater hurdles to those politicians, even male politicians, seeking office, who have not served in the military (Elshtain 1987). Former generals are looked upon as prime presidential material, and some American politicians have run for office on the basis of their war records. Women, though, have traditionally been employed as spies, special agents, and in special intelligence units (Steans 1998). There is little need to emphasize that this type of employment might fit nicely with traditional gendered views of women as perhaps devious, cunning, and able to fool men through the use of sexual favours. Not for nothing has the reputation of Mata Hari exercised such a keen fascination.

Yet, any positive view of the way in which men have been treated after serving their country in war must be contested. Veterans of the Vietnam conflict, especially those drawn from the African American community in the United States, might find it difficult to recognize their treatment as that of heroes or to find that their combat experiences advanced them socially (Sherry 1995). The recent controversies over the level of compensation for those killed and maimed in conflicts such as the First and Second Gulf Wars also do not point to a necessarily glorious post-war life for those who have served, particularly those who are not drawn from the officer class. Recent reports from both wars in Iraq have demonstrated that war, or rather occupation duty after war in a hostile environment, is proving extremely stressful for young soldiers and has longer-term psychological implications. There is a recent and worrying rise in the number of army suicides, as, for example within the UK armed forces.

Despite the increasing evidence of the toll that soldiering exerts on the individual, to die in combat for one's country was at least in certain narratives of war regarded as an honour and was one that was revered within many cultures. The construction, though, of a male security state is not accidental. As Cynthia Enloe (1993: 253) points out, militarism has not been 'kept going by merely drawing on a type of civilian masculinity ... rather it requires drill sergeants ... and men's willingness to earn their manhood credentials by soldiering: it also requires women to accept particular assumptions about mothering, marriage and unskilled work [as well as policies, written and unwritten] to ensure certain sorts of sexual relations'. Enloe's formulation is important because arguably it helps explain why, even though women are increasingly integrated into many state institutions, certainly in Western societies, the highest level of the security apparatus remain predominantly the preserve of men. This is certainly true of most militaries across the globe.

It is not just at the highest levels, that of the presidents and the generals, that scholars claim that there is a linkage between man, war, and the state. The relationship between the bearing of arms and citizenship has a long history in Western political thought. Judith Hicks Stiehm argues that we in the West have traditionally held militarized conceptions of citizenship and that different categories of citizenship arise from the classes of those excluded from military service. The very young, the old, the disabled, in some societies the homosexual, are barred from combat (Hicks

Stiehm 1983, 1989). This is odd in many ways, but for our purposes it has meant historically that the fittest in society were slaughtered. As Nicolai has argued:

> Children and old men are protected by Government, but besides them the blind, deaf and dumb, idiots, hunchbacks, scrofulous and impotent persons, imbeciles, paralytics, epileptics, dwarfs and abortions—all this human riff-raff and dross need have no anxiety, for no bullets will come hissing against them, and they can stay at home and dress their ulcers while the brave, strong young men are rotting on the battle-field.
>
> Pick (1993)

Within such a rubric, women have been excluded along with the infirm from battle. In the United States and within other NATO countries, as the women's movement grew, demands escalated from the inclusion of women into the military to an insistence on the right to participate in combat.

Those pushing for the placement of women in combat have argued that, apart from the issue of political rights, those males who serve in the US military enjoy a range of economic benefits, such as free medical care and cheap loans, which are denied to women. Yet there is much that is culturally and socially sensitive here. In the words of one American official, 'a woman POW is the ultimate nightmare'. The sagas of Melissa Rathbun-Nathy, captured by the Iraqis during the Gulf War (Nantais and Lee 1999) and Jessica Lynch, taken prisoner by the Iraqis in the second Gulf War (both eventually rescued), clearly illustrate the headache that the capture of female soldiers creates in the upper echelons of Western military apparatuses.

Despite this, the decades following the end of the Cold War saw an increase in women's recruitment. Further, the restrictions on women's ability to take part in combat operations, especially in the case of counterinsurgency operations where women have been sent to the frontline in places like Afghanistan as part of cultural teams, have ended. The increasing integration of women is not only indicative of changes in the combat environment but also, as Saskia Stachowitsch (2012) shows, demonstrative of the link between gendered foreign policy discourses and their effects on security practices. Stachowitsch (2012: 317–18) illustrates how during President Clinton's first term domestic and foreign policy conditions favoured integration and equality. However, when the administration's foreign policy choices of cooperation and compromise were accused of 'feminizing' the army, the drive for equality and integration was abandoned. During George W. Bush's presidency, the goal of saving the Afghan and Iraqi women led to the recruitment of more women. However, the drive for their recruitment was not connected with civil rights or equality issues. Following Obama's election, the focus shifted. The drive for equality for women and sexual minorities in the armed forces was of paramount importance. This was coupled with new peace-building approaches which eventually led to the revaluation of the role of female service members in war zones (Stachowitsch 2012: 318) and their deployment in the operations described above.

However, these improvements for women's inclusion in the armed forces which have a knock-on effect on their civil rights and status as equal citizens, seem to be undercut by new developments in security practices. Since the wars in Iraq and Afghanistan, security has become increasingly privatized. This privatization and deregulation of the armed forces has been steadily excluding women from jobs in the security sector partly because the main labour markets that Private Military Companies (PMCs) use for recruitment are the army and police—sectors where women are underrepresented. Further, the fact that women are excluded by law from combat makes it less likely that they will be recruited. As a result the women who work for PMCs are usually employed as secretaries and personal assistants. Finally, where the state has been increasingly involved in a push for gender integration and equality in the military, with the combat exclusion zone lifted in most democratic states and women literally on the frontline, the state has been unable to enforce these policies in the private sector. As a result, the security sector is arguably being re-masculinized while it is also being de-democratized (Stachowitsch 2013).

Although we have seen the equation of women with peace is not one based on fact but on powerful discourses, it would be difficult to ignore the role women played in movements such as that at **Greenham Common** during the 1980s and in Washington more recently to protest against the torture of detainees in Guantanamo. Female voices often lead those protests that are against the stationing of foreign troops or missiles in local areas. As Elshtain's (1987) discussion of 'beautiful souls' always reminds us, the long tradition that seemingly demonstrates that women and peace are interconnected is based on the assumption that females as the bearers of children or the potential bearers of children are necessarily more anti-war than men. These anti-war and now anti-torture movements have habitually treated the military apparatus of the state, especially the military component, as an expression of male aggression (Alonso 1993). Within this rubric, mothers are life affirming, and biology of the female kind negates male militarism. While the 'peace' women of the 1980s can justifiably claim that they did in fact influence the military debate through their actions of 'chaining themselves to fences outside nuclear bases, dancing on missile silos and jumping into convoy jeeps as they pass by', the problem was, as Christine Sylvester points out, that all these activities can be discounted by those in power. In her words, 'peace camps do not lead us to the edge of war. They do not stockpile weapons and hurtle us into arms races. . . . They do not matter' (Sylvester 1996). Those linkages between men and war and women and peace are important, even if, as we have seen, so often they are ill-founded. They imply, as the American academic Bell Hooks (1995) has argued, that women by virtue of simply being women have played little or no role in supporting and upholding the militarism of the state. Women have in this one-dimensional version of historical events been merely observers of and objects in war.

Women have, however, always been engaged in the business of war. For some scholars this is important, because it means that the history of war and indeed histories generally have been told in such a way that it is just that: 'his story'. Women and their stories or narratives are therefore absent from a number of textbooks or what are regarded as the important studies of war. More recently, academics have concentrated in growing numbers on the telling of female histories, and we do now have a number of works that tell some of the stories of women as victims of war—for example, monographs and scholarly works that tell the stories of mass rape in war or examine the gendered effects of war (Stiglmayer 1994).

The woman as 'victim' is, as we saw earlier, an important thread in the stories of war. Indeed, in 1990 an estimated 90 per cent of war casualties were civilians, the vast majority women and children, but contemporary scholarship has uncovered numerous examples where women have supported the role of men in war and participated in civil war and war itself. The tales of these women shed fascinating light on the work of the female in war, revealing female experiences as soldiers, special agents, nurses, surgeons, laundry women, cooks, and prostitutes (Isaksson 1988). They do not suggest that men and women are different in some absolute way. It may also be that such formulations ignore the contribution that many men have made to peace movements and to pacifism. Individual men have often sought to avoid combat and most conscript armies have been dogged by desertion and so-called cowardice brought about by the trauma of war. As we move into the twenty-first century, and know about the problems of trauma in war amongst even very brave and honourable people, it is difficult to see how long we can sustain the idea of war as either heroic or the natural place for a human regardless of gender.

KEY POINTS

- The importance of gender as a topic in international security studies is now accepted.
- Feminist scholars introduced and answered the question of where are the women in security. They also alerted us to the idea that the experiences of women in relation to the state, state militaries, and conflict may be very different from those of men.
- The traditional literature on security has, when it has engaged with issues of gender, treated women as upholders of peace.
- Western militaries now utilize women on the frontline of combat and the utility of women is widely accepted in Counter Insurgency Operations. The US Marine Corps, for example, created Female Engagement Teams for work in Iraq and Afghanistan and US Special Operations Command has deployed women as part of frontline units in cultural support teams (CTS).

Practical context II: civilian life

For some, of course, women are seen (as they have always been seen) as the 'weaker'—sometimes termed the 'fairer'—sex, and so will continue to be second-class citizens dependent on men for protection in the international environment, both in a domestic context and also ironically within the armed services themselves. In many contemporary societies the state has conscripted its young men for service in the armed forces, but women have usually been excluded. The overall effect is therefore to 'arm' men and 'disarm' women. There are, to the minds of some feminist scholars, important consequences of the exclusion of the female from the bearing of arms: one is to render women dependent on men for their protection. To walk a woman 'home' in the dark is a metaphor for how the female must need a protector to survive outside the alleged security of home and hearth. This is why feminists who recognize the threat posed to women (and indeed men) by violence in the street talk of the need to 'take back the night' rather than to look for a 'hero' to walk you home. Both culturally and in institutional terms this function of protection has been linked to masculinity.

There are, of course, some pragmatic reasons for this at a state level. After all, the slaughter of women on the battlefield along with men would prejudice future generations. The phrase 'women and children' is one commonly used to symbolize the place of the female within the community—note a subordinate one, linking women with 'dependants'. It is an important place, because of biology and the continual demands of the state on its female and child-bearing constituencies. Women have been used by virtue of their biology to promote certain security goals. Not the least of these has been the demand to breed for empire or the national interest. Although this may seem a rather crude formulation, it is central to understanding how states and societies after war reproduce their populations and survive. Not for nothing did Stalin demand an increase in the birth rate after the Second World War (see Case Study 11.1). In the Russian population, women were encouraged to have a high number of children as the Soviet state sought to recover from the ravaging of its population in the years of war (Kennedy-Pipe 2004). In certain states, women were denied access to birth control or abortion to promote and achieve a certain rate of reproduction (Buckley 1989). Arguably the most intimate of human activities for women were less important than the demands of male political and religious elites that women provide a functional and biological service to the state. This role of women as 'breeders' remains imperative for the health of many wealthy industrialized societies. In other places around the globe, the control of population and resources rests precisely on the control of population growth. President Obama has, much to the delight of feminist lobbies, revoked former President Bush's ban on contraceptive supplies to the world's largest family-planning organization, Marie Stopes International. Bush's legislation had prejudiced the health care of women in a number of countries, including Malawi, Ghana, Sierra Leone, Tanzania, Uganda, and Zimbabwe. The very essence of a state or a community rests upon the ability to produce the next generation safely and the ability of women to look after their health and have access to contraception, and when necessary adequate maternity care.

CASE STUDY 11.1 Breeding for the state? Russia

In 1944, as victory against Germany became apparent, the Soviet authorities turned their attention to increasing the birth rate. This was an acute pressure because of the heavy wartime losses. Some twenty-four million Soviet people had died during the war, with the result that there was a very large preponderance of women left in the population. By 1946 women outnumbered men by almost twenty-six million. Because relatively few men were available to marry, the Soviet authorities encouraged women to have illegitimate children. Small allowances were made by the state to single mothers or these women could place their children in state homes without cost. Effectively, as Mary Buckley has shown, the state took over the financial role of the father. This was designed to prevent single women who had children by married men from disrupting his existing family and to encourage them to return to work after giving birth. The state also promoted the idea of very large families, with the introduction of decorations for motherhood. Motherhood Glory went to mothers of seven, eight, and nine children. After bearing ten children, women became 'Heroine Mother'.

These measures were designed to address the population of surplus females and male population loss. Children were needed to address gaps in the labour market. So too were women. Despite maternity leave and some state benefits, women were also expected to return to the workplace after childbirth. The so-called women question (the emancipation of women), which had been highlighted after the Revolution by both Trotsky and Lenin, was therefore subordinated to the demands of a state recovering from war and the decimation of the male population. This problem for Russia has not gone away. After the fall of Communism from 1991 onwards, the population fell by 4 per cent. By 2011 the then Prime Minister, Vladimir Putin, revealed plans to boost the Russian birth rate by at least 25–30 per cent compared to the 2006 rate. By the end of 2012, his programme of financial incentives appeared to have had some success and for the first time in the post-Cold War world, births had narrowly overtaken deaths and the population had grown by 200,000. While growing birth rates were tied to an overtly nationalistic agenda, this demonstrated that women and biology were deemed key to the survival of Russia (Buckley 1989; Alpern Engel 1992).

However, as noted earlier, women's importance for the reproduction and survival of the state has not meant that women have been protected from physical, psychological, and emotional violence. On the contrary, patriarchy, which equates women to dependants and allows the state to 'protect' and control them, is also a crucial source of vulnerability. According to the World Health Organization, 35 per cent of women experience violence at the hands of an intimate partner (WHO 2013). In her work, Jacqui True (2012) argues that the gendered global (and domestic) political economy heightens women's vulnerability to violence. For example, the globalization of the sex and domestic labour industries has left women vulnerable around the world, while their labour is exploited not only by criminal gangs but also by their own states. True (2012) argues that in order to understand women's vulnerability to violence, we need to take into consideration the gendered political economy by clearly showing how women's economic inequality, which is produced through gendered discourses, constrains women's choice, leaving them vulnerable to violence.

KEY POINTS

- Looking at women and their place in contemporary and historical conflicts helped bring about recognition that there are specific female issues relating to state control of biology and reproduction.
- Women are intimately affected by state policy on contraception, abortion, and marriage. Female biology is crucial to states' existence.
- Patriarchy has been a crucial ingredient in the construction of the global political economy, which sidelines women and constrains their opportunity for action, making them vulnerable to violence.

Practical context III: the post-conflict environment

Moving away from the peace/war dichotomy allows us to examine the gender-specific insecurities women face in the grey area of post-conflict reconstruction and peace building. Work examining the Balkan Wars in the early 1990s and the first Gulf War has revealed a degree of violence perpetrated against women by soldiers returning home from the trauma of conflict. Indeed, violence against women in general is on the increase in times of post-conflict reconstruction and when men return from war (True 2012). A claim might be made that violence against women is more prevalent both in militarized societies and within military families and that the idea that women and children are, as a matter of course, protected by male soldiers should be re-examined (Human Rights Watch 1999).

The same may be said of the post-revolutionary environment. This has become an issue of increasing importance for feminist security studies scholars in connection with the Arab Spring. As we saw, the place of women in any given social order is crucial for the security of the state and the regime. This is usually accompanied by patriarchal discourse which determines who or what the idealized 'woman' and 'man' may be. The regimes that were eventually swept up by pro-democracy demonstrators were key examples of this. At the start of the revolutions, women of these regimes (in the main educated, professional, and Westernized) took to the streets to protest against the regimes, despite the fact that these regimes had made much of the positive and protected treatment of women within their society (Johansson-Nogués 2013). In response, the regimes resorted to violence of a gendered kind. Perhaps unsurprisingly, the end of the revolutions did not bring about an increase in female political rights. Instead, the post-revolutionary order brought additional restrictions on the rights of women and a concomitant rise in violence. Elisabeth Johansson-Nogués (2013) argues that the levels of violence we are currently witnessing in states like Egypt may be interpreted as a symptom of the hyper-masculine militarized mode which the new regimes are in. This is a mode characteristic of violent circumstances like war and revolution and their aftermath. The gendered violence in the aftermath of the Arab Spring is related to forceful attempts to remake the categories of ideal woman and man. Now the ideal woman is not professional and empowered but confined in the home. What remains constant in this account is the fact that militarism outlives war and in militarized societies women remain vulnerable to violence.

KEY POINTS

- Theorists have usually discussed gender and security by referring to war and peace. However, it is becoming increasingly obvious that we need to pay attention to the post-war/conflict environment.
- In post-conflict militarized environments women are often the victims of what has been increasingly accepted as hyper-militarized masculine violence.

Multiple perceptions, same realities?

We in the West have had the luxury of being able to acknowledge the problems of humankind and war at something of a distance. Indeed, since the revolution in military affairs (RMA) there has been a gradual erosion of the state's military demands on its peoples: a trend accelerated in the Western world by the decline of communism. In many democracies, the notion of the soldier as citizen has simply died. Even if we do not yet live in a post-heroic culture, as Edward Luttwak (1995) has claimed, war as trial by national survival is almost certainly dead. We, or certainly those in the Western world, live in a world where war is at a distance, our own casualties are minimized, and, as the wars in Iraq and Afghanistan proved, controversial. Wars at a distance from our civilian engagement have changed the way in which modern militaries fight and the way in which civilian populations respond. As we saw during the Kosovo conflict of the late 1990s, liberal states were able to wage a successful war against Serbia without having to suffer a single conflict fatality. The increased use of drone strikes seems to merely follow this trend. This use of 'virtual war', to misuse Ignatieff's term, solved the problem of men, women, and war (Ignatieff 2001). If actual combat could be avoided, then male and female soldiers could wage war on equal terms.

As the nature of war has changed after the Cold War, however, from one of war conducted by mass armies through defence by nuclear deterrence to 'virtual war', the role of both men and women in relation to conflict has changed. We in the West can engage in mass killing through technology with few apparent costs to ourselves. This might, except at the margins, mean that debates over the relative fitness of men and women for war are irrelevant, although the decade-long war in Afghanistan has surely brought home to Western audiences the costs to troops fighting counter-insurgencies. Yet there is a problem here, and it is one that is raised in much of the security literature on women and war and development and security. The problem is, to put it bluntly, that, while gender and war in the West may have been about the 'right to fight' or the right to object to state policies fought in the name of national politics, in most of the rest of the world, men and women have far fewer choices. In many parts of the globe, campaigns for women to be allowed to fight and die in national armies would seem bizarre. While war may be sanitized for those of us living in the West, women (and indeed men and children) in war zones such as Afghanistan, Sri Lanka, Iraq, or Latin America are victims of, are witnesses of, may participate in, but almost certainly seek to remove themselves from, war and violence. This may even take the form of suicide. Self-immolation by women has been a feature of Afghan life since 2001. Conflict in these cases is rarely about the historical contract between the individual and the central authorities but a battle for individual, familial, or communal survival in a local patch. Add into this the complexities of what are now known as soft security issues, **AIDS**, illegal trading of people, and economic hardship, and our understanding of gender as a divide between men and women must be elaborated upon to provide a more complex picture of what it means to a man or a women in a specific time and place.

KEY POINTS

- The 9/11 wars have once again reminded us of the complexity of what happens to men and women once conflict begins.
- We have, at the beginning of the twenty-first century, become keenly aware of the challenges of ensuring human rights for men and for women in post-conflict situations.

Conclusion

The traditional literature on security largely ignored the issue of gender. It was implicit in most of the literature on war and security that gender produced different roles for men and women. In short, boys would have 'toys' (weapons) and girls would have 'dolls'. Women as a category were ignored and on the whole were regarded either as unfit for service in war or as unsuited for leadership or in some cases even citizenship. While men were warriors, women were either ignored or depicted as passive in terms of security issues. Quite often even the role of women as victim was regarded as irrelevant to the business of state security. Women did, however, serve the purposes of nationalist causes, with nationalism often presented in highly gendered and female terms. Female symbols of statehood were and remain a characteristic of many modern states. The figure of the woman as mother to the nation is a familiar one (see Case Study 11.1).

Feminist and critical security investigations into the state, war, and security allowed us in the 1980s and 1990s to go beyond the rather simple categories of men/warrior/protector and women/mother/protected. What the feminist literature did was to alert us to a series of consequences that state security policies had for women. More recent writings on the subject have also alerted us to the effect of gendered and racial discourses for the security of both men and women in the war zones of Iraq and Afghanistan and the other greyer combat zone of the war on terror, from Abu Ghraib to Waziristan.

Looking beyond the insecurities of war and combat and focusing on 'peace' we can also see that patriarchy allowed states to control the biology of women to construct certain state policies. Women might be coerced or persuaded to produce children for the state. They might, for example, not be allowed access to abortion or contraception depending on the whim or needs of the central authorities. Perhaps more importantly, though, the feminist and gender literature allowed us to rethink notions of security that have dominated the realist understandings of international relations. It allowed us to ask key questions that include the questioning of core certainties of international relations such as the notion of state power. What does power actually mean for men and women, both within the state and outside? What might citizenship mean for men and women? What might war mean? Crucially, how do men and women relate to issues of security? Do they in fact define and interpret security differently? In a more positive fashion, we also learnt that women might organize themselves to protest against state policy and certain facets of nationalism. However, there are still areas of huge contestation. One needs only think about the issue of religion. Many states have 'liberated' women from what may be deemed traditional religious values such as the wearing of the veil. Yet, what may be radical shifts in the daily lives of women inevitably complicate their identities in various social situations and does not necessarily lead to women having a choice in either their public or private lives (see Corcoran-Nantes 2005).

Perhaps, the most telling and pertinent feature of recent literature is that 'gender' is a way of unlocking security concerns, allowing us to see that gender as a category is a social construction. That is, the way men and women act or react may be a product of sexual difference but may be a product of gender, while at the same time it is also a product of circumstance. We should ask, therefore, how both men and women in different contexts relate to local, regional, and international security apparatus. Is it the case that security policies, as some feminists have claimed, always privilege men and always discriminate against women? Or is it that we need to understand that men are not always or simply leaders, warriors, or the oppressors of women and women are not always the victims of security apparatus?

'Gender' and 'security' are terms that require, for a proper understanding of either, to be related. But, of course, this does not mean that either is reducible to the other nor that either does not have a role independent of the other. Gender—in all its forms and with all its complexities—affects many things other than security, and security—in its turn, and however it is understood—is dependent on many things other than gender. But, as we hope to have shown, trying to understand either without an appreciation of the role of the other results in an impoverished understanding of both. Understanding, of course, does not necessarily lead to any change in practice, but it is an assumption that governs any reasoned (and reasonable) politics that it must be a first step.

? QUESTIONS

1. What does gender mean?
2. What difference does it make to any understanding of security to ask where are the women?
3. Should armies admit women to the frontline?
4. Why does rape occur in every conflict zone?

5. Are men natural warriors?
6. How have the wars in Iraq and Afghanistan highlighted the complexities of the gender question in international relations?
7. What can be done to ensure the safety of the vulnerable in post-conflict situations?
8. What role can and should international organizations play in ensuring the physical and mental health of women in places of conflict?
9. Who are the upholders of peace?
10. For what reasons do women become agents of violence?

FURTHER READING

- Bloom, Mia (2007), 'Female Suicide Bombers: A Global Trend', *Daedalus*, 136/1: 94–102. Perhaps the first account of the phenomenon of female suicide bombers by an expert on terrorism. Bloom catalogues and analyses the rise of women perpetrating violent acts through suicide.
- Enloe, Cynthia (1989), *Bananas, Bases and Beaches: Making Feminist Sense of International Politics*, London: Pinter. This is in many ways one of the original and still most important readings of feminist international relations. Enloe was amongst the first to pose and answer the question 'Where are the women in international politics?' Enloe alerted us to the fact that women occupy multiple roles in security, diplomacy, trade, and local and regional politics.
- Enloe, Cynthia (2000), *Maneuvers*, Berkeley and Los Angeles: University of California Press. Professor Enloe continued her mission of uncovering the effects of militarization on women in a global context. She argued that women everywhere are affected by the presence and ethos of military institutions and the processes of militarization. Security of the female individual and community is therefore compromised and undermined by the needs of the military.

IMPORTANT WEBSITES

- **http://www.womenwarpeace.org** The United Nations Security Council in its October 2000 resolution on Women, Peace, and Security noted the 'need to consolidate data on the impact of armed conflict on women and girls'. This website is the response to this. It is a portal that provides data on the impact of armed conflict on women and girls.
- **http://www.unicef.org/emerg/files/women_insecure_world.pdf** Women in an Insecure World is part of the Geneva Centre for the Democratic Control of Armed Forces and has as its main objective the empowerment of women as security sector actors.
- For an analysis of global trends and violence against women and girls, see **www.womenforwomen.org**.
- **www.warchild.org.uk** Provides details of women and children in conflict and post-conflict regions.

Visit the Online Resource Centre that accompanies this book for lots of interesting additional material: www.oxfordtextbooks.co.uk/orc/collins4e/

12

Securitization

Ralf Emmers

Chapter Contents

Reader's Guide

The chapter introduces, assesses, and applies the Copenhagen School and its securitization model. The School widens the definition of security by encompassing five different sectors—military, political, societal, economic, and environmental security. It examines how a specific matter becomes removed from the political process to the security agenda. The chapter analyses the act of securitization by identifying the role of the securitizing actor and the importance of the 'speech act' in convincing a specific audience of the existential nature of a threat. It argues that the Copenhagen School allows for non-military matters to be included in security studies while still offering a coherent understanding of the concept of security. Yet the chapter also stresses the dangers and the negative connotations of securitizing an issue as well as some shortcomings of the model. While the chapter is conceptually driven, it relies on a series of illustrations to apply the securitization model.

Introduction

The Copenhagen School emerged at the Conflict and Peace Research Institute (COPRI) of Copenhagen and is represented by the writings of Barry Buzan, Ole Wæver, Jaap de Wilde, and others (Wæver 1995; Buzan et al. 1998; Buzan and Wæver 2003). The Copenhagen School has developed a substantial body of concepts to rethink security, most notably through its notions of **securitization** and **desecuritization**. The

School has played an important role in broadening the conception of security and in providing a framework to analyse how an issue becomes securitized or desecuritized. It is part of a broader attempt to reconceptualize the notion of security and to redefine the agenda of security studies in the light of the end of the Cold War.

The Copenhagen School has developed its approach to security in numerous writings, most notably in *Security: A New Framework for Analysis* (Buzan et al. 1998). In this volume, Buzan, Wæver, and de Wilde start by defining international security in a traditional military context. 'Security', according to them, 'is about survival. It is when an issue is presented as posing an existential threat to a designated referent object (traditionally, but not necessarily, the state, incorporating government, territory, and society)' (Buzan et al. 1998: 21). With this point in mind, the Copenhagen School identifies five general categories of security: military security as well as environmental, economic, societal, and political security. The security survival logic is therefore maintained as well as extended beyond military security to four other categories.

The dynamics of each category of security are determined by **securitizing actors** and **referent objects**. The former are defined as 'actors who securitize issues by declaring something, a referent object, existentially threatened' (Buzan et al. 1998: 36) and can be expected to be 'political leaders, bureaucracies, governments, lobbyists, and pressure groups' (Buzan et al. 1998: 40). Referent objects are 'things that are seen to be existentially threatened and that have a legitimate claim to survival' (Buzan et al. 1998: 36). Evidently, the referent objects and the kind of existential threats that they face vary across security sectors. Referent objects can be the state (military security); national sovereignty, or an ideology (political security); national economies (economic security); collective identities (societal security); species, or habitats (environmental security) (Buzan et al. 1998).

The Copenhagen School adopts a multi-sectoral approach to security that represents a move away from **traditional security** studies and its focus on the military sector. Four of the five components account for non-military threats to security. In addition to widening the definition of security beyond military issues, the Copenhagen School deepens security studies by including non-state actors. A crucial question, though, is whether the concept of security can be broadened to such an extent without losing its coherence. There is a risk of overstretching the definition of security, with the result that everything, and therefore nothing in particular, ends up being a security problem. A loose and broad conceptualization of security can lead to vagueness and a lack of conceptual and analytical coherence. In other words, the redefinition and broadening of the concept of security need to be matched by the development of new conceptual tools. This is where the Copenhagen School with its securitization and desecuritization model has sought to contribute to the debates by developing an analytical framework to study security. The Copenhagen School raises the possibility for a systematic, comparative, and coherent analysis of security.

KEY POINTS

- A narrow interpretation of security concentrates on the state and its defence from external military attacks. In response to this narrow definition of security, other approaches to security studies have called for a widening and deepening of security to include non-military threats.
- The Copenhagen School stresses that security is about survival. A security concern must be articulated as an existential threat. The School maintains the security-survival logic found in a traditional understanding of security.
- Yet the Copenhagen School broadens the conception of security. It identifies five general categories of security: military, environmental, economic, societal, and political security. The School thus broadens the concept of security beyond the state by including new referent objects such as societies and the environment.
- The dynamics of each security category are determined by securitizing actors and referent objects.
- It is important, however, to preserve the conceptual precision of the term security. This is where the Copenhagen School contributes to the security studies literature. It provides a framework to define security and determine how a specific matter becomes securitized or desecuritized.

Securitization model

Two-stage process of securitization

The Copenhagen School provides a spectrum along which issues can be plotted (see Figure 12.1). It claims that any specific matter can be **non-politicized**, **politicized**, or **securitized** (Figure 12.1). An issue is non-politicized when it is not a matter for state action and is not included in public debate. An issue becomes politicized when it is managed within the standard political system. A politicized issue is 'part of public policy, requiring government decision and resource allocations or, more rarely, some other form of communal governance' (Buzan et al. 1998: 23). Finally, an issue is plotted at the securitized end of the spectrum when it requires emergency actions beyond the state's standard political procedures.

The Copenhagen School argues that a concern can be securitized—framed as a security issue and moved from the politicized to the securitized end of the spectrum—through an act of securitization. A securitizing actor (for example, government, political elite, military, civil society) articulates an already politicized issue as an existential threat to a referent object (for example, state, groups, national sovereignty, ideology, economy). In response to the existential nature of the threat, the securitizing actor asserts that it has to adopt extraordinary means that go beyond the ordinary norms of the political domain. Buzan, Wæver, and de Wilde argue, therefore, that securitization 'is the move that takes politics beyond the established rules of the game and frames the issue either as a special kind of politics or as above politics. Securitization can thus be seen as a more extreme version of politicization' (Buzan et al. 1998: 23). The Copenhagen School notes that desecuritization refers to the reverse process. It involves the 'shifting of issues out of emergency mode and into the normal bargaining processes of the political sphere' (Buzan et al. 1998: 4). For example, the end of the Apartheid regime in South Africa represents an illustration of the desecuritization of the race question in South African society and of its reintroduction into the political domain.

An act of securitization refers to the accepted classification of certain and not other phenomena, persons, or entities as existential threats requiring emergency measures. The Copenhagen School relies on a two-stage process of securitization to explain how and when an issue is to be perceived and acted upon as an existential threat to security. The first stage concerns the portrayal of certain issues, persons, or entities

Figure 12.1 Securitization spectrum

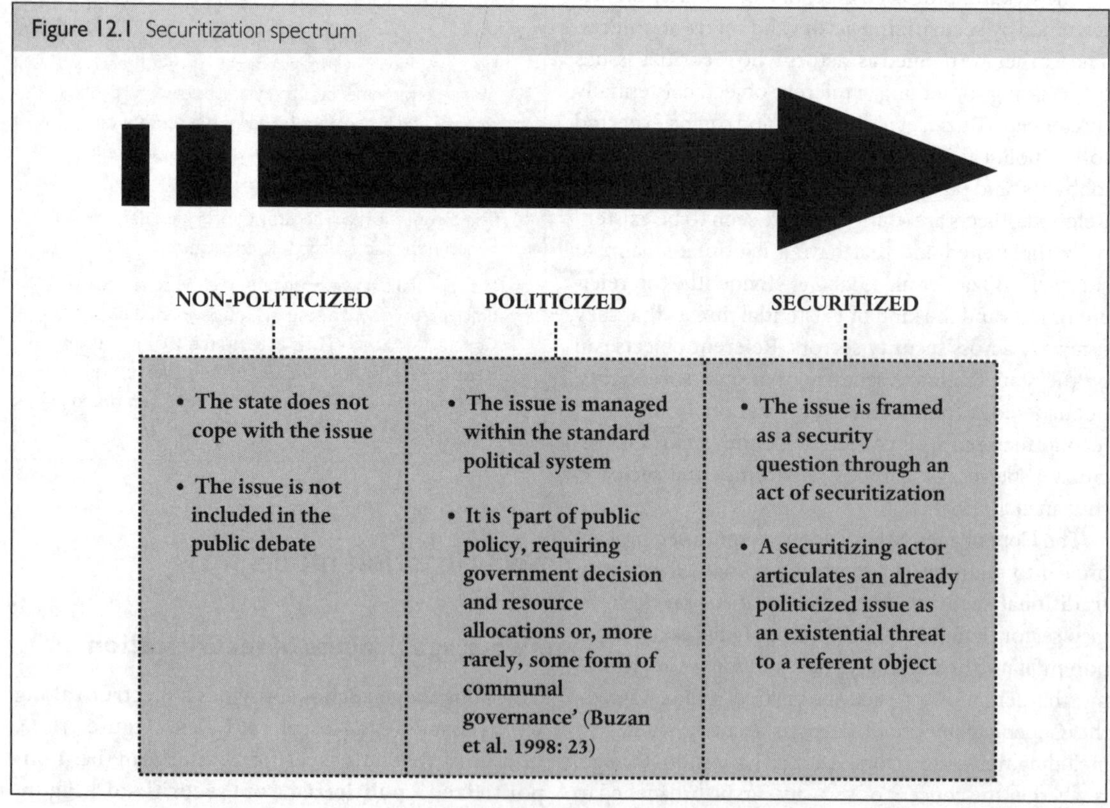

as existential threats to referent objects. The initial move of securitization can be initiated by states but also by non-state actors such as trade unions or popular movements. Non-state actors are thus regarded as important players in the securitization model. Yet securitization tends to be a process dominated by powerful actors that benefit from privileged positions. Indeed, the move of securitization depends on, as well as reveals, the **power** and influence of the securitizing actor, which as a result often happens to be the state and its elites (Collins 2005).

The use of a language of security does not mean, however, that the issue is automatically transformed into a security question. Instead, the consensual establishment of threat needs to be of sufficient salience to produce substantial political effects. The second and crucial stage of securitization is completed successfully only once the securitizing actor has succeeded in convincing a relevant **audience** (public opinion, politicians, military officers, or other elites) that a referent object is existentially threatened. Only then can **extraordinary measures** be imposed. Because of the urgency of the accepted **existential threat** to security, constituencies tolerate the use of counteractions outside the normal bounds of political procedures.

Central to the two-stage process of securitization is the importance of the '**speech act**'. The latter is defined as the discursive representation of a certain issue as an existential threat to security. The Copenhagen School considers the speech act to be the starting point of the process of securitization. An issue can become a security question through the speech act alone, irrespective of whether the concern represents an existential threat in material terms. A securitizing actor uses language to articulate a problem in security terms and to persuade a relevant audience of its immediate danger. The articulation in security terms conditions the audience and provides securitizing actors with the right to mobilize state power and move beyond traditional rules. As discussed, the security concern must be articulated as an existential threat (Buzan et al. 1998). This significant criterion enables the Copenhagen School to link a broadly defined security concept to the question of survival and thus to the reasoning found within a traditional approach to security studies. This avoids a broad and loose conceptualization of security that could too easily become meaningless. The adherence to the idea of an existential threat to limit what constitutes security and to maintain coherence reflects a realist stand in the securitization model.

KEY POINTS

- The referent objects can be individuals and groups (refugees, victims of human rights abuses, and so on) as well as issue areas (national sovereignty, environment, economy, and so on) that possess a legitimate claim to survival and whose existence is ostensibly threatened.
- The securitizing actors can be the government, political elite, military, and/or civil society. They securitize an issue by articulating the existence of threat(s) to the survival of specific referent objects.
- The desecuritizing actors reconstitute an issue as no longer an existential threat, thereby moving it from the securitized realm into the ordinary public arena.
- Securitizing actors use the language of security (speech act) to convince a specific audience of the existential nature of the threat.

Successful act of securitization

Governments and political elites have a certain advantage over other actors in seeking to influence audiences and calling for the implementation of extraordinary measures (Collins 2005). In a democratic system, a government benefits from the legitimacy of having been elected by the electorate. This gives it a significant advantage when seeking to convince an audience of the need for emergency actions in response to an existential threat. In democratic societies, the audience still has the right, however, to reject the speech act—namely, the representation of a certain issue as an existential threat.

An important question to examine is whether an act of securitization is more likely to succeed in authoritarian states where the military plays a central role in national politics (Anthony et al. 2006). The formulation of threat perceptions and the decision-making process are often dominated in undemocratic societies by the military as well as by bureaucratic and political elites. The influence of social pressure and aspirations on the securitization or desecuritization of political matters remains limited. Yet this is not to say that an audience is not part of the securitization move or that it is not expected to authorize the adoption of emergency measures, but, rather, that the audience excludes the wider population and consists solely of political elites and some state institutions such as the military. In such a context, political elites can abuse extreme forms of politicization to achieve specific political objectives and consolidate their grip on power. While the wider population may reject the speech act and consider the emergency measures adopted as a result to be illegitimate, the securitization act is nevertheless successful, having convinced a more restrictive audience on the existential nature of the threat (Collins 2005).

It should be clear by now that the Copenhagen School regards security as a socially constructed concept. In that sense, the School is rather constructivist in its approach (Balzacq 2010). What constitutes an existential threat is regarded as a subjective matter. It very much depends on a shared understanding of what constitutes a danger to security. A person in authority first needs to speak the language of security and demand the adoption of emergency measures. The discourse of the securitizing actor has to be articulated in a fashion that convinces an audience. In other words, a collective has to accept a specific issue as an existential threat to a referent object. Consequently, every act of securitization involves a political decision and results from a political and social act. Only in a successful case will standard political procedures no longer be viewed as adequate to counter the threat.

In contrast to a realist approach to security studies that focuses on the material nature of the threat, the Copenhagen School focuses on the processes by which an issue is securitized, or made to be perceived as a threat. The School predicts that an act of securitization can either succeed or fail depending on whether a separate audience accepts the discourse. As a result, it naturally asks why some acts tend to fail while others succeed. The Copenhagen School also examines why some questions are securitized in the first place while others are not. It argues that this will not just depend on material factors.

Ultimately, the securitization model occupies a unique position within the security studies literature. While on the one hand the concept's use of language and perception might lead one to conclude that the approach is wholly constructivist in nature, its concurrent adherence to the realist notions of 'existential' threats and survival suggests instead that the concept of securitization resides within the nexus of constructivism and realism. Hence, rather than highlighting a tension between the two schools of thought, the securitization model could be seen as a synthesis of realism and constructivism.

KEY POINTS

- The act of securitization is successful only once the relevant audience has been convinced of the existential threat to the referent object.
- Governments and elites have an advantage over other actors when seeking to influence an audience.
- What constitutes security is a subjective matter.
- Every process of securitization involves a political and security act.
- An act of securitization can either fail or succeed depending on the persuasiveness of the discourse.
- The securitization model is a middle ground or compromise between realism and constructivism.

Extraordinary measures and motives for securitization

The Copenhagen School asserts that a successful act of securitization provides securitizing actors with the special right to use exceptional means. It indicates, however, that the success of the process does not depend on the adoption of such actions. It is natural to ask what is meant by 'extraordinary measures'. The latter go beyond rules ordinarily abided by and are therefore located outside the usual bounds of political procedures and practices. Such measures are put in place to specifically address a critical incident or a crisis and they can include emergency powers as well as measures that are not legislated. As such, extraordinary measures are expected to respond to a specific issue that is posing an existential threat to a referent object. The adoption and implementation of extraordinary measures involve the identification and classification of some issue as an enemy that needs to be tackled urgently. The types of measures to be adopted in response will obviously depend on the circumstances and the context of the threat. An existential threat to the environment, a sector of the economy, or a state ideology will demand different emergency responses (Collins 2005).

Some shortcomings of the Copenhagen School's interpretation of extraordinary measures should be mentioned. One can rather easily anticipate the types of emergency measures to be introduced by a state. Yet it is less clear what would form an extraordinary measure for a non-state actor after it has successfully convinced an audience of the existential nature of a threat. For instance, what would constitute an extraordinary measure that goes beyond standard political procedures for non-governmental organizations such as Greenpeace and Christian Aid? Moreover, one may question the significance of a securitization process when it does not go hand in hand with actions and policies to address the ostensible threat. According to the securitization model, transforming an issue into a security question requires only the audience's acknowledgement that it is indeed a threat. The adoption of extraordinary means is not a requirement. Buzan, Wæver, and de Wilde (1998: 25) specifically indicate that 'we do not push the demand so high as to say that an emergency measure has to be adopted'. This means that a securititizing actor can make successful speech acts while still deciding to address the existential threat through standard political procedures rather than extraordinary measures (Collins 2005). Yet it can be argued that a complete act of securitization really consists of and demands both discursive (speech act and shared understanding) and non-discursive (policy implementation) dimensions (Emmers 2004). In this case, a security act would therefore depend on successful speech acts (discursive dimension) that persuade a relevant audience of the existential nature of the threat as well as the adoption by the securitizing actor of emergency powers (non-discursive dimension) to address the so-defined threat.

A series of motives and intentions can help us explain a securitizing act and the subsequent implementation of extraordinary measures (Anthony et al. 2006). Securitizing injects urgency into an issue and leads to a sustained mobilization of political support and deployment of resources. It also creates the kind of political momentum necessary for the adoption of additional and emergency measures. The securitization of an issue can thus provide some tangible benefits, including a more efficient handling of complex problems, a mobilizing of popular support for policies in specific areas by calling them security relevant, the allocation of more resources, and so forth. These achievements might not be obtained if the same problems were regarded only as political matters.

Yet it is crucial to highlight the danger of securitization. The process can be abused to legitimize and empower the role of the military or special security forces in civilian activities. This is particularly relevant in emerging democracies or countries where the division between the military and civilian authority is blurred. With the growing articulation of issues as threats in a post-9/11 context, an act of securitization can lead to the further legitimization of the armed forces in politics as well as to the curbing of civil liberties in the name of security in well-established democratic societies. Elites can use a securitizing act to curtail civil liberties, impose martial law, detain political opponents or suspected terrorists without trial, restrict the influence of certain domestic political institutions, or increase military budgets (Anthony et al. 2006). Few checks and balances are normally imposed on implemented emergency measures opening the door for possible abuse. In undemocratic societies, the greater public is not invited to speak out and is thus unable to prevent the dangers associated with an act of securitization. To highlight the potential danger linked to an act of securitization, Kyle Grayson (2003) uses a Frankenstein's Monster analogy. This metaphor for securitization helps us understand how powerful the securitizing actor can become as a result of the process as well as the loss of control that arises from a strategy that opens the door to extraordinary security actions.

Keeping Grayson's Monster metaphor in mind, it is not surprising that the Copenhagen School does not regard an act of securitization as a positive value or as a required development to tackle specific issues (Williams 2003). It argues instead that societies should, as much as possible, operate within the realm of normal politics where issues can be debated and addressed within the standard boundaries of politicization. Consequently, a process of desecuritization is described by Buzan and Wæver as particularly important to reintroduce a matter into a standard politicized level. Risks to society and abuse of authority can be prevented by desecuritizing an issue and reincluding it into the normal political domain. This logic also applies to inter-state relations, where a process of desecuritization can facilitate a shift from conflict to cooperation (Aras and Polat 2008).

KEY POINTS

- A successful act of securitization provides securitizing actors with the right to use exceptional means.
- What constitutes an extraordinary measure is not always well defined.
- A series of motives and intentions can explain an act of securitization.
- An act of securitization can lead to excesses and abuse of power. It can easily be abused by authoritarian regimes and/or in the name of security.
- Desecuritization can be beneficial, as it reintroduces an issue into a politicized sphere.

Empirical research and limitations of the securitization model

The Copenhagen School provides a framework to determine how, as well as by whom, a specific matter becomes securitized or desecuritized. Since its initial conceptualization as an approach to security studies, much attention has been given to its application to empirical research. Numerous studies have sought to understand the dynamics of securitization and desecuritization empirically. Significantly, the securitization model has been applied to a broad range of issues, including health (Elbe 2006; Kelle 2007; Sjostedt 2008; Jin 2010; Seckinelgin et al. 2010), transnational crime (Emmers 2003; Jackson 2006; Emmers et al. 2008), and international institutions (Haacke and Williams 2008; L. Jones 2011) among others. Conversely, some studies have focused on the absence of particular issues, including gender and culture, in the Copenhagen School and its securitization model (Hansen 2000). Questions that have been explored empirically include why some moves of securitization succeed in convincing an audience while others fail to do so. Attention has also been given to analysing why some issues are articulated and treated as existential security threats while others are not. In other words, empirical studies on the path that leads to the securitization of public issues have sought to achieve a better understanding of the transition from the politicized to the securitized end of the spectrum and vice versa. Finally, empirical studies have given attention to assessing the policy effectiveness of extraordinary measures and to the unintended consequences that they might provoke.

Beyond its immediate application to particular issues and areas of research, various empirical studies have examined whether the Copenhagen School can be applied outside Europe or to non-liberal democracies (Wilkinson 2007; Vuori 2008). The securitization model has indeed been criticized for being Eurocentric. This Eurocentricism is less obvious though in the case of *Security: A New Framework for Analysis* (Buzan et al. 1998), which seeks to provide a broad theoretical approach to security studies. Still, the notion of societal security, for example, which is at the core of the Copenhagen School and emphasizes society rather than the state as the primary referent object (Tow 2001), very much derives from a European experience. It refers to borderless societies that are said to exist in Europe as a result of political and economic integration. Societal security, which is examined in Chapter 15, is linked to the construction of a collective European identity and should be dissociated from state security, which relates to the preservation of national sovereignty and territorial integrity. The existence of a similar sense of community in many other regions or parts of the world is disputable.

Another area of research touches on the blurred distinction between the political and security realms (Anthony et al. 2006). The Copenhagen School needs further to define and clarify the boundaries between politics and security. The School defines securitization as an extreme version of politicization, which contributes to the possible confusion and overlap along the spectrum of depoliticized, politicized, and securitized issues. As it stands, the model may not be able sufficiently to dissociate an act of securitization from a case of severe politicization. The distinction that may exist between these processes can be blurred depending on the political context and existing circumstances. For instance, the separation between the political and security domains traditionally remains indistinct in undemocratic societies. Moreover, matters that are articulated in security terms even by democratically elected governments may continue to be located within the political domain and addressed through standard political procedures. Despite the use of speech acts, solutions for the resolution of non-military challenges are frequently found in the realm of politics. Furthermore, and as will be discussed in the next section, more needs to be said about the political motives to securitize an issue. Politicians can use the language of security towards public matters in order to boost their popularity and enhance their chances of re-election. Taking a tough stance on sensitive questions such as undocumented migration, for example, can help them win support among the electorate. Such examples of securitization could be regarded, therefore, as illustrations of politicization.

Finally, the securitization model raises some important questions about the role of academia. Are academics and analysts meant to be and act solely as observers or as advocates—securitizing or desecuritizing actors in their own right—when studying a securitizing move? The Copenhagen School expects analysts to distinguish themselves from a securitization act and the role of the securitizing actor. Yet the distinction may be obscured by a variety of factors. For example, ever since the terror attacks in the United States on 11 September 2001, terrorist experts have been widely present in the media and sometimes even in contact with intelligence agencies. It can be argued, therefore, that such repeated interventions blur the separation between academic analysis and politics and transform the analyst into a separate and influential securitizing actor that is part of the securitizing move.

> **KEY POINTS**
>
> - The securitization model has been applied empirically to better understand the dynamics of securitization.
> - The Copenhagen School is often viewed as Eurocentric, reflecting European security concerns and questions.
> - The boundaries between securitization and politicization are sometimes blurred.
> - The securitization model raises questions about the role of scholars and analysts.

Cases of securitization

Securitization of undocumented migration

The securitization of undocumented migration has become a recurrent event. Migration is a complex social phenomenon that is influenced by economic, political, socio-cultural, historical, and geographical factors (see Key Quote 12.1). Economic determinants, especially poverty and economic disparities, are the prime motivation for migrants to leave their countries of origin. They are in pursuit of better opportunities to earn an income and improve their quality of life. Besides the phenomenon of economic migration, political circumstances also explain the movement of populations. Inter-state wars, domestic conflicts of ethno-nationalist origin, and authoritarian regimes with appalling human rights records create waves of political refugees leaving their countries of origin in the hope of escaping persecution and violence. Migrants face restrictive immigration policies and reduced-legal immigration opportunities. This leads to a growing reliance on illegal methods either to enter or to remain in a specific country, including overstaying the expiry of a valid tourist visa or work permit. Since the 1990s, the issue of undocumented migration has also been increasingly linked to organized criminal groups, which now largely control the smuggling and trafficking of people. It is estimated by the United States State Department that as many as 900,000 people might be trafficked annually across international borders.

Undocumented migration can be articulated by politicians and perceived by specific audiences as representing a threat to the political, societal, economic, as well as cultural security of a state and its society (Graham 2000). See Key Quotes 12.1. Undocumented migration is said to undermine the security of national borders and thus to be a threat to the national sovereignty of a state (political security). It can also have a negative effect on the fabric of a society and its economic welfare by affecting social order and increasing unrest and crime rates (societal security). Moreover, migrants are often portrayed as a threat to the lifestyle and culture of the receiving country. In addition to being blamed for contributing to a rise in crime and other social problems, undocumented migrants are sometimes described as economic migrants who are claiming asylum to take advantage of national social benefits or take away jobs from the local population (economic security). Hiring undocumented workers tends to be much cheaper for local employers, as the latter do not have to cover their welfare or medical costs. Viewed as cheap labour, undocumented migrants are regarded as threatening employment opportunities. In reality, they mostly end up doing low-skilled jobs that nationals refuse to do. Finally, the arrival of immigrants from a common ethnic or religious group can be perceived as causing a shift in the racial composition of a country and diluting its cultural identity.

> **KEY QUOTES 12.1 Migration**
>
> 'Then Australian Immigration Minister Philip Ruddock said "whole (Middle East) villages are packing up to come to Australia and the nation was facing 'a national emergency'".'
>
> *O'Connor (2002)*
>
> 'Discussing strip searches of children, then Australian Prime Minister John Howard told Melbourne radio station 3AW: "It sounds stark and authoritarian, but if you are dealing with situations where people are using children in an exploitive way—which sometimes occurs—then I think that kind of thing is justified."'
>
> *Way and Polglaze (2001)*
>
> 'The then leader of the UK Conservative Party Michael Howard spoke on asylum and immigration on 22 September 2004: "And we have lost control of our asylum and immigration system. At a time when Britain faces an unprecedented terrorist threat, we appear to have little idea who is coming into or leaving our country."'
>
> *BBC News (2004)*

The handling of the undocumented migration issue by the John Howard government in 2001 represents an interesting case of securitization (Emmers 2004). Undocumented migration had started to have a significant political impact in Australia since the late 1990s. Pauline Hanson and her political party, the One Nation Party, transformed the immigration issue into a popular political rallying point. Hanson had proclaimed her extreme views on immigration, the Aborigines, and asylum-seekers. She won a seat in the Australian federal parliament as an independent candidate in 1996 and created the One Nation Party in 1997. The John Howard government first adopted a hard line on undocumented migration in the summer of 2001 over the *Tampa* incident. The *Tampa*, a Norwegian freighter, had rescued 460 Afghans on their way to Australia to claim asylum. Approaching its territorial waters, the Australian government refused the right of entry to the *Tampa* and ordered the ship to turn away. After the ship had failed to obey, Howard ordered units of the Special Air Service (SAS) to take control of the ship and prevent it from reaching Christmas Island or mainland Australia. A military operation had thus been undertaken to avoid asylum-seekers from coming to Australia.

The Australian Prime Minister John Howard, used the migration theme in his re-election campaign in November 2001, together with the issue of terrorism in a post 9/11 environment. The prime minister explained that he did not want undocumented migrants who had been smuggled into Australia to jump ahead of other people recognized as genuine asylum-seekers by the Australian authorities. The smuggling of undocumented migrants into Australia was also described as a threat to the national sovereignty and territorial integrity of the state. The government indicated that it could not give the impression that it was losing control over its borders, control that is so essential to national sovereignty. Finally, after the terrorist attacks of 9/11, the Australian authorities were concerned that terrorists might be among the migrants smuggled into Australia. The questions of terrorism and undocumented migration were therefore to some extent intertwined in public discussions.

The referent objects in this case of securitization were the national sovereignty and territorial integrity of Australia (military and political security), the fabric of society (societal security), and economic welfare (economic security). The securitizing actor was the John Howard government. The audience consisted of Australian public opinion (Emmers 2004). Despite a lot of domestic debates and fierce criticism, the audience generally accepted the interpretation of events set forward by the securitizing actor and acknowledged the need to implement extraordinary measures to respond to the threat. Opinion polls suggested that a majority of Australians supported Howard's hard line on undocumented migration. While migration was certainly not the sole reason for success, his conservative coalition was re-elected for a third term in office in November 2001. In other words, the securitizing actor used a discourse of security that convinced an audience of the threat posed by the smuggling of undocumented migration into Australia.

Beyond the use of rhetoric, the Howard government adopted and implemented a series of extraordinary measures to reduce the number of asylum-seekers reaching Australia (Emmers 2004). Such measures included the automatic detention of asylum-seekers in camps while waiting for their applications to be processed and the interception of ships carrying asylum-seekers off the coast of Australia and their diversion to Pacific Islands for processing. The Australian government built immigration detention centres both on its territory and abroad. Asylum-seekers were interned on the Australian territory of Christmas Island, a remote island in the Indian Ocean located about 1800 kilometres from Western Australia. Offshore refugee centres were also built on Mauru and on Manus Island, in Papua New Guinea, to detain asylum-seekers until their applications were processed. Finally, the Australian Federal Police (AFP) and the Australian Defence Force (ADF) increased their capabilities to ensure border and domestic security against people smuggling, terrorism, and other threats.

Securitization of drug trafficking

The securitization of the illicit trafficking and abuse of drugs has become a recurrent event. Drug trafficking is a transnational criminal activity and is probably the largest international crime problem in the world. The global trade of illicit drugs is believed to be worth as much as US$400 billion a year. Drug trafficking is connected to other categories of transnational crime. It is the prime generator of money laundering and is linked to arms smuggling (drug dealers often outgun police forces), organized crime, corruption, illegal migration, and, in some cases, terrorism. Drug trafficking is viewed as a threat to societal security by increasing drug consumption and addiction, raising the level of violent crime, affecting the health of consumers, spreading HIV/**AIDS** through intravenous drug use, and undermining family structures. In addition to its social consequences, drug trafficking has significant economic and political effects. It creates shadow economies, distorts financial institutions, undermines national economies, and fuels the problem of money laundering. It also erodes the rule of law, promotes corruption, and undermines border security. This is examined in detail in Chapter 26.

The so-called war on drugs waged by Thailand in 2003 is an example of a securitizing act (Emmers 2004). The consumption of illicit drugs in the country is a dramatic problem that primarily involves young adults. The most serious trend in Thailand has been the rapid increase in the use of synthetic drugs. Besides the health and social consequences of illicit drug consumption, many in Thailand view the drug-trafficking activities coming from Burma as a significant national security issue. In response, the then Thai Prime Minister, Thaksin Shinawatra, declared war on drugs in February 2003, vowing to the Thai population to eliminate the narcotics problem within three months (see Key Quote 12.2). The prime minister stated at an anti-drugs event in late March 2003: 'The drugs problem is a threat to national security. Thus my government has declared war on drugs and placed drugs eradication as the nation's most urgent agenda' (BBC News 2003).

In this case of securitization, the referent objects were the national sovereignty and territorial integrity of Thailand (military and political security), the integrity and stability of the political system (political security), the Thai population (societal security), and the economic development and prosperity of the country (economic security). The securitizing actor was the Thai Prime Minister Thaksin Shinawatra and his government. See Key Quotes 12.2. Finally, the audience consisted of Thai public opinion (Emmers 2004).

Opinion polls indicated that the audience generally accepted the articulation of drug trafficking as a threat to Thailand's national security and its society as well as the need for it to be addressed through extraordinary measures. Repeated pollsters indicated strong public approval of the anti-drugs campaign. The audience therefore accepted the interpretation of events set forward by the securitizing actor and acknowledged the need for emergency action. According to the Copenhagen School, this indicates a successful act of securitization—the securitizing actor had used a discourse of security and an audience had been convinced by the existential threat posed by drug trafficking to the referent objects.

The war on drugs led to the implementation of extreme measures as well as to a series of abuses (Emmers 2004). The interior ministry, the police, and local authorities published blacklists of suspected drug producers, traffickers, and dealers. The blacklists were widely criticized in the media and by non-governmental organizations because of their lack of accuracy. This led to concern that the police might accuse innocent people of being drug producers or traffickers. It was also reported that more than 2,500 people had been killed primarily between February and April 2003. The Thai government blamed inter-gang warfare for most of the killings. Thaksin announced: 'It is bandits killing bandits' (quoted in Cochrane 2003: 35). Most of the killings were not investigated, nor did they lead to arrests. Human rights groups argued that a 'shoot-to-kill policy' had been put in place. They suspected the police of taking matters into their own hands and executing alleged traffickers as part of the war-on-drugs campaign. Despite domestic and international criticism of the extra-judicial killings, repeated polls indicated that Thai public opinion generally supported the implementation of extraordinary measures.

KEY POINTS

- The illicit trafficking and abuse of drugs has recurrently been securitized.
- Narcotics are viewed as a threat to political, societal, economic, and health security.
- Thailand declared war on drugs in 2003. The Thai population (audience) generally accepted the articulation of drug trafficking as a threat to Thailand and its society.
- The implementation of extraordinary measures led to abuses.

The war in Iraq and the failure of securitization

We have so far noted two cases of a completed act of securitization. This is not to say, however, that all moves of securitization succeed in convincing a specific audience on the existential nature of a threat. In fact, as mentioned, the Copenhagen School anticipates that some speech acts will fail to do so. Various

KEY QUOTES 12.2 Thaksin and the War on Drugs

'I am serious about taking action against drug traffickers. Government officials, police in particular, must take action too as these traffickers destroy youths' lives, ruin the economy and damage the country.'
Nation *(2004)*

'We must go after all traders and producers. They are not suitable to be part of our society. They deserve to be put in jail. Drug traders who fight back must be dealt with decisively.'
Tunyasiri (2003)

'Although we have destroyed most of the drug networks it does not mean that the drug problem is totally wiped out. They are like germs: they'll resurrect themselves when our body is weak.'
Agence France Presse *(2003)*

'But increasingly problems such as terrorism, in all kinds of form, the trafficking of narcotic drugs, or even the SARS epidemic have equally threatened our security, especially our national economic security. The latter represents the kind of non-traditional threats to security that could strike at the very heart of any nation. Because what these threats often aim at is to destroy the economic confidence of a nation. Confidence, being the most important component of a successful economy, once destroyed or even seriously impaired, could drive the whole economy to total collapse.'
Shinawatra (2003)

empirical studies have examined the attempt by US President George W. Bush and British Prime Minister Tony Blair to securitize the Saddam Hussein regime as a means to justify the war in Iraq (Roe 2008; Hayes 2011). It can be argued, however, that the attempt failed to convince the international community of the existential threat posed by Saddam Hussein. Alternatively, the international community might have been convinced that the Iraqi regime constituted a security threat but disagreed with the adoption of extraordinary measures to secure regime change in Iraq (see Roe 2008 in the context of the United Kingdom).

In his State of the Union address on 29 January 2002, President Bush had already characterized Iraq together with North Korea and Iran as an 'axis of evil' (see Key Quote 12.3). The US administration later sought to justify the removal of Saddam Hussein through military force by linking the issue of international terrorism to the threat of the proliferation of weapons of mass destruction (WMD). The language of security was therefore utilized to justify the need for the implementation of emergency and extraordinary measures (the immediate use of military force to dispose of a foreign regime). See Key Quotes 12.3. In the meantime, critics of the American position questioned Iraq's WMD capabilities and the accuracy of its immediate threat to international peace and stability. The WMD capabilities of Iraq were also said to be less than those of Libya, North Korea, or Iran.

Opponents to the use of military force called for a diplomatic resolution to the crisis through efforts at the United Nations (UN). The UN Security Council adopted, in November 2002, a new resolution that allowed UN inspectors to go back to Iraq and search for WMD after a four-year absence. In early 2003, Mr Hans Blix, head of the UN weapons inspectors, pointed out that Iraq had failed to cooperate pro-actively. Yet he also announced that, in the two months of inspections in Iraq, his team had not found any WMDs, or, in the parlance of the time, a 'smoking gun'. In the meantime, the military build-up continued in the Gulf, with the US and British military sending more and more troops and equipment.

The opposition to the war was not limited to a diplomatic level but was characterized instead by a broad popular movement. Although the United Kingdom was a key member of the US coalition, the wider UK population did not accept the government's speech act describing Saddam Hussein's regime as an existential threat to international peace. This was indicated by opinion polls as well as by massive and repeated demonstrations against the war. Aware that they would not be able to get a UN mandate to attack Iraq, the United States and the United Kingdom launched Operation Iraqi Freedom on 20 March 2003. The opposition to the war remained particularly strong in most parts of the world. Even after the start of the hostilities, the US administration and the British government failed to convince the wider international community of the necessity and legitimacy of the conflict. The continuing demonstrations against the war reflected these elites' lack of legitimacy and perceived abuse of power.

KEY QUOTES 12.3 Bush and the Iraq War

'Iraq is the latest battlefield in this war. Many terrorists who kill innocent men, women and children on the streets of Baghdad are followers of the same murderous ideology that took the lives of our citizens in New York, in Washington, and Pennsylvania. There is only one course of action against them: to defeat them abroad before they attack us at home.'

President Addresses Nation, Discusses Iraq, War on Terror, Fort Bragg, North Carolina. 28 June 2005, http://georgewbush-whitehouse.archives.gov/news/releases/2002/10/20021007-8.html

'The threat comes from Iraq. It arises directly from the Iraqi regime's own actions—its history of aggression, and its drive toward an arsenal of terror. Eleven years ago, as a condition for ending the Persian Gulf War, the Iraqi regime was required to destroy its weapons of mass destruction, to cease all development of such weapons, and to stop all support for terrorist groups. The Iraqi regime has violated all of those obligations. It possesses and produces chemical and biological weapons. It is seeking nuclear weapons. It has given shelter and support to terrorism, and practices terror against its own people. The entire world has witnessed Iraq's eleven-year history of defiance, deception and bad faith.'

President Bush Outlines Iraqi Threat, Remarks by the President on Iraq Cincinnati Museum Center–Cincinnati Union Terminal, Cincinnati, Ohio. 7 October 2002, http://www.whitehouse.gov/briefing-room/

'While there are many dangers in the world, the threat from Iraq stands alone—because it gathers the most serious dangers of our age in one place. Iraq's weapons of mass destruction are controlled by a murderous tyrant who has already used chemical weapons to kill thousands of people. This same tyrant has tried to dominate the Middle East, has invaded and brutally occupied a small neighbour, has struck other nations without warning, and holds an unrelenting hostility toward the United States.'

President Bush Outlines Iraqi Threat, Remarks by the President on Iraq Cincinnati Museum Center–Cincinnati Union Terminal, Cincinnati, Ohio. 7 October 2002, http://www.whitehouse.gov/briefing-room/

Some scholars have made the assertion that the Iraq War was a successful case of securitization given that the political leaders involved, primarily George W. Bush and Tony Blair, managed to convince a key audience (i.e. the US Congress and the UK Parliament) of the use of extraordinary measures (i.e. engaging in war). Indeed, the speech act was specifically designated to convince the US and UK legislature. Hence, one can argue that the act of securitization was completed because the securitizing actor was successful in convincing its formal or target audience. One must note, however, that the Bush administration and their allies had failed to obtain support and approval from other relevant audiences, including the UN Security Council and the broader international community. Securitizing actors should seek to convince as wide an audience as possible and garner both formal and moral support from their public opinions as well as from domestic and international institutions (Balzacq 2005). A failure to do so affects the credibility of the securitizing act. In the case of the Iraq War, whereas the US Congress and UK Parliament had provided formal support by authorizing the use of force, the broader international community remained unconvinced, as exemplified by the 15 February 2003 anti-war protests in which millions of people in up to sixty countries took part in rallies and marches to demonstrate their opposition to military action against Iraq. The failure to convince this wider audience proved detrimental and suggests that the process of securitization may have failed to move beyond its first stage.

KEY POINTS

- Moves of securitization can fail. This results from the audience rejecting the speech act articulated by the securitizing actor.
- A distinction can be made between a formal and a moral audience.
- US President George W. Bush and British Prime Minister Tony Blair arguably failed to convince the international community of the existential threat posed by Iraqi President Saddam Hussein.
- Members of the coalition sought to justify the military removal of Saddam Hussein linking the issues of international terrorism and the proliferation of WMD.
- The linkage was not accepted by most other members of the UN Security Council, nor by the wider international community.

Conclusion

The Copenhagen School, and its securitization model, is a framework for security studies that encapsulates both state security and **non-traditional security** concerns. It allows for non-military matters to be included in security studies while offering a coherent understanding of the concept of security. It provides a framework to determine how, why, and by whom a specific matter becomes securitized, and thus succeeds in distinguishing security and non-security threats. The securitization and desecuritization model makes it possible to adopt a broader conceptualization of security without losing the central coherence of the term. In that respect, the Copenhagen School greatly contributes to the security studies literature.

The Copenhagen School structures its securitization model around a series of salient questions and steps. First, it asks who the securitizing actors might be—those who initiate a move of securitization through the speech act. These include not only policy makers or bureaucracies, but also transnational actors (international institutions, non-state actors, civil society), and even individuals. Second, who or what is to be protected? States and governments are no longer the sole referent objects of security, as individuals, communities, economies, ecosystems, and others are all alternative referents for security. Third, from what kinds of threats are the referent objects to be protected? The security concern must be articulated as an existential threat, thus linking the concept of security to the question of survival. Fourth, who decides on what is a security issue? The act of securitization is completed only once a relevant audience (public opinion, politicians, military officers, or other elites) is convinced that the so-called security issue represents an existential threat to the referent object. Finally, what means are to be used to tackle the existential threat? Once the act of securitization is completed, extraordinary measures can be imposed that go beyond rules ordinarily abided by. The emergency measures are thus located outside the normal bounds of political procedures.

Nonetheless, the chapter has also stressed the dangers of securitization, particularly in an undemocratic political system where the wider population is unable to reject an illegitimate speech act and the emergency measures adopted as a result. Even in democratic societies, there is the risk of an act of securitization leading to the curbing of well-established civil liberties in the name of security. This is especially relevant in a post-9/11 context and the growing articulation of issues as existential threats. The pejorative and possibly negative connotations of securitizing an issue have been stressed through several illustrations as well as the preference for a desecuritizing approach. Finally, the chapter has highlighted some of the shortcomings of the Copenhagen School and its securitization model. These include the Eurocentric nature of the Copenhagen School and the blurred distinction between securitization and politicization.

? QUESTIONS

1. Why are some issues considered as security questions while others are not?
2. How is a process of securitization completed?
3. Is an act of securitization generally dominated by powerful actors? Why?
4. Is securitization more likely to succeed in authoritarian states? Why?
5. What are the benefits of securitizing or desecuritizing an issue?
6. Assess the dangers of securitization.
7. What are some of the shortcomings of the securitization model?
8. How is drug trafficking a national security problem?
9. Did the process of securitization fail in the case of Iraq? Why?

FURTHER READING

- Doty, R. L. (1999), 'Immigration and the Politics of Security', *Security Studies*, 8/2–3: 71–93. The article offers 'lenses' for understanding security, arguing that a one-dimensional understanding of security is inadequate for both scholars and policy makers.
- Hansen, L. (2000), 'The Little Mermaid's Silent Security Dilemma and the Absence of Gender in the Copenhagen School', *Millennium: Journal of International Studies*, 29/2: 285–306. This paper presents a critique of the Copenhagen School by raising gender issues and other blind spots of securitization.
- Kenney, M. (2003), 'From Pablo to Osama: Counter-Terrorism Lessons from the War on Drugs', *Survival*, 45/3: 187–206. The author looks at lessons from the war on drugs and suggests the need for policy makers to address the 'demand side' of terrorism in the war on terror.
- Matthews, J. T. (1989), 'Redefining Security', *Foreign Affairs*, 68/2: 162–77. This essay argues for a redefinition of national security that incorporates resource, environmental, and demographic issues.
- Rudolph, C. (2003), 'Security and the Political Economy of International Migration', *American Political Science Review*, 97/4: 603–20. The article examines how migration affects the security of four advanced industrial states, namely the United States, Germany, France, and the United Kingdom.
- Salehi, R. and Ali, S. H. (2006), 'The Social and Political Context of Disease Outbreaks: The Case of SARS in Toronto', *Canadian Public Policy*, 32/4: 373–85. This paper addresses the impact of government policies and politics on the diffusion as well as transmission of the Severe Acute Respiratory Syndrome Coronavirus (SARS-S-CoV) within a local Toronto context.

IMPORTANT WEBSITE

- **http://www.rsis.edu.sg/research/nts-centre/** This website contains information about the Centre for Non-Traditional Security Studies at the S. Rajaratnam School of International Studies (RSIS), Nanyang Technological University, Singapore. It is an information hub for policy makers and academics working on non-traditional security and offers analytical tools by analysing the dynamics of securitization and desecuritization.

Visit the Online Resource Centre that accompanies this book for lots of interesting additional material: www.oxfordtextbooks.co.uk/orc/collins4e/

PART 2

Deepening and Broadening Security

13

Military Security

Michael Sheehan

Chapter Contents

Reader's Guide

This chapter examines the continuing importance of military security. It notes that international relations has historically seen security almost entirely in terms of the military dimension, before going on to review the impact of the broadening of the concept of security on approaches to the study of its military dimension. It then analyses the key aspects of the traditional approach to military security and some of the most common ways in which states have sought to acquire it historically, such as war, alliances, and, more recently, nuclear deterrence. The chapter then reflects on some of the difficulties in acquiring military security, and ways in which its pursuit can sometimes reduce, rather than increase, security, before concluding with a reminder of the continuing centrality of military security, even within a significantly broadened understanding of security as a multifaceted concept.

Introduction

Attention to issues of military security has always been central to the discipline of international relations. A preoccupation with the study of war after 1919 was foundational to the emergence of International Relations as a university discipline in the first place. The catastrophe of the Second World War, and the almost immediate outbreak of the Cold War meant that in the subsequent decades, security was defined very narrowly, being seen almost entirely in terms of 'national' or military security. Although Buzan (1991a: 7) has argued that security is an 'essentially contested concept', this was not really the case during the Cold War, during which there was a consensus that it related to military threats to the state posed by the military capabilities of adversaries. In practice, during this period, security studies was synonymous with strategic studies. States were seen as entities that provided 'collective goods' to their citizens, of which the most important was freedom from external attack (Kapstein 1992: 14).

Even with the emergence of a broader understanding of security at the end of the Cold War, a focus on military security remained fundamental and it was one of the five core sectors of the broader security conception advocated by the Copenhagen School. In this wider, sectoral understanding, military security was defined as 'the two-level interplay of the armed offensive and defensive capabilities of states, and states perceptions of each other's intentions' (Buzan et al. 1998: 51). This, however, is more a description of the method for attaining military security, rather than a description of the objective or desired outcome, which is covered in an earlier assertion that the military security agenda revolves largely around 'the ability of governments to maintain themselves against internal and external military threats, but it can also involve the use of military power to defend states or governments against non-military threats to their existence' (1998: 50).

The tendency to focus on the means, rather than the ends, of military security is typical in security studies. However as Baldwin has noted, Clausewitz's statement that war was a continuation of politics was an insistence that 'military force should be understood in the context of the purposes it serves' (1995: 103).

In this regard, military security is clearly the focus of strategic studies, that is, the study of the relationship between the pursuit and possession of military power and the achievement of political objectives, and of the use of military force to advance one's own political agenda and frustrate those of other states or substate actors. Thus, while military power can be used to supplement policing, emergency service, and intelligence capabilities in dealing with non-military threats, its distinctive identity as a security sector refers to the use, or threatened use of national and allied military capabilities to achieve political-military goals in international relations, and to frustrate the efforts of other national or international actors to impose their own political agenda through the threat or use of their military capabilities.

Approaches to military security

Military issues continue to be paramount, because 'a state and its society can be, in their own terms, secure in the political, economic, societal and environmental dimensions, and yet all of these accomplishments can be undone by military failure' (Buzan 1991b: 35). Military forces capable of defending the country and supporting its foreign policy remain central to state security. It therefore remains a priority in terms of the attention paid to it by International Relations as an academic discipline.

In the traditional approach, security is a military phenomenon, military capabilities take priority in governments' budgetary allocations, and the projection and **deterrence** of military force is central to understanding the workings of international politics. The absolute primacy given to the pursuit of military security for most of the Cold War period needs to be explained, because prior to the Second World War, and even during the first few years of the Cold War, this was not an automatic assumption of international relations scholars. During this period, security was seen as one among several goals pursued by states and the importance attached to it could vary from state to state, depending on their circumstances. In addition, international relations analysts did not automatically assume that the use of the military instrument should be prioritized over the other instruments of influence available to states, such as diplomacy and economic inducements. Military power was seen as a tool to be used, either in isolation, or more usually, in combination with other techniques, only when it was clear that alternative approaches were unlikely to succeed.

As the Cold War progressed, however, the increasingly dominant realist paradigm promoted the pursuit of security as the primary duty of governments, and the view that military security took priority over all other goals. The justification for this prioritization was a set of interrelated arguments that gave a special status and meaning to military security and did so in such a way that it clearly trumped all other state objectives and forms of security. In the first place, military security challenges were seen as being of a fundamentally distinctive and immediately threatening character because they involved the threat or use of force (Buzan 1983: 76). If insecurity is seen as being defined by perceived threats to cherished values, then deliberate military attacks on a state's population or infrastructure clearly represent an immediate and unambiguous security threat. The reality of such dangers is seen in the fact that in the past two centuries more than a quarter of the states in the international system have ceased to exist at some point, making the requirement to prioritize military security an obvious one for states (Fazal 2004).

Second, the existence of military security was seen as being necessary in order to allow other forms of security such as economic or societal security to be pursued behind its protective shield. Such military security was also vital because it made possible the political independence that allowed governments the freedom to choose between competing goals, including which security goals they wished to pursue, and with what resources. A state that was dominated by or occupied by another would no longer be in a position to independently make such critical choices.

Third, the death and destruction endured by a state in wartime could frustrate the pursuit of other goals, but also undo the historic achievements it had already made (Buzan 1991b: 35). For all these reasons, realists argued that it made sense for governments to give military security absolute priority.

In an early realist contribution to the study of national security, Arnold Wolfers (1962: 150) noted that threats can result from a psychological construction as well as an empirical reality. Wolfers pointed out that 'security, in an objective sense, measures the absence of threats to acquired values, in a subjective sense, the absence of fear that such values will be attacked'. His insight was not followed up for several decades, which was unfortunate, since it opens the analysis to a more social-constructivist understanding of security in all its forms. Military insecurity can be an objective reality which states must acquire capabilities to address. But it is also subjective. For example, Finland would not be alarmed by Swedish defence acquisitions, whereas it might well be by a similar build-up by Russia. Similarly, the armed forces of the United States do not alarm Canada. Historical experience and contemporary political relations contextualize the meanings of these actions for the different states. In a real sense the notion of 'security' has no meaning in and of itself. It is a 'floating signifier', a socially constructed understanding that has a particular meaning only in relation to other assumptions and understandings. During the Cold War, for example, the superpowers saw their adversary as a primary and absolute military threat and this shaped how they interpreted all other developments in international relations, legitimized a very particular international order, and influenced their interpretation of their own ideological and ethical ideas and behaviour.

It is possible to study military security through non-realist analytical lenses, however. Rather than making the realist assumption that the structural realities of the international system are a given, which define the need for particular forms of military capability and policy, it is possible to adopt a social-constructivist approach, which sees all human reality as the product of human interaction and capable of being interpreted in different ways, and altered by human actions. In this approach, cultural factors and **norms** become central to the analysis (Adler and Barnett 1998). It is also important to be aware that the security of the state is an essential, but not always sufficient, condition for making its citizens secure.

Snyder (1977) introduced the concept of **strategic culture** in understanding the way that countries formulate and implement military-security policies. In contrast to the structuralist approach of neorealism, Snyder argued that societies' beliefs and historical behaviour patterns are crucial for understanding their policy decisions. Factors such as the continuing influence of national myths and social and political norms (Wendt 1996) help shape the boundaries of what a government considers vital or not, acceptable or not, achievable or not, urgent or not, and influences the manner in which governments seek to implement their policy choices.

In the post-9/11 world, ontology is changing. In the past forty years, the major powers have seen their military security challenged by non-state actors, such as terrorist organizations, rather than by the military forces of other states. In their wars on terror, both the United States and Israel have deployed their armed forces abroad in large-scale military operations: the USA in Afghanistan (post-2001) and Israel in Lebanon (2006) and Palestine (2009), where the operations were directed not against the armed forces of those states, or to secure the territory, but in pursuit of sub-state **insurgent** or terrorist forces (Al-Qaeda, Hisbollah, and Hamas). In Colombia, US forces have been operating against insurgent forces linked with the international drugs trade. This is a very different use of military capability from the realist state-to-state logic, although the use of military forces in the counter-insurgency role has a long historical pedigree. Prior to the development of national police forces in the nineteenth century, the military were the only force the state had at its disposal for such purposes.

Constructing 'military security' as solely relative to threats to a state or population emanating from the armed forces of other states is also problematic because in many parts of the world, the 'military security' threat facing a population, and sometimes facing the national government, is not the armed forces of neighbouring states, but those of the state itself. The 'threat' to states such as Argentina, Chile, Greece, South Korea, Nigeria, Pakistan, and many others in recent decades has been military coups against the national government, followed by long periods of brutal military dictatorship. In these circumstances, the 'military insecurity' felt by a population would originate from the actions of its own national armed forces rather than those of another state. The cosy assumption that a state needs to maximize its own military capabilities to face external threats safely takes no account of these realities. In 1948, Costa Rica abolished its armed forces in recognition of the fact that they, not those of other countries, were the real threat.

Focusing on the population rather than the state is typical of the social constructivist approach, which highlights the implications of notions of 'identity' for military security. Where realism sees identities as essentially fixed, the social constructivist approach sees them as being more fluid, and this has important implications for the use of force in international relations. Conflict can be the forge in which national identity is formed, rather than a struggle between pre-existing rival identities, as Campbell (1998b) argues was the case during the Bosnian War in the early 1990s. Campbell (1992) in fact insists that the state itself is constructed through the practice of pursuing militarized security against real or imagined external threats.

The social constructivist approach to security is useful because, in Onuf's words (1989), the international system is 'a world of our making'. The meaning that governments and individuals attach to events is crucial—for example, President George W. Bush seeing the 9/11 attacks as part of a war rather than a terrorist attack requiring a policing response, or the way in which the understanding of 'child soldiers' has evolved in recent decades, or whether the conflict in Bosnia was a 'civil war' or an 'invasion'. The socially constructed meanings societies give to events shape the way they respond to them, and interpretations of 'national interest' are crucial in underpinning national security policies.

Governments can choose to 'securitize' certain issues and not others (see Chapter 12 for more on securitization). The decision about whether or not to place an issue within the military-security discourse will reflect the political objectives of those promoting the move. Militarization (in the conceptual sense), like theory, is 'always for someone and for some purpose'. It is not a politically neutral step; it will be taken because it advances the objectives of an influential group within the national polity.

KEY POINTS

- Military security has historically been prioritized by governments ahead of other objectives.
- Military security has both an objective and a subjective dimension.
- While realist approaches have dominated the study of military security, other approaches, such as constructivism, can also be employed.

Traditional military-security studies

Prior to the expanding of the definition, security was understood in overwhelmingly military terms and was seen as meaning 'military protection against the threats posed by the armed forces of other states'. It was further assumed that the referent object of security, the thing that needed to be made secure, was the state. Thus, military security was about identifying actual and potential military threats from other states, and coping with them, either by acquiring sufficient levels of appropriate military capability oneself, or by allying with other states that possessed such a capability. The ultimate mechanism for maintaining security was the resort to war. Thus Lippmann (1943: 51) argued that 'a nation is secure to the extent to which it is not in danger of having to sacrifice core values, if it wishes to avoid war, and is able, if challenged, to maintain them by victory in such a war'. The study of military security is, therefore, the central concern of strategic studies, and one of the central concerns of security studies. In this regard, one can think of security studies as a subset of international relations, and strategic studies as a subset of security studies, the latter focusing solely on the military dimension of security in terms of the threat and use of force to achieve political objectives.

For traditionalists, the requirement for governments to focus their attention on military rather than other forms of security was seen as being a result of the structure of the international system. For traditional realists, the key element of the system is that it is an anarchy—that is, there is no world government. States are therefore obliged to produce their military security through their own efforts, and these efforts will seem threatening to other states in the system, causing them to respond in kind, and triggering an arms race spiral as a result of this '**security dilemma**' (see Key Quotes 13.1). This produces what Snow (1991: 1) called the 'violent peace'. John Herz (1950: 158), who originated the term 'security dilemma', argued that it had crucial domestic as well as international implications because it resulted in 'power-political, oligarchic, authoritarian and similar trends and tendencies in society'. In this regard it has implications for the other security sectors as well, particularly political and societal security.

This was important, because the **traditional security** approach assumed that the domestic political order was stable and essentially peaceful, whereas there was an arena of 'necessity, contingency and violence beyond the state' (Dalby 1992b: 105). In reality, the boundaries of military security are themselves necessarily somewhat fluid. Since the perception of a 'threat' implies the recognition of vulnerabilities, military security must encompass internal elements such as actual or potential insurgencies and terrorism, ideological division, nationalist pressures, in fact any 'national weaknesses that might be exploited by an enemy' (Freedman 1992: 754). Moreover, states tend to define 'threats' not just in terms of existential dangers to the country, but also of actions by other states or actors which frustrate certain foreign policy objectives.

KEY QUOTES 13.1 The security dilemma

'When states seek the ability to defend themselves, they get too much and too little—too much because they gain the ability to carry out aggression; too little because others, being menaced, will increase their own arms and so reduce the first state's security. Unless the requirements for offence and defence differ in kind or amount, a status quo power will desire a military posture that resembles that of an aggressor. For this reason others cannot infer from its military forces and preparations whether the state is aggressive. States therefore assume the worst. The other's intentions must be co-extensive with his capabilities.'

Jervis (1991: 92–3)

As well as this specific ontology (understanding of what it was that was being studied), traditional military security studies also operated with a very particular positivist epistemology (or understanding of what constituted legitimate knowledge). This was based upon empiricism, naturalism, and objectivism (Smith 1996: 18). A 'scientific objectivism' was held to be characteristic of the way that military security issues were studied (Wyn Jones 1996). Military security theorists assumed that the scientific method was applicable both to the natural and the social worlds (naturalism), and that it was possible for security analysts to remain objective by distinguishing between 'facts' and 'values' (objectivism). Finally, analysis, following the scientific method, would proceed through empirical validation or falsification. The 'real world' would be investigated, without bias or ideology influencing the results. As outlined by Walt (1991: 222), 'security studies seeks *cumulative* knowledge about the role of military force. To obtain it, the field must follow the standard canons of scientific research.' The study of military security is in this sense seen as a search for 'truth'.

Although security realism is often contrasted with idealism, there are idealistic elements within the realist world view in this regard. As Reus-Smit (1992: 17) notes, many traditional security specialists effectively see the state as an 'idealized political community', where the survival and well-being of the population as a whole is aggregated into a minimalist notion of state security. It is this assumption that allows Buzan (1991a: 328), for example, to claim that 'national security subsumes all other security considerations'. For critics such as Booth (1991: 320) this is illogical, since it gives priority to 'the security of the means as opposed to the security of the ends'.

Military power is relative to the situation in which a state tries to use it. It was a fatal error by Iraq under Saddam Hussein to think that, because its army performed well against Iran, it was capable of standing up to the forces of the United States. How much military capability is deemed to be enough depends partly on what threats exist, and partly on what a state wishes to do with its military capabilities, both in terms of its overall defence strategy and on whether it sees the security of other states as also crucial to its own security, and thereby feels a need for power projection capabilities.

For most of the Cold War period, therefore, thinking about security in the heavily armed states of the developed world focused not on security in a broad sense, but rather on what were seen to be the requirements for maintaining the **balance of power** in the nuclear age, through policies of deterrence, **alliance** formation, and force projection. These ideas were reflected in the writings of key scholars such as Kissinger (1956), Brodie (1959), and Schelling (1960b).

More recently, contributors to realist thinking have divided into somewhat different *contemporary* realist approaches that have differing assumptions on the implications of the security dilemma for military security. Offensive realism operates with a traditional interpretation of the security dilemma, in which rivalry and conflict are inevitable. Defensive realists, in contrast, do not assume that the international anarchy always leads to conflict. It can often produce relatively peaceful areas of the world, where states do not face any insurmountable military security threats, so that major external military dangers are seen as exceptional and unusual, rather than the norm (Rose 1998: 149).

KEY POINTS

- Traditional security approaches focused on military threats posed to the state in an environment characterized by the security dilemma.
- Security specialists used a positivist methodology, emphasizing the scientific method.
- Post-Cold War realists have divided into groups with differing assumptions about the implications of the security dilemma.

War

States acquire and maintain military capabilities ultimately because they face the possibility of war. The problem of war has always been foundational to the study of international relations and central to security studies. Security studies has always operated with a Clausewitzian perspective on war: that war is not a social aberration or mass psychological disorder, but rather is simply a rational instrument of policy, in the same way as diplomacy or economic sanctions. It is a continuation of politics by other means. War, according to Clausewitz, is a political activity, 'intended to compel our opponent to fulfil our will'. It is simply a brutal form of bargaining.

This was a major reason why planning for massive use of nuclear weapons during the Cold War was so controversial. The absolute destruction of *both* sides' populations and infrastructure that would be likely in such a war broke with the Clausewitzian logic of war as a rational instrument of policy that had dominated Western thinking about warfare for a century. An unlimited level of violence and destruction meant that war was no longer a political act because there was no longer a clear linkage between the level and type of violence being employed, and the political objectives being pursued.

In the 1970s, and again in the 1990s, it became fashionable in some academic circles to argue that war was on the decline and the use of military force as a foreign-policy instrument was increasingly unattractive for states. Most of this writing originated in America and Western Europe, two areas of the international system that had certainly become less dangerous environments since the end of the Second World War.

Advocates of this logic argued that foreign-policy objectives had become more intangible, that there was less emphasis on territorial expansion and more emphasis on trade. States now sought to win friends and influence people, rather than to invade and occupy their territories. Nuclear weapons had proved to be effectively unusable, great powers had failed dismally to achieve their military objectives in wars in Vietnam (the USA) and Afghanistan (the USSR), and the international system seemed dominated by states with major constraints on their armed forces, such as Germany and Japan. Some went so far as to suggest that, at least between the major powers, war was becoming obsolete.

Certainly war is a risky option to resort to. Of all wars occurring between 1815 and 1910, 80 per cent were won by the governments that started them. But 60 per cent of the wars between 1910 and 1965 were lost by the initiating state. But, in the post-Cold War period, war does not seem to have lost its salience for military security. The debates about it have rather been concerned with the nature of the wars that have taken place and the implications of revolutionary developments in military technology.

The changing character of military capabilities clearly has encouraged an evolution in the *forms* of warfare characteristic of engagements between the major powers. The period 1861–1945 was characterized by the move to full-scale industrialization of warfare and the consolidation of the modern nation state. These two processes led to the emergence of a form of warfare in which all the human and material resources of the state were mobilized to support the war effort, and the entire human and material resources of the opponent were deemed legitimate targets in wartime. The catastrophic consequences of these logics were seen in the Second World War and the advent of nuclear weapons led to the emergence of the belief that this form of unrestrained great power warfare was no longer a cost-effective instrument of policy. Military security could not be attained with such a suicidal method. The major powers reacted to this situation not by abstaining from war altogether, but by avoiding direct military conflict between each other, and developing new forms of limited war to allow them to pursue their military security objectives.

One area of debate has concerned the question of whether or not a 'revolution in military affairs' (RMA) has been underway in the post-Cold War period. The term revolution suggests a sudden and radical break with the past, and it has been suggested that the technological superiority of American military forces revealed in the 1991 Gulf War showed that just such a revolution had occurred. This interpretation placed great emphasis on technological developments. However, sceptics such as Lambert have cautioned against overemphasizing the significance of technological change, while underestimating the importance of changes in doctrine and organization.

Kaldor and Münkler have engaged with the issue of whether the wars typical of the post-Cold War period differ in form sufficiently from previous eras that they can be termed 'new wars'. While Kaldor (1999), argues that such wars are indeed a new phenomenon, Münkler (2005) disagrees, arguing that such a view lacks historical depth, but that a 'new terrorism' is the central challenge facing contemporary states.

In the 'new wars' thesis, identity politics are central to the explanation of political violence. Kaldor argues that the conflicts typical of the post-Cold War period have been struggles to control the state in order to assert a particular understanding of national identity. A feature of such conflicts is that they are internal to the state, taking the form of insurgencies and civil wars. They therefore lend themselves to a constructivist analysis, rather than a traditional analysis of military security.

KEY POINTS

- War remains a legitimate instrument of national policy for states.
- War between the major powers risks consequences that have dramatically reduced its attractiveness.
- Technological and doctrinal changes may be driving a revolution in military affairs.
- Since 1991, the dominant form of warfare has been intra-state rather than inter-state.

Alliances and neutrality

One method of acquiring military security is to become a member of a military alliance. Security analysis has thus historically also paid attention to the issues relating to the attractiveness or otherwise of alliance membership, usually linking it to structural realist explanations of international politics (Waltz 1979; Gilpin 1981). Most of the scholarly analysis of alliance theory was conducted during the Cold War, but there has been a smaller literature since then exploring the implications of unipolarity for alliance systems and tracking the changes in alliance forms since 1991. Historically, alliances have been seen as a way to overcome national resource constraints in order to maximize military security. States will seek membership of an alliance if they believe that their own resources are inadequate to maintain their sovereignty and security, and will make common cause with states that share their goals, or at least perceive similar threats. Alliance formation is particularly notable when a potential hegemonic power threatens the other states in the system. Alliance theories are therefore often linked to balance-of-power theory. While some scholars argue that states automatically ally to 'balance' against a threatening state (Walt 1987), others argue that states are just as likely to 'bandwagon'—that is, to ally with the likely winning hegemon. In practice, the reasons for joining alliances vary widely.

More powerful states may also create alliances in order to extend their protective umbrella over weaker friendly states. Alliances are often seen by members not so much as essential tools for balancing against a potential hegemon, but rather as mechanisms for exercising influence over allies, whose own military security policies may increase the dangers to their allies—for example, by drawing them into confrontations or expeditionary commitments against third parties. They allow states to restrain or exert pressure on states within the alliance framework (Osgood 1968; Ikenberry 2000). While the idea that states prefer to join alliances with states that share common cultures or ideologies appears logical, such 'affinity theories' have not been confirmed by detailed studies of alliance formation (Russett 1971; Walt 1987).

The obligations assumed as members of an alliance vary significantly between organizations, although definitions of alliances normally require that they involve a formal commitment by the participating states (Miller and Toritsyn 2004/2005). Because of its size and longevity, NATO can sometimes be seen as a 'typical' alliance (see Case Study 13.1). In reality it is a very unusual alliance, completely unlike most others in history. Alliances vary in terms of issues that cause them to be created, the situations in which military commitments are triggered, the degree of military integration that takes place within the alliance, the numbers of allies, the geographical scope of the alliance, and many other factors.

Most military alliances are assembled for the purpose of waging war, and end when the war is concluded. Their purpose is to coordinate the allies' common war effort to maximum effect. Integration of forces is unusual. NATO is unusual, both in that it is a peacetime alliance and in that it has remained in existence for sixty years, outlasting the disappearance of all its original reasons for being created. Alliances tend to have brief existences because they require the harmonization of many conflicting interests, which becomes more difficult over long periods, particularly if there is not an overwhelming sense of commonly perceived external threat. In the post-Cold War period, the emergence of a unipolar international system has raised questions about whether or not alliances would remain a typical response to military insecurity, and to what extent they were being replaced by more ad hoc coalitions (Menon 2003; Campbell 2004), as well as how alliances might evolve in the new strategic geography of the post-Cold War world (Hansen 2000).

Critics of alliances argue that they contribute little to a state's military security, and are destabilizing for the international system. Wright (1965: 774) argued that they simply generate opposing alliances and are incompatible with collective security, since they promote a selective response to acts of aggression. However, Kegley and Raymond (1982) found that on balance alliances make a positive contribution to peace and security as long as the alliance structure is flexible and when alliance commitments are considered binding by the member states.

Nevertheless, a state is likely to avoid alliance membership if it feels strong enough to maintain its security unaided, or if it feels that its sovereignty will be compromised by alliance membership, or that the obligations and risks involved outweigh the potential benefits. Many states have historically sought security, not by joining alliances, but, on the contrary, by declaring neutral or non-aligned status. Occasionally **neutrality** is forced upon a state. Austria's neutral status was not a national political choice, but rather the price imposed by the superpowers in return for ending their military occupation and restoring Austrian sovereignty in 1955. Finnish neutrality was a conscious choice by Finland's government, but one taken in the knowledge that any other option would be likely to trigger a renewed Soviet invasion after 1945. Other states, such as Sweden, have seen neutrality as providing more security, sovereignty, and freedom than entry into a military alliance dominated by one or more of the great powers (Joenniemi 1988: 53). Neutrality does not come cheaply. Because they do not have access to the military capabilities of allied states, neutral countries typically have to maintain large armed forces and institute systems of national service.

Neutrality is a legal status. A neutral state must remain outside military alliances in peacetime, and refrain from activities that might seem to align it too closely with the members of any existing alliances. In return, its neutral status will (or at least should) be accepted by the belligerent states in wartime. In the post-Cold War period, collective security organizations have become more prominent than collective defence bodies, but, given that the systemic factors promoting

CASE STUDY 13.1 NATO

The North Atlantic Treaty Organization (NATO) was created in 1949 with the signing of the Washington Treaty. NATO is a military alliance that has expanded in the post-Cold War period and by 2009 comprised twenty-eight countries from North America and Europe. It was originally created as an insurance against a revival of German militarism after the Second World War and as a collective defence initiative against the perceived threat from the Soviet Union.

The key clause of the Washington Treaty is Article 5, which declares that each ally will treat an attack against one Ally as an attack against all and respond with its own military forces as if it itself had been attacked. Article 4 of the treaty ensures consultations among Allies on security matters of common interest. The NATO members routinely consult each other on security matters, a habit that has become ingrained over six decades since 1949. In the post-Cold War period, NATO expanded its remit and geographical zone of operations, to allow it to become a collective security organization, operating in counter-insurgency warfare in Afghanistan, as well as peacekeeping in Kosovo.

Although its longevity and political influence encourage a perception of NATO as a 'typical' alliance, in reality NATO is historically unique. In terms of the length of time it has existed, the fact that it has done so in peacetime, rather than wartime, the degree of military integration among its members, and a number of other factors, NATO is an institution without precedent or parallel in recorded human history.

alliance formation have changed little in the post-Cold War period, alliances are likely to remain important mechanisms by which states pursue military security (Snyder 1997: 78).

KEY POINTS

- Military security can be pursued unilaterally by relying on one's own capabilities, multilaterally via alliance membership, or unilaterally via a policy of neutrality.
- States join alliances to compensate for their own relative military weakness.
- Alliances vary significantly in terms of their membership, objectives, and obligations.
- Some states have historically preferred to remain neutral rather than join alliances.

Deterrence

For most of the Cold War period, not only did 'security' studies in the developed world focus almost exclusively on military security, but within that focus there was an enormous, if perhaps understandable, emphasis on the study of the issue of nuclear deterrence (see Key Quotes 13.2). The stress on deterrence occurred despite the fact that nuclear weapons were never actually employed in war during the Cold War.

Early writers on nuclear weapons believed that they would be a 'powerful inhibitor to aggression' and would lead military security policies to become designed to avert wars rather than to win them (Brodie 1946: 73). In practice, the impact of nuclear weapons was more complicated. They did act as an inhibitor of full-scale war between the nuclear-armed great powers during crises (Kennedy 1969), but had no impact on those states (the vast majority) that did not possess such weapons. The existence of nuclear weapons certainly encouraged superpower diplomatic caution during the Cold War, and also encouraged the superpowers to pursue **arms control**. But it also encouraged the development of a balance-of-power system that tried to limit the propensity for superpower military engagement worldwide, and stabilized a nuclear balance where the superpowers constantly strengthened themselves so as not to have to fight.

In terms of generating a sense of security, military power can serve a number of ends. Where feasible, defence is the goal that all states aim for first. If defence is not possible, deterrence is generally the next priority. The defensive use of military power revolves around two purposes. The first is to ward off an attack. Should this not succeed, the second purpose is to minimize the damage to oneself if attacked.

The deterrent use of military power works with a different logic. Deterrence is based upon the threat of retaliation. It seeks to prevent an adversary from doing something by threatening him with unacceptable punishment if he does it. The threat of retaliation or punishment is directed at the adversary's population or industrial infrastructure. It is effective only if the adversary is convinced you have both the will and the power to carry out the threat. Hence deterrence can be judged successful only if the retaliatory threat has not had to be carried out.

Nuclear weapons have paradoxically made those that possess them more militarily secure than any previous states in history, and more militarily insecure than any other states in history. Everything depends on the effectiveness of deterrence. Robert Art (1980: 22) argues that nuclear security buys conventional power projection capability: 'precisely because security can be bought so cheaply with nuclear weapons is each superpower able to use the bulk of its defence dollars on conventional forces, which can be readily employed and more finely tuned'.

Deterrence produces security not by physically obstructing a certain course of action, as defence does, but by threatening a response that makes the action seem disproportionately costly and therefore unattractive in the first place (Morgan 2006: 79–81). In practice, this is not entirely straightforward. Deterrence will work only if the threatened state clearly possesses the capability to inflict overwhelming retaliation, successfully convinces the adversary that it would be certain to do so if attacked, and is able to communicate clearly what is and is not acceptable within its deterrence doctrine. All these requirements are problematical in various ways. There are additional issues related to commitments to allies. Against a fellow nuclear-armed state, the willingness to use nuclear weapons is tantamount to committing suicide. Such a 'passive' deterrent threat may be credible when one's own population is threatened, but an 'active' deterrent threat, to follow the same course in defence of an ally, is much more difficult to make credible.

There are also clear moral issues. Actually to carry out the threat of retaliation is for a state to commit genocide against its enemies. This would be in breach of all existing laws of war, and the moral codes of all the world's major religions. Given social norms against **blackmail** and violent intimidation of other people, and particularly those who threaten violence against children, the old, or the helpless, it is debatable whether even the *threat* to use nuclear weapons is morally acceptable. Such issues spawned a large and lively scholarly literature (see, e.g., Elshtain 1992).

Michael McGuire argues that the 'theology' of deterrence encouraged the development of an arcane language that disguised the brutal realities of nuclear weapons' 'countervalue' rather than, say, city-targeting strikes. It also assumed a particular kind of worst-case analysis, where an enemy course of action needed only to be conceivable for it to be included in the threat assessment. Finally, because 'retaliation' actually meant genocidal mass murder of civilian populations, deterrence encouraged continual efforts to paint the adversary as a people deserving of such a terrible fate (McGuire 1986: 24–9). This critique is another example both of the importance of cultural determinants of military security thinking, and of the potential disjuncture between 'state' and 'population' logics when pursuing military security.

A number of authors have argued that the characteristics of the nuclear balance of power since the end of the Cold War are so different from the 1945–91 period that the world has now entered the Second Nuclear Age (Gray 1999; Walton 2013). In this new era, it is argued, the number of nuclear-weapons states will continue to increase, but the stability of deterrent relationships will decrease, so that a failure of deterrence and an outbreak of nuclear war becomes more likely.

KEY POINTS

- Nuclear deterrence theory dominated Cold War security studies.
- Nuclear deterrent relationships can increase and decrease security simultaneously.
- Deterrence has very different moral implications from policies based upon defence.
- The Cold War was the First Nuclear Age. The post-Cold War period may represent a Second Nuclear Age, with different implications for the pursuit of military security.

KEY QUOTES 13.2 Deterrence and defence

'Defence is possible without deterrence and deterrence is possible without defence. A state can have the military wherewithal to repel an invasion without also being able to threaten devastation to the invader's population or territory. Similarly, a state can have the wherewithal to credibly threaten an adversary with such devastation and yet be unable to repel his invading force. Defence, therefore, does not necessarily buy deterrence, nor deterrence defence. A state that can defend itself from attack, moreover, will have little need to develop the wherewithal to deter. If physical attacks can be repelled or if the damage from them drastically minimized, the incentive to develop a retaliatory capability is low. A state that cannot defend itself, however, will try to develop an effective deterrent if that be possible.'

Art (1980: 7)

Cooperative security and arms control

Traditional approaches to military security assume that the existence of international anarchy leads inevitably to the security dilemma. However, a number of scholars such as Wendt (1992: 407), have argued that while the anarchy may indeed exist, it is not inevitable that it should produce a security dilemma, and might indeed encourage cooperation among states. The operation of the security dilemma is a result of the practices of states, not of the structure of the system, and practices can change.

One example of states seeking to circumvent the difficulties of the security dilemma is through practices of cooperative security such as the pursuit of arms control and disarmament. A feature of the search for military security in the Cold War period was the pursuit of arms control. It was recognized that a purely adversarial relationship between nuclear-armed states was far too dangerous and that therefore efforts should be made to negotiate agreed constraints on military capability in certain areas, particularly with regard to weapons of mass destruction.

Arms control is a distinctive approach to the pursuit of military security because it involves both the deliberate acceptance of self-restraint in regard to the acquisition and deployment of weapons, and because it operates on the assumption that it is both possible and profitable to pursue security cooperatively with a potential military adversary. In the post-Cold War period, it has been increasingly associated with the concept of cooperative security, defined as 'a commitment to regulate the size, technical composition, investment patterns, and operational practices of all military forces by mutual consent for mutual benefit' (Larsen 2009: 3).

Classical disarmament theory assumed that weapons, rather than being a route to security, were a cause of insecurity. They were seen as both deepening tensions between states, and making them more likely to resort to the use of force in times of crisis (Claude 1964: 262–3). The solution was therefore to reduce armaments, thereby reducing tension. Booth (1975: 89) described this approach by paraphrasing Clausewitz as 'a continuation of politics by a reduction of military means'. Arms control is a more conservative approach to building military security, though it can lead to disarmament in the longer term. Arms controllers did not see weapons as producing insecurity merely by their existence. On the contrary, they believed that weaponry was a normal and acceptable part of international relations. The arms control community therefore promoted the creation and maintenance of balances of power in which arms control would complement unilateral force improvements as the route to military security (Lefever 1962: 122).

Arms control as an approach to military security sought to distinguish between 'those kinds and quantities of forces and weapons that promote the stability of the balance of power and those which do not; to tolerate or even to promote the former and to restrict the latter' (Bull 1961: 61). Thus while disarmament always implies weapon reductions, arms control may simply freeze numbers, or even increase them through mutual consent. Schelling and Halperin (1961: 2) defined the objectives of arms control as being 'reducing the likelihood of war, its scope and violence if it occurs, and the political and economic costs of being prepared for it'. In practice, however, subsequent decades of experience with arms control demonstrated that these objectives often conflicted with one another. Increasing the number of survivable nuclear weapons may make war less likely, but increases the cost of preparing for it, and the death and destruction if it occurs. Developing complex verification regimes reduces the likelihood of war, and the death and destruction if it occurs, but still increases the cost of being prepared for it.

One problem that policy makers encountered in subsequently implementing arms control was that politicians and the general public expected agreements to produce lowered numerical balances, what Krepon (1984: 130) called 'optical parity'. But, as Schelling (1985–6) pointed out, this reflected a shift from a concern with the *character* of weapons to an obsession with numbers. Bertram also argued that what is important is 'who could do what' rather than 'who had what'. But, from the point of view of economics and public perceptions, numbers are clearly important. Nevertheless, the arms control approach led to the conclusion of a large number of important agreements during the Cold War period, which can be held to have had a significant stabilizing function.

In the post-Cold War period, arms control lost momentum. A number of agreements were signed

CASE STUDY 13.2 The 'New START' Treaty

The New START Treaty between the Russian Federation and the United States was signed in Prague in April 2010 and entered into force in February 2011. It has a lifespan of ten years, but can be extended for a further five. It superseded the 1991 START Treaty signed at the end of the Cold War which reduced superpower strategic nuclear delivery systems to 1,600 each with a total of 6,000 warheads per country. New START reduces delivery systems to 700 each (with 100 in permitted non-operational reserve) and 1,550 deployed nuclear warheads. This represents a huge reduction from the 12,000 warheads each, on 2,500 delivery systems permitted under the 1979 SALT II Treaty. Unlike SALT and START, the New START has no sub-limits; each country can choose for itself how it wishes to divide its permitted total between inter-continental ballistic missiles (ICBMs), submarine-launched ballistic missiles (SLBMs), and bombers. New START continues the verification techniques pioneered in earlier treaties and also has mandates for eighteen on-site inspections per year. Every six months, the two countries exchange an updated database of their strategic nuclear holdings and facilities, and there is a continuous process of 'notifications' of treaty-relevant information to the other country. The treaty also obliges the signatories to hold 'exhibitions' showing new weapon systems, such as the US B-2A bomber and Russian RS-24 missile.

The USA and Russia have seven years in which to complete the New START reductions. By the end of the process US–Russian nuclear warheads will have fallen to their lowest level since the 1950s.

in the first half of the 1990s, but these represented the tidying-up of the Cold War agenda. They nevertheless established an important framework for cooperative security, particularly in Europe, and the implementation of the Chemical Weapons Convention and the START nuclear treaties led to massive reductions in the numbers of weapons held in each category (see Case Study 13.2). Nevertheless, arms control became less central both to the practice of military security after 1991 and to scholarly debates about the best way to sustain such security. The very different international political environment called for what Daalder (1993) described as 'threat deconstruction'. However, while progress largely halted in some areas, arms-control thinking was applied to some new areas, such as light weapons and to the issue of conventional weapons proliferation. Efforts to contain the proliferation of nuclear weapons also continued, with a new 'counterproliferation' emphasis on activities such as interdiction of transfers of components of weapons of mass destruction to hostile states and terrorist organizations and a renewed emphasis on defensive capabilities. This was evident in the 2002 United States National Security Strategy Document and in the 2003 Proliferation Security Initiative. An increasing number of intergovernmental organizations are involved in ad hoc initiatives to identify and block transportation of treaty-limited materials, so that the traditional term of 'arms control' may no longer accurately reflect state practices, which are more typically focused on more varied and flexible international security initiatives.

KEY POINTS

- Arms control has become an important cooperative dimension of efforts to acquire military security through mutual restraint.
- Arms control does not challenge the central role of weaponry and military power in the international system, but focuses on problems produced by specific weapon systems and relationships.
- In the post-Cold War period arms control lost much of its political salience, but remains a useful tool for pursuing security.

The cost of military security

Analysts of international relations have reflected not only on the nature of security and alternative military strategies for maximizing it, but also on the fact that some of these strategies can be self-defeating, or generate security problems in other dimensions of the broader security agenda. Military security is of a different moral order to the other security sectors. The right of a people to defend their independence and way of life by maintaining and, if necessary, employing military capabilities is recognized under international law. However, as Klaus Knorr (1970: 50) said 'military power is ultimately the power to destroy and kill, or to occupy and control, and hence to coerce', and it therefore has rather different implications to the pursuit of environmental security for example.

There are also economic and political issues. Military power can be acquired only by enormous effort in terms of the commitment of manpower and economic resources. All states struggle to acquire and maintain what they consider to be adequate military forces, and democratically elected governments therefore face particular difficulties in deciding upon the appropriate level of military capability. There are two main reasons for this. In the first place, such capability is extremely expensive to acquire, and high levels of defence spending may be unpopular, especially during a long period of peace. Defence spending generates 'opportunity costs', the value of the social good a government could not invest in because it chose to spend the money on military capabilities. When President Eisenhower was asked the cost of the latest American bomber, he replied that the cost was 'a modern brick school in more than thirty cities, or two fully equipped hospitals'.

Acquiring military security is neither simple nor straightforward. One issue that overlaps with issues of economic security is the question, not so much of how much military capability does a state *need* to be secure, but how much can it *afford*? States often acquire less military capability than they would ideally like. The costs of acquiring such capability are real. The demand for security is a normative demand; it is the pursuit of a particular value. As Wolfers (1962: 150) noted, security is a value 'of which a nation can have more or less and which it can aspire to have in greater or lesser measure'.

The pursuit of military security requires states to make sacrifices in terms of spending on other social, or even security, goals that they might have. State resources are relatively scarce, and therefore the decision to spend resources on acquiring military security means such decisions are inevitably a subject for political judgement, and like any other area of government spending, they are subject to the law of diminishing marginal utility.

Second, the concentration of military power that a government feels is required to defend a democracy against its enemies in certain ways poses an inherent threat to the very values it is designed to protect. A state can become dangerously 'militarized' by such efforts. And the *use* of military force may damage democratic values, since it represents an undemocratic mechanism—the resort to force and violence to resolve disputes, rather than using dialogue and compromise, as would be expected in the domestic democratic context. In wartime civil rights are invariably weakened, and normally abhorrent practices such as the use of torture may be condoned.

Efforts to acquire military security may generate security problems of their own. Increasing the size of national armed forces may trigger an arms race with other states, for example, and require modified policies, such as the addition of arms-control initiatives. Historian Paul Kennedy has argued that in pursuing maximum levels of military power, states may fatally overstretch themselves and that historically this has been a key cause of the collapse of imperial powers (Kennedy 1988). Acquiring substantial military capabilities may also encourage states to pursue military options when non-violent instruments still had the capacity to succeed. The use of force is seen both as legitimate for states and as a threat to the stability of the system, but the perception of the possibility of military threats from external actors ensures that states continue to maintain such capabilities.

The inhibitions in the use of violence between states are considerable, and they rest on the most basic kind of self-interest. Violence is seldom the most effective way of settling disputes. It is expensive in its methods and unpredictable in its outcome. However no state (with the exception of Costa Rica) has yet found it possible to dispense with armed forces. The capacity of states to defend themselves, and their evident willingness to do so, provides the basic framework within which the business of international negotiations is carried on. Every new state since 1945 has considered it necessary to create armed forces.

KEY POINTS

- Military security is expensive to acquire.
- The 'costs' of doing so are social as well as economic.
- Acquiring military capability can have consequences that threaten as well as secure a state's values.

Conclusion

The expansion of the concept of security has moved the focus of security studies away from a purely military understanding. Nevertheless, military security remains an absolutely crucial dimension of security as a whole. Governments continue to invest considerable resources in attempting to acquire it, and analysts of international relations seek to understand military security both in its own right and in relation to efforts to increase security in the non-military realms. Military security is extremely expensive to acquire, and the opportunity costs in terms of the human security agenda are profound. Efforts to increase military security can have unintended counter-productive consequences in the military or other fields. Questions about how much, and what kind of, military capability to seek in relation to perceived threats remain at the heart of the study of security.

QUESTIONS

1. Why is it important to study military security?
2. Are governments correct in prioritizing military security?
3. To what extent is the requirement for military security produced by the international anarchy and the security dilemma?
4. Has the end of the Cold War invalidated the arguments for security policies based on nuclear deterrence?
5. In what ways can military security be said to have objective and subjective reality?
6. How useful is arms control as a means of achieving military security?
7. What are the strengths and weaknesses of the traditional realist approach to military security?
8. To what extent can the military-security environment be said to be 'socially constructed'?
9. Is war becoming obsolete as an instrument of national policy?
10. In what ways can the pursuit of military security leave a state perceiving itself as less secure?

FURTHER READING

- Baylis, John, Wirtz, James J., and Gray, Colin S. (eds) (2015), *Strategy in the Contemporary World*, 5th edn, Oxford: Oxford University Press. An excellent collection of essays on the relationship of military power to international security.
- Biddle, Stephen (2004), *Military Power: Explaining Victory and Defeat in Modern Battle*, Princeton, NJ: Princeton University Press. A good recent study of the issues involved in attempts to use force to increase military security in conventional terms.
- Freedman, L. (2004), *Deterrence*, Cambridge: Polity Press. A brief and effective study that provides a clear and well-structured explanation of the nature and history of nuclear deterrence.
- Kaldor, M. (1999), *New and Old Wars: Organised Violence in the Global Era*, Cambridge: Polity Press. Kaldor offers a controversial take on the nature of war in the post-Cold War era. Some of her arguments are disputable, but the book is provocative, thoughtful, and worthy of study.
- Larsen, Jeffrey A. and Wirtz, James J. (eds) (2009), *Arms Control and Cooperative Security*, Boulder, CO: Lynne Rienner. A very useful collection of essays on the utility and future of arms control in the contemporary international system.
- Locke, Edward (2010), 'Refining Strategic Culture: Return of the Second Generation', *Review of International Studies*, 36/1: 685–708. An interesting and valuable survey of recent scholarship on the subject of strategic culture.

- Minear, L. and Weiss, T. G. (1995), *Mercy under Fire: War and the Global Humanitarian Community*, Boulder, CO: Westview Press. A very good study of the complexities of using traditional military capabilities in humanitarian interventions.

- Sloan, E. (2002), *The Revolution in Military Affairs*, Montreal: McGill-Queens Press. A good survey of the issues involved in the RMA debate.

IMPORTANT WEBSITES

- **http://www.armscontrol.org** The Arms Control Association is a national non-partisan membership organization that seeks to build public understanding of and support for effective arms-control policies. It produces the journal *Arms Control Today* and its website provides information on a range of issues relating to military security.

- **http://www.defense.gov** The web portal for the United States Department of Defense, a crucial resource for understanding contemporary US defence policy and thinking.

- **http://www.fas.org** The website of the Federation of American Scientists. Provides excellent resources on the military capabilities and policies of key states.

- **http://www.sipri.org** The website of the excellent Stockholm International Peace Research Institute.

Visit the Online Resource Centre that accompanies this book for lots of interesting additional material: www.oxfordtextbooks.co.uk/orc/collins4e/

14

Regime Security

Richard Jackson

Chapter Contents

Reader's Guide

This chapter examines the unique security dilemma facing many developing countries. It begins with an explanation of the security threats facing states with weak institutional and coercive capacity and lack of national cohesion—what are called weak states—before going on to look at the kinds of security strategies that weak-state elites typically adopt to try and manage their predicament. Referred to as an 'insecurity dilemma', and in contrast to the **security dilemma** facing strong, developed states, the problem faced by weak states is a security environment in which the primary threats to security originate from internal rather than external sources. The chapter goes on to examine a number of competing theoretical explanations for how the weak state predicament arose and why it persists. It concludes with a brief discussion of international attempts to build security in weak states, and the long-term prospects of transforming weak states into strong states.

Introduction

By any measure of security, the disparity between the wealthy, developed countries of the **global North** and the rest of the world could not be greater. Citizens of the small group of highly developed nations face no real threat of major war and enjoy abundant food supplies, economic prosperity, comparatively low levels of crime, and enduring political and social stability. Even the threat of terrorism is relatively minor compared to the everyday risks of accident or disease.

By contrast, the majority of people living in developing countries face profound security challenges, including perennial threats of **intra-state war** and communal violence, terrorism, poverty and famine, weapons proliferation and crime, political instability, social breakdown, economic failure, and, at its most extreme, complete **state collapse**. At the most basic level of physical security, between twenty million and thirty million people have lost their lives in more than 100 intra-state wars in developing regions since 1945. Around 90 per cent of the victims were civilians, and tens of millions of people were displaced by the fighting, many of whom have remained refugees for decades after. There are between twenty and forty intra-state wars ongoing in any given year, all of them in developing countries. In a great many more developing nations serious internal political violence, such as military coups or rebellions, ethnic or religious violence, campaigns of terrorism or riots and disorder, is a constant threat.

In addition, half a million people are killed every year by light weapons, frequently during criminal violence and almost all in developing countries. Added to these military threats, an estimated 40,000 people die every day from hunger and tens of millions of others die annually from diseases such as influenza, HIV/**AIDS**, diarrhoea, and tuberculosis. Tens of millions more suffer from chronic poverty, lack of employment opportunities, inadequate health, and environmental ruin. There is, in other words, a profound disjuncture between the kinds of security enjoyed by the small group of developed nations and the kind of security environment inhabited by the majority of the world's population. The effects of the Ebola outbreak in 2014, in which thousands of people from West Africa died compared to less than a handful of Western victims, illustrates the security disparity. From a global perspective, insecurity is actually more the norm than security.

This situation provides us with important reasons for trying to understand the nature and consequences of insecurity in the developing world. Empirically, we need to understand why so many wars and bouts of major political violence since 1945 continue to take place in the developing world, and why most of them originate from internal rather than external sources. Conceptually, there is an urgent need to find appropriate theories and concepts that can accommodate the unique character of the security situation facing these countries, not least to facilitate more appropriate and more effective international security policies. From a normative perspective, there are clear humanitarian reasons to try and deal with the immense suffering caused by the lack of basic security in the world's 'zones of instability'. Finally, enlightened self-interest dictates that we make a real effort to resolve the fundamental inequality in security between the developed and developing worlds. Globalization means that insecurity in any part of the world cannot be contained within increasingly porous national borders; security is, to a large extent, interdependent. In many ways, terrorism, gun crime, illegal migration, the drugs trade, infectious diseases and environmental damage are all spill-over effects of persistent structural insecurity in the developing world.

In this chapter we shall try to make sense of the profound security challenges facing developing countries and the unique security dilemma they find themselves trapped in. We shall examine the nature of the main security threats facing developing nations, the key security strategies that they have adopted to deal with these threats, and the domestic and international causes of their security predicament. The argument we wish to advance in this chapter is that, unlike the developed nations of the global North, the primary security threats facing **weak states** are potentially catastrophic and originate primarily, although not exclusively, from internal, domestic sources. They include, among others, the threat of violent transfers of **power**, insurgency, secession, rebellion, genocide, warlordism, and, ultimately, state collapse and anarchy.

Moreover, these internal threats are rooted in the fundamental conditions of statehood and governance, thereby creating an enduring 'insecurity dilemma' (Job 1992) for ruling elites: the more elites try to establish effective state **rule**, the more they provoke challenges to their authority from powerful groups in society. In this context, **regime security**—the condition where governing elites are secure from violent challenges to their rule—becomes indistinguishable from **state security**—the condition where the institutions, processes, and structures of the state are able to continue functioning effectively, regardless of the make-up of the ruling elite. For weak states, the domestic sphere is actually far more dangerous and threatening than the international sphere.

Given this inversion of the accepted conception of the classical security dilemma (in which military threats originate primarily from other unitary states in an anarchic international system), it is not surprising that the weak state **insecurity dilemma** has received little attention in the orthodox security studies literature. By focusing on a limited number of states (the great powers and developed countries), a limited set of military threats (Soviet expansionism, foreign invasion, nuclear proliferation, rogue states, international terrorism), a limited array of security strategies (national defence, deterrence, arms control, alliances), and employing a restricted conception of security (externally directed 'national security'), the security challenges facing the majority of the world's population have been largely sidelined in academic studies. Widening and deepening our understanding of security therefore necessitates a new set of diagnostic tools that allows us to get to grips more fully with the security challenges facing the vast majority of the world's people and the unique kind of states they inhabit.

KEY POINTS

- There is a profound disjuncture between the security challenges facing developed and developing countries.
- There are important empirical, conceptual, normative, and self-interested reasons to attend to the security of developing regions.
- Weak states face a unique set of security challenges that originate primarily from internal sources.
- Orthodox approaches to national security are limited in what they can tell us about the conditions of security in weak states.

The weak-state insecurity dilemma

The unique insecurity dilemma facing weak states is largely a function of the structural conditions of their existence. Weak states lack the most fundamental of state attributes—namely, effective institutions, a monopoly on the instruments of violence, and consensus on the idea of the state. Consequently, as incomplete or 'quasi-states' (Jackson 1990), they face numerous challenges to their authority from powerful domestic actors and manipulative external actors. In order to understand how this condition of insecurity arises in the first place, we need to examine the primary structural characteristics of weak states and the nature of the internal security threats they face.

Weak states

Assessing state strength can be a difficult and controversial exercise; scholars tend to apply different measures. Thomas (1987) associates state strength/weakness with institutional capacity and distinguishes between two forms of state power: despotic power and infrastructural power. Despotic power refers to the state's coercive abilities and the exercise of force to impose its rule on civilians. By contrast, infrastructural power refers to the effectiveness and legitimacy of the state's institutions and its ability to rule through consensus. States may be 'weak' or deficient in one or both of these capacities, but, as a general rule, strong states have less need to exercise coercive power because their infrastructural power makes it unnecessary. Paradoxically, the more a weak state exercises coercive power, the more it reinforces its 'weakness' and corresponding lack of infrastructural power.

In contrast, Buzan (1991a) argues that states consist of three primary components: a physical base, institutional capacity, and the 'idea of the state'. For Buzan, state strength/weakness rests primarily in the less tangible realm of the 'idea of the state' and the extent to which society forms a consensus on, and identifies with, the state. Weak states, therefore, 'either do not have, or have failed to create, a domestic political and social consensus of sufficient strength to eliminate the large-scale use of force as a major and continuing element in the domestic political life of the nation' (Buzan 1983: 67).

Migdal (1988) provides a counterpoint to both these formulations. He defines state strength in terms of state capacity, or 'the ability of state leaders to use the agencies of the state to get people in the state to do what they want them to do' (Migdal 1988: xvii). But then he reverses attention to how society and groups within it tolerate, permit, or resist the development of the state. He argues that most developing societies end up in a state/society standoff where the state confronts powerful social forces with substantial coercive force, which in turn provokes violent resistance—as occurred in Libya and Syria during the uprisings in 2011. In Migdal's view, weak states are less the issue than strong societies. This internal **balance of power** between state and society can often militate against the emergence of prototypical Western-style nation states.

In summary, three dimensions of state strength appear to be important: (1) infrastructural capacity in terms of the ability of state institutions to perform essential tasks and enact policy; (2) coercive capacity in terms of the state's ability and willingness to employ force against challenges to its authority; and (3) national identity and social cohesion in terms of the degree to which the population identifies with the nation state and accepts its legitimate role in their lives.

Empirically, it can be seen that most developing nations are weak or deficient on most, if not all, of these dimensions. Or, they have overdeveloped coercive capacities but lack infrastructural capacity and social consensus. As a consequence of these fundamental deficiencies, weak states typically display all or many of the following characteristics: institutional weakness and an inability to effectively enact national policy or perform basic state functions such as tax collection and providing law and order; political instability, as evidenced by coups, plots, rebellions, terrorist campaigns, protests and frequent violent changes of government; the centralization of political power in a single individual or small elite who command the machinery of government to run the state in their own interest; unconsolidated or non-existent democracies; ongoing economic crisis and structural weakness; external vulnerability to international actors and outside forces; intense societal divisions along class, religious, regional, urban–rural, and/or ethnic lines; lack of a cohesive or strong sense of national identity; and an ongoing crisis of legitimacy for both the government of the day and the institutions of state in general, often expressed in widespread protests, boycotts, strikes, disorder, or disengagement.

The most important characteristic of weak states is their frequent inability to establish and maintain a monopoly on the instruments of violence. Even in states with well-developed coercive power, civilian governments do not always retain the absolute loyalty of the armed forces and face a constant threat of military intervention—as occurred in Egypt in July 2013. For most weak states, however, the armed forces are ill equipped, poorly managed, and prone to factional divisions. At the same time, a range of social actors—rival politicians with their own private armies, warlords, criminal gangs, locally organized militias, armed and organized ethnic or religious groups, and private security companies or mercenaries—are often powerful enough to resist the state's attempt to enforce compliance. In such a situation, even the most minimal requirement of statehood—the monopoly on the instruments of violence—is largely out of reach.

At the other end of the scale, and in complete contrast, it is suggested that *strong states* have the willingness and ability to 'maintain social control, ensure societal compliance with official laws, act decisively, make effective policies, preserve stability and cohesion, encourage societal participation in state institutions, provide basic services, manage and control the national economy, and retain legitimacy' (Dauvergne 1998: 2). Strong states also possess high levels of socio-political cohesion that is directly correlated with consolidated participatory democracies, strong national identities, and productive and highly developed economies—although these are not immune to crisis and social protest. Most importantly, strong states exist as a 'hegemonic idea', accepted and naturalized in the minds of ordinary citizens such that they 'consider the state as natural as the landscape around them; they cannot imagine their lives without it' (Migdal 1998: 12).

Crucially, the notion of weak and strong states is not a binary measure but rather a continuum along which states in the real world fall. Moreover, it is a dynamic condition. States can move back and forth along the continuum over time given sufficient changes to key factors: weak states can become strong by building a strong sense of national identity, for example; and strong states could potentially weaken through increased social conflict brought on by immigration or austerity measures, for example. Most states in developing regions fall towards the weak end of the state-strength continuum.

KEY POINTS

- The key dimensions of state strength/weakness are infrastructural capacity, coercive capacity, and national identity and social cohesion.
- Weak states are typically characterized by institutional weakness, political instability, centralization of power, unconsolidated democracy, economic crisis, external vulnerability, social divisions, lack of national identity, and an ongoing crisis of legitimacy.
- The most important characteristic of weak states is their lack of a monopoly on the instruments of violence.
- State strength or weakness is a dynamic continuum along which states can move; it is possible for weak states to become strong states, and vice versa.

Threats to weak states

Because of their debilitating structural characteristics, weak states face a number of internal and external security challenges. *Internally*, weak states face the continual threat of violent intervention in politics by the armed forces. Such interventions can take the form of *coups d'état*, mutiny, rebellion, or revolt over pay and conditions. There have been literally hundreds of coup attempts in Latin America, Asia-Pacific, and the Middle East, and nearly two-thirds of Africa's states have experienced military rule since independence. Military rulers still govern numerous developing countries, while in others, such as Pakistan, the military retain a powerful behind-the-scenes influence.

Weak states also face serious threats from **strongmen**, individuals, or groups who exercise a degree of coercive and/or infrastructural power in their own right and who challenge the authority of the state. They may be semi-legitimate actors such as politicians or traditional and religious leaders who nonetheless command large followings and private access to weaponry. Alternatively, they may be criminal gangs or **warlords**—charismatic individuals who command private armies and enforce a kind of absolutist rule in areas under their control, primarily for the purposes of pursuing illegal commerce. Examples of such strongmen include the drug cartels in Mexico, Colombia, Myanmar, and Afghanistan, and some of the rebel leaders in Africa during the 1990s, such as Charles Taylor, Foday Sankoh, and Jonas Savimbi. If the state fails to accommodate or placate such groups, they may launch a violent challenge to the regime.

In other cases, weak states face challenges from various social groups such as protestors, ethnic groups, religious movements, ideological factions, or local militias who organize for self-defence. Owing in large part to pre-existing divisions, the inability of the state to provide adequate welfare, and the tendency to employ excessive coercion, a great many ethnic groups in weak states have organized politically and militarily to protect their interests. Gurr's (2000) *Minorities at Risk* project found more than ninety ethnic minorities were either actively engaged in violent conflict with the state or at medium-to-serious risk of significant political violence. Similarly, in a number of Middle Eastern and Asian countries, such as Algeria, Egypt, Saudi Arabia, Pakistan, Indonesia, and Thailand, religious groups have launched violent challenges to the state. Ideologically driven groups also continue to threaten weak states, from the Maoist insurgency in Nepal to the Zapatistas in Chiapas, Mexico. It is a sad fact that virtually all armed groups in weak states—state armies, warlord factions, and local, ethnic, and religious militias—employ large numbers of child soldiers. Into this mix, the so-called Arab Spring, which began in early 2011, has seen broad-based democracy movements challenging, sometimes violently, established rulers in countries across the Middle East and elsewhere.

A final internal threat can come from the steady erosion of state institutions and processes. Increasing lawlessness and the eventual collapse of governmental institutions can create a power vacuum in which the ruling elite simply becomes one of several factions struggling to fill the void and claim the formal mantle of statehood. At various times during the conflicts in Liberia and Somalia, for example, several different factions claimed to be the legitimate government at the same time, despite lacking the necessary control of territory or governing institutions required for formal recognition. In the final analysis, any of these threats—military intervention in politics, warlords and strongmen, ethnic demands for secession, protest movements, or state collapse—may lead to sustained bouts of all-out intra-state war.

Because of their internal fragility, weak states also face a variety of *external* threats. Lacking the infrastructural or coercive capacity to resist outside interference, weak states are vulnerable to penetration and intervention by other states and groups. Powerful states may directly invade or may sponsor a coup or rebellion in order to overthrow a regime, such as the American invasions of Grenada, Panama, Afghanistan, and Iraq, NATO's support for the Libyan rebels in 2011, and French intervention in numerous African states over several decades. Alternatively, the provision of significant quantities of arms and military assistance to rebel movements, such as American support to UNITA in Angola and Soviet support for the Vietcong in Vietnam, can pose a serious threat to the ruling elite. Often, support for rebel factions or coup plotters can come from sources closer to home, such as rival neighbouring states. A great many regional rivals—such as India–Pakistan, Uganda–Sudan, Somalia–Ethiopia, Iran–Iraq—have threatened each other in this manner. In addition, very small weak states can be threatened by the tiniest of external groups: mercenary coups and invasions have been launched against the Seychelles, the Maldives, the Comoros, and Guinea-Bissau, sometimes by no more than a few dozen men. In most cases, the coups were thwarted only through assistance from powerful allies such as France or India.

A related external threat comes from the spill-over or contagion of conflict and disorder from neighbouring regions. Lacking the necessary infrastructural capacity to control their borders effectively, weak states can often do little to prevent the massive influx of refugees, fleeing rebels, arms smuggling, or actual fighting. Major external shocks like this can seriously threaten the stability of the weak state. The Rwandan genocide in 1994 spilled over into Zaïre, a weak and failing state; the shock eventually led to the overthrow of the Mobutu regime, invasion by several neighbouring states and large-scale factional fighting (see Case Study 14.1).

Related to this, weak states are threatened by the uncontrollable spread of small arms and light weapons. In the hands of warlords, criminals, and private militias, these weapons pose a real challenge to the authority of the state and can intensify existing conflicts and seriously undermine peace efforts. Light, portable, durable, and easy-to-use (even by children) small and light weapons are easily obtained through legal and illegal channels, and, once in use, have a tendency to spread throughout the region. An estimated $5 billion worth of light weapons are traded illegally every year to the world's conflict zones, killing an estimated half a million people per year in criminal activity and civil violence.

KEY POINTS

- Internally, weak states are threatened by military factions, rival 'strongmen' such as warlords or criminals, rebellions from minorities, institutional collapse, protest and disorder, and ultimately, intra-state war.
- Externally, weak states are threatened by interference from powerful international actors, contagion and spill-over from neighbouring states, and the small arms trade.

The weak-state 'insecurity dilemma'

The combination of state weakness and internal threats creates a security challenge unique to weak states. It is distinctive because it arises from meeting *internal* threats to the regime in power, rather than *external* threats to the existence of the nation state. The inability of the state to provide peace and order creates a contentious environment where each component of society—including the ruling elite or regime—competes to preserve and protect its own well-being. This creates a domestic situation similar to the neorealist conception of structural anarchy where groups create insecurity in the rest of the system when they try to improve their own security. To distinguish this internally oriented condition from the classical *security dilemma*, it is helpful to think of it as an **insecurity dilemma**. This condition of insecurity is self-perpetuating because every effort by the regime to secure its own security through force provokes greater resistance and further undermines the institutional basis of the state and the security of the society as a whole.

In a sense, the weak-state insecurity dilemma is caused by an initial and profound lack of 'stateness', in particular, the inability to establish a monopoly on the instruments of violence. This failure can be both normative—in the sense that the state has failed to convince the population that armed resistance is wrong or counterproductive—and practical—in that the state cannot physically disarm and control all its rivals. Either way, the lack of a political and institutional centre with a monopoly of force creates an insecurity spiral—a semi-permanent situation of 'emergent anarchy'—where armed groups are forced to engage in self-help strategies.

Thus, within the weak-state context, where ruling elites use the machinery of government primarily to secure the continuation of their rule, the concept of *national security*—the security of a whole socio-political entity, a nation state with its own way of life and independent self-government—is wholly inapplicable. In practice, the idea of **state security**—the integrity and functioning of the institutions and idea of the state—and **regime security**—the security of the ruling elite from violent challenge—become indistinguishable. Because of the fusion of state and government, when a particular regime is overthrown, as the Siad Barre regime was overthrown in Somalia in 1991, the entire apparatus of the state collapses too. In this sense, weak-state security *is* regime security.

KEY POINTS

- The weak-state insecurity dilemma is primarily an internal condition based on the contradiction between societal and state power.
- It is engendered by a lack of 'stateness', most importantly, the failure to establish a monopoly on the instruments of violence.
- The weak-state insecurity dilemma transforms national or state security into regime security.

Security strategies in weak states

The structural characteristics of weak states and the unique insecurity dilemma in which they are trapped severely constrain the range of policy options open to ruling elites. Essentially, the conditions of governance create a semi-permanent condition of 'crisis politics' or 'the politics of survival' (Migdal 1988) in which short-term strategies of regime security substitute for long-term state-building policies.

Elite security strategies

Weak-state elites typically employ an array of internal and external strategies aimed at regime survival. *Internally*, elites employ a combination of carrot-and-stick approaches to challengers. First, lacking both infrastructural capacity and wider social legitimacy, weak-state elites are often forced to rely on coercive power and state intimidation to secure continued rule. This entails creating or expanding the security forces, spending large sums of the national income on military supplies, and using violence and intimidation against real and perceived opponents of the regime. This is perhaps the most common survival strategy of weak-state elites, and it is reflected in the appalling human rights record seen in a great many developing countries. Typically, regimes try to suppress opposition or protest through the widespread use of torture and imprisonment, assassination and extra-judicial killings, disappearances, the violent suppression of political expression, forced removals, destruction of food supplies, and, in extreme cases, genocide, mass rape, and ethnic cleansing—as seen in Libya, Syria, Bahrain, and elsewhere during the Arab Spring.

A key dilemma for elites is that the instruments of coercion—the armed forces—can themselves develop into a threat against the regime. For this reason, elites sometimes deliberately weaken the armed forces by creating divisions, establishing elite units such as presidential guards, and fomenting rivalry between different services. Such divide-and-rule strategies are also used against other potential sources of opposition, such as state bureaucracies, religious groups, traditional authorities, and opposition politicians. From this perspective, the deliberate undermining or hollowing-out of state institutions can be a rational and effective means of preventing the rise of potential centres of opposition to the regime.

On the other side of the ledger, elites sometimes find it easier to try and create positive inducements for supporting the regime. Typically, this entails the establishment of elaborate patronage systems, whereby state elites and various social groups are joined in complex networks of mutual exchange. In this way, corruption acts as a form of redistribution and a means of integrating the state in an informal power structure. Such systems may extend to strongmen in a form of **elite accommodation** (Reno 1998). Warlords or political leaders with private armies may be permitted control over a particular area, have state resources diverted their way, or be given exclusive control over a particular commercial activity, for example, in exchange for an agreement not to try and overthrow the regime or encroach on its other activities. In the settlement ending the war in Sierra Leone, the warlord leader of the rebel Revolutionary United Front (RUF), Foday Sankoh, became Minister for Mines in an attempt to buy his loyalty. Ethnic manipulation or 'the politics of identity' is another typical strategy in weak states. In what is a form of divide and rule borrowed from colonialism, elites will sometimes deliberately foment inter-communal conflict as a means of preventing the emergence of united opposition to the regime. At other times, it is simply a method of rooting a regime's power base in what is seen to be a reliable source of support. Thus, elites will favour certain groups in the allocation of state resources, oppress minorities viewed as hostile, create minority scapegoat groups during times of unrest, and appoint members of the elite's own ethnic group to positions of power. Such strategies are frequently successful, as ethnic consciousness is usually well developed and readily exploitable in many developing societies.

A final internal strategy involves the careful manipulation of democratic political processes. Because of their external vulnerability, a great many weak states have been forced by international donors—developed states and international financial institutions (IFIs) such as the IMF and World Bank—to begin the process of democratic reform. Alternatively, pressures stemming from widespread protest and demands for democratic reform—such as the social movements seen in the Arab Spring—can also force regimes to make concessions. A great many weak-state rulers have successfully managed the transition to multi-party democracy and retained control of the state, primarily through careful manipulation of internal opponents and external perceptions. Typically, this involved monopolizing and controlling the media, the co-option

KEY QUOTES 14.1 Private military companies

'Private military companies—or PMCs, as the new world order's mercenaries have come to be known—allow governments to pursue policies in tough corners of the world with the distance and comfort of plausible deniability. The ICIJ [International Consortium of Investigative Journalists] investigation uncovered the existence of at least 90 private military companies that have operated in 110 countries worldwide. These corporate armies, often providing services normally carried out by a national military force, offer specialized skills in high-tech warfare, including communications and signals intelligence and aerial surveillance, as well as pilots, logistical support, battlefield planning, and training. They have been hired both by governments and multinational corporations to further their policies or protect their interests.

Some African governments are little more than criminal syndicates—warlords such as Charles Taylor, the president of Liberia, or more sophisticated elites, such as the rulers of Angola. But to sell diamonds and timber and oil onto the world market requires foreign partners.

The people doing the extracting, the bribing, the arms dealing, and the deal-making are South African, Belgian, American, Israeli, French, Ukrainian, Lebanese, Canadian, British, Russian, Malaysian, and Syrian. They are a class of entrepreneur that operates beyond borders, often unaccountable to shareholders and unfettered by the regulation they would encounter in their own countries. They have become influential political players in the countries in which they operate.'

van Niekerk (2002)

of opponents, setting up fake parties to split the vote, gerrymandering, ballot rigging, candidate and elector disqualification, and manipulating the electoral rules. Constructing the outward appearance of democracy without any substantial concessions can actually function to bolster regime security by giving it a degree of international legitimacy. The partial transition in Egypt following the ousting of President Mubarak in 2011 is arguably an example of this process—even though the military reversed the results less than two years later.

In addition to these internal strategies, weak-state elites also look to form alliances with powerful *external* actors as a means of bolstering regime security. An increasingly prevalent strategy has been to employ foreign mercenaries or private military or security companies as force multipliers. There are nearly a hundred **private military companies (PMCs)** operating in 110 states around the world (see Key Quotes 14.1). Often working closely with oil and mineral companies, the industry is thought to be worth as much as $100 billion per year. Weak states employ private security contractors, because they see them as being more effective and reliable than many national militaries. With superior weapons and training, these private armies have often proved to be decisive in securing weak-state survival against various internal threats, although this tactic failed in Libya's civil war in 2011. In Angola and Sierra Leone, the notorious PMC Executive Outcomes turned the tide against rebel forces, recapturing diamond mining areas in the process.

More formally, weak states seek out alliances with powerful states that can help to guarantee regime survival. During the Cold War, many weak states obtained military support from one or other of the superpowers in exchange for political and strategic assistance in the East–West confrontation. In Africa, at least twenty countries entered into defence agreements with France; subsequent military intervention by French troops was decisive in keeping several West African regimes in power, including Zaïre/DRC (see Case Study 14.1), Togo, Ivory Coast, and Mali. At present, the war on terror is providing weak states with another opportunity to bolster their internal security: in exchange for cooperation in fighting terrorism, the United States provides countries like Pakistan, Yemen, Saudi Arabia, Indonesia, and Uzbekistan (see Case Study 14.2) with vital military and economic assistance. External intervention of this kind can be crucial for keeping internal rivals at bay and ensuring regime security.

Finally, weak-state elites sometimes join together with other weak states in regional defence arrangements designed primarily to prop each other up. For example, under new multilateral security agreements, both the **Economic Community of West African States (ECOWAS)** and the **Southern African Development Community (SADC)** have since 1990 intervened a number of times in member states to overturn coups or secure governments from overthrow by rebel forces. In March 2011, Saudi Arabia sent troops to Bahrain to protect the regime from an uprising. Thus, the creation of regional security architecture, including regional peacekeeping forces, can function as a strategy of mutually reinforcing regime security.

Security outcomes

The perennial conundrum facing weak-state elites lies in the contradiction between ensuring the short-term security of the regime and the long-term goal of state making. Many of the security strategies described are, in the long-run, self-defeating, as they further undermine the foundations of the state, provoke even more serious opposition from social groups, and delay genuine state consolidation. For most weak-state elites, however, there is no way out of this dilemma; if they neglect regime security in favour of more genuine state-building activities such as strengthening state institutions and forging a sense of national identity, they are just as likely to be overthrown in a coup or toppled by a protest movement. Thus, with few genuine alternatives, elites have to persist with policies that could eventually lead to complete state disintegration and collapse.

KEY POINTS

- Internal security strategies include repression and military expansion, employing mercenaries and private military companies, using divide-and-rule strategies, deliberately undermining state institutions, patronage politics and elite accommodation, identity politics, and democratic manipulation.
- External security strategies include employing private military companies and mercenaries, entering into external defence agreements with Great Powers, and joining in regional defence organizations.

Ultimately, of course, a key outcome of these strategies is that the weak state, or rather the regime, becomes the greatest single threat to the security of its own people. In weak states, individual citizens often

CASE STUDY 14.1 Anatomy of a weak state: the Democratic Republic of Congo

The central African state of the Democratic Republic of Congo (DRC) has always been a weak state. It has suffered from tremendous insecurity since its founding, and ruling elites have employed all the classic regime security strategies to avoid being toppled.

At independence in 1960, Congo was poorly prepared for full statehood, with irrational national boundaries, underdeveloped state institutions, poor infrastructure, a fragile economic base, and only 100 university graduates to fill the civil service. In the first four years of independence, the country was plunged into civil war, with three main factions vying for power and the mineral-rich Shaba province attempting to secede. Order was established only with the help of a large-scale United Nations Operation. In 1965, Mobutu Sese Seko took power in a military coup.

Throughout his rule, Mobutu faced numerous threats to his regime: military rebellions, dissident movements, attempts at secession, mercenary revolts, invasions and violent disputes, and conflict spill-over from neighbouring states. Cobalt and copper-rich Shaba province was invaded by mercenaries and exiled dissidents on four occasions.

Following the pattern of weak-state rules, Mobutu employed a number of classic regime security strategies. He employed mercenaries to subdue the country in the first years of his rule, bribed opposition politicians to join the government, suppressed opposition movements, engaged in identity politics, hollowed out state institutions to prevent the rise of potential opponents, and split the armed forces into several factions to avoid coups and rebellions. Externally, he allied with the United States, providing a conduit for arms transfers to Angola's UNITA rebels. In exchange, he received massive amounts of military and economic aid, which he then used to manage internal opposition. French paratroopers and American logistical support helped Mobutu to defeat an invasion of Shaba in 1978.

In 1996, a rebel alliance led by Laurent Kabila and backed by Rwanda emerged in the east of the country in the chaos engendered by the spill-over of the 1994 Rwandan genocide. Within a few months, and despite employing a mercenary army, Mobutu's regime collapsed. The Kabila-led alliance soon fell apart, however, and full-scale civil war broke out in 1998. Rwanda and Uganda intervened on the side of different rebel factions, while Angola, Namibia, and Zimbabwe sent troops to support the Kabila government. Africa's 'first world war' raged until peace accords were signed in 2003, leading to elections and the withdrawal of most foreign occupying forces. However, Rwandan troops intervened again in 2009, further violent rebellions occurred in 2012 and 2013, and major protests broke out in early 2015—despite the holding of national elections in 2011 and the continued presence of UN peacekeepers. The UN estimates that more than five million people have lost their lives in the conflict. Despite a recognized central government, the DRC continues to exist as a semi-collapsed state, with various warlords, ethnic militia, criminal enterprises, and foreign entrepreneurs engaged in large-scale looting, trade monopolization, and the exploitation of minerals.

face a much more serious threat from their own governments than they do from the governments of other states. Instead of ensuring individual and social security, the continual use of coercion makes the state the primary threat to security. Moreover, the threat is affected on several levels: repression and identity politics threatens their physical survival through the spread of violent conflict; and deliberately undermining state institutions and patronage politics threatens their welfare and livelihood.

KEY POINTS

- The long-term effect of elite security strategies is to reinforce insecurity for both the regime itself and the wider population.
- In extreme cases, elite security strategies can lead to complete state collapse.

Explaining insecurity in weak states

There are different theories about the causes of weak-state or regime insecurity. Taken together, they can tell us a great deal about how conditions of insecurity evolve and persist. State-making theories explore the origins of the weak-state insecurity dilemma in the initial state-construction process. Warlord politics theories explore the impact of neoliberal globalization and the end of the Cold War on the choices facing weak-state elites. The combination of the inherited structural features of statehood and the nature and processes of the international context explain a great deal about why weak states find it so difficult to escape from their insecurity dilemma.

State-making theories

Observing weak-state insecurity, scholars like Ayoob (1995) have suggested that these conditions represent a predictable stage in the long-term state-building

CASE STUDY 14.2 Anatomy of a weak state: Uzbekistan

The Central Asian country of Uzbekistan gained its independence from the Soviet Union in 1991. From 1924 to 1991, Uzbekistan had been governed as an outlying colony in the Soviet Empire. Consequently, at independence it shared many of the weaknesses of other postcolonial and post-Soviet states, such as an externally oriented, dependent economy, weak national institutions, overdeveloped coercive capabilities, a legitimacy crisis, and a history of authoritarianism.

President Islam Karimov, a former Communist Party boss, has ruled Uzbekistan since its independence from the Soviet Union in 1991. Throughout this period, the Karimov regime has been under constant threat from dissidents and anti-government campaigners, crime syndicates and drug traders, a small-scale terrorist campaign, opposition Islamic groups, and spill-over from the conflicts in Afghanistan and Tadjikistan.

Karimov has clung to power using a variety of regime security strategies, most commonly severe repression against real and potential opponents. Despite nominal constitutional protections, the government has banned public meetings and demonstrations, restricted the independent media, arrested thousands of opposition political and religious supporters, and used horrific torture and murder to suppress dissents. Uzbekistan presently has the worst human rights record in the former Soviet Union. Other internal strategies used by Karimov to maintain power have included the clever manipulation of elections and referendums, rewriting the constitution to centralize all power in the president, and endemic corruption among government officials.

Externally, Karimov's primary strategy was to ally the regime with the United States in the War on Terror. In 2002, the two countries signed a Declaration of Strategic Partnership. In return for hundreds of millions of dollars of economic and military support, Uzbekistan provided the USA with military bases from which to conduct missions in Afghanistan, coercive interrogation facilities for terrorist suspects in the controversial rendition programme, and diplomatic support for US policies in the United Nations.

However, the US–Uzbek partnership came under severe strain following the military crackdown against anti-government demonstrators in the city of Andijan in May 2005, when hundreds of unarmed civilians were killed and injured. Following US criticism of the appalling human rights situation in Uzbekistan, and the imposition of sanctions by the European Union, Karimov ordered the closure of US military bases in the country. In response to the deterioration in relations with the USA, Karimov turned instead towards building closer relations with Russia, a strategy of some success for a number of years. Since 2008 however, relations with the West have once again improved, and by early 2015, Uzbekistan was maintaining fragile relationships with Russia, its neighbours, and the West.

process from which strong states will, in time, emerge. Taking a historical view, they argue that the European experience proves that state building is a long and traumatic process, taking several centuries to complete and involving a great deal of bloodshed. Typically, it entailed sustained and bloody conflict between a centralizing state and powerful social forces before a monopoly on violence was achieved and disparate groups of people were welded into a single national identity. Significantly, representative institutions emerged only gradually, after a powerful central state and a cohesive sense of national identity had been established.

The argument is that what has been observed in developing countries since the mid-twentieth century is a similar process of state consolidation to that experienced by European states in past centuries, but with additional obstacles that were absent during the European experience. For example, today's weak states have to cope with the ongoing effects of colonial rule, which includes: the imposition of alien doctrines and institutions of statehood; irrational territorial boundaries and the lack of organic national identity; societies divided along class, religious, and ethnic lines; stunted and dependent economies; and an entrenched culture of political violence.

The contemporary state-building process is also constrained by a shortened time frame. Unlike European states, weak states today are expected to become effective, fully functioning, democratic states within a few decades. Moreover, they are expected to do it without the violence, corruption, and human rights abuses that accompanied the European state-building process. Established international **norms** and rules, such as the protection of minority and human rights and the right of self-determination (which often encourages ethnic rebellion), also complicates the state-building process. A particularly problematic norm is the inviolability of statehood. Once a state achieves independence and is admitted to the United Nations, its status cannot be revoked or its territory subsumed into another state, no matter how unviable it proves to be in practice. Thus, unlike European entities such as Burgundy and Aragon, which could not complete the state-building process and were absorbed into larger, more viable units, today's weak states must struggle on indefinitely.

In short, according to this approach, we can expect weak states to experience a great deal more bloodshed and violence over an extended period until stronger, more representative states emerge. Until then, they will remain 'quasi-states'—states possessing the nominal features of statehood, such as international recognition, but lacking the infrastructural capacities to create and secure a sense of genuine national identity (Jackson 1990).

KEY POINTS

- Scholars like Ayoob suggest that the conditions of insecurity in weak states are an expression of the historical state-building process.
- The European state-building process was similarly bloody and long.
- Weak states face the state-building process in an environment constrained by the experience of colonialism, a shortened time frame, and problematic international norms.

Warlord politics

During the Cold War, many weak states maintained a semblance of stability and integration through various forms of elite and social accommodation. The primary means of accommodation was the construction of a patrimonial or *redistributive state*—a system of patronage where state resources were distributed to supporters through complex social and political networks. The redistributive state was frequently maintained by direct superpower assistance, loans and development assistance from international financial institutions, and periods of high commodity prices that supplied its primary national income. Temporary disruptions to the stability of the weak-state redistributive system came from sudden falls in commodity prices, wider economic shocks (such as the oil shocks), and the sudden loss of superpower support (which could be compensated for by switching to the other superpower, as Somalia did in the 1970s). In many cases, these shocks resulted in serious internal violence.

The end of the Cold War signalled a period of profound transformation in the international system. A major consequence of the end of superpower conflict was the decline of military and economic support for many weak states. At the same time, international financial institutions began to demand changes in the economic and political policies of weak states—what are called 'conditionalities'—in exchange for continuing loans and assistance. In keeping with the global trend of privatization and deregulation, weak states were forced by lenders and investors to sell off and downsize government bureaucracies. These developments severely disrupted the redistributive state and forced rulers to find new ways of accommodating rival strongmen and restless social groups.

Somewhat paradoxically, elite strategies have since involved the deliberate creation of state collapse and social disorder. This entails hollowing out state institutions, fragmenting the armed forces, and creating parallel informal armed groups, thereby spreading the means of violence even further into society. The logic of 'disorder as a political instrument' is that, within the context of a collapsing state, elites can pursue forms of commercial activity that are not possible under normal circumstances, such as trading in illegal commodities, looting, protection rackets, coercive monopolies, and the like. Thus, exploiting the shadow markets engendered by neoliberal globalization, and in alliance with local strongmen and multinational companies, weak-state elites have created a new kind of political economy, what Reno (1998) has called 'warlord politics'. Crucial in this enterprise is the ability to employ private companies to perform state roles, especially the task of providing regime security.

As an alternative political-economic system, warlord politics provides elites with several advantages. It permits commercial activity and accumulation in the grey or shadow regions of the global economy, tapping into resources that would otherwise be unavailable to weak-state elites and that are desperately needed to buy protection from rivals. In this sense, warlord politics facilitates the process of elite accommodation needed to keep regimes safe from violent overthrow. It also inhibits the emergence of mass social movements because civil society finds itself trapped between a rapacious state and well-armed networks of strongmen pursuing their own illiberal agendas.

In short, warlord politics represents an innovative response to rapid global change that permits the survival of the regime under harsh new conditions. From this perspective, state collapse and widespread disorder are not a temporary aberration in the normal functioning of the state, but a new form of regime security forced on weak-state elites by changes in the wider international system.

KEY POINTS

- The end of the Cold War, economic crises, and the adoption of conditionalities by IFIs severely disrupted the redistributive state.
- Weak-state elites responded by developing new and innovative forms of political economy based on shadow and predatory commercial activities called 'warlord politics'.
- Warlord politics works to control internal threats from strongmen and mass movements.

Conclusion: prospects for the weak state

In this chapter, we have examined the conditions of insecurity that affect the majority of the world's states. We have suggested that the insecurity dilemma facing developing countries is both profound and unique, and is rooted in the fundamental structures and processes of incomplete statehood. The conditions of insecurity in weak states are the result of three interrelated factors: the historical state-making process; the structures and processes of the present international system; and the security strategies employed by weak-state elites. In the context of profound internal threats and constraining external conditions, national security becomes a matter of maintaining short-term regime security. The pursuit of regime security, however, is itself a profoundly contradictory process; short-term policies of regime security undermine the more important state-building project—and the security of the state and society.

From this perspective, weak-state insecurity appears to be an inescapable condition. There have been very few clear-cut cases where weak states have made a successful transition to state consolidation and genuine national security. The fundamental security challenge facing weak states lies in achieving greater levels of stateness and moving towards improved levels of genuine state strength. The challenge, therefore, lies in the willingness and ability of weak-state elites to substitute short-term regime security strategies for long-term state-building strategies.

Should regimes choose to take the state-building project seriously, the process will undoubtedly be long and difficult, not least because a number of entrenched internal and external obstacles to effective statehood remain. These include: the continued distorting effects of colonialism; the processes of neoliberal globalization and the imposition of external conditionalities; small arms proliferation; continuing external intervention by powerful actors and processes; the existence of constraining international norms; and debilitating internal conditions such as poverty, social division, weak institutions, and the like. The global war on terror launched in the wake of 9/11 has also had a negative effect on the state-building project, as the fight against terrorism has largely diverted international attention and resources from poverty eradication, democracy promotion, and peace-building activities. Weak-state elites have also been able to brand their internal enemies as terrorists, and, just as during the Cold War, receive large-scale military support in exchange for cooperation in the fight against terrorism (see Case Study 14.2). In other words, the new war on terror has allowed weak-state elites to re-prioritize regime security over state building and receive vital international support for their efforts.

As during the Cold War, the problems of weak-state insecurity take a low priority on international agendas compared to the interests of the Great Powers. So far, solutions to the weak-state security dilemma have not moved far beyond the establishment of multi-party democracy and free markets. It is sometimes argued that forceful 'regime change' and perhaps even a liberal or benign recolonization, such as occurred in Germany and Japan after the Second World War, is the only effective long-term solution. Others stress the need for humanitarian intervention to protect the security of civilians and promote human rights. They argue that 'cosmopolitan peace-keeping' (Kaldor 1999) and so-called peace-building missions are required to transform violent domestic politics in weak states into long-term peace and stability. In practice, both approaches are based on a similar liberal perspective, which envisages a minimal state devoted to protecting individual and market freedoms. The main problem is that, thus far, despite decades of effort, no case of enforced neo-liberalization, through either conditionalities, regime change, or peace building, has succeeded in transforming a weak state into a strong state.

Given the enormous challenges facing weak states, and recognizing the fundamental inequities of the state project itself and the failure thus far to reform illiberal weak states, some radical commentators have suggested that state building should be abandoned in favour of alternative forms of political organization based on either smaller units—city states or ethnic groups, for example—or larger units—such as regional organizations like the European Union. The first option, sub-state political organizations, seems impractical in regions that are awash with weapons, criminal gangs, and poverty; the case of Somalia, which has been without a functioning central government since 1991, is informative in this regard. The second option, regional organization, is similarly not without its limitations. While it has had a modicum of success in the European Union, in regions characterized by weak states, underdevelopment, and instability, such as Africa or Latin America, regional processes are severely constrained in what they can achieve.

In the end, overcoming the internal and external obstacles to state building in the developing world will require tremendous political will and resources, the emergence of local actors capable of building peaceful and prosperous communities, and the elaboration of alternative and innovative approaches to state-building assistance. More importantly, it will require fundamental reform of international economic and political structures, including the international trade in weapons. Given the present preoccupation with international terrorism and the lack of enthusiasm by the world's developed states for debt relief, development, and curbs on the small arms trade, the short-to-medium-term future of the weak state looks as bleak as it ever was, although the international movement for greater democratic participation exemplified in the Arab Spring and emerging approaches to local peace building may offer some hope. (For more on the arms trade see Chapter 24.)

? QUESTIONS

1. In what ways are orthodox approaches to security limited in their explanation of the weak-state insecurity dilemma?
2. What are the primary differences between weak and strong states?
3. Outline the main internal and external security threats facing weak states.
4. What makes the security dilemma in weak states unique?

5. What are the differences, if any, between national security, state security, and regime security in the weak-state context?
6. What domestic and international strategies do weak-state elites adopt to try to manage their security challenges?
7. What are the main internal and external obstacles to state building for weak states?
8. What impact has the end of the Cold War and the onset of globalization had on the weak-state security predicament?
9. Is abandoning the state-building project in favour of alternative forms of political organization a feasible solution to the weak-state security dilemma?
10. What role should the international community play in the state consolidation process?
11. How might the global democracy movement seen in the Arab Spring affect the process of state consolidation and the quest for greater security in developing countries?

FURTHER READING

- Ayoob, Mohammed (1995), *The Third World Security Predicament: State Making, Regional Conflict, and the International System*, Boulder, CO: Lynne Rienner. Provides an informative analysis of the weak-state security predicament in its internal, regional, and international dimensions.
- Buzan, Barry (1991), *People, States and Fear: An Agenda for International Security Studies in the Post-Cold War Era*, 2nd edn, Boulder, CO: Lynne Rienner. A seminal reformulation of security beyond its traditional focus to include the security predicament facing the majority of weak states in the world.
- Holsti, Kalevi J. (1996), *The State, War, and the State of War*, Cambridge: Cambridge University Press. An empirical analysis of contemporary warfare, which demonstrates that internal war within weak states has been the primary form of international conflict since 1945.
- Job, Brian (ed.) (1992), *The Insecurity Dilemma: National Security of Third World States*, Boulder, CO: Lynne Rienner. A very useful collection of essays from leading experts on some of the key dimensions of security in developing states.
- Kaldor, Mary (1999), *New and Old Wars: Organised Violence in a Global Era*, Cambridge: Polity Press. A provocative and original statement on the changing nature of warfare and the need for new approaches to peacekeeping in weak states.
- Musah, Abdel-Fatah and Kayode Fayemi, J. (eds) (2000), *Mercenaries: An African Security Dilemma*, London: Pluto. Provides a fascinating collection of essays on the security dilemma associated with the intervention of mercenaries in Africa's weak states.
- Reno, William (1998), *Warlord Politics and African States*, Boulder, CO: Lynne Rienner. Provides a compelling analysis of how weak-state elites have adapted governance strategies to the opportunities and constraints of neoliberal globalization.
- Rich, Paul B. (ed.) (1999), *Warlords in International Relations*, London: Macmillan. An insightful collection of essays by leading experts on the role of warlords, the small arms trade, private military contractors, and other security challenges facing weak states.
- Thomas, Caroline (1987), *In Search of Security: The Third World in International Relations*, Boulder, CO: Lynne Rienner. An original formulation of the weak-state security predicament.
- Zartman, I. William (ed.) (1995), *Collapsed States: The Disintegration and Restoration of Legitimate Authority*, Boulder, CO: Lynne Rienner. An important collection of essays on the nature, causes, and consequences of weak-state decay and collapse.

IMPORTANT WEBSITES

- **http://www.iansa.org** The International Action Network on Small Arms is a global network of civil society organizations working to stop the proliferation and misuse of small arms and light weapons. The website contains resources on all aspects of small arms proliferation and international efforts to regulate the trade.
- **http://www.iss.co.za** The Institute for Security Studies is a leading research institution on all aspects of human security in Africa. The website contains news, analysis, and special reports on all aspects of security in Africa.
- **http://www.systemicpeace.org/inscrdata.html** The Integrated Network for Societal Conflict Research (INSCR) programme at the Center for International Development and Conflict Management, the University of Maryland, coordinates major empirical research projects on armed conflict, genocide, and politicide, minorities at risk, regime types, and state failure. The website has links to all the major projects and datasets.

Visit the Online Resource Centre that accompanies this book for lots of interesting additional material: www.oxfordtextbooks.co.uk/orc/collins4e/

15

Societal Security

Paul Roe

Chapter Contents

Reader's Guide

This chapter explores the concept of societal security. It starts by looking at how society came to be conceived as a referent object of security in its own right. It then goes on to discuss the so-called Copenhagen School's understanding of both society and societal identity, showing how societal security is tied most of all to the maintenance of ethno-national identities. In looking at threats to societal security, through examples such as the former Yugoslavia and Northern Ireland, the chapter discusses a number of those means that can prevent or hinder the reproduction of collective identity, and, in turn, at how societies may react to such perceived threats. The concept of a societal security dilemma is then introduced to show how societal security dynamics can spiral to produce violent conflict. The chapter concludes by considering some of the main critiques of the concept as an analytical tool.

Introduction

Throughout the 1980s and early 1990s, significant moves took place designed to take security studies beyond the confines of the dominant realist and neorealist paradigms. For the most part, such moves were made possible by the winding down and eventual end to the Cold War. The decreasing threat of nuclear war opened the way for the emergence of other, non-military conceptions of security. For example, writing at the end of the 1980s, Jessica Tuchman Mathews (1989: 162–77) suggested that international security be rethought to include resource, environmental, and demographic issues. Mathews, together with a number of like-minded others (see, e.g., Ullman 1983; Booth 1991), came to be known as the 'wideners': those wishing to broaden the concept of security out of its military-centric confines. One such widener was Barry Buzan.

The term 'societal security' was first introduced by Buzan in *People, States and Fear* (1991a). In the book, societal security was just one of the sectors in his five-dimensional approach, alongside military, political, economic, and environmental concerns. In this context, societal security referred to the sustainable development of traditional patterns of language, culture, religions, and national identities, and customs of states (1991a: 122–3). Each one of Buzan's five sectors was formulated within the confines of an essentially neorealist framework: all the dimensions remained as sectors of national—that is, state—security. 'Society' was just one section through which the state might be threatened. Furthermore, threats in the military sector were seen as primary: as the priorities given to each dimension depended on their relative urgency, Buzan argued that military security was still the most expensive, politically potent, and visible aspect of state behaviour (1991b: 35). Hence: 'A state and society can be, in their own terms, secure in the political, economic, societal and environmental dimensions, and yet all of these accomplishments can be undone by military failure' (1991b: 37).

Although recognizing Buzan's vital contribution to the 'broadening' of international security, a major contention was that introducing more sectors of state security was simply not enough. While security studies was indeed beginning to move away from its preoccupation with military issues, it was still very much **state-centric** in its focus. What was required, therefore, were other referent objects of security: that international security should be 'deepened' as well as broadened brought with it a refocusing on what, or indeed who, should be secured, from the individual through to the global level. (For a fuller discussion of human versus state security, see Chapter 10.) Set against this, the concept of 'societal security' came to mark out a distinct third, and indeed middle, position; one that was reluctant to consider notions of either human or global security, but one that was also in agreement that the realist and neorealist approach to international security had become just too narrow. As a result, this middle position began to talk about the security of other collectivities, or 'societies'.

A duality of state and societal security

In the 1993 book *Identity, Migration and the New Security Agenda in Europe*, Ole Wæver, together with Buzan, Morten Kelstrup, and Pierre Lemaitre, suggested that 'societal securities' had become increasingly important vis-à-vis concerns over state sovereignty in contemporary, post-Cold War Europe. Most crucially, the writers claimed that Buzan's previous five-dimensional approach to international security had now become untenable as a context for societal security. They suggested a reconceptualization: not five sectors relating to the state, but instead a duality of state and societal security. Although society was retained as a dimension of state security, it also became a referent object of security in its own right.

The key to this reconceptualization was the notion of *survival*. While state security is concerned with threats to its sovereignty—if a state loses its sovereignty, it will not survive as a state—societal security is concerned with threats to its identity—if a society loses its identity, it will not survive as a society. States can be made insecure through threats to their societies. But state security can also be brought into question by a high level of societal cohesion. This relates to those instances where a state's programme of homogenization comes into conflict with the strong identity of one or more of its minority groups. For example, during the 1990s the 'Romanianness' of the Romanian state was compromised as the large Hungarian minority in the Transylvania region of the country further asserted its 'Hungarianness'. In other words, the more secure in terms of identity these societies are, the less secure the states containing them may feel. For Wæver (1993: 25) and his collaborators, in this way **traditional security** analysis had created 'an excessive concern with state stability', and thus had largely removed any sense of 'the "security" of societies in their own right'.

> **KEY QUOTES 15.1 The importance of societal security**
>
> 'In the West and the East, at the centre and the periphery, cultural identity and societal security have become the central theme of political attitudes and conflicts.'
>
> *Hassner (1993: 58)*
>
> 'With the increasing intertwining of security and identity, a new agenda has emerged, both for policy-makers struggling with the dilemmas and uncertainties of post-Cold-War Europe, and for academics trying to make sense analytically and conceptually of this changed continent . . . exploring the interface between security and identity can shed considerable light on the structural dynamics and underlying trends of contemporary European politics.'
>
> *Aggestan and Hyde-Price (2000: 1)*

As a concept, societal security was conceived very much as a reaction to events in Europe, in both the East and in the West. In the West, the process of European Union (EU) integration meant that political loyalties were increasingly being shifted, either upwards to the EU level itself, or downwards to the level of the regions, thus weakening the traditional link between state and society. Meanwhile, in the East, the collapse of some of the former socialist countries showed starkly the conflict between adherence to the state (Federal Yugoslavia) or adherence to its constituent groups (Serbs, Croats, Bosnian Muslims). As an analytical tool, the concept has therefore mainly been employed very much in a European context (see, e.g., Huysmans 1995; Herd and Lofgren 2001; Roe 2002). However, its applicability arguably goes much further, in particular to those 'weak states' in parts of South East Asia and sub-Saharan Africa. More will be said about this in the conclusion to this chapter. (See Key Quotes 15.1 for more on the importance of societal security.)

> **KEY POINTS**
>
> - To begin with, societal security was just a sector of state security. This is where the state can be destabilized through threats to its language, culture, religion, and other customs.
> - The societal security concept was (re)conceived in the light of the processes of integration in Western Europe and disintegration in Eastern Europe.
> - Societal security was reconceptualized as a referent object of security in its own right.
> - Societal security concerns the maintenance of collective identity: if a society loses its identity it will not survive as such.
> - Societal security represents a middle way between notions of individual and global security.

Society and societal identity

Put simply, society is about identity: it is about the self-conception of collectivities and individuals identifying themselves as members of that collectivity. Thus, societies are units constituted by a sense of collective identity. Wæver (1993: 17) defines collective identity as simply 'what enables the word *we* to be used'. In this sense, however, a 'we' identity can vary a great deal as to the kind of group to which it applies, the intensity to which it is felt, and the reasons that create a sense of it. Moreover, societies are composed of, and support a multitude of, different identities. That is to say, societies are multiple-identity units. How, then, is it possible to talk about a society's identity?

According to Anthony Giddens (in Wæver 1993: 19), there are two main ways to think about society. The first one is something fixed that has boundaries marking it off from other similar units. The second one is something that is constituted by social interaction; society is viewed rather as a fluid concept, referring more to a process than to an object. For Wæver (1993: 19), however, defining society as a process arguably reduced it to more or less any classification of 'we'—a view of society that cannot easily be employed in the analysis of international security. The interest for the so-called Copenhagen School, as in particular Buzan and Wæver came to be known, was in 'societies operating as units in the international system', where their reactions to threats against their identity have politically significant effects. Accordingly, Wæver distinguished between society and 'social group'. Here, societal security is concerned with the security *of* society as a whole, but not the security of groups *in* society (social group).

Wæver (1994: 8) notes that security action is 'always taken on behalf of, and with reference to a collectivity . . . that which you can point to and say: "it has to survive, therefore it is necessary . . ."'. From this there are two main points to keep in mind. The first one is that for the collectivity there are distinctive kinds of behaviour that cannot be reduced to the individual level. Like state security, societal security must be approached as the security of societies having more than, and thus being different from, the sum of their constituent individual and social groups. Thus, society is viewed as an entity possessing a reality of its own. The second one, following on from the first, is that societies must also be seen as having the right to survive. For example, while farmers might be considered as a distinct social group, the argument is a difficult one to make that 'farmers' also constitute a significant entity operating alongside the state in political terms. Moreover, the argument that farmers automatically have some kind of right always to be farmers is a difficult one to sustain, as farms are routinely allowed to go out of business for a number of reasons. (However, when farming, as in the case of France in particular, is tied very closely to a particular notion of collective identity—in this instance 'Frenchness'—then farmers may become part of a societal security agenda: farms in France going out of business represent a loss of what it means to be French.)

Such difficulties over defining society can be tackled further by pinning the relationship between society and **societal identity** to a more easily definable unit. Wæver refers to Giddens' view that, as 'units', modern societies are most often nation states or based on the idea of the nation state. Indeed, Wæver (1993: 19) claims that the nation is a special case of society characterized by: attachment to territory, or at least a sense of homeland; a continuity of existence across time, from past generations to the present; and a sense of being one of the entities that make up the social world. In this way, though, the idea of nation and state are often blurred. Buzan, Wæver, and a further collaborator, Jaap de Wilde (1998: 121), recognize all too well that the problem with *societal* is that the related term *society* is often used to refer to the state population. Taking the example of Sudan, they emphasize that 'Sudanese society is that population contained by the Sudanese state but which is composed of many societal units (e.g. Arab and black African). This is not our use of societal; we used societal for communities with which one identifies.' Thus, while, on the one hand, nation can be defined in relation to 'citizenship', on the other hand, it can also be defined in terms of 'ethnicity'. And this distinction is often characterized by the terms 'civic nation' and 'ethnic nation'.

Nations perform a number of roles—most prominently, the marking of borders, thereby staking claim to control a territory. For much of the time, though, the concept of nation is underpinned by common cultural (more often than not ethnic) bonds. Nations are, in this regard, very much a response to the need for identity. Belonging to a distinct culture tells us 'who we are', and it is this process of self-identification that is key to nations.

Although nationality and ethnicity are indeed often mingled, nation and ethnic group can be distinguished in the following terms: a nation strives for a state of its own, whereas an ethnic group acts within the state as it exists. Anthony D. Smith (1993: 48–62) suggests that an ethnic group constitutes a nation when it has become 'politicized': when the group is not only bound by a distinct culture, but also begins to act as a cohesive political unit. Smith's formulation is a useful one—although it must be kept in mind that politicized ethnic groups do not always strive for statehood. Nations, therefore, are often predicated on ethnicity. Shared ethnic origins provide nations with some sort of legitimacy over claims for territory and political autonomy. Thus, with regard to society, Wæver duly employs the label 'ethno-national' group.

Perhaps the only rival to ethno-national identity as a political mobilizer is religion. Religion possesses the ability to reproduce its 'we' identity more or less unconsciously across generations. It is also able to generate a feeling of self-identification, which can be as intense as that of nationalism. Moreover, where religious and ethno-national identities reinforce each other (e.g. Catholic Croats, Orthodox Serbs), this can produce very defined and resilient identities.

Wæver (1993: 23) concludes that the main units of analysis for societal security are 'politically significant ethno-national and religious entities', and accordingly defines societal security as 'the ability of a society to persist under changing conditions and possible and actual threats. More specifically, it is about the sustainability, within acceptable conditions for evolution, of traditional patterns of language, culture, association, and religion and national identity and custom.'

But just what 'possible and actual threats' might Wæver be referring to? The next section tackles this question.

KEY POINTS

- Societies are units formed by a sense of collective identity, where collective identity is defined as what enables the word 'we' to be used.
- For security analysis, societies are different from social groups. Societies have a reality of their own, they can operate as units in the international system, and they are invariably seen as having the right to survive.
- Nations and states are sometimes difficult to distinguish. Societies may be nation states, but do not always refer to state population.
- Society most often equates to ethno-national group, although religious groups may also be relevant units for analysis.
- Societal security can be defined as the maintenance of distinct ethno-national and religious identities.

Threats to societal identity

Objective definitions of threats to societal security are as problematic as they are for states. Indeed, perhaps more so. Given the sometimes fluid nature of collective identities, not all changes to it will necessarily be regarded as threatening. Some change will be seen as the natural process by which groups respond to meet changing historical conditions. Nevertheless, some processes invariably carry with them the potential to harm societal security.

Threats to societal security exist when a society perceives that its 'we' identity is being brought into question, whether this is objectively the case or not. Those means that can threaten societal identity range from the suppression of its expression to interference with its ability to reproduce itself across generations. This, according to Buzan (1993: 43), may include 'forbidding the use of language, names and dress, through closure of places of education and worship, to the deportation or killing of members of the community'. Threats to the reproduction of a society can occur through the sustained application of repressive measures against the expression of identity. If the institutions that reproduce language and culture, such as schools, newspapers, museums, and so forth, are shut down, then identity cannot easily be passed on from one generation to the next. Moreover, if the balance of the population changes in a given area, this can also disrupt societal reproduction.

As a referent object of security, society can be harmed through all of Buzan's five dimensions: societal, military, political, economic, and environmental. And, while some of the sectors are talked about at greater length in Chapters 13, 14, 16, and 17, it is worth describing here their specific relationship to societal identity.

The five sectors of security

Buzan et al. (1998: 121) have divided threats in the societal sector of security into three main categories: **migration**, **horizontal competition**, and **vertical competition**. In cases of migration, the host society is changed by the influx of those from outside; by a shift in the composition of the population. Think of examples in the early 2000s in the UK, where immigrants, particularly from countries such as Pakistan, India, and Bangladesh, have been accused of intensifying the formation of ghettos in major conurbations such as Greater London and the West Midlands, and where fears have likewise grown over competition for often scarce local resources such as education and health care. Horizontal competition refers to groups having to change their ways because of the overriding linguistic and cultural influences of others. For example, in the Soviet Union many of the republics were 'Russified'; Russian language and culture came to dominate over Latvian, Estonian, Ukrainian, and Kazakh identities, to name but a few. Finally, vertical competition refers to those instances where, because of either integration or disintegration, groups are pushed towards either wider or narrower identities, as was the case in the former Yugoslavia.

In the military sector, it is invariably the case that an external military threat will threaten the society or societies within the state. Here, threats to societal security can arguably be seen mainly in terms of depopulation—where enough members of the society are killed (or sometimes deported) either to hinder or to prevent collective identity being transmitted from one generation to the next.

However, some societies within invaded states may not always view armed aggression as a threat. Some minorities may be liberated either from their own regimes or from occupation by a foreign power. Besides, while external military aggression will invariably threaten state sovereignty, it may not necessarily pose a concomitant danger to the society's identity. Take, for example, Nazi Germany's invasion of France in

1940. There was an obvious potential to threaten both the French state and French society. However, while French sovereignty was indeed violated, for the most part French society remained relatively secure: French identity was not, to any significant extent at least, intentionally suppressed. Contrast this with Hitler's prior invasion of Poland in 1939: hand in hand with the military threat to the Polish state was also a political–societal threat to Polish identity: the Poles' Slavic identity coupled with the Nazi's policy of *Lebensraum*. As such, except when invasion is specifically designed towards the harming of state populations, such threats are mainly directed against either the maintenance of political autonomy (puppet states) or the survival of the incumbent regime (regime change).

Military threats to societies may also come from internal aggression. Perhaps the clearest example of this is when a regime, representing one ethnic group, uses its armed forces to suppress other minorities (for more on this see Chapter 14).

In the political sector, threats to societies are most likely to come from their own government, usually in the form of the suppression of minorities. And in this way political and military threats to societal identity will be closely linked. Political threats can often be mitigated by the state itself: for example, certain legislation can be introduced in order to protect societal identity. However, when the state machinery is overwhelmingly controlled by a dominant society, then not only might the state be unwilling to provide societal security, but it may itself be posing the threat.

The economic sector of security is for the most part characterized by how the capitalist system can undermine cultural distinctiveness by generating global products (televisions, computers, and computer games), attitudes (materialism and individualism), and style (English language), thereby replacing traditional identities with contemporary 'consumer' ones.

In the environmental sector, threats to societies can occur especially when identity is tied to a particular territory. This is certainly the case when culture is adapted to a way of life that is strongly conditioned by its natural surroundings. Threats to the environment may thus endanger the existence of that culture and sometimes the people themselves. For example, the loss of huge swathes of the Amazon rainforest has seriously affected many of its indigenous peoples in terms of their traditional existence as hunter-gatherer communities. In addition to deforestation, pollution, climate change, and desertification also pose similar threats to societal security.

In *Identity, Migration and the New Security Agenda in Europe* (1993), migration was as much a concentration for Wæver et al. as horizontal and vertical competition. In their chapter in the book describing the possible links between migration and societal security, Martin Heisler and Zig Layton-Henry (1993: 162) conclude the following: 'The capacity of social, economic, political and administrative institutions to integrate large numbers of immigrants, and the resistance of some immigrant communities to assimilation, affects the stability of society and therefore the ability of receiving states' governments to govern.' In subsequent works on the concept, migration was largely overshadowed by questions of state disintegration—predominantly in Eastern Europe and the former Soviet Union—as a focus for cases of societal insecurities. More recently, though, migration to the UK and other parts of Europe has again brought to the fore a societal security agenda made particularly salient by the concomitant rise of the political, sometime extreme, right in a number of countries.

Immigration and the rise of the political right

Within the scholarly literature, writers such as Jef Huysmans came to recognize how migration was increasingly subject to a discourse of security; a process of securitization, within parts of the EU space: Huysmans (2000: 758) noting that migration 'is identified as being one of the main factors weakening national tradition and societal homegeneity'. In this way, Huysmans (2000: 758) highlights how migrants are often subject to exclusion from the national community 'not just as aliens[,] but as aliens who are dangerous to the reproduction of the social fabric'.

Security discourses concerning immigration have tended to take three main forms. The first is concerned with state (national) security; in particular, with the question of territorial integrity. For example, the French port of Calais has been subject to a great deal of attention, with many reported cases of migrants having illegally entered into the UK from there. Moreover, some writers have also pointed to the conflation of the dangers posed by migrants and by terrorists (see, e.g., Huysmans and Buonfino, 2008, with reference to parliamentary debates in the UK in the post 9/11 period), with control over borders again being a focal point.

The second discourse is located within the economic sector of security and, in a recent, and sometimes continuing period of austerity for many European countries, has been much more sustained than that of territorial integrity—although also linking itself to certain notions of sovereignty. Familiar in many such cases has been talk of migrants 'taking our jobs' and abusing welfare and social service provisions. Often in keeping with an anti-EU rhetoric, many right-wing parties, including the UK Independence Party (UKIP), have made swift and significant electoral gains in expounding policies that promise to curtail, and even reverse, the number of immigrants. For example, UKIP's policy proposals have consistently rested largely on the message that Britain is being overwhelmed by immigration and the UK government is powerless to act as long as the country remains in the EU. In one such campaign, UKIP posters warned that '29 million Romanians and Bulgarians' were coming to take British jobs. UKIP leader Nigel Farage has also made links between economic migration and criminality. In an interview with the *Guardian* newspaper, Farage (Wintour 2014) explained that it was not only a question of numbers, but the kind of people who were arriving: 'People hate talking about this, but if you look at the Met crime figures for Romanian arrests, there have been 28,000 in London in the last five years. Is there a problem? Yeah. There is a problem.'

The third discourse, and of most immediate concern for this chapter, is a societal one. Although the economic discourse has been prominent, societal security concerns have consistently also been manifest. In a societal security discourse, the immigrant brings with him or her traits and forms of behaviour that are not only strange to the national community but which, if brought by sufficient numbers, are also said to dilute or extinguish completely certain traditions and practices. In some cases, right-wing parties have often attempted to downplay questions of societal security for fear of being branded racist; and this has arguably been the case with UKIP. Still, certain pronouncements have made more than clear these kind of societal insecurities. When questioned as to whether he thought certain parts of Britain are a foreign land, Nigel Farage (Wintour 2014) replied that on a recent train journey from London's Charing Cross station '[i]t was not until we got past Grove Park that I could hear English being audibly spoken in the carriage. Does that make me feel slightly awkward? Yes it does. I wonder what is really going on.' (Although winning just one parliamentary seat, the strong resonance of UKIPs rhetoric was reflected in the 2015 General Election, in which the party secured 12.6 per cent of the popular vote.)

Still, some other right-wing parties elsewhere have been far less guarded about questions of identity. In Sweden's 2014 elections, standing on an overt anti-immigrant platform, the extreme-right Sweden Democrats took 13 per cent of the vote. At times, the party's rhetoric has been fiercely racist; in particular, attacking Muslim migrants as a threat to the nation's culture. In a rebuke to notions of multiculturalism, Niclas Nilsson, the party's local leader in the town of Kristianstad, complained (Crouch 2014): 'Swedish people don't feel at home any more. The problem we have is basically with the Muslims. They have difficulty assimilating . . .'. He went on to express his fears that higher birth rates among Muslim immigrants will inevitably lead to a dilution of the nation's 'Swedishness'.

While in the case of immigration, such rhetoric is arguably often the stuff of mere scaremongering, in instances of horizontal, and certainly sometimes vertical competition, societal insecurities may indeed sometimes correspond with very real dangers to collective identities: as was demonstrated only too starkly in the wars in the former Yugoslavia.

Genocide, 'culturecide', and the Yugoslav wars

If carried out on a large enough scale, many such threats to societal security come to correspond with the definition of genocide as set out under the terms of the 1948 UN Genocide Convention. According to Article 2 of the Convention, genocide refers to acts that intend to destroy, physically or biologically, 'national, ethnical, racial or religious groups'. This was highlighted only too starkly during the conflict in Rwanda (see Case Study 15.1) and the wars in the former Yugoslavia. The now well-known horrors of **ethnic cleansing** saw the intentional killing, violence (including sexual) against, and deportation of peoples on the part of all parties to the Yugoslav conflicts, although such acts were perpetrated most by the Bosnian Serb army and paramilitaries. We can think not only of the 1995 massacre of an estimated 8,000 Bosnian Muslim men and boys at Srebrenica, but also of the existence of many camps in towns, such as Foca,

KEY QUOTES 15.2 The effects of cultural cleansing

'You have to understand that the cultural identity of a population represents its survival in the future. When Serbs blow up the mosque of a village and destroy its graveyards and the foundations of the graveyards and mosques and then level them off . . . no one can ever tell this was a Muslim village. This is the murder of a people's cultural identity.'

Boeles (1990)

'In extreme circumstances, systematic discrimination threatens communal groups' most fundamental right, the right to survival. Many groups also face cultural discrimination and the risk of de-culturation or so-called cultural genocide in the form of pressures or incentives to adopt a dominant culture, or denial of cultural self-expression.'

Gurr (1993: 6)

where women were imprisoned and subjected to rape and other forms of sexual violence.

In addition to ethnic cleansing, however, what some have termed cultural cleansing was also a prevalent practice. By contrast, **cultural cleansing** is perpetrated not against members of the group as such, but against manifestations of group culture. This involved the deliberate destruction of churches, mosques, libraries, and monuments across much of Bosnia-Hercegovina and parts of Croatia, and was intended to wipe out hundreds of years of history from the former Yugoslavia. It is what some writers have described as 'culturecide', and it strikes right against the very core of societal identity (see Key Quotes 15.2).

Culturecide, or 'cultural genocide', is not a part of the Genocide Convention, although Raphael Lemkin (1944), who is seen as being the originator of the term 'genocide', did propose a cultural component to it. Lemkin argued that the destruction of cultures was every bit as disastrous as the physical destruction of nations. Although not clearly defined, the UN's 1994 Draft Declaration on the Rights of Indigenous Peoples does use the term 'cultural genocide'; amongst other provisions, Article 7 calls for prevention against the deprivation of 'cultural values' and against any imposed forms of 'assimilation or integration by other cultures'. Indeed, the term 'cultural genocide' (culturecide) is used regularly by politicians, scholars, and human- and minority-rights activists to describe threats to societal security. For example, in 2008 the Dalai Lama accused China of cultural genocide, referring to ethnic Chinese immigration into Tibet and the restrictions placed on Buddhist worship.

CASE STUDY 15.1 The Rwandan genocide

The 1994 genocide in Rwanda was provoked by the assassination of the country's president, Juvenal Habyarimana, in April of that year. Over the course of the following three months, up to as many as three-quarters of a million Tutsis are estimated to have been killed by Hutu militias, the most notorious of these being the *Interahamwe*.

Historically, Tutsis, who at the time of the genocide made up around 15 per cent of Rwanda's population, had been privileged over Hutus by the country's aristocracy and, in this way, the difference between the two groups was as much economic and social as it was ethnic. However, under Belgian administration a strict system of racial classification served both to exaggerate and to reinforce ethnic difference: Tutsis were considered superior by virtue of being seen as more 'white' looking by their colonial rulers. Following an uprising in 1959 and the establishment of an independent republic in 1961, the new, Hutu-dominated government retained racial classification as a means of subordinating the Tutsi minority. Government suppression resulted in the flight of tens of thousands of Tutsis from Rwanda, and culminated in an invasion by Tutsi rebels from neighbouring Uganda in 1990.

From a societal security perspective, perceived ethnic differences were used by the majority Hutus to reinforce grievances over the privileges historically enjoyed by the minority Tutsis: Tutsis were murdered and expelled because of their ethnic identity, and not just because of their prior economic and social standing. The ideology of 'Hutu Power' articulated a culturally defined disdain for, and superiority over, Tutsis: Tutsis were portrayed as foreigners, and Hutu propaganda frequently depicted them as cockroaches and rats. Moreover, as in the former Yugoslavia, the majority of rapes perpetrated by Hutu militias against Tutsi women were carried out with the express intention of trying to destroy Tutsi culture.

Skjelsbaek (2001: 219)

Against perceived threats through all five dimensions of security, societies can react in two ways. First, by trying to move the threat onto the state's security agenda—and actions taken by states to defend their societies are quite common. However, second, societies can also choose, or may be forced, to defend themselves through non-state means. As Buzan (1993: 56–7) enquires: 'What happens when societies cannot look to the state for protection . . .?' Unable to turn to the regime to guarantee their survival, societies will have to provide for their own security; they will be in a self-help situation. Just how societies help themselves is the matter of the next section.

KEY POINTS

- Objectively defining threats to societal security is difficult, especially as some changes to group identity will be seen as a natural response to shifting historical circumstance.
- Societal identity can be threatened from the suppression of its expression through to interference with its ability to reproduce itself across generations.
- Ethnic cleansing; the deliberate killing, violence against, and deportation of members of one society by another, and cultural cleansing, the systematic destruction of institutions and symbols designed to promote and maintain group identity, are two prominent manifestations of threats to societal security, and were widely employed, for example, during the wars in the former Yugoslavia.
- Societies can be threatened through all five of Buzan's sectors of security, although the societal and military dimensions are perhaps the most important.
- States often take measures to defend their own societies. But, in multi-ethnic states in particular, societies may find themselves in self-help situations, where they are compelled to provide for their own security.

Defending societal identity

Perhaps most evidently, societal identity can be defended using military means. This is particularly the case if identity is linked to territory: the defence of the historic homeland. If the threat posed by one group to another is military (armed attack from a neighbouring society), then some kind of armed response is invariably required. However, in such a scenario, societal security dynamics are likely closely to resemble those of armed aggression between states: defending societal identity becomes much the same as defending state sovereignty. Therefore, in order to show how societal security can be used as a distinct (from state security) analytical tool, the remainder of this section turns its attention to the intra-state level of analysis, and to multi-ethnic states where societal insecurities are most often apparent.

While some societies (as states or quasi-states) may very well have an army or at least some kind of militia that can be utilized for defence, the vast majority of intra-state groups possess no such exclusive means of protection. For them, members of the group will either make up part of the state's armed forces as a whole, or have military forces composed of the same ethnic group in a neighbouring state. Facing a threat in identity terms, such groups are therefore left with two main options: first, they can try to form their own militia/defence force as a means of protection, although this can prove to be extremely difficult; or, second, they can try to defend their identity using non-military means.

Non-military means of defence

At the intra-state level, the vulnerabilities felt by many groups may often derive not so much from armed aggression as from demographic processes and political-legal means designed to deprive societies of beliefs and practices vital to the maintenance of their culture. Returning to the example of ethnic cleansing, Robert Hayden (1996: 784) highlights how, for example, such threats to societal identity can be shaped very much by demographic considerations: 'Within areas in which the sovereign group is already an overwhelming majority, homogenization can be brought about by legal and bureaucratic means, such as denying citizenship to those not of the right group.' In more mixed areas, however, Hayden goes on, homogenization requires more drastic measures such as killing and physical expulsion. And, although it is only the attempted extermination of the minority group in this regard that has been widely recognized as ethnic cleansing, 'it is important to recognize that legal and bureaucratic discrimination is aimed at bringing about the same result: the elimination of the minority'.

When the nature of the threat is non-military (legal, bureaucratic), countervailing measures are also likely to be so. In the *Identity, Migration* book, Wæver et al. (1993: 191) suggest that for threatened societies 'one obvious line of defensive response is to

> **KEY QUOTES 15.3 The project of cultural nationalism**
>
> '[C]ultural nationalists establish . . . clusters of cultural societies and journals, designed to inspire spontaneous love of the community in its different members by educating them to their common heritage of splendour and suffering. They engage in naming rituals, celebrate national cultural uniqueness and reject foreign practices, in order to identify the community to itself, embed this into everyday life and differentiate this against other communities.'
>
> *Hutchinson (1994: 124)*

strengthen societal identity'. This can be done, Wæver (1995: 68) notes succinctly, by defending culture 'with culture'; and consequently 'culture becomes security policy'. The idea of defending culture with culture is a slightly tricky one to unpack, but John Hutchinson provides a useful starting point. Hutchinson (1994) describes the project of what he calls **cultural nationalism**. Cultural nationalism is designed to generate a strong feeling of self-identification. It emphasizes various commonalities such as language, religion, and history, and downplays other ties that might detract from its unity. In this sense, cultural nationalism celebrates what is special about our *identity* (see Key Quotes 15.3). Self-identification, as such, often takes place because societal identity has been threatened: 'Our present identity has become too weak. We therefore need to change it and make ourselves strong again.'

Defending societal identity through cultural nationalism can be seen in the case of relations between the Protestant and Catholic communities in Northern Ireland.

In Portadown, the Protestant Orange Order has struggled to maintain what it sees as its historic right to march down the predominantly Catholic Garvaghy Road. Likewise, many of the town's Catholic inhabitants have protested, claiming that the march is highly provocative. For the Orange Order, not to march is tantamount to surrender: 'We have been walking down this road for generations. Why should we stop now?' In this way, the right of the Orange Order to march is inextricably bound up with the maintenance of its Protestant identity: it is the right to express who *we* are, where *we* come from (and indeed, where *we* are going). It is a societal security requirement. However, for the Catholic community, the march is a celebration of the Protestant victory at the 1690 Battle of the Boyne, and thus represents a serious attack on their own identity. As Michael Ignatieff (1993: 169) points out, the victory of William of Orange over the Catholic King James 'became a founding myth of ethnic superiority. . . The Ulstermen's reward, as they saw it, was permanent ascendancy over the Catholic Irish.'

In the face of what many Protestants have come to see as the erosion of their ascendant status in the province, Orange Order marches are a cultural-nationalist strategy aimed at strengthening their identity: the celebration of the self.

In perhaps more concrete terms, collective identity can be strengthened when cultural nationalist strategies are manifest as **cultural autonomy**. Cultural autonomy entails the granting of certain rights in relation to the means of cultural reproduction: the control of one's own schools, newspapers, religious institutions, and so forth.

Similarly, societal groups may also employ 'ethnic' or '**political nationalism**' as a means of defence. Unlike cultural nationalism, political-nationalist projects have an explicit territorial element to them. Political nationalism, as manifest in political autonomy, often involves self-government along a wider range of issues, such as the ability to control some of its own legal and financial affairs (for example, as with the Basques in Spain). In this way, political autonomy usually equates to some kind of autonomous region within the state. In its most extreme expression, though, and if threats to societal identity are seen as particularly severe, political-nationalist projects may seek outright independence outside of the existing state structure.

In this way, the concept of societal security and questions of human and minority rights become closely linked. Both Will Kymlicka (2001) and Gwendolyn Sasse (2005) have discussed the implications of framing minority rights as a security issue: Kymlicka argues that using the language of (societal) security effectively prevents thinking about the provision of minority rights in terms of justice, while Sasse shows how actors, such as the OSCE's High Commissioner for National Minorities (HCNM), are increasingly cognizant of the balance between security and rights- (or justice-) based concerns. Similarly, Paul Roe (2001, 2004) has talked about the role of the HCNM in mitigating societal security dilemmas (see the following section), and has also made the argument that societal security concerns are an inherent quality of minority rights provisions (see Key Quotes 15.4).

KEY QUOTES 15.4 Societal security and minority rights

'"First of all, a minority is a group with linguistic, ethnic or cultural characteristics which distinguish it from the majority. Secondly, a minority is a group which usually not only seeks to maintain its identity but also tries to give a stronger expression to that identity" . . . Or, in the language of the Copenhagen School, being a minority, and thus pursuing minority rights, is a matter of societal security.'

Roe (2004: 288)

KEY POINTS

- Military means may often be used to defend societal identity. This is particularly the case when identity is linked to territory.
- At the intra-state level, however, many societal groups may have no such means of armed protection. Forced to provide for their own security, such groups are compelled to employ non-military countermeasures.
- Cultural-nationalist strategies can be used to defend societal security. When manifest as cultural autonomy, this involves the control over those institutions that are responsible for cultural reproduction, such as schools and churches.
- Political-nationalist strategies are also a means of defending collective identity. Political autonomy, however, is more territorially based and thus involves a much greater measure of self-government within the state.
- Secession is the most extreme form of defence for societal security.

In the book *Identity, Migration*, Buzan (1993: 46) suggests that, by analogy with relations between states, it may be possible to talk of **societal security dilemmas**, and that societal security dilemmas might

KEY QUOTES 15.5 The two sides of ethnicity

'On the one hand, ethnicity . . . is often perceived as backward and dangerous. On the other hand, [some] authors tend to view ethnicity as . . . the self-expression of the threatened and the marginalised. Ethnicity can be both positive and negative. Of course, the divisive nature of contemporary ethno-nationalism, its violent boundary makings, its exclusiveness, etc., must also be viewed as considerable challenges to the modern international system, as well as potentials for violence and wars. One must not forget, however, that ethnicity has also a potential for internal group solidarity and loyalty.'

Lindholm (1993: 24)

explain why some ethnic conflicts 'come to acquire a dynamic of their own'. Paul Roe (2002; 2005) has since developed the concept of the societal security dilemma; applying it to explain instances of ethnic violence between Serbs and Croats in Croatia (1990) and Hungarians and Romanians in Romania (also 1990). The societal security dilemma describes a situation where the actions of one society, in trying to strengthen its collective identity, causes a reaction in a second, which, in the end, weakens the identity of the first.

While the intention here is not to discuss the societal security dilemma at any great length, it is worth noting, still, how Roe (2005) sees the concept as being driven by the two sides of nationalism; cultural (positive) and ethnic (negative). By analogy with the inherent ambiguity of arms in the (state) security dilemma, nationalism can also be viewed as such in that it is both malign (political)—often characterized with the annexation of territories and the disintegration of states—and benign (cultural)—mostly seen as working within existing state structures (see Key Quotes 15.5).

Conclusion

Thus far, the chapter has shown the importance of societal security concerns and how the concept can be used profitably as an analytical tool. However, the Copenhagen School has not been without its critics. And in this concluding section some of the major contentions are considered.

The charge of reification

A first, and perhaps most fundamental, criticism concerns the Copenhagen School's view of the construction of collective identity. In a comprehensive critique of the societal security concept, Bill McSweeney (1996: 82) charges Wæver, Buzan, and their fellow collaborators with reification. He claims that both 'society' and 'identity' are treated as 'objective realities, out there to be discovered': seen in objectivist terms, societies and societal identities are 'things' that somehow naturally exist. McSweeney (1996: 85) takes a more constructivist view in which society is rather a fluid entity: 'Identity is not a fact of society; it is a process of negotiation . . .'. If, in this way, society is subject to constant construction and reconstruction, the question becomes whether societies, like states, can be seen as objects around which security dynamics can be observed. In a direct response to McSweeney's contentions, Buzan and Wæver (1997) refute the charge of objectivism, arguing that theirs is also a constructivist approach. Unlike McSweeney, though, they claim that, while societal identities are indeed socially constructed, once constructed they can also be regarded as, at least temporarily, fixed. In a subsequent review of the societal security concept, Tobias Theiler (2003: 254) talks of the Copenhagen School's 'persuasive defence', and agrees that when 'beliefs and institutions become deeply sedimented' they 'change only very slowly'. As an analytical tool, therefore, societal security is useful in accounting for specific events in specific places at specific times. An example of this is Graeme P. Herd and Joan Lofgren's study (2001) of societal security concerns between the Baltic States and their Russian minorities during much of the 1990s.

Nevertheless, more poststructural writings, such as the work of David Campbell (1992), contend that the construction of collective identities is made possible only through reference to external threat; what Campbell calls 'discourses of danger'. That is to say, societal identity exists not prior to the identification of threat but as a very consequence of it. Indeed, as Michael C. Williams (2003: 519) argues: 'A successful securitization of identity involves precisely the capacity to decide on the limits of a given identity . . .'. This serves to highlight the criticism that the Copenhagen School have failed to theorize the relationship between threat and collective identity construction.

Who speaks for society?

A second major criticism concerns the separation between state and society. In particular, the question arises as to who speaks for society if not the state. Certainly, where state and society coincide, in the case of relatively homogenous nation states, societal security concerns are invariably articulated by the government or by major political parties, the very same voices that speak on behalf of the state. In such an instance, to the observer state security and societal security may very well appear as pretty much one and the same. However, while the voice may indeed often be the same, the 'grammar' may nonetheless be different: state security concerns come hand in hand with the language of sovereignty, while societal security concerns come hand in hand with the language of identity. The point here is essentially tied to the Copenhagen School's notion of securitization, which is discussed at length in Chapter 12. For the purposes here, though, what is important to keep in mind is that, although state and society may be coterminous, *how* the referent object is threatened gives rise to different responses.

Sometimes, though, as has already been discussed, states and societies do not coincide. And in these instances the voices of state security and societal security may be different. For minority groups, societal security concerns are not always voiced from within the government, unless minority political parties are part of the ruling coalition. Minority groups may at least have some kind of representation within the legislature. If not, though, such societies will be forced to articulate their concerns outside the state apparatus. In this regard, cultural elites (writers, poets, academics) can try to mobilize their societies against the government (majority group).

The dangers of speaking societal security

From this second criticism comes a third, and it concerns the political implications of voicing societal security. As Williams (1998) points out, although, on the one hand, McSweeney charges the Copenhagen School with objectivism, on the other hand, he also notes how the societal security concept is dangerously subjectivist too. Politicians can use perceived threats to societal security to legitimize racists and xenophobic political agendas. For example, defending 'our' identity against 'theirs' can serve to characterize immigrant communities as dangerous Others who must either be assimilated or expelled (see Key Quotes 15.6). There is certainly a risk here, but a risk that Wæver (1999: 337) believes is worth taking: 'This danger [of giving rise to fascist and anti-foreigner voices] has to be offset against the necessity to use the concept of societal security to try to understand what is actually happening.' This is what Jef Huysmans (2002) has called the 'normative dilemma' of writing security.

> **KEY QUOTES 15.6 Legitimizing racism and xenophobia**
>
> 'What if [Jean-Marie] Le Pen manages to manufacture a majority consent, verified by polls or other measurement techniques, around the idea of racism and xenophobia, or if the IRA creates a "collective identity" which incorporates intense anti-British sentiment into a symbol of Irish solidarity? Such hypothetical developments are not wildly improbable, and would immediately present a serious security problem in France and Ireland'.
>
> *McSweeney (1996: 87–8)*

Applying the concept elsewhere

While not really a substantive criticism of societal security, a final point worth considering is whether the concept has a potentially wider application outside Europe. As was mentioned, the Copenhagen School's thinking about societal security was very much a response to the European Security agenda of the 1990s—to the processes of Western integration and Eastern disintegration. So what about elsewhere?

As an analytical tool, societal security is particularly effective for understanding the security concerns of multi-ethnic states: relations between the regime (majority group) and the country's minority groups. And this is the focus of the so-called Third World Security School (see, e.g., Job 1992; Ayoob 1995). For many countries in the developing world, the greatest threats are often internal. During the process of nation building, where minority identities are assimilated into the majority, state regimes may often require minority groups to give up all, or part, of their cultural distinctiveness. These ethnic differences, together with the state's inability to provide for certain sections of its people, cause the population to express its loyalty elsewhere. And it is this lack of cohesion between the state and its societies that defines the state as 'weak'. Weak states provide propitious conditions for the study of societal insecurities (see, e.g., Collins 2003; Caballero-Anthony et al. 2006), and serve to locate the concept more firmly in the peace studies tradition where the provision for 'identity needs' (Galtung 1990) are, alongside other social and economic freedoms, critical to the realization of social justice.

QUESTIONS

1. In what ways does societal security mark a departure from more traditional thinking about security? Cannot realist and neorealist approaches adequately capture the dynamics of nationalism and ethnic conflict?
2. What is the difference between society as a sector of security and society as a referent object?
3. How far can 'societies' be seen as rational, instrumental actors?
4. Is there a clear distinction to be drawn between societies and 'social groups'?
5. In what way might societies be said to have a right to survive?
6. Are societies, as the Copenhagen School claim, all about identity?
7. How can multi-ethnic states threaten the societal security of their minority groups? How can minorities try to counter these threats?
8. How differently does, for example, a map of Europe look seen through a societal security rather than a state security perspective?
9. Is the Copenhagen School right in saying the European security agenda has become increasingly concerned with questions of group identity?

FURTHER READING

- Aggestam, L. and Hyde-Price, A. (eds) (2000), *Security and Identity in Europe*, London: Macmillan. Excellent coverage of key issues facing European security; including NATO enlargement, EU integration, and the wars in the Balkans.
- Buzan, B., Kelstrup, M., Lemaitre, P., Tromer, E., and Wæver, O. (1990), *The European Security Order Recast: Scenarios for the Post-Cold War Era*, London: Pinter. Precursor to the *Identity, Migration* book, this is the Copenhagen School's exploration of the new, emerging European security agenda through Buzan's five dimensions.

- Katzenstein, P. J. (ed.) (1996), *The Culture of National Security: Norms and Identity in World Politics*, New York: Columbia University Press. Perhaps the most important edited collection concerning the impact of norms and identity on security and foreign policy and behaviour.
- Lapid, J. and Kratochwil, F. (eds) (1999), *The Return of Culture and Identity in IR Theory*, Boulder, CO: Lynne Rienner. Edited volume that covers the 'constructivist turn' in international relations from the Copenhagen School to postmodern and poststructural approaches.
- McSweeney, B. (1999), *Security, Identity, and Interests: A Sociology of International Relations*, Cambridge: Cambridge University Press. Provides excellent critiques of existing constructivist approaches to security and identity.
- Roe. P. (2005), *Ethnic Violence and the Societal Security Dilemma*, London: Routledge. One of the few books that successfully combines questions of identity with traditional security studies scholarship.
- Weldes, J., Laffey, M., Gusterson, H., and Duvall, R. (1999), *Cultures of Insecurity: States, Communities, and the Production of Dangers*, Minneapolis: University of Minnesota Press. Introduces sociological and anthropological approaches in examining the cultural production of insecurity in local, national, and international contexts; from the Korean War, to the Cuban Missile Crisis, to the conflicts in the Middle East.

IMPORTANT WEBSITES

- **http://www.ciaonet.org** Provides access to a wide range of working papers, journals, and policy briefs, including previous COPRI works.
- **http://www.systemicpeace.org** Official website of the Center for Systemic Peace. Contains datasets, project reports, including Ted Robert Gurr's *Minorities at Risk* and an extensive library of bibliographical references for works that examine violent conflicts from both a human and societal security perspective.
- **http://www.hrw.org** Excellent resource for news releases, publications, reports, and event lists concerning human and minority rights in Europe and elsewhere.

Visit the Online Resource Centre that accompanies this book for lots of interesting additional material: www.oxfordtextbooks.co.uk/orc/collins4e/

16

Environmental Security

Jon Barnett

Chapter Contents

Reader's Guide

This chapter discusses the concept of environmental security. It explains the way environmental security has both broadened and deepened the issue of security. It describes the evolution of the concept as a merger of international environmental agreements, efforts by the peace movement to contest the meaning and practice of security, the proliferation of new security issues in the post-Cold War era, recognition that environmental changes pose grave risks to human well-being, and the growing community of research practice that seeks to build peace through natural resource management. The chapter examines the different meanings of environmental security, and then it explains four major categories of environmental security problems—namely, the way environmental change can be a factor in violent conflict, the way environmental change can be a risk to national security, the way war and preparation for war can damage the environment, and the way environmental change can be a risk to human security. It explains how environmental security can mean different things to different people and can apply to vastly different referent objects in ways that sometimes have very little to do with environmental change.

Introduction

In its most basic sense, **insecurity** is the risk of something bad happening to a thing that is valued. For example, people who value their jobs are concerned about the risk of unemployment, families who value having enough to eat are concerned about the regular supply of food, and governments that value **power** are concerned about losing office. So, security can apply to many different things that are valued (referent objects such as jobs, health, or organizations) and refer to many different kinds of risks (unemployment, lack of food, a change of government). The environment has also been seen as a referent object of security, and **environmental change** has been seen as a security risk. These connections between the environment and security fall under the heading of **environmental security**, and this chapter provides an overview of this concept.

Environmental security is one of a number of 'new', **non-traditional security** issues that have served to deepen and broaden the concept of security. It helps to deepen security, as it entails considering not just the security of states, but also the security of 'the environment' and its many nested subsystems. It broadens security by considering risks other than war—principally the risks posed by environmental change—to the things that people value. Further, like the concepts of human security and gender security discussed in this book (see Chapters 10 and 11), environmental security is sometimes a *critical* security project in that it is used to ask questions about who and what is being secured—and from what risks—by orthodox security policies (see also Chapters 7 and 8 of this book).

Like security studies more generally, environmental security has entailed much research of a more practical kind. There have been numerous attempts to assess the extent to which environmental change causes violent conflict within and between countries (this is examined in the fourth section of this chapter). There are explanations of the ways in which environmental change may undermine national security (explained in the fifth section of this chapter). There have been investigations of the ways in which war and preparations for war affect the environment (discussed in the sixth section of this chapter). Finally, there has been a growing body of research that investigates the linkages between environmental change and development issues such as poverty and human security (as explained in the seventh section of this chapter). These research endeavours have influenced policy development in some countries, in intergovernmental organizations such as the United Nations and NATO, and in non-governmental organizations such as the World Conservation Union and Greenpeace.

KEY POINTS

- The environment can be both an object to be secured and a source of risk.
- Environmental security means different things to different people.
- Environmental security has contributed to both a broadening and a deepening of security.
- Environmental security has both critical and applied dimensions.

The origins of environmental security

Environmental security emerged as an important concept in security studies because of four interrelated developments beginning in the 1960s. The first of these was the growth of environmental consciousness in developed countries. A number of events stimulated and sustained the growth of the environmental movement at this time. Notable among these was the publication in 1962 of Rachel Carson's widely read book *Silent Spring* (also serialized in the *New Yorker*), which explained the impacts of the pesticide DDT on animals and the food chain. Carson was among the first of many people whose use of print and electronic media have created and sustained awareness of environmental issues; others include notable personalities such as David Attenborough, Jacques Cousteau, and David Suzuki.

The number of environmental non-governmental organizations—of which there are now more than 100,000 worldwide—also seriously began to grow in the 1960s. From an international relations perspective, a notable development was the creation of large international environmental non-governmental organizations such as the World Wildlife Fund (1961), Friends of the Earth (1969), and Greenpeace (1971). Their functions have grown to include networking across countries, research, awareness raising, policy development and monitoring, capacity building, fund raising, and lobbying at local, national, and

BACKGROUND 16.1 Major multilateral environmental agreements

1946 International Convention for the Regulation of Whaling
1963 Treaty Banning Nuclear Weapon Tests in the Atmosphere, in Outer Space and under Water
1971 Convention on Wetlands of International Importance especially as Waterfowl Habitat (Ramsar)
1972 Convention on the Prevention of Marine Pollution by Dumping of Wastes and Other Matter (London Convention)
1972 Convention for the Protection of the World Cultural and Natural Heritage
1973 International Convention for the Prevention of Pollution for Ships, 1973, and Protocols (MARPOL)
1973 Convention on International Trade in Endangered Species of Wild Fauna and Flora (CITES)
1979 Convention on Long-Range Transboundary Air Pollution
1982 United Nations Convention on the Law of the Sea
1983 International Tropical Timber Agreement
1987 Montreal Protocol on Substances that Deplete the Ozone Layer
1989 Basel Convention on the Control of Transboundary Movements of Hazardous Wastes and their Disposal
1992 Convention on Biological Diversity
1992 United Nations Framework Convention on Climate Change
1996 Comprehensive Nuclear Test Ban Treaty
1997 Kyoto Protocol to the United Nations Framework Convention on Climate Change
2000 Cartegena Protocol on Biosafety to the Convention on Biological Diversity
2001 Stockholm Convention on Persistent Organic Pollutants
2013 Minamata Convention on Mercury

international forums. Their issue agenda is similarly broad, extending beyond conservation to include environmental justice, gender inequities, genetic engineering, indigenous rights, nuclear non-proliferation, poverty alleviation, sustainable energy technologies, and waste management. A growing number of non-governmental organizations of various scales and in various locations are incorporating environmental security issues into their work, including the African Centre for Technology Studies, the Institute for Environmental Security, the International Institute for Sustainable Development, the Stockholm Environment Institute, and the Worldwatch Institute.

The 1970s also saw the beginning of international summits on environmental issues, and a proliferation of international agreements on environmental issues. According to the United Nations Environment Programme (itself established in 1972), there are now over 500 multilateral environmental agreements, most of which were signed after 1972 (see Background 16.1). The first major global environmental summit was arguably the **United Nations Conference on the Human Environment (UNCHE)** held in Stockholm in 1972. It initiated a number of intergovernmental investigations, meetings, and agreements on global environmental problems. These merged at times with parallel investigations into development and common security, and culminated in the 1987 report of the World Commission on Environment and Development (WCED) entitled *Our Common Future*. The WCED report popularized the term 'sustainable development', and it introduced the term 'environmental security' (see Key Quotes 16.1). It set the scene for the watershed United Nations Conference on Environment and Development (UNCED) held in Rio de Janeiro in 1992, which has had follow-up conferences in 1997, 2002, and 2012.

The second major development leading to the emergence of environmental security was attempts from the 1970s onwards by a number of scholars to critique orthodox security discourse and practices by highlighting their inability to manage environmental risks to national and international security. This is the initial critical use of the concept of environmental security. Among the first attempts to do this were Richard Falk's *This Endangered Planet* (1971), and Harold and Margaret Sprout's *Toward a Politics of Planet Earth* (1971) (see Key Quotes 16.2). Both books argued that the international political system needs to comprehend and collectively to respond to common environmental problems, as they pose threats to international stability and national well-being. These ideas about environmental interdependence and **common security** have remained key themes of environmental security studies.

It was not until 1983, when Richard Ullman published an article titled 'Redefining Security', that the idea that environmental change might cause war was seriously proposed. Ullman defined a national security threat as anything that can quickly degrade the

KEY QUOTES 16.1 Environmental security

'A comprehensive approach to international and national security must transcend the traditional emphasis on military power and armed competition. The real sources of insecurity also encompass unsustainable development . . .'

'Environmental stress can thus be an important part of the web of causality associated with any conflict and can in some cases be catalytic.'

'Poverty, injustice, environmental degradation and conflict interact in complex and potent ways.'

'As unsustainable forms of development push individual countries up against environmental limits, major differences in environmental endowment among countries, or various stocks of usable land and raw materials, could precipitate and exacerbate international tension and conflict.'

'Threats to environmental security can only be dealt with by joint management and multilateral procedures and mechanisms.'

WCED (1987: ch. 11)

KEY QUOTES 16.2 Environment and security

'We need to revamp our entire concept of "national security" and "economic growth" if we are to solve the problems of environmental decay.'

Falk (1971: 185)

'The thrust of the evidence is simply that the goal of national security as traditionally conceived—and as still very much alive—presents problems that are becoming increasingly resistant to military solutions.'

Sprout and Sprout (1971: 406)

'Neither bloated military budgets nor highly sophisticated weapons systems can halt deforestation or solve the firewood crisis.'

Brown (1977: 37)

'The pressure engendered by population growth in the Third World is bound to degrade the quality of life, and diminish the range of options available, to governments and persons in the rich countries.'

Ullman (1983: 143)

'Conflict over resources is likely to grow more intense.'

Ullman (1983: 139)

'If a nation's environmental foundations are depleted, its economy will steadily decline, its social fabric deteriorate, and its political structure become destabilized. The outcome is all too likely to be conflict, whether conflict in the form of disorder and insurrection within the nation, or tensions and hostilities with other nations.'

Myers (1986: 251)

'It is thus inescapable that any concept of international security must in the last analysis be based on this obligate relationship of humankind with its environment.'

Westing (1986: 195)

'Climate change not only exacerbates threats to peace and security. It is a threat to international peace and security.'

UN Secretary-General Ban Ki-moon (UN Security Council, 20 July 2011)

'Climate change will impact every country on the planet. No nation is immune . . . climate change constitutes a serious threat to global security, an immediate risk to our national security. And make no mistake, it will impact how our military defends our country.'

Remarks by the President of the United States at the United States Coast Guard Academy Commencement (20 May 2015)

quality of life of the inhabitants of a state, or that narrows the choices available to people and organizations within the state. A number of environmental scientists have also argued that environmental degradation will induce violent conflict (see Key Quotes 16.2).

These early arguments for the connections between the environment and security were very much of peripheral concern to Western security institutions occupied with the 'hard' business of winning the Cold War. For the United States and its allies, security meant national security from the military and ideological threat of the Soviet Union and its allies, and the principal strategy to achieve this was to build and to maintain military superiority. However, one notable event troubled this pure vision of security. In 1973 the Organization of Petroleum Exporting Countries (OPEC) restricted oil exports, leading to a quadrupling of the price of oil on world markets. This showed that the industrial capacity that underpinned the military superiority of the West was vulnerable to the dictates of the suppliers of energy. This event firmly established the idea of energy security in mainstream security planning.

A shift in the strategic landscape is the third reason why environmental security is now an important concept in security studies. The end of the bipolar world order created by the Cold War created something of a 'vertigo' for security policy and security studies, and for a few years the old ways of thinking about security became less obviously relevant (O'Tuathail 1996). This 'vertigo', combined with the growing environmental consciousness of people in developed countries, the call for common security approaches in *Our Common Future*, and preparations for the UNCED Rio conference, created the intellectual and policy space for environmental security to enter the mainstream as one of a suite of 'new' security issues (Dalby 1992a). So, from 1989 onwards there were many more publications and studies on environmental security, including in prominent security journals. These were to have some influence on policy, particularly in the United States (Barnett 2001). In the first decades of the twenty-first century climate change and increasing instability in world food and energy markets are issues that foreign and security policy makers in many countries consider to be security issues.

The fourth reason why environmental security has become an important concept in security studies is because of the growing recognition that environmental changes do not merely pose risks to ecosystems; they also pose risks to human well-being. It is now well understood that environmental change poses real risks to human security by undermining access to basic environmental assets such as productive soils, clean water, and food; by contributing to violations of civil and political rights such as to the means of subsistence and health; and by restricting people's access to the economic and social opportunities they need to develop meaningful lives (Matthew et al. 2009). As this recognition has grown, environmental security has become an important concern of environmental and development studies, and this has resulted in increased dialogue between security, development, and environmental researchers and policy makers.

KEY POINTS

- Environmental security emerged as an important concept in security studies because of:
  - the development of environmentalism in developed countries after the 1960s;
  - attempts to contest the meaning and practice of security from an environmental standpoint;
  - changes in strategic circumstances, in particular the end of the Cold War;
  - growing recognition of the risks environmental changes pose to human security.
- There are now a large number of multilateral environmental agreements.
- Both political scientists and environmental scientists have contributed to the development of the concept of environmental security.

Major interpretations of environmental security

Since the early 1990s, environmental security has been an important concept in security studies and increasingly also in environmental studies. Yet the meaning of environmental security is ambiguous, perhaps because of the vagueness of the words *environment and security*. The basic meaning of **environment** is the external conditions that surround an entity, but it can be more accurately defined as the living organisms and the physical and chemical components of the total Earth system (Boyden et al. 1990: 314). **Security** is also an all-encompassing yet vague concept, which has perhaps been best defined by Soroos (1997: 236) as 'the assurance people have that they will continue to enjoy those things that are most important to their survival and well-being'. The ambiguity of these words has given rise to many different meanings of environmental security.

Six principal approaches to environmental security can be discerned from the literature (see Table 16.1). First, environmental security can be seen as being about the impacts of human activities on the environment. This interpretation of environmental security—sometimes also called 'ecological security'—emphasizes at least implicitly that it is ecosystems and ecological processes that should be secured, and the principal threat to ecological integrity

Table 16.1 Six key interpretations of environmental security

Name	Entity to be secured	Major source of risk	Scale of concern
Ecological security	Natural environment	Human activity	Ecosystems
Common security	Nation state	Environmental change	Global/regional
Environmental violence	Nation state	War	National
National security	Nation state	Environmental change	National
Greening defence	Armed forces	Green/peace groups	Organizational
Human security	Individuals	Environmental change	Local

THINK POINT 16.1 Human impacts on . . .

Land

- In the past 40 years nearly one-third of existing cropland has been abandoned because of erosion.
- 25 per cent of all land is affected by some form of land degradation.

Forests

- In the decade 2000–2010, 13 million hectares of natural forests were cleared each year.
- Between 2000 and 2010, an average of 7.4 million hectares of forests were cleared each year in Africa and South America.

Biodiversity

- Over 1,100 species of mammals, 1,300 species of birds, and 1,900 species of amphibians are threatened with extinction).
- It is estimated that approximately 27,000 species are lost every year.

Freshwater

- More than 1 billion people do not have access to safe drinking water, contributing to the death of 2 million children each year.
- Approximately half of the world's wetlands were lost during the twentieth century.

Coastal and marine areas

- Approximately 20 per cent of the world's mangroves have been lost since 1980.
- Approximately 75 per cent of the world's coral reefs are threatened from the combination of local impacts and climate change.

The atmosphere

- Concentrations of CO_2 have increased by over 40 per cent since 1750.

UNEP (2002, 2005); UNDP (2006); FAO (2010); Secretariat of the Convention on Biological Diversity (2010); WRI (2011); CDIAC (2014).

is human activity (see Think Point 16.1). In this view, humans are secured only in so far as they are part of the environment (Pirages and DeGeest 2004). Recognizing that human activities are now powerfully changing the biosphere, Dalby, (2009) extends the notion of ecological security to talk of 'anthropocene security', which he says is 'security in terms of ecological understandings of humanity as a new presence in the biosphere that we are already changing quite drastically' (2009: 172). Such formulations of security differ radically from mainstream security discourse and policy, and have so far had little influence on either.

The second key approach to environmental security focuses on common security. The causes and impacts of some environmental problems are not confined to the borders of nation states. Some problems, such as ozone depletion and climate change, are very 'global' in nature in that they are caused by cumulative emissions of gases from many countries, which in turn affect many countries. However, to say that these problems are 'global' is not to say that all countries are equally responsible for them, or that all countries and communities are equally at risk from them (see Case Study 16.2 and Think Point 16.2). Other environmental

! THINK POINT 16.2 The environmental impacts of armed forces

- In the 1980s, the US military was the largest holder of agricultural land in the Philippines.
- The US nuclear weapons programme was conducted in thirty-four states and covered 2.4 million acres of land; clean-up costs are expected to be in the order of US$200–300 billion.
- Nuclear tests have been carried out at seven sites in the South Pacific, making four islands completely uninhabitable and causing above-average cancer levels in residents of the Marshall Islands.
- The former Soviet Union dumped up to 17,000 containers of nuclear waste and up to 21 nuclear reactors into the Barents and Kara seas.
- The US military generates more toxins than the top five US chemical companies combined.
- In the United States in the 1980s, there were 26 US military bases with significant toxic hazards; clean-up costs were estimated to be over US$400 billion.
- Worldwide use of aluminium, copper, nickel, and platinum for military purposes exceeded the combined demand for these materials in all the developing countries.
- One-quarter of the entire world's jet fuel is consumed by military aircraft.
- The US military–industrial complex may be responsible for at least 10 per cent of the US total CO_2 emissions, making it responsible for some 2–3 per cent of total global emissions, or more than those of all Australia, Finland, Sweden, and New Zealand combined.

Renner (1991); Seager (1993); Heininen (1994); Dycus (1996).

problems, such as acid rain, smoke haze, and water scarcity and pollution, are often caused by, and impact on, more than one country. This means that groups of countries with similar environmental problems cannot easily unilaterally achieve environmental security, and so their common national security interests require collective action. This is the rationale behind the many treaties discussed in the previous section. However, while many environmental problems are to some degree 'common', no two countries have exactly the same interests, and all have sovereign rights. For these reasons multilateral environmental agreements have not significantly halted environmental degradation. The four other major approaches to environmental security are each discussed in the following sections.

KEY POINTS

- Both 'environment' and 'security' are ambiguous concepts.
- Interpretations of environmental security differ according to the entity to be secured, the source of risk to that entity, and the solutions proposed.
- Most interpretations of environmental security do not require much change in security thought and practice because they are concerned with the nation state and/or the risk of armed conflict.
- The ecological security and human security approaches to environmental security challenge the security **policy community** to consider alternative objects of security, and alternative security risks.

Environmental change and violent conflict

The connections between environmental change and violent conflict have been a central and long-standing concern of environmental security studies. The critical questions, which have yet to be conclusively answered, are whether environmental change contributes to violent conflict, and, if so, to what degree and in what ways.

Early writing on the connections between environmental change and violence borrowed heavily from realist international relations theory and focused largely on resource scarcity and conflict between states. Gleick (1991), for example, argued that there were clear connections between environmental degradation and violence, suggesting that resources could be strategic goals and strategic tools, and that resource inequalities could be a source of conflict. The early contributions from Ullman and Myers (see Key Quotes 16.2) also canvassed the possibility of inter-state war caused by resource and environmental problems. The possibility of war between countries with shared water resources was often highlighted (see Case Study 16.1). The idea that environmental change may cause wars between countries has been critiqued by researchers such as Deudney (1990) and Barnett (2001), as well as by liberal theories about the ways complex interdependence and trade mitigate against resource wars, and by subsequent waves of research on environmental conflicts (see Peluso and Watts 2001).

CASE STUDY 16.1 Water wars?

The idea that countries might fight over water has been widely discussed by academics, politicians, and in the media. For example, for Thomas Naff (1992: 25), 'the strategic reality of water is that under circumstances of scarcity, it becomes a highly symbolic, contagious, aggregated, intense, salient, complicated, zero-sum, power-and prestige-packed issue, highly prone to conflict and extremely difficult to resolve'.

Most commentators suggest that a future water war is most likely to occur in the Middle East, a region already rife with religious, ethnic, and political tensions. Attention was first drawn to the problems of shared waterways and water scarcity in the region by the Egyptian Foreign Minister Boutros Boutros-Ghali, who later became Secretary-General of the United Nations, who reportedly observed that 'the next war in our region will be over the waters of the Nile, not politics' (cited in Gleick 1991: 20).

There are 261 major river systems that are shared by two or more countries. Yet this geographical misfit between water and national boundaries does not necessarily imply that states will fight over water. Indeed, Priscoli and Wolf (2009) demonstrate that, despite rapid population growth and increased demand for water for agriculture, industry, and cities in the twentieth century, there have been only a handful of minor skirmishes over international water, in contrast to the more than 400 treaties concerning water. Countries, it seems, are more likely to cooperate than fight over water, including in the Middle East (Allan 2002; Tir and Ackerman 2009). Despite evidence to the contrary, the risk of water wars continues to be overstated by some academics, politicians, journalists, and NGOs, who each have their reasons for wanting to promote the problem (Katz 2011).

Population growth and its links to environmental degradation and subsequent violent conflict were also a theme of early writing on environmental violence (see, e.g., Myers 1987). Yet the linkages between both population growth and environmental change, and environmental change and violent conflict, are not overly straightforward. Poverty and technology are critical additional variables. In low-income and technology-poor societies more people means more consumption of natural resources for food, fuel, and shelter, but it can also mean more labour, and this can stimulate innovation, and lead to more environmentally sustainable forms of production and consumption. In high-income and high-technology societies people consume up to a hundred times more resources and energy than people in developing countries. For example, while India had 17 per cent of the world's population in 2007, it produced only 4.7 per cent of the world's carbon dioxide emissions in 2004, whereas the United States, with 4.6 per cent of the world's population in 2007, produced 22 per cent of all greenhouse gas emissions in 2004 (World Bank 2009b). These differences imply that the aggregate number of people is not as important as the amount of resources they consume and the volumes of waste they produce.

The relationship between population, environmental change, and violent conflict was most systematically explored by the Project on Environment, Population, and Security at the University of Toronto. The Toronto Project carried out numerous case studies to investigate the links among population growth, renewable resource scarcities, migration, and conflict. These studies examined cases where there had been violent conflict, and then they sought to determine the influence of environmental factors in the generation of those conflicts. At around the same time another project—the Zurich-based Environment and Conflict Project (ENCOP) directed by Guenther Baechler (1999)—also conducted case studies on the linkages between environmental degradation and violence. Common findings of both projects are that: unequal consumption of scarce resources contributes to violent conflicts; violent conflicts where environmental scarcity is a factor are more likely in low-income resource-dependent societies; and, when mechanisms that enable adaptation to environmental scarcity fail, violent conflict is a more likely outcome. Both Homer-Dixon (1999) and Baechler (1999) find that environmental change is not an immediate cause of conflict, but it can at times be an exacerbating factor. Both also find that environmental change is unlikely to be a cause of war between countries.

Since the Toronto and ENCOP Projects there have been three further developments in environmental violence research. The first of these has been a series of quantitative analyses of aggregated data to test the relationships between various environmental and social variables such as resource scarcity/abundance, population growth, and income inequality. These studies have tentatively shown that 'strong states' tend to be less prone to internal conflicts, whereas states undergoing significant economic and political transitions are relatively more prone to internal violent conflict (Esty et al. 1999). A number of them suggest that it is the abundance of natural resources as much as their scarcity that drives armed conflict (Collier 2000; de Soysa 2000). They have also shown that poverty is an important causal variable in internal wars. Because these studies are constrained by the quality of data they use, and lack detailed field-based observations, their findings are inevitably somewhat uncertain (Conca 2002). In more recent times there has been a flurry of research seeking to quantify the influence of climate on violent conflict, leading to a significant (and still inconclusive) debate about the validity of methods and evidence in research of this kind. There is no robust theory that can explain the causal pathways between climate variability and violent conflict (Adger et al. 2014). Most researchers agree that changes in climate will not directly cause conflict between states, but may increase the risk of conflict within states only under certain circumstances. Climate change is therefore often referred to as a 'threat multiplier'.

The second new development in environmental violence research seeks to learn from peaceful responses to environmental change rather than from instances of violence. This is an important approach if the goal of research is to help prevent conflicts, because understanding what works to promote peace is as important as understanding what causes violent outcomes. Early research in the field focused on cooperation between states over shared resources such as rivers and seas (Conca and Dabelko 2002). It has since evolved into a significant and growing research and policy community on environmental peace building. This initiative is advancing theories, evidence, and a community of practice on the ways in which managing resources can build trust and cooperation between rival groups, and help to sustain peace and build resilience in communities affected by violent conflict (Jensen and Lonergan 2012). This research endeavour serves as a useful reminder that cooperation among people and groups is also an outcome of common environmental problems, and that careful policies and practices can promote peaceful outcomes from environmental change (Unruh and Williams 2013)

The final new approach to environment and violence research involves detailed field-based studies of places that have experienced environmental problems and forms of violence (Schnurr and Swatuk 2012). These studies have stressed the importance of unequal outcomes of social and environmental changes. For example, inadequate distribution of the returns from resource extraction activities has been a factor in violence in West Kalimantan (Peluso and Harwell 2001), the Niger Delta (Watts 2001), and Bougainville island (Böge 1999). They show that a range of intervening economic, political, and cultural processes that produce and sustain power are seen as more important in causing (and preventing and resolving) violent conflict than the actual material environmental changes that take place.

KEY POINTS

- There are no strong causal relationships among population growth, environmental change, and violent conflict.
- Environmental change is not an immediate cause of conflict, but it can at times be an exacerbating factor.
- Environmental change is unlikely to be a cause of war between countries.
- Groups experiencing common environmental problems can also cooperate to address those problems.

Environmental change and national security

Most interpretations of environmental security take existing theories of national security, and then factor in environmental issues. Regardless of whether or not environmental change may cause violent conflict within or between states, in many less subtle ways it can undermine national security.

Environmental change can weaken the economic base that determines military capacity. In some developed countries, and in most developing countries, natural resources and environmental services are important to economic growth and employment. Income from and employment in primary sectors such as agriculture, forestry, fishing, and mining, and from environmentally dependent services like tourism, may all be adversely affected by environmental change. It has been widely reported, for example, that China's rapid economic growth—which has funded its military modernization programme—is ecologically unsustainable because of water shortages, water pollution, and land degradation. So, in some cases, if the natural capital base of an economy erodes, then so does the long-term capacity of its armed forces. Because it exposes people to health risks, environmental change can also undermine the human development that Sen (1999) considers important for economic growth. It can also weaken the legitimacy and stability of ruling regimes by decreasing the income they gain from resource-based rents or taxes, thereby undermining their ability to provide welfare, employment, and key services (Kahl 2006). In other words, if economic development can be ecologically unsustainable, then national security can be similarly unsustainable.

Climate change too is seen to be a risk to the territorial integrity of states. For example, cyclones are likely to be more intense under climate change, raising the prospect of more events of the kind that occurred when hurricane Katrina struck New Orleans in 2005, killing more than 1,000 people, displacing over 500,000 people, and causing damage valued at over US$100 billion. Climate change also poses risks to critical infrastructure such as those required for producing and distributing energy, water, and food, and for transport and trade (Adger et al. 2014). It also poses risks to military facilities such as naval yards and training grounds (Dabelko 2009).

While many of the environmental problems countries face are principally caused by internal developments within those countries, some problems are largely beyond their control. Examples of this include the impacts of global emissions of ozone-depleting substances on rates of skin cancer in southern latitudes, the legacies of nuclear-weapons tests conducted during colonial times in French Polynesia and the Marshall Islands, the impacts of the Chernobyl nuclear reactor accident in 1986 on East European countries, the impacts of forest fires in Indonesia on air pollution in Malaysia and Singapore, and the impacts of global emissions of greenhouse gases on low-lying countries and countries with high climatic variability (for example, a 45-cm rise in sea level will potentially result in a loss of 11 per cent of Bangladesh's territory, forcing some 5.5 million people to relocate) (see Case Study 16.2). Transboundary flows differ from traditional external security threats in that they are uncontrolled and most often unintended; in this respect they are 'threats without enemies' (Prins 1993).

However, understanding environmental problems as national security issues is not unproblematic. Daniel Deudney (1990) offers three reasons why linking environmental issues to national security is analytically misleading. First, he argues that military threats are different from environmental threats in that military threats are deliberately imposed and the cause of the threat is easily identifiable, whereas environmental threats are accidental and their causes are often uncertain. Second, Deudney argues that linking environmental issues to national security may not have the effect of mobilizing

CASE STUDY 16.2 Climate change and atoll countries

Atolls are rings of coral reefs that enclose a lagoon that contains small islets with a mean height above sea level of approximately 2 metres. There are five countries comprised entirely of low-lying atolls: Kiribati (population 85,000), the Maldives (population 309,000), the Marshall Islands (population 58,000), Tokelau (population 2,000), and Tuvalu (population 10,000).

Climate change is likely to cause sea levels to rise by between 9 and 88 cm by the year 2100. Atoll countries are highly vulnerable to sea-level rise because of their high ratio of coastline to land area, lack of elevated land, soft coastlines, relatively high population densities, and low incomes to fund response measures. Also, climate change is likely to result in more intense rainfall events and possibly more intense droughts. The combined effect of these changes on atoll societies is likely to include coastal erosion, increases in flooding events, freshwater aquifers becoming increasingly contaminated with saline water, and decreasing food security because of reduced harvests from agriculture and fishing. The World Bank estimates that by 2050 Tarawa atoll in Kiribati could face an annual damages bill equivalent to 13–27 per cent of current Kiribati GDP.

This combination of changes in mean conditions and extreme events driven by climate change may mean that atoll countries are unable to sustain their populations, a possibility with even a moderate amount of climate change. This danger to the sovereignty of the atoll countries is arguably greater than anything any single country could impose; indeed, nuclear testing in the Marshall Islands and severe fighting in Kiribati during the Second World War had relatively minor impacts compared to the risks posed by climate change. This risk that climate change poses to national sovereignty is a very clear case of national (and human) environmental insecurity. Thus, in 2011, the President of Nauru, speaking on behalf of the Pacific small island states, told the United Nations Security Council that for small islands climate change was as great a security threat as nuclear proliferation.

Barnett and Adger (2003).

BACKGROUND 16.2 The 1998 National Security Strategy (United States)

The 1998 National Security Strategy was the first major national security policy statement to include environmental issues in a significant way. Here are some excerpts:

- 'The same forces that bring us closer increase our interdependence, and make us more vulnerable to forces like extreme nationalism, terrorism, crime, environmental damage and the complex flows of trade and investment that know no borders' (White House 1998: iii).
- 'We seek a cleaner global environment to protect the health and well-being of our citizens. A deteriorating environment not only threatens public health, it impedes economic growth and can generate tensions that threaten international stability. To the extent that other nations believe they must engage in non-sustainable exploitation of natural resources, our long term prosperity and security are at risk' (White House 1998: 5).
- 'Crises are averted—and US preventative diplomacy actively reinforced—through US sustainable development programs that promote voluntary family planning, basic education, environmental protection, democratic governance and the rule of law, and the economic empowerment of private citizens' (White House 1998: 8).
- 'The current international security environment presents a diverse set of threats to our enduring goals and hence to our security . . . [including] terrorism, international crime, drug trafficking, illicit arms trafficking, uncontrolled refugee migrations and environmental damage [which] threaten US interests, citizens and the US homeland itself' (White House 1998: 10).

more attention and action on environmental problems, but, rather, it may serve to strengthen existing security logic and institutions. There are reasonable grounds to consider that this has been the case—for example, a 2007 study by the CNA Corporation argued that climate change 'poses a serious threat to America's national security' and concluded that part of the solution was that the US 'Department of Defense should enhance its operational capability' (CNA Corporation 2007: 6, 8; see also Background 16.2). Deudney's third argument against environmental security is that environmental change is not likely to cause wars between countries (as discussed in the previous section). So, while there is some basis for considering environmental problems as national security problems, the problem remains one of interpretation—of what constitutes national security, of whom it is for, and of how it is to be achieved.

KEY POINTS

- Environmental change can put at risk the quality and quantity of resources available to a country.
- Environmental change can put at risk the economic strength of many countries.
- Environmental change poses risks to population health in many countries.
- Some environmental risks come from beyond a country's borders, and are unintentional.
- Linking environmental issues to security issues may not help solve environmental problems.

Armed forces and the environment

Linking environmental change with security inevitably means addressing the linkages between the most important of security institutions—the military—and the environment. It is when considering the role of militaries that some of the most profound contradictions with the concept of environmental security are raised. The goal of most militaries is to win wars, and so they train for and sometimes fight wars with devastating consequences for people and the environment. This contrasts considerably with the goals of the environmental movement to achieve sustainable development and peace.

Warfare almost always results in environmental degradation. The use of nuclear weapons in Japan, defoliants in Vietnam, depleted uranium ammunition in Kuwait and Kosovo, the burning of oil wells in Kuwait, the destruction of crops in Eritrea, and the draining of marshes in south-eastern Iraq are all examples of the direct impacts of war on the natural environment. In most cases the consequences of these impacts last well beyond the end of fighting (Austin and Bruch 2000).

Warfare also has indirect—but in many ways more extensive—impacts on the environment. In many cases, spending on fighting is sustained by resource extraction, and in some cases it is resources that are the principal source of conflict. For example, timber in Cambodia and Burma, gems in Afghanistan, and diamonds in Sierra Leone have all been sources of income for armed groups. In these kinds of conflicts, control over and extraction of resources is of paramount concern and the environmental and social impacts of extraction are not considered. Violent conflict almost always involves denial of territory to opponents, sometimes with associated environmental impacts. Landmines are often used, and there are now over 100 million landmines lying in 90 countries denying access to land for productive purposes. Countries particularly affected include Angola, Afghanistan, Cambodia, and Iraq.

War also affects economic development in ways that impact indirectly on the environment. Money spent on weapons, for example, is money that could have been spent on social and environmental activities. War deters foreign investment and aid, disrupts domestic markets, and often results in a decline in exports. It depletes and damages the labour force, creates a massive health burden, and destroys productive assets such as factories and communications and energy infrastructure. War often results in increased foreign debt, increased income inequality, reduced food production, and a reduction in GDP per capita. It also creates refugees and internally displaced people. Famines are also increasingly caused by war. The East African famine in 2011–12, which killed between 50,000 and 100,000 thousand people, was largely caused by disruptions to food supplies and livelihoods due to ongoing warfare in Somalia.

These environmental, economic, and social effects of war all negatively impact on people's access to the kinds of resources they need to develop themselves in ecologically sustainable ways. They also reduce the amount of economic resources available to governments and communities to implement environmental policies and programmes, restrict access to the kinds of technologies needed for sustainable economic growth, suppress educational attainment and restrict the policy learning necessary for understanding and responding to environmental problems, damage the infrastructure needed to distribute resources such as water, electricity, and food efficiently and equitably, and weaken the institutions and social cohesion necessary for a society to manage its environmental problems. So, armed forces wage war, and war is extremely bad for environmental security.

As well as causing major environmental impacts in times of war, in times of peace militaries also cause environmental damage. They may indeed be the single largest institutional source of environmental degradation in the world. This raises serious questions about the possibility of militaries having a positive role in environmental protection and recovery. Despite this, in the 1990s the United States Department of Defense (DOD) claimed it made a positive contribution to environmental security, through, for example, supporting 'the military readiness of the US armed forces by ensuring continued access to the air, land and water needed for training and testing' and contributing to 'weapons systems that have improved performance, lower cost, and better environmental characteristics' (Barnett 2001: 79). This, and other responses by the United States, suggests that what the DOD is securing through these 'environmental security' measures is its own capacity to wage wars.

The idea that environmental change may be a cause of armed conflict also has implications for armed forces. If environmental change is likely to make for a more unstable international environment through environmentally induced wars, for example, then this suggests that armed forces are still required to help manage these negative effects. In this way, arguments about the threats environmental change poses to security help to justify existing security institutions like the armed forces, even though they may have significant environmental impacts.

KEY POINTS

- Armed forces have very different goals from the environmental movement.
- War causes environmental damage.
- War is harmful to sustainable development.
- Armed forces are major consumers of resources and major polluters.

Environmental change and human security

The concept of environmental security refers to a sector of security (the environment) rather than a referent object to be secured. Thus, it is possible to talk of the environmental security of the international system, of nation states, and, as explained in this section, of people (human security) (see also Chapter 10). The environment is one of the seven sectors identified in the United Nations Development Program's (UNDP 1994) early definition of human security (the others being economic, food, health, personal, community,

CASE STUDY 16.3 Environmental change and food security

Food security arises when all people at all times have access to a sufficient quantity of safe and nutritious food necessary for an active and healthy life. It is a function of the availability of food (food production plus imports less exports), people's ability to access the food that is available (people get food by growing it themselves, buying it, or receiving it as a gift), and the ability of people to safely prepare food (which is usually about having access to clean water and energy for cooking), as well as their bodies' ability to utilize food (people suffering from severe diarrhoea, for example, typically do not absorb nutrients from food as well as healthy people). Largely because of poverty and the resultant inability to buy food, in 2010 there were over 900 million people in the world who were chronically hungry (FAO 2011).

While food prices and poverty remain the primary drivers of food insecurity, environmental change can undermine food security in many different ways. Land degradation and declining rainfall can cause declines in food production, as can overfishing and depletion of fish stocks, both of which mean lower food availability in producing regions and in the places to which they may export. It can also affect people's ability to access food as long-term or sudden decreases in food production can cause both job losses among people who work in food production and increases in food prices. Damage to food distribution and storage infrastructure due to extreme events can also undermine people's ability to access food. Environmental change can also undermine people's ability to utilize food, as it may lead to increased contamination of fresh water, depletion of local fuel sources (such as fuelwood), and increasing illnesses, so decreasing the ability of people's bodies to absorb nutrients.

Ericksen (2008).

and political security), and so for some time now environmental change has been identified as a human security issue.

Whereas the ways in which environmental change threaten the welfare of the international system and states are somewhat ambiguous and hypothetical, the ways in which it affects the welfare of individuals and communities are obvious (see Case Study 16.3). People are environmentally insecure in all sorts of ways, and for all sorts of reasons. Broadly speaking, the determinants of environmental insecurity are: where people live and the nature of environmental changes in those places; how susceptible people are to damage caused by environmental changes; and people's capacity to adapt to environmental changes. For example, subsistence farmers in the mountains of East Timor rely almost exclusively on their own farm produce for food, they earn very little, if any, money (on average less than US$0.55 cents per day), their farms do not have irrigation, the soils they farm are not very fertile and are eroding, infrastructure for storing and transporting food is not well developed, agricultural productivity is low, and rainfall is variable. So, in seasons where the rain fails, food production falls, and farmers have no ability to supplement their diet with other food sources because they cannot afford to purchase food. As a result, hunger and malnutrition are widespread in East Timor in drought years. In this case, the environmental insecurity of Timorese farmers is a function of the physical properties of their environments—they live in steep mountainous areas with thin soils and variable rainfall, and they also depend on farming as their only source of livelihood; if they had alternative sources of income, they could afford to buy food. The capacity of East Timor's farmers to adapt to land degradation and water shortages is constrained by poverty: if they had more money, they could afford to invest in irrigation systems, soil-erosion control programmes, food storage systems, tractors, and fertilizers to increase production so that food would not be scarce during drought years. The causes of this environmental insecurity of Timorese farmers lie not so much in the environmental characteristics of where they live, but rather in the deep rural poverty caused by twenty-five years of violent occupation of East Timor by the Indonesian armed forces.

A comparison between Timorese farmers and Australian farmers underlies the ways in which human environmental insecurity is more socially created than naturally determined. Australian farmers live in similar environmental conditions (thin soils and variable climate), but they eat little if any of their own production, which is instead sold on markets, irrigation is widely available, food transport and storage systems are modern and efficient, fertilizers and pesticides are easily afforded, high levels of government support are available, and there is a wide array of options for off-farm income. Therefore, when drought strikes Australia, farmers do not go hungry; at worst they lose some livestock and some income. For both Timorese

THINK POINT 16.3 Inequality and environmental insecurity

Inequalities in consumption

- The wealthiest 20 per cent of people in the world receive 83 per cent of all income.
- The wealthiest 1 per cent of people in the world receive 21 per cent of all income.
- The poorest 20 per cent of people in the world receive 1 per cent of all income.
- 2.4 billion people live on less than US$2/day.
- The wealthiest 20 per cent of people in the world:
  - consume 58 per cent of all energy resources;
  - consume 84 per cent of all paper;
  - own 87 per cent of the world's vehicles.
- The poorest 20 per cent of people in the world:
  - consume 4 per cent of all energy resources;
  - consume 1.1 per cent of all paper;
  - own less than 1 per cent of the world's vehicles.

Inequalities in pollution

- The average person in a developed country causes as much pollution as 30 people in developing countries.
- The wealthiest 20 per cent of people in the world produce over half of all carbon dioxide emissions; the poorest 20 per cent produce 3 per cent.

World Bank (2008); Ortiz and Cummins (2011); Chen and Ravillion (2012); Anand and Segal (2014).

and Australian farmers, climate variability is likely to increase because of climate change, and, while it will be difficult for Australian farmers to adapt to sustain their existing income levels, for Timorese farmers it may well be even more difficult for them to maintain enough food to keep their children healthy.

Environmental change therefore does not undermine human security in isolation from a broad range of social factors, including poverty, the degree of support (or discrimination) communities receive from the state, the effectiveness of decision-making processes, and the extent of social cohesion within and surrounding vulnerable groups. These factors determine the capacity of people and communities to adapt to environmental change so that the things that they value are not adversely affected. In terms of environmental change, for example, upstream users of water, distant atmospheric polluters, multinational logging and mining companies, regional-scale climatic processes, and a host of other distant actors and larger-scale processes influence the security of individuals' use of natural resources and services. Similarly, in terms of the social determinants of insecurity, larger-scale processes such as warfare, corruption, trade dependency, and economic liberalization affect people's sensitivity to environmental changes and their capacity to adapt to them. Finally, past processes such as colonization and war shape present insecurities, and ongoing processes such as climate change and trade liberalization shape future insecurities.

Understanding human environmental insecurity therefore requires understanding the larger-scale past and present processes that create wealth in some places and poverty in others, and environmental change in some places and not in others. Think Point 16.3 describes some of the existing levels of inequality that generate environmental security for some people, and environmental insecurity for others. Therefore, even though the focus of human security is the individual, the processes that undermine or strengthen human security are often extra-local. Similarly, then, the solution to human environmental insecurity rests not just with local people, but also with larger-scale institutions such as states, the international system, the private sector, civil society, and consumers in developed countries. In this respect, even an approach to environmental security that focuses on human security cannot avoid taking into account nation states and their security policies.

KEY POINTS

- Environmental security is an important component of human security.
- Physical changes in the environment are only one aspect of people's environmental insecurity; other factors are the extent to which people rely on the environment for their welfare, and the ability of people to adapt to environmental changes.
- Not all people are equally environmentally insecure.
- People who are environmentally insecure are also often insecure in other ways.

Environment or security?

Security is a power word. When a problem is identified as a security issue it can lead to state monopolization of solutions (see Chapter 12) (Wæver 1995). Environmentalists have used environmental security to 'securitize' environmental problems—to make them matters of 'high' politics that warrant extraordinary responses from governments equal in magnitude and urgency to their response to more orthodox security threats. They have also used environmental security to highlight the opportunity costs of defence spending, and the environmental impacts of military activities, including war. This is the 'political rationale' of environmental security (Soroos 1994).

This securitizing move has to some degree raised the profile of environmental issues among foreign and security policy makers and agencies, so that there is a general recognition that environmental changes can in some sense be considered as security issues. These changes relate mostly to a broadening of the issue of security, but there has arguably been little real change in policy and action in terms of the referent object of environmental security. The focus of much of the research and writing on environmental security on environmental violence, on environmental threats to national security, and on greening the armed forces suggests that it is the environmental security of the state that still matters most for the security policy community. Indeed, the concept of environmental security and its messages of impending danger may have helped security institutions to appropriate environmental issues in ways that help to maintain national security business as usual.

For the environmental and peace movement, therefore, environmental security has not lead to the trade-offs between military security and environmental security that they hoped for, nor has it lead to increased resources committed to solving environmental problems. Instead, environmental problems have been incorporated into mainstream security discourse and policy; the emphasis has been placed on environmental change as a cause of violent conflict rather than human insecurity; and on addressing environmental threats from other places as opposed to attending to domestic causes of environmental change. In this respect, much that is called 'environmental security' has had little to do with the environment, and much to do with security.

Despite all these arguments, there are some good reasons for continuing to use the concept of environmental security. It has gained some purchase with development agencies, as it helps to capture the environmental dimensions of social vulnerability. It communicates the critical nature of environmental problems better than standard concepts like sustainability or vulnerability. Environmental security can also serve as an integrative concept to link local (human security), national (national security), and global (international security) levels of environmental change and response. Further, in that it involves merging international relations with development studies and environmental studies, environmental security helps produce new fusions of knowledge and awareness. It offers a common language that facilitates the exchange of knowledge among people from diverse arms of government, civil society, and academia across both the developed and developing worlds. Finally, environmental security still helps to contest the legitimacy of the dominant security paradigm by pointing to the contradiction between simple state-based and military approaches to national security, and the complex, multi-scale, and transboundary nature of environmental flows.

KEY POINTS

- Environmental security has in some ways 'securitized' environmental problems.
- Environmental security may have helped secure security.
- Environmental security helps create new coalitions of actors and interests.

Conclusions

Environmental security has been one of the key new security issues that has helped to broaden the meaning of security in the post-Cold War period.

It is the product of: efforts by the environmental movement to raise the profile of environmental issues and contest the practices of national security; the increasing recognition that environmental problems demand common security approaches and the growth in multilateral environmental agreements; and the strategic vacuum created by the end of the Cold War.

Therefore, despite some twenty years of prior thinking about the connections between the environment and security, it was not until the 1990s that the concept of environmental security came to prominence and featured regularly in academic journals, in the speeches of politicians and security bureaucrats, and in the work of environmental organizations.

There are many different interpretations of environmental security because there are many different approaches to security and an even broader range of approaches to environmental change. At two ends of the spectrum of views are those people who follow the orthodox national security paradigm, who understand environmental security as being about the ways in which environmental change might be a cause of armed conflict between countries; and environmentalists, who tend to see environmental security as being about the impacts of human activities—including military activities—on the environment. Somewhere in the middle ground are those who are concerned about the ways in which environmental change undermines human security.

The most influential interpretations of environmental security are those that fit well the orthodox security paradigm. In particular, arguments that environmental change may be a cause of violent conflict between and within countries, and suggest that environmental problems in other countries are threats to national security, have all largely been accepted by the security-policy community and the armed forces—especially in the United States. So, environmental security is still largely understood to be about threats to the nation state rather than to the environment per se, to other states, or to individuals. This suggests that, while environmental security may have broadened the meaning of security, it has been less successful in deepening it. This is not to say, though, that for some countries environmental change is not a major security problem, as the example of climate change and atoll countries shows.

The growing attention paid to environmental change as a human security issue does not fit so well with the Western security-policy community. It does, however, have some appeal to the development-policy community and to environmental groups and organizations. In the future it is likely that the concept of environmental security as human security will become more central in the fields of environmental studies and development studies, and figure more prominently in their respective policy domains. Research and policy will extend to include the impacts of environmental change on women and children, on livelihoods, and on human development. There may also be more research and policy development on institutions for cooperation on common environmental problems at a range of scales.

In the same way that environmental security did not gain much purchase with the security-policy community during the Cold War, it received far less attention in the years immediately following the 9/11 attacks in the United States. This suggests that environmental security is a second-order security problem, which is considered only in times when more conventional dangers from armed aggression do not dominate national security concerns. The immediate future of the environment as a security issue may therefore be determined by the relevance of other security problems. However, in the longer term, environmental issues may well become paramount security concerns, as the impacts of certain environmental problems seem set to increase—for example, concentrations of greenhouse gases in the atmosphere are ever increasing and so, therefore, will sea levels and the intensity of climatic hazards such as cyclones, floods, and droughts; problems of nuclear waste have not been dealt with and the stockpile is still growing; and water demand is increasing but supply is relatively fixed. So, the relevance of environmental security will most probably increase until such time as truly common and cooperative approaches implement serious reforms to achieve forms of social organization that are ecologically sustainable. In this sense, current practices of national security are a significant barrier to achieving environmental security for all people.

? QUESTIONS

1. Is environmental security about the impact of humans on the environment, or about the impact of environmental processes on things that people value?
2. What reasons explain why there has been so much effort devoted to finding connections between environmental change and violence?

3. What are the implications of calling environmental problems security issues?
4. Can armed forces enhance environmental security?
5. What kinds of environmental problems are national security issues? For what reasons?
6. What kinds of environmental problems are human security issues? For what reasons?
7. What causes someone to be environmentally insecure?
8. How is it that the securitization of environmental issues may have helped to secure security?
9. How could the human security and national security approaches to environmental security be reconciled?
10. What are the most appropriate policies to provide environmental security? Who should implement them?

FURTHER READING

- Barnett, J. (2001), *The Meaning of Environmental Security: Ecological Politics and Policy in the New Security Era*, London: Zed Books. A critical examination of different approaches to environmental security which promotes a human security approach.
- Jensen, D. and Lonergan, S. (eds) (2012), *Assessing and Restoring Natural Resources in Post-Conflict Peacebuilding* Abingdon: Routledge. One of an important of a series of edited books that explain environmental peace building.
- Dalby, S. (2009), *Security and Environmental Change*, Cambridge: Polity Press. A critical geopolitical perspective on environmental security.
- Floyd, R. (2010), *Security and the Environment: Securitisation Theory and US Environmental Security Policy*, Cambridge: Cambridge University Press. A critique of environmental security informed by the theory of the Copenhagen School.
- Homer-Dixon, T. (1999), *Environment, Scarcity, and Violence*, Princeton, NJ: Princeton University Press. Summarizes the author's highly influential work on environmental scarcity and violence.
- Kahl, C. (2006), *States, Scarcity and Civil Strife in the Developing World*, Princeton, NJ: Princeton University Press. A widely acclaimed empirical study of the relationship between resource scarcity and political instability.
- Matthew, R. , Barnett, J., McDonald, B., and O'Brien, K. (eds) (2009), *Global Environmental Change and Human Security* Cambridge MA: MIT Press. A collection of essays outlining various dimensions of the relationship between environmental change and human security.
- Peluso, N. and Watts, M. (eds) (2001), *Violent Environments*, Ithaca, NY: Cornell University Press. A collection of detailed field-based qualitative case studies of environmental disputes.
- Schnurr, M. and Swatuk, L. (eds) (2012), *Natural Resources and Social Conflict* Basingstoke: Palgrave Macmillan. A collection of cases that show how environmental struggles are influenced by broader political and economic processes.
- WCED (1987), *World Commission on Environment and Development, Our Common Future*, Oxford: Oxford University Press. A foundational report on the environment and common security.

IMPORTANT WEBSITES

- **http://www.wilsoncenter.org/ecsp** The Environmental Change and Security Program at the Woodrow Wilson International Center for Scholars is a major centre for environmental security studies in the United States. The site contains a wealth of information, including the influential Environmental Change and Security Project Report.

- **http://www.environmentalpeacebuilding.org** The environmental peacebuilding initiative seeks to promote research and practice on the ways in which natural resource management can build peace and assist in recovery from conflict. The website has excellent news and events services, and many publications and policy briefs that can be downloaded for free.
- **http://www.envirosecurity.org** The Institute for Environmental Security is an international NGO. This website is a good source for up-to-date information on events and publications in the area of environmental security.
- **http://www.unep.org** The United Nations Environment Program provides leadership on environmental issues within the UN system. Among other things, this site contains information about global environmental issues, summits, and treaties.

Visit the Online Resource Centre that accompanies this book for lots of interesting additional material: www.oxfordtextbooks.co.uk/orc/collins4e/

17

Economic Security

Gary M. Shiffman

Chapter Contents

Reader's Guide

This chapter provides an economic framework for analysing and countering organized violence. The systematic use of violence can mean many things, so for the purpose of study, we simplify organized violence into three categories: warfare, crime, and insurgency. The many and various decision makers involved in combating organized violence have different goals and face different constraints. However, looking closely at some aspects of economics as a science provides insight into some common attributes of criminals, terrorists, and insurgents. Understanding these dynamics informs the kinds of countermeasures policy makers, analysts, and operators will use in their efforts to promote security.

Introduction

When looking through the economic lens, we see issues of security evolve in complex yet easily understandable ways. Technologies provide new opportunities for people to do bad things, yet simultaneously allow for people to counter these bad actors and make the world a better and more secure place.

This evolving game of 'cat and mouse' will continue into the future. Despite the evolution of technology and economic growth and development, human nature does not change. People behave with purpose and meaning in ways that are understandable and largely—but not completely—predictable. Fortunately, economics—a science of human behaviour and decision making—allows us to take a scientific approach to security studies and understand the ever-evolving global security environment. This chapter summarizes and provides a brief history of economic thought and applies economic theory to security studies. Through various case studies, this approach provides the reader with an understanding of how states leverage traditional economic tools to influence, alter, and deter another actor's behaviour.

Economic science of security

Economics is the science of individuals making decisions in conditions of scarcity. When readers previously encountered this topic, perhaps in an introductory economics course at school or university, they learned to associate economics with trade balances, gross domestic product (GDP), and interest rates. While it is true that economists work on each of these issues, this chapter will instead focus on 'microeconomics' and use this material as the foundation for explaining the mechanisms of macroeconomic policies to advance national security. Specifically, this chapter applies economic concepts such as supply and demand, substitution, institutions, and rationality to the observable world of freedom and security.

Overview of economic theory

Social science explains that human inclination for improvement through social interaction allows us to anticipate human actions and reactions. Furthermore, social science does not differentiate human decision making between 'bad actors' and 'good'. Tyrants, drug kingpins, terrorists, insurgents, and democratic leaders alike seek some combination of wealth, power, and justice. According to philosopher Ludwig von Mises:

> Human action is purposeful behavior. Or we may say: Action is will put into operation and transformed into an agency, is aiming at ends and goals, is the ego's meaningful response to stimuli and to the conditions of its environment, is a person's conscious adjustment to the state of the universe that determines his life.
>
> von Mises (1949: 11)

The science of economics helps us understand human action as related to resource allocations (e.g. 'guns versus butter') and conflicts over resources (i.e. water, oil, food, diamonds, etc.), grievances (e.g. ethnic, religious, national), or political control. Economic theory begins in eighteenth-century Scotland with Adam Smith, whose work led to the creation of the academic and professional field of Economics. Smith's work primarily focused on human nature, morality, virtue, and other dynamics of individual decision making. He published *The Theory of Moral Sentiments* and addressed issues such as human judgement, approbation, virtue, and what he defined as 'systems of moral philosophy' (Smith 1790). Almost two decades later, Smith published the fifth edition of his most famous work, *An Inquiry into the Nature and Causes of the Wealth of Nations* (Smith 1776/1904). *Wealth of Nations* remains concerned with fundamental human nature and how individuals make decisions, but also addresses wealth creation and why some have more wealth than others. Thus, at its foundation, economics is a science that provides insights into human decision making and can be applied to any domain of human interaction.

Economists see humans acting with purpose and tending to exchange in order to achieve goals. Smith cites the division of labour as an example of this phenomenon. In Book I of the *Wealth of Nations*, Smith provides insight into the economist's view of human nature by describing the process of pin making. Smith observes how one person can make up to 20 pins per day, but ten people can make 48,000 pins per day, therefore increasing the productivity of one worker from 20 to 4,800, 1/10th of 48,000:

> This division of labour, from which so many advantages are derived, is not originally the effect of any human wisdom, which foresees and intends that general opulence to which it gives occasion. It is the necessary, though very slow and gradual, consequence of a certain propensity in human nature which has in view no such extensive utility; the propensity to truck, barter, and exchange one thing for another.
>
> Smith (1776/1904: I.I.3)

He suggests here that this division of labour does not come from choice, but from human nature itself; it is not a learned behaviour, but intrinsic to the human condition. If purposeful human action is to be the foundation for a science of behaviour, it must apply universally—not be subject to language, religion, or other socio-cultural volatility, and be verifiable through observation. Therefore, when we say that every human has a propensity to trade, 'every human' applies to every individual throughout the world and throughout history. This specific human trait does not change with place and time. As with any rule, we can find exceptions. In social science modelling, we call people 'rational actors'. Economic theory and its models assume the individual to be 'sane' and 'rational'. While not everyone fits this description, most do. The literature exploring the topic of rationality and the economic actor is rich (Kunreuther and Slovic 1978; Kahneman 2002; Smith 2003).

The significance of this observation of purposeful action describing human nature is threefold and can be applied to national security problem solving. First, we now understand an aspect of human nature that can be associated with anyone in the world. We can apply this insight to world leaders, terrorists, insurgents, and tyrants, as well as democrats and friendly monarchs. As security operators, policy makers, or analysts, we know something about every actor whose behaviour we might seek to stop, influence, or just understand. Second, this insight into human nature does not depend upon cultural or religious assumptions, but provides the base upon which these analytic layers rest. Socio-cultural knowledge and other popular human terrain factors play important roles in helping us understand security environments, as suggested in the discussion on 'incentive vectors'. Third, this understanding of the universal and unchanging aspect of human nature comes from observation, and so modelling an individual's actions and reactions can occur where we can observe prior actions and reactions. Economists work from observed human behaviour—we *know* people exchange because we can *see* people exchange. Many disciplines from across the social sciences assume esoteric topics—such as the afterlife and the supernatural—that cannot be observed yet still provide important insights into human action. However, Smith's basic assumption of human nature—the propensity to truck, barter, and exchange—simply comes from observation. We do not require any religious or other socio-cultural viewpoint. Understanding fundamental human nature begins with observing the human tendency to trade.

Smith operationalizes the observed trait, explaining why individuals trade, in the same chapter. He notes:

[M]an has almost constant occasion for the help of his brethren, and it is in vain for him to expect it from their benevolence only. He will be more likely to prevail if he can interest their self-love in his favor, and show them that it is for their own advantage to do for him what he requires of them. Whoever offers to another a bargain of any kind, proposes to do this. Give me that which I want, and you shall have this which you want, is the meaning of every such offer; and it is in this manner that we obtain from one another the far greater part of those good offices which we stand in need of. It is not from the benevolence of the butcher, the brewer, or the baker, that we expect our dinner, but from their regard to their own interest. We address ourselves, not to their humanity but to their self-love, and never talk to them of our own necessities but of their advantages.

Smith (1776/1904: I.I.2)

The economics of security starts with the observed phenomena of the division of labour and trade, and with the argument that this occurs naturally and universally throughout history and human terrain. In order to trade, individuals need other people; we cannot trade in the absence of others. In fact, trade and the benefits of trade increase with the number of participants in a given market. A manufacturer requires suppliers, workers, and customers. Likewise, in order to overthrow a ruler, an insurgent requires the help and support of others—suppliers, workers, and constituents. To succeed, any leader, democrat or **autocrat**, relies upon others almost all of the time. Adam Smith tells us the key element of any exchange: 'give me that which I want, and you shall have this which you want'. Self-interest motivates exchange of goods and services, including in the marketplace for political power.

Knowing something about human nature, we can better articulate our observations, anticipate people's actions and reactions, explain significant security events—such as the collapse of the Soviet Union or the actions of a regional warlord—and influence global security. In exchange, people reveal their preferences through the choices they make. If a person pays one dollar for a bottle of water, and we observe the act, then we can make inferences about the person. Assuming she was sane and rational and was not coerced to buy that water, we know that, at that place and time, she preferred a bottle of water to a dollar. Since human nature wires us to move towards goals ('self preservation and propagation of the species'), behaviour is not random, and we can know someone's preference through their actions.

To apply economics to security studies by understanding revealed preferences and asking how we compel people to change behaviour, again we refer to Adam Smith's statement: 'It is not from the benevolence of the butcher, the brewer, or the baker, that we expect our dinner, but from their regard to their own interest.' All humans act to maximize their own interests. For example, during the Cold War, Mikhail Gorbachev did not predicate his decision to reform Soviet economic policies on simple altruism. By renouncing the Brezhnev Doctrine in 1988—a doctrine that mandated that no Eastern European country could renounce communism without forceful Soviet intervention—and dissolving the Soviet Union, Gorbachev essentially eliminated his own job. However, while Gorbachev's decision tarnished his domestic gains, he ultimately maximized his international reputation and, consequently, his overall gain. He was awarded the Nobel Peace Prize in 1990 'for his leading role in the peace process which today characterizes important parts of the international community'. He is hailed as an international hero and has earned a nice living through speaking engagements and public appearances.

Ironically, Gorbachev's decision to dissolve the Soviet Union was intended to promote his personal interests as much as Russian Premier Vladimir Putin's decision to annex Crimea in 2014 was motivated by his desire to further his own interests. While the effect of each man's political decision produced an inverse effect—Putin's annexation of Crimea earned him international condemnation but domestic acclaim—these decisions reveal both leaders' preferences for maximum political 'goods': power and prestige. Regardless of their desired end state, humans behave in predictable ways: we seek goals, betterment, and the attainment of 'good' things while avoiding 'bad' things, and we seek to increase our ability to reach these goals through interaction with other humans. To develop tools for security policy, we further dissect the decision-making dynamics (see Think Point 17.1).

Looking at human action and behaviour reveals much about an individual's perceived goals and constraints and can therefore maximize our understanding of what is needed for security policy. We do not

! THINK POINT 17.1 Profile: The decisions and constraints of US and Russian leaders

Russian President Vladimir Putin's decision to annex Crimea in February 2014 further complicated strained US–Russian and EU–Russian relations and brought him condemnation from leaders throughout the world. He framed his actions in nationalistic rhetoric. For example:

'there is not a single weakness for us there. Start with the fact that for Russians—and I mean the ethnically Russian part of our multinational people, the Christian Russian people—is a sacred place. . . . The original baptismal font of Russia is there.'

(RT Network (http://rt.com/news/203467-putin-speech-crimea-)

Pragmatically, President Putin seems to have gained more than he lost in making this move. He increased his domestic political power and his place as an important figure in the history of Russia. He faced little domestic opposition. The military move proved low cost: Russia already had a strong military presence in the area and controlled nearly all of the region's energy resources. Putin also had access to timely and accurate information about troop movements, politicians, and popular opinion in Eastern Ukraine and Crimea, while Russian Special Forces were able to obfuscate ground reports, complicating information gathering for both the Ukrainian government and international journalists. Time was also to President Putin's advantage. He has served as either Russia's prime minister or president since 1999 and will likely seek a fourth presidential term in 2018. He faces little political opposition, and Russia's six-year presidential term allows Putin to pursue his desired agendas without fearing re-election in the near term. In short, President Putin can afford to play a long game; it is tough to oppose a strong leader who appears to be in power for a long time to come. Ultimately, the cost for Putin to annex the Crimea and interfere in Ukrainian politics was low, and the gains seem high. His actions make sense.

Conversely, President Barack Obama originally intended to maximize his personal legacy by reforming domestic issues, such as health care, extricating US troops from wars in Iraq and Afghanistan, and avoiding United States' involvement in another lengthy conflict. He faced significant constraints, discouraging him from any type of intervention in Ukraine or Crimea. For example, the US military was stretched thin after thirteen years of a two-front war. Mobilizing US assets to the Crimea would require significant material, personnel, and money that the Department of Defence did not anticipate. Domestically, President Obama also faced stark opposition from Congress, and the perceived wisdom was that the American people feared US 'boots on the ground' in another costly foreign conflict. As a democratically elected leader in his second term in office, President Obama had a limited window of opportunity to pursue his own foreign and domestic policy agendas until his term expires in 2016. Overall, any military intervention in the Crimean crisis would have been a costly endeavour for President Obama and awarded him very few advantages. Instead, President Obama imposed sanctions against Russia in conjunction with the European Union in order to condemn Putin's actions while minimizing his own relative costs.

know if Putin cares that Crimea is the 'baptismal font'. We do know that Putin and Obama believed that the rhetoric they used supported their positions. We know they are **political entrepreneurs** taking actions that seem to benefit their positions. Getting beyond rhetoric and observing behaviours-as-revealed-preferences leads us to a true science for security policy.

Five vectors of economic incentives

To understand and change the behaviour of a criminal, terrorist, or tyrant, we must offer something in exchange or propose something that they might prefer. We can offer a 'good' or the avoidance of something 'bad', but a bargain must be proposed, and the incentives must be sufficient to gain acceptance. That any individual will respond to incentives, in a nutshell, encapsulates economics. By extension, understanding a system of incentives allows us to observe how targeted policies can alter the actions of an individual, and therefore an organization or government. In this sense, our understanding of macro events arises from the ground of human decision making. The following five vectors of economic incentives identify the forces acting on human behaviour and explain why an actor may respond to externally proffered incentives.

Goals

People inherently seek to maximize for themselves and their future generations. They want to survive and improve life for self, offspring, family, community, nation, country, and world, but do not pursue all goals equally. Think in terms of concentric social circles around a person; the closer someone is to this centre, the stronger the kinship and sense of shared future, and the greater the inclination to modify actions for some other's benefit. Consider your own extra-curricular activities at university. Whether you play a sport, volunteer for the community, support campus social events, or participate in professional or academic organizations, your dedication to each of these communities differs across the spectrum for self and for others. Yet your involvement in these activities is predicated on the belief that these organizations will help you maximize your own personal gains. For example, participation in campus events—such as fundraisers or conferences—intended to increase the prestige of a particular university benefits students at that institution, since graduating from a reputable school can increase a graduate's likelihood of obtaining a good job. As a result, your personal gains overlap with other members of your college community; this sense of a shared future creates a kinship between fellow students and alumni alike. Even community service, which many consider to be an altruistic activity, serves individuals as a way to maximize their goals. High school students frequently perform community service to enhance their profile in college applications, while members of a city may volunteer to help increase their property value or improve the community for their children. If you believed that your participation in any one of these activities did not improve your life in any way, this would affect your level of participation and engagement with these groups.

This basic premise applies universally. Even world leaders who implement policies that ostensibly provide for the common good pursue goals that will specifically enhance their own personal legacy and enable them to remain in power. Russian president Vladamir Putin and US president Barak Obama each pursued policies perceived to promote personal goals, but as Think Point 17.1 demonstrated, each leader pursued his individual goal in a very different manner.

Resource constraints

Resource constraints, or wealth constraints, limit the amount of resources to be spent on some good. We each make our individual choices within respective systems of constraints. One may want expensive cars but have only enough wealth to allow a choice from inexpensive models. Tools such as sanctions constrain wealth, and tools such as economic aid and trade promotion increase wealth. These foreign policy actions influence the decision making of others and can be effective tools of security policy.

Institutional constraints

Beyond goals and wealth constraints, our analysis must also consider the institutions in which individuals take action. Douglas North offers the following well-established definition:

> Institutions are the humanly devised constraints that structure human interaction. They are made up of formal constraints (e.g., rules, laws, constitutions), informal constraints (e.g., norms of behaviour, conventions, self-imposed codes of conduct), and their enforcement characteristics. Together they define the incentive structure of societies and specifically economies.
>
> North (1994: 360)

Institutional constraints consist of the man-made rules that structure and govern behaviour, guiding decision making. These include formal rules, such as laws and regulations, but also informal rules, such as cultural norms of behaviour. Since theft is illegal and this law is strictly enforced in my community, I cannot steal. In one's home, one may face a prohibition on eating candy after brushing teeth; although the law does not prohibit late-night candy, the norms of my household do.

Policy makers can seek to influence the institutions of others through formal rule making, such as laws; statements of policy at international institutions, such as a United Nations Security Council Resolution; or transparency and moral suasion, such as the 'name-and-shame' policies designed to identify individuals providing financial support to terrorists.

Information

Information plays a significant role in decision making, and therefore must comprise an important part of security analysis and policy-making. Although theory asserts that people act in their own best interests, 'rational action' depends on the information available and how that person perceives that information. For example, if you pay US$30,000 for a car, you prefer the car to the money, and the dealer prefers the money to the car, otherwise the exchange would not occur. You base your decision to hand over $30,000 on assumptions about the condition of the car, but you have imperfect information. With perfect information, people do not overpay for cars; in the absence of information, an individual may rationally purchase a 'lemon' (see Akerlof 1970).

Information is an economic good, and the provision and denial of information can influence economic decision making. Although we believe that most actors are rational, the 'rational' response to certain information is affected by each person's perspective and by how the information is presented or framed. Since people make choices based on what they perceive to be in their best interests, our analysis must consider what might be influencing this perception. In turn, by manipulating the information available and the way that information is presented, we can manipulate the way a person perceives a situation and the way that they see their goals and constraints. **Prospect theory** considers how people make decisions not based on objective analysis, but on their perception of a situation (Kahnemann 2002). For example, in a classic experiment, subjects were asked to place their arm into cold water twice. The first time, they held their hand in the water for 60 seconds at 14 degrees Celsius; the second time, they submersed their hand for 60 seconds at 14 degrees Celsius followed by 30 seconds at 15 degrees Celsius. When asked which experience was the least unpleasant and the one which they would prefer to repeat, most people preferred the 90 second option. Why would people prefer 90 seconds of pain over 60 seconds? The answer lies in framing. Participants remembered the last 30 seconds of the experiment most clearly. Since those final 30 seconds felt a little better in the second experiment compared with the first, they remembered the entire experience as better and so preferred it, even though the first 60 seconds were identical in each case.

Time

Decisions are also affected by a person's view of the 'time horizon', or how far one looks into the future. An individual's time horizon can change based on age, health, and goals, for example. Leaders are likewise influenced by their time horizon. All policies, such as monetary and fiscal sanctions and trade agreements made by policy makers, must consider a leader's demonstrated perspective when offering incentives or threatening sanctions.

As we move to economic tools of security, we bring forward economic science and the five vectors of economic incentives: goals, wealth constraints, institutional constraints, information, and time. To assess or craft policies, we must disaggregate the decision-making process and identify the system of incentives.

KEY POINTS

- Economics—a science concerned with how individuals make decisions—can help us understand security issues.
- People possess the propensity to exchange with others; and, through the division of labour, people become better off.
- Institutions are the man-made rules that constrain behaviour, which can be formal and/or informal.
- Scarcity requires choice. You cannot have everything, and you cannot have it now.
- To change the behaviour of an adversary, we must offer incentives, taking into account the five vectors of economic incentive.

Economic tools of security policy

By this point in the chapter it is clear that economics is not the study of money and wealth, but of exchange and value—of individuals making decisions in conditions of scarcity. But it seems the most natural way for people to think of value is to denominate it in terms of money. Therefore, in the policy-making communities and in the media, the concepts of economics and money are often conflated. Although you know the difference, for the purpose of our discussion of 'economic' instruments, or tools, we will accept the common shorthand and refer to economic policies as those relating to wealth. A policy that impacts another's creation, holding, and loss of wealth is an economic instrument. A policy that further seeks to advance a national security goal by impacting the wealth of another is an economic instrument of security policy. Economic tools can fit simply into four common categories: sanctions, trade, finance, and aid. A portmanteau category, 'new or non-traditional' can prove a useful fifth category, to ensure no orphan policies clutter discussions. The world outside of academia tends to ignore our neat theoretical lines, so let us not consider these five groupings as mutually exclusive, but a powerful and time-tested structure allowing understanding of economic theory as applied to global security.

Economic theory applied to specific economic instruments of national policy allows powerful views into the appropriate as well as misguided expectations. Policy makers often use economic instruments to achieve security policy goals—goals other than wealth creation or loss. For example, US leaders prioritized the investment of time and resources in concluding bilateral trade agreements with relatively small economies such as Jordan and Oman for reasons other than GDP growth of the US economy. Bilateral trade agreements can provide foreign policy power. Beyond wealth, economic tools provide a system of resources and constraints that, if properly constructed, can allow for the influence of the decisions of leaders. We address each class of tool here.

Sanctions

Economic sanctions are the politically motivated denial, or threat of denial, of normal economic relations with the intent of changing behaviours. At a minimum, economic sanctions aim to disassociate one economy with another. The tools have evolved significantly since the end of the Cold War, becoming more targeted on individual actors and less on blanket condemnations of an entire population. However, focusing on economic sanctions remains a difficult challenge. The tool will continue to improve as policy makers appreciate the system of incentives acting on an individual's self-interest and the propensity of humans—more specifically, political leaders—to engage in exchanges.

Imagine two countries, A and B, with Leader A and Leader B respectively the recognized political leaders of each. If Leader A ceases all trade in goods and services with B for political reasons, she has instituted a broad sanction. She may choose this policy to promote regime change in B, or simply to disassociate with a regime that engages in gross violations of human rights. This pattern has characterized economic sanctions since the Cold War, but success at causing regime change appears limited. For example, US president John F. Kennedy instituted a broad economic embargo against Fidel Castro's Cuba in 1962 following the Cuban nationalization of all US-person owned property in Cuba. Although the policy goal of regime change did not come about, many remain in support of the policy fifty years later with no expectation that the sanctions will bring about regime change. Alternatively, imagine Leader A denying normal economic relations with only the family and business associates of Leader B. This targeted sanction represents a trend in sanctions policies over the past fifteen years. For example, US policies following the 9/11 attacks on the United States sanction specific people and businesses from transacting in the United States; these sanctions target a small group of individuals when compared to an embargo of an entire country, and intend to target those who supported the 9/11 attacks. (For further reading on sanctions, see Drezner 1998; Haass 1998; Elliott et al. 2008; and Shiffman and Jochum 2011.)

Sanctions serve important purposes. From a political viewpoint, sanctions exert economic power to advance peace and freedom. Morally, they can deny economic participation in egregious evils. Militarily, they may isolate dangerous regimes and weaken threats to regional and global security. These arguments comprise most rhetorical justifications for sanctions policies.

Political leaders intend sanctions to prompt target governments to either comply with some requirement or suffer the consequences. In Saddam Hussein's Iraq, the choice was to verify disarmament or struggle with growing economic deprivation. In Castro's Cuba, the choice was to advance democratic reforms or miss benefits associated with trade and investments with the United States.

However, broad economic sanctions have proven fairly limited in altering behaviour. When intended to cripple a target country's economy, they generally fail because dictators do not seek national wealth only. Power is key. Dictators balance maximizing regime revenue and minimizing security costs to remain in power. They welcome economic growth when it funds the regime's security needs and controls society; they reject growth when it promotes the emergence of formidable power struggles such as a middle class eager to advance political reform and openness.

Moreover, sanctions may actually solidify a dictator's power. Dictators can turn to other partners for trade and investment when facing unilateral sanctions. This is why untargeted unilateral sanctions have little economic impact (Shiffman and Jochum 2011). Multilateral sanctions such as those imposed by the United Nations (UN) may have loopholes that can paradoxically help a dictator sustain power. UN sanctions imposed against Saddam's Iraq in 1990 were intended to pressure him to disarm. Saddam manipulated the sanction to bolster his regime—resources flowed solely to the military and elite—while a propaganda campaign blamed sanctioning powers, especially the USA, for the population's economic hardships. Throughout the Arab world and elsewhere, sanctioning powers received blame as the instigator for Saddam's actions.

Sanctions can remain a credible policy tool as long as policy makers understand the costs and likely benefits of the policy. If they set an achievable goal in an achievable timeline, and can manage the constraints, then they may understand how a sanction will impact the target leader's decision making.

Dictators are human, however, and not all dictators are alike, so we need to study each individual we seek to influence and determine individual goals, wealth and institutional constraints, information deficits, and time horizons. All people possess the same human nature, but exhibit different behaviours due to differences across the incentive vectors. Ronald Wintrobe (1990) suggests a simplifying typology: totalitarian, tyrant, tinpot, and 'timocrat', and Shiffman and Jochum (2011) further develop the model (Figure 17.1).

Starting near the bottom left of the diagram, a *tinpot* seeks to steal the wealth of the people he governs and usually governs in a location with a history of frequent changes in government (i.e. coups, overthrows, or even elections). Therefore, tinpots seek wealth and face few institutional constraints to theft, but face the challenge of staying in power and alive. The tinpot, then, acts under a short-term time horizon, unaware of when, for example, a general will seek to assassinate him or the populace will move to overthrow him.

Figure 17.1 Typology of autocracy

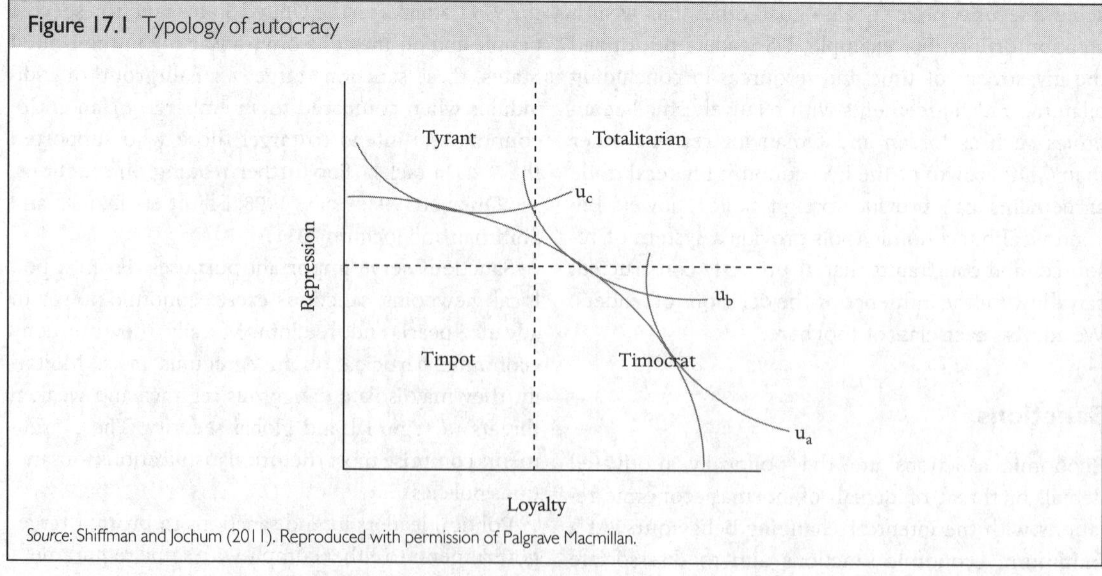

Source: Shiffman and Jochum (2011). Reproduced with permission of Palgrave Macmillan.

The tinpot takes money for personal gain and does not invest more than absolutely necessary in the economic engine of the country's economy. The *totalitarian*, by contrast, seeks power, and uses the wealth from the economy to invest in the tools of remaining in power. Specifically, the totalitarian uses wealth to buy the loyalty of those closest to him in power to avoid a coup or assassination. He also purchases the instruments of repression to keep the population from uprising. He invests in the productive means of the economy, since his income and wealth are tied to that of the economy, but never to the detriment of his relative power over others. He has a long time horizon, seeking to rule until death, and even put his family into power once he passes away. Like the totalitarian, tyrants and timocrats also invest heavily in the institutions of power, seeking to remain in power for long periods of time. The difference lies in their choice of tools. The *tyrant* will invest more heavily in repression, and less on loyalty, preferring to be feared rather than loved. The *timocrat*, by contrast, seeks support and loyalty from those around him, and so invests in his generals and senior officials, as well as in the population. The timocrat is also known as the 'benevolent dictator'—the king that seeks the love and admiration of the entire kingdom.

Political leaders (autocrats and democrats alike) must spend money to stay in power. In democracies, electoral candidates dedicate vast sums of spending on political activities to receive votes in future elections. The autocrat, however, faces the added complexity of the 'dictator's dilemma' (Wintrobe 1990; see Think Point 17.2).

Based upon our economic analysis, a policy that seeks to alter the leader's wealth constraint might provide the greatest opportunity to influence the decision making of the leader. A good case study that most clearly represents a tyranny using Wintrobe's typology is the Democratic People's Republic of Korea (DPRK), or North Korea, led by the Kim dynasty. (See Background 17.1.) The Great and Dear Leaders each reveal a preference for maximizing power in order to stay in power, and to do so over an indefinite time horizon. The Leaders display near total control over the domestic political levers of power. The biggest challenge facing any dictator is transition; the Kims managed to handle succession twice—first in 1994, then again in 2011. Beyond the domestic aspiration to rule forever, the Kims have shown an interest in regional power through the development of nuclear weapons. A nuclear weapons-armed ballistic missile arsenal in North Korea would alter regional and global dynamics in significant ways. Can we use economic tools to change the behaviour of the Kim dynasty and the DPRK government?

In order to increase regional power, the Kim dynasty needs wealth, and North Korea is a poor country. Based upon economic analysis, a policy that seeks to alter the leader's constraints will provide the greatest opportunity to influence the decision making of the leader; see Table 17.1.

American presidents had made agreements—entered into exchanges—with Kim Jong Il on several occasions. In 1994, US President Bill Clinton's administration negotiated the Agreed Framework, where the United States provided 500,000 tons of oil and

BACKGROUND 17.1 North Korea: quick facts

1948 Founded by Kim Il Sung (the 'Great Leader')

1994 Kim Il Sung declared 'President for Life' following his death. His duties were assumed by his son, Kim Jong Il (the 'Dear Leader')

2011 Upon the death of Kim Jong Il, his duties transferred to his son, Kim Jong Un

According to the CIA World Factbook (Central Intelligence Agency 2012): 'After decades of economic mismanagement and resource misallocation, the DPRK since the mid-1990s has relied heavily on international aid to feed its population. North Korea's history of regional military provocations, proliferation of military-related items, long-range missile development, WMD [weapons of mass destruction] programs, including tests of nuclear devices in 2006 and 2009, and massive conventional armed forces are of major concern to the international community.'

! THINK POINT 17.2 The dictator's dilemma

Dictators remain in power by convincing all potential future challenges for power: 'If you challenge me, I will win and you will pay a price for the failed attempt. However, to convincingly threaten any and all challenges, I require people loyal to me; someone must support and carry out my acts of repression. Therefore, I must also rely on the loyalty of some people; otherwise, I cannot maintain power.' The dictator must simultaneously use repression and loyalty as tools to stay in power.

Table 17.1 Goals and constraints for Kim Jong Il, and perhaps Kim Jong Un

Goal	Remain in power and increase power regionally
Institutional constraint	Strong power at home; very little support internationally
Wealth constraint	Significant; poor economy
Information	Domestic calculations probably well informed; internationally, however, the isolated regime may make decisions based upon incomplete and inaccurate information
Time horizon	Current leader's father and grandfather sought indefinite power; new leader may be the same, but 'revealed preferences' as yet unknown

two so-called light-water nuclear reactors—significant wealth to President Kim Jong Il's regime. In exchange, President Kim promised to close the nuclear reactor at Yongbyon, a reactor capable of producing weapons-grade plutonium. What was the trade? Wealth for security. The exchange makes sense. Kim wanted to remain in power and his wealth constraint perhaps most significantly challenged this goal. The United States and its allies wanted to prevent or slow down the DPRK nuclear weapons programme. Both sides got what they wanted—or so it seemed.

In 2002, Kim Jong Il admitted to cheating on the Agreed Framework, and continued to develop weapons-grade plutonium and a ballistic missile capability. Recall that we inferred a second Kim goal of regional power; additional concessions were made to Kim in exchange for further promises and inspections. In 2007, Kim was again caught and confirmed violating agreements related to nuclear materials, so President Bush struck another agreement. The US will lift trade sanctions in exchange for further guarantees on the cessation of the DPRK nuclear programme. Again, this agreement tendered wealth for security. In each of these instances, however, Kim received the wealth immediately, therefore maintaining control over the institutions of power inside North Korea, while the US and allies received only promises regarding future behaviour—promises not kept. As recently as 2012, with the installation of Kim Jong Un, President Obama has agreed to provide 240,000 metric tons of food to Kim in exchange, once again, for promises to stop enriching uranium and conducting nuclear tests.

Trade

Trade, when voluntary, makes all parties to the exchange better off. Trade creates wealth. In the previous section, we addressed sanctions as the denial of trade; in this section, we discuss trade promotion in goods and services. If I am thirsty and have $1, and I exchange that dollar for a bottle of water, then I have exactly what I preferred—a bottle of water to a dollar. If I valued the dollar more than the water, I would not buy the water. So, after the exchange, if I have something I value in excess of $1, I have increased my wealth. If the vendor valued the bottle of water more than $1, she would not sell it to me for that amount. Trade makes all participants better off—wealthier. Aggregating the actions of many, one can surmise that nations engage in trade to become better off. Trade, therefore, is an economic 'good'—something that people want.

However, when we look at the world, we do not see free trade everywhere. Some leaders oppose this economic good. A leader makes choices in his or her own interest; if one does not engage in trade, one must consider some trade as 'bad' for the decision maker.

Both democrats and autocrats benefit from trade, but both can also be seen opposing free trade in the world. Dictators may not favour free trade if it increases the power of political opposition and makes insurrections more likely, since this decreases a dictator's ability to sustain power. Democratic leaders must take positions that serve some constituencies more than others. For example, free trade may make the country better off over time, but harm a local community or trade union in the short term. In comparison with the long-term benefits of trade, constituencies and politicians can make decisions based upon short-term horizons. A worker may need a job to afford this month's rent, and his views on trade will reflect this short-term imperative. Furthermore, large national corporations may oppose trade agreements with other nations if their companies are left out of the deal or if their intellectual property is threatened by this agreement. Politicians want votes and campaign dollars for their next election; consequently, we can observe domestic interests hindering free trade. In spite of clear long-term benefits, we see people rationally opposing free trade. Case Study 17.1 offers an excellent example by way of the Free Trade Agreement between India and Japan.

Access to the US marketplace is a good; countries wish to increase trade with the United States in order to become richer. Once established, the withdrawal of economic engagement becomes a sanction—a tool used to influence a leader's behaviour. Thus, a US President can employ trade agreements as a powerful tool to advance national security. The United States' implementation of the Free Trade Agreement (FTA) with South Korea (KORUS FTA) in 2012 presents an example of trade agreements as a security tool. While both nations stand to gain considerable wealth from this trade agreement, KORUS FTA is perhaps more successful because it demonstrates the US political leaders' commitment to maintaining stability and prosperity throughout the Asia-Pacific region. This agreement not only sends a powerful signal to North Korean leaders that the United States rewards its allies, but also grants US political leaders further influence with South Korean leadership and the ability to leverage South Korea's economic benefits to advance security for the US and its allies against an increasingly expansionist Chinese government (Office of US Trade Representative 2012).

Export controls protect technological advantages, maintain security, and further foreign policy objectives. Policy makers may regulate or prevent the sale of technology and goods to certain countries for security reasons. For example, the US Department of State controls the sales of munitions, the US Department of Commerce controls dual use technology (items that can have both civilian and military applications), and the US Treasury Department oversees trade embargoes. Import restrictions, on the other hand, protect a country's businesses from certain unfair advantages of imported foreign goods. They include a number of policies such as anti-dumping, countervailing duties, and safeguards. Policy makers restrict imports for three main reasons: as an intervention to correct some market failure and make trade *fair*; as a way of limiting access to the US domestic market for a particular trade benefit; and as a remedy to influence the behaviour of other policy makers.

Finance

The exchange of money influences national security and creates opportunities to leverage world leaders and events. The international financial system supports the international trade today, as well as trade across time, which involves trading something today for something tomorrow.

In finance, people benefit from access to the market in two ways: first, from the ability to trade weak currency for strong currency; second, from the ability to finance today's consumption with tomorrow's income—otherwise known as debt and equity.

Most of the domestic currencies traded in the world today hold no intrinsic value. Unlike a gold coin, which retains value when melted down, a US dollar, for example, holds no value when ripped into pieces. We call this a **fiat currency**. Euro banknotes have a value because people expect the national central banks within the Eurozone and the European Union to protect that value. Entire economies work upon the faith that central banks will preserve the value of the currencies. But not all central banks exercise the same degree of responsibility, so some currencies hold their value better than others. In business, you want to use a currency that holds value.

People trade different currencies as products in the global economy. Just as one can trade in commodities (such as oil or cars), so it is possible to trade dollars, euro, pesos, etc. We expect individuals to hold money that retains or grows in value and avoid money that loses value. Just like trade in goods and services, this

CASE STUDY 17.1 India–Japan Comprehensive Economic Partnership Agreement

In 2011, Japanese Foreign Minister Seiji Maehara and Indian Commerce Minister Anand Sharma finalized a Free Trade Agreement (FTA) entitled the India–Japan Comprehensive Economic Partnership Agreement (IJCEPA). The trade agreement removes the 10 per cent tax India previously placed on Japanese batteries, technology, and auto parts and eliminates Japanese taxes on Indian tea and agricultural products (Ministry of Foreign Affairs of Japan 2014). However, the IJCEPA not only opens the door for further Japanese investment in India, a promising and rapidly growing international market, but also marks the beginning of a Japan and Indian economic security agreement intended to minimize China's influence in the Pacific.

insight into currencies gives analysts explanatory power over observed events, and allows policy makers to find tools of influence in international finance.

When people trade across time, often one party purchases debt from another. Debt is a promise to pay in the future for what you receive now. You can think of debt as a trade across time; you gain value today in exchange for a value in the future. One can purchase a car or home because of access to the debt market. Interest rates reflect the cost of the exchange. For example, US$1 today in exchange for US$1.10 in one year is a 10 per cent annual interest rate. Like all other forms of trade, individuals desire access to the market, which provides that opportunity for voluntary exchange and an increase in wealth. Access to debt markets is an economic good. In terms of security policy, therefore, offering access to credit—or denying it—can provide significant incentives to a foreign leader to change behaviour. (See Case Study 17.2, which illustrates the effectiveness of post-9/11 counterterrorist financing.)

Aid

People may support giving aid out of compassion, but national security decision makers also understand the significant national security power derived from providing and denying development assistance grants and loans (see Case Studies 17.3 and 17.4). As an economic

CASE STUDY 17.2 Counterterrorist financing post-9/11

Following the 11 September 2001 **(9/11)** attacks in the United States, the Treasury Department created the Office of Terrorist Financing and Intelligence (OTFI) and adopted a three-pronged security strategy. First, to deter individuals from supporting terrorist groups, it instituted a 'name-and-shame' programme to publicly identify individuals known to provide financial support to terrorist groups. Second, the US Treasury stepped up efforts to 'block' the assets of those involved in supporting international terrorism. By Executive Order 13224 (2001), the US President asserted the authority to 'freeze' assets, money, and real property, denying access to the owners of the assets if the owner engages in or supports acts of international terrorism. Finally, the US President instituted policies to deny access to American banks to those engaged in or supporting international terrorism. Therefore, identified individuals, groups, or states, could not trade in US dollars, or borrow money in US funds. In addition to these domestic efforts, the US attained international support for these policies, with many countries and the UN adopting mirroring policies, seen for example in UN Security Council Resolution 1267 (1999) regarding the situation in Afghanistan. In summary, leaders can (1) apply the tools of international finance to deny access to a person's or a country's own assets; (2) deny someone the ability to conduct transactions in a specific currency; and (3) deny access to the debt market (the ability to borrow or lend money).

CASE STUDY 17.3 World Bank Development Assistance to Uganda

In February 2014, the World Bank postponed a health-care loan to Uganda a few days after Ugandan President Yoweri Museveni signed an anti-gay bill into law that imposed life sentences for those guilty of 'aggravated homosexuality'. World Bank President Jim Yong Kim rejected the $90 million loan in an attempt to alter Museveni's behaviour and encourage him to embrace a policy of social inclusion. Furthermore, Jim wanted to protect the $1.94 billion that the World Bank had already invested in Ugandan social projects and claimed that Museveni's restriction on sexual rights could negatively impact Uganda's 'competitiveness by discouraging multinational companies from investing or locating their activities in those nations' (Jim Yong Kim 2014).

Ultimately, Jim's postponement of the World Bank loan had little impact on Museveni's resolve because he significantly overestimated Museveni's concern for his citizens. The Ugandan people—not President Museveni—are the ones most significantly impacted by the cancellation of health-care loans. Consequently, denying aid to the Ugandan people does nothing to influence Museveni's personal incentive vectors. Additionally, as the leader of a hybrid semi-authoritarian/semi-democratic state, Museveni's ability to remain in power largely depends on his ability to quell all internal and external opposition. Shortly after the World Bank decision, one of Museveni's spokesmen claimed that, despite Western pressure, President Museveni would continue to assert Uganda's independence. This independence proved to be costly; after the cancellation and postponement of Western loans, Uganda's shilling currency fell to its lowest level in two years. Still, Museveni continued to support the anti-homosexuality laws, despite Uganda's declining GDP. If remaining in power is Museveni's immediate goal, and securing his place in history his long-term goal, accommodating Western demands would make Museveni appear weak and could potentially encourage opposition leaders to contest Museveni's claim to power, both now and in the history books.

CASE STUDY 17.4 Somalia

The US relationship with Somalia, although complicated, presents a clear example of the use of aid for national security interests. In fact, aid can be seen as a barometer of US–Somali relations through the years. Aid, or Official Development Assistance (ODA), in its many forms from states or other international actors is almost always distributed with some motive beyond the humanitarian. In the twentieth century, the USA and the Soviet Union (USSR) used aid as a powerful tool of influence during the Cold War. This was especially the case on the African continent, where the superpowers backed supporters, who sometimes engaged in proxy wars.

Somalia, under the leadership and influence of General Mohamed Siad Barre, aligned itself with the Soviet Union during the Cold War, and received military and economic assistance in exchange. In the late 1970s, however, the USSR under Leonid Brezhnev ceased providing aid to Somali leaders and populations and decided instead to back a more socialist regime in Ethiopia, the Derg. US leaders in the Ford and Carter administrations saw this as an opportunity and began backing Somalia against the Ethiopians in a war that broke out in the Ogaden border regions of the two countries.

This shift in aid donors to Somalia began a long and complicated relationship of aid from the United States to Somalia. Beginning in the early 1990s, President George H. W. Bush used aid for Somalia during and after the Somali civil war to give preference to 'warlords' whom US policy makers thought were serving their best interests in the region. President Bill Clinton backed the United Nations in one of the first militarized aid distribution schemes that ended in the infamous 'Black Hawk Down' incident. More recently, Somalia has received aid in a variety of indirect forms to avoid directly sending actual US-backed aid workers into the country. This aid is sent to refugee camps in Somalia and Ethiopia not only with the intent to help a needy people, but also to curb radicalization of extremist sympathizers to the terrorist group al-Shabaab. Like many insurgencies and terrorist organizations before it, al-Shabaab provides services and 'aid' to win the hearts and minds of the Somali people. The US administrations of Presidents George W. Bush and Barack Obama, wishing to win hearts and minds away from extremist organizations, counter the influence of al-Shabaab with US aid that provided food and medical services, and other social support.

good—something that leaders in the developing and poorest countries desire—aid money can incentivize individual decision making and therefore advance national security. For example, Leader A communicates to Leader B this message, 'Stop abusing ethnic or religious minorities in your country, and we will give you foreign assistance and encourage others to do the same.'

In addition to the quid-pro-quo of money for action, some argue that ending poverty promotes global security. USAID's document 'Foreign Aid in the National Interest' (United States Agency for International Development 2002) argues that security increasingly relies on the prosperity of the rest of the world. If he agreed, Leader A would communicate to Leader B: 'Use these funds for economic growth, and we will provide more. If you squander these funds, we will cut you off from further assistance.'

KEY POINTS

- Economic policies can provide effective national security tools by working through the vectors of incentives to influence the decisions of leaders.
- Sanctions intended to influence the actions of an adversary must decrease wealth, and therefore the options available to the adversary.
- The size and nature of the market in which an economy can trade influences the ability to create wealth. Trade policies can entice leaders to change behaviours in exchange for access to markets or trade preferences, and advance security.
- Access to banking and finance markets, like those for goods and services, represents an economic good, and policy makers can incentivize security-promoting behaviours in others by providing and denying access to debt and equity.
- To the extent that poverty promotes insecurity, economic policies that alleviate poverty can increase security. And economic policies must take into account the incentives of not only the leaders, but also the populations it is intended to influence.

Conclusion

This chapter explains economics as a science of human decision making, and a social science critical to understanding threat and policy-making environments to improve actions taken to promote security. People are inclined to trade to gain wealth, which allows for a suite of economic security policies. By analysing an individual's actions and considering their system of incentives (goals and constraints [resource, institutional, information, and time]), policy makers can utilize economic tools to create agreements that are mutually beneficial, win leverage with foreign leaders, and improve the living conditions of people throughout the world. By considering the economic science of human behaviour, we can describe and forecast the actions and preferences of people whose backgrounds and beliefs seem widely different from our own, and thereby create more effective security policy.

QUESTIONS

1. What does Adam Smith's moral philosophy teach us about fundamental human nature and how does economic science help us understand the variety of behaviours observed among individuals?
2. Are violent criminals, terrorists, and insurgents economic actors who seek economic goods just like most people in the world?
3. Provide an example of how a market allows individuals to increase wealth for the self and others. How can violence be placed into market terms?
4. What institutional rules, other than laws, might impact a political leader's decision to engage in acts of war?
5. In what ways can we think of economic policies as 'bargains' in which one leader offers a deal or a trade to another? Can you provide an example?
6. Like Smith's butcher, brewer, and baker, do terrorists require support from others? Can you pick a terrorist and describe their vectors of incentives as you understand them from publicly known or revealed preferences?
7. When would economic sanctions denying market access for good, services, or finance likely bring about a desired policy objective?
8. What is the difference between high-quality currency and low-quality, and how is currency an economic good capable of being used to as a tool to change behaviour?
9. Beyond the goods and services exchanged in a market, how can you describe access to debt markets and international financial institutions as an economic good and tool for security policy?
10. How would you craft a new development assistance grant programme to a foreign country to maximize your country's security goals?

FURTHER READING

- Berman, E. (2009), *Radical, Religious, and Violent: The New Economics of Terrorism*, Cambridge, MA: MIT Press. Using economic theory, this book explains how radical religious sects can run such violent, deadly terrorist organizations.
- Dam, K. (2001), *The Rules of the Global Game*, Chicago, IL: University of Chicago Press. An academic and veteran policy maker, Ken Dam explains the political economy of Washington, DC providing insight into the democratic process of decision making.
- Easterly, W. (2001), *The Elusive Quest for Growth: Economists' Adventures and Misadventures in the Tropics*, Cambridge, MA: MIT Press. Former World Bank economist, Easterly makes clear the importance of economic incentives, and why ignoring them can lead to failed policies.

- Shiffman, G. and Jochum, J. (2011), *Economic Instruments of Security Policy: Influencing the Choices of Leaders*, 2nd edn, London: Palgrave Macmillan. This book provides a deeper exposition on the economics of security studies with an emphasis on the political economy of autocracy. Specifically, it provides a technical model of the political economy of totalitarianism, contrasted with that of other forms of political leadership.
- Smith, A. (1904), *An Inquiry into the Nature and Causes of the Wealth of Nations*, E. Cannan, ed., Library of Economics and Liberty, London: Methuen. 2 vols. Available from: http://www.econlib.org/library/Smith/smWN.html. The definitive source text on economics; a free version is available online at this link.
- Shapiro, J. (2013), *The Terrorist's Dilemma: Managing Violent Covert Organizations*, Princeton, NJ: Princeton University Press. This book provides the best comprehensive view of terrorist organizations as businesses with leaders subject to economic influences in much the same way that country leaders and corporate executives are.

IMPORTANT WEBSITES

- **www.EconomicInstruments.org** This site specifically provides links to information on two courses and a book on the general topic of economic instruments of security policy.
- **http://www.ustr.gov/trade-agreements/free-trade-agreements** The Office of the United States Trade Representative lists all countries with which the USA presently has trade agreements. This site also provides current information concerning newly introduced FTAs, which have not yet been fully implemented.
- **http://sdnsearch.ofac.treas.gov/** The US Treasury Department's Sanctions List Search provides a great resource for searching the many US sanctions lists. General information on US sactions programmes can be found at http://www.treasury.gov/resource-center/sanctions/Pages/default.aspx.

Visit the Online Resource Centre that accompanies this book for lots of interesting additional material: www.oxfordtextbooks.co.uk/orc/collins4e/

18

Globalization, Development, and Security

Nana K. Poku and Jacqueline Therkelsen

Chapter Contents

Reader's Guide

This chapter proposes that globalization is a neoliberal ideology for development, promoted by key international financial institutions, which deepens inequality between and within nations on a global scale, resulting in increased global insecurity through a growing sense of injustice and grievance that may lead to rebellion and radicalization. The authors argue that, ultimately, the globalization ideology for development services the interest of its advocates, the elites of the core capitalist economies that dominate the international financial institutions, at the expense and immiseration of the majority of people in developing economies and the weaker segments of their own societies. The chapter is set out in three stages: first, it presents the case for conceptualizing globalization as a neoliberal ideology for development; second, it provides evidence to demonstrate the harmful effects of the ideology on societies, particularly across the developing world, and; third, it explores the connection between uneven globalization and global insecurity through two case studies: the Egypt uprising in 2011, and the collapse of the Greek economy in 2010.

Introduction

To its advocates, **globalization** encapsulates new technology, supported by more open policies designed to create a world more interconnected than ever before. This spans not only growing interdependence in economic relations, such as trade, investment, finance, and the organization of production globally, but also social and political interaction among organizations and individuals across the world. For the leading globalizers, the process is apolitical with unrivalled productive capacity, which, if unhindered by state regulations or fear, can deliver unprecedented material progress for the poor. In what follows, we argue the world is far from realizing this potential and the current phase of globalization is generating unbalanced outcomes, both between and within nations. Indeed, the euphoria the process has generated, and continues to generate, serves to disguise the very real social and economic inequalities that are not merely leftovers from the past, but are the result of the **ideology** at the heart of the process. This is an ideology indebted to the epistemological insights of classical economic liberalism, with its emphasis on open markets, limited government intervention, de-controlled pricing systems, liberalized trade and investment and privatizing areas of the economy previously controlled by the state.

We set the argument out in three stages. In the first stage, we present the case for conceptualizing globalization as an ideology for **development**, highlighting the key actors involved and the key policies being promoted. In the second stage, we draw on a growing body of evidence demonstrating the harmful effects of the ideology on societies and communities, particularly across the developing world. The final section makes the case for why uneven globalization may pose the greatest risk to global security. We argue that wealth is being created through globalization, but too many people across all countries are not sharing in its fruits; nor do they have any voice in shaping the process. For the three-quarters of the world's population caught on the barren side of the globalization fence, the process has not met any of their basic needs; many live in the limbo of the informal economy without formal rights, decent livelihoods, or the legitimate prospect of better futures for their children. While poverty is a pervasive feature of most societies, past and present, and can push some individuals towards desperate acts of violence in their struggle for survival, it is the notion of unjust inequality that brings to the disadvantaged a sense of grievance. It is out of this grievance that radicalization and rebellion is likely to gain ferment, with untold ramifications for national and international security.

Globalization as a neoliberal ideology for development

Globalization as a concept

The late Susan Strange rated the notion of globalization as the 'worst of all the vague and woolly words' in the discipline of International Relations, as it refers to 'anything from the Internet to a hamburger' (Strange 1986). Yet, it would be misguided to argue there is nothing new about contemporary globalization. Quantitatively, most manifestations of global connectivity have reached unprecedented levels during the past half-century (Scholte 2005). While the eventual picture remains in doubt, the principal agents of such change are evident enough, such as globalizing corporations emerging from a rapid process of super-mergers, techno-scientific networks, and the aesthetic architects of mass culture. At the same time, there is also a shrinking of the world brought about by the third technological revolution that has enabled us to travel both vicariously and instantaneously to almost all regions of the world (Allen and Hammett 1998). Similarly, economic activities are no longer focused at the local level and the objective is no longer to serve a limited population with immediate needs (Dicken 1992). Socio-economic activities are geared towards producing commodities that satisfy the desires of absent others who, in all likelihood, one will never meet. Globalization has, therefore, radically altered the manner in which we conduct our lives (McGrew and Poku 2007). Such processes are further strengthened by a trend towards large-scale corporate mergers designed to create enterprises with genuinely global scale and reach (Dicken 1992). Globalization is a response to changing configurations in global relations—new connectivities as well as new divisions—generating the need for an original approach to grasp those changes. Moreover, it is a process driven by economics.

The neoliberalism of globalization

Reflecting its economism, regulators of trade, finance, and industry have held pride of place in policy-making around contemporary globalization. Among global governance organizations, for instance, the international financial institutions (IFIs), the World Trade Organization (WTO), and the Organisation for Economic Co-operation and Development (OECD) have overshadowed agencies such as the International Labour Organization (ILO) and the United Nations Educational, Scientific and Cultural Organization (UNESCO) on questions of managing globalization. Viewed in this way, it becomes possible to imagine globalization as an ideology seeking to remodel the world in an image that serves the mindsets of its advocates. This mindset reflects an intellectual lineage that connects with nineteenth-century classical economic liberalism (see Key Ideas 18.1).

Cultural, ecological, geographical, political, and psychological aspects of globality are generally approached as functions of, and subordinate to, economics, if they are considered at all. Indeed, liberalism tends to treat economics in isolation from other dimensions of social relations. In particular, the doctrine supposes that economic policies in world politics could be a culturally and politically neutral matter of technical expertise. A key aspect of economic liberalism is that it was also the central ideology behind European colonialism. In *The Wealth of Nations* (1776), Adam Smith considered colonialism to be economically beneficial to both the colonial powers and the colonies, and he was only opposed to the exclusive (monopolistic) trade conditions that some metropolitan countries established with their colonies. Smith noted, 'The *exclusive* trade of the mother countries tends to diminish ... both the enjoyments and industry of all those nations in general' (A. Smith 1776: 467; emphasis added).

The contemporary version of liberalism (popularly referred to as **neoliberalism**) emphasizes certain micro-foundations of traditional neo-classical economics, such as the efficiency of market competition, the role of individual consumers in determining economic outcomes, and criticisms of distortions associated with government intervention and regulation of markets (Saad Filho and Johnston 2005).

Neoliberal articulations of globalization not only claim to capture the nature and extent of complex and inter-related political, economic, social, and technological processes that are extending and deepening relations between countries and peoples across the world, but also involves normative statements and judgements about the perceived benefits and, following from this, appropriate responses and policy prescriptions. Neoliberal ideology, as embodied in *The Washington Consensus* (see Background 18.1), has

KEY IDEAS 18.1 Classical economic liberalism

Classical economic theory was developed in the late eighteenth and nineteenth centuries through the work of political economists such as Adam Smith (1723–90) and, later, David Ricardo (1770–1823). Smith's *The Wealth of Nations* (1776) was a critique of mercantilism, the dominant economic theory of the time. According to E. H. Carr (1945: 5), 'the aim of mercantilism ... was not to promote the welfare of the community and its members, but to augment the power of the state, of which the sovereign was the embodiment ... wealth was the source of power, or more specifically of fitness for war'. Wealth (bullion) was brought in by exports, and heavily controlled by government, who intervened in economic life to encourage the export of goods and restrict imports. During this time, society, and thereby export markets, were seen as static, and the only means for a nation to expand its markets was to capture existing markets from other nations, for example by waging trade wars. Mercantilism, then, was viewed by classical economic theorists as a source of international conflict and a promotion of government and aristocracy at the expense of societal welfare. Instead, they suggested market capitalism would better promote general welfare through the efficient allocation of scarce resources within society. The market should be free from government interference as it would be managed through a self-regulating mechanism Smith called an 'invisible hand'. This self-regulation was based around a belief in human nature as essentially self-interested and materialistic. Internationally, free trade was promoted as a more peaceful means of generating wealth, and according to the theory of comparative advantage, each national economy would benefit more from free trade than from pursuing nationalism and self-sufficiency. Free market ideas dominated the United Kingdom and United States economies of the nineteenth century, and included the doctrine of laissez-faire, which dictated the state should have no economic role, in the belief that unrestrained pursuit of profit by individuals would result in benefit for society as a whole. Laissez-faire theories were not seriously challenged until the depression years of the 1930s, but in the late twentieth century, they saw a revival through neoliberalism (Burchill 2001; Heyward 2003).

BACKGROUND 18.1 The 10 Steps of *The Washington Consensus*

1. Fiscal Discipline: budget deficits of no more than 2 per cent of gross domestic product (GDP).
2. Public Expenditure Priorities: redirect what is left of reduced public expenditures away from domestic industry and towards poverty-reduction priority areas of the budget, especially towards primary health and education, and infrastructure.
3. Tax Reform: broadening the tax base, cut marginal tax rates, improve tax administration.
4. Financial Liberalization: reforms towards market-determined interest rates, abolition of preferential interest rates for privileged borrowers, and achievement of a moderately positive real interest rate.
5. Exchange Rates: a unified exchange rate (for trading) set at a level sufficiently competitive to induce a rapid growth in non-traditional exports, and managed so as to assure exporters that competitiveness will be maintained in the future.
6. Trade Liberalization: change quantitative trade restrictions with tariffs, and then progressively lower these tariffs until a uniform low tariff in the range of 10 per cent (or at most around 20 per cent) is achieved.
7. Foreign Direct Investment: abolish restrictions on entry of foreign firms; establishing 'national treatment' for foreign investors, i.e. no beneficial subsidies or taxes or other support for domestic firms.
8. Privatization: state enterprises should be privatized.
9. Deregulation: abolish regulations on entry of new firms or competition laws that favour domestic firms; ensure that any remaining regulations are 'justified' by safety, environmental, or financial oversight needs.
10. Property Rights: promote legal reforms to secure property rights without excessive costs and to regularize the informal sector.

generated consensual guidelines through terms and concepts, which circumscribe what can be thought and done and has given intellectual respectability to ideas that support the deregulation of markets and the 'rolling back' of the state (Murphy 2000). States are presented as being increasingly subject to the disciplines of the global market, compelled to adjust to the realities of technological changes and intensifying economic interdependence that make it impossible to de-link from the global economy. Governments, international development agencies, and other multilateral economic institutions, like the World Bank and International Monetary Fund, have played a major role in devising development strategies, grounded in neoliberal economic principles, promoting marketization and moves towards free trade and export-led growth strategies. Increasingly, it is the IMF, the WTO, and the World Bank who 'make the rules', favouring the adoption of neoliberal, pro-market policies (O'Brien et al. 2000).

A neoliberal ideology for development

That other societies outside of Europe now participate in the neoliberal globalization process does not make it any the less ideological, or devastating in its consequences, but merely points to changes in the global configuration of power and class. In this sense, the preoccupation in globalization discourse with the benefits of interdependence is a distraction from confronting new forms of colonialism. Unlike the old forms, with their emphasis on domination, subjugation, and exploitation, under globalization the process is driven through policies and systems designed to distance its perpetrators from unseemly motivation. Nothing exemplifies this more than the promotion of neoliberal ideology to the developing world by the chief advocates of globalization: the IMF and World Bank. For these institutions, the causes of underdevelopment reside squarely within the affected countries, rather than resulting mainly or at least in part from the structure of the global economy. Hence, the remedy lies not in large-scale redistribution of wealth or structural transformation of the way international trade and finance regimes operate, but rather in domestic reform. The desperate need of developing countries for aid in the final decades of the twentieth century provided the context in which to force domestic policy changes, and the oil crisis of the 1970s was the catalyst for this.

In 1973, the Organisation of Petroleum Exporting Countries (OPEC) dramatically increased the price of oil, undermining growth rates in many economies around the world. Oil-producing nations, of course, gained from the price rise, and proceeded to invest their profits in Western banks. These banks, which also needed to make a profit, lent the money on to developing nations at low interest rates. Many poor countries who were suffering in the wake of the oil price rise were glad of this injection of foreign finance. In 1979, OPEC raised the price of oil again, but by this time in the developed world (in particular the United States and United Kingdom), governments with a new economic agenda (monetarism) had come to power. They believed the high levels of inflation coupled with stagnation in economic growth witnessed during the 1970s were due to reckless government spending. They believed the solution was to cut government expenditure and reduce demand in the economy overall, and one of the most important tools used to reduce demand was to raise interest rates.

These economic changes had two immediate, practical effects. First, the recession induced by the demand-reduction policies being implemented in the industrialized world not only hurt the populations of those countries, it also affected people in the developing nations, because it lowered demand for developing-country exports. Second, the rise in interest rates also meant developing countries had to make much higher levels of debt repayments. Many countries now had great difficulties in keeping to repayment schedules and, as private commercial banks, alarmed at the prospect of countries defaulting on their debt, withdrew from lending new money, the World Bank and IMF stepped in to bail countries out with new loans. However, these loans came with conditions attached—known collectively as **Structural Adjustment Programmes** (SAPs).

Structural adjustment programmes and loans

As more and more developing countries faced greater difficulties servicing their huge debts from the 1970s, pressure to adopt SAP policies grew strong, as a wide range of bilateral and multilateral donors insisted upon economic reform as a condition for the disbursement of funds and for rescheduling the debt. By the end of 1985, twelve of the fifteen debtors designated as top-priority debtors, including Argentina, Mexico, and the Philippines, had submitted to SAPs (Cavanagh et al. 1985). Over the next decade, Structural Adjustment Loans (SALs) proliferated as the economies of more and more developing countries came under the surveillance and control of the World Bank and the IMF.

Later, in the 1990s, the SAPs evolved into a broader package of policies, involving governmental expenditure cuts, de-controlled prices, liberalized trade and investment and privatizing areas of the economy previously controlled by the state, and the other elements of what came to be called *The Washington Consensus*, largely because they were championed most vigorously by the United States Treasury Department (Klein 2008). Although there are many variations of SAPs at country level, at heart they all share the same logic, namely, the need to maintain fiscal discipline whilst discouraging protectionism. Implicit is the assumption that postcolonial development, with its heavy emphasis on state-led growth, had failed the developing world (Collier and Institute of Economic Affairs (Great Britain) 1998). Structural adjustment, therefore, was designed to roll back the state, which included privatizing public enterprises, dismantling trade barriers, abolishing state-marketing boards, removing price controls, and liberalizing exchange rates (see Tables 18.1 and 18.2).

These measures were meant to help countries resolve balance of payments problems, reduce inflation, and to prevent future economic crises by promoting longer-term structural reforms—particularly those

Table 18.1 IMF adjustment policies

IMF macroeconomic adjustment (stabilization) policies	Economic objectives
Devaluation	To promote exports and reduce demand for imports by raising their prices
Public spending reduction on: wages; employment; investment; subsidies; etc. *Tax increases*: taxes on incomes; taxes on spending	To reduce the budget deficit and thus: slow down the growth of government debt; slow down the growth of the money supply; reduce overall demand, and thus demand for imports
Tighter monetary and credit policies and higher interest rates	To reduce overall demand, and thus demand for imports; to limit or reduce the rate of inflation

Table 18.2 World Bank structural adjustment policies

World Bank structural adjustment policies	Economic objectives
Reducing the role of the state: restricting government spending; privatization; deregulation of markets *'Getting the prices right'*: freeing interest rates; freeing exchange rates; freeing wages; freeing prices; agricultural produce price increases; parastatal price increases; subsidy reductions; tax reforms; cost recovery *Opening the economy*: trade reform; foreign investment reform *Institutional strengthening and capacity building*	To increase economic efficiency, and thus improve long-term economic performance

pertaining to the public sector. Often, the reforms led to periods of economic austerity as government expenditure was drastically reduced and market forces were unleashed. The World Bank euphemistically called this process 'crossing the desert', and argued that short-term pain was necessary for long-term success in economic growth and improvements in the quality of life (Poku 2006). The 'short-term pain' provoked a storm of criticism, especially from African governments and non-governmental organizations (NGOs). They were joined by international agencies, such as the United Nations Children's Fund (UNICEF) who, in 1987, made a fundamental challenge to the adjustment paradigm by publishing *Adjustment with a Human Face—A Multi-Country Study of the Effects of IMF Policies on Children*. In response, both the World Bank and the IMF said they would prioritize the social sectors and poverty reduction concerns in their policies and even admitted their initial attempts in the early 1980s to push through adjustment, whatever the price, caused unnecessary hardship (World Bank et al. 1989).

From 1980 to 2000, growth in most developing countries implementing neoliberal policies declined significantly compared to the preceding 20 years. As the UNDP's Jan Vandemoortele concludes, 'If the 1980s were the "lost decade for development", the 1990s were the "decade of broken promises"' (Vandemoortele 2003: 1). The failings lie in the belief that markets will correct deficiencies of states by promoting growth. A report by the **United Nations Conference on Trade and Development (UNCTAD)** (2011a) suggests developing countries, despite a massive increase in their openness to trade over the last twenty years, are earning less. This is attributed to a number of reasons, such as their continued concentration on production of primary commodities, which (with the exception of oil) are subject to the challenges of **commodity** price volatility (see Think Point 18.1); and also the failure of most developing countries to shift their production into technology-intensive products. They lack the necessary finance and technological expertise, as well as human capacity, and they are unable to attract **foreign direct investment** to remedy this. Where they have moved from primary commodities into manufactured exports, the latter have been resource-based and labour intensive, thus adding little value. Moreover, the export drive, undertaken simultaneously by so many developing countries, itself contributes to price decreases.

Looking to the future, given the surfeit of labour in these poor countries, the picture grows even more worrying as we can foresee a race to the bottom with low wages being used as an enticement in the highly competitive market to attract foreign direct investment. This point is evidenced in the experience of the relatively developed region of southern Europe, where foreign investment through European Union membership has solved some problems for some people at some points, only to create other problems at a later date. This example also shows that trade cannot be divorced from issues of finance and attendant instabilities of global financial markets, which contributed to millions being thrown below the poverty line in 2011 with the collapse of the Greek economy (see Case Study 18.1). Investors continually seek out the location where they can make the greatest profit, and this results in capital and export production being moved from one location to another, with all the attendant difficulties for local populations in terms of insecure employment opportunities.

THINK POINT 18.1 Commodity price volatility

Commodity prices have historically been amongst the most volatile of international prices and they tend to follow general business cycles of boom and bust. High commodity price volatility, if not properly managed, can have negative development implications on commodity-dependent developing countries (CDDCs), mainly because of volatile and uncertain revenue flows, which can complicate not only fiscal management, but also budgetary and long-term planning. High-price volatility also undermines CDDCs' development efforts as it could discourage investment, widen trade deficits, and aggravate household poverty, particularly as commodity sectors generally constitute the major source of livelihoods of large sections of the population in low-income and least-developed countries (LDCs). (UNCTAD 2011b: 2–9)

The legacy of structural adjustment programmes

Today, there are scant signs the structural adjustment policies are achieving their desired objectives: macroeconomic stability and growth. Amid the bitter recriminations between the concerned parties—developing countries, NGOs, and the institutions of global economic governance—it is not clear whether the lack of effective results stems from an unwillingness to undertake reforms on the part of the developing countries, or the unsuitability and impracticality of the adjustment policies being recommended for their economies. The combined effects of SAP policies on the developing world has been to push millions of people already on the margins of vulnerability to adopt coping mechanisms that expose them to greater risk of disease and death (see Table 18.3). In Africa, for example, Nguyuru H. I. Lipumba (1994) observes that the dominant view among African intellectuals is that structural adjustment programmes are part of the continent's problems, not the solution.

KEY POINTS

- The advocates of globalization point to its benefits, but three-quarters of the world's population do not share in these benefits. The current phase of globalization is generating increased social and economic inequalities, between and within states.
- Much of this inequality is as a result of the neoliberal predominance in the current phase of globalization, which promotes open markets and limited government intervention, which favours the advanced capitalist economies and disadvantages developing economies.
- This neoliberal predominance on a global scale is created and maintained by the international financial institutions, and, in this way, it becomes possible to imagine globalization as an ideology seeking to remodel the world in an image that serves the mindsets of its advocates. This supports the idea of the current phase of globalization as an ideology for development and a new form of colonialism.
- Many developing countries received conditional loans from the World Bank and International Monetary Fund in the 1970s, 1980s, and 1990s, under the structural adjustment programmes of these institutions. The neoliberal-based loan conditions caused great and unnecessary hardship in developing countries and there is still no evidence they achieved their objectives for macroeconomic stability and growth.

Neoliberalism and the fostering of inequality

The rising inequality between and within nations

This uneven distribution of global investment patterns, with its associated selectivity and polarization of societies, has given rise to the following: a growing gap between the rich and poor within and between nations, in particular between North (the developed world) and South (the developing world); the destruction of quality jobs and their replacement by casualization and temporary jobs; growing unemployment, in particular in developing countries, which goes hand in hand with poverty; and mass migration in pursuit of adequate standards of living. As a result, a true process of immiseration is now observable in many parts of the world, particularly within developing countries. The facts of global inequalities are truly staggering: the richest 25 million Americans have an income equal to that of almost two billion people, while the assets of the world's three richest men, even after the recent fall in the value of stock markets, is greater than the combined income

Table 18.3 Impact of common structural adjustment measures on the poor

Intended result	Policy	Common impact on the poor
Reduced budget deficit, freeing up money for debt servicing	Reducing government expenditure	Reduced health, education, and social welfare spending and the introduction of cost-recovery and user fees put health care and education beyond the reach of many ordinary people. Public-sector redundancies and salary freezes lead to fewer teachers and doctors
Increased efficiency	Privatization of state-run industries	Massive redundancies and increased unemployment with no social security provision push families deeper into poverty
Increased exports, boosting foreign exchange reserves needed for debt repayment	Currency devaluation and export promotion	Cost of imports soar, including vital resources such as imported medicines; moreover, export prices fall because many countries are promoting the same exports under SAPs, so countries are still in no better position
Reduced inflation	Raising interest rates	Farmers and small companies can no longer afford to borrow money and are forced to reduce production or go out of business
Increased efficiency in food production	Removal of price controls	Basic food prices rise, putting even greater pressure on already stretched household budgets

of the world's Least Developed Countries with a population of more than one billion (World Bank 2011).

Christine Lagarde, managing director of IMF, who clearly believes integration into the global economy has huge potential for the developing world, concedes 'there is clear evidence that far too many of the world's people have been left behind' (Lagarde 2011). Most obviously, global welfare inequalities have mushroomed alongside the noted advancements in technological development and the rapid expansion of trade and investment. Whether inequality is measured in terms of disparities among states or between specific social groups; by gross domestic product or per capita national income; by relative levels of wealth and poverty; by the degree of influence states and non-state actors exercise in international institutions and decision-making bodies; in terms of access to food and health care, or the distribution of life chances more generally, the world is a grossly unequal place and, if anything, is becoming more so as we move on in the twenty-first century. At a conceptual level, it is possible to identify at least two dimensions of inequality at the heart of globalization: inequality between nations and inequality within nations.

Inequality between nations

Inter-national inequality refers to the differential impact of globalization on regions and states across the globe. A fifth of the world's people live in the highest income countries that have 86 per cent of the world's gross domestic product, 82 per cent of the world's export markets, and 68 per cent of foreign direct investment (FDI) (World Bank 2011). For what constitutes FDI, see Background 18.2. The bottom fifth of the population have about 1 per cent in each category. Nor have increased levels of growth and prosperity across the globe improved the situation for the poorest of the world's peoples. For example, the WTO has facilitated globalization, but greater openness in world trade is correlated negatively with income growth among the poorest 40 per cent of the world's population (World Bank 2009a).

The polarized nature of foreign investment provides yet another example of international inequality resulting from uneven globalization. At the beginning of the 2000s, the North held over three-quarters of the accumulated stock of FDI and attracted 60 per cent of new FDI flows (World Bank 2005). Moreover, insofar as FDI went to the developing countries (the global South), it was concentrated in ten countries, with China alone accounting for more than one-third. Thus foreign investment resources are being concentrated on those countries, such as Thailand, Indonesia, Colombia, Malaysia, and Taiwan, which are performing most strongly in global trade. Eight countries that accounted for 30 per cent of developing country GDP

BACKGROUND 18.2 Foreign direct investment

Foreign direct investment (FDI) occurs where an entity, for example an individual, public or private enterprise, a government, or groups of entities, owns at least 10 per cent of a foreign (i.e. non-resident) enterprise, with the aim of developing a long-term relationship between investor and enterprise. The OECD proposes that FDI forms an essential part of the rapidly evolving process of international economic integration, creating direct, stable, and long-lasting links between economies. Furthermore, the OECD argues that FDI encourages the transfer of technology and knowledge capacity across borders, and enables the host economy to market its products more widely, internationally. Lastly, under the right policy environment, FDI, as an additional source of funding for capital investment, can be used to support enterprise development (OECD 2009).

absorbed around two-thirds of total FDI. At the other extreme, the forty-eight Least Developed Countries received around $800 million in FDI in 1995—roughly the same size as flows into Brazil, and less than 1 per cent of the total transfer to developing countries (World Bank 2011).

Inequality within nations

While International Financial Institutions (IFIs) continue to hold great store by the potential contribution of trade liberalization to development, the reality is far less certain. A UNDP study, for example, notes '... there is no convincing evidence that trade liberalization is automatically or always associated with economic growth, let alone poverty reduction or human development' (UNDP 2004: 4). Moreover, even if growth occurs, it does not necessarily and inevitably translate into development for people in general, even if it does for their states or select interests within them. Branko Milanovic (2002) questions long-held assumptions of international trade theory that say increased openness will result in more equal income distribution within poor countries. Milanovic found, in countries with a low per capita income level, such as in sub-Saharan Africa, it is the rich who benefit from trade openness, while in countries where average income has risen, such as Chile or the Czech Republic, openness seems to be related to the rise in income of the poor and middle class relative to the rich. In China, global economic integration has been accompanied by more acute rural–urban polarization, and also by unemployment for previously secure workers in restructured state-owned enterprises (Cook and Jolly 2001).

The pattern of inequality across the globe continues to reveal significant divisions between North and South, but when the focus shifts to inequalities between social groups, the picture begins to look more complex. It is estimated that the bottom 50 per cent of global wealth holders together possess barely 1 per cent of global wealth, compared with the richest 10 per cent of the world's population, holding 88 per cent of global wealth, and the top 1 per cent owning a staggering 44 per cent of global assets (Credit Suisse 2012: 10). This stark division of wealth cannot simply be understood in terms of North–South relations. There are incidences of severe poverty in the North, while pockets of wealth exist in even the poorest countries. In the United States since the 1970s, virtually all income gains have gone to the highest earning 20 per cent. This decline in income for the vast majority of the American population has also had important implications for poverty trends. The US poverty rate rose from 14.3 per cent in 2009 to 15.1 per cent in 2010, reaching its highest point since 1993 (Berube 2011). This trend in the United States is evident in many other industrialized states. Across the global geopolitical landscape, the overall patterns of resource distribution have tended to shift since the 1960s from the shape of an egg to a pear. In other words, fewer people have occupied the top, and more people have slipped towards the bottom. One seventh of the world's population, or 925 million people, are malnourished (World Food Programme (WFP) 2012a), with 75 per cent of the hungry people living in developing countries (WFP 2012b); some 2 billion people, around 30 per cent of the world's population, are anaemic, contributing to 20 per cent of all maternal deaths (WHO 2012); and 884 million people still use unsafe drinking water sources, exposing them to waterborne sickness (UNICEF 2012). Our globalized world is one in which, for many people, finding food to eat and a supply of clean drinking water is a part of their daily struggle of existence, consuming many hours of labour.

KEY POINTS

- The uneven distribution of global investment patterns has given rise to a growing gap between the rich and poor within and between nations, rising unemployment, and mass migration in pursuit of adequate standards of living, leading to a process of immiseration, particularly in developing countries.
- Inequality between nations here refers to the differential impact of globalization on regions and states across the globe, for example in terms of gross domestic product, access to export markets, and foreign direct investment. This also translates into related degrees of influence in international institutions and decision-making bodies, that shape the forces and impacts of globalization.
- Inequality within nations here refers to unequal wealth distribution between social groups which, in the poorest countries, appears to be deepened through trade liberalization, challenging long-held assumptions of international trade theory that say increased openness will result in more equal income distribution within poor countries.
- Industrialized states are also experiencing increasingly unequal wealth distribution while pursuing neoliberal economic policies and practices, with growing numbers falling into poverty.

Global inequality as a threat to global security

The advancement of the industrialized states' neoliberal agenda through globalization as an ideology for development has failed to deliver the promised macroeconomic stability and growth, with intended trickle down benefits. Instead, globalization continues to increase the gap between rich and poor, between and within states, and the barren side of the fence becomes ever more crowded. Globalization, thereby, services the interest of its advocates, the elites of the core capitalist economies, at the expense and immiseration of the majority of people in developing economies—arguably a form of neo-colonialism—and the weaker segments of their own societies. At the point where desperation meets grievance is where rebellion and radicalization are likely to ferment. Recent examples of the revolutionary uprisings in Egypt in early 2011, and the murmurs of radicalization in Greece in 2010 and ongoing in response to IMF-imposed austerity measures, provide useful case studies of neoliberal economies to demonstrate how this insecurity can manifest in the real world, and will be explored further. Globalization's incitement of rebellion and radicalization may have untold ramifications for national and international security to come.

Anti-neoliberal revolution

Hosni Mubarak's Egypt, along with Zine al-Abidine Ben Ali's Tunisia, was considered to be at the forefront of instituting neoliberal policies in the Middle East. However, the rhetoric of Egypt's political economy during the Mubarak era did not match the reality, as was the case in every other neoliberal state from Chile to Indonesia (Armbrust 2011). In Egypt, the unfettering of markets and agenda of privatization were unevenly applied, and the most vulnerable members of society suffered most at the hands of neoliberalism. As Walter Armbrust (2011) observed, 'Organized labor was fiercely suppressed. The public education and the health-care systems were gutted by a combination of neglect and privatization. Much of the population suffered stagnant or falling wages relative to inflation. Official unemployment was estimated at approximately 9.4 per cent last year (and much higher for the youth who spearheaded the January 25th Revolution), and about 20 per cent of the population is said to live below a poverty line defined as $2 per day per person'. Meanwhile, the wealthy and well-connected profiteered from the neoliberal political agenda as Egypt reallocated public resources for the benefit of a small and already affluent elite. Privatization provided windfalls for favoured and connected individuals, who purchased state-owned assets for much less than their market value, or who monopolized rents from such diverse sources as tourism and foreign aid.

On the 25 January 2011, a popular uprising began in Egypt of mainly non-violent civil resistance in the form of demonstrations, marches, labour strikes, and civil disobedience, lasting eight days. The millions of protesters came from a variety of social, economic, and religious backgrounds, but were united in seeking the resignation of the unelected president of thirty years, Hosni Mubarak. While demands may have been expressed as regime change and desire for democracy in Egypt, implicit in these demands was an expectation of greater social and economic justice. A large element of what motivated millions of people to join the hundreds of dedicated activists on the streets in protest, eventually overwhelming the state security forces, was economic grievances that are intrinsic to neoliberalism (Armbrust 2011; Bogaert 2011).

Armbrust suggests these grievances cannot be reduced to absolute poverty, for revolutions are never carried out by the poorest of the poor; indeed, in the years leading up to the revolt, only 10 per cent of Egypt's population of 74 million had any disposable income, which had sparked bread riots in 2008. The protesters, rather, rebelled against the erosion of a sense that some human spheres should be outside the logic of markets. Under Mubarak, state provision of education and health care suffered greatly and wages in the private sector in particular were allowed to fall far below adequate standards. The protesters rejected the structural adjustments, austerity measures, and privatization that had put the middle and working classes in Egypt increasingly under pressure, mainly due to the cutback of income redistribution mechanisms and rising job insecurity (Bogaert 2011).

A neoliberal response

While the revolution brought regime change, Maya Mikdashi (2011) suggests observers should not be too quick to applaud the defeat of neoliberalism in Egypt. She notes that, rather than demanding the end of neoliberal market practices, protesters demanded only the reform of those practices and sought more equal economic opportunities. The international advocates of neoliberal globalization are only too eager to assist with this 'reform'. As Naomi Klein argued in *The Shock Doctrine* (2008), the free-market fundamentalism promoted by economist Milton Friedman (and highly influential in the United States in particular) is predicated on restructuring economies following catastrophic disruptions, natural or manmade, including revolutions. The restructuring takes advantage of a moment of profound societal dysfunctionality or 'shock', as a normally functioning society or political system would not vote for, or accept it. Furthermore, the restructuring is couched in appealing language; in the case of Western intervention in Egypt, assistance is offered in the language of supporting a transition to democracy and freedom.

While the Egyptian economy is already structured around neoliberal principles, the Western neoliberal globalization ideology continues to strive for the neoliberal utopia, and is pushing for both economic and institutional restructuring towards greater neoliberalism, as a solution to the revolutionary discontent. Adam Hanieh (2011) suggests that at the core of the Western governments and IFI interventions in Egypt is an attempt to accelerate the neoliberal programme instituted under the Mubarak regime. The IFI assistance packages appear to heed the call of protesters by promoting measures such as employment creation and infrastructure expansion among other popular demands, but these are in fact premised upon the classic neoliberal policies of privatization, de-regulation, and opening to foreign investment. Hanieh further observes the aid packages promised to Egypt do not in any way represent a break from the logic encapsulated in previous economic strategies for the region. Debt relief and loans are all conditional on the fulfilment of neoliberal reforms.

Importantly, despite the claims of democratic transition, the institutions of the Egyptian state had long been remodelled within this neoliberal drive as an enabling mechanism of the market. This is part of a change in developmental strategy from the IFIs since the 1990s, emphasizing the link between the functioning of the markets and their institutional governance. The new strategy promotes the rule of law, decentralization, good governance, and other such measures with the supposed aim of reducing rent-seeking capabilities of the well-connected and ensuring greater transparency in economic affairs, but with the explicit aim of advancing legitimacy for neoliberalism (Soederberg 2005). The result was a tailoring of public institutions to the needs of the private sector, while removing any ability of the state to intervene in the market. Hanieh proposes that 'Egypt is, in many ways, shaping up as the perfect laboratory of the so-called post-Washington Consensus, in which a liberal-sounding "pro poor" rhetoric—principally linked to the discourse of democratization—is used to deepen the neoliberal trajectory of the Mubarak-era.'

The sour and perverse outcomes of the various 'Arab Spring' revolts might serve to further entrench neoliberal interests. It remains unclear how much of the revolutionary spirit of 2011 was determinedly anti-neoliberal, but it has since become clear that the hopes invested in a popularly driven scaling back or wholesale rejection of neoliberalism (Joya 2011) were misplaced. At the same time, the fragility and vulnerability of states which have endured the sociopolitical and socio-economic dislocations of revolution on top of already tensioned and fractious state–society relations, grossly inequitable economies, and dependence on global capital are highly susceptible to the application of 'shock doctrine' tactics.

Some facets of the international interest and enthusiasm voiced for the 'Arab Spring' were politically naïve or intensely self-interested. Revolutions have a propensity to become violent—and once they do, their trajectories become very difficult to direct, control or even predict; and political opportunists of every stripe see their moment to act, exposing and exacerbating differences and grievances that stable

CASE STUDY 18.1 The Greek Economic Crisis

The economic crisis in Greece since 2009 provides a good example of the devastating effects of neoliberal policies on recipient societies. It was the first of five sovereign debt crises in the Eurozone arising from poor economic governance, corruption, and declining investor confidence in government fiscal policy. The outcome was a desperate need for fiscal stimulus to reenergize an economy with declining growth indicators. When European finance ministers approved another US$74 billion in aid (bailout) to Greece in June 2015, it was hoped, as with previous instalments, that it would soften Greece's fiscal adjustment programme — the severest in history — and the country would gradually recover.

Inside Greece, however, economic recovery has felt far less assured, with overextended and overtaxed citizens not sharing the enthusiasm for the country's grim economic outlook. Indeed, the bailout is widely seen as the source of economic and social despair, threatening to reduce a proud nation to the brink of destitution. Ironically, neoliberals will argue that, though painful, Greece's adjustment has been successful and will yield longer-term benefits and prosperity to the Greek people. For example, the government deficit has been cut from 15.6 per cent of GDP in 2009 to an estimated 7 per cent in 2015. By the end of 2015, the government could theoretically record an annual primary surplus—all very much in line with the expectations of the bailout conditionalities.

However, the social cost of the bailout reform has been staggering. 2015 marked the sixth year of Greece's depression during which the country has lost more than a quarter of its GDP. Moreover, the dynamic is far worse than what the piecemeal policies prescribed by the 'troika'—the International Monetary Fund, the European Union, and the European Central Bank—could possibly remedy. Personal income has been in freefall since 2010, and it is unlikely that wages will recover for many years. At the same time, the country's output has regressed to levels last seen nearly two decades ago, before the country joined the European Project, and as the country's debt sustainability is being put to the test, so is its society's ability to withstand hardship.

At the same time as the Greek welfare state is being gutted, the expectations, income, and quality of life for an entire generation are being adjusted downward. The same generation that became accustomed to cheap credit following Greece's accession to the Eurozone in 2002 is now trying to learn to live on far less. Unemployment has surpassed 30 per cent according to the OECD, or 39 per cent according to the World Bank. Over 60 per cent of unemployed Greeks have been without work for more than a year. Youth unemployment, meanwhile, which clocks in at 65 per cent, has already surpassed rates in most countries with similar labour force participation rates. Analysis of previous crises by the International Labour Organization showed that the average recovery time for youth employment during crises in countries where the pre-crisis employment level was eventually attained is eleven years, while in many countries employment only achieved a new trough.

With joblessness on the rise and the middle class squeezed from all directions, the 'new poor' of Greece are fast rising. The percentage of Greek households at risk of falling into poverty increased to 26.4 per cent in 2014 from 20.1 percent in 2013—the fourth worst in Europe behind Bulgaria, Romania, and Spain. As the recession has only deepened since then, it is inevitable that the number of poor Greeks will rise accordingly. Since the beginning of the crisis, Greece's suicide rate has more than doubled, from three to nearly seven suicides per 100,000 citizens.

As the economic position of ordinary Greeks deteriorates, we are left with an increasingly polarized society lurching between the extremes of neo-Conservatism and neo-Marxism with attendant rise in intolerance, xenophobia, and crime. The election of the Syriza coalition government in January 2015 on an outspokenly anti-austerity platform was an important if not necessarily commanding development. In the years leading up to the election, the Greek population has shown its opposition to the effects of the bailout measures with waves of civil and political disobedience, riots, and protests. Though emboldened by these events, the related negotiations between the Syriza government and Troika were conducted in poor faith with both sides blaming the other. Yet for ordinary Greeks, the outcome was to be the most far-reaching invasion of sovereignty by neoliberalism in modern times. Greek public assets are being forcibly sold to foreign investors with virtually all the means for the Greek government to generate income also being liquidated to private enterprises. At one stage in the negotiations, the Times reported that the German Finance Ministry suggested moving the titles to Greek assets to an 'external fund' in Luxembourg so that Athens could not renege on their sale. This would have further eroded the already weakened sovereignty claims of the Greek state.

(if sometimes oppressive) conditions tend to hold in check: witness Libya and Syria since 2011. Once popular anti-neoliberalist ideals are lost to factionalism, the ensuing social and economic ferment can eventually create propitious circumstances for the re-application of neoliberal disciplines—and another unhappy cycle of human insecurity can begin. The extent of north African regional insecurity now extending into Sudan, together with the impacts of the global financial crisis since 2008 clearly indicates the manner and extent to which neoliberalism's consequences have global implications, current and impending.

While rebellion and revolution either caused or catalysed by the strictures of neoliberalism is one challenge to security, radicalization is another. The crisis in the neoliberal global financial system, which began in 2008, and the ensuing recession have wrought havoc with national economies and individual livelihoods alike. Widely considered the worst financial crisis since the Great Depression of the 1930s, the current crisis has resulted in the collapse of large financial institutions around the world, the bailing out of banks by national governments, the failure of key businesses and decline in consumer wealth. Importantly, many countries are struggling to fund public services and service their debts, and a number of European Union countries are facing a sovereign debt crisis where their governments are unable to pay back their debts on time and in full, with potentially devastating implications for the European economy, and globally. In response, many European nations implemented austerity measures to counter this debt crisis. Three European countries, Greece, Ireland, and Portugal, have so far accepted large, relatively high-interest, bail-outs from other governments, the European Commission, and the International Monetary Fund to prevent sovereign default on their debt, with conditions for reduction on public spending. Greece, the worst affected, also provides a stark case study of radicalization in the face of the failure of neoliberalism.

KEY POINTS

- The advancement of the industrialized states' neoliberal agenda through globalization as an ideology for development has failed to deliver the promised macroeconomic stability and growth, with intended trickle down benefits.
- While poverty is a pervasive feature of most societies, past and present, it is the notion of unjust inequality that brings to the disadvantaged a sense of grievance. It is out of this grievance that radicalization and rebellion is likely to gain ferment, with untold ramifications for national and international security.
- Recent examples of the revolutionary uprisings in Egypt in early 2011, and the murmurs of radicalization in Greece in 2010 and ongoing in response to IMF imposed austerity measures, provide useful case studies of neoliberal economies to demonstrate how this insecurity can manifest in the real world.
- The global response to the revolutionary uprisings and radicalization appears to be the imposition of still more neoliberal policies, but the question remains of what the consequences will be for global security.

Conclusion

This uneven distribution of global investment patterns with its associated selectivity and polarization of societies has given rise to a series of modern phenomena, all indelibly associated with globalization, key among which are: a growing gap between the rich and poor within and between nations—in particular between North and South; the destruction of quality jobs and their replacement by casualization and temporary jobs; growing unemployment, in particular in the developing countries, which goes hand in hand with poverty (Wallace 1999), and; mass migration in pursuit of adequate standards of living (Allen and Hammett 1998). As a result, a true process of immiseration is now observable in many parts of the world, particularly within developing countries.

The liberal global governance network which determines the rules of the world trading system is essentially undemocratic, unaccountable and lacking in transparency (McGrew and Poku 2007). The IMF, World Bank, and WTO are, of course, heavily influenced by the states that exercise most power within them, and they, of course, are the core capitalist states. The structure of global trade directly impacts on security of the vulnerable billions, and their governments and the people themselves have no voice to affect this. All too often, corporate actors have had a hand in setting the global trade agenda, in drafting WTO agreements, and generally exercising a role that is not open to most developing countries due to their low level of financial and human resources.

Without more extensive representation in the governance of trade, it is unlikely that all-important job creation will be prioritized, and this is one of the mandates of the WTO Charter. Yet, in security terms, this is imperative, and demands action. Without employment opportunities, individuals, households, communities, sub-state regions, countries, and entire world regions are denied the chance to fulfil basic needs within the marketplace. As many as 200 million people in 2012 are classified as unemployed by the ILO (2012), and this is a push factor in migration, with the majority of migrants being unskilled. The ILO (2012: 9) urges that 'to generate sustainable growth while maintaining social cohesion, the world must rise to the urgent challenge of creating 600 million productive jobs over the next decade, which would still leave 900 million workers living with their families below the US$2 a day poverty line, largely in developing countries'.

A number of conclusions can be drawn from the discussion above. First, trade liberalization has been promoted beyond the core capitalist states by the 'Group of 7' (G7) (seven of the world's largest economies) and by unrepresentative, undemocratic global governance institutions, which they dominate. Second, it is difficult to test the validity of the assumption that free trade promotes growth and development, when politically motivated, self-interested protectionism characterizes the trade policies of core states, thus denying export opportunities to the rest, while simultaneously forcing them to liberalize and dumping on them heavily subsidized products, thus crippling local production outside of the core. Third, the fact that core capitalist states are unwilling to play by free market rules must prompt us to reflect on the reason for this reluctance. The answer is that to go down this road would be hugely destructive of sections of their domestic societies. In other words, G7 governments are well aware that capitalist markets based purely on profit do not work well for societies, hence their unwillingness to implement them.

? QUESTIONS

1. What are the key theories, assumptions and goals behind neoliberalism?
2. What are the key features of neoliberalism in the global economic system?
3. What are the key differences between neoliberal theory and its implementation?
4. What is the role of international financial institutions in promoting neoliberalism as an ideology for development?
5. How has neoliberal globalization impacted differently on developed and developing countries?
6. How has neoliberal globalization impacted differently on the wealthier and poorer segments of society?
7. How does global inequality increase global insecurity?
8. Compare and contrast neoliberalism with alternative theories for development.

FURTHER READING

- Goodale, Mark and Nancy Postero (eds) (2013), *Neoliberalism interrupted: Social Change and Contested Governance in Contemporary Latin America*, Stanford, CA: Stanford University Press. This book contains very good recent case material on neoliberalism and its impacts
- Glenn, John (2008), *Globalisation: North–South Perspectives*, Oxford: Routledge. This book provides a very good introduction to globalization and its impacts across the developed and developing world.
- Klein, Naomi (2008), *The Shock Doctrine: The Rise of Disaster Capitalism*, London: Penguin. This book is a thought-provoking read that explores the very visible 'hand' of capitalism.

- McGrew, Anthony and Poku, Nana K. (2007), *Globalisation, Development and Human Security*, Cambridge: Polity Press. This book contains a series of essays by leading scholars on the challenges that globalization is posing for development.
- Scholte, Jan Aart (2005), *Globalization: A Critical Introduction*, 2nd edn, Basingstoke: Palgrave Macmillan. This is an excellent and highly accessible book, exploring the dimensions of globalization, and the rise of superterritoriality.

IMPORTANT WEBSITES

- **http://hdr.undp.org/en/reports/global/hdr2010/** Human Development Report 2010—The Real Wealth of Nations: Pathways to Human Development.
- **http://www.brettonwoodsproject.org** The Bretton Woods Project focuses on the World Bank and the IMF to challenge their power, open policy space, and promote alternative approaches. They do this because they see these institutions as influential funders, proponents, and enforcers of economic and development policies, and global opinion formers.
- **http://www.jadaliyya.com/pages/index/Reports** *Jadaliyya* is an independent ezine produced by ASI (Arab Studies Institute). *Jadaliyya* provides a unique source of insight and critical analysis that combines local knowledge, scholarship, and advocacy with an eye to audiences in the United States, the Arab world, and beyond. The site currently publishes posts in both Arabic and English.
- **http://www.oecd.org/site/0,3407,en_21571361_49041236_1_1_1_1_1,00.html** Organisation for Economic Cooperation and Development—Perspectives on Global Development 2012: Social Cohesion in a Shifting World.
- **http://www.oecd.org/finance/financial-markets/financialmarkettrends-oecdjournal.htm** Organisation for Economic Cooperation and Development—Financial Market Trends and Policies.
- **http://data.worldbank.org/topic/economic-policy-and-external-debt** World Bank—Economic Policy and External Debt data.
- **http://data.worldbank.org/topic/poverty** World Bank—Poverty data.
- **http://www.imf.org/external/data.htm** International Monetary Fund—Data and Statistics.

Visit the Online Resource Centre that accompanies this book for lots of interesting additional material: www.oxfordtextbooks.co.uk/orc/collins4e/.

PART 3

Traditional and Non-Traditional Security

19

Coercive Diplomacy: Countering War-Threatening Crises and Armed Conflicts

Peter Viggo Jakobsen

Chapter Contents

Reader's Guide

Nowadays states rarely resort to war to defeat each other or to address war-threatening crises and armed conflicts. Instead, coercive diplomacy has emerged as their strategy of choice when persuasion and other non-military instruments fall short. Coercive diplomacy involves the use of military threats and/or limited force (sticks) coupled with inducements and assurances (carrots) in order to influence the opponent to do something it would prefer not to. States use coercive diplomacy in the hope of achieving their objectives without having to resort to full-scale war. This chapter presents the strategy of coercive diplomacy and its requirements for success and shows how states have employed it to manage crises and conflicts during the three strategic eras that the world has passed through since the end of the Cold War.

Introduction

War understood as the sustained use of organized violence by two or more actors in pursuit of political objectives has been the single most important factor shaping the formation and evolution of the state system that we live in today (Tilly 1975). The study of inter-state war has also traditionally been the disciplinary heart of both International Relations and Security Studies. This is no longer the case. Since the Second World War, the number of inter-state wars has declined steadily, and major war among nuclear armed great powers is now placed on the endangered species list by an increasing number of scholars. No such war has ever been fought, and great powers have not fought major wars against each other since the United States and China clashed during the Korean War (1950–53).

Interstate wars still occur. The United States went to war with Afghanistan in 2001 and Iraq in 2003, and Russia fought an armed conflict with Georgia in 2008. The latter is not counted as a war in most statistics, since it did not cross the threshold of at least 1,000 battle-related deaths per year, which is the generally accepted criterion for classifying an armed conflict as a war. Most contemporary armed conflicts crossing this threshold occur within the borders of existing states between a government and non-state actors or between non-state actors supported by external states. A total of 115 such **intra-state** wars took place in the 1989–2006 period compared to seven inter-state wars (Harbom and Wallensteen 2007: 624). In 2013, seven intra-state wars were active compared to zero inter-state wars (Themnér and Wallensteen 2014: 541–42).

It is hotly debated why this shift has occurred and whether it is irreversible (Human Security Report Project 2013). What is indisputable is that states primarily use their armed forces to coerce other actors to do something against their will instead of imposing defeat upon them. The difference may seem subtle, but it makes a fundamental difference to international security whether military force is used to render an opponent defenceless or to (threaten to) hurt it so much that it becomes willing to accept a negotiated agreement that it would not otherwise have agreed to. In the latter situation, threats and use of limited military force become a bargaining tool aimed at coercing the opponent to agree with the coercer's demands at a time when it still has the capacity for continued resistance. This shift from **brute force** to **coercive diplomacy** has profound implications for contemporary crisis and **conflict management**. These implications are the focus of this chapter.

The use of coercive diplomacy has grown since the invention of the nuclear bomb created the risk of mutually assured destruction (MAD) in the event of war (see Chapter 20 in this textbook). Since then, the nuclear-armed great powers have increasingly resorted to coercive diplomacy in order to manage their disputes and pressure each other to make concessions that could not be obtained by diplomatic negotiations alone. When the Soviet Union in 1948 wanted to throw the Western powers out of their occupation sectors in Berlin, it opted for a blockade out of fear that the use of force might trigger a US nuclear response. The Soviet attempt to coerce the Western powers out of Berlin failed because they succeeded in supplying their sectors from the air through the winter.

The Cold War between the Soviet Union and the United States (1947–89) was one long coercive duel in which each superpower bloc used military threats to deter the other from using force. This was accomplished through the formation of alliances (the North Atlantic Treaty Organization (NATO) and the Warsaw Pact) and the creation of large conventional and nuclear forces. Fear that the use of conventional weapons might escalate to nuclear exchanges and MAD naturally put a premium on war avoidance throughout this period.

The collapse of the Soviet Union and the subsequent US–Soviet cooperation in the United Nations Security Council with respect to reversing the Iraqi annexation of Kuwait in 1990–91 ushered in a new era in which great power-led coalitions used coercive diplomacy to manage intra-state wars and stop mass violations of human rights. The so-called **humanitarian interventions** (see Chapter 22) launched in the course of the 1990s in Liberia, Northern Iraq, Bosnia, Somalia, Rwanda, Kosovo, East Timor, and Sierra Leone thus involved the collective use of coercive diplomacy to stop mass violations of human rights and undo their consequences, for instance to allow refugees to return to their homes in Kosovo in 1999 (see Case Study 19.3).

The attacks on the World Trade Center and the Pentagon on 11 September 2001 (**9/11**) marked the start of the so-called **Global War on Terror** in which the United States, supported by allies, relied heavily on coercive diplomacy in its efforts to influence states and non-state actors to stop their involvement in terrorist activities (see Chapter 21) or their efforts to acquire Weapons of Mass Destruction (WMD).

With the withdrawals of US ground forces from Iraq and Afghanistan and the death of Al-Qaeda leader Osama bin Laden, the world has entered a new strategic era likely to be characterized by a number of regional great power duels resembling the global one fought by the Soviet Union and the United States during the Cold War. Russia and the Western powers have used coercive diplomacy against each other in their efforts to manage the crisis triggered by the overthrow of the Ukrainian President Yanukovich in February 2014 (see Case Study 19.5). China and the United States are also increasingly using coercive diplomacy to resolve their differences in the East and South China Seas.

The central role played by coercive diplomacy in the management of crises and conflicts since the end of the Cold War is often overlooked for two reasons. The first is that activities involving the use of military threats and **limited force** in order to influence actors to do something against their will are referred to by a bewildering array of names, such as armed suasion, coercive inducement, counter-insurgency, gunboat diplomacy, humanitarian intervention, peace enforcement, peaceful persuasion, robust peacekeeping, and smart power (Jakobsen 2011). The second is the widespread tendency to view diplomacy and the use of military threats/limited force as mutually exclusive alternatives employing different instruments and serving very different ends. Thus, the use of military threats and limited force is commonly regarded as evidence that diplomacy has failed and as undermining the prospects for diplomatic success. This view ignores conclusions drawn by practitioners across the centuries that military threats and limited force used in support of diplomatic negotiations can enhance the scope for resolving crises and conflicts short of war in situations when diplomatic instruments such as persuasion, inducements, and assurances alone prove ineffective. Frederick the Great is attributed with the statement that 'diplomacy without military power is like music without instruments'; American President Theodore Roosevelt believed in speaking softly while carrying a big stick; and UN Secretary-General Kofi Annan found that: 'if diplomacy is to succeed, it must be backed both by force and by fairness' (Annan 1998).

Critics counter that coercive diplomacy has a poor track record and that its potential for peaceful conflict resolution and war avoidance is hard to realize (Ganguly and Kraig 2005). Although they have a point, it is well documented that, with respect to resolving war-threatening crises and armed conflicts short of war, strategies coupling sticks and carrots work better than strategies relying solely on carrots or sticks (Art and Cronin 2003; Jakobsen 2010, 2011, 2012).

The remainder of this chapter will present the strategy of coercive diplomacy and its requirements for success and show how states have employed it to manage crises and conflicts during the three strategic eras that the world has passed through since the end of the Cold War.

KEY POINTS

- Inter-state wars have become rare since the end of the Second World War and great powers have not fought major wars against each other since the Korean War.
- States have increasingly resorted to coercive diplomacy in order to resolve war-threatening crises and armed conflicts short of war.
- Since the end of the Cold War, coercive diplomacy has been used to manage mass violations of human rights, terrorism, the proliferation of weapons of mass destruction, and most recently great power confrontations.
- The importance of coercive diplomacy in contemporary crisis and conflict management is often overlooked and its potential for peaceful conflict resolution is difficult to realize.

What is coercive diplomacy?

Coercive diplomacy seeks to resolve crises and armed conflicts short of full-scale war. Actors resort to coercive diplomacy when diplomacy falls short. Coercive diplomacy couples military threats and limited use of force (sticks) with inducements and assurances (carrots) in order to influence an adversary to visibly change its behaviour and do something against its will. It is employed to stop actions already undertaken by the adversary such as ethnic cleansing or military attacks, or to initiate target action. Use of sticks and carrots to coerce states to give up parts of their territory would be an example of the latter category. It is the combination of sticks and carrots that sets coercive diplomacy apart from military coercion in its pure form relying solely on sticks and diplomacy relying solely on non-coercive instruments.

Coercive diplomacy differs from deterrence, which relies on military threats to coerce adversaries to refrain from doing something. Deterrence was the cornerstone of the Western strategy employed against the Soviet Union during the Cold War. The Western states threatened to respond to a Soviet attack by using nuclear weapons in the hope that it would convince the Soviet leadership that an attack on the Western states would be too costly. If a deterrent threat fails to prevent an attack, the coercer has to consider whether to respond by threatening to use force to influence the enemy to stop the attack, to use limited force to this end, or to use full-scale or **brute force** to defeat the attack (Schelling 1966).

The use of threats and limited force counts as coercive diplomacy; the use of brute force to defeat the attacker does not. Coercive diplomacy is employed in order to avoid or limit the use of force. It is an influence strategy that is intended to obtain compliance from the adversary without defeating it first. It leaves an element of choice with the target; it has to make a decision whether to comply or to fight on. Full-scale or brute force, on the other hand, aims at defeating the adversary. It seeks not to influence but to control by imposing compliance upon the adversary by depriving it of any say in the issue at hand (Freedman 1998: 16).

The 2001–2 Afghanistan War illustrates this important difference. The United States initially threatened to attack the Taliban regime unless it handed over Al-Qaeda's leadership and closed their training camps. In return for compliance, the United States promised not to overthrow the regime. When the Taliban failed to comply, the US used limited force, bombing air fields and communications centres to signal resolve, and threatened further escalation. When this failed to elicit compliance, the United States escalated to brute force, bombing frontline positions and providing combat support to the Northern alliance in order to overthrow the regime. At that stage, the American strategy changed from influence to control (see Case Study 19.1).

CASE STUDY 19.1 Failure in Afghanistan

Pre-9/11 context

At the time of the 9/11 attacks, the United States was already engaged in a coercive diplomacy campaign against the Taliban regime. Cruise missiles had been employed in an attack on Al-Qaeda targets in 1998, and the following year, sanctions were imposed in an attempt to coerce the Taliban to extradite Osama bin Laden. The Taliban flatly refused to force him out or hand him over to an 'infidel nation' (Crenshaw 2003: 328).

US response to the 9/11 attacks

On 20 September 2001, the United States issued a public ultimatum to the Taliban demanding the immediate handover of the Al-Qaeda leadership and closure of their training camps. These demands were accompanied by threats of force and an offer to leave the Taliban regime in place. While the credibility of the threats were enhanced by military preparations, strong international support, and successful coercion that cut the Taliban off from Pakistani support, the Taliban had reason to question the American offer to leave the regime in place. The Taliban response was defiant. It engaged in counter-coercion and refused to hand over Osama bin Laden and associates. The United States then began to bomb military air fields, command centres, air defence systems, and leadership residences. The United States also began to provide support to the Northern Alliance, the Afghan groups that were fighting the Taliban.

Escalation to brute force and failure

On 11 October 2001, the United States offered to end its use of force in return for compliance. Now regime change had been added to the list of US demands. The Taliban regime had to go, but prospects of participation in a future Afghan government were held open for moderate members of the existing regime. Continued non-compliance then led the United States to bomb Taliban frontline positions and provide direct combat support to the Northern Alliance. This caused the Taliban regime to quickly collapse.

Was the Taliban impossible to coerce?

The Taliban had no reason to doubt American resolve, and threat credibility could not have been higher. Their failure to comply may consequently have stemmed from the belief that the USA would seek their overthrow whether they complied or not, religious/ideological beliefs ruling out compliance, an inability to comply, or a combination of the three. If the Taliban effectively depended upon financial and military support from Al-Qaeda for regime survival, as US intelligence concluded (Woodward 2001), it may simply not have been able to comply with US demands.

The distinction between limited force and full-scale/brute force is crucial, because resort to brute force means that coercive diplomacy has failed. It is important to understand that this distinction is not based on the number of bombs dropped on the adversary. The distinction rests on the purpose for which force is used and the element of choice left to the adversary. Coercive diplomacy uses limited force as a bargaining tool. It is used to increase the costs of non-compliance and to threaten with more of the same unless compliance is forthcoming. It always leaves room for the adversary to decide whether to comply or not. Brute force does not leave such a choice; its purpose is to defeat the adversary. The resort to brute force means that diplomacy has been abandoned and that the coercer has lost faith in negotiation and decided to impose its will by force.

Following this logic, use of force, regardless of the amount employed, will be limited in nature as long as it does not, and is not intended to, render the opponent defenceless or settle the dispute at hand (e.g. conquer the disputed territory or destroy a disputed WMD facility). It also follows that isolated use of conventional air and sea power will usually count as limited use of force because it generally cannot achieve decisive results on its own unless the objective in question is the elimination of facilities, individuals, or weapons. Similarly, the use of land power that stops short of settling the dispute or defeating the adversary will also count as limited force. Conversely, the use of air and sea power in support of land offensives aimed at achieving decisive outcomes such as regime change counts as full-scale use of force (see Case Studies 19.1 and 19.2).

The proposed definition of limited force has two components that are directly observable and easy to measure: (a) communication of limited intent to the adversary; and (b) use of force that does not achieve decisive outcomes. The drawback is that it allows for major use of air and sea power. For this reason, coercive diplomacy scholars have typically defined limited force as 'demonstrative' or 'symbolic' use, meaning 'just enough force of an appropriate kind to demonstrate resolution and to give credibility to the threat that greater force will be used if necessary' (George and Simons 1994: 10; Art and Cronin 2003: 9). The problem with such definitions is that they are impossible to operationalize and measure in real time. 'Just enough' and 'appropriate kind' can only be known after the fact.

The practical implication of adopting the proposed definition is that the scope for coercive diplomacy success is broadened. NATO's 78-day air campaign in the Kosovo conflict becomes a success since NATO relied on air power only, refrained from supporting Kosovo Albanian ground forces directly, and never expressed

CASE STUDY 19.2 Brute force success in Libya

The context

In early 2011, the wave of popular protests sweeping the Arab world triggered an armed rebellion in Libya. To prevent the Qaddafi regime from massacring civilians in rebel-held areas, the UN Security Council authorized the imposition of a no-fly zone on 19 March. UN resolution 1973 called for a cease-fire, avoided taking sides in the conflict, and ruled out the deployment of an occupation force.

Total objectives

Although NATO paid lip-service to the UN resolution, it quickly became apparent that leading alliance members wanted to do more than merely protect civilians and create the conditions for a cease-fire. On 15 April 2011, British Prime Minister David Cameron, US President Barack Obama, and French President Nicolas Sarkozy stated in a joint op-ed that it was impossible to 'imagine a future Libya with Qaddafi in power'.

Brute force

Their desire for regime change was also evident in NATO's military operations. The target list drawn up by the Alliance to protect civilians went beyond military forces attacking civilians to include all types of military equipment, units, and communications facilities wherever they could be found. NATO aircraft directly supported rebel forces attacking Qaddafi held areas, and France and the United Kingdom and a number of Arab countries supplied the rebels with weapons and deployed special forces, which trained the rebels and helped them conquer the capital city of Tripoli in August.

Not coercive diplomacy

Coercive diplomacy only allows for limited use of force that seeks to influence the adversary to comply. Yet leading NATO members wanted Qaddafi removed and actively helped the rebels to achieve this. The fall of the Qaddafi regime was therefore a success for brute force in pursuit of a total objective (regime change).

a desire to defeat the Serbs (see Case Study 19.3). By contrast, the conventional definition employed by Art, George, and others codes this case as a failure since 78 days of bombing can hardly be characterized as 'demonstrative' or 'symbolic'.

The distinction between coercive diplomacy and full-scale use of force cannot be made solely on the basis of communicated intent and how force is used, however. When coercive diplomacy is used as part of an escalation sequence, which culminates in brute force, as was the case in the 1991 Gulf War, the 2001–2 Afghanistan War, and the 2003 Iraq War, it has to be determined whether the coercer was pursuing a peaceful solution or merely using threats and limited force in order to legitimize the resort to brute force that followed. One way to do this is to consider whether the coercer deliberately made demands that it knew that the adversary could not meet, and whether the adversary was denied sufficient time to comply. If that is the case, the conclusion must be that the coercer preferred war to adversary compliance. If the Bush administration preferred regime change to compliance in order to get rid of Saddam Hussein once and for all, the American use of threats in the run-up to the 2003 Iraq war does not constitute coercive diplomacy.

KEY POINTS

- Coercive diplomacy seeks to resolve crises and armed conflicts short of full-scale war.
- Coercive diplomacy couples threats and limited force (sticks) with inducements and assurances (carrots) in order to influence adversaries to visibly change their behaviour and do something they would prefer not to do.
- Coercive diplomacy is an influence strategy that leaves the choice between compliance and defiance to the adversary.
- Full-scale or brute force is a control strategy that deprives the adversary of any choice by forcing compliance upon it.
- Escalation from limited to brute force means that coercive diplomacy has failed.
- The definition of limited force hinges on the intent communicated to the adversary and the nature of the military operations; not the amount of force employed.
- Use of threats and limited force constitute coercive diplomacy only if the coercer prefers compliance to full-scale war.

Requirements for success

To succeed, a coercer has to do four things: (1) communicate (through words or actions or both) its demands to the adversary; (2) signal willingness and capability to punish non-compliance so hard that the costs will exceed any conceivable gains; (3) offer compensation (carrots) to reduce the cost of non-compliance; and finally (4) use confidence-building measures to assure the adversary that compliance will not trigger new demands in the future.

Translating these requirements into successful policies is anything but easy. Successful use of coercive diplomacy requires a favourable context and a well-executed strategy. This has led some scholars to propose comprehensive checklists identifying all the factors that are likely to affect the use of coercive diplomacy such as a favourable balance of military power, an asymmetry of interest favouring the coercer, domestic and international support backing the use of coercive diplomacy, internal disagreements within the target leadership, clear demands and so on (George et al. 1971; George and Simons 1994; Blechman and Wittes 1999; Art and Cronin 2003; Jentleson and Whytock 2005/06). Such checklists (see Key Ideas 19.1) have the advantage of highlighting the complexities and dangers that the use of coercive diplomacy involves. It always entails a risk of escalation to full-scale war, the very outcome it is employed to prevent, because it is affected by the interaction of factors that the coercer cannot control or fully comprehend in the midst of an evolving confrontation. It also underlines the importance of understanding the context and the adversary's domestic politics, mind-set, and objectives. The drawback is that the high number of explanatory factors makes such frameworks hard to use. It is impossible to discern which of the many factors actually cause success or failure in a given case (Jakobsen 1998).

These weaknesses have motivated other scholars to focus on the policy challenge facing the coercer; that is, how sticks and carrots can be combined most effectively. This strand of research has led to the identification of a number of actions that states must undertake to maximize the scope for success (see Key Ideas 19.2).

Parsimonious frameworks like Jakobsen's *ideal policy* (Key Ideas 19.2) are designed to determine the probability of coercive diplomacy success in a given crisis or to explain coercive diplomacy outcomes post

KEY IDEAS 19.1 George and Simons' checklist of factors influencing the use of coercive diplomacy

Contextual variables

1. Global strategic environment.
2. Type of provocation.
3. Image of war.
4. Unilateral or coalitional coercive diplomacy.
5. The isolation of the adversary.

Conditions favouring success

1. Clarity of objective.
2. Strength of motivation.
3. *Asymmetry of motivation.*
4. *Sense of urgency.*
5. Strong leadership.
6. Domestic support.
7. International support.
8. *Opponent's fear of unacceptable escalation.*
9. *Clarity concerning the precise terms of settlement of the crisis.*

Note: *Italicized* factors are deemed 'particularly significant' for success.

George and Simons (1994: 271–4, 287–8, 292).

KEY IDEAS 19.2 Jakobsen's *ideal policy* identifying the minimum conditions for success

1. A threat of force to defeat the opponent or deny him his objectives quickly with little cost.
2. A deadline for compliance.
3. An offer of inducements for compliance.
4. An assurance to the adversary against future demands.

Jakobsen (1998).

hoc with as few explanatory factors as possible. The expectation is that coercive diplomacy will fail if the *ideal policy* is not implemented, as this will make it rational for the adversary not to comply. Implementation of the *ideal policy* is not sufficient for success, however. A coercive diplomacy attempt meeting the requirements of the *ideal policy* may still fail because of factors outside the coercer's control, such as misperception or miscalculation by the opponent, or because the opponent prefers to fight and lose to preserve honour rather than complying with the coercer's demand. This is not expected to happen very often and there is a strong empirical correlation between *ideal policy* implementation and coercive diplomacy success (Jakobsen 2010). The principal weakness of this framework is the black-boxing of the opponent, and the assumption that the probability of success can be assessed by looking solely at the adversary.

The choice of framework will depend on the policy or research objective in question and the information available to the analyst. It may not always be necessary or possible to obtain the detailed understanding of the adversary that a framework like George and Simons' requires (see Key Ideas 19.1). The most important thing, therefore, is to have a clear understanding of the strengths and limitations of the various frameworks and choose the one that is best suited for the analytical purpose at hand.

KEY POINTS

- The theoretical requirements for coercive diplomacy success are easily identified.
- They are hard to translate to successful policies because success hinges on contextual and perceptual factors outside the coercer's control as well as the ability of the coercer to combine sticks and carrots effectively.
- George and Simons propose a comprehensive framework capturing all the factors that affect the use of coercive diplomacy.
- Jakobsen's *ideal policy* framework identifies four minimum conditions that the coercer's strategy must meet to maximize the prospects for success.
- The choice of framework should be determined by the research/policy objective and the data at hand.

The challenge of defining success

Coercive diplomacy succeeds when the communication of a threat or use of limited force produces compliance with the coercer's demands. Non-compliance

CASE STUDY 19.3 Costly success in Kosovo

The context

Kosovo had long been regarded as a powder keg when violence broke out in the spring of 1998. The Serbian security forces responded to the armed bid for independence launched by the Kosovo Liberation Army (KLA) with excessive use of force, which immediately drew international condemnation and mediation aimed at ending the violence.

Half-hearted coercion

NATO governments threatened to undertake air strikes in June 1998 unless the fighting ended and Serbian forces were withdrawn from Kosovo. Threat credibility was, however, undermined by Russian opposition and internal disagreements within NATO. The situation was complicated further by KLA insistence on independence and their unwillingness to meet American negotiators. Western governments consequently settled for a symbolic deployment of fifty observers and turned a blind eye as the Serbs attempted to defeat the KLA.

Temporary success

In October 1998 the implementation of a coercive strategy meeting the requirements of the *ideal policy* paved the way for a deployment of 2,000 unarmed observers in Kosovo. To obtain Serbian compliance, NATO postponed its deadline twice and allowed more than 20,000 Serbian personnel to remain in Kosovo. The underlying sources of conflict were not addressed, and, since the KLA was not party to the agreement and vowed to fight on, few believed that the agreement would end the violence.

Escalation to limited use of force

Continued fighting resulted in peace negotiations, the failure of which resulted in a NATO ultimatum demanding that the Serbs sign the proposed peace agreement or face air strikes. The proposed agreement gave NATO unimpeded access to all of Serbia, involved a deployment of a large NATO force in Kosovo, and a referendum on the future status of Kosovo that could only lead to independence. The Serbs were not offered any inducements or assurances, and the context was not conducive to coercive diplomacy success: China and Russia opposed the use of force, forcing NATO to attack without a UN mandate, several NATO members had questioned the wisdom of resorting to force, and the United States had publicly ruled out the use of ground forces. Against this background it is hardly surprising that Serbian President Milosevic failed to comply. By ruling out the use of ground forces, NATO guaranteed Milosevic that Kosovo would not be taken from him unless he agreed to hand it over, and this left him with considerable leverage.

Explaining Serbian compliance after 78 days of bombing

Milosevic's resistance paid off. The final agreement made no mention of a referendum on Kosovo's future, it affirmed Serbia's sovereignty and territorial integrity, NATO was not granted access to Serbia proper, and the NATO force deployed in Kosovo had a UN mandate and Russian participation. In addition to these inducements and assurances, three other factors account for Milosevic's decision to comply. The first was NATO's ability to maintain its unity and escalate its bombing campaign, the second was a credible threat to invade if the bombing failed, and the third was the loss of Russian support. Taken together these new factors meant that the requirements of the *ideal policy* had been met.

equals failure. In practice, four factors complicate the task of defining success. First, most studies of coercive diplomacy define success in binary terms: coercive diplomacy either fails or succeeds. The problem with this approach is that success in most cases is a question of degree. As pointed out by Schelling (1966), coercive diplomacy is a form of bargaining and resolving a conflict short of full-scale war usually requires compromises on both sides. Coercers usually settle for partial compliance or reduce their demands in order to avoid full-scale war. To give an example, Serbia complied with NATO's demands regarding Kosovo only after NATO had lowered its demands. This has led some to claim that Serbia was not coerced by NATO, and that Serbian compliance resulted from NATO's concessions and the loss of Russian support (see Case Study 19.3).

The Kosovo case also illustrates a related second problem: that it will often be difficult to isolate the effect that the threat of force/use of limited force had in a specific case. This matters because coercion only takes place when compliance results from fear of the stick. This was undoubtedly the case in Kosovo, as Serbian compliance (and Serbia's loss of Russian support) would not have been forthcoming in the absence of NATO's air campaign. The stick does not have to be sufficient for success, however, since it would be wrong to regard a case where both inducements and sticks prove necessary for compliance as a coercive

Table 19.1 Measuring success

Strategies	Diplomacy	Coercive diplomacy (CD)		War
Instruments	Persuasion and inducements	Threats and inducements	Limited force and inducements	Full scale/brute force
Degree of success	CD unnecessary	Cheap CD success	Costly CD success	CD failure

diplomacy failure. The question to ask is consequently whether the stick was necessary for success in a given case. A threat of force/use of limited force should never be studied in isolation. The analytical challenge is to examine how the threat of force/use of limited force interacted with the other policy tools employed (e.g. economic sanctions, inducements, and assurances) and whether it proved necessary in order to influence the adversary to comply (Byman and Waxman 2002: 31).

Third, the price of success must be weighed against the amount of coercion employed. Ideally, coercion should not be required at all to solve disputes. But, if the threshold from persuasion to coercion is crossed, the degree of successfulness is negatively correlated with the amount of coercion and inducement required for compliance. When the threshold between limited and brute force is crossed, coercive diplomacy fails. The challenge, in short, is to obtain compliance without having to use brute force.

Finally, it is important to distinguish between tactical/temporary and strategic/lasting success. Coercive diplomacy often takes the form of a protracted bargaining process involving a series of inconclusive coercive diplomacy exchanges resulting in tactical/temporary successes followed by new acts of non-compliance. Western use of coercive diplomacy in Bosnia from 1992 to 1995 is a case in point. It involved seven major coercive diplomacy exchanges each involving (1) acts of aggression committed by the Bosnian Serbs; (2) a response from the Western powers in the form of a demand coupled with a threat of force; and (3) the response to this threat from the Bosnian Serbs. Three of these exchanges can be considered tactical/temporary successes because Western threats coerced the Serbs to back down and comply with Western demands (Jakobsen 1998: 79–109). From a strategic perspective, they cannot be considered successes, however, because compliance did not last for long.

This said, it is important to reiterate that coercive diplomacy should not be studied in isolation. Studies clearly show that coercive diplomacy rarely generates lasting successes by itself. Threats and use of limited force coupled with carrots and assurances can achieve tactical successes and buy time, but if they are not followed up by diplomatic efforts addressing the underlying drivers of the conflict, the target is most likely to engage in hostile action again in the future (Jakobsen 2011). The failures to stop the Iranian and North Korean nuclear programmes are cases in point. Coercive diplomacy has achieved a number of tactical successes in the form of temporary suspensions of these programmes over the years, but they remain in existence because subsequent diplomatic efforts have failed to address the underlying factors driving them.

These considerations produce the operationalization of success depicted in Table 19.1. Coercive diplomacy successes resulting from the use of military threats and inducements are classified as cheap successes, whereas successes resulting from the use of limited force count as costly ones. Escalation to brute force equals failure.

KEY POINTS

- Coercive diplomacy succeeds when a threat or limited use of force is necessary for compliance.
- Escalation from limited to brute force represents failure.
- Coercive diplomacy success usually requires compromises from both sides.
- Success is negatively correlated with the amount of coercion and inducements required for compliance.
- It is important to distinguish between temporary and lasting successes.
- Coercive diplomacy can achieve temporary success and buy time.
- Lasting success will usually require subsequent negotiations successfully addressing the drivers of the conflict.

The importance of the strategic context

During the Cold War, the risk of nuclear escalation war resulted in crisis and conflict management strategies emphasizing deterrence and war avoidance. This changed with the collapse of the Soviet Union and the establishment of a more cooperative relationship between the five great powers in the UN Security Council (China, France, Russia, the United Kingdom, and the United States). These changes made it possible to use coercive diplomacy as a collective tool to reduce the human suffering resulting from the growing number of internal wars that erupted in the early 1990s. While most of these so-called humanitarian interventions were led by Western great powers, the Security Council also welcomed an intervention led by Nigeria to stop the civil war raging in Liberia in 1990.

It proved difficult to use coercive diplomacy for humanitarian purposes. The asymmetry of motivation (see Key Ideas 19.1) generally favoured the targets as Western coercers proved reluctant to threaten and use force on the scale required to make non-compliance too costly. Such reluctance undermined early attempts to coerce the military leadership in Haiti and the Serbs in Bosnia and Kosovo. It took a series of humiliations in all three cases before the Western powers became sufficiently motivated to threaten and use force in a way that met the *ideal policy* requirement. When that happened, coercive diplomacy contributed to lasting successes in all three cases (Jakobsen 1998: 70–129; Case Study 19.3).

The 9/11 attacks removed the reluctance to use force and the fear of casualties that had shaped the conduct of Western, and especially American, coercive diplomacy in the 1990s. National interest replaced humanitarian sentiment as the principal driver of US foreign policy as the Bush Administration declared war on terrorist groups and 'rogue' states sponsoring terrorism and seeking to acquire WMD (White House 2002). The American willingness to use brute force to change regimes altered the strategic context fundamentally.

Yet the American preference for brute force proved short-lived, because the quick defeat of the regimes in Afghanistan and Iraq were followed by insurgencies that imposed unacceptable costs upon the United States. Coercive diplomacy consequently became the strategy of choice with respect to stopping suspected WMD programmes and (support for) terrorism. The fall of Saddam Hussein contributed positively to these efforts by creating a fear of regime change in Tripoli that American and British negotiators exploited to put together a package of carrots and assurances that convinced Qaddafi that it was in his own best interest to give up his WMD programmes (see Case Study 19.4).

From the point of taking office in 2009, the Obama Administration tried to coerce Iran to give up its nuclear programme using a combination of economic sanctions, carrots, and assurances, and although it has succeeded in getting a negotiated agreement with the Iranians; its implementation remains elusive. US-led efforts to coerce North Korea to give up its nuclear programme relying primarily on economic sanctions have not had any discernible effects. In neither case has the United States been able to create the sense of urgency in the mind of the targets that is required for success.

In its war on terror, the US has relied heavily on drones to monitor and attack terrorist groups. The extensive use of drone attacks in Pakistan had a dual coercive objective: to coerce militant groups to stop their attacks on US and NATO personnel in Afghanistan and to coerce the Pakistan government to terminate its support for these groups. The drone attacks did not achieve any of these objectives.

Following two 'asymmetric' decades where the great powers primarily used coercive diplomacy against lesser ones, the crisis triggered by Russia's annexation of the Crimea and China's growing assertiveness over sovereignty issues in the East and South China Seas herald the coming of a new strategic era defined by symmetric great power confrontations. During the Ukraine conflict, Russia used both deterrence and coercive diplomacy in order to influence Ukraine and the Western EU/ NATO members to comply with its demands. The Western powers responded in kind, using a wide array of political and economic sanctions to coerce Moscow to withdraw from the Crimea and to stop its economic and military support for Ukrainian separatists. They also enhanced NATO's military presence in Eastern Europe in order to deter Russia from attacking or destabilizing NATO member states (see Case Study 19.5).

In the East and South China Seas, China has stepped up its use of coercive diplomacy using a combination of civilian and military instruments in order to coerce

CASE STUDY 19.4 Cheap success in Libya

Pre 9/11 context

By 2001, the United States had used coercive diplomacy against Libya for more than 30 years. Since 1979, the United States had imposed sanctions and used air power against Libya on a number of occasions. Libya hit back, conducting a series of terrorist attacks against American targets, which culminated with the blowing up of two civilian airliners in 1988/89. This made Libya an international pariah and the UN imposed comprehensive sanctions in 1992 to coerce it to hand over two suspects to stand trial. The US/UN sanctions regime helped deepen an economic crisis that led to public dissatisfaction as well as elite pressure on the regime to change its policies. It consequently agreed to do so in 1999, but a UN weapons embargo and a ban on international flights remained in place to pressure Libya to pay compensation to the victims' families. US sanctions also continued due to concern over Libya's human rights record and its pursuit of WMD.

Why Libya gave up its WMD in 2003

9/11 and the fall of Baghdad increased the pressure on Qaddafi to agree to a deal, by creating the necessary sense of urgency and fear of military escalation. Serious WMD negotiations got underway in early 2003. Initially, Qaddafi was only prepared to discuss his chemical programme, but in October 2003, the interception of a ship en route to Libya with centrifuge parts made it impossible for him to continue to deny his nuclear programme. It took another two months and clever use of inducements and assurances to convince him to give it up. He got all the inducements he craved: US sanctions lifted, a return of US oil companies to resurrect his ailing oil industry, normalized diplomatic relations, recognition as an international statesman, and, most important of all, US guarantees against regime change. Qaddafi's fear of regime change was so pronounced that he kept demanding security guarantees right up to the moment when the official WMD renunciation was made in December 2003.

The United Kingdom acted as an honest broker, assuring him that the United States would keep its promises, and the implementation of the agreement was designed as a quid-pro-quo process where each verified step of dismantlement was rewarded with removal of US restrictions. This gave both parties an interest in sticking to their word. Finally, at Tripoli's insistence, the International Atomic Energy Agency monitored the dismantlement process to make it harder for Washington to renege on its promises.

The 2003 negotiations succeeded because sticks, inducements, and assurances were employed in a mutually reinforcing manner meeting *ideal policy* requirements. This may serve as an explanation as to why Qaddafi complied with US requests at this point, which had not been the case previously, despite his signalled interest in negotiations.

Jakobsen (2012).

CASE STUDY 19.5 Ukraine—caught in the midst of a great power coercive duel

During 2013, Russia became concerned that its plan for a Eurasian Economic Customs Union would be undermined if the Ukraine signed an association agreement with the EU. Moscow consequently used a combination of economic sanctions, threats, and inducements offering cheap loans and gas to coerce the Ukrainian government not to do so. The Ukrainian government complied but its decision triggered violent demonstrations, causing its downfall in February 2014. When the new Ukrainian government announced its intention to strengthen links with the EU and ban Russian as an official language, Russia annexed the Crimean peninsula, massed thousands of soldiers on the border to eastern Ukraine and provided economic and military support, including manpower, to Ukrainian rebels attempting to take over government buildings in the main cities of eastern Ukraine. These efforts were combined with export embargoes and threats to cut off Ukraine's and Western Europe's gas supplies. Russia also threatened to intervene elsewhere to protect Russian minorities at risk and significantly stepped up its patrols close to NATO air space. A series of simulated air strikes on NATO countries were also undertaken to demonstrate capability and willingness to escalate.

Russia's actions had two coercive objectives. They sought to deter the Western powers from intervening militarily and the new Ukrainian government from launching offensives to retake its lost territory. In addition, Moscow also sought to coerce the new Ukrainian government to stop its rapprochement to the EU and NATO, and to grant greater autonomy to the eastern areas under Russian-supported rebel control.

(continued)

CASE STUDY 19.5 (continued)

Mixed results

Russia successfully deterred the Ukrainian government from attempting to take back the Crimea but the latter continued its rapprochement with the West and attacked the rebels in eastern Ukraine. In response, Russia stepped up its military support for the rebels. This escalation paid off as it coerced the Ukrainian government to accept a ceasefire agreement on 5 September 2014, which left a large swathe of territory in eastern Ukraine under rebel control. While low-level fighting continued for the remainder of the year, the September agreement remained the most likely basis for a political settlement.

Russia also succeeded in deterring the Western powers from providing military support to the Ukrainian government but it failed to deter them from engaging in counter-coercion. To deter destabilization of its member states, NATO stepped up air patrols over Baltic air space, established a new rapid-reaction force, and decided to deploy more soldiers and heavy equipment in Eastern Europe. The EU and the United States imposed economic sanctions and threw Russia out of the G-8 in order to coerce it to withdraw from the Crimea and to deter additional violations of Ukrainian sovereignty. Western sanctions were expanded as Russia failed to comply with these demands, and Russia retaliated by imposing sanctions on Western countries as well.

Limited, costly success

By the end of 2014, both Russia and the West could claim some limited coercive successes. Russia had coerced the Ukraine and the West to acquiesce to its annexation of the Crimea and the establishment of rebel/Russian-controlled areas in eastern Ukraine. In addition, the implementation of an EU association agreement with the Ukraine has been postponed for a year. These gains came at high costs, however. Western sanctions had thrown the Russian economy into recession and the rouble into freefall. These costs and threats of additional punishment, including US provision of military assistance to the Ukraine, likely coerced Russia not to grab more territory in Eastern Ukraine. The rebel area constitutes but a tiny part of what Putin has referred to as Novorossia (New Russia), and Russian forces have not forged a corridor connecting mainland Russia to Crimea, let alone Odessa and Transnistria, as many observers feared (Dreyer and Popescu 2014).

Mutual fear of escalation

Both Russia and the West have exercised restraint and displayed the common interest in war avoidance that one expects in direct confrontations between nuclear-armed great powers. Western leaders made clear throughout the crisis that they had no intention of intervening militarily or providing military equipment to the Ukrainian government. They were also slow to impose sanctions on Russia, hoping that threats would suffice to coerce Russia to stop its military involvement in eastern Ukraine. Likewise, Russia consistently tried to keep its military involvement in eastern Ukraine under the radar, using soldiers without markings on their uniforms and denying direct involvement. It also refrained from grabbing as much territory as it would have liked and from using more force than required to prevent defeat of the rebels.

Brunei, Japan, Malaysia, the Philippines, Taiwan, and Vietnam to accept its territorial claims. These states have responded by enhancing their military capabilities, and several of them have sought closer cooperation with the United States. The US has enhanced its military presence in the region and is asserting its right to patrol and fly over international waters in order to coerce China to stop its coercive tactics (Cronin et al. 2014; Dutton 2014).

More great power confrontations involving the use of coercive diplomacy are to be expected as the world moves towards a multipolar order. Rising great powers such as Brazil and India can also be expected to resort to coercive diplomacy when their demands for a greater say in the running of regional affairs are resisted by other (great) powers.

KEY POINTS

- Use of coercive diplomacy is shaped by the strategic context.
- In the 1990s, coercive diplomacy was employed frequently as a collective tool to address humanitarian crises.
- In the 2000s, the US relied heavily on coercive diplomacy to counter WMD proliferation and terrorism.
- In the 2010s, the great powers are increasingly using coercive diplomacy against each other.

Conclusion

The decline in inter-state war has given coercive diplomacy a more prominent role in the management of war-threatening crises and armed conflicts. Coercive diplomacy is an attractive strategy, because it can stop and/or reverse acts of military aggression, mass violations of human rights, terrorism, and attempts to acquire WMD with limited or, at the best of times, no use of force.

The conditions for success are clear in the abstract. Coercive diplomacy succeeds when the coercer (1) communicates (through words or actions or both) its demands to the adversary; (2) signals its willingness and capability to punish non-compliance so hard that the costs will exceed any conceivable gains; (3) offers compensation (carrots) to reduce the cost of non-compliance; and finally (4) uses confidence-building measures to assure the adversary that compliance will not trigger new demands in the future.

These conditions have proven hard to meet in practice. It is a paradoxical feature of coercive diplomacy that the prospects of cheap success are highest when the coercer is willing to go all the way and use brute force if need be. Yet it is often hard for policy makers to signal willingness to go to war in a situation where they would prefer not to and have resorted to coercive diplomacy in the hope of avoiding this very outcome.

It is also difficult to frighten and reassure the adversary at the same time. The coercer must create fear of uncontrollable escalation and a sense of urgency in the mind of the adversary and convince it that compliance will not lead to further demands in the future. It is no easy task to use threats or limited force without hardening the adversary's motivation to resist, and equally hard to offer inducements and assurances to prevent this without appearing weak.

That success ultimately rests on perceptual, psychological, and emotional factors adds to the difficulty. Since success hinges on cooperation from the adversary, there is always a risk that misperception or miscalculation will defeat even a well-executed strategy meeting all the *ideal policy* requirements for success. Adversaries finding themselves in what they may perceive as no-win situations will be prone to wishful thinking.

This makes coercive diplomacy a high-risk and hard-to-use strategy. It is a low-cost strategy when it succeeds, but failure may be very costly, as the coercer then faces the grim choice of backing down or executing his threat. This is a situation that coercers have faced often since the end of the Cold War. A study of thirty-six Western coercive diplomacy exchanges (1990–2008) counts only three cheap successes in which a threat of force coupled with inducements and assurances proved sufficient for compliance, and the number of lasting successes was six (Jakobsen 2010).

While this success rate is less than encouraging, it is not surprising considering that states only resort to coercive diplomacy in the small number of cases where diplomacy falls short, and the stakes are so high that they are willing to contemplate the use of force. States only resort to coercive diplomacy in situations where the risk of war is real, in the hope of avoiding it or keeping the use of force as limited as possible.

States will continue to use the strategy to manage crises and armed conflicts despite the difficulties involved. The resort to coercive diplomacy will increase in the future because the number of actors willing and capable to do so is rising. The rise of new regional great powers and the proliferation of militant non-state actors with regional/global reach, such as Al-Qaeda, the Islamic State, and al-Shabaab, will increase the number of challenges that status quo-oriented actors will employ coercive diplomacy to resolve. They will do so for the same reasons that have motivated states to use coercive diplomacy since the end of the Cold War: an interest in war avoidance, fear of (nuclear) escalation, a reluctance to put troops in harm's way to stop mass violations of human rights, and a strong determination to threaten and use force to protect national security.

Since coercive diplomacy will remain a central crisis and conflict management tool, practitioners and scholars must devote more attention to it. Our understanding of the strategy remains wanting in several respects. It must be improved if we want to realize more of the potential for peaceful conflict resolution that coercive diplomacy does hold.

QUESTIONS

1. Why has the Western use of coercive diplomacy increased since the end of the Cold War?
2. What is coercive diplomacy and how does it differ from brute force?
3. Consider the pros and cons of the definition of limited force employed in this chapter.
4. How do you determine whether the coercer wants to avoid the use of brute force or is using coercive diplomacy to legitimize it?
5. What does coercive diplomacy success require?
6. List the strengths and weaknesses of the comprehensive and parsimonious coercive diplomacy frameworks presented.
7. Why is it difficult to define coercive diplomacy success?
8. How have changes in the strategic context affected the use of coercive diplomacy since the Cold War?
9. Why is coercive diplomacy risky and hard to use?
10. Why will coercive diplomacy continue to be used in the future?
11. How can our understanding of coercive diplomacy be improved?

FURTHER READING

- Art, R. J. and Cronin, P. M. (eds) (2003), *The United States and Coercive Diplomacy*, Washington, DC: United States Institute of Peace. Applies a refined version of George's theory to eight new cases.
- Byman, D. L. and Waxman, M. C. (2002), *The Dynamics of Coercion: American Foreign Policy and the Limits of Military Might*, Cambridge: Cambridge University Press. Discussion of success and how to study coercion in combination with other instruments plus discussion of contemporary contextual challenges.
- Freedman, L. (ed.) (1998), *Strategic Coercion: Concepts and Cases*, Oxford: Oxford University Press. Discusses strategic coercion, coercive diplomacy, and compellence and contains eight case studies.
- George, A. L., Hall, D., and Simons, W. E. (1971), *The Limits of Coercive Diplomacy: Laos, Cuba, Vietnam*, Boston: Little, Brown. The initial formulation of George's theory applied to three cases.
- George, A. L. and Simons, W. E. (eds) (1994), *The Limits of Coercive Diplomacy*, Boulder, CO: Westview. Refined version of 1971-theory applied to seven cases.
- Jakobsen, P. V. (1998), *Western Use of Coercive Diplomacy after the Cold War: A Challenge for Theory and Practice*, Basingstoke: Macmillan Press. Develops and tests the *ideal policy* concept in three cases and identifies the conditions under which Western governments are most likely to threaten and use force.
- Jakobsen, P. V. (2011), 'Pushing the Limits of Military Coercion Theory', *International Studies Perspectives*, 12/2 (May): 153–70. Review of the field and practical suggestions for improving our theories and making them more policy relevant.
- Jakobsen, P. V. (2012), 'Reinterpreting Libya's WMD Turnaround—Bridging the Carrot–Coercion Divide', *The Journal of Strategic Studies*, 35/4 (August): 489–512. Develops a 3C framework (coercion, carrots, and confidence-building) and shows how all three components were necessary to coerce Libya to give up its WMD programmes peacefully.
- Schelling, T. C. (1966), *Arms and Influence*, New Haven: Yale University Press. A rational theory of compellence (coercive diplomacy) is presented and distinguished from deterrence and brute force.

IMPORTANT WEBSITES

- **http://www.crisisgroup.org** High-quality analysis of current and potential armed conflicts.
- **http://www.globalsecurity.org** Useful background information on armed conflicts past and present.
- **http://www.rand.org** Excellent studies of coercion and air power.

Visit the Online Resource Centre that accompanies this book for lots of interesting additional material: www.oxfordtextbooks.co.uk/orc/collins4e/

20

Weapons of Mass Destruction

James J. Wirtz

Chapter Contents

Reader's Guide

Since the late 1990s, policy makers everywhere have been deeply concerned about the possibility that weapons of mass destruction—chemical, biological, nuclear, and radiological weapons—are not only becoming fixtures in the arsenals of states, but might fall into the hands of terrorists. This chapter explains how these weapons work and the effects they might have if used on the battlefield or against civilian targets. It describes how they have been used in war and how they have shaped the practice of international politics.

Introduction

Although many observers hoped that the danger posed by weapons of mass destruction (WMD)—chemical, biological, nuclear, and radiological weapons—would fade with the end of the Cold War, these armaments continue to pose a worldwide threat. Some progress has been made in terms of rolling back WMD proliferation. Iraq no longer menaces its neighbours with its chemical arsenal, and its efforts to acquire nuclear and biological weapons have been thwarted. Libya has also abandoned its nuclear weapons programme. Following the Russian-American negotiation of the Framework for the Elimination of Syrian Chemical Weapons on 13 September 2013, the regime of Bashar al Asad agreed to the orderly destruction of its chemical arsenal. The international community has bolstered the non-proliferation regime by undertaking a series of diplomatic efforts, for example the **Chemical Weapons Convention**, the **1972 Biological and Toxin Weapons Convention**, the Proliferation Security Initiative, and the **2002 Moscow Treaty**. In his April 2009 speech delivered in Prague, Czech Republic, President Barack Obama embraced nuclear disarmament as a long-term policy objective for the United States, a sentiment that was echoed in the United Kingdom's October 2010 *Strategic Defence and Security Review*. Despite these concerted efforts, however, several state and non-state actors find WMD to be an attractive part of their arsenals. Black-market trade in nuclear materials, technology, and know-how is increasing. In 2004, revelations that the Pakistani scientist A. Q. Khan might have provided information about gas centrifuges (used to produce weapons-grade uranium) and nuclear-bomb designs to North Korea, Iraq, Iran, Libya, and Syria sent a shockwave through the non-proliferation community (Clary 2004; Albright and Hinderstein 2005). Indigenous nuclear programmes are also making existing proliferation safeguards obsolete (Braun and Chyba 2004). For some states, WMD provide a way to offset their inferiority in conventional armaments compared to stronger regional rivals or the United States and its allies. Leaders of these regimes probably hope that the threat of chemical, biological, or nuclear warfare might deter stronger opponents contemplating attack, defeat those opponents once battle has been joined, or even, as in the case of Syria, eliminate domestic opponents (Lavoy et al. 2000; Nikitin et al. 2013). Weapons of mass destruction also serve as status symbols that highlight the 'success' of otherwise dubious regimes.

If the threat posed by WMD proliferation to state actors is of increasing concern, then the possibility that these weapons could fall into the hands of terrorists or even individuals is alarming. A chemical weapons attack against a major sporting venue could kill thousands of people, while a successful anthrax attack might place hundreds of thousands at risk. A 'dirty bomb', a device that uses high explosives to spread radioactive contamination, could poison scores of city blocks. It would be extraordinarily difficult for even a well-funded terrorist organization to construct a primitive gun-type nuclear weapon, but international terrorist networks, domestic terrorist organizations, or even individuals have the resources and materials to construct and use chemical, biological, and radiological weapons. Weapons of mass destruction have been used in terrorist attacks, albeit with relatively limited effects. In 1995, for instance, Chechen rebels planted a radiological source (caesium-137) in Moscow's Izmailovsky Park, probably to show Russian authorities that they had the capability to make a 'dirty bomb'. The **Aum Shinrikyo** (Aum Supreme Truth) cult experimented with several toxic substances before launching their **Sarin** attack against the Tokyo subway in 1995 that injured thousands of people. In the wake of the 9/11 terrorist attacks against the World Trade Center and Pentagon, some person or group in 2001 used the US postal system to mail letters contaminated with **anthrax**, which was probably derived from materials supplied to US weapons laboratories.

Weapons of mass destruction vary greatly in terms of their availability, lethality, and destructive potential, and the ease with which they can be manufactured and employed. High-yield, lightweight nuclear weapons are some of the most sophisticated machines ever manufactured by humans, while some chemical and biological weapons have been available for centuries. What separates WMD from conventional weapons, created from chemical-based explosives, however, is their potential to generate truly catastrophic levels of death and destruction. A small nuclear weapon can devastate a city: the fission device that destroyed Hiroshima produced an explosive blast (yield) that was equivalent to about 20 kilotons (kt) of trinitrotoluene (TNT). A smallpox attack against an unprotected (unvaccinated) population could kill 30 per cent of its victims and leave survivors horribly scarred for life. Because of their ability to strike terror worldwide, these weapons are attractive as political instruments.

The remainder of this chapter will first describe the technology that underlies nuclear, chemical, and biological weapons, and explain how they are constructed. What is reassuring about this overview is the fact that, while these weapons can be extraordinarily destructive, state and non-state actors would have to overcome significant technical hurdles before they could maximize their destructive power. The chapter will also describe their destructive effects, the systems used to deliver them, and the history of their use in war. It will then outline the impact these weapons have on national defence policy and international security.

Nuclear weapons

The design and development of nuclear weapons were based on advances in theoretical and experimental physics that began at the start of the twentieth century. By the late 1930s, Leo Szilard, a physicist who escaped Nazi persecution by fleeing to the United States, realized that it might be possible to construct an 'atomic bomb'. Unlike conventional (chemical) explosions, which are produced by a rapid rearrangement of the hydrogen, oxygen, carbon, and nitrogen atoms that are components of TNT, for example, Szilard suggested that a nuclear explosion could be created by a change in atomic nuclei themselves. If an atom of **uranium-235**, for instance, is fragmented into two relatively equal parts, the remaining mass of the two new atoms would have less mass than the original atom. The lost mass would be instantaneously converted into energy. Nuclear weapons are so powerful because, as Albert Einstein predicted, under certain conditions mass and energy are interchangeable ($E = MC^2$). The difficult aspect of setting off this interchange would be to create a device that would sustain a nuclear reaction for a fraction of a second before it is destroyed in the resulting nuclear explosion.

Szilard's opinion was not widely shared among American scientists or government officials, so he enlisted the aid of his friend, Albert Einstein, to bring the issue to the attention of President Franklin D. Roosevelt. In a letter dated 2 August 1939, Einstein informed Roosevelt that it was theoretically possible to construct an atomic bomb and that the Nazis might be hard at work constructing such a device. It took the USA's entry into the Second World War to launch a full-scale project to construct a nuclear weapon: the UK–US **Manhattan Project**, which began in September 1942. The first nuclear (fission) device was ready for testing at Alamagordo New Mexico on 6 July 1945. It was quickly followed by the detonation of 'Little Boy' over Hiroshima on 6 August 1945 and 'Fat Man' over Nagasaki on 9 August 1945.

Fission weapons all share similar components: fissile material (for example, U-235 or plutonium); chemical explosives; non-fissile materials to reflect neutrons and tamp the explosion; and some sort of neutron generator to help initiate the nuclear reaction. Weapons also need triggers, a mechanical safety, arming, and firing mechanisms. There are two basic types of fission weapons. 'Little Boy' was a gun-type fission device. This is the simplest and least efficient nuclear weapon design (the design requires a relatively large amount of fissile material to produce a relatively small blast). In a gun design, two sub-critical masses of U-235 are fired down a barrel, striking each other at extremely high velocities producing a fission reaction. Gun-type devices, however, are rugged and have a relatively high probability of 'going critical'—that is, producing a nuclear detonation. The second design, an implosion-type device, uses high-explosive lenses to compress the fissile material—'Fat Man' utilized plutonium—until it reaches criticality. Implosion devices are relatively difficult to manufacture and assemble because the shaped charges that compress the fissile material need to be manufactured to critical tolerances and detonated with more than split-second timing. The physics and engineering behind the design and manufacture of nuclear weapons are widely available. What is far more difficult is to acquire the highly enriched uranium (U-235) and plutonium. These materials are under safeguards, and their production and storage are monitored by the **International Atomic Energy Agency (IAEA)** and the declared and undeclared nuclear-weapons states themselves (Table 20.1).

A fusion weapon is a three-stage bomb that uses an implosion device to trigger a fission reaction, which in turn detonates a fusion reaction (a process whereby one heavier nucleus is produced from two lighter nuclei). When the nuclei of light elements are combined, the resulting heavier element has less mass than the two original nuclei, and the difference in mass is instantaneously translated into energy. Often referred to as a thermo-nuclear weapon, or a hydrogen bomb, fusion

Table 20.1 Nuclear-weapons states

Country	Fission device	Fusion device
United States	1945	1952
Soviet Union	1949	1953
United Kingdom	1952	1957
France	1960	1966
PRC	1964	1967
Israel	1967?	1973?
India	1974	1998?
Pakistan	1998	1998?
North Korea	2006	
Iran	?	

weapons can be relatively small and lightweight, and pack virtually unlimited destructive force. During the Cold War, large nuclear weapons had yields in the millions of tons—megatons (mgt)—of TNT. On 31 October 1952, for example, the United States tested its first fusion device (Test Mike) at Eniwetok atoll in the Pacific Ocean. It produced a yield of about 10 mgt, which is equivalent to 10,000 kt. The most powerful nuclear weapon ever detonated was the Tsar Bomba (King of Bombs), which was a reduced-yield test of a 100-mgt bomb design. A product of Soviet science, the device was detonated with a 50-mgt yield on 30 October 1961 at the Mityushikha Bay Test range, Novayua Zemlya Island, producing a flash so bright that it was visible 1,000 km away. Bombs in the multi-megaton range generally have limited military utility since their destructive radius often exceeds the size of potential urban or military targets.

Nuclear-weapons effects

Compared to the devices we encounter in our everyday lives, nuclear weapons operate at the extremes of time, pressure, and temperature. The entire explosive process of a hydrogen bomb, for example, occurs over the period of a few thousand nanoseconds (a nanosecond is 1 / 100,000,000 of a second). Pressure within a fusion bomb core can reach up to 8,000,000,000 tons per square inch and temperatures exceeding those found on the surface of the sun (6,000°C). Nuclear weapons introduce galactic scale forces into a terrestrial environment, producing devastating consequences.

Nuclear-weapons effects are shaped by a variety of factors, including the weapon's explosive yield, its height of detonation, weather conditions, and terrain features. For example, an airburst occurs when the nuclear fireball does not touch the ground. Airbursts distribute the explosive blast and the radiation burst produced at detonation over a relatively wide area. Raising the height of burst lowers the pressure generated immediately below the detonation, but covers a larger area with somewhat lower overpressure. A ground burst maximizes the overpressure against a specific target—a missile silo or a command and control complex. A ground burst produces a great deal of fallout, because the fireball irradiates and lofts dirt and debris high into the atmosphere. Nuclear weapons can also be driven deep beneath the earth's surface in an effort to couple their explosive power more efficiently to the ground to destroy deeply buried and hardened targets.

All nuclear weapons produce similar effects, although the balance between these effects can be altered somewhat by design. An average nuclear weapon (about 100 kt) detonated in the atmosphere will deliver 50 per cent of its energy as blast, 35 per cent as thermal radiation, and about 15 per cent in gamma and residual radiation. A so-called neutron bomb, for instance, shifts some of the energy involved in a nuclear detonation from blast into radiation effects. Not all nuclear effects, however, are known or well understood. In the aftermath of a US high-altitude test of a 1.4 mgt weapon in 1962, for example, scientists were surprised to learn that the resulting electro-magnetic pulse (EMP) burned out street lights and fuses and opened circuit breakers 800 miles away in Oahu (Hansen 1988: 87). In the 1980s, scientists and analysts also debated whether a full-scale nuclear exchange would plunge the world into nuclear winter (Turco et al. 1990). By contrast, nuclear blast and thermal effects can be predicted with great precision.

The best-known and most important nuclear-weapons effects are EMP, a thermal-light pulse, blast, and fallout. EMP and the thermal-light pulse are produced at the instant of detonation. Electro-magnetic pulse occurs when **gamma radiation** interacts with matter (for example, the atmosphere)—a process known as the Compton effect. EMP produces a high-voltage electrical charge, which is harmless to humans, but can destroy electronic systems that are not specifically shielded against its effects. EMP effects are maximized by detonating weapons at relatively high altitudes (100,000 feet). In theory, a single high-altitude nuclear detonation could temporarily knock out most electronic systems in a medium-sized country. Thermal-light pulse, which lasts about two seconds, can cause flash blindness and fire. A 1-mgt airburst could produce flash blindness in individuals 53 miles away on a clear night and 13 miles away on a clear day. This airburst would cause first-degree burns on unprotected skin 7 miles away, second-degree burns at about 6 miles away, and third-degree burns at about 5 miles away.

A shockwave (a sudden rise in atmosphere pressure) and dynamic overpressure (wind) follow a few seconds behind the thermal light pulse. At about one mile away, a 1-mgt airburst will produce 20 lb per square inch (psi) overpressure and 470 mph winds, pressure sufficient to level steel-reinforced concrete structures. At 3 miles away, overpressure reaches 10 psi, producing winds of about 290 mph, sufficient to destroy most commercial structures and private residences. At 5 miles away, winds reach about 160 mph and overpressure reaches 5 psi, enough to damage most structures and subject people caught in the open to lethal collisions with flying debris. Blast effects were generally used by military planners to calculate casualty rates in a nuclear attack: it was estimated that about 50 per cent of the people living within 5 miles of a 1-mgt airburst would be either killed or wounded by blast effects (see Figure 20.1).

Individuals can be exposed to the fourth nuclear effect, radiation, either in the initial nuclear detonation or from fallout, which is irradiated debris picked up by the nuclear fireball and lofted into the atmosphere. A REM (roentgen-equivalent-man) is a measure of radiation energy absorbed by living creatures: 600 REM is likely to produce lethal radiation sickness in an exposed population, while a dose of 300 REM would produce lethal radiation sickness in about 10 per cent of an exposed population (United States Congress 1979).

A dirty bomb uses chemical high explosive to disperse radioactive material. It relies primarily on radiation to produce a lethal effect. A dirty bomb's lethality thus would be governed by how far radioactive materials might be lofted by the conventional chemical explosive and the radioactivity of the material used in the bomb. Many observers believe that the explosive blast produced by a dirty bomb, not the radioactive material it disperses, would cause the greatest amount of actual damage. Panic set off by even a limited dispersion of radioactive material, however, might be more costly in terms of the disruption it causes than the actual casualties or damage to property produced by the detonation of a dirty bomb.

Methods of delivery

Nuclear weapons have taken a variety of forms over the years. Early weapons were relatively large and heavy; only four-engine bombers were capable of lifting them. With the advent of thermonuclear (fusion) weapons, the size and weight of weapons began to decrease as their yields increased. Nuclear 'warheads' were soon mounted on cruise missiles, medium-range ballistic missiles, and eventually intercontinental ballistic missiles (ICBMs) and submarine-launched ballistic missiles (SLBMs) that were launched beneath the surface of the ocean from nuclear-powered submarines. By the 1970s, multiple independently targetable re-entry vehicles were being installed aboard US and Soviet ICBMs, giving both superpowers the ability to strike up to a dozen targets with one missile. Nuclear warheads were soon available for air-to-air missiles that were to be fired by aircraft to knock down incoming bombers, artillery shells, and even man-portable demolition charges. Neutron warheads were created to arm interceptor missiles that were part of the Safeguard Anti-Ballistic Missile System, which was developed by the United States in the 1970s. Both superpowers also investigated the possibility of deploying Fractional Orbital Bombardment Systems (FOBS)—that is, parking nuclear weapons in orbit so

Figure 20.1 Percentages of population killed (as a function of peak overpressure)

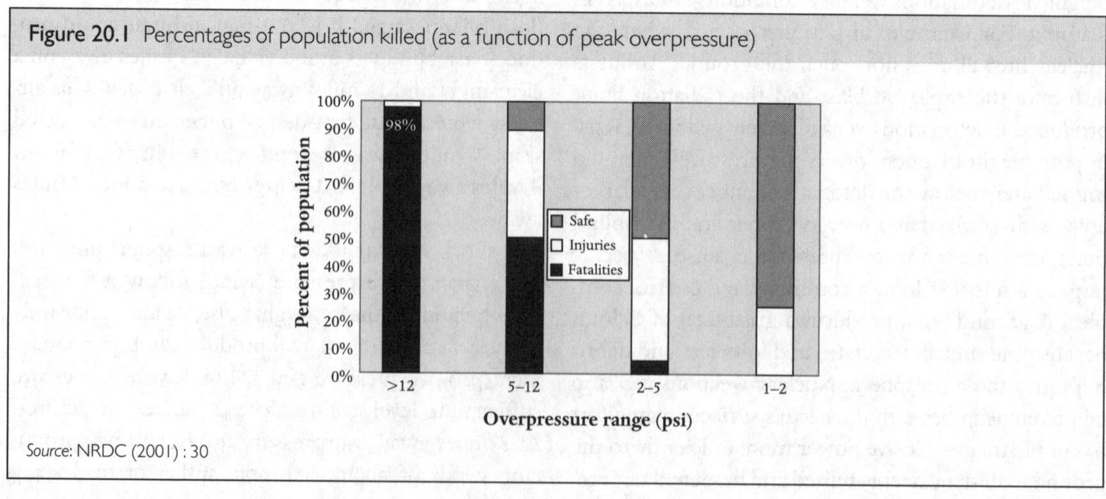

Source: NRDC (2001) : 30

that they could be armed and targeted following an alert from ground-control stations. Mercifully, officials on both sides of the Cold War divide thought better of living literally with a sword of Damocles over their heads, and in the 1967 Outer Space Treaty they banned the placement of nuclear weapons in space.

Methods of delivery sometimes help to characterize the way analysts view nuclear weapons. For instance, analysts describe delivery systems and the nuclear weapons associated with them as survivable (unlikely to be destroyed before they are used), reliable (likely to reach their targets without malfunctioning), accurate (likely to detonate near their target), or as likely to penetrate the target (evade air or missile defences). Weapons deployed on ballistic missiles carried by submarines that operate at sea are seen as desirable because they are highly survivable, although the cost involved in deploying nuclear weapons in this way is extremely high. It is less expensive to deploy warheads on land-based ICBMs and because of fixed communications they can be launched more quickly than their submarine-based counterparts, but these weapons are potentially more vulnerable to attack. ICBMs deployed in the United States have an additional drawback: using them to attack targets in the Middle East, for instance, would require a polar trajectory and over flight of Russia, a fact that might produce unintended and quite catastrophic consequences. Piloted bombers allow a human to reassess target options or fly routes that respect neutral air space, but it can take many hours to deliver weapons from aircraft and they are vulnerable to attack while on the ground. Nuclear weapons can also be placed on air-launched, ground-launched, or sea-launched cruise missiles to attack areas protected by heavy air defences, but it is unlikely that policy makers would be willing to trust this sort of 'robot' weapon in anything other than the direst circumstances. Because of various arms control agreements, Russians and Americans are also not free to develop new delivery systems or deploy them as they please.

Today, officials are worried about the possibility that terrorists might somehow manufacture or acquire a nuclear weapon or a radiological device. Although a missile or airborne attack is possible, there is much concern that a weapon might be smuggled into a country in one of the thousands of marine shipping containers that travel the world's oceans every day. There is also a possibility that a weapon's components could be shipped separately and assembled on site. Local police forces and national intelligence agencies also closely monitor efforts to sell radioactive materials on the black market. In 1998, for instance, Mamdough Mamud Salim, an Al-Qaeda operative, was arrested after attempting to buy 'enriched uranium' in Western Europe (Boureston 2002). Nuclear or radiological weapons manufactured by terrorists would probably be relatively crude, suggesting that they would be relatively large and difficult to transport. Small, man-portable nuclear devices (for example, atomic demolitions) were manufactured by the superpowers during the Cold War, which has raised concerns that these weapons might find their way onto the black market. In September 1997, for instance, the CBS news programme *Sixty Minutes* reported that former Russian National Security Adviser Aleksander Lebed claimed that the Russian military had lost track of 100 'suit-case bombs', each with a yield of about 10 kt. Russian officials confirmed that such devices had been constructed, but it remains unclear if they have been secured or destroyed.

Impact on international politics

Despite the fact that seventy years have passed since nuclear weapons emerged on the world scene and that they played a dominant role in the Cold War standoff between the North Atlantic Treaty Organization (NATO) and the Warsaw Pact, debate continues about their impact on world politics (Paul et al. 1998). Disarmament advocates bemoan the failure of the existing nuclear powers to reduce their reliance on nuclear weapons, the failure of the US Senate to ratify the **Comprehensive Test Ban Treaty**, and the decision of the George W. Bush administration to withdraw from the **1972 Anti-Ballistic Missile Treaty**, which in their mind threatens a new round in the arms race. They are also concerned that the non-proliferation regime is slowly losing ground, as several states continue to press ahead with covert and overt programmes to develop nuclear weapons. Others see the cup as half full. The United States and Russia have greatly decreased the size of their deployed nuclear forces—the 2002 Moscow Treaty cuts Russian and American nuclear forces to about 20 per cent of the level they reached during the Cold War. The New START Accords, which were signed on 8 April 2010, further cut the Russian and US nuclear arsenals, limiting each side to only 1,550 deployed strategic warheads. The international community has also taken a series of steps to address the issue of non-compliance with non-proliferation norms and to imbed international non-proliferation norms into domestic laws. United Nations Resolution 1540, for instance, obliged all nations to criminalize trafficking in WMD and to establish domestic controls over the export and use of materials that could be used in WMD programmes. Resolution 1540 extends the reach of existing international efforts to combat nuclear proliferation. The Global Initiative to Combat Nuclear Terrorism, announced jointly by President Bush and President Vladimir Putin in July 2006, refocuses international efforts in the battle against nuclear terrorism. It is a multinational effort to coordinate policy and transmit best practices.

Scholars are divided about the impact of nuclear weapons on world politics (Sagan and Waltz 2003). Some believe that a nuclear arsenal helps to deter attack by other states armed with conventional and nuclear weapons. The ability to retaliate with nuclear weapons after suffering an attack—known as a secure second-strike capability—is especially desirable, because it can effectively eliminate an opponent's potential gain produced by using nuclear weapons first, a situation known as crisis stability. Because even a few nuclear weapons can cause catastrophic destruction, and it is virtually impossible to defend against the effects of nuclear weapons, these scholars believe that they are truly revolutionary weapons that force militaries to concentrate on preventing, not fighting, wars (Brodie 1946). Some, focusing on Soviet–American relations during the Cold War, suggest that peace is the logical outcome, especially if potential enemies obtain secure second-strike capabilities: it is not logical for officials to engage in conflicts if they know in advance that a nuclear exchange will devastate, if not completely destroy, their country (Jervis 1989).

By contrast, proliferation pessimists worry that the superpower Cold War experience was at best an anomaly, and at worse a situation that often teetered on the brink of disaster. They worry that human frailty, communication failures and misperception, bureaucratic snafus, or psychological or technological breakdowns in a crisis can cause failures of deterrence, leading to inadvertent or accidental nuclear war. Others point to normal accidents—the inability to anticipate all human–machine interaction in complex systems—as a potential path to accidental nuclear war, especially because nuclear warning and command and control systems interact intensively during a crisis. Proliferation pessimists also point out that there is no guarantee that all militaries and governments will be good stewards of their nuclear arsenals. Those who possess nuclear weapons might take risks that expose their arsenals to sabotage, loss through theft, or accidental or inadvertent use. Some governments might use their newly found weapons not for deterrence purposes, but instead for purposes of intimidation or aggression. They might gravitate towards nuclear war-fighting strategies that seek to introduce nuclear weapons quickly and massively on the battlefield in an attempt either to pre-empt an adversary's use of nuclear weapons or to end a conflict with a quick knock-out blow.

Two divergent trends thus characterize the role of nuclear weapons on the international stage. Some states—the United Kingdom, France, the United States, and China—have embraced modest nuclear modernization programmes or have taken steps to reduce the size of their nuclear arsenals or their reliance on nuclear weapons in their foreign and defence policies. Sometimes ageing weapons systems are not replaced—the United States will no longer deploy nuclear-armed air launched cruise missiles as part of its strategic deterrent. Sometimes modernization programmes are minimized—in the UK the pace and scale of the Trident submarine replacement programme has been slowed, culminating in nearly a 30 per cent reduction in the number of nuclear weapons deployed on a day-to-day basis. In these states, nuclear weapons programmes can no longer be considered as a 'growth industry'. In other states—Iran, North Korea, Pakistan, and India—nuclear weapons are apparently viewed as desirable national assets. Tehran seems intent on acquiring a nuclear arsenal despite international opposition. Pakistan is enhancing its stockpile of fissile material and is undertaking a host of development and modernization programmes to improve its short-, medium-, and intermediate-range ballistic missile delivery systems and is acquiring various types of cruise missiles. Allegations in 2014 that Russia has violated the 1987 Intermediate-Range Nuclear Forces Treaty by flight testing a ground-launched cruise missile within the 'prohibited range' of 500 km and 5,500 km are also calling Russian nuclear ambitions into question. It is unclear which of these trends—nuclear armament or disarmament—will ultimately come to dominate world politics.

> **KEY POINTS**
>
> - A gun-type fission device is a relatively simple, reliable, and rugged nuclear weapon design that would be attractive to terrorist organizations or states developing a nuclear programme.
> - Fusion weapons are highly complex devices that can produce enormous destructive energy from relatively small, light-weight packages.
> - Primary nuclear effects are electromagnetic pulse, thermal-light energy, blast, and radiation.
> - Although the risk of nuclear Armageddon has receded since the end of the Cold War, concerns are increasing that terrorists might acquire and detonate a dirty bomb or a gun-type device.
> - Scholars continue to debate whether nuclear weapons are a source of peace in world politics or an unjustified risk to international security.

Chemical weapons

Although poisons and chemicals have been used in war since ancient times, chemical weapons emerged in the late 1800s as part of the modern chemical industry. Scholars debate whether chemical weapons should be considered a weapon of mass destruction, because large quantities of chemical weapons often have to be used on the battlefield to have a significant effect against a prepared opponent, and these weapons have to be expertly employed to produce massive casualties. On 20 March 1995, for instance, the Aum Shinrikyo cult launched a Sarin attack against the Tokyo subway system that resulted in twelve deaths. By contrast, the Al-Qaeda attack against the Madrid train system on 11 March 2004 used conventional explosives and killed nearly 200 innocent civilians. What worries analysts, however, is that any state with a chemical industry could quickly convert production processes from civilian use to weapons manufacturing and that even readily available household products can be mixed to create relatively dangerous concoctions. Weapons can be created from commonly available chemicals using well-understood technologies. Household insecticides, for example, are simply 'watered-down' nerve agents.

The first significant employment of chemical weapons occurred in the First World War, as both sides sought a way to break through the stalemate of trench warfare. On 22 April 1915, German units unleashed a cloud of chlorine gas (an asphyxiating agent) against allied lines at Ypres, Belgium, but failed to exploit the gap created in the French lines. Petrified by the sight of corpses that exhibited no obvious causes of death, attacking German soldiers refused to advance. The Germans introduced mustard gas (a blistering agent) on the battlefield on 12 July 1917. The Allies also developed their own blister agent, Lewisite, but it was just reaching the battlefield as the First World War came to an end. Although chemical weapons caused only about 4 per cent of the casualties suffered by all sides during the First World War, the use of gas on the battlefield affected societies everywhere as **veterans** related stories of helpless soldiers struggling to put on gas masks as they chocked to death or were blinded by blister agents. This imagery, best exemplified by the painting of a field dressing station in Arras, France, made by the American artist John Singer Sargent, highlighted the horror and cruelty of gas warfare (see Figure 20.2).

Figure 20.2 John Singer Sargent, *Gassed* (1918)

Source: Reproduced with permission from the Art Archive/Imperial War Museum

Although the Italians employed mustard agent against Ethiopia in 1935 and the Japanese attacked Chinese troops with chemical weapons in the 1930s, chemical weapons were not used extensively on Second World War battlefields. Many speculate that Adolf Hitler, a mustard-gas casualty in the First World War, was personally reluctant to be the first to introduce these weapons in Europe (although this apparent aversion did not stop the Nazis from using Zyclon-B, a prussic-acid-based substance used as a pesticide and disinfectant, to kill thousands of victims in gas chambers). In fact, only one major chemical-weapons incident occurred during the war. On 2 December 1943, a Nazi air raid on the harbour in Bari, Italy, damaged a merchant ship carrying 2,000 100 lb M 47A1 bombs filled with mustard agent. The accidental release of agent affected thousands of allied soldiers and civilians. It was not until the Iran–Iraq War, however, that chemical weapons were again employed on the battlefield. In 1982, Iraqi units, hard pressed by far more numerous Iranian forces, dispensed mass concentrations of the riot control agent CS to break up opposing formations. By 1983, Iraq was using mustard agents on the battlefield and continued experimenting with more lethal agents and concoctions. In a February 1986 strike against al-Faw, the Iraqis employed a mixture of mustard and tabun (a nerve agent) against the Iranians, which resulted in thousands of casualties. Saddam Hussein's murderous regime also attacked its own citizens with chemical weapons. On 16 March 1988, Iraqi forces sprayed a mixture of mustard and nerve agents over the Kurdish village of Halabja, killing more than 10,000 civilians. Additionally, in late 2012, the Syrian regime used chemical weapons against opposition groups in a series of small-scale attacks, which culminated on 21 August 2013 when Sarin (a nerve agent) rained down on Ghouta, a suburb of Damascus.

Chemical-weapons effects

Chemical weapons vary in terms of their lethality, their complexity, and the way they cause injury and death. They also vary in terms of their persistence: some disperse quickly, allowing attacking troops to move through an area, while 'area denial agents', which might be used to attack an airfield to reduce the tempo of flight operations, might persist for a long time. Traditionally, chemical weapons have been characterized as blood agents, choking agents, blister agents, nerve agents, and incapacitants.

Blood agents, which are generally based on hydrocyanic acid (HCN), interfere with the body's ability to transport oxygen in the blood. Because cyanide has been used as a poison throughout history, several countries experimented with using this agent as a weapon. Owing to its high volatility—it evaporates quickly, making it hard to create a lethal concentration over a battlefield—most states long ago abandoned it as a toxic agent for military use.

Choking agents—phosgene and chlorine—get their name from the fact that their victims literally drown in the fluids produced when the tissues lining the lungs interact with the agent. Choking agents produce hydrochloric acid when they are inhaled, causing blood and fluid to infiltrate the lungs. Phosgene, which reacts with water in the body to produce hydrochloric acid, is a common industrial chemical that is more toxic than chlorine. Most of the deaths caused in the First World War by chemical weapons were caused by phosgene.

Blister agents are primarily intended to generate serious casualities in an opposing force, thereby placing enormous demands on supporting medical services. Before the development of more lethal nerve agents, sulphur mustard was considered to be the chemical weapon of choice. It exists as a thick liquid at room temperature, but can be suspended in air (that is, turned into an aerosol that can be inhaled) by using a conventional explosive. It can also be used to contaminate people, terrain, or equipment. Although the exact reason why mustard agent is an extreme irritant is not well understood, it causes severe blistering on exposed skin and mucous membranes. It can also cause temporary blindness. Long-term effects from a single moderate exposure to mustard agent are not usually lethal. The effects of mustard can sometimes take several hours to develop; Lewisite, another blister agent, works more rapidly than mustard.

Nerve agents are by far the most lethal chemical weapons. Invented during the 1930s as insecticides, they entered Nazi and Allied military inventories in the Second World War but were not used in combat. The name 'nerve agent' reflects the fact that these chemicals interfere with the body's neurological system by irreversibly inactivating acetyl cholinesterase (AChE), which 'deactivates' the neurotransmitter acetylcholine. Nerve agents bind to the active site of AchE, making it incapable of deactivating acetylcholine. Without an ability to deactivate acetylcholine, muscles fire continuously and glandular hypersecretion occurs (for example, excess saliva), leading to paralysis and suffocation. Second-generation nerve agents, G- (German) series agents (GA) Tabun, (GB) Sarin, (GD) Soman, (GF) Cyclosarin, are considered to be non-persistent agents. G-series agents are all water- and fat-soluble, and can enter the skin and cause lethal effects. Third-generation V Series—VX, VE, VG, VM—nerve agents, a product of British science, are persistent agents that are about ten times more lethal than Sarin. Less is publicly known about fourth-generation A-series agents (also known as 'Novichok' agents), a product of Soviet science. Exposure to high aerosol concentrations of nerve agents causes prompt collapse and death.

Incapacitants are used for riot control (CS or tear gas) or for personal protection (CN or mace). They are less toxic than other chemical weapons and usually do not produce lethal effects when used in the open at a proper concentration. Vomiting agents (adamsite) have been developed for use in combat. Both Soviet and US scientists also experimented with psychochemicals (that is, lysergic acid diethylamide [LSD] and BZ) in an effort to cause altered states of situational awareness. BZ was weaponized by the United States, but it was dropped from its arsenal because its effects were unpredictable. In October 2002, Russian security forces used an opiod form of fentanyl in an attempt to incapacitate Chechin separatists who were holding 800 hostages in a Moscow theatre. Owing to either a lack of prompt medical attention or an overdose of fentanyl, 126 people died from this 'incapacitant'.

Methods of delivery

Chemical weapons are delivered from either a line or a point source. Bombs, artillery shells, missile warheads, or parcels, for instance, are all point sources, because they deliver chemical weapons to a specific location. A line source, which is generated by a series of dispensing devices, a crop duster, or even a moving crop sprayer, creates a cloud or 'line' of gas that drifts towards the target. Wind, temperature, and terrain can affect the lethality and persistence of an agent. For example, a gallon of VX is sufficient to kill thousands of people, but only if individuals are brought into contact with the correct amount of agent to cause casualties. Agents can be blown off target, diluted by rain, or even solidify, if the temperature drops too low.

Because proper dispersal is the key to employing chemical weapons, analysts are most concerned about their use in closed venues such as sporting arenas or large buildings with ventilation systems that could be subject to tampering. Aum Shinrikyo targeted the Tokyo subway because of the large numbers of people who travel daily through its contained spaces and choke points. The cult experimented with a suitcase mechanism to deliver Sarin aerosol in the subway: two small electric fans were used to disperse the chemical agent after it was released from vials stored inside the suitcase. To conduct the actual attack, however, the cult relied on a far simpler method: they punched holes in plastic bags containing Sarin and simply allowed the agent to evaporate in the subway cars.

Impact on international politics

By the 1970s, NATO militaries began to view chemical weapons as a deterrent, not as a weapon they preferred to use on the battlefield. Chemical weapons pose obvious difficulties in terms of transportation and handling, and most military observers agree there are safer and more efficient ways to hold targets at risk. Thus the preferences of military professionals helped to foster a taboo against the use of chemical weapons in war, a restraint codified in the **1925 Geneva Protocol for the Prohibition of the Use in War of Asphyxiating, Poisonous, or Other Gases, and of Bacteriological Methods of Warfare**. Although the Geneva Protocol banned first use of chemical weapons, it did not prevent states from stockpiling chemical munitions. The Chemical Weapons Convention (CWC), which entered into force on 29 April 1997, makes it illegal for signatories to possess or employ chemical weapons, with the exception of small samples used to test protective equipment. States party to the CWC are required to declare their existing stocks of chemical weapons, to identify facilities that were once involved in chemical-weapons production, and to announce when their existing stocks will be completely destroyed. The Organization for the Prohibition of Chemical Weapons (OPCW) is authorized to verify compliance with the CWC and can undertake challenge inspections when demanded by states parties (Larsen 2002).

While 148 nations have ratified the CWC, about twenty countries, some of which maintain a large chemical arsenal (for example, North Korea), have not signed the treaty. Most military analysts believe that these large arsenals would only have a modest effect on well-equipped and trained troops on the battlefield. In their view, a chemical arsenal is the 'poor man's' weapon of mass destruction, because it is based on old, relatively simple, and inexpensive technologies that have limited military utility. Nevertheless, if employed deliberately against relatively defenceless civilian populations, these weapons wreak havoc. Approximately 1,500 people died in the Syrian attack on Ghouta in August 2013—witnesses uploaded ghastly images of many victims writhing in agony onto the world wide web.

Analysts are most concerned that terrorist organizations or even individuals might gain access to poisonous chemicals that are part of industrial processes and attack urban targets. Iraqi use of chemical weapons in war is considered an anomaly. The fear is that Aum Shinrikyo's Sarin attack might be a harbinger of things to come.

KEY POINTS

- There are five types of chemical weapons: blood agents, choking agents, blister agents, nerve agents, and incapacitants.
- Chemical agents can be persistent or non-persistent and can be delivered from a point or a line source.
- State and non-state actors with access to even a rudimentary chemical industry can acquire chemical weapons.
- The nearly universal Chemical Weapons Convention bans the manufacture or use of chemical weapons and allows signatories to possess only small amounts of agents for research into defensive equipment and prophylaxis.

Biological weapons

Biological weapons (BW) make use of living organisms or toxins to sicken or kill humans, animals, and plants. These organisms and toxins all occur in nature, which makes it difficult to differentiate natural disease outbreaks from a BW attack. BW is probably the most potentially destructive weapon known to humans in the sense that a single organism or infected individual can affect millions of human beings, although scientists debate the degree of difficulty any state or non-state actor might encounter in infecting large numbers of people quickly. Although extremely contagious diseases are generally not lethal, some (smallpox, for example) are easily transmitted and produce high **morbidity**. Sometimes, diseases that are considered relatively mundane can be extremely lethal: the 1918–19 Spanish Flu killed upwards of forty million people, striking hardest among healthy adults between the ages of 20 and 40.

Disease has been a part of war throughout history. Until recently, most people died in war from illness, not from wounds suffered in combat. Deliberate use of disease as a weapon of war, however, has been sporadic, producing mixed results. In 1346, Mongol invaders hurled the corpses of soldiers who had died from bubonic plague into the besieged city of Kaffa in a deliberate effort to spread disease. The Mongols did not know, however, that the causative bacteria of plague, *Yersinia pestis*, is spread by fleas that feed only on live hosts. At the end of the Seven Years War (1756–63), British forces apparently provided American Indians with smallpox-infected blankets, although it is difficult to determine whether or not they succeeded in infecting anyone, because smallpox was already endemic in the Americas and had decimated Indian populations about 200 years earlier. During the First World War, German saboteurs apparently succeeded in infecting horses used by the allies with glanders. During the Second World War, the Japanese filled glass bombs with plague-infected fleas to spread disease, and Japanese scientists working in the infamous Unit 731 conducted biological warfare experiments on prisoners of war.

Although the United States, the UK, and Canada conducted research into the weaponization of **anthrax**, **tularemia**, **Q-fever**, **Venezuelan equine encephalitis**, and anti-agricultural agents, biological weapons were generally viewed in the West as lacking military utility. By contrast, Soviet researchers concentrated on perfecting a variety of biological agents during the Cold War and exploited the emerging science of genetic engineering better to weaponize naturally occurring diseases. According to Ken Alibek (2000), who was a leading figure in Biopreperat, the Soviet Union's complex of biological weapons facilities, Soviet science worked with a variety of bacteria (for example, an antibiotic-resistant strain of anthrax), viruses (for example, smallpox) and even haemorrhagic fevers (for example, Ebola). Although the 'Soviet' biological weapons programme apparently ended in Russia in the early 1990s, experts still debate what motivated the Soviets to undertake such an extensive BW programme. The Soviets probably saw their BW programme as a counter to the precision, global-strike complex that was emerging in NATO in the 1970s or as a way to retard Western recovery following an all-out nuclear exchange. The Soviets apparently loaded several SS-18 intercontinental ballistic missiles with plague in an attempt to provide Western survivors of a nuclear war with an additional reason to envy the dead.

Biological weapons effects

Although naturally occurring diseases have been a scourge of humankind, not every disease provides the basis for an effective biological weapon. An agent's storage, delivery, mode of transmission, and its very resilience (that is, how long can it survive in the environment) can shape its effects on a target population. Military professionals believe that most biological weapons are simply too unpredictable in their effects to be a reliable weapon. Because they are easy to manufacture and can be potentially highly lethal in small quantities—any basic medical laboratory has the capability to cultivate a biological agent—biological agents might be attractive and available to terrorists. Relatively large industrial facilities are needed to produce militarily significant quantities of chemical weapons, but relatively small fermenters used to make legitimate vaccines, for instance, could be quickly converted to produce biological agents.

There are three varieties of biological agents: bacteria, viruses, and toxins. As an area attack agent, anthrax is probably the best-known bacterial agent (see Table 20.2). Its spores are extremely hardy (they can live for literally hundreds of years) and it can be spread quickly across large areas. Anthrax is not contagious, so its effects can be relatively contained and focused on specific targets. It also can be genetically engineered to be resistant to most antibiotics and it can be formulated with inert matter better to form an aerosol. These qualities make anthrax the agent of choice for many biological-weapons programmes. The cutaneous form of anthrax occurs in the animal industry and can be treated relatively easily; by contrast, the inhalation form of the disease is extremely dangerous. By the time the victim begins to show symptoms of inhalation anthrax, a near-lethal dose of toxins produced by the anthrax bacteria has already built up in the body. The Aum Shinrikyo cult attempted to disperse anthrax in Tokyo in 1996; they failed because they used a non-toxic vaccine strain of the virus. The terrorist who sent anthrax through the US mail in autumn 2001, however, used a deadly 'Ames' strain, which US weapons laboratories employ to test defensive equipment and prophylaxis (Stern 2000).

Although haemorrhagic fevers—Marburg, Lassa fever, or Ebola—are viral agents that could serve as potent weapons, policy makers are most worried about the threat posed by smallpox (see Table 20.3). As smallpox was eradicated as a naturally occurring disease, global vaccination programmes were terminated, leaving entire generations unprotected against the disease for the first time in hundreds of years. Smallpox is an airborne virus that is about as contagious as the flu, but it has a lethality of about 30 per cent in its ordinary form (rarer malignant and haemorrhagic forms of smallpox are 100 per cent lethal). Smallpox vaccination can stop the disease, even if administered a few days after exposure, but, to prevent a pandemic, potentially millions of doses of vaccine need to be made quickly available. Reintroduction of general inoculation programmes, however, have not been advocated by public health

Table 20.2 Possible biological warfare agents: bacterial and rickettsial agents

Agent/disease	Organism	Lethality	Onset	Symptoms	Target
Anthrax	*Bacillus anthracis*	80 per cent lethality, non-contagious	1–5 days	Pulmonary form: chest cold symptoms, respiratory distress, fever, shock death	Area attack
Brucellosis	*Brucella*	3–20 per cent lethality, non-contagious	5–60 days	Fever, headaches, pain in joints and muscle fatigue	Area attack
Plague	*Yersinia pesstis*	80 per cent lethality, contagious	2–3 days	High fever, headache, extreme weakness, haemorrhages in skin and mucous membranes	Area attack
Tularemia	*Francisella tularensis*	50 per cent lethality, contagious	2–10 days	Chills, fever, headache, loss of body fluids	Area attack
Q Fever	*Coxiella burnettii*	2 per cent lethality, non-contagious	10–40 days	Fever, headache, cough, muscle and joint pain	

Table 20.3 Possible biological warfare agents: viral agents

Agent/disease	Organism	Lethality	Onset	Symptoms	Target
Smallpox	Variola virus	2–49 per cent lethality, contagious	7–17 days	Severe fever, small blisters on skin, bleeding on skin and mucous	Area attack
Viral encephalitis	Eastern Equine Encephalitis (EEE) virus	80 per cent lethality, non-contagious	1–14 days	Headache, general aches and pains, photophobia	Area attack
Viral haemorrhagic fevers	Ebola	80 per cent lethality, contagious	4–21 days	Subcutaneous haemorrhage, bleeding from body orifices, headache, fever, stupor, convulsion	Area attack

authorities, because the smallpox vaccine itself leads to about fifty instances of side effects per one million people vaccinated. The impact of a smallpox outbreak, however, cannot be underestimated. The 'Dark Winter' exercise run by the US Federal Emergency Management Agency in June 2001 was based on a smallpox outbreak in the American Midwest. Within 30 days, over 300,000 people in twenty-five states and ten foreign countries had already contracted the disease. Smallpox truly has the capability of creating a global catastrophe.

Although toxins are not living organisms and are in fact a by-product of metabolic activity, they are generally discussed as a biological weapon. Toxins are probably best thought of as a poison, which is often used to attack specific individuals. Like chemical weapons, individuals have to be brought into direct contact with the toxin to suffer from its effects. Toxins, however, can be extremely lethal. Ricin, which is made from castor bean, kills by inhibiting protein synthesis within cells. Used as an assassination weapon—the Bulgarian dissident Georgy Markov was killed by a Ricin injection in 1978—it can kill within three days. Because it can be made easily from readily available materials, many analysts believe that terrorists will seek to use ricin. In 2003, for instance, British officials arrested a terrorist who was plotting to smear Ricin on the door handles of cars and buildings in London. In 2008, a man was sickened by the Ricin he had stockpiled in a Las Vegas hotel room. In 2004, Victor Yushchenko was badly disfigured from a toxin attack (see Think Point 20.1).

Methods of delivery

Biological agents are generally delivered in the form of an infectious aerosol. Precise preparation of the aerosol is crucial because the agent has to be the proper size to infect a host by lodging in the small alveoli of the lungs. Vectors—lice, fleas, mosquitoes—transmit disease in nature, but it would be difficult to use this mode of transmission as a military weapon because it is inherently difficult to control. Terrorists might attempt to infect individuals surreptitiously with a disease such as smallpox, but the disease is difficult to grow in vitro and the terrorists themselves would have to be vaccinated to work with the virus. Because smallpox vaccine is not readily available, seeking vaccine might allow public health officials to detect some nefarious scheme. The difficulty of controlling infectious diseases should also give terrorists pause. Unleashing highly contagious diseases can backfire, because a pandemic does not respect religious, political, or cultural boundaries, although public health services in rich countries are far more likely to cope with an outbreak of infectious disease than poorer countries whose health care systems are already stretched to breaking point.

Impact on international politics

Following revelations in the early 1990s about the Soviet biological weapons programme and renewed concerns about biological warfare following the 1991 Gulf War, policy makers devoted renewed attention to strengthening the **1972 Biological and Toxin Weapons Convention** (**BWC**) by devising an inspection protocol similar to the verification mechanism embedded in the CWC. By late 2001, however, negotiations over an inspection protocol for the BWC reached an impasse. Officials concluded that it was too difficult to devise an inspection regime that could provide any significant insight into what was being manufactured in the tens of thousands of medical laboratories around the planet and that, regardless of the efforts of inspection teams, it was simply

! THINK POINT 20.1 Who poisoned Yushchenko?

Although toxins could be employed against troops in the field or against large groups of individuals in sporting arenas or transportation systems, history suggests that they often serve as an exotic weapon for assassination. In the latest example of attempted 'toxin assassination', Austrian doctors reported in December 2004 that Ukrainian presidential candidate Victor Yushchenko was suffering from dioxin poisoning. Yushchenko apparently developed symptoms—fatigue, pain, and disfiguring chloracne—quickly after he had apparently ingested TCDD dioxin in his food. The concentration of dioxin in Yushchenko's body, the second highest ever recorded, was as least 1,000 times more than is found in most people. Some observers speculate that dioxin was used because it would disfigure and sicken Yushchenko, literally making him an unattractive candidate to the Ukrainian electorate. Campaigning in extreme pain, and badly disfigured by dioxin, Yushchenko went on to ride the 'Orange Revolution' in Ukraine that followed the electoral fraud in the November 2004 presidential elections. He took office as the Ukraine's President on 23 January 2005 (see Figure 20.3).

Figure 20.3 Who poisoned Yushchenko? This combination image shows the changing face of Ukraine's opposition leader Viktor Yushchenko in file photos taken on 4 July 2004 (left) and 1 November 2004 (right)

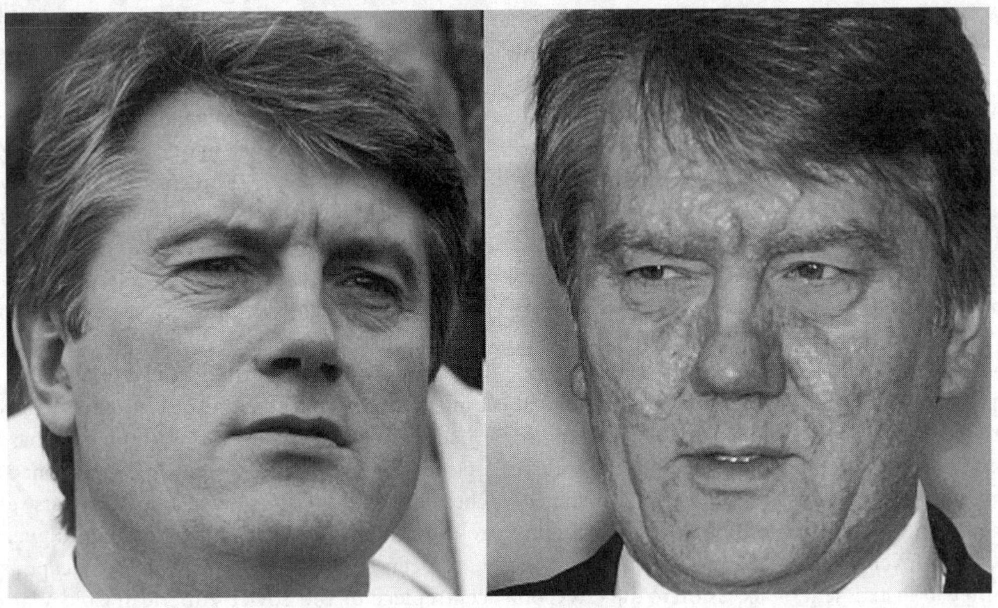

Source: Reproduced with permission from Reuters/Gleb Garanich and Vasily Fedosenko.

too easy to conceal work on biological agents. Efforts instead shifted from the diplomatic realm to strengthening domestic criminal laws against the manufacture or possession of biological weapons or agents and improving international health monitoring to spot the outbreak of infectious diseases (see Table 20.4).

KEY POINTS

- Biological weapons are derived from naturally occurring diseases and can be manufactured in medical laboratories.
- Biological weapons vary in terms of their lethality and whether or not they are contagious.
- Anthrax is a biological agent of great concern because it is a hardy, non-contagious agent that can be used to contaminate large areas. It can potentially directly infect many people quickly.
- The revolution in genetic engineering has been used to weaponize naturally occurring diseases.

Table 20.4 Possible biological warfare agents: toxins

Agent/disease	Organism	Lethality	Onset	Symptoms	Target
Botulinum Toxin	*Clostridium botulinum*	80 per cent lethality, non-contagious	1–5 days	Blurred vision, photophobia, paralysis	Proximity attack
SEB Toxin	*Staphylococcus aureus*	2 per cent lethality	1–6 hours	Headache, sudden fever, nausea, vomiting	Proximity attack

Conclusion

In some respects, the WMD threat has greatly receded since the end of the Cold War. The number of deployed Soviet (Russian) and American strategic nuclear warheads has been reduced by 80 per cent since the 1990s, and US tactical nuclear weapons have largely been withdrawn from service. The threat of Armageddon produced by a massive nuclear exchange is now only a remote possibility. The International Non-Proliferation Regime has survived the 1998 Indian and Pakistani nuclear tests and a *de facto* nuclear test ban remains in place, despite the fact that the US Senate failed to ratify the Comprehensive Test Ban Treaty. The CWC and BWC not only provide a basis in international law to stop the spread of these deadly chemical and biological agents, but they also serve as a useful diplomatic framework for devising new ways to stop the spread and use of these weapons. The OPCW, for instance, quickly swung into action to eliminate Syria's chemical weapons inventory once the regime in Damascus submitted its instrument of accession to the CWC on 14 September 2013.

Although Iranian efforts to develop a nuclear weapon and the fact that North Korea has a nascent nuclear arsenal continue to dominate headlines, officials today are most concerned by the prospect that WMD is escaping the control of state actors. The biological and medical sciences are undergoing a period of revolutionary development based on advances in genetics and genetic engineering. These capabilities are now widely available to researchers and manufacturers. This raises the possibility that new biological weapons will inevitably find their way into the hands of individuals or non-state actors. The so-called renaissance in nuclear energy, the turn towards nuclear power as an answer to global warming and peak oil, also creates opportunities for more state and non-state actors to gain access to radiological materials and know-how. The emerging challenge is to devise ways to safeguard these nuclear, biological, and chemical technologies and materials in both a domestic and an international setting so that they cannot be diverted to nefarious purposes. Since the First World War, the use of WMD in war has been episodic. Nation states have mostly abandoned their chemical and biological arsenals. Terrorists' efforts to use chemical, biological, or radiological weapons have been largely ineffective. Nuclear weapons, the centrepiece of the Soviet–American Cold War competition, have been used on the battlefield twice. Lingering questions remain. Is there a taboo against the use of weapons of mass destruction? Will the quest to obtain nuclear weapons trump international trends that foster nuclear stasis or even disarmament among the great powers? Have we all just been incredibly lucky?

? QUESTIONS

1. Why might nuclear weapons be a source of stability in international relations?
2. Why do you think that the use of weapons of mass destruction in war is relatively rare?

3. Why would terrorists be attracted to chemical, biological, radiological, or nuclear weapons?
4. What effect would another use of nuclear weapons have on world politics?
5. Toxins are often used against what type of target?
6. Which variety of WMD is most destructive? Which is most easily manufactured?
7. What steps should governments take to prevent WMD terrorism?
8. Is direct action or international negotiation the best way to counter the spread of WMD?
9. Do you think Aum Shinrikyo's experience with Sarin will be emulated by other groups or individuals?
10. Do you think that weapons of mass destruction serve as status symbols in world politics?

FURTHER READING

- Bernstein, Jeremy (2008), *Nuclear Weapons: What You Need To Know*, New York: Cambridge University Press. This volume offers a fascinating account of how scientific puzzles and technical hurdles were overcome in the quest to build nuclear weapons.
- Croddy, Eric A. and Wirtz, James J. (eds) (2005), *Weapons of Mass Destruction: An Encyclopedia of Worldwide Policy, Technology, and History*, 2 vols, Santa Barbara, CA: ABC-Clio. A handy reference on WMD.
- Freedman, Lawrence (2003), *The Evolution of Nuclear Strategy*, 3rd edn, New York: Palgrave Macmillan. This is the best single volume on the history of nuclear arsenals and the strategic thinking that guided nuclear strategy.
- Pant, Harsh V. (2012), *Handbook of Nuclear Proliferation*, New York: Routledge. Provides an overview of various national policies on nuclear weapons.
- Sagan, Scott D. and Waltz, Kenneth (2003), *The Spread of Nuclear Weapons: A Debate Renewed*, 2nd edn, New York: Norton. Provides an engaging debate between proliferation optimists and pessimists.
- Schell, Jonathan (1982), *The Fate of the Earth*, New York: Knopf. This is probably the best description of the existential threat posed by the widespread use of nuclear weapons.

IMPORTANT WEBSITES

- **http://www.cdc.gov** Center for Disease Control and Prevention. The Center provides information on diseases.
- **http://www.ucsusa.org** Union of Concerned Scientists. Established in 1969, this is an independent non-profit alliance of more than 100,000 citizens and scientists concerned by the misuse of science and technology in society.
- **http://www.nps.edu/Academics/Centers/CCC/** Center on Contemporary Conflict. Launched in 2001, the CCC conducts research on current and emerging security issues and conveys its findings to US and Allied policy makers and military forces.
- **http://nuclearweaponarchive.org** Nuclear Weapons Archive. The purpose of this archive is to illuminate the reader regarding the effects of these destructive devices, and to warn against their use.
- **http://cns.miis.edu** Center for Nonproliferation Studies, Monterey Institute of International Studies. The Center strives to combat the spread of weapons of mass destruction (WMD) by training the next generation of non-proliferation specialists and disseminating timely information and analysis.

- **http://www.fas.org/index.html** Federation of American Scientists. Formed in 1945 by atomic scientists from the Manhattan Project, the FAS conducts research and provides education on nuclear arms control and global security, conventional arms transfers, proliferation of weapons of mass destruction, information technology for human health, and government information policy.

Visit the Online Resource Centre that accompanies this book for lots of interesting additional material: www.oxfordtextbooks.co.uk/orc/collins4e/

21

Terrorism

Brenda Lutz and James Lutz

Chapter Contents

Reader's Guide

This chapter analyses the threat that terrorism poses for countries and the world. Efforts to deal with terrorism can be considered within the framework of terrorism as warfare, terrorism as crime, and terrorism as disease. Which of these views is adopted often determines what kinds of countermeasures countries will use in their effort to deal with terrorism. Terrorism is a technique of action available to many different groups; security measures that work with one group may not be effective with others. As a consequence, dealing with terrorism in today's world can be a very complex process indeed.

Introduction

Terrorism has become an important phenomenon, as well as a major security issue for many countries. The attacks of 9/11 on the World Trade Center in New York City and the Pentagon near Washington, DC highlighted the great damage that such attacks could cause. Since that time, large-scale attacks on tourist facilities in Bali in 2002 and again in 2005, on the commuter trains in Madrid in 2004, on a Russian middle school in Beslan in 2004, the suicide bombings in London in 2005, the Christmas attacks in Mumbai in 2008, the attack in Norway in 2011 by a lone gunman, and the Boston Marathon bombings in 2013 all demonstrate the continuing threat that terrorism can pose. Further, continuing terrorist campaigns that persist over time, such as the attacks in Afghanistan or Iraq since the US invasion, have claimed many victims. It is not only the spectacular attacks that constitute a threat. Continuing attacks by a variety of dissident groups in Turkey between 1975 and 1980 left at least 5,000 dead and 15,000 injured (Bal and Laciner 2001: 106). This cumulative casualty toll is heavier than that sustained on 9/11. Such casualty lists have demonstrated the continuing vulnerability of people everywhere to terrorism, and more recently concern has grown that terrorists might use weapons of mass destruction (biological, chemical, radiological, or nuclear).

Terrorism is a technique that has been around for millennia and used by different groups. Zealots in Judea in the first and second centuries CE, the Assassins in the twelfth and thirteenth centuries, the Sons of Liberty in colonial America, and Fascists and Nazis after World War I are among the historical examples. The more pressing concern for governments today is the organizations that are currently threats. Groups have adapted to changing circumstances. During the Cold War, terrorist groups often gained the support of the Soviet Union or the United States or their respective allies. Today, there are no competing superpowers, and overt support for terrorist groups can generate a massive military response, as the **Taliban** regime in Afghanistan discovered. As a consequence, terrorist organizations have developed networks that provide mutual assistance. Groups like **Al-Qaeda** in some respects have network structures (see Case Study 21.1). Other terrorist groups have also developed linkages with criminal organizations, especially those involved in drug trafficking. These loosely connected international networks can be more difficult to attack and defeat.

While terrorism and terrorists have been analysed from a variety of theoretical perspectives, one of the most useful has been proposed by Peter Sederberg (2003), who suggests that terrorism can be viewed from three perspectives. The first perspective is to think of terrorism in the context of an enemy to be defeated in war. The war analogy presumes that the use of military methods can be successful and that it is possible to achieve victory. A second perspective for dealing with terrorists is to rely on normal police techniques. The criminal analogy has two quite important implications. First, it suggests that terrorism, like crime, will not disappear; it can only be contained. Second, this approach is a reactive one—criminals are normally caught after they commit their crimes. The third perspective is to consider terrorism as a disease, emphasizing both symptoms and underlying causes. It assumes that there is a need for long-term strategies

CASE STUDY 21.1 Al-Qaeda and the global Jihad network

Al-Qaeda (the Base) provides the most prominent contemporary example of a terrorist group organized as a network. Before 9/11 Al-Qaeda had a core of planners and close associates of Osama bin Laden and groups in individual countries that cooperated with this central group. Al-Qaeda, in turn, often provided financial and technical assistance to national groups in Muslim countries, especially those opposed to more secular and pro-Western governments or those groups opposed to Western influences that come with globalization and modernization. Al-Qaeda provided technical and financial support for the first attack on the World Trade Center in 1993. It was much more centrally involved in the attacks on the US embassies in East Africa in 1998 and the 9/11 attacks on the World Trade Center and the Pentagon. Once Afghanistan was invaded, Al-Qaeda maintained some of these network characteristics, but it also became a form of global leaderless resistance. Since 2002, the **global jihadist** movement has involved both network and leaderless resistance characteristics (Sageman 2008). The Madrid commuter train bombings of 2004, for example, involved participation by Al-Qaeda agents. The London transit attacks in 2005, the Boston Marathon bombings in 2013, and probably the 2007 bombing attempt at Glasgow airport, although they were inspired by Al-Qaeda, were undertaken independently by local groups of extremists who saw their attacks as part of the broader global jihad against the West. The network character of Al-Qaeda has been demonstrated by the adherence of groups elsewhere in the world to the organization. Al-Qaeda in the Arabian Peninsula in Yemen became a branch operation of the group, as has **Al Qaeda in the Islamic Maghreb (AQIM)**. AQIM has brought together remnants of terrorist groups in the region as a franchise of the larger organization. The death of Osama bin Laden, while a blow to the global jihad, had not caused a serious disruption to such a decentralized network of terrorist groups and individuals. Al-Qaeda and the global jihad have been precursors of the **Islamic State in Iraq and Syria (ISIS)** that has appeared to promote the idea of Islamic revival and a new Muslim state.

that address the basic causes, even if there can be successes along the way in treating symptoms. The three perspectives, although not mutually exclusive, represent dominant ways in which terrorism is viewed. They are important for analysing the phenomenon and for government officials who make choices in terms of how to deal with terrorist activity. Which perspective is adopted will suggest mechanisms for dealing with terrorism. Before 9/11, authorities in the United States largely dealt with acts of terrorism from the criminal perspective. Terrorists were caught (although it took time in some cases) and brought to trial (although not always convicted). Normal police techniques, including the use of informers and the infiltration of agents into potentially dangerous groups (like the **Ku Klux Klan** in the United States in the 1960s), drew upon conventional practices. After 9/11, however, the war analogy became dominant for the administration of President Bush, and references to the global war on terrorism appeared regularly. Others have suggested reforms and policy changes to deal with the causes of terrorism, but that has never been the main strategy adopted by the United States. In Europe, the crime analogy was also prevalent for many years. More recently there has been greater concern with addressing causes and trying to prevent the radicalization of individuals who might become recruits for terrorist groups.

KEY POINTS

- Terrorism was a problem long before the 9/11 attacks.
- Terrorism can be viewed as a problem to be resolved by military means (war on terrorism), by normal police techniques (terrorism as crime), or as a medical problem with underlying causes and symptoms (terrorism as disease).
- How terrorism is viewed will help to determine which policies governments adopt to deal with terrorism.

Concepts and definitions

There are a number of key concepts that are essential to any discussion of terrorism. The first is selecting a workable definition. A second concern involves targets and techniques, including the increasing concern about the danger that weapons of mass destruction present. A third key issue involves the prevalence of terrorism. Finally, it is useful to distinguish among some basic types of terrorist groups, including ethnic, religious, and ideological.

Definition of terrorism

There has been a multitude of definitions used for terrorism, partially because of disagreements among commentators or analysts and partially because some definers seek to exclude groups that they support or to include groups that they wish to denounce. Courts and police agencies require definitions that permit prosecution and incarceration; political leaders may have different needs and agendas. A working definition that is relatively neutral recognizes the basic fact that terrorism is a tactic used by many different kinds of groups. It includes six major elements. Terrorism involves (1) the use of violence or threat of violence; (2) by an organized group; (3) to achieve political objectives. The violence; (4) is directed against a target audience that extends beyond the immediate victims, who are often innocent civilians. Further (5), while a government can be either the perpetrator of violence or the target, it is considered an act of terrorism only if one or both actors is not a government. Finally, (6) terrorism is a weapon of the weak (Lutz and Lutz 2013: 8–9).

This definition excludes kidnappings for financial gain and excludes many acts by individuals. Organization is essential for a successful campaign to bring about the political goals that are being sought. While the exact political objectives vary, they can include changes in government policies or practices, changes in government leaders or structures, demands for regional autonomy or independence, or a mix of such political issues. Although organization is necessary for any chance of a successful campaign, individuals may operate in loose affiliation with a group. Individual dissidents may receive suggestions from leaders who maintain their distance from the operatives in the field in an organizational form that has come to be known as **leaderless resistance**. In such circumstances, individuals or small groups operate as part of a broader movement, even though they may not have direct links with a leadership. Groups as different as animal rights organizations, the American militia movement, and global jihadists have relied on leaderless resistance tactics (Joosse 2007). Anders Breivik, the Norwegian right-wing extremist who planted a bomb in Oslo and went on a shooting rampage against members of the youth wing of the Labour Party, drew inspiration from those opposed to increasing Muslim populations in Europe and their local leftist, political allies. Similarly, the Tsarnaev brothers in Boston may have seen themselves as Islamic militants battling the West.

Terrorism has a target audience that goes well beyond the immediate victims. Ultimately terrorist violence is a form of psychological warfare that undermines opposition to the terrorists' goals (Chalk 1996: 13). The violence generates fear in a target audience by attacking individuals who are representative of the larger group. This group can consist of members of the elite, supporters of the government, members of a particular ethnic or religious community, or the general public. Civilians are often chosen as targets, because they are more vulnerable than members of the security forces; furthermore, their deaths or injuries heighten the level of insecurity in the larger audience. It is often suggested that terrorist targets are chosen at random, but in fact terrorists usually pick their targets very carefully in order to influence an audience. The media often become important for this aspect of terrorism, since media coverage is very important for spreading fear, or at least in reaching the target audience more quickly, although target populations will usually become aware of attacks even when media attention is limited. Finally, terrorism is also a weapon utilized by the weak. Groups that can win elections or seize control of the government will do so; groups that cannot hope to win their objectives in other ways, however, may resort to terrorism.

Although terrorism can involve governments as targets or perpetrators, it does not include cases during cold and hot wars, even when governments use actions designed to instil terror. These government-to-government attacks are a different security issue and are not included in definitions of terrorism, even if they involve massacres, atrocities, war crimes, or even genocide. Governments, however, are often the targets of dissident terrorists. While governments usually oppose terrorists attacking their citizens, at times political leaders may tolerate terrorist attacks by private groups against enemies, potential dissidents, or unpopular minorities (ethnic, religious, cultural, or ideological). The government may fail to investigate or prosecute the perpetrators of the violence. In other cases governments may provide active support and in extreme cases even form death squads to attack their enemies while maintaining at least an illusion of deniability. Even though this governmental involvement in terrorism is quite important, it will not be the focus of this chapter, since the violence does not begin as a security concern (although violent groups that are tolerated may later challenge the government, as occurred with the **Fascists** in Italy).

Techniques and targets

The range of techniques available to terrorists is varied, but most activities are variations of standard practices—bombings, kidnappings, assaults including assassinations, and takeovers of buildings, planes, or ships, invariably with hostages. Bombs can be used to damage property or in efforts to inflict casualties, sometimes in large numbers. Car bombs have increasingly become a favourite device for terrorist groups because of the damage that they can do. Kidnapping frequently provides a publicity bonanza for terrorist groups. In some cases, ransoms from kidnappings have provided an important source of funding for terrorist organizations, and in other cases terrorists have been able to gain some concessions from governments in return for the release of the victims. Assaults are usually directed at individuals who represent a particular group (politicians, police, military personnel, journalists, and so on). Sometimes the intent is to wound, while in other cases the goal is the assassination of the individual or individuals. No one assassination is likely to bring about the changes the terrorists desire, but a campaign of such assassinations generates greater fear. Hostage situations in airline hijackings or the capture of buildings demonstrate the vulnerability of society and generate publicity for the terrorist cause. Even when governments refuse to make major concessions, they will often at least publicize a list of demands by the terrorists or publish other kinds of communiqués.

Weapons of mass destruction (WMD) have become a special security concern for governments. There is a great fear that some terrorist groups will use biological, chemical, nuclear, or radiological (dirty) weapons to cause more casualties. To some extent, terrorist groups have already gained a psychological edge simply because of the fear of their use. There have been only a few such attacks to date. **Aum Shinriyko**, the Japanese cult, attempted to use nerve gas in the Tokyo subway system to cause mass casualties but failed. The anthrax attacks in the United States after 9/11 generated great fear, but there were only a few deaths. A single bomb might have killed more people, but the use of anthrax made the attacks more terrifying. Most terrorists, however, still prefer to stick to the tried-and-true techniques, at least until the utility of a new technique, such as car bombs, has been demonstrated.

One deadly technique that has been increasingly used by terrorists is suicide attacks. Such attacks can be more deadly since casualties will be maximized. Some attacks have been devastating, as with the airliners on 9/11 and bombers in Israel. Suicide attacks as a technique were first used on a large scale by the Liberation Tigers of Tamil Eelam (LTTE) in Sri Lanka, more commonly known as the **Tamil Tigers**. They were responsible for more suicide attacks than all other groups combined between 1980 and 2000 (Radu 2002). Such attacks have increased in various parts of the Middle East, Chechnya, and elsewhere in the twenty-first century. Many of these attacks have inflicted large numbers of casualties, while others have been directed against important political figures. The increased use of suicide attacks by all kinds of terrorist organizations is one indication of how successful such tactics have been in gaining publicity and heightening fear in target audiences. Suicide attacks send a clear message about the commitment of organizations and individuals. Perhaps the greatest danger in the future is that a suicide attack might be combined with the use of biological, chemical, or radiological weapons. If the persons involved in the use of these weapons are willing to die in the effort, many of the problems involved in using WMD will have been reduced.

Terrorists have great flexibility in choosing their targets. If one target is too carefully protected, they can simply shift to another. Some other individual, building, or large gathering of people will serve to send the message that everyone in the target audience is vulnerable. The ability to find vulnerable targets may be greater in democratic states, since government security is likely to be weaker than in equivalent authoritarian societies. There are limitations on how much a democratic state can monitor its citizens and visitors. Democracies also provide greater publicity for the cause, since the media face few, if any, restraints. Further, even if the terrorists are caught, they will be tried in some type of impartial judicial setting where proof of guilt must be established. Of course, it is not only democratic countries that are vulnerable. Security forces may be weak in a variety of non-democratic political systems providing terrorist groups with opportunities to operate relatively freely.

Prevalence of terrorism

Terrorism has been present in the world for centuries. Tables 21.1 and 21.2 draw upon the Global Terrorism Database maintained at the University of Maryland. This database incorporates material from earlier databases. The data include both domestic and international terrorist incidents designed to achieve social, economic, or political objectives. The levels of terrorism were relatively low prior to 2001 but increased in that year. They declined briefly after 2001 but increased significantly after 2003, reflecting turmoil in Iraq and increasing instability in Afghanistan after US resources were diverted to Iraq. It is obvious that since the beginning of the twenty-first century, terrorism has increased. The years 2007 and 2012 have particularly high levels of fatalities. Latin America, West Europe, and North America (except in 2001) had relatively low levels in terms of incidents and fatalities in the first decade of the twenty-first century. Terrorist activities in Asia and in the Middle East and North Africa have been particularly high, with violence in sub-Saharan Africa showing more recent increases. The continuing violence in Afghanistan, Pakistan, Iraq, Israel/Palestine, and India as well as internal conflicts in the Congo, Sierra Leone, Liberia, and Guinea has contributed to these higher levels.

KEY POINTS

- Statistics indicate that terrorism increased significantly after 9/11 and remains at higher levels than in earlier years.
- Domestic terrorism is often not as newsworthy as international actions, but it accounts for a majority of terrorist attacks.
- Terrorist groups can be very flexible in their choice of targets.
- Terrorist groups often find that democratic states or weaker authoritarian political systems are more inviting targets.
- Some groups may be willing to use weapons of mass destruction, but most terrorist organizations continue to rely on conventional weapons for their attacks.

Table 21.1 Terrorist incidents, by region, 1998–2013

Year	Region							
	Africa	Asia[1]	East Europe[2]	Latin America	West Europe	Middle East	North America[3]	Total
1999	140	323	151	138	227	296	55	1,330
2000	182	608	229	160	239	252	40	1,264
2001	161	581	260	232	228	353	45	1,860
2002	118	441	111	161	119	310	34	1,294
2003	67	482	107	125	121	295	33	1,230
2004	35	468	53	47	56	488	12	1,159
2005	57	766	85	52	98	796	24	2,193
2006	110	1,179	64	55	95	1,123	12	2,648
2007	269	1,179	64	48	70	1,311	19	2,960
2008	354	2,137	225	142	157	1,469	26	4,510
2009	273	2,454	152	169	181	1,313	13	4,555
2010	309	2,383	266	147	132	1,398	23	4,658
2011	468	2,312	67	51	51	1,536	9	4,494
2012	894	3,540	150	112	180	1,983	24	6,883
2013	740	4,872	131	156	230	3,775	26	9,930

[1] Includes Australasia and the Pacific islands.

[2] Former communist countries of Eastern Europe and successor states of the Soviet Union in Europe and Asia.

[3] United States, Canada, and Mexico.

Source: START (2014).

Types and causes of terrorism

Terrorism has been widespread, and there is no single cause that explains outbreaks of this kind of violence. It is a complex phenomenon with many facets. Linked with the causes of terrorism are the motivations of the various organizations involved in the violence, motivations that provide some clues as to the underlying causes. These motivations can be used to categorize groups in terms of their objectives. The basic types are religious, ethnic or nationalist, and ideological. Additionally, there are groups that are more difficult to place into any particular category given the complexity of their motivations.

Categories

Religious groups obviously come to mind in the twenty-first century, given their prevalence in recent years. Al-Qaeda is the most prominent example since 2000, with the global nature of its attacks, but it is not the only such group in operation. There are other Islamic groups, some with linkages to Al-Qaeda and the broader global jihadist movement, that have been active in Indonesia, India, Pakistan, Israel and the Occupied Territories, Russia, Algeria, the Philippines, and other countries. Religious terrorism, however, has not been limited to Islamic organizations; extremists' groups in other religious traditions have also used the

Table 21.2 Terrorist fatalities, by region, 1998–2013

Year	Region							
	Africa	Asia[1]	East Europe[2]	Latin America	West Europe	Middle East	North America[3]	Total
1999	784	938	469	287	11	635	5	3,129
2000	962	1,536	275	438	37	555	5	3,808
2001	1,040	1,511	286	572	45	910	3,003	7,367
2002	813	1,484	476	366	9	1,123	4	4,275
2003	483	1,088	338	196	5	974	2	3,086
2004	321	1,802	674	127	195	2,534	0	5,653
2005	378	1,548	169	153	58	3,636	2	5,944
2006	953	3,045	61	100	4	4,959	2	9,124
2007	1,262	3,710	61	77	16	6,747	25	11,898
2008	1,340	3,643	111	100	3	3,324	18	8,539
2009	1,226	4,162	193	137	13	2,903	6	8,640
2010	715	3,657	241	58	5	2,583	4	7,173
2011	1,129	3,254	109	24	71	2,356	0	6,943
2012	1,980	5,208	149	121	10	3,614	14	11,096
2013	2,944	6,493	138	81	5	8,939	55	18,655

The exact number of fatalities occurring in some attacks is unknown.

[1] Includes Australasia and the Pacific islands.

[2] Former communist countries of Eastern Europe and successor states of the Soviet Union in Europe and Asia.

[3] United States, Canada, and Mexico.

Source: START (2014).

technique. The violent anti-abortion activities in the United States are based in Christian viewpoints. Christian beliefs were used to justify ethnic cleansing activities against Muslims in Bosnia. There was a guerrilla struggle in the Indian **Punjab** in the 1980s and 1990s that pitted **Sikhs** against Hindus. The Sikh uprising was in part a reaction to extremist Hindu groups in India that sought to reclaim the subcontinent for their religion and to drive out foreign religions, especially Islam and also Christianity. Jewish extremists, justifying their actions by religious beliefs, have used terrorist tactics against Palestinians, and a Jewish extremist assassinated prime minister Yitzak Rabin for making concessions to the Palestinians. Aum Shinrikyo was attempting to cleanse Japanese society of its impurities. Many religious groups are too weak to impose their views in other fashions, and terrorism then becomes the weapon that they use.

Groups defined by their ethnic or linguistic identifications are another broad category (see Case Study 21.2). The Basque **Euzkadi ta Askatasuna** (ETA—Basque for Homeland and Freedom) has been seeking independence for the Basque region of Spain since 1959, and began using violence to achieve that goal in 1968. Until their defeat, the Tamil Tigers sought independence (or at least autonomy) for those areas

CASE STUDY 21.2 Palestinian Liberation Organization (PLO)

The struggle between the Israelis and the Palestinians is often seen as a religious conflict, but it was for many years primarily a clash of nationalisms. Most of the initial Jewish settlers who engaged in terrorism were largely secular, and the original Palestinian resistance movements were overwhelmingly secular as well. Only in the 1990s did Palestinian dissidents take on overtly religious objectives, such as the creation of an Islamic Palestinian state in all of the Occupied Territories and Israel. The **Palestinian Liberation Organization (PLO)** always focused on Palestinian nationalism and stressed secular themes, so that it could appeal to both Muslim and Christian Palestinians. It was an umbrella organization that included many different Palestinian nationalist groups, but it never included avowedly Islamic groups. **Fatah**, the organization led by Yasser Arafat, was one of the most important organizations, but others like the **Popular Front for the Liberation of Palestine (PFLP)** combined leftist ideology with Palestinian nationalism. For them, the Palestinians were an oppressed Third World people battling against the evils of global capitalism and its Israeli representatives in the Middle East. After the defeat of the Arab armies in the 1967 war, the PLO shifted to terrorism as the remaining hope for creating a Palestinian homeland. Some groups, such as the PFLP among others, left the PLO (temporarily or permanently) because of disputes over the course of action to be followed—for example, when terrorist attacks were limited, when they were discontinued, and when the agreement to create the Palestinian Authority was made in Oslo. The PLO and Fatah have been displaced to some extent by **Hamas** and the Palestinian **Islamic Jihad** which have a much more religious orientation that drives their activities.

of Sri Lanka where Tamils are a majority. Turkey has faced significant terrorist attacks from Kurdish separatist groups. A large number of anti-colonial groups in the past were ethnically based and used terrorism as one tactic in their efforts to gain independence. Algerian nationalists mounted a major urban terrorism campaign against the French in the late 1950s to supplement guerrilla activities. Greek Cypriots also used urban terrorism and guerrilla attacks against the British in the same period.

Other terrorist groups have drawn their ideas from ideologies. There was a wave of terrorist violence in Europe in the 1970s and 1980s rooted in various leftist and Marxist ideologies. The **Red Brigades** in Italy, the **Red Army Faction** in Germany, and other groups in Europe were joined by Japanese groups, the **Weathermen** in the United States, and organizations in Latin America. The leftist wave was on the wane by the last part of the 1980s, when the collapse of communism in East Europe and the Soviet Union weakened the surviving groups even further. Some leftist groups have survived and have continued to be active in Nepal, India, Mexico, and the Philippines. Terrorist groups based in right-wing ideologies have also been present. Such groups were relatively weak in the years after the Second World War, but a great number of them appeared in the 1990s in Western Europe. These groups have often been opposed to foreign influences, a large state, or leftist ideas. They have frequently targeted migrants and foreign workers, especially those from the Middle East, South Asia, or sub-Saharan Africa where cultural, ethnic, and religious differences reinforced each other. Anders Breivik identified with these views. Such groups have their counterparts in the United States with **xenophobic** and anti-black groups. The Ku Klux Klan was once one of the largest of such groups (see Case Study 21.3). It was severely weakened in the 1960s and 1970s, but its place has been taken by a large number of smaller groups espousing some of the same racist and anti-foreign ideas. When groups from the left and right have battled each other, more conservative governments tolerated the violent right-wing groups that targeted members of the left.

Some groups are more difficult to categorize. A number of right-wing groups in the United States incorporate Christianity into their ideologies (sometimes in unusual ways). The **Irish Republican Army (IRA)** in Northern Ireland has mobilized support on the basis of Irish versus British nationalities, but the role of religion in the struggles in the province cannot be denied. Ideology has also appeared in this struggle since the **Irish National Liberation Army** (**INLA**) shared the ethnic Irish basis of the IRA, but also included a Marxist-Leninist ideological component. In Colombia, there were some straightforwardly Marxist-Leninist terrorist groups that operated in the country, but others such as the **Revolutionary Armed Forces of Colombia** (**FARC**) joined forces with drug cartels. In Peru in the 1980s and 1990s, dissident organizations combining leftist ideology with an ethnic appeal to the Indian communities that have been ignored by the Europeanized elite of the country developed links with the drug groups in that country.

CASE STUDY 21.3 The Ku Klux Klan (KKK)

The KKK is a classic American terrorist group that propounded racist and right-wing views in the 1950s and 1960s. It tried to terrorize Black Americans and their white supporters during the civil rights struggle of those years. Lynchings, murders, and bombs were used in failed attempts to dissuade people from agitating for equal rights. This period, violent though it was, resulted in hundreds of deaths. The most active period for the KKK was in the 1920s, when the KKK combined its racist orientation with opposition to the presence of Catholics, Jews, and Orientals. It was also opposed to the arrival of new immigrants (many of whom were Catholic or Jewish). In these years, the KKK had significant strength outside the Southern states; in fact, Indiana (in the Midwest) at one time had the largest membership of any state branch. The overall level of violence by racist and anti-foreign groups, including the KKK, was greater in this period with lynchings and murders totalling in the thousands (Hofstader 1970: 65). Many of the dead were Black Americans, but members of other groups were also victims. Whites were at times the main targets, as they were considered more dangerous by the KKK because they had been contaminated by foreign ideas (Tucker 1991: 5). The KKK eventually declined, partially as a consequence of scandals that involved the leaders, including the leader of the Indiana chapter (Chalmers 1965: 167–70).

Drug cartels have become an increasing threat in Mexico. Thousands have died. While some of the violence reflects battles among competing criminal groups, in other cases the intent of the violence has been to intimidate government officials, the police, or the general public. These criminal groups eventually could start to cooperate with anti-government organizations. Drug organizations have cooperated with terrorist groups in many other countries as well, and there are increasing connections between criminal organizations and terrorist groups.

Causes

The causes of terrorism are in many ways similar to the causes of most other forms of political violence (such as riots, rebellions, coups, and civil wars). Individuals in a society become so discontented or frustrated with their inability to bring about what they see as necessary changes since other means of seeking change have failed that they resort to violence. The dissidents have a perception that society and the political system discriminate or are unfair. What is ultimately important are the perceptions of the dissidents, although greater levels of exploitation may drive larger numbers to attempt violent change.

There are some specific factors, however, that can contribute to outbreaks of terrorism. Many regard terrorists as mentally deranged or otherwise suffering from psychological problems. There is little evidence that such a situation actually exists. From the evidence available, terrorists appear to be no more likely to suffer from psychological disorders than members of the general population. Poverty has been suggested as an underlying cause of terrorism, but analyses have indicated that poverty is not linked to terrorist outbreaks. Terrorism is not prevalent in poorer countries, and terrorists are not more likely to come from the poorer sections of individual societies. While poverty may in fact be a contributing factor in many cases, there is no compelling evidence that terrorism is linked to poverty in any systematic way. The general characteristics of a political system can be a factor. Democracies with their limitations on the security forces provide opportunities for terrorists. Limited political participation and repression by government forces can also breed the necessary popular discontent for violence, but states with strong security forces and firm control of their societies can usually prevent terrorists from operating. Dissidents and potential dissidents can be jailed, suspects can be tortured, families can be held hostage, and convictions can be guaranteed in the courts (if trials occur). When the Soviet Union was a strong centralized system, terrorism was virtually unknown. The successor states are weaker, and some, like Russia, have faced significant terrorist problems. It is the inability of the government of Colombia to function effectively in many parts of the country that has provided significant opportunities for guerrillas and terrorists, as well as the drug cartels, to survive and prosper. Similarly, the weak state in Yemen has permitted groups like **Al-Qaeda in the Arabian Peninsula** opportunities to operate, while the lack of an effective government in Somalia has also provided opportunities for terrorist groups to operate.

The processes involved with globalization have also contributed to outbreaks of terrorism. With faster communications and transportation, outside forces—usually Western—intrude into local societies.

Economies are disrupted, and, even if winners outnumber losers, there are still losers. Further, local cultures, including religious components, are threatened by globalization, especially when it has been accompanied by secularization. Terrorism in many cases can be seen as a reaction to globalization. Leftist groups around the world have opposed the spread of capitalism and all its evils. Secular globalization also leads to religious and ethnic fragmentation (Ramakrishna and Tan 2003: 3–4). Many religious groups (Christian, Jewish, Muslim, Hindu) are opposed to the secularism that comes with modernity (Pillar 2001: 65). Right-wing, ethnocentric groups have opposed the dilution of their cultures by the outside ideas that accompany migrants, guest workers, and refugees. It is perhaps ironic that some Muslims in the Middle East feel threatened by the intrusion of European or Western values at the same time that extremist groups in Europe feel threatened by individuals from Middle Eastern cultures with Islamic ideas. Terrorism rooted in ethnic differences can also reflect the intrusion of outside forces, and groups like the Irish and the Basques fear the submergence of their language and culture into a larger ethnic identity (Dingley and Kirk-Smith 2002).

Ultimately, there are a number of underlying causes that combine in different ways in different circumstances to create the conditions that are conducive to outbreaks of terrorism. For example, globalization can lead to changes in societies that increase poverty and weaken governments. The appearance of new democracies is a consequence of globalization and the spread of new ideas. The presence of democratic systems, however, has only been associated with more terrorism in some circumstances (Lutz and Lutz 2010). Thus, although it is possible that the creation of new democracies may eventually lead to less terrorism sometime in the future, in the short term, the appearance of new democratic systems may provide additional opportunities for terrorist groups to appear.

KEY POINTS

- There is no one cause of terrorism.
- Terrorism is a technique that is available to different kinds of groups pursuing different types of objectives.
- Terrorism is not unique to Islam or the Middle East.
- Globalization and responses to it can be linked to fresh outbreaks of terrorism.

Security measures

Leaders and governments facing terrorist attacks have to defend against these attacks. Since there is no one overwhelming cause or source of terrorism, both because it is a technique that can be used by different groups for different objectives and, because different factors cause terrorism, countermeasures become more difficult. Sederberg's threefold typology is relevant as a point of reference, because some security or counterterrorism measures are more in keeping with viewing terrorism as war, others fit terrorism as crime, and yet others are more relevant for the disease analogy. Counterterrorism measures can also be considered within the scope of prevention, response to attacks, international collaboration, and the effects of security measures on civil liberties.

Prevention

Prevention is normally associated with the concept of terrorism as war or crime. All governments will practise prevention—repression from the terrorist perspective—seeking to arrest or eliminate those actively involved in the violence. Security forces want to attack the terrorists before they strike (war) or to arrest them after the attack (crime). Clearly, whichever concept of battling terrorism is chosen helps to determine security policies. The war conceptualization, for example, permits a stronger pre-emptive response. In actual fact, however, the military and police functions do not have a precise dividing line. Police forces dealing with dangerous criminals (terrorist or otherwise) may shoot first and ask questions later. In both the warfare and criminal models, there may be a desire to capture terrorists to elicit further intelligence, sometimes by offering shorter sentences to a captured terrorist in exchange for information. Informers inside the terrorist groups can be key assets for the security forces for gathering intelligence. The use of informers is difficult in the case of small groups; they are usually too cohesive for effective infiltration. Larger organizations are easier to penetrate and thus gain information, but it is unlikely that all the operations of larger groups can be stopped by intelligence gathering except with the passage of time. Similarly, loose network groups such as Al-Qaeda and right-wing extremist groups in the United States and Europe are difficult to dismantle because of any single intelligence coup, although actions based on successful intelligence gathering can weaken them, as was the case with the raid on bin Laden's compound in Pakistan.

Greater physical security measures are another preventive option that has merit. Not every possible target can be protected of course, but key installations, including potential sources of materials for weapons of mass destruction can be secured. In other cases security can be enhanced for many potential targets, even if all attacks cannot be prevented. Some terrorist activities might be foiled, and in other cases some members of the dissident groups may be captured or killed as a consequence of improved security. These preventative measures will not stop determined terrorists, who will seek other, more vulnerable targets (see Think Point 21.1). Increased security, of course, will mean increased costs, and the money spent on physical security and target hardening is not available elsewhere in the economy, which could result in important lost economic opportunities.

Responses

Responses to terrorist attacks vary, either explicitly or implicitly, if terrorism is seen as warfare, crime, or disease. If the war analogy holds, retaliation and punishment become the norms. Pre-emptive strikes against training facilities or at headquarters, or even the assassinations of key individuals in the terrorist organizations including strikes by drones are potential responses. Removal of key leaders is seen as one way to destroy a terrorist organization, although such decapitation may work in one case but in others may actually make the situation worse (Cronin 2009: 31–4). The United States and its allies have attempted to follow this strategy against Al-Qaeda, albeit with less than complete success. In their confrontations before the **Oslo Accords**, Israel and the PLO basically viewed their struggle in terms of covert warfare. Even though Israel considered the PLO and other Palestinian groups to be terrorists and consciously refused to consider Palestinians as soldiers, the context of the struggle was one of warfare. Israel has continued the same approach in dealing with attacks by Hamas and Islamic Jihad.

Arrest, capture, trial (fair or otherwise), and incarceration of suspected or known terrorists reflect the crime perspective. The ultimate goal of police forces is to deter action by demonstrating that criminals will be caught and punished. The same goal is present with terrorists; capture and punishment are inevitable. While the warfare analogy can attempt to deter terrorism by guaranteeing a quick, deadly response, deterrence is more central to a justice system. Pre-emptive strikes and assassinations are not normally part of the arsenal of crime fighting unless a government unleashes death squads as a form of state violence or permits groups allied with the government to attack in this fashion. In such circumstances, governments have shifted from the crime perspective to one closer to the warfare analogy. One form of pre-emption available in a normal criminal context is detention of suspects—sometimes for lengthy periods (but not indefinite ones), and perhaps judicial harassment of suspects. Hostage situations are one area where terrorism is frequently treated as crime. Police forces are usually better equipped and trained to deal with these kinds of situations. Even rescue attempts are not foreign to typical police practice, although some military units train for rescue operations. The war response might be more difficult for the hostages, since a military response might see them as potential casualties of a conflict with terrorists rather than considering their safety as the prime objective.

! THINK POINT 21.1 Security and the law of unintended consequences

Sometimes improved security can have unintended, and negative, consequences. In the 1960s and 1970s, the United States and other countries suffered through a wave of airline hijackings. Individuals from a variety of groups (and loners with no cause but a desire for publicity) skyjacked airliners and issued communiqués justifying their actions. Many of the aircraft were flown to Cuba or Algeria, where the hijackers received asylum in return for releasing the planes and passengers. In response to the hijackings, airport security was improved so that hijackings virtually ceased. Groups could no longer use this tactic to publicize their cause; therefore, some organizations shifted to planting bombs that destroyed airliners to raise public awareness of their objectives. The terrorists even developed sophisticated bombs that would begin a countdown to detonation only when a certain altitude was reached. Eventually baggage security at airports improved so that only an occasional bomb could be successfully placed on planes, but not before a number of airliners had been destroyed in mid-flight. In some ways, the use of airliners on 9/11 was a response to the difficulties of placing bombs on aircraft. It is clear that defensive security precautions can be important, but committed terrorists can find new techniques (Enders and Sandler 2006: 5). These new techniques may be more deadly than the methods that were replaced. Even if new techniques do not appear, terrorist organizations can find population groups or other targets that are now vulnerable.

If terrorism is viewed as a disease, the range of responses will change. Since diseases have both symptoms and causes, this perspective requires that some of the responses related to the war and crime views be applied. Terrorist violence, as a symptom, will need to be dealt with by arrest or prevention. The disease perspective, moreover, logically leads to efforts to deal with the underlying causes. Reform packages may become part of the government response in an effort to reduce the appeal of the terrorist groups within the population. If ethnic or religious discrimination is present, laws forbidding discrimination may be passed. If poverty is perceived to contribute to terrorism, then government programmes to reduce poverty in a region or group may be instituted (at least if the funds are available). If the terrorists are operating in a colonial situation, then the ultimate reform is for the colonial power to grant independence. Of course, it has been argued that reforms will simply encourage the terrorist to continue the violence because they are being rewarded. As one leader of a terrorist group argued, more was won by a few months of violence than by years of peaceful politics (Ash 2003: 63). Under these circumstances reforms may become concessions that fuel the violence rather than a mechanism for ending it; yet, there has been no compelling or consistent evidence that concessions encourage terrorists to continue to use violence to gain even more (Crenshaw 1998: 255). Like other counterterrorist approaches, sometimes concessions will work and sometimes they will make the situation worse.

There are other reasons why reforms cannot eliminate the presence of terrorism. Demands by the terrorist dissidents for the establishment of a religious state, a leftist government, the repression of a minority, or removal of all foreigners or foreign elements may not be acceptable to the majority. The leftists in the 1970s and 1980s in Europe wanted to do away with the international capitalist system, yet most Europeans wanted to continue to receive the benefits of capitalism. The spread of globalization or the intrusion of outside values and new cultures cannot be prevented. In other cases, extremist groups in the same country may have mutually incompatible goals. Extreme Jewish settler groups in Israel want complete control of the West Bank and all Palestinians to leave; Hamas wants to create an Islamic state in the whole of Israel, the West Bank, and the Gaza Strip. No Israeli government can meet the demands of both groups. In Turkey in the 1970s, dissident terrorists from the left and the right attacked the Turkish government. There was no programme available that could meet the demands of both sides. In circumstances such as these, even a government or political leaders otherwise amenable to reforms will have to rely on other options.

Outbreaks of terrorism had led to emphasizing counterterrorism and counter-insurgency (COIN) techniques to deal with dissidents. The US armed forces have reconstructed their COIN techniques after their experiences in Afghanistan and Iraq. The new COIN techniques in theory place the focus on 'winning the hearts and minds' of local populations (the disease approach) but ultimately implementation has relied on either military force or the police and security forces to actively deal with terrorists (treating terrorism as war or crime). Effective COIN operations normally require a long time line to be effective with established dissident campaigns (Wayne 2008: 15). Political necessity often leads governments to focus on short-term and tangible outcomes. One consequence is that notwithstanding the emphasis on dealing with underlying causes the actual practices still largely focus on preventing operations or catching the terrorists after the fact.

International measures

International cooperation among countries is another important counterterrorist technique. Intelligence agencies operate best on their own soil or in their own region; national intelligence agencies are not equally effective everywhere. Collaboration among intelligence agencies, as has occurred in the European Union, therefore, will contribute to the prevention of terrorism. International cooperation can also provide the necessary support for reforms that reduce the severity of terrorism. Sanctions against countries aiding terrorists have worked in the past, but in the second decade of the twenty-first century there are few state sponsors that can be targeted. Military action was effective in toppling the Taliban regime in Afghanistan and ending its support for Al-Qaeda, and this military action had widespread international support (unlike the invasion of Iraq in 2003). While cooperative international sanctions do not always work, it is important to note that they have not always failed.

A great deal of international diplomacy has involved attempts to define terrorism so that all countries could then take steps to eliminate terrorist groups. These efforts have faltered because countries often support or sympathize with dissidents who use violence against repressive governments. Governments in the developing world have wanted to avoid situations where anti-colonial struggles are labelled as terrorism. Most countries have not favoured too strict a definition, since they want the flexibility to avoid extradition or punishment of some political dissidents. The United States would not have considered anti-Saddam Hussein dissidents as terrorists had they attacked members of his regime. There have been some successes in the international sphere. Certain types of actions, such as air piracy, have been outlawed, and most members of the United Nations have signed these treaties and conventions (Pillar 2001: 77–9). These partial agreements are a positive step in the process of containing terrorism by defining certain actions as crimes. When global agreements are not possible, diplomacy can achieve agreements among smaller groups of countries, providing for greater cooperation and bilateral arrangements that automatically prohibit asylum for individuals associated with certain organizations. The United States and the United Kingdom, for example, eventually signed a bilateral agreement making it easier to extradite suspected IRA members from the United States.

Civil liberties in peril

A final concern that has appeared with counterterrorism efforts in many countries is the potential threat that such measures can have for civil liberties. Democracies cannot routinely use torture, threaten the families of suspects, guarantee convictions, maintain intrusive surveillance of individuals, or kill suspected terrorists, while authoritarian states do not worry about civil liberties. There are also limits on intelligence gathering and pre-emptive actions in democracies. Increased security measures can lead to infringements on the rights of citizens or foreign residents. In the United States, the **Patriot Act** has permitted lengthy detention of non-citizens on only suspicion of terrorism, more intensive surveillance techniques, limited access to lawyers for nationals, and deportation of non-citizens, with little opportunity to defend themselves. In addition, persons captured overseas have been placed in indefinite detention at the **Guantanamo Naval Base** in Cuba with initially virtually no access to legal assistance. Recent cases before US courts including the Supreme Court have provided the prisoners with some ability to challenge their detention. Others captured outside of the United States have been sent to countries where suspects have few or no rights and thus can be subjected to vigorous interrogation. There have also been efforts to establish special tribunals to try suspected terrorists that would be expected to operate in ways to make conviction of suspects more likely than would be the case in normal courts. In Northern Ireland, IRA intimidation of jurors led to the use of courts without juries, and preventative detention for IRA suspects was also introduced. Special terrorism laws passed in the United Kingdom increased the danger of wrongful convictions. Even without special legislation, judges and juries may be quick to assume the guilt of suspected terrorists. Germany, France, and Australia—like the United Kingdom and the United States—passed new legislation after the events of 9/11, giving government security forces greater powers to detain and interrogate those suspected of terrorism (Haubrick 2003). India has infringed on the civil rights of citizens in its struggles with Sikhs in the Punjab, dissidents in Kashmir, and opposition groups elsewhere in the country. While Israel has generally respected the rights of its own citizens, its treatment of Palestinian suspects has been much less concerned with civil rights. Even though emergency laws and procedures may be necessary in especially serious situations of terrorist challenges, such laws should be temporary and subject to frequent review in democracies (Wilkinson 2006: 62).

In such circumstances, there is always the danger of convicting innocent people (see Case Study 21.4). There is also a danger that suspect communities will be created. Individuals may be targeted for investigation (profiled) because of their religion or ethnicity or political beliefs. The general public may also effectively undermine individual rights by their suspicions. Civil liberties are in the least danger if terrorism is viewed as a disease where the root causes need to be treated. The crime model provides for some threat to civil liberties, but defenders of civil liberties frequently deal with the police and criminal justice system and politicians aware they are under scrutiny. The greatest danger comes when governments regard the battle against terrorism as warfare because most democratic countries permit greater restrictions on the rights of individuals during wartime. As a consequence, viewing the struggle with terrorism as war tends to bring with it the idea that temporary personal sacrifices of liberties may be necessary in the interest of victory. Ultimately, civil liberties in democratic societies can be in jeopardy. 'Overreaction and general repression ... could destroy democracy far more rapidly and effectively than any campaign by a terrorist group' (Wilkinson 2006: 61).

KEY POINTS

- Detection and prevention of terrorist attacks will not always be possible, since terrorists have choices among vulnerable targets.
- Dealing with terrorism within the context of warfare is more likely to result in pre-emptive actions.
- Considering terrorism within the disease perspective places greater emphasis on reforms than either the crime or the war perspective.
- International cooperation for dealing with terrorism would appear to have natural limits, and any global agreements on a meaningful definition of terrorism are unlikely.
- The greatest threat to civil liberties in democracies comes in those contexts where the battle against terrorism is seen as being equivalent to war.

CASE STUDY 21.4 Miscarriages of justice with Irish defendants

In 1974, IRA attack teams set off bombs in Woolwich in London and Guildford in Surrey that killed off-duty service personnel (and others). A month later two pubs in Birmingham were bombed. These bombings led to the passage of the **Prevention of Terrorism Acts** (Temporary Provisions)—initially renewed and then given permanent status—which provided for longer detention of IRA suspects for questioning and other changes that facilitated intelligence gathering. Four suspects (the Guildford Four) were arrested, convicted, and imprisoned on shaky evidence and coerced confessions. Their arrests also led to the arrest and conviction on weak forensic evidence of seven more suspects (the Maguire Seven). The bombings in Birmingham resulted in the conviction of six individuals (the Birmingham Six) with weak evidence and coerced confessions. Sixteen of the seventeen individuals were Irish, and the seventeenth was the English girlfriend of one of the suspects. The special interrogation procedures available to the authorities under the terrorism legislation permitted over-zealous police officers to coerce confessions and manipulate evidence to convict the individuals whom the police thought were guilty. Juries were clearly inclined to believe the police and be doubtful of the Irish suspects. While there is no evidence that the police, the courts, or the government had a concerted policy to manufacture convictions, the climate of fear and the desire to convict someone for the bombings contributed to these miscarriages of justice and the imprisonment of these seventeen innocent persons (Lutz et al. 2002).

Conclusion

It is clear that terrorism will remain a major security threat for years to come. The ethnic, religious, and ideological disputes that have fuelled terrorism in the past have not disappeared. While ideological terrorism has declined with the end of communism, it has not disappeared as right-wing groups and fewer leftist groups continue to operate. Ethnically and religiously inspired terrorism remains very important. Groups that cannot attain their goals through the electoral process or government takeovers will often adopt terrorism as a technique. Globalization will continue to disrupt economic, political, social, religious, and cultural systems. Weak states will be inviting targets for attacks or provide terrorists with convenient bases. Government repression will generate opposition. Connections between terrorists and criminal groups could increase.

Providing security against terrorism will not be easy. There are too many targets. Terrorists have the advantage of being able to choose targets that are not defended. No one countermeasure will defeat terrorism—it has multifaceted causes and is a technique that can be used by many different groups. Success against one group will not guarantee success against another. There is no magic bullet that will guarantee success against all types of groups or even most terrorist organizations. Groups come from different backgrounds, have different kinds of support, and seek different objectives. Under these circumstances it would be amazing if there was one countermeasure that always worked. In some cases, normal police methods will be very successful. Treating terrorism as crime, for example, could be quite appropriate when terrorists have links with drug cartels. Considering terrorism as war is relevant in cases where the dissident groups combine terrorism with guerrilla activities, as has been the case with the resurgent Taliban in Afghanistan or the Islamic State in Iraq and Syria (ISIS) in those countries. In other cases there may be some value in governments considering reforms as one means of weakening support for the dissidents or as a compromise to end violence. Looking at terrorism from the perspective of war, crime, or disease is useful for analysis and for pinpointing problems that can occur when one or the other of these particular approaches is taken, but many terrorist groups do not fit neatly into any one situation. The necessary response will often be a mixture of elements involving all three, and determining the appropriate mix of security programmes and responses to terrorism will never be easy. Security measures for dealing with terrorist threats are likely to require flexibility, and government security forces will have to change techniques in different circumstances.

QUESTIONS

1. Is terrorism likely to become more prevalent or less prevalent around the world?
2. Which areas of the world are most vulnerable to terrorism and why?
3. What other categories of terrorism might be added to the religious, ideological, and ethnic varieties?
4. What role do media outlets play in international terrorism and domestic terrorism?
5. What techniques might be most effective in dealing with different kinds of terrorism? Why?
6. Does the appearance of leaderless resistance styles of terrorism or network systems create special problems for countermeasures?
7. Is terrorism best dealt with as war, crime, or disease in your country?
8. What counterterrorism measures would be most effective in dealing with terrorism in your country?
9. What changes (if any) will occur in the next decade in how terrorist groups operate? How will ways of providing security against terrorism change?
10. Are efforts to defeat or contain terrorism a great threat to civil liberties?

FURTHER READING

- Bjorgo, Tore (ed.) (2005), *Root Causes of Terrorism: Myths, Reality, and Ways Forward*, London: Routledge. This volume provides a comprehensive survey of the types of terrorism (ethnic, religious, ideological, criminal) and techniques with reference to recent events.
- Cronin, Audrey Kurth (2009), *How Terrorism Ends: Understanding the Decline and Demise of Terrorist Campaigns*, Princeton, NJ: Princeton University Press. Cronin provides an excellent summary of the ways in which terrorist groups can be defeated or reintegrated into the political system. The analysis clearly indicates that no one method is superior in all cases.
- Enders, Walter and Sandler, Todd (2006), *The Political Economy of Terrorism*, Cambridge: Cambridge University Press. This book is a compilation of the authors' earlier work. It involves some empirical assessment of terrorism, but it also contains excellent overviews on key topics as well.
- Hoffman, Bruce (2006), *Inside Terrorism*, rev. and expanded edn, New York: Columbia University Press. The new edition of this book, like its predecessor, is one of the best introductions to the topic of terrorist groups and terrorism.

- Kegley, Charles W., Jr (ed.) (2003), *The New Global Terrorism: Characteristics, Causes, Controls*, Upper Saddle River, NJ: Prentice Hall. This collection of short articles is still one of the best compilations of works in the field; it covers virtually all the basic issues from a variety of perspectives.
- Lutz, James and Lutz, Brenda (2013), *Global Terrorism*, 3rd edn, London: Routledge. This textbook uses case studies to provide historical and geographical depth to the discussion of terrorism. While terrorism in the Middle East and by extremist Islamic groups is covered, the book clearly avoids concentrating on these topics to the exclusion of others.
- Tan, Andrew H. T. (2006), *The Politics of Terrorism: A Survey*, London: Routledge. This volume is an excellent source of information. It contains chapters by individual authors on the various types of terrorism or techniques that are used as well as a very useful compilation of the types of groups that have been operating on some of the key terrorist incidents.
- Tucker, Jonathan B. (ed.) (2000), *Toxic Terror: Assessing Terrorist Use of Chemical and Biological Weapons*, Cambridge, MA: MIT Press. This volume documents various attempts to use chemical and biological weapons by terrorist groups. Most ended in failures, although the attacks by Aum Shinrikyo in Japan have been an obvious exception. The conclusions drawn from the book about the relative danger of such attacks remain valid today.
- Wilkinson, Paul (2006), *Terrorism versus Democracy: The Liberal State Response*, 2nd edn, London: Routledge. Wilkinson provides an overview of terrorism and terrorist groups and then discusses the effects that terrorism has had on Western democracies.

IMPORTANT WEBSITES

- **http://www.comw.org/rma** Project on Defense Alternatives, Revolution on Military Affairs (RMA)—maintained by the Commonwealth Institute, Cambridge, MA. This website provides access to papers and other works dealing with terrorism, including some papers (from conferences or as working papers) that are not readily available elsewhere.
- **http//www.start.umd.edu/gtd** National Consortium for the Study of Terrorism and Responses to Terrorism (START), Global Terrorism Database. This database contains information on incidents and casualties by country, region, type of attack, and group from the 1970s forward. This database is a continuation of materials that were first collected at St Andrews and then incorporated into the National Memorial Institute for the Prevention of Terrorism. It is the best source for such information.
- **http://www.nctc.gov/** This is the website of the National Counterterrorism Center (NCTC). This centre took over incident reports from the State Department and has published a number of annual reports in recent years with useful data. The volumes for individual years are more readily accessed with a search engine with the search term 'Reports on Incidents of Terrorism'.

Visit the Online Resource Centre that accompanies this book for lots of interesting additional material: www.oxfordtextbooks.co.uk/orc/collins4e/

22

Humanitarian Intervention

Alex J. Bellamy

Chapter Contents

Reader's Guide

This chapter provides an overview of the debate between those who believe that the protection of civilians from genocide and mass atrocities ought to trump the principle of non-intervention in certain circumstances and those who oppose this proposition. This has become a particular problem in the post-Cold War world where the commission of atrocities in places like Rwanda, Bosnia, and Darfur prompted calls, in the West especially, for international society to step in to protect the victims with military force if necessary. Although it might seem morally appealing to intervene to protect populations from death and destruction, humanitarian intervention causes problems for international security by potentially weakening the rules governing the use of force in world politics. Since the end of the Cold War, a broad international consensus has emerged around a principle called the '**Responsibility to Protect**' (**R2P**). The R2P holds that states have a responsibility to protect their populations from genocide and mass atrocities and that the international community has a duty to help states fulfil their responsibilities and use various measures to protect populations when their own states are manifestly failing to do so. In 2011, the principle helped the UN Security Council authorize the use of force against a sovereign state for human protection purposes for the first time in its history.

Introduction

'Humanitarian intervention' refers to the use of military force by external actors for humanitarian purposes, usually against the wishes of the host government. There have been several humanitarian interventions since the end of the Cold War (see Table 22.1). In the 1990s, **genocide** in Rwanda (1994) killed at least 800,000, war in the former Yugoslavia (1992–5) left at least 250,000 dead, and forced thousands more to flee. Protracted conflicts in Sierra Leone, Sudan, Haiti, Somalia, Liberia, East Timor, the Democratic Republic of Congo (DRC), and elsewhere killed millions more. This century, conflict in the Darfur region of Sudan cost the lives of around 250,000 people and forced more than three million people from their homes (Coebergh 2005). In what Mary Kaldor (1999) famously described as 'new wars', civilian deaths are a direct war aim, not an unfortunate by-product (see Slim 2008). Although most of these wars involved non-state militia groups, sometimes the worst perpetrators of crimes against civilians are states and their allies. According to one study, in the twentieth century around forty million civilians were killed in wars between states, whilst nearly six times that number were killed by their own governments (Rummel 1994: 21).

Historically, genocides perpetrated by states against sections of their own populations have ended in one of two ways: either the perpetrators succeed in destroying their target group or they are defeated in battle. This cold fact is borne out by recent cases. The 1994 Rwandan genocide ended with the defeat of the Rwandan government and *Interehamwe* militia at the hands of a rebel group known as the Rwandan Patriotic Front (RPF). The rate of killing in Darfur has declined from its peak in 2003–4 primarily because the *Janjaweed* militia and their government backers largely succeeded in forcing their enemies into exile. A combination of NATO airpower and local armed resistance prevented the Qaddafi regime in Libya from perpetrating a massacre in Benghazi in 2011. When it was confronted by armed opponents the government of Syria refused to back down, resulting in a protracted civil war that has cost the lives of some 200,000 people.

Facts like this pose a major challenge to international security. For liberals and realists, security is best pursued through a society of sovereign states that enjoy exclusive jurisdiction over a particular piece of territory and rights to non-interference and non-intervention that are enshrined in the Charter of the United Nations. Article 2(4) of the **United Nations Charter** (UN Charter) forbids the threat or use of force by states in their dealings with one another and Article 2(7) prohibits the UN from interfering in the domestic affairs of its member states. There are only two exceptions to the ban on the use of force contained in Article 2(4): Article 39 gives the UN Security Council the right to authorize military action in cases where it identifies a 'threat to international peace and security' and Article 51 recognizes that all states have an inherent right to use force in self-defence.

From this perspective, the security of the state is considered important, and worth protecting, because states provide security to individuals. It should be clear from the preceding paragraphs, however, that this assumption is problematic. In the past, threats to human security have tended to come more from an individual's own state than from other states. This raises the question of whether there are circumstances in which the security of individuals should be privileged over the security of states. Should a state's right to be secure and free from external interference be conditional on its fulfilment of certain responsibilities to its citizens, not least a responsibility to protect them from mass killing?

If we think that there are circumstances in which the use of force for humanitarian purposes is legitimate, we are then confronted by a range of practical questions about the utility of force in promoting humanitarian objectives. It is widely accepted that, although it sometimes provides the only means of protecting civilians from grave harm, military force is a relatively blunt humanitarian instrument. It is much better, and cheaper, to prevent humanitarian catastrophes in the first place than to intervene and rebuild afterwards (Carnegie Commission 1997). Sometimes, as in Somalia in 1993 and Kosovo in 1999, armed intervention seems to make the situation worse. There are also claims that the potential for foreign intervention might encourage rebels to take up arms and provoke their government to attack the civilian population (Kuperman 2008).

In recent years, important progress has been made towards building an international consensus on some of these questions. Most notably, the R2P principle adopted by over 150 world leaders in 2005 and reaffirmed by the UN Security Council several times since (most recently in Resolution 2150 (2014)) attempts to reconcile the twin concerns of state sovereignty and human security by setting out the responsibilities that states have towards their own citizens, and

Table 22.1 Interventions for ostensibly humanitarian reasons, post-Cold War era

Place	Date	Intervener	UN Authority?	Consent?	Type of intervention	Outcome
Liberia	1990–7	ECOWAS–Nigeria	No—but later welcomed by UN	Initially, but ECOWAS then forcibly engaged with the Charles Taylor faction controlling most of the territory	Active combat against anti-government rebels	ECOMOG defeated Taylor in 1992, but Taylor elected president in 1997 elections
Iraqi Kurdistan	1991	USA, UK, France	Ambiguous	No—but little resistance	Establishment of safe area and no-fly zone	Kurds protected from Iraqi army
Somalia	1992–3	USA/UN	Yes	No government to seek consent from	Secure delivery of humanitarian relief, disarmament of warlords	Humanitarian relief delivered, but warlords resisted disarmament, prompting withdrawal after USA sustained casualties
Bosnia-Hercegovina	1993–5	NATO	Yes	Bosnian government consented, Yugoslav government/Bosnian Serbs did not	Limited airstrikes followed by deployment of rapid reaction force; large-scale air operations in 1995	Bosnian Serbs and Yugoslav government accepted Dayton peace accord
Haiti	1994	USA	Yes	Yes; Haitian military leaders backed down prior to deployment of US forces	Deployment to restore elected government	Peacekeepers deployed to maintain order and disarm rebels
Rwanda	1994	France	Yes	Pre-genocide government had collapsed	Creation of safe areas at the end of genocide	Safe areas saved some lives, but the perpetrators of the genocide allowed to flee to safety in the DRC, destabilizing that country
Kosovo	1999	NATO	No	No—intervention opposed	Aerial bombardment to coerce compliance with the Rambouillet accords	After 78 days, Yugoslavia conceded and permitted deployment of KFOR

(continued)

Table 22.1 (continued)

Place	Date	Intervener	UN Authority?	Consent?	Type of intervention	Outcome
East Timor	1999	Australian-led coalition	Yes	Yes—Indonesia granted consent after economic pressure used	Deployment of peacekeepers to deter and end militia violence	Militia withdrew or laid down arms; INTERFET handed over to UN transitional administration
Liberia	2002	ECOWAS—Nigeria	No	No—intervention in support of rebels after they had made significant advances	Deployment of peacekeepers in support of new government	Handed over to UN Mission to Liberia (UNMIL)
Democratic Republic of Congo	2003	EU–France	Yes	The government consented, but not the armed groups that controlled the town and its environs	Deployment of forces to prevent genocide in the town of Bunia after Ugandan withdrawal	Atrocities in Bunia deterred but pushed into countryside in Ituri province; handed over to UN Mission (MONUC)
Georgia	2008	Russia	No	No	Deployment of forces and airstrikes in response to Georgian assault on disputed territory of South Ossetia	Georgians forced to withdraw; Russia created buffer zone; strongly criticized by the West
Cote d'Ivoire	2011	France/UN	Yes	Consent of the recognized winner of the presidential election, but not of the defeated sitting president	Limited use of helicopters against 'government' forces in order to protect civilians	Gbagbo captured by supporters of the newly elected President and the regime transitioned to allow Ouattarra to assume presidency
Libya	2011	NATO-led (also Jordan, Qatar)	Yes	No	NATO and allies conduct air strikes to secure a no-fly zone and protect civilians	National Transitional Council forces defeat the regime and establish new government

Notes

1. The table is illustrative not definitive.

2. For the purposes of this table, 'humanitarian intervention' is taken to mean the use of military force for ostensibly humanitarian purposes; 'ostensibly humanitarian' means that the principal justification offered was humanitarian.

3. Although humanitarian justification properly understood included only those cases where force is used without the consent of the host state, for illustrative purposes cases have been included where consent was in doubt (e.g. Liberia), where military and economic coercion was required to seecure consent (Haiti and East Timor, respectively), and where the government gave consent but did not control the territory under question (e.g. Congo).

international society's responsibility in cases where states struggle or fail to meet their responsibilities. By situating the potential for humanitarian intervention within a broader continuum of measures such as early warning and capacity building designed to prevent crises erupting in the first place, the R2P also addresses some of the practical problems associated with humanitarian intervention. In 2008, the principle was used to stem the tide of mass atrocities in Kenya after a disputed election there, without the need for armed intervention. Three years later, the UN Security Council specifically referred to R2P in its resolutions on Libya (Resolutions 1970 and 1973), the second of which authorized the use of force. This was the first time in which the Security Council had ever authorized the use of force for humanitarian purposes against a functioning sovereign state and suggests that consensus is sometimes possible about when and where to use force for humanitarian purposes, even if this is rare. Since Libya, the Security Council has referred to R2P in a number of resolutions dealing with crises in places such as Central African Republic, Mali, Somalia, South Sudan, and Yemen. It is now common for the Council to authorize the use of force by UN peacekeepers to protect civilians from harm, though this type of operation requires the consent of the state involved and should be distinguished from humanitarian intervention without such consent.

KEY POINTS

- Westphalian sovereignty rests on the assumption that sovereign states provide the best avenue for protecting human security and that international security is dependent on rules that prohibit states from interfering in one another's affairs. In the twentieth century, however, states were responsible for many genocides and mass atrocities, often targeting their own citizens.
- Genocides tend to end with either the military defeat of the perpetrators or their victory. Often, the only way to halt genocide and mass atrocities is to use military force against the perpetrators. This use of force, referred to as 'humanitarian intervention', challenges the basic principles of Westphalian sovereignty and raises practical dilemmas.
- Progress has been made towards reconciling the divergent principles connected to humanitarian intervention and addressing the practical challenges, through the R2P principle. This made international consensus on intervention in Libya possible in 2011 and has enabled new types of UN peacekeeping focused on protecting civilians.

The case for humanitarian intervention

Usually associated with liberalism and cosmopolitanism, the case for intervention is typically premised on the idea that external actors have a *duty* as well as a *right* to intervene to halt genocide and **mass atrocities**. For advocates of this position, the rights that sovereigns enjoy are conditional on the fulfilment of the state's responsibility to protect its citizens. When states fail in their duties towards their citizens, they lose their sovereign right to **non-interference** (Caney 1997: 32; Tesón 1998, 2003: 93). There are a variety of ways to arrive at this conclusion. Some liberal cosmopolitanists draw on the work of the German philosopher Immanuel Kant to insist that all individuals have certain fundamental rights that deserve protection (Caney 1997: 34). Some advocates of the Just War tradition arrive at a broadly similar position but ground their arguments in Christian theology. Paul Ramsey (2002: 20), for instance, based his argument on St Augustine's injunction that military force be used to defend or uphold justice and maintained that intervention to end injustice was 'among the rights and duties of states until and unless supplanted by superior government'.

Political leaders who adopt this position often argue that today's globalized world is so integrated that massive human rights violations in one part of the world have an effect on every other part. This social interconnectedness, they argue, creates moral obligations. One of the leading proponents of this view was former British Prime Minister Tony Blair. Shortly after NATO began its 1999 intervention in Kosovo, Blair (1999) gave a landmark speech setting out his 'doctrine of the international community'. Blair maintained that enlightened self-interest created international responsibilities for dealing with egregious human suffering, because, in an interdependent world, 'freedom is indivisible and when one man is enslaved who is free?' He also maintained that sovereigns had international responsibilities, because problems caused by massive human rights abuse in one place tended to spread across borders.

A further line of argument is to point to the fact that states have already agreed to certain minimum standards of behaviour and that humanitarian intervention is not about imposing the will of a few Western states upon the many, but about protecting and enforcing the collective will of international society. Advocates of this position argue that there is a customary right (but not duty) of intervention in supreme humanitarian emergencies (Wheeler 2000: 14). They argue that there is agreement in international society that cases of genocide, mass killing, and ethnic cleansing constitute grave humanitarian crises warranting intervention (see Arend and Beck 1993; Tesón 1997; Donnelly 1998). They point to state practice since the end of the Cold War to suggest that there is a customary right of humanitarian intervention (Lepard 2002; Finnemore 2003). In particular, they point to the justifications offered to defend the American-, French-, and British-led intervention in Northern Iraq in 1991 to support their case. In that case, the British argued that they were upholding customary international law, France invoked a customary 'right' of intervention, and the USA noted a 're-balancing of the claims of sovereignty and those of extreme humanitarian need' (see Roberts 1993: 436–7).

This movement towards acceptance of a customary right of humanitarian intervention was reinforced by state practice after Northern Iraq. For instance, throughout the UN Security Council's deliberations about how to respond to the Rwandan genocide in 1994, no state argued that either the ban on force (Article 2(4)) or the non-interference rule (Article 2(7)) prohibited armed intervention to halt the bloodshed (see Barnett 2002), suggesting that armed intervention would have been legitimate in that case. What stood in the way of intervention in Rwanda was the fact that no government wanted to risk the lives of its own soldiers to save Africans. Throughout the 1990s, the Security Council expanded its interpretation of 'international peace and security' and authorized interventions to protect civilians in safe areas (Bosnia), maintain law and order and protect aid supplies (Somalia), and restore an elected government toppled by a coup (Haiti) (see Roberts 1993; Morris 1995; Findlay 2002). Since 2000, the Security Council has on several occasions mandated peacekeepers to protect civilians under threat in the Democratic Republic of Congo, Burundi, Côte d'Ivoire, Liberia, and Darfur (see Holt and Berkman 2006), although it has usually insisted on receiving the consent of the host government.

Although appealing, several aspects of this defence of humanitarian intervention are problematic. First, it is not self-evident that individuals *do* have universal and fundamental human rights. Parekh (1997: 54–5), for example, argues that liberal rights cannot provide the basis for a theory of humanitarian intervention because liberalism itself is rejected in many parts of the world. Realists argue that rights are meaningful only if they are backed up with the **power** to enforce them. Second, critics argue that any norm endorsing the use of force to protect individual rights would be abused by powerful states, making armed conflict more frequent by relaxing the rules prohibiting it but without making humanitarian intervention any more likely (Chesterman 2001; Thakur 2004).

Above all, however, is the charge that advocates of humanitarian intervention exaggerate the extent of global consensus about the use of force to protect human rights. From this perspective there is a gap between what advocates would like to be the norm and what the norm actually is. The putative 'golden era' of humanitarian intervention in the 1990s included the world's failure to halt the Rwandan genocide, the UN's failure to protect civilians sheltering in its 'safe areas' in Bosnia, and the failure to prevent the widely predicted mass murder that followed East Timor's referendum on independence in 1999. The world stood aside as Congo destroyed itself, taking four million lives, and—more recently—failed to halt the mass killing in Darfur. Moreover, closer inspection of the relevant cases from the 1990s suggests that world leaders were much more hesitant than implied by advocates of humanitarian intervention. The 1991 intervention occurred in the wake of the first Gulf War, the 1992–3 intervention in Somalia occurred only after the state had effectively ceased to exist, military intervention in Bosnia was endorsed by the Bosnian government, the 1994 intervention in Haiti was finally conducted with the (albeit heavily coerced) consent of the country's military leaders, the French intervention in Rwanda in the same year occurred after the Rwandan Patriotic Front had defeated government forces and the *Interehamwe* militia, and peacekeepers were deployed in Darfur with the consent of the Sudanese government. We should, therefore, avoid the temptation of thinking that there was a 'rash' of humanitarian interventions in the post-Cold War era (Finnemore 2008: 197). Before the Libyan intervention in 2011, which is discussed in more detail later, the only example of humanitarian intervention against the wishes of the sovereign state in the post-Cold War era was the 1999 NATO intervention in Kosovo, and this was done without authorization from the UN Security Council and proved to be highly controversial.

Finally, with only a few partial exceptions, humanitarian interveners themselves have chosen not to justify their actions by reference to a norm of humanitarian intervention (see Wheeler 2000). This is principally because they are wary of making it easier for other states to justify the use of force—just as Russia did, for example, when it claimed to be acting as a 'peacekeeper' when it invaded Georgia in 2008.

KEY POINTS

- Liberals argue that all humans enjoy fundamental human rights and that this creates a right and duty to intervene in cases where fundamental human rights are abused on a massive scale. This moral duty is reinforced by globalization, which connects individuals.
- The post-Cold War era saw the development of a customary norm of humanitarian intervention, as international society responded to humanitarian emergencies in Iraq, the Balkans, Somalia, Rwanda, Haiti, East Timor, and elsewhere.
- Critics argue that the idea of fundamental human rights has little empirical purchase, that humanitarian intervention destabilizes international security, and that advocates overstate the progress made towards a new norm of humanitarian intervention in the post-Cold War era.

The case against humanitarian intervention

Nowadays, only a handful of states—often those with atrocious human rights records themselves (such as Cuba, Iran, Venezuela, Zimbabwe)—are prepared to argue that humanitarian intervention is *never* warranted. Even China, Russia, and India—states usually associated with defending the principle of non-intervention—have accepted that intervention might sometimes be necessary. When it came to Libya in 2011, all three chose to abstain in the Security Council's vote on authorizing the use of force when they could have conspired to defeat the resolution and prevent intervention. By and large, therefore, contemporary opposition to humanitarian intervention focuses on the questions about who can *legitimately authorize* intervention, *in what circumstances*, and the effectiveness of using military force for humanitarian purposes.

Opponents of humanitarian intervention maintain that international peace and security requires something approximating an absolute ban on the use of force outside the two exceptions set out by the UN Charter—Security Council authorization (Chapter VII) and self-defence (Article 51). The starting point for this position is the assumption that international society comprises a large number of diverse communities each with different ideas about the best way to live. The world is made up of democratic states of different types (e.g. social democracies in Scandinavia, authoritarian democracy in Russia, and market democracy in the USA), states organized according to religious principles (e.g. Iran), monarchies (e.g. Tonga and Saudi Arabia), dictatorships and communist states (e.g. China and Cuba), and each state houses communities with very different cultural values. According to this view, international security is based on rules—the UN Charter's rules on the use of force first among them—that permit the peaceful coexistence of these very different types of states and societies (see Jackson 2002). Given these disagreements, it is important that the use of force is governed by rules and that no single group of states has a right to impose its own preferences on others.

From this perspective, a general right of humanitarian intervention would open the door to abuse. Historically, states have shown a predilection towards 'abusing' humanitarian justifications to legitimize wars that were anything but humanitarian in nature. Most notoriously, Hitler insisted that the 1939 invasion of Czechoslovakia intended to protect Czechoslovak citizens whose 'life and liberty' were threatened by their own government (in Brownlie 1974: 217–21). Some commentators have argued that the United States and UK abused humanitarian justifications in an ill-fated attempt to legitimize the 2003 invasion of Iraq (see Bellamy 2004; cf. Morris and Wheeler 2006). Similar claims could also be made about Russia's use of humanitarian arguments to justify its 2008 invasion of Georgia (see Case Study 22.1). It was precisely because of the fear that states would exploit any loophole in the ban on the use of force that the delegates who wrote the UN Charter in 1944–5 issued a comprehensive ban with only two limited exceptions. According to Simon Chesterman (2001: 231), without this general ban there would be *more war* in world politics but not necessarily more humanitarian interventions. 'On balance', Thomas Franck and Nigel Rodley (1973: 278) warned in 1973, 'very little good has been wrought' in the name of humanitarian intervention.

It is also important to note that a majority of states oppose a general right of humanitarian intervention—seeing it as a dangerous affront to another core

CASE STUDY 22.1 The misuse of humanitarian justifications: Russia's 2008 intervention in Georgia

In August 2008, Russia responded to Georgian incursions into the disputed territory of South Ossetia, which was formally part of Georgia, with a large military intervention. Backed up by the aerial bombardment of key Georgian cities, including Georgia's capital Tblisi, Russian forces pushed the Georgian army out of South Ossetia and another disputed territory, Abkhazia, and established a buffer zone over twenty miles inside Georgia proper. Russia's foreign minister, Sergei Lavrov, accused Georgia of committing 'genocide' in South Ossetia and argued that its intervention was a legitimate exercise of its 'responsibility to protect', a principle being widely used by the UN.

These justifications, however, were rejected by analysts and won little support from international society, with even China refusing to support Russia's position despite calls for it to do so. First, although the Organization for Security and Cooperation in Europe (OSCE) has suggested that Georgian forces probably did fire the first shots, there is no empirical evidence to support Russia's claims that Georgia was committing 'genocide'. Whilst it is likely that individual war crimes were committed during the short war, it seems that Georgian, Russian, and South Ossetian forces all committed crimes to some extent. As such, the claim that Georgian crimes justified the intervention is as dubious as America's claim that the invasion of Iraq was justified by that country's possession of weapons of mass destruction. Second, the Global Centre for the Responsibility to Protect argued that the scale of Russia's assault on Georgia far exceeded that which was necessary to protect South Ossetians. In particular, Russian forces entered Georgia proper, attacked ports and cities that were unrelated to South Ossetia, and used force in the other disputed territory of Abkhazia. This suggests that the protection of South Ossetia was not Russia's principal objective. Third, the Global Centre argues that R2P does not give legal cover for armed intervention absent a Security Council resolution (GCR2P 2008).

For these reasons, Russia's intervention in Georgia seems to be a clear case of 'abuse'. The Russian government specifically invoked R2P and used humanitarian justifications to justify armed intervention, but its claims were not supported by the evidence. The situation in South Ossetia was not as Russia described it, and, even if it were, Russia's use of force went well beyond that necessary for human protection purposes.

principle, the right to self-determination. The General Assembly's 1970 Declaration on Principles of International Law Concerning Friendly Relations stated categorically:

> No state or group of states has the right to intervene, directly or indirectly, for any reason whatever, in the internal or external affairs of any other state. Consequently, armed intervention and all other forms of interference or attempted threats against the personality of the state or against its political, economic and cultural elements, are in violation of international law.
>
> UN General Assembly, Declaration on Principles of International Law Concerning Friendly Relations (1970)

Finally, realists especially claim that humanitarian intervention should be avoided because it does not work and is an inappropriate use of armed force. It does not work, they argue, because foreign intervention tends to prolong wars and create unstable peace. For realists, war is the ultimate test of strength, and stable post-war peace is produced by the victory of one side over the other, which then forces actors to realign their behaviour in accordance with the new distribution of power. Because foreign intervention reduces the proportion of wars that end in outright victory, it leaves behind an unstable peace that is likely to reignite (Luttwak 1999). Realists also argue that armed force should only ever be used in the national interest and that humanitarian intervention is therefore imprudent.

There are a number of problems with these positions as well, however. First, the overriding assumption that states protect their citizens' rights and cultural differences does not hold in every case, as the examples offered at the beginning of this chapter attest. Second, this perspective underestimates the wealth of customary practice suggesting that sovereignty carries responsibilities as well as rights (see Tesón 1997). Third, although there are a few notorious historical cases, the fear of abuse is exaggerated (Weiss 2004: 135). It is fanciful to argue that denying a state recourse to humanitarian justifications for war would make them less war-prone. It is highly unlikely that either Hitler in 1939 or Bush and Blair in 2003 would have been deterred from waging war by the absence of a plausible humanitarian justification. Fourth, the critics of humanitarian intervention overlook the wide body of international law relating to basic human rights and the consensus on grave crimes such as genocide (see Scheffer 1992; Mertus 2000). Finally, the realist claim that intervention produces unstable peace is not supported by empirical studies, which show that well-equipped peace operations can significantly reduce the likelihood of war reigniting (Fortna 2008).

In summary, almost all governments recognize that crimes such as genocide and mass killing are a legitimate concern for international society. Some governments, international officials, activists, and analysts argue that sovereigns have a responsibility to protect their citizens from mass killing and other abuses, and, when they fail to do so, others acquire a right to intervene. A majority of the world's governments, however, argue that this responsibility does not translate into a right of humanitarian intervention without the authority of the UN Security Council because that would contradict other cherished principles, including the rule of non-aggression and the right to self-determination. Since the end of the Cold War, the UN Security Council has authorized collective intervention to protect populations from mass killing. In this sense, there is a norm of UN-sanctioned humanitarian intervention (Wheeler 2000) and there is evidence that the Security Council is growing more willing to act to prevent mass atrocities and protect vulnerable populations. This presents a dilemma about what to do in cases where some governments believe that intervention is warranted to save people from genocide and mass atrocities but where there is no consensus in the Security Council. This dilemma was exposed by NATO's decision to intervene in Kosovo in 1999. The debate sparked by this case provided a catalyst for a fundamental rethink of the way that international society conceptualizes the relationship between sovereignty and human rights.

KEY POINTS

- There is broad consensus that there are circumstances in which the use of force for military purposes might be justified, but critics argue that humanitarian intervention is legitimate only as a last resort, in the very worst of cases, and only when authorized by the UN Security Council.
- The rule of non-intervention is important because it protects weak states from strong states and preserves cultural diversity.
- A general right of humanitarian intervention is likely to be abused by states that would use humanitarian arguments to justify self-interested acts of war. This would damage international security without a corresponding improvement in human security.

The Responsibility to Protect

The Responsibility to Protect principle arose out of the controversies surrounding the international community's response to genocide and mass atrocities in Rwanda and the former Yugoslavia. In Rwanda, in 1994, the world lacked the political will to intervene to end a genocide that cost the lives of 800,000 people in 100 days. In Bosnia, in 1995, UN peacekeepers stood aside as more than 7,500 men and boys from the UN's 'safe area' of Srebrenica were massacred. In 1999, the crisis in Kosovo posed a different challenge stemming from NATO's decision to intervene without a mandate from the UN Security Council. The questions surrounding NATO's intervention in Kosovo prompted UN Secretary-General Kofi Annan to argue that 'state sovereignty, in its most basic sense, is being redefined by the forces of globalization and international co-operation'. He continued, 'the state is now widely understood to be the servant of its people, and not vice versa. At the same time, individual sovereignty—and by this I mean the human rights and fundamental freedoms of each and every individual as enshrined in our Charter—has been enhanced by a renewed consciousness of the right of every individual to control his or her own destiny' (Annan 1999: 2). Annan also pointed to three critical concerns. First, intervention should be understood broadly to cover measures short of armed force that could be used to prevent and halt humanitarian emergencies. Second, sovereignty alone was not the principal barrier to effective action to protect human rights. Just as significant, Annan argued, was the way in which member states defined their national interests. Third, international society should make a long-term commitment to rebuild states and societies once a conflict was over.

Together with Francis Deng, a former Sudanese diplomat and UN Secretary-General's specialist on internally displaced people, Annan pointed towards a new way of thinking about sovereignty as responsibility. The Canadian government then created the International Commission on Intervention and State Sovereignty (ICISS), chaired by Gareth Evans and Mohammed Sahnoun, to develop a way of reconciling sovereignty and human rights (see Evans 2008). The Commission's report, released in late 2001, was premised on the notion that, when states are unwilling or unable to protect their citizens from grave harm, the principle of non-interference 'yields to the responsibility to protect' (ICISS 2001: xi). The concept of R2P that it put forward was intended as a way of escaping the logic of 'intervention versus sovereignty' by focusing not on what interveners were entitled to do ('a right of intervention') but on what was necessary to protect civilians threatened by genocide and mass atrocities. Influenced by Annan and Deng, the ICISS argued that the R2P was about much more than just military intervention. Appropriate responses to humanitarian emergencies included non-violent measures such as diplomacy, sanctions, and embargoes, and legal measures such as referring crimes to the International Criminal Court. Furthermore, in addition to the 'responsibility to react' to massive human suffering, the ICISS insisted that international society also had responsibilities to rebuild polities and societies afterwards.

At the 2005 World Summit (see Key Quotes 22.1) over 150 world leaders adopted a declaration affirming the R2P, which was itself subsequently reaffirmed by the UN Security Council in 2006 (Resolution 1674) and 2009 (Resolution 1894).

According to the UN Secretary-General, Ban Ki-moon, who succeeded Kofi Annan in 2007, the R2P rests on three pillars:

1. the responsibility of the state to protect its own populations from genocide, war crimes, ethnic cleansing and crimes against humanity;

2. the international community's commitment to assist states in meeting these obligations;

3. the international community's responsibility to respond in a timely and decisive manner when a state is manifestly failing to protect its population, using Chapters VI (peaceful means), VII (coercive means authorized by the UN Security Council) and VIII (regional arrangements).

Ban Ki-moon (2008); Luck (2008)

The approach adopted by the UN Secretary-General has been described as 'narrow but deep' (Luck 2008: 1). The R2P applies only to a narrow category of cases (genocide, war crimes, ethnic cleansing, and crimes against humanity) but requires a deep commitment from states. International society is expected to shoulder the responsibility of preventing genocide and mass atrocities by helping states to build the necessary capacities, developing early warning systems and being prepared to act 'upstream' of an outbreak of violence with a range of diplomatic, humanitarian, legal, and other peaceful measures. Heeding the concerns of states such as Russia and China, the R2P insists that military intervention be authorized by the UN Security Council and rules out unilateral force.

The World Summit's declaration on the R2P received a mixed reception. Simon Chesterman argued

KEY QUOTES 22.1 Responsibility to protect and the 2005 World Summit

'138 Each individual state has the responsibility to protect its populations from genocide, war crimes, ethnic cleansing and crimes against humanity. This responsibility entails the prevention of such crimes, including their incitement, through appropriate and necessary means. We accept that responsibility and will act in accordance with it. The international community should, as appropriate, encourage and help States to exercise this responsibility and support the United Nations in establishing an early warning capability.'

'139 The international community, through the United Nations, also has the responsibility to use appropriate diplomatic, humanitarian and other peaceful means, in accordance with Chapters VI and VIII of the Charter of the United Nations, to help protect populations from war crimes, ethnic cleansing and crimes against humanity. In this context, we are prepared to take collective action, in a timely and decisive manner, through the Security Council, in accordance with the Charter, including Chapter VII, on a case-by-case basis and in cooperation with relevant regional organizations as appropriate, should peaceful means be inadequate and national authorities are manifestly failing to protect their populations from genocide, war crimes, ethnic cleansing and crimes against humanity. We stress the need for the General Assembly to continue consideration of the responsibility to protect populations from genocide, war crimes, ethnic cleansing and crimes against humanity and its implications, bearing in mind the principles of the Charter and international law. We also intend to commit ourselves, as necessary and appropriate, to helping States build capacity to protect their populations from genocide, war crimes, ethnic cleansing and crimes against humanity and to assisting those which are under stress before crises and conflicts break out.'

'140 We fully support the mission of the Special Adviser of the Secretary-General on the Prevention of Genocide.'

United Nations (2005c)

that 'what we're seeing is a progressive redefinition of sovereignty in a way that would have been outrageous sixty years ago' (in Turner 2005). Others were more equivocal. John Bolton, the American Ambassador to the UN and a well-known UN-sceptic, described the R2P as 'a moveable feast of an idea that was the High Minded *cause du jour*' and said of the World Summit Outcome Document: 'I plan never to read it again. I doubt many others will either' (Bolton 2007: 213–14).

To what extent has the R2P advanced and replaced debates about humanitarian intervention? One group of critics complain that the principle amounts to little more than an assault on state sovereignty. They argue that it is little different from the interventionist doctrines put forward by liberals in the 1990s and has all the negative connotations associated with humanitarian intervention (e.g. Chandler 2005). A second group of critics make the opposite point. Michael Byers (2005), for example, argued that the 2005 World Summit Outcome Document watered down the original R2P concept to such an extent that the new principle would not advance the humanitarian intervention debate or protect threatened populations.

Whilst the first group of critics ignore the fact that the R2P has been adopted by world leaders of all stripes and carefully limits the scope for armed intervention, the second group focus too heavily on the question of armed intervention and underestimate the potential impact of the commitment to the R2P. Thus, whilst we need to be mindful of the principle's limitations, as the UN Secretary-General's special adviser, Edward Luck, has pointed out, there are several good reasons for thinking that the R2P is likely to make a lasting impact on international peace and security (see Key Ideas 22.1). To get a sense of the strengths and limitations of the new principle, it is worth considering three prominent cases where it has been employed: first, in relation to Darfur, the international community has struggled to protect civilians in the face of a complex conflict in a difficult context where the host government (Sudan) has presented innumerable obstacles (Case Study 22.2); second, in relation to Kenya, where R2P helped frame a diplomatic response to an escalating crisis that helped stem the tide of mass atrocities; third, in relation to Libya, where R2P was used to support a raft of measures designed to prevent mass atrocities and, when they failed, was used to support armed intervention (Case Study 22.3).

KEY IDEAS 22.1 The impact of the responsibility to protect

1. R2P is a politically potent concept based on a consensus produced by one of the largest gatherings of heads of state ever seen.
2. The Outcome Document specifically points to the prevention of genocide, war crimes, ethnic cleansing, and crimes against humanity.
3. The Outcome Document points to the kinds of tools, actors, and procedures that could form the basis for operationalizing the R2P.
4. The process of negotiating the Document and forging consensus required compromise by both sides of the intervention debate and produced a shared conception of sovereignty as responsibility that bridges the divide.

Based on Luck (2008: 3)

The Security Council's increasing tendency to use R2P and the fact that the use of R2P in both Côte d'Ivoire and Libya in 2011, has increased concern among some states that the principle might be abused or that states who are authorized to use force for R2P purposes might exceed the terms of their mandate. This is what Secretary-General Ban Ki-moon called the 'risk of relevance'—that as R2P is actually used in practice, difficult questions about implementation are raised. In response to some of the concerns raised about the way in which NATO went about enforcing Resolution 1973, Brazil advanced a new principle of 'Responsibility whilst Protecting', or RWP, that would help guide the implementation of R2P. RWP emphasizes the role that should be played by non-coercive measures and insists that the Council should properly debate and evaluate the likely outcomes of using force and that those given mandates to use force by the Security Council should be accountable to the Council and at least provide regular updates. Although some R2P advocates and sceptics welcomed the Brazilian initiative, others opposed it, and Brazil decided not to proactively promote the concept.

One of the immediate consequences of the controversies sparked by Libya appeared to be the Security Council's inability to respond effectively to the mounting crisis in Syria from 2011. Although Russia's refusal to cooperate with the West on Syria appeared to be a reaction to Libya, there were a

CASE STUDY 22.2 Darfur

At the time of writing, the situation in Darfur remains the only case in which UN Security Council has invoked the R2P Security Council Resolution 1706 (2006), which called for the creation of a large peacekeeping force to protect civilians in Darfur, and specifically referred to the R2P principle. However, the UN and African Union have encountered serious obstacles in their effort to translate R2P from words to deeds in this case, leaving some analysts to argue that R2P has 'failed' its first test (e.g. de Waal 2007).

The conflict began in earnest in 2003, after a few years of sporadic fighting over land and access to water between some of the different groups. In April 2003, rebel groups captured the border town of Tine and attacked al-Fashir airport. The government responded by 'outsourcing' the counter-insurgency to local militia leaders. In return for their military support, the government basically gave the militia a free hand to attack civilians, steal livestock, and destroy homes. The war they waged was primarily a war of genocide on the civilian population designed to curb support for the rebel groups, occupy land, secure access to water, and steal booty. The consequences are well-known. Over 250,000—and by some estimates as many as 400,000—civilians have been killed. Another 2.5 million have been forcibly displaced and either live rough or in one of the 230 refugee camps for displaced people that dot the countryside in Darfur and Chad. The violence has decreased since 2003–4, but in many regions this is only because the government's janjaweed militia succeeded in seizing the land and driving out or butchering their civilian targets.

The international response to the crisis in Darfur is best described as tepid. With the West unwilling to commit troops to a peacekeeping operation and the Security Council unable to agree on measures such as targeted sanctions and a no-fly zone, the African Union (AU) dispatched a small force (AMIS) to monitor a ceasefire in 2004. The ceasefire collapsed almost as soon as it had been signed and the small AMIS force, which numbered 7,000 at its peak (covering an area the size of France), proved utterly incapable of protecting civilians or preventing other breaches (Williams 2006). The West now focused its efforts on getting a UN peacekeeping force deployed. This required a peace agreement, and the USA led an effort to deliver such an agreement. However, the process did not receive high-level support in the West and resulted in an agreement being forced through against the will of several rebel leaders. As a result, the rebel groups began to fracture and the violence persisted. Although the UN got its peace agreement, with violence persisting member states remained unwilling to commit troops and the Sudanese government refused to grant its consent. In the end, a compromise was reached whereby the UN entered into an agreement with the AU to deploy a 'hybrid' operation managed by both organizations. In the absence of additional resources, however, the new UNAMID mission mainly comprised rebadged AMIS peacekeepers. Progress was made, however, on other aspects of the international community's engagement with Darfur—the Security Council imposed limited sanctions on the Sudanese government and referred the matter to the International Criminal Court.

There are three main reasons why the international response to the atrocities in Darfur has been so tepid. First, the situation in Darfur is highly complex and there is little agreement about the most appropriate type of response. Even among activists there is no agreement on the best course of action. Some focus on the need to get sufficient numbers of peacekeepers into Darfur, whilst others argue that this is a distraction from the main game of securing a political settlement and delivering humanitarian aid (see Flint and de Waal 2008). Second, the crisis in Darfur is not a political priority for the West. Western priorities are focused elsewhere, in Afghanistan, Iraq, and the Balkans. As such, they are reluctant to commit the resources and political capital needed to lead on Darfur. Third, many states—particularly China and several Arab states—have actively blocked coercive measures on the grounds that they impinge on Sudanese sovereignty (see Williams and Bellamy 2005).

The Darfur case suggests that a lot more work is needed to figure out the best way of translating R2P from words to deeds in real-world cases, both in terms of the measures that are necessary to protect populations from harm and in terms of the politics of consensus building.

number of factors at play: not least, Russia has a long-standing alliance with Syria and a naval base there, is concerned about the spread of Islamism to its southernmost regions, and both Russia and China have maintained—not implausibly—that weakening Damascus would only erode regional stability. After Syrian security forces began opening fire on unarmed demonstrators, prompting an escalation of the conflict into civil war, Western states pushed for targeted sanctions and other measures. Russia resisted, however, arguing that the West wanted regime change and would abuse any

CASE STUDY 22.3 Libya

The Responsibility to Protect (R2P) played an important role in shaping the world's response to the threat of atrocities in Libya. In particular, in Resolution 1973 the UN Security Council authorized the use of 'all necessary means' to protect civilians in harm's way. Resolution 1973 is important because it is the first time that the Security Council has authorized the use of force for human protection purposes against the wishes of a functioning state. On 22 February 2011, the UN's High Commissioner for Human Rights, Navi Pillay issued a statement in which she reiterated that the state 'has an obligation to protect the rights to life, liberty and security'. She continued, 'Protection of civilians should always be the paramount consideration in maintaining order and the rule of law. The authorities should immediately cease such illegal acts of violence against demonstrators. Widespread and systematic attacks against the civilian population may amount to crimes against humanity.' This early activism was part of the catalyst for the adoption of Resolution 1970 (26 February 2011) which condemned attacks on the civilian population which it deemed may amount to crimes against humanity, demanded an immediate cessation of violence, established an arms embargo and travel ban, and referred the matter to the prosecutor of the International Criminal Court. With Qaddafi showing little sign of backing down, the Secretary-General intervened personally by calling the Libyan leader to persuade him to comply with the resolution. When that too failed, the onus was placed squarely on the Council to determine the next step.

However, Libya might be exceptional for two reasons, suggesting that whilst consensus might sometimes be possible in the Security Council, it is likely to be rare. First was the extraordinary clarity of the threat of mass atrocities. Not since Rwanda has a regime signalled its intent to commit crimes against humanity so clearly. With direct echoes of Rwanda, Qaddafi told the world that 'officers have been deployed in all tribes and regions so that they can purify all decisions from these cockroaches' and 'any Libyan who takes arms against Libya will be executed'. These overt threats to commit mass atrocities that explicitly employed the language used by Hutu genocidaires to incite the 1994 Rwandan genocide, coupled with evidence that Qaddafi's regime had already targeted civilians and the regime's long track record of abuses, left no room for doubt about the likely consequences of a successful government crackdown. Second, the timeframe was extremely short. The rapidity of rebel gains and subsequent losses in early March 2011, which left the stronghold of Benghazi vulnerable to Qaddafi's forces and their promised retribution, left little time to try measures short of force. The Council's first resolution on Libya, Resolution 1970 bundled a variety of punitive measures together, when slower moving events might have facilitated a more graduated approach to coercive inducement. At the time Resolution 1973 was presented to the Council the fall of Benghazi was days, if not hours, away. Having endorsed the R2P principle, states such as China and Russia that might have opposed the use of force could not come up with plausible alternative ways of protecting civilians in the face of Qaddafi's record and his public utterances. As a result, they abstained and allowed the Council to authorize the use of force.

Other factors, unlikely to be often repeated also helped to generate both the will to act and international consensus. Qaddafi's regime had few friends in the region and it was the League of Arab States' call for a no-fly zone, supported by the Organization of the Islamic Conferences that proved to be a diplomatic game-changer. Without their support, China and Russia would have probably vetoed Resolution 1973. Also significant was the fact that the USA, UK, and France declared that they would only intervene if authorized to do so by the Security Council—a prerequisite for R2P as agreed by member states. The Obama Administration's obvious reticence about intervention and the insistence on a UN mandate reassured states that would otherwise have been critical of 'Western interventionism'.

The military action ultimately proved to be successful—the feared massacre in Benghazi was averted and the Qaddafi regime removed from power. However, serious concerns were raised about the conduct of military operations. Critics complained that NATO effectively used R2P to pursue a 'regime change' agenda, that its use of force went well beyond that which was necessary to protect civilians, that it deliberately targeted Qaddafi and his family and caused excessive civilian damage. France's decision to drop arms to anti-Qaddafi groups was particularly controversial, because the Security Council had imposed an arms embargo on the country. These concerns created a significant backlash. Although the Security Council remained willing to use R2P after Libya—referring to the principle in relation to the situations in Yemen and South Sudan—states such as Russia, China, and India argued that the Libyan experience made them less willing to contemplate the use of coercive measures in relation to crises in Syria and Yemen.

mandate for its own purposes. In 2012, the Council agreed to support a peace plan brokered by Kofi Annan, but neither side of the war in Syria complied with its agreement and the plan broke down. When Russia and China vetoed a draft resolution imposing sanctions on the Syrian government for failing to comply with its agreement, Annan resigned as UN/Arab League mediator. A further draft resolution, referring the situation in Syria to the International Criminal Court was also vetoed by Russia and China on the grounds that it would destabilize the situation and make it more difficult to negotiate an agreement. The Security Council was, however, able to reach a consensus on the need to disarm Syria's chemical and biological weapons, after a chemical weapons attack on the town of Houla left hundreds dead. However, that was the limit of the Council's consensus and the UN's General Assembly expressed its disappointment in a resolution which 'deplored' the Council's failure in Syria. In 2014, the rise of the 'Islamic State' in Iraq and Syria seemed to pose a greater threat to stability than did the Syrian government, prompting a relaxation of pressure for tough measures against Damascus.

KEY POINTS

- The R2P principle attempts to replace the debate about humanitarian intervention with a new consensus based on the principle of sovereignty as responsibility and duties to prevent genocide and mass atrocities, react appropriately to them, and rebuild states and societies afterwards.
- The R2P rests on three pillars: (1) each state's responsibility to protect its own populations; (2) the international community's commitment to help states fulfil their responsibility; (3) the international community's responsibility to take timely and effective measures, using Chapters VI, VII, and/or VIII of the UN Charter, when a state is manifestly failing in its R2P.
- Critics argue that the R2P is either simply a reincarnation of liberal arguments in favour of humanitarian intervention or a piece of meaningless rhetoric that will make little difference in practice.
- R2P has been increasingly used since 2005 and has given rise to different sorts of responses—including peacekeeping, preventive diplomacy, and military force.
- The use of R2P in practice has given rise to debate about implementation. Brazil has suggested the concept of 'responsibility whilst protecting' to guide this debate.

Conclusion

The R2P is an attempt to reconfigure the relationship between sovereignty and human rights and replace the debates about humanitarian intervention covered in the first part of the chapter with a new consensus that focuses on protecting populations from genocide and mass atrocities. It has succeeded in winning a consensus among states about its meaning and scope, and the debate is now turning to difficult questions about practical implementation. This in itself though is a significant change in world politics because it was traditionally assumed that international security required strict adherence to the principles of sovereignty and non-interference and that, in cases where the security of states and individuals collided, the former should be privileged. With the end of the Cold War, however, many states and activists began to question whether states that committed grave abuses should be allowed to use sovereignty to shield themselves. The international community began to become more actively involved in humanitarian crises but two problems quickly emerged: those associated with the lack of political will and those associated with profound disagreements about the circumstances in which a state should lose the protections of sovereignty. R2P arose as an attempt to resolve these two problems.

But, if sovereignty is understood as a responsibility to protect, then the role of international society becomes one of enabling and supporting sovereigns in discharging their responsibilities to their citizens. The R2P holds that this is not just a matter of charity but a matter of responsibility, because the very foundations of sovereignty and international society are individual human rights. As a result, international society has a responsibility to ensure that sovereigns fulfil their duties by preventing and reacting to cases of genocide, mass killing, and ethnic cleansing and helping to rebuild societies afterwards. This responsibility was acknowledged at the 2005 World Summit and reaffirmed by the UN Security Council, but there remains much work to be done to ensure that all this makes a difference to those in need and succeeds in replacing the debate about humanitarian intervention. In the wake of the UN-authorized NATO-led intervention in Libya and the failure to respond adequately to the crisis in Syria, the challenge now is for states to work through practical issues about how best to protect populations.

? QUESTIONS

1. Why do liberals think there is a moral duty to help endangered populations in far-away countries? Is their argument plausible?
2. To what extent does international security depend on the UN Charter's rules on the non-use of force (Article 2(4)) and non-interference in the domestic affairs of sovereigns?
3. What is the likelihood that a right of humanitarian intervention would be abused by powerful states to justify aggressive war? Does the R2P increase or reduce that likelihood?
4. Should armed intervention always be authorized by the UN Security Council? Why?
5. To what extent do you think that the R2P principle replaces humanitarian intervention?
6. Is the R2P principle just 'hot air' or a rehashed version of the liberal defence of humanitarian intervention?
7. What needs to be done in order to translate the R2P from words to deeds?
8. What was the significance of the 2011 interventions in Côte d'Ivoire and Libya?
9. Why has the UN failed to respond adequately to the crisis in Syria?
10. Should the power of veto on the UN Security Council be limited when it comes to responding to genocide and mass atrocities?
11. What are the strengths and weaknesses of 'responsibility whilst protecting'? To what extent does it help bridge different opinions on the use of force for protection purposes.
12. Has the theory and practice of humanitarian intervention evolved since the end of the Cold War?

FURTHER READING

- Bellamy, A. J. (2009), *Responsibility to Protect: The Global Effort to End Genocide and Mass Atrocities*, Cambridge: Polity Press. Presents an account of the emergence of the R2P and the challenges of translating it from words to deeds.
- Chesterman, S. (2001), *Just War or Just Peace? Humanitarian Intervention and International Law*, Oxford: Oxford University Press. An excellent account of the legal issues relating to humanitarian intervention.
- Evans, G. (2008), *The Responsibility to Protect: Ending Mass Atrocity Crimes Once and for All*, Washington: Brookings Institution. A powerful defence of the R2P and insider's account of the ICISS experience.
- ICISS (2001), International Commission on Intervention and State Sovereignty, *The Responsibility to Protect*, Ottawa: IDRC. Report making a landmark contribution to the field.
- Macqueen, Norrie (2011), *Humanitarian Intervention and the United Nations*, Edinburgh: Edinburgh University Press. A very useful assessment of the UN's track record on humanitarian intervention.
- Weiss, T. G. (2007), *Humanitarian Intervention: Ideas into Action*, Cambridge: Polity Press. A compelling introduction to the theory and practice of humanitarian intervention.
- Welsh, J. (ed.) (2004), *Humanitarian Intervention and International Relations*, Oxford: Oxford University Press. A superb collection that covers the ethical, legal, and political dilemmas provoked by humanitarian intervention.

- Wheeler, N. J. (2000), *Saving Strangers: Humanitarian Intervention in International Society*, Oxford: Oxford University Press. Remains the best account of humanitarian intervention in the 1990s and earlier.

IMPORTANT WEBSITES

- **http://www.un.org** The website of the UN; contains information about Security Council and General Assembly debates on humanitarian intervention and the responsibility to protect, as well as the organization's work on conflict prevention, peacekeeping, peace building, and human rights.
- **http://www.responsibilitytoprotect.org** The website of the World Federalist Movement's project on R2P; contains an excellent archive of reports and other documents.
- **http://www.globalr2p.org** The website of the Global Centre for the Responsibility to Protect, which aims to advance the principle through research and outreach.
- **http://www.r2pasiapacific.org** The website of the Asia-Pacific Centre for the Responsibility to Protect.
- **http://www.reliefweb.int** A UN-run website that provides information to humanitarian agencies in the field.

Visit the Online Resource Centre that accompanies this book for lots of interesting additional material: www.oxfordtextbooks.co.uk/orc/collins4e/

23

Energy Security

Sam Raphael and Doug Stokes

Chapter Contents

Reader's Guide

This chapter examines growing concerns over global energy security, as accelerating demand for fossil fuels by industrialized economies is matched by increasing uncertainties over future energy reserves. With a particular focus on the politics of oil (as the key global energy source), it will assess the ways in which increasing energy *insecurity* amongst the world's major powers will impact upon international security more broadly, and will discuss different understandings of the likelihood of future 'resource wars' and a new era of geopolitical rivalry. The chapter will also examine the impact that the search for energy security by states in the global North has upon the human security of communities in the oil-rich global South. Finally, the chapter will examine the central role played by the United States in underpinning global energy security in the post-war era, and the impact that this has had for oil-rich regions.

Introduction

'Energy security' is a term in vogue. The intersection of a number of trends—rising global demand for energy, fears of dwindling supplies, increased instability in many of the energy-rich regions, and concerns about the potential future devastation wrought by climate change—ensures that the sources, locations, and stability of world energy supplies have become a common subject for debate. For the purposes of this chapter, we will define 'energy security' as follows:

Energy security exists when there are energy sources large enough to meet the needs of the political community (the energy demands), which include all military, economic, and societal activity. Those sources must be able to deliver such quantities of energy in a reliable and stable manner, and for the foreseeable future. As soon as these conditions are not met, there exists a problem of energy (in)security.

This is our definition of 'energy security', but it captures—we think—what is meant by the term when used by academics and politicians alike.

Many communities live in conditions of energy *insecurity*. Across the global South in particular, regular shortages of energy supply are a fact of life, even where abundant local sources of energy exist (as daily power cuts in post-invasion Baghdad demonstrated). Such insecurity has a significant effect on the quality of life for many, with health, education, and transport services often severely affected. In contrast, for most of those living in the industrialized and rapidly industrializing states of the North, the existence of robust infrastructure ensures that the problem of energy security manifests differently. For these societies, the existence of stable energy supply at a *state* level is usually sufficient to ensure enough energy for the entire population. For example, as long as the United Kingdom receives a supply of energy to meet the overall demand of its citizens, the existence of a high-quality national grid within the UK ensures that any one community can almost always be guaranteed reliable and sufficient supply.

Over recent decades, government officials, analysts, and academics alike have identified energy security as a growing problem, affecting states in the North as much as, if not more than, those in the South. Indeed, given the rapid industrialization of large regions of the globe, and the transformation of lead economies into those dependent upon copious amounts of fossil fuels, energy security has become elevated to a key political and economic problem of modern times. Moreover, this problem intersects with a range of wider security concerns covered elsewhere in this book. The existence of reliable supplies of energy clearly underpins economic activity, and can be seen as a prerequisite for any significant degree of *economic security*. In attempting to ensure the stability of supplies, core powers are increasingly militarizing their approach to energy security. This, as we shall see, may have significant consequences for *international security*, as inter-state cooperation threatens to break down into a struggle over the control of key energy reserves. Likewise, this militarization often has a profound impact upon the *human security* of those living in oil-rich regions in the South, as the use of armed force is used to 'stabilize' energy-rich areas. Oil wealth has other impacts upon states in the South, with *regime security* often becoming intimately bound up with the collection of oil 'rents' (a method of income generation that allows governments to become politically insulated from their citizens). This process often leads to negative consequences for *development and security*, as oil wealth fails to filter down to the wider population. And lastly, of course, the huge reliance of the world on fossil fuels as a source of energy, and the likely continuation of this fact, will ultimately impact widely upon us all, as understood through the lens of *environmental security*.

Overall, then, the problem of energy security intersects with a host of other security issues, and is rising up the agenda of international politics as governments are increasingly concerned over the quantity and reliability of their state's energy sources. And, given the causes of this problem, discussed in the next section, it is likely to be a central security issue well into the twenty-first century.

KEY POINTS

- The degree of energy security experienced by each political community is measured by the reliable and stable supply of enough energy to meet the energy demands of the present, and into the near future.
- Many communities live in a state of energy insecurity, although the problem tends to manifest differently in the global North, as compared to the South. Robust energy infrastructure in industrialized economies means that energy security here is best considered at the state level.
- For energy-intensive economies of the North, the search for energy security is intimately wrapped up with notions of economic security, and may affect the wider dynamics of international security, with the potential for inter-state conflict over key resources in the future.
- For oil-rich regions in the South, the drive to achieve energy security by the core powers has an impact upon the human security of local communities, whilst oil wealth often insulates leaders from the wider population, with consequences for notions of regime security and development.

The problem of energy security

At one level, the growing problem of energy (in)security is simple to explain. Demand for energy use is growing—and in all likelihood will continue to grow for the foreseeable future—whilst it is not at all clear that reliable and stable sources of supply will continue to match this. This leads to a growing 'energy gap' between demand and supply, which in turn exacerbates concerns amongst leaders over the sources of future supply. The vast majority of global energy consumption is sourced from fossil fuels, whether oil, coal, or natural gas, with the remainder made up from nuclear and renewable sources. And, in particular, oil is crucial to the workings of industrialized and industrializing economies, providing the basis for much of the world's transportation, industrial production, and commercial activity.

Oil consumption is set to rise significantly over the coming decades. Whereas the world consumed 84 million barrels per day (bbl/d) in 2005, forecasts show that this will rise to 120 million bbl/d by 2040 (an increase of almost 50 per cent).[1] Crucially, those states currently responsible for the majority of the world's energy consumption—the industrialized states of North America, Europe, East Asia, and Australasia that make up the Organization for Economic Cooperation and Development (OECD)—are actually set to *decrease* their oil consumption by 2040, as energy demands from economic growth are met by other sources. It will be a meteoric rise in demand by the newly emergent major economies of the non-OECD that will primarily account for increased global consumption. These regions of the world consumed 34 million bbl/d in 2005, just 40 per cent of the world's total. By 2040 consumption is forecast to more than double, to 75 million bbl/d, representing at that stage over 60 per cent of total consumption. In particular, the rapid growth of the Chinese and Indian economies is drastically changing the energy map of the world: by 2040 they are projected to be responsible for over 20 per cent of the world's consumption, with Chinese use of oil projected to outstrip that of the United States for the first time in 2035. It is unsurprising, therefore, that some have referred to an emerging 'Chindia Challenge', destined to exacerbate the coming problem of energy insecurity (Klare 2008).

[1] Unless otherwise stated, all data in this section are drawn from the authoritative *International Energy Outlook 2014*, a publication from the US Department of Energy (see Energy Information Administration (EIA) 2014).

As will be explored next, the geographical distribution of world energy stocks and the location of the largest energy consumers creates what we will call an 'energy–security nexus', whereby energy security becomes irretrievably entwined with the foreign and security policies of both the established great powers and rapidly 'rising' states.

The energy–security 'nexus'

Some powerful states in world politics, such as Russia, Canada, and the UK do not require large volumes of imported oil to sustain the demand from their domestic economies. Moreover, recent developments in hydraulic fracturing in North America ('fracking') has increased the global reserves of both oil and gas, and led many analysts to speculate that the USA—historically the world's largest importer—could become energy independent in the future. Imports are a growing concern for other powers. China and India need to import over half of their oil requirements, whereas members of the older and established G8 such as Japan, France, Germany, and Italy are almost wholly reliant on foreign oil. Moreover, reliance amongst some is set to grow, as increased demand from powerful states is not matched by rises in domestic production. For China, for example, oil consumption is forecast to triple between 2005 and 2040, from under 7 million bbl/d to 20 million bbl/d. Domestic oil production, however, is set to rise from 3.8 million bbl/d to 5.7 million bbl/d. The resulting 'energy gap' for China will therefore grow massively: the economy will need to increase oil imports from under 3 million bbl/d in 2005 to over 14 million bbl/d in 2040, more than *quadrupling* the amount of oil needing to be imported into the country.

This fact ensures that controlling the conditions under which this resource is produced, exported, and delivered to consumers has become a key strategic concern for powerful states. And this is not just the case for growing oil importers: as we will explore later on, global economic interdependence and the current distribution of power in the international system means that the US and other core powers will continue to remain involved in global energy security whilst remaining sensitive to sudden oil price shocks likely precipitated by rapid geopolitical change in oil-rich regions. In the postcolonial era, where formal notions of imperial control no longer frame North–South relations, political, economic, and even military intervention in oil-rich regions by the world's great powers has continued to play itself out on the ground. In particular, the *stability and friendly orientation* of key oil-producing states and regions is a central concern for strategists, and foreign and security policies have often reflected this fact. In regions where instability is often endemic, and where there exists a range of forces seeking to challenge existing geopolitical configurations, these powers have often acted to bolster those governmental and non-governmental forces considered 'friendly'. Billions of dollars of economic and military assistance have been granted to oil-rich regimes by the great powers, often in direct competition with one another for influence. Ensuring that enough oil keeps on flowing—and that local governments are sufficiently responsive to the needs of the larger economies—is a priority for consuming states.

Attempts to exert control over energy reserves in the South have consequences for the extent to which cooperation between core powers can be sustained. Indeed, the potential for an emerging set of geopolitical rivalries over this form of control has implications for international security more broadly. What these implications might be depends largely upon the theoretical framework employed. In the next section we will briefly explore competing understandings of the role played by energy in international politics, and the consequences of growing energy insecurity for international security.

KEY POINTS

- Growing concerns over energy security derive from rapidly increasing global demand for energy (with oil consumption set to rise by 50 per cent by 2040), allied to rising fears over the size of key energy stocks and the likelihood of being able to exploit them in the future. The emerging 'Chindia Challenge' is especially significant in this regard, given the huge rises in energy consumption forecast for the Chinese and Indian economies.
- An energy–security 'nexus' exists, whereby a central priority for core powers becomes ensuring that friendly and stable governments exist in the oil-rich South. This objective is a key determinant of foreign policy, and influences the nature of diplomacy and assistance.
- This strategy has potential consequences for international security, as larger states compete over the politics of control with regards to producing states. It also has consequences for those living in the oil-rich South, particularly given that the core powers often support non-democratic regimes in the name of 'stability'.

Energy security and IR theory

Liberalism and energy security

According to received liberal wisdom, the spread of liberal democracy in the post-Cold War era, tied to free-market capitalism, has ensured that many more regions now benefit from an order that has brought peace and stability to the West since 1945. Processes of globalization are accelerating, and a vastly increased set of interlinkages between states ensures that national interests are increasingly subsumed by the logic of transnational economic cooperation. The potential for inter-state competition has consequently reduced, and many liberals now see war between the major powers as an obsolete phenomenon.

On this reading, the increasing reliance by the core powers upon the oil reserves in the global South is unlikely to lead to major conflict. International energy markets—which dictate production levels, major transit routes, and prices—mediate relations between producers and consumers, as well as between major consumers. The interests of all core powers are highly enmeshed, as the energy security of each state cannot be divorced from that of others. All major players want to maximize the stability of the flow of oil onto the market, and to minimize fluctuations over the prices that everyone pays. Moreover, this common interest is not dependent on where each state physically receives its oil from; it is the stability of the overall market that is of concern.

For liberals, then, the interconnected nature of today's global economy ensures that energy security for one is dependent upon energy security for all, and that all core powers have the same interests in maintaining and extending the conditions under which this market operates. As long as this economic order exists, conflict between major powers over energy reserves is highly unlikely. We can read this liberal logic into the US management of oil-rich Iraq after 2003. China is now one of the biggest players in Iraq, with some of the largest oil deals in human history signed between the Iraqi state and Chinese state-owned oil companies such as China National Petroleum Corp. Continued US military and diplomatic engagement in the country plays out alongside a shared US–Sino interest in stability in Iraq, given a mutual need for stable suppliers of energy to international markets.

Realism and energy security

In contrast to liberals, realist thinkers are increasingly sceptical about the durability of the current liberal order, and point to several disturbing trends that may signal a return to an era of greater geopolitical confrontation. 'Resource wars', in particular over energy sources, present a clear possibility for a breakdown in international cooperation, as states begin to compete (and eventually conflict) over the control of major reserves. For Michael Klare, the key thinker in this regard, we are witnessing

> the energy equivalent of an arms race to secure control over whatever remaining deposits of oil and natural gas are up for sale on the planet, along with reserves of other vital minerals. This resource race is already one of the most conspicuous features of the contemporary landscape and, in our lifetimes, may become *the* most conspicuous one—a voracious, zero-sum contest that, if allowed to continue along present paths, can only lead to conflict among the major powers.
>
> Klare (2008: 30)

In this light, energy scarcity was said to lead to future disruptions in the global system and the potential emergence of a 'new international energy order', characterized less by liberal free-market trading than by statism and neo-mercantilism. This realist understanding does well to explain recent moves by powers outside the liberal core—most noticeably China—to circumvent the international market in energy. For Beijing, such moves are driven by a sense of deep concern about the sheer degree of American dominance over Persian Gulf oil, which will allow Washington to control the flow of oil during any period of heightened Sino–US tension. As a result, Chinese planners are pursuing direct, bilateral deals with oil-rich regimes across the world, which results in the trade of oil outside the global marketplace.

In particular, realists point to the strategic rivalries at play in the Caspian Basin. Since the scale of the reserves became clear in the mid-1990s, Russia, China, and the USA have been vying for influence over the oil-rich regimes of Central Asia and the Caucasus. Military and economic aid has flowed from each power, and the issue of pipeline routes have become key. In this context, a strategic priority for Washington has been to loosen Moscow's traditional dominance of the region through pushing for the construction of westward-pointing pipelines, bypassing Russian territory to reach international markets. In return, Moscow and Beijing have been working to minimize American influence in the region. Clearly, such rivalry presents a challenge to the current liberal order, and may signal the beginning of intensified inter-state competition and conflict. The 2008 Russian invasion of Georgia (a key oil-transit state), the Russian annexation of Crimea in 2014, and continued tensions over Ukraine have led to sanctions imposed on Moscow, including on its all-important energy sector. These developments are, for some, a harbinger of a new age of resource competition played out through force of arms.

Historical materialism and energy security

From a historical-materialist (HM) perspective, liberal and realist accounts miss a central aspect of the picture. Indeed, one cannot understand the importance of energy and its influence on international politics without placing it within the context of the development of global capitalism, and without exploring the role of key states in defending and expanding this economic system. Oil remains the lifeblood of the current order—an order that is based upon an unequal distribution of wealth and **power** in favour of global economic elites. In this regard, those who benefit most from the prevailing order are driven to ensure that the flow of energy under favourable conditions continues to underpin their position in the global system.

There are disputes from within the HM tradition over exactly how and why control of oil supplies is sought by leading capitalist states. In what we will call the 'blood-for-oil' thesis, intervention by core capitalist powers in oil-rich regions is designed to serve specific corporate interests, especially those of 'Big Oil'. In this reading, the capitalist state is little more than an instrument for ruling economic elites, with foreign policy subsumed under a logic of profit maximization. Ian Rutledge (2006: 65) provides a clear example of this form of analysis when he describes figures such as US Vice President Dick Cheney as a 'single-minded representative of oil capitalism', and someone who 'would not hesitate to mould US foreign policy into a form conducive to the business opportunities and profit maximisation so earnestly sought after by the huge energy multinationals of which his own company was a leading representative'.

In contrast to such 'instrumentalist' accounts, others working within the HM tradition have stressed the 'relative autonomy' of capitalist states, whereby they act primarily for the interests of the capitalist world order *as a whole*, rather than for the interests of specific capitalists (such as the oil sector). Such accounts stress the managerial role assumed by core powers (and by Washington in particular), whereby they work to ensure the smooth operations of a global economy beneficial to all. In this reading, overt competition over the world's oil stocks will continue to be overwhelmingly pacified, as rival centres of power opt to work within the framework of the liberal international economic order. Within this, international oil companies (IOCs) are granted the freedom to make independent commercial decisions over where to invest, with the role of capitalist states one of maintaining an international environment required for private capital to operate with security and profits.

On this reading we are not, in the face of increased tension between major powers, seeing a return to widespread geopolitical rivalry, especially given that the global hegemon (the USA) and many other key states remain dedicated to an order based on a largely positive-sum, open-door trading regime. For the capitalist core, by far the most preferred future scenario is a China (and Russia and India) that remains pacified and subordinated within the liberal economic order.

KEY POINTS

- The likelihood of increased international competition and conflict over energy reserves depends upon the theoretical framework employed, with realists generally pessimistic about the future sustainability of the liberal economic order.
- A key question in this regard is how core powers will begin to relate to each other as energy stocks dwindle: will they continue to cooperate through current open-door trading regimes, or will they retreat behind nationalist barriers? And what will this mean for the likelihood of inter-state conflict?
- Historical materialists stress the importance of control of the world's energy reserves to the development of global capitalism, and examine how and why core capitalist states have worked to ensure this control is maintained.

Energy security and human insecurity

Of all the regions in the global South, oil-rich zones are often some of the most unstable. **Dutch disease**—whereby substantial oil income drives up exchange rates, slowing overall growth and 'hollowing out' non-oil sectors—affects many oil-rich economies. In parallel, these regions tend to have a set of *political* problems that have the potential to exacerbate existing instabilities and generate new ones. In particular, as the economist Joseph Stiglitz (2003) has made clear: 'Control over natural resource wealth provides leaders with little incentive to share power, and gives leaders the means with which to buy legitimacy rather than earn it through elections.' Authoritarian state forms can be more easily sustained in oil-rich regions, given that the centralization of wealth works to insulate the ruling strata from popular pressure for reform. The prevalence of non-democratic governance can be seen across the oil-rich Middle East, Caspian Region, and West Africa, where the power of corrupt dictatorships is largely based upon the huge wealth generated through the energy sector.

In turn, the reduction of legitimate political space for most of the population, combined with often vast inequalities in wealth distribution (as the oil 'rents' are retained within a small circle of economic and political elites), can easily breed domestic unrest. Across the oil-rich South, a wide variety of social and political forces have arisen to challenge the current distribution of power, and the conditions under which energy stocks are released onto international markets. Most of these adopt peaceful means of protest, although increasingly these have been matched by armed campaigns against the prevailing order, as groups turn to violence in order to achieve their goals. Attacks on energy infrastructure and foreign oil workers have increased, and these have often tied in with wider insurgent campaigns for greater autonomy and control over resources. The ideological base supporting these movements is highly dependent on each situation, ranging from leftist groups in Colombia to ethno-nationalist groups in the Niger Delta (see Case Study 23.1), to Al-Qaeda-affiliated groups in Saudi Arabia.

Regardless of the specificities of each case, these forms of resistance all—to varying degrees—present a major challenge to the security of oil operations

CASE STUDY 23.1 Oil and resistance in the Niger delta

The extraction and exportation of oil in the Niger delta has generated significant internal instability within Nigeria, as extreme poverty combines with widespread environmental degradation as a direct result of oil operations. A wide range of groups in the delta have been active in the region. Particularly high profile has been the peaceful campaign by the Ogoni community, which coalesced in the early 1990s around the Movement for the Survival of the Ogoni People (MOSOP). Consisting of a collection of trade unions, church bodies, women's associations, and student unions, MOSOP (1990) declared that 'over 30 years of oil mining have led to the complete degradation of the Ogoni environment', and that 'we as a people must through all lawful and non-violent means fight for social justice and fair play for ourselves and our progeny'. The group has been key in organizing mass protests against oil operations on Ogoni land—acts of popular expression that led ultimately to the execution of nine Ogoni activists by the Nigerian state (including, infamously, MOSOP's President, Kenule Saro-Wiwa).

In addition to lawful means of protest, groups in the delta have taken to direct action. Oil facilities and platforms have been occupied. In May 1998, for example, over 100 unarmed Ijaw Youth Council members occupied Chevron's Parabe oil platform in order to demand more local employment and greater efforts to clear up pollution. This was followed by the release of the Kaiama Declaration in December 1998, which stated the group's intent to 'cease to recognise all undemocratic decrees that rob our peoples/communities of the right to ownership and control of our lives and resources', and demanded 'the immediate withdrawal from Ijawland of all military forces of occupation and repression by the Nigerian state' (Ijaw Youth Council 1998). This tactic was repeated by 600 Itsekiri women in 2002, who peacefully occupied ChevronTexaco's Escravos export terminal for ten days, shutting down around 25 per cent of the country's production (International Crisis Group 2006a: 15).

Increasingly, however, such peaceful protests have been matched by armed campaigns in the delta. Two groups in particular—the Movement for the Emancipation of the Niger Delta (MEND) and the Niger Delta People's Volunteer Force (NDPVF)—have emerged in recent years, and use armed force explicitly as part of a campaign to seize 'total control' of the Niger delta's oil wealth. MEND, for example, is explicitly fighting for 25–30 per cent of oil revenues to be returned to local communities in the delta (International Crisis Group 2006b: 3–5). It aims to achieve this by halting the current activities of the oil sector. By attacking oil workers and facilities, MEND has declared that: 'It must be clear that the Nigerian government cannot protect your workers or assets. Leave our land while you can, or die in it. Our aim is to totally destroy the capacity of the Nigerian government to export oil' (BBC News 2006b).

in the region, and therefore to the energy security of consuming states. As with other forms of foreign investment, the confidence and smooth operation of oil capital is deeply affected by political instability. In this sense, conditions in much of the oil-rich South give rise to grave concern for those powers reliant upon a steady flow of energy from these regions, not least because it may adversely affect the commercial decisions of IOCs about where to invest. This has translated into a focus by these states on 'critical infrastructure protection', in order to ensure the smooth operation of the oil sector in the face of 'terrorist' threats. Organizations such as NATO have emphasized that 'protecting energy infrastructure at home only provides a partial response to the challenge posed by energy security', and that European and North American dependence on foreign energy supplies ensures that they have 'an interest in enhancing protection of energy infrastructure in producing and transit countries, and of energy routes worldwide' (NATO 2007).

This interest has seen a rise in military assistance provided to oil-rich states. However, and of key importance in relation to the impact on human security, this aid is not simply designed to provide static defence for oil infrastructure. It is also provided in order to ensure a wider stability of prevailing social orders, where these are considered favourable for energy-consuming states. In other words, given the presence of forces in the oil-rich South who would overturn existing forms of governance, and who may alter the terms under which oil is supplied to the major powers, it often becomes important for those powers to support incumbent regimes in their fight against sources of 'instability'. The rationale for militarized intervention in this regard has been clearly spelt out by policy analysts in the field:

> It is . . . reasonable to ask who, among present-day occupants of the international stage, would like to see a great deal changed? To which the immediate answer would obviously be the ramshackle assemblage of rogue

states and revolutionary movements whose machinations consume such a disproportionate share of time and attention from the defense establishments around the world . . . military planners and civilian strategists are [inclined] to point to the potential threat that terrorists and other disenfranchised groups pose to global energy markets; and indeed they have good reason to.

Moran and Russell (2008)

This focus on the threat posed to international energy markets by 'disenfranchised groups' in the South has led to the provision of a particular form of military assistance by the core powers. Alongside pipeline protection and anti-kidnapping training, local security forces are being equipped to *actively* deploy against a wide range of armed and unarmed groups. Frequently refracted through the lens of 'counter-insurgency' or 'counterterrorism', this aid has often had grave consequences for those sections of civil society pushing for change (however moderate). Groups that in some way challenge the rule of incumbent elites in oil-rich regions are often recast as 'terrorist' or 'subversive' threats, thereby legitimating the use of armed force in response. Indeed, a cursory examination of the human rights records of security forces in the oil-rich South leaves no doubt of the effects on human security of their campaigns to ensure regime security (and, indirectly, global energy security).

In parallel, IOCs have often resorted to the employment of force in order to guarantee the security of their investments. On the ground, this has been carried out through close cooperation with both host-nation security forces and **private military companies (PMCs)**. PMCs are employed by oil corporations throughout the global South to protect specific installations, create localized zones of stability to allow operations to continue unimpeded, and even to influence the wider dynamics of conflict in the region. In this way, they 'act as 'investment enablers', providing clients with robust security that make otherwise extremely risky investment options safe enough to be financially viable. In the midst of conflict, they create localized stability that reduces costs and increases investment values' (Singer 2003: 80–1). Throughout the oil-rich South, such operations have led to extensive human rights abuses. Indeed, according to John Ruggie (2006) in his work for the UN, the extractive sector 'utterly dominates' the record of documented abuses by transnational corporations in the South, accounting for most of the 'allegations of the worst abuses, up to and including complicity in crimes against humanity, typically for acts committed by public and private security forces protecting company assets and property; large-scale corruption; violations of labour rights; and a broad array of abuses in relation to local communities, especially indigenous people'. In many cases, the outsourcing of security requirements to private companies is used to ensure 'plausible deniability' in the face of any abuses that result.

KEY POINTS

- The drive to maximize and stabilize the flow of oil onto international markets has profound implications for populations in producing states, as oil wealth insulates ruling elites from the need to ensure political accountability and a fair distribution of economic resources.
- Ongoing social injustice has spurred many groups to challenge the prevailing order, through both peaceful protest and armed insurgency. Although motivated by a wide range of ideological commitments, such movements present a common threat to the interests of oil corporations, local economic and political elites, and the energy-consuming states of the global North.
- Often supported by one or more of the major powers, and working alongside oil corporations, non-democratic governments in oil-rich regions routinely deploy their security forces to ensure 'stability' is maintained.
- 'Stability' in this context refers to the absence of challenge to the status quo, and the pursuit of this objective has severe ramifications for human security in the regions. Operating through the lens of 'counter-insurgency' or 'counterterrorism', local security forces often engage in repeated human rights violations in order to remove threats.

Energy security and the United States

As the global hegemon, the United States has long been concerned with ensuring the security of the world's energy supplies. This has translated into a post-war strategy of political, economic, and military intervention in oil-rich regions, precisely in order to stabilize and maximize global energy production. In this section, we will begin to unpack the logic behind this strategy, before briefly examining the record of intervention by Washington.

In addition to the substantial reliance on foreign sources of oil, an important component of American grand strategy is premised upon establishing and retaining control of major oil reserves. In other words, there is a geostrategic, as well as an economic logic driving concerns over 'energy security'. The Pentagon is by far the largest single consumer of oil in the world; for example, in 2012, the US military consumed 350,000 barrels of oil—80 per cent of the US government's entire energy consumption.

Moreover, the USA plays a key role in stabilizing global oil production that in turn provides the USA with an often subtle form of control over other great powers. Zbigniew Brzezinski, President Carter's former National Security Adviser and close adviser to the Obama administration, captured this wider, structural logic when he argued:

> America has major strategic and economic interests in the Middle East that are dictated by the region's vast energy supplies. Not only does America benefit economically from the relatively low costs of Middle Eastern oil, but America's security role in the region gives it indirect but politically critical leverage on the European and Asian economies that are also dependent on energy exports from the region.
>
> Zbigniew Brzezinski (2003–4: 8)

It is in this context that US control over the Persian Gulf has long been considered so important and helps partially explain the US's abiding national security interests in the region. In particular, Saudi Arabia remains central for US strategic planners, given that it holds more than 20 per cent of the entire global stock of oil and—along with other regional producers—over 80 per cent of the world's '**excess production capacity**' (EIA 2011). The EIA estimates that OPEC surplus crude oil production capacity, concentrated in Saudi Arabia, will average three million bbl/d in 2015, ensuring that the US continues to have significant national security interests in the region (Energy Information Administration 2014).

US hegemony, oil, and intervention in the Middle East

The centrality of oil from the Middle East has long been understood by US planners. As early as 1944, for example, a report by the Office of Strategic Services (the forerunner of the CIA) concluded that, in relation to the Middle East, Washington's key national interests were 'oil, airbases and future markets', whilst the US State Department urged a 'substantial and orderly expansion of production in Eastern Hemisphere sources of supply, principally the Middle East' (Klare 2004: 30; Layne 2006: 47–8). In particular, the United States has long worked to forge close relations with Saudi Arabia. President Roosevelt committed the United States in 1945 to secure the Saudi monarchical dictatorship from external and internal threat, in return for an agreement to export oil cheaply onto international markets. This strategic posture was concretized with the 1951 deployment of the United States Military Training Mission (USMTM): a large-scale, Pentagon-led advisory mission still in position in the 2000s. Militarizing the relationship between the Saudi state and people has been a long-term goal of the USA, which has worked continuously (and alongside a wide range of PMCs) to 'stabilize' the regime from internal 'subversion' (see Case Study 23.2).

This long-standing strategy towards Saudi Arabia was matched, before 1979, by a strategy to ensure the 'stability' of Iran, as the second significant oil state of the region. This played itself out through a CIA-sponsored coup against the democratically elected president, Mossadegh, after he moved to nationalize Iranian oil reserves and pull away from American and British influence. With a pro-US regime installed, Iran became the largest single purchaser of American arms in the world, and between 1972 and 1977 US military sales to Iran reached a staggering $16.2 billion (Bill 1988: 202).

However, this 'twin-pillar' strategy suffered a calamitous setback in 1979, with the Iranian Revolution and the Soviet invasion of Afghanistan both ensuring that powerful counter-hegemonic forces were present in the region. In response, the outgoing Carter administration swiftly announced a clear commitment to retain Washington's primacy in the Persian Gulf, through a policy of *direct intervention* in the face of any major threat to the flow of oil. To give teeth to his new doctrine, Carter ordered the formation of a Rapid Deployment Force (RDF) that could speedily assemble for forward power projection in the region. This force was later upgraded by Ronald Reagan to a full-scale regional command, US Central Command (CENTCOM). This has since been the central vehicle through which US power is exercised across the Persian Gulf. CENTCOM provides the key instrument for applying overwhelming military force throughout the region at any point that supplies appear threatened—a function acknowledged by its Commander-in-Chief, Anthony Zinni (1998): the command's military strategy towards

CASE STUDY 23.2 US counter-insurgency assistance and PMCs: stabilizing the Saudi regime

The United States has long worked to ensure the stability of the Saudi regime, given that it has provided the best means through which to access the country's oil reserves. Security assistance to Saudi Arabia has been designed explicitly to insulate the Saudi monarchy from internal unrest, given that—in President Reagan's words—'there is no way we could stand by and see [the country] taken over by anyone that would shut off that oil' (Maynes 1995: 105). This has been achieved primarily through the training and arming of the Saudi Arabian National Guard (SANG), a **paramilitary** force designed to consolidate the rule of the Saudi dictatorship and highly trained in internal warfare and counter-insurgency (CI) techniques. And central to the provision of US expertise in this regard has been the activities of private military companies (PMCs), which have been deployed *en masse* by Washington. Contracts between the Saudi regime and US-based PMCs run into billions of dollars, and have resulted in 35,000–40,000 private security personnel deploying to the country at any one time in order to buttress the military and internal security forces (Wells et al. 2001). Central to this assistance effort has been the Vinnell Corporation, which has been paid hundreds of millions of dollars to train the SANG, including the provision of CI doctrine, operational training in small-unit tactics and advanced infantry manœuvres, and equipment. As one Vinnell official told *Time* (1975): 'We are not mercenaries because we are not pulling triggers. We train people to pull triggers. Maybe that makes us executive mercenaries.' This relationship continues to be central to US planning, with huge sums dedicated by the Pentagon to bolstering Saudi internal security. In just one example, the Pentagon notified Congress in October 2005 of the possible provision of $918 million of equipment to support the modernization of the SANG. The package included 144 armoured personnel carriers, water cannon vehicles, command, control, and communications equipment, and tens of thousands of assault rifles with grenade launchers, as well as scopes and sights for sniper weapons systems. According to US officials, the SANG 'needs these defense articles so that it can effectively conduct security and counterterrorism operations' (Defense Security Cooperation Agency 2005). This trend has continued, with a 2013 request for up to $4 billion for further modernization of SANG's equipment, parts, training and logistical support.

Although increasingly wrapped up in the language of 'counterterrorism', assistance to the SANG has been designed to provide the means for the Saudi regime to suppress any domestic challenge to its rule, with overt activity by unionized workers or political activists targeted through widespread imprisonment and torture. Stabilizing the pro-US regime and keeping the oil flowing has required the continual policing of the Saudi population and the severe suppression of any significant protests. This has included the crushing of dissent over oil revenues by workers in 1978, the slaughter of over 400 people in protests against the Saudi authorities in 1987, right through to the 2007 imprisonment of 700 people who, according to the Saudi Ministry of the Interior, 'were not involved in terrorist acts' but were simply suspected of 'harbouring extremist thoughts' (Human Rights Watch 2007). US security assistance has continued even after the Arab Spring with the US concluding a $30 billion arms sale with Saudi Arabia in late 2011. This is driven in large part to help the **balance of power** in the region between the Sunni Saudis and the Shiite Iranians. More recently, the SANG were used to put down an uprising in neighbouring Bahrain as part of the so-called 'Peninsula Shield Force'.

the region was, he said, 'basically energy driven', with the significant oil deposits in the region 'one of the prime considerations in determining our interests'.

These interests have underpinned US strategy towards the region throughout the post-Cold War era, and explain Washington's response to the Iraqi invasion of Kuwait in August 1990, as well as the continued presence of significant numbers of US troops in the region throughout the 1990s. As the leaked draft of the 1992 Defense Planning Guidance made clear, in the Persian Gulf 'our overall objective is to remain the predominant outside power in the region and preserve US and Western access to the region's oil' (Tyler 1992). Ultimately, after the election of Bush and the attacks of 9/11 had provided a window of opportunity for US strategists, this objective translated into the campaign against Saddam Hussein, in order to remove a key threat to US power in the region. Although US officials strenuously denied that oil factored into the strategic planning surrounding regime change in Iraq, this logic was clearly at play. Indeed, the continuing centrality of this interest has been acknowledged by the former Chairman of the US Federal Reserve, Alan Greenspan:

> If Saddam Hussein had been head of Iraq and there was no oil under those sands, our response to him would not have been as strong as it was in the first Gulf War. And the second gulf war is an extension of the first. My view is that Saddam, looking over his 30-year history, very clearly was giving evidence of moving towards controlling the Straits of Hormuz, where there are 17, 18, 19 million barrels a day [passing through. Given that,] I'm saying taking Saddam out was essential.
>
> Woodward (2007)

US strategy of diversification

Continuing instability in the Persian Gulf, not ameliorated by the invasion and occupation of Iraq and continued instability in the region following the rise of various non-state actors such as the so-called 'Islamic State' in Iraq and Syria, has led to rising levels of concern amongst US planners as to the sheer vulnerability of an American economy, and a wider global position, which are both ultimately reliant on the steady flow of oil from this region. This is especially the case given the physical concentration of oil production and transportation from the Persian Gulf, which ensures that high-profile targets exist for those forces wishing to reduce export levels. This was brought home in dramatic style after the failed suicide bombing of the Abqaiq oil-processing plant in Saudi Arabia in February 2006. Had this been successful, output from a site through which two-thirds of the country's oil passes would have been drastically affected, with overall exports from Saudi Arabia potentially halved for up to a year (BBC News 2006a). Likewise, almost all this oil travels through the 21-mile-wide Strait of Hormuz, which is clearly vulnerable to closure or severe disruption. In this way, the beating heart of US power rests upon an exceptionally fragile set of conditions. This has been acknowledged by key US officials, with former US President George W. Bush (2007) clear that this dependence 'leaves us more vulnerable to hostile regimes, and to terrorists—who could cause huge disruptions of oil shipments, and raise the price of oil, and do great harm to our economy'. With tensions between the USA and Iran, in particular on the rise, the prospect of the Strait being closed is particularly acute.

As a result of this vulnerability, US planners have pursued a dual approach to ensure the highest possible degree of global (and, by extension, American) energy security. On the one hand, as we have seen, the USA has sought to entrench its dominance over the Persian Gulf. On the other hand, however, Washington has increasingly pursued a policy of **energy diversification** away from the Persian Gulf. Through this, US planners aim to supplant Middle Eastern oil supplies with those from other oil-rich regions within the South, with increasing efforts to cultivate new sets of relationships with alternative oil suppliers. Focusing on states in the Caspian Basin, West Africa, and Latin America—regions that together are thought to hold around 220 billion barrels of oil (not significantly less than Saudi Arabia)—Washington has increased the amount of military and economic assistance provided to oil-rich regimes. Employing this strategy, the USA has worked to establish its hegemony over these zones, so as to stabilize and maximize production levels, and to integrate local political economies within the wider US-led order.

As in the Persian Gulf, this strategy has relied upon an explicit militarization of state–society relations through extensive levels of security assistance, and a reorientation of local security forces away from concerns over external security and towards the provision of internal defence. As one key report from the Center for Strategic and International Studies declared: 'Stability in petroleum exporting regions is tenuous at best', and is threatened by a wide range of domestic forces, including 'pipeline sabotage in Nigeria, labour strikes in Venezuela. . . . and civil unrest in Uzbekistan and other [former Soviet Union] states' (Cordesman and Al-Rodhan 2005: 8). Ensuring domestic stability, often through the use of counter-insurgency training and equipment, has become a central means by which the USA attempts to maintain energy production in these regions. Needless to say, this has continued to have profound implications for local populations, as vocal elements from civil society are recast as subversive threats to 'peace and stability'.

KEY POINTS

- The USA has adopted a lead role in the post-war era in ensuring an adequate degree of global energy security. This has translated into extensive military deployment in oil-rich regions, and a wide array of interventions in order to stabilize friendly political and economic orders.
- The strategy has been pursued to secure enough oil for the American economy, but also to secure American primacy vis-à-vis friendly and rival powers. In this way, there is a geostrategic logic to US energy interventions, running alongside a purely economic logic.
- This logic has fed into a long-standing strategy of ensuring US dominance in the Persian Gulf, through the provision of military and economic aid to allied states, and through the presence and use of huge numbers of US troops. The invasion of Iraq in 2003 can be best understood as an implementation of this overall post-war strategy (albeit under the guise of a uniquely unilateralist and militarist American administration).
- Increasingly, the USA is attempting to supplant its dominance over the Persian Gulf with the integration of other oil-rich zones within the US-led order. Again, this is being largely achieved through the militarization of state–society relations in those regions, in order to stabilize energy production. And again, this has consequences for the human security of those in the wider oil-rich South.

Conclusion

As we have seen, energy security involves a complex nexus of geopolitical, economic, and strategic concerns, which link together distant regions of the globe, and disparate security concerns. Rising demand for energy, and the likelihood that this will continue to be met by fossil fuels, are matched by increasing uncertainties over the size and stability of remaining stocks. This will, almost inevitably, lead to a rising prominence of concerns over energy security, and an increasing possibility of intensified inter-state competition (and even conflict) over energy reserves. As we have examined, there exist a number of different theoretical approaches to understanding the nature of the current energy order, and these emphasize different aspects of the coming challenge. Liberal theorists stress the positive-sum nature of US oil hegemony, the openness of the market mechanism, and the ways in which the liberal order serves to pacify resource rivalry. In contrast, realist theorists tend to stress the inherent likelihood of a return to geopolitical tensions as a result of increased oil demands, and the strong potential for major powers to direct their strategic primacy towards a more 'mercantilist' direction. Finally, historical-materialist theorists stress the close interrelationship between energy security and the maintenance of a capitalist economic order, and consider the likelihood of future conflict through this lens.

Unsurprisingly, each of these approaches reveals important dimensions of contemporary and future global energy security. The global oil regime *is* a liberal one, in the sense that major powers can and do participate within it to the benefit of all. The nature of continued US military and diplomatic engagement in Iraq illustrates that the hegemon does not seek to parlay its influence into an outcome that would purely benefit US energy needs or oil corporations, with the Chinese and other great powers cutting multi-billion deals with the post-Saddam Iraqi state. As such, talk of a new 'Great Game', and the inherent likelihood of conflict and rivalry, is perhaps overblown. However, it is also true that increased economic turbulence as a result of the 2008 global financial crisis could see the gradual erosion of the liberal logic and the re-emergence of strategic rivalries. The effects of the crisis are still being felt with ongoing instability in Europe with a now resurgent Russia and an energy-dependent Western Europe. Moreover, the 2011 Arab Spring portends broader changes that are still as yet unpredictable, with the ongoing Syrian civil war and the rise of non-state actors such as the so-called 'Islamic State' increasing regional instability. The broad-based revolutions in the Middle East and North Africa have yet to affect the oil-rich Saudi Kingdom, but a number of lesser oil-rich regimes have been toppled, such as Qaddafi's Libya. It is still not clear what kind of regime will emerge, if these will prove as amenable to the energy interests of the great powers, and indeed what kind of leverage these powers can bring to bear given the fluidity of change in the region.

? QUESTIONS

1. What is meant by 'energy security'?
2. Why do medium-term projections paint a picture of increased future energy insecurity?
3. How might the problem of energy security impact upon wider aspects of international security?
4. How does the quest for energy security by states in the North generate human insecurity for people in the South?
5. In what ways have movements in the South attempted to resist what they see as the exploitative nature of current energy ownership and production structures?
6. How likely is a return to an era of geopolitical rivalry, driven by so-called resource wars?
7. Why does the USA have such a long record of military intervention in oil-rich regions of the global South?
8. What is military assistance to oil-rich states in the South primarily designed to achieve?
9. What role did oil play in the 2003 invasion of Iraq?

FURTHER READING

- Klare, M. (2004), *Blood and Oil: How America's Thirst for Petrol is Killing Us*, London: Penguin. A penetrating critique of America's drive to control energy reserves, both in the Middle East and more widely. It argues that this strategy is, in fact, generating insecurity for the United States.
- Klare, M. (2008), *Rising Powers Shrinking Planet: The New Geopolitics of Energy*, New York: Metropolitan Books. In this highly readable book, Klare outlines his vision for an emerging new international energy order, based on a rejection of the free-market order and a return to statism and neo-mercantilism.
- Layne, C. (2006), *The Peace of Illusions: American Grand Strategy from 1940 to the Present*, Ithaca, NY: Cornell University Press. Using detailed empirical analysis, this book lays out a convincing argument as to the continuity of American strategy in the post-war era. Although ranging far wider than oil, his analysis has direct relevance for thinking about the US role in underpinning global energy security.
- Leech, G. (2006), *Crude Interventions: The United States, Oil and the New World (Dis)Order*, London: Zed Books. Focusing on the effects of US intervention in the oil-rich South, this volume charts the degree to which abusive regimes are supported by the West (and the USA in particular), and the complicity of these powers in the human rights violations that result.
- Stokes, D. and Raphael, S. (2010), *Global Energy Security and American Hegemony*, Baltimore: Johns Hopkins University Press. In this book, we chart the long-standing American strategy to control oil-rich zones in the South, and the ways in which this control translates into the wider US objective of maintaining its primacy within the current liberal order. We pay particular attention to the attempt by US planners to 'stabilize' oil-rich zones, through the provision of military assistance to counter threats to its interests. Detailed case studies of Latin America, the Caspian Basin, and West Africa examine Washington's current strategy of energy diversification, and the consequences this has for the peoples living in these regions.

IMPORTANT WEBSITES

- **http://www.eia.doe.gov** The Energy Information Administration. An agency of the US Government, housed within the Department of Energy, the EIA provides official energy statistics (including production, export, and consumption data for all forms of marketed energy), in-depth country briefs, and authoritative forecasts up to 2040.
- **http://www.energybulletin.net** Energy Bulletin. A clearing house for information regarding energy security and the upcoming peak in global energy supply. Organized by energy source, region, and issue, this site gathers many useful and respectable analyses of the issue.
- **http://www.gwu.edu/~nsarchiv** National Security Archive, an independent, non-governmental research institute located at the George Washington University. Collects, analyses, and publishes declassified documents on US foreign policy, obtained through the US Freedom of Information Act. Many of these are published online, and provide a fascinating insight into US interventions in the Middle East and other oil-rich regions.
- **http://www.business-humanrights.org/** Home Business and Human Rights Resource Centre, a UK- and US-based charity dedicated to providing information on the human rights impacts—positive and negative—of corporate activities. A very detailed section on the energy sector, with over 4,800 entries searchable by company, countries, or issue. Publishes media articles, first-hand accounts, UN reports, and sought responses from corporations.

Visit the Online Resource Centre that accompanies this book for lots of interesting additional material: www.oxfordtextbooks.co.uk/orc/collins4e/

24

The Weapons Trade

Suzette R. Grillot

Chapter Contents

Reader's Guide

This chapter provides an overview of the international weapons trade. A history of the global arms trade is provided, highlighting the various ways in which the trade in defence and military equipment has shifted throughout the years until the present day. The chapter outlines the ways in which weapons are illicitly traded and addresses the connections between legal and illicit arms markets. Finally, the chapter addresses the many attempts that have been made in recent years to control the international arms trade, as well as prospects for its future regulation. What emerges is a rather complex picture of the global arms trade that requires attention to numerous facets involving both weapons supply and demand.

Introduction

The international trade in military equipment is a large and profitable, but also potentially dangerous and deadly, enterprise. Billions of dollars of weapons—large and small—as well as ammunition and spare parts are produced, sold, exported, imported, transported, smuggled, used, and even misused on a daily basis around the world. The international arms trade not only consists of legal transfers between governments and militaries, but also involves the illicit trade of weapons and military items among less reputable governments, groups, and individuals. One cannot analyse the weapons trade without considering the various actors involved. From weapons producers, suppliers, transporters, **middlemen**, **gunrunners**, and individual traders to national militaries, insurgents, terrorists, corrupt governments, and various others, the international trade in arms, ammunition, and military equipment is multi-faceted and complex. Moreover, numerous governments, groups, and individuals are involved in controlling the arms trade, adding an additional layer of complexity. The international weapons trade, after all, is difficult to manage and control. Yet, unrestricted flows of weapons pose significant threats and result in dangerous consequences for international, national, and human security. A complete understanding of the international weapons trade, therefore, requires complete attention to the entirety of the arms market—from supply to demand, use to misuse, and consequences to control.

This chapter provides a general, but comprehensive, overview of the international weapons trade. It begins with a discussion of the arms trade in historical perspective and notes the ways in which the international trade in military equipment has shifted, changed, and evolved over the years. The chapter then focuses on the most recent arms trade trends. Next, the chapter addresses the connections between the legal and illicit arms markets, before discussing the many attempts that have been made in recent years to control the international arms trade.

History and shifting dynamics of the defence trade

The international trade of defence and military items is not new. Weapons of all kinds, sizes, and uses have been important commodities for centuries. Nevertheless, the international production and transfer of defence and military goods increased substantially in the fifteenth and sixteenth centuries (Pearson 1994: 10–11). It was primarily in Europe that weapons were produced and traded throughout this time period, but production and trade did extend to the Middle East, Asia, Africa, and elsewhere. From the mid-1500s until the mid-1600s there was a significant increase in arms trade networks as capitalist economic systems began to grow and technological advances in the production of firearms, gunpowder, and cannons emerged (Pearson 1994: 11; Krause 1995: 48–21). The weapons trade then slowed and stabilized until the industrial revolution of the 1800s; throughout this industrial period laissez-faire economic activity flourished, meaning that few if any regulations hampered the development, production, trade, and transfer of just about any kind of commodity imaginable, including weapons (Krause 1995: 53, 58, 60–1; Stoker and Grant 2003).

The devastation, destruction, and death resulting from the First World War changed the perception and, therefore, the operation of the international arms trade. The production and transfer of weapons came to be seen by some as a 'bloody business' and a significant cause of war in the wake of the First World War (Brockway 1933). This did not, however, lead to a reduction in the weapons trade—quite the contrary. The twentieth century, in fact, was a period of significant growth and change for the international arms trade—and governments were very clearly in the driver's seat (Stanley and Pearton 1972: 8).

Throughout the twentieth century, four general trends in the global weapons trade were evident. First, the arms trade shifted from being considered a matter of private enterprise to a process that was government controlled (Stohl and Grillot 2009: 16–17). Major governments, such as the United States, the UK, France, and Germany, began to play a more active and important role in guiding the production of weapons and directing their export. Governments developed credit and financing programmes to those who sought to buy weapons made in their respective countries and created laws regarding weapons production, licensing, and trade to enhance domestic, if not international regulation of arms transfers. Because of the significance of weapons and their role in protecting national sovereignty and providing for the national defence, governments also began to view weapons transfers as an important aspect of foreign policy. The arms trade, therefore, was often used as a diplomatic tool to potentially enhance national **power** and capability in faraway lands (Pierre 1982). In fact, arms transfers have been an important method for governments to promote their own power and improve their security environment (Morrow 1993).

The second general trend of the twentieth century weapons trade is its significant growth in volume (Stohl and Grillot 2009: 17–21). In 1950, approximately $7 billion worth of weapons and defence equipment was being transferred internationally. This value exploded to about $20 billion by the mid-1950s. By the early 1980s, weapons sales were valued at about $45 billion. Several factors account for such growth.

This time period was considered to be the height of the Cold War standoff between the United States and its Western allies and the Soviet Union and its Eastern allies. The 'West' and the 'East' both engaged in major military build-ups throughout this time. Moreover, there was a substantial increase in technology throughout this period of the twentieth century and a dramatic increase in the economic wealth of the West in particular that led to enhanced weapons production and trade. Because domestic production and consumption of weaponry was more and more expensive, due to technological advancements making weapons more sophisticated and lethal, profits from weapons exports became more and more important to finance domestic defence capabilities. And as weapons production increased and more profits were being made, weapons production and trade became more extensively tied to domestic economies and employment of the citizenry (Krause 1995: 31–2).

A third trend of the twentieth century weapons trade is the growth in the number and variety of weapons producers and suppliers (Stohl and Grillot 2009: 21–2). Earlier in the twentieth century, weapons were produced in relatively few countries. Major suppliers were, of course, the USA, the Soviet Union, the UK, France, Germany, and China. By 1970, however, a number of other countries were beginning to produce defence and military items. By 1990 more than forty countries were exporting weapons around the world. Countries such as India, Israel, South Africa, Brazil, North Korea, South Korea, Egypt, and Argentina have joined the ranks of global arms producers and traders (Brzoska and Ohlson 1986).

Finally, a fourth weapons trade trend of the twentieth century is the shift in weapons recipients (Stohl and Grillot 2009: 22–3). Throughout most of the twentieth century, weapons were primarily produced by, exported to, and imported by developed countries. Members of the North Atlantic Treaty Organization (NATO), for example, were the primary recipients of weapons manufactured in and traded by Western countries and among Euro-Atlantic partners. The Soviet Union and its allies in Eastern Europe were major weapons producers and exporters among and within the Soviet Bloc. By the 1970s, however, defence and military equipment of all kinds were being exported to and imported by numerous countries outside of the United States and Europe. Countries in Asia, South Asia, the Middle East, Africa, and Latin America emerged in the late twentieth century as major recipients of weapons. In 1970, for example, these regions received an approximate $6 billion in weapons imports. Ten years later, by 1980, that number had nearly tripled (Edmonds 1981).

The history of the international arms trade, therefore, is characterized by significant change and growth throughout the twentieth century in terms of government involvement and control, a significant increase in amounts and volume, the expansion of weapons suppliers and shifts in weapons recipients. By the end of the twentieth century, however, the global weapons trade was set to change even more. With the end of the Cold War, the changing nature of violent conflict, and the impact of international terrorism in the twenty-first century, recent trends in the global weapons trade are quite varied and continue to be a moving target.

KEY POINTS

- Weapons have been developed, traded, and used throughout much of human history.
- Historically speaking, the international defence trade increased substantially in the fifteenth, sixteenth, and seventeenth centuries.
- Governments became more involved in the defence trade during the twentieth century—both in directing and regulating the arms trade.
- Despite the role of government, the defence trade increased significantly in volume throughout the twentieth century.
- In the late twentieth century there was a tremendous growth in the number of weapons suppliers and a shift in the types of weapons recipients.
- After the First World War, the defence industry was questioned as a 'bloody business'.

Contemporary trends in the weapons trade

In the post-Cold War period, three significant trends are evident in the global weapons trade (Stohl and Grillot 2009: 24–31). First, there was an initial reduction in global arms sales throughout the 1990s, but the trade then rebounded and increased significantly after 11 September 2001. From a high of about $45 billion in the mid-1980s, the value of the international arms trade fell to about $25 billion in the mid-1990s and then to approximately $20 billion in the late 1990s.

What might help us understand this decline in the weapons trade? One factor is that domestic economies had been pushed to their limits in terms of defence spending throughout the Cold War era—particularly in the Soviet Union and within the Soviet Bloc. Concerns about domestic economic well-being, therefore, were elevated to the extent that weapons production for domestic consumption decreased substantially. Moreover, in the post-Cold War period there was an initial pause in the potential for global conflict, especially between the United States and the Soviet Union. Therefore, a decrease in arms sales emerged due to decreased demand for defence and military equipment in both the East and the West (Pearson 1994). After the terrorist attacks of **9/11**, however, arms sales increased substantially as the United States targeted its arms transfers to relevant parties involved in the **Global War on Terror** (Stohl and Grillot 2009: 34–6). By 2011, US arms sales alone totalled more than $65 billion, resulting in the USA becoming the world's primary weapons producer and supplier to the rest of the world (Grimmett and Kerr 2012). Nonetheless, the USA was not the only country to increase its weapons production and exports after 9/11. An overall increase in weapons transfers emerged in countries such as Russia, China, India, Pakistan, the UK, Germany, France, and others as well. Furthermore, no continent went untouched as defence and military items were exported in significant quantities to countries throughout the Middle East, Asia, Africa, and Latin America. Overall, the total value of the global weapons trade in 2011 was more than $85 billion, with more than 60 per cent of arms transfers being received by developing countries (Grimmett and Kerr 2012) (see Tables 24.1 and 24.2).

Table 24.1 Global arms sales: primary weapons suppliers and recipients, 2004–2011

Weapons supplier	Value of weapons sales (in billions of US dollars)	Percentage of total sales
United States	220.608	44
Russia	83.323	17
France	41.96	8
UK	27.037	5
China	17.808	4
Germany	22.068	4
Italy	14.278	3
Other European Countries	48.259	10
Others	27.109	5
Weapons recipient	**Value of weapons imported (in billions of US dollars)**	**Percentage of total sales**
Saudi Arabia	75.7	21
India	46.6	13
UAE	20.3	6
Egypt	14.3	4
Pakistan	13.2	4
Venezuela	13.1	4
Brazil	10.9	3
Algeria	10.3	3
Israel	9.5	3
South Korea	9.2	2
All other developing countries	145.168	39

Source: Grimmett and Kerr (2012).

Table 24.2 Primary weapons exporters and their recipients

	Percentage of supplier sales to recipients in each region			
Supplier to recipient	Latin America	Africa	Asia	North Africa and the Middle East
United States	3.0	0.6	22.0	39.0
Russia	2.0	9.0	62.0	15.0
France	2.0	0.0	39.0	40.0
UK	0.0	0.5	13.0	72.0
China	0.0	23.0	45.0	18.0

Source: SIPRI (2012).

Along with this noteworthy surge in the global weapons trade in the post-Cold War period came an important (and perhaps ironic) intensification of government control to prevent the spread of weapons (especially weapons of mass destruction) to countries and end-users of potential concern. In fact, this second trend in the contemporary weapons trade began initially after the Gulf War in 1991 when it became clear that Iraq had procured weapons capability that was considered in violation of international arms and **export control** agreements (Stohl and Grillot 2009: 31–3). Government efforts, particularly at the behest of the United States, to establish appropriate weapons transfer policies and procedures regarding the licensing and control of arms exports expanded (see section on Controlling the weapons trade) throughout the 1990s and 2000s, as did transnational interaction and cooperation on the issue. Such growth in defence trade controls, however, corresponded with the largest increase in international arms transfers in history.

A final trend relevant for the contemporary weapons trade is the changing nature of violent conflict in recent years and the different motivations for engaging in the international arms trade (Betts 2012). During the Cold War era, violent conflict was often characterized in terms of the East-versus-West rivalry of the Soviet Union and the United States. The various wars that emerged throughout the Cold War period—in Korea, Vietnam, and elsewhere—were largely seen as offspring of the global standoff between two large enemies in the East and West. After the Cold War, however, the violent conflicts that emerged in Southeastern Europe, Africa, Asia, the Middle East, and other regions were primarily civil wars, many involving non-state actors, and regularly characterized as ethnic, nationalist, and/or religious conflicts. While Cold War conflicts were principally ideological in nature—a democratic, capitalist West versus a non-democratic, communist East—post-Cold War conflicts have been fundamentally caused and motivated by a broad range of factors, including ethnicity, nationalism, religion, ideology, resources, corruption, failed or weak states, terrorism, insurgency, **narco-trafficking**, and so on. Death and destruction due to armed conflict in the post-Cold War period has certainly continued. Such conflict has influenced the weapons trade in that smaller and lighter weapons are more often in demand. Moreover, contemporary conflict has had a considerable impact on the illicit and illegal trade of defence and military items as many of the territories, regions, and non-state actors involved in violent conflict today are not considered legitimate recipients of government-sponsored arms transfers (see Case Study 24.1).

Although international commodities such as oil and agricultural items are much more valuable and account for a much greater share of today's global trade—approximately $2 trillion per year—the weapons trade, which accounts for less than 1 per cent of the overall international market, remains an important and potentially deadly aspect of the global economy. This is particularly the case when considering we can only know so much about the global weapons trade, and what we do know accounts primarily for the legal trade in military goods. The **illicit** arms market is, on the other hand, a growing aspect of global trade—and we currently know relatively little about its specifics and value. However, we do know that illicit arms flows are a key aspect of today's weapons trade.

CASE STUDY 24.1 MANPADS and terrorism

Man-portable air defence systems (MANPADS) are one of the many types of weapons that terrorists seek and use to terrorize civilian populations. MANPADS are rather sophisticated missiles that are launched from a small and light delivery system that rests on a shoulder. Weighing only about 30 pounds and being approximately four feet long, the missiles launched from surface to air can reach a height of approximately 10,000 feet. These weapons seek and destroy their targets by using infrared technology to detect the heat emanating from an aircraft engine. And not only military aircraft are at risk—so are passenger jets and cargo planes. An Israeli airliner, for example, was attacked with a MANPAD missile in East Africa in 2002 and a cargo plane that was also carrying civilians was threatened over Baghdad in 2005 (United States Department of Homeland Security 2005; see also Small Arms Survey 2011).

In the wake of recent conflict in the Middle East, many experts are concerned that terrorists and insurgents have and will continue to acquire thousands of MANPADS that remain missing, especially in Libya. Prior to the beginning of Libya's civil war in 2011, the country was known to possess approximately 20,000 such weapons systems. Many of these weapons were targeted for destruction with NATO airstrikes, but thousands have never been found and pose a risk to civilian and other airlines in the future (Chivers 2011; Lekic 2011). Because MANPADS are relatively small, light, and easy to conceal and smuggle, officials and experts alike believe it is important to do more to establish better stockpile security measures and arms control efforts to prevent such weapons from being illicitly traded and ultimately used in terrorist attacks (US Department of Homeland Security 2005).

KEY POINTS

- Throughout the 1990s, there was a significant decline in the global weapons trade.
- After 9/11 the international arms trade rebounded and increased substantially.
- The United States is the world's primary weapons producer and exporter.
- Government efforts to control the international weapons trade grew after the Gulf War in 1991.
- The changed nature of armed conflict in recent years also had an impact on the global weapons trade.

The illicit arms trade

It is estimated that approximately $5 billion of weapons are exchanged illicitly on the black market each year (Mandel 2011: 97). About $1 billion of those weapons are **small arms** and light weapons (Stohl et al. 2006: 12). In fact, more than 800 million pieces of small arms are in circulation around the world in any given year as they are easy to hide, conceal, and smuggle (Small Arms Survey 2007: 39). Large weapons systems, however, are also illicitly traded, particularly in grey market arms deals—transfers that involve government authorities, or individuals working on their behalf, to exploit often ambiguous and vague arms export control requirements and abuse legal loopholes. Governments also engage in covert transfers and skirt the line between what is legal and illegal by violating domestic and international expectations of what is an acceptable weapons transfer (Stohl and Grillot 2009: 94). Whether arms transfers are considered black or grey, or involve either large or small weaponry, both forms of illicit trade are considered by many to be a significant problem resulting from the very large and complicated global weapons market.

What we can ultimately know about the illicit weapons trade, however, is limited. In fact, the value of the illicit arms market may actually be higher than estimated given our lack of knowledge of such transactions. By nature, these weapons exchanges are secret and underground. Therefore, identifying, targeting, and prosecuting the illicit weapons trade is extremely difficult—and preventing it is even more troubling. What we can and do know, however, is that the illicit arms market is not only fuelled by the global arms supply, but by very local and specific interests in weapons acquisition and use. While grey market transfers between and/or involving government authorities, but occurring on the margins of the law where loopholes are exploited, are often the result of foreign and security policy concerns, black market, or illegal, arms deals are driven by demand. Three factors in particular fuel the demand for weapons that are traded on the black market. First, inhabitants of territories or governments of countries that face arms and other embargoes must acquire their defence and military items through black market channels. There is a US embargo on Iran, for example, that prevents the country from purchasing American military equipment. The Iranian government, therefore, turns to black and/or grey market opportunities to acquire spare parts for their US-made fighter jets that were purchased long ago (Levitt 2009).

Second, countries or territories involved in violent conflict, with or without being embargoed, often find that they cannot acquire the kinds of numbers of weapons they desire to engage in war. Violence and conflict, therefore, fuels the demand for weapons that in turn enhances black market opportunities. Armed conflict in the Balkans, throughout Africa, and in various locations in Asia and Latin America have particularly increased black market forces and the illicit defence trade worldwide (Atwood et al. 2006).

Finally, the growth in international organized crime, as well as general instability and insecurity around the world have contributed to the global illicit arms trade. Transnational crime has, in fact, exploded in the past twenty years with major advancements in communications and electronic exchanges. The Internet alone has significantly enhanced opportunities for illicit and criminal activities of all kinds—including weapons trafficking—and has substantially increased the ability for criminals to **launder** their dirty money. International **crime syndicates** operate all around the world, and with such crime comes violence. International crime, therefore, has contributed to and fuelled the need for an illicit arms market (Naim 2006).

Although the illegal demand for weapons leads to illicitly traded defence and military equipment, it is important to note that relatively few weapons are actually illicitly produced. Legally produced and originally legally traded and procured weapons, therefore, are the primary source of illicitly traded arms. In fact, there are a number of ways that legal weapons find their way into an illicit market (Stohl and Grillot 2009: 100–7). First, weapons once produced legally under **licence** from original manufacturers may continue to be produced even after the licences expire or are revoked. Once a specific enterprise is licensed to operate and weapons manufacturing begins, in other words, it is often difficult to cease production at that specific location and/or re-orient the production line (Stohl et al. 2006: 53).

Second, weapons and defence items that were produced legally may enter an illicit market due to the corrupt and illegal activities of government officials. Bribes are often paid to border guards or customs officials in certain parts of the world, for example, to divert arms shipments or to overlook false documentation regarding their ultimate destination (Small Arms Survey 2001: 176). Third, individual gun owners themselves contribute to illicit arms markets when they engage in secondary sales without completing the necessary paperwork or background checks. Approximately 75 per cent of the weapons available around the world in any given year are, in fact, owned and traded by individuals—not by governments or police forces (Small Arms Survey 2007: 43). Individual activities regarding the legal purchase and then illegal re-sale or re-distribution of weapons significantly contribute to the overall illicit defence trade.

Fourth, theft and looting of official military or police weapons stockpiles contribute to the global illicit arms market (Stohl et al. 2006: 14). This is particularly the case in regions where weapons depots are not well secured, as well as in areas where significant instability and insecurity are pervasive throughout society. In Albania in the mid-to-late 1990s, for example, a government-run pyramid scheme led to an economic collapse that resulted in the looting of more than 500,000 government weapons (Saferworld 2005: 6). These guns led then to a significant increase in violence and crime in Albania, but also found their way into an illicit arms market that fuelled conflict throughout the Balkan region and elsewhere. Fifth, legally produced and procured weapons end up being traded illicitly because of weak legislation governing weapons production, transfer, trans-shipment, and delivery verification (Stohl et al. 2006: 15). Weapons manufacturers operate in dozens of countries around the world, all of which do not necessarily create, implement, and enforce strong rules, regulations, and laws to prevent the inappropriate transfer of defence items. Arms export laws in many countries, in fact, may exist only on paper and are in effect useless when it comes to combating illicit arms transfers. Customs checks on the export, import, trans-shipment, and delivery of defence and military goods, for example, are a necessary legal component of a strong arms trade system, but Customs officials are often unable, due to a lack of resources, or unwilling, due to corruption or multiple responsibilities, to effectively ensure that arms shipments are indeed legal and legitimate (Lumpe 2000: 107).

CASE STUDY 24.2 The 'Merchant of Death'

Few contemporary gunrunners are as notorious as Victor Bout. The subject of Douglas Farah and Stephen Braun's 2007 book, *Merchant of Death*, as well as the feature film *Lord of War*, Bout is the quintessential arms broker responsible for illicitly trading and transferring perhaps billions of dollars' worth of weaponry around the world throughout the 1990s and 2000s. Ukrainian born and a former officer in the Soviet Army, Victor Bout used his numerous military contacts in the post-Cold War era to supply weapons to various rebels, insurgents, and terrorists in Africa, Asia, and Latin America. In violation of many international arms embargoes, Bout supplied weapons to the Democratic Republic of Congo, Angola, Sierra Leone, and Libera, among numerous others. While earning multiple millions of dollars for his services, he delivered arms with impunity across borders for nearly twenty years. In March of 2008, Bout was arrested in Bangkok, Thailand and charged with delivering approximately $5 million in arms to the Colombian terrorist organization FARC (Fuerzas Armadas Revolucionarias de Colombia or the Revolutionary Armed Forces of Colombia). After being extradited to New York in November 2010, he stood trial and was convicted of 'conspiracy to kill Americans, conspiracy to kill U.S. government officers and employees, conspiracy to acquire and use antiaircraft missiles, and conspiracy to provide material support or resources to a designated foreign terrorist organization' (Lynch 2011). In 2012, Bout was sentenced to twenty-five years in prison.

Sixth, gun shows and international arms fairs contribute to illicit arms markets because rules and regulations about weapons procurement and re-sale or re-export are not necessarily relevant or acknowledged at such events. In the United States, for example, background checks that are typically required when purchasing weapons at reputable gun shops are not required or regularly performed at gun shows. Individuals with criminal backgrounds or criminal intent, therefore, may legally purchase weapons at gun shows and then illegally trade or transfer them thereafter. Large weapons deals are often completed at international arms fairs, with more attention being paid to specific price-tags and economic gain and less attention to the details of the deal regarding re-export, redistribution, or ultimate end-use of the weapons (Stohl et al. 2006: 15).

Finally, gun buy-back programmes can contribute to the illicit arms trade. Gun buy-back activities have been relatively popular in collecting old and unnecessary weapons from what might be perceived to be an over-militarized society. Providing financial reward for turning over old or used weapons, however, has sometimes had the effect of infusing cash into the hands of those who then buy bigger or better weapons on the **black market**. Some argue, therefore, that guns-for-development projects are more effective than cash-for-guns programmes in areas where illicit arms markets and a certain demand for weapons among the population are prevalent.

In addition to all of the ways in which legal weapons supplies contribute to the illicit defence trade—and in addition to all the reasons why certain segments of society may turn to illicit arms markets for their weapons—another significant factor contributing to the illicit arms trade is the gunrunner or the middleman (Stohl and Grillot 2009: 107–12). The role of the gunrunner is, in fact, critical (see Case Study 24.2). Because governments sometimes do not want to be involved in certain weapons transfers, and because certain parties desire access to defence and military items of all kinds, well-connected gunrunners and middlemen work to connect weapons supply with weapons demand. As with any other commodity, there are those entrepreneurial few who engage their respective market and work to turn a profit by distributing items from those who make them to those who want them. The arms industry is no exception. Therefore, the role of the individual gunrunner in illicitly smuggling, transporting, and ultimately delivering weapons to individuals, groups, or governments that are not eligible or able to manage the transactions on their own is an important one regarding the operations and perpetuation of the illicit arms trade (Lumpe 2000).

Ultimately, it is important to note that the illicit arms trade is extensively connected to other illicit markets and activities. The illicit trafficking of drugs, humans, counterfeit goods, and contraband of all kinds is clearly linked to the illicit trafficking and trade of weapons and defence items. In fact, traffickers do not necessarily specialize in any one commodity, but engage in the illicit trade of multiple products and then launder their money through legitimate enterprises as a result. The illicit weapons trade, therefore, is often connected to other forms of illicit activities and generally contributes to international criminal activity more broadly (Naim 2006).

KEY POINTS

- Although the bulk of the weapons trade is legal and above-board, a certain amount involves illegal and illicit arms transfers on both the black and grey market.
- What we know about the arms trade in general is limited, but our lack of specific knowledge regarding the illicit defence trade is particularly limited.
- Legally produced and procured weapons may be re-routed into illicit markets in a number of ways.
- Individual gunrunners or middlemen play a significant role in facilitating and perpetuating the illicit defence trade.
- The illicit trade in weapons is often connected to other forms of illicit activity such as drug and human trafficking.

Controlling the weapons trade

Given the significant real and potential effects of the weapons trade, both legal and illicit, governments, international organizations, and concerned citizens have worked diligently to try and establish proper procedures, codes of conduct and best practices for the appropriate transfer of defence and military items. In fact, governments have attempted to control the flow of weapons since the Middle Ages (Harkavy 1975). Many early control efforts, however, focused on disarmament rather than the control of trade. Once weapons build-ups were evident and violent conflict resulted, government authorities sought to reduce stockpiles with disarmament agreements. Ultimately, most of these control efforts, including disarmament discussions in the late 1800s, were less than successful. Once governments took a greater role in guiding weapons production and trade in the early twentieth century, they also enhanced their efforts in controlling weapons transfers. Numerous discussions about weapons production and trade occurred at the League of Nations, for example. Nonetheless, it was not until after the Second World War and the advent of the Cold War that the most powerful states around the world began to take arms control agreements and procedures more seriously (Pierre 1982). Despite such attention to the arms trade, however, the twentieth century can be seen as a period of significant militarization and extreme growth in the defence trade. Regardless, there are a number of important national, regional, and international arms trade control measures that influence the extent and character of weapons transfers today.

Regarding national control measures, most of the major weapons suppliers—and many of the second-tier exporters—have developed a wide array of laws, regulations, and rules governing their arms production and transfers. Moreover, many governments have established a large network of bureaucratic agencies that manage and oversee the weapons trade. The US arms export and control system, for example, is particularly elaborate and involves hundreds of individuals working in various agencies within the Departments of Defence, State, Commerce, Treasury, and Homeland Security. Defence trade control measures in the UK, France, and Germany are similarly intricate and complex. Russia and China, two other major weapons producers and exporters, however, have relatively rudimentary arms trade control policies and procedures in place—and other suppliers, such as Argentina, Brazil, Egypt, and India, operate with fairly basic rules and regulations in place (Stohl and Grillot 2009: 52–73).

What are the specific elements of a comprehensive national defence trade control system? The strongest national arms control efforts include several important activities. First, governments should create and implement laws that outline the legal limits of the weapons trade, as well as who should be charged with overseeing the legal process and how such efforts should be funded. Second, governments should establish licensing procedures to authorize certain arms producers and exporters to engage in the weapons business. Moreover, specific arms transfers should be licensed by appropriate government authorities so that any given transfer may be examined, scrutinized, and officially certified. Third, governments should outline specific arms control lists that detail what is and is not subject to export licensing or prohibited for transfer. Fourth, authorities should establish export criteria that guide the transfer of arms, such as not exporting weapons to known human rights abusers, terrorist organizations, or unstable regimes. Fifth, interagency coordination should be delineated so that multiple government players are involved in defence trade decisions. Such interagency processes prevent any one party from dominating and controlling arms transfer activities.

Sixth, governments should establish and authorize appropriate customs and border control officials and procedures. After all, it is at the points of entry and exit in each country that weapons shipments can be checked, double-checked, and verified for accuracy regarding their origin and final destination. Seventh, delivery verification procedures should be created to confirm that weapons transfers have indeed reached their final and authorized destination. Eighth, governments should include in their arms trade rules, laws, and regulations specific criminal and civil penalties for their violation—and should ensure that such violations are policed, investigated, prosecuted, and enforced. Ninth, internal and external transparency measures should be established, as well as opportunities for public oversight, so that defence trade activities are open to examination and public consideration. Tenth, governments should ensure that weapons producers mark their defence items with a unique marking so that arms found in locations where they should not be can be traced through the arms transfer process to learn more about and, hopefully, how to prevent illicit trade. Eleventh, government police and military forces should establish appropriate weapons stockpile security measures to prevent theft and looting. Twelfth, national authorities should seek to collect and destroy old, outdated, and excess weaponry in a safe and controlled manner. And finally, governments should work together to develop regional and international cooperative procedures to prevent unauthorized arms transfers. Ultimately, the weapons trade is a transnational enterprise involving the cross-border movement of important commodities. Cooperation across borders, therefore, is an absolute requirement for strong and effective defence trade control efforts (Stohl and Grillot 2009: 170–5).

In terms of regional and international cooperation regarding the international weapons trade, there have been many discussions and many agreements. Some, however, have been more successful than others in facilitating international defence trade controls. Moreover, global arms trade controls remain somewhat of a controversial topic given the legitimacy of the trade and perceived and real differences among governments about what can and should be controlled. Nonetheless, a number of arms control agreements have emerged over the past several decades that are worthy of attention.

A few arms control agreements during the latter part of the twentieth century set the stage for a changed arms control environment and focus during the early twenty-first century. In the late 1970s, the United States and Soviet Union participated in the *Conventional Arms Transfer Talks* in light of the Cold War military build-up and the perception that the arms trade was moving so swiftly that no one could control it. The Talks failed to produce an agreement and hopes of addressing a growing global trade in military and defence items were dashed (Pierre 1982: 140).

In 1980, the *United Nations Convention on Prohibitions or Restrictions on the Use of Certain Conventional Weapons Which May Be Deemed to be Excessively Injurious and Have Indiscriminate Effects* (known as the CCW) was signed, and several additional protocols have since been added. According to the agreement, governments would not develop or transfer incendiary weapons, weapons that are indiscriminate in nature, and certain explosives that would undoubtedly injure civilian populations. In the mid-1990s, blinding lasers were added to the list of weapons that should not be produced or exported (Arms Control Association 2007). Despite the development of such agreements, the CCW has suffered from a lack of implementation among member states, particularly regarding explosives. Debates about cluster munitions, for example, have hampered solid implementation of the agreement (Stohl and Grillot 2009: 141–3). States did, however, ultimately address cluster munitions in another venue and at the insistence of non-governmental organizations that campaigned to prevent the future production, transfer, and use of such weapons. The result was the *Convention on Cluster Munitions*, which 'prohibits all use, stockpiling, production and transfer of Cluster Munitions' (CCM 2008).

Perhaps one of the most significant international arms control efforts established to date is the *United Nations Register of Conventional Arms*. The UN Register was created in 1991 as an effort to heighten transparency in the defence trade. UN member states agreed to voluntarily record arms transfer information in the Registry so that they could collectively monitor weapons flows and prevent destabilizing military build-ups. Until 2006, the Registry only included large military and defence equipment, but thereafter small arms and light weapons were added to the Registry process (United Nations Department for Disarmament Affairs 2007). Although many states participate in the Registry and provide arms transfer information, because the process is voluntary many states also do not contribute. As a defence trade control measure, therefore, the UN Arms Registry is only as effective as the number of governments that participate.

By the late 1990s, numerous governments, international organizations, and non-governmental groups began to highlight the problems associated with illicit arms trafficking. As a result several international and regional agreements have been developed to address the illegal defence trade. In June 2001, for example, UN member states signed the *Protocol Against the Illicit Manufacturing of and Trafficking in Firearms, Their Parts and Components and Ammunition*. A few months later, in July 2001, UN members adopted the *Programme of Action to Prevent, Combat and Eradicate the Illicit Trade in Small Arms and Light Weapons in All its Aspects*. Various follow-up agreements, such as the 2005 *Marking and Tracing of Weapons Accord* and the current attempts to develop a global *Arms Trade Treaty* indicate that the international community is indeed considering, contemplating, and coming to terms with the need to control the global trade in defence and military items (Stohl and Grillot 2009: 147–52, 153–4). Moreover, numerous regional arms control agreements targeting illicit weapons production, trafficking, and trading have been signed over the past several years.

In 1997, the Organization of American States (OAS) established the *Inter-American Convention Against the Illicit Manufacturing of and Trafficking in Firearms, Ammunition, Explosives, and Other Related Material*. Also in the late 1990s, the OAS adopted the *Model Regulations for the Control of the International Movement of Firearms, Their Parts and Components and Ammunition* and the *Model Regulations for the Control of Brokers of Firearms, Their Parts and Components and Ammunition*. The European Union (EU) created the *EU Code of Conduct on Arms Exports* in 1998 and the *Common Position on the Control of Arms Brokering* in 2003. The Organization for Security and Cooperation in Europe (OSCE) signed its *Document on Small Arms and Light Weapons* in 2000, as well as the *Handbook of Best Practices on Small Arms and Light Weapons* and *Document on Stockpiles of Conventional Weapons* in 2003. In 2001, the Economic Community of West African States (ECOWAS) established the *Declaration of a Moratorium on Importation, Exportation, and Manufacture of Light Weapons in Africa* and the Southern African Development Community (SADC) signed its *Firearms Protocol*. Finally, the *Nairobi Declaration for Prevention, Control and Reduction of Small Arms and Light Weapons* was adopted in 2004 and the Central American Integration System *Code of Conduct on the Transfer of Arms, Ammunition, Explosives and Other Related Material* was signed in 2005. In less than ten years, therefore, nearly every region of the world had established at least one agreement requiring signatories to enhance their efforts to control the flow of relevant defence items, particularly the illicit trade in small arms and light weapons.

In addition to inter-governmental arms control activities, non-governmental actors and organizations have significantly increased their role throughout the 1990s and beyond in controlling the global weapons trade. Even well before the 1990s, in fact, organizations such as the Federation of American Scientists and Stockholm International Peace Research Institute (SIPRI) have highlighted concerns about the uncontrolled international trade in defence and military items. These groups were later joined by non-governmental organizations such as the International Campaign to Ban Landmines (see Case Study 24.3), the International Action Network on Small Arms, the Small Arms Survey, the Control Arms Campaign, and the Cluster Munitions Coalition, among numerous others. Ultimately, all of these non-governmental actors seek to raise public awareness about the causes and consequences of an uncontrolled defence trade and are working directly with governments and international organizations to enhance global arms control efforts.

Despite all of the governmental and non-governmental activities to control the international arms trade, challenges remain. With a very large global supply of defence and military equipment, numerous and diverse weapons producers, and multiple players and interested parties, the international defence trade is a very complex system. From legitimate and legal trade to illegitimate and illicit transfers, many obstacles must be overcome in order to effectively check the global flow of weapons. Moreover, a complete ban on weapons production and trade is never an option. Some middle ground must, therefore, be found to address both the global supply and local demand of deadly defence items. The best arms control process will ideally allow for the legal, legitimate, and limited manufacturing and trading of defence equipment while the illicit flow of weapons is managed, minimized, and, hopefully, prevented. Governments, non-governmental organizations, multi-national corporations that produce weapons, and concerned citizens must do more to ensure such an outcome.

KEY POINTS

- Governments have attempted to control the weapons trade since the middle ages, but arms control efforts were primarily enhanced throughout the twentieth century.
- Effective national arms trade controls involve a number of important elements from legislative processes, arms control lists, and export criteria to border and customs control, delivery verification, and international, regional, and interagency cooperation.
- Several global and regional arms control agreements and activities have emerged over the past two decades to prevent the unchecked flow of defence and military items.
- Non-governmental organizations have also increased their role in global weapons trade activities.

CASE STUDY 24.3 The International Campaign to Ban Landmines

One of the most successful non-governmental organizations (NGOs) involved in arms control activities has been the International Campaign to Ban Landmines (ICBL). In October 1992, six NGOs (Handicap International, Human Rights Watch, Medico International, Mines Advisory Group, Physicians for Human Rights, and Vietnam **Veterans** of America Foundation) created the ICBL to raise awareness about the indiscriminate effects of landmines, particularly in Africa, Asia, the Middle East, and Latin America. The organization quickly grew to more than 1,000 NGOs in nearly 100 countries. Highlighting the humanitarian consequences of landmine use, the network of NGOs ultimately organized and hosted the Diplomatic Conference on an International Total Ban on Anti-Personnel Landmines on 18 September 1997 in Oslo, Norway. Shortly thereafter, on 3 December 1997, 122 government representatives met in Ottawa, Canada to sign the Convention on the Prohibition of the Use, Stockpiling, Production and Transfer of Anti-Personnel Mines and on Their Destruction. One week later the Director of the ICBL, Jody Williams, received the Nobel Peace Prize. By 2012, 162 countries had become party to the Treaty, but a few important countries, such as China, Russia, and the United States, remain outside the agreement. As an international agreement, the Mine Ban Treaty remains one of the most unprecedented international conventions to date given the significant role a non-governmental organization played in making the ban happen. Many argue that if the ICBL had not campaigned for a landmine ban, it is unlikely to have occurred (Rutherford 2010). Therefore, other NGOs have taken notice and enhanced their efforts regarding arms control today. From small arms and light weapons to cluster munitions, NGO networks like the ICBL are actively working with and placing pressure on governments to do more to limit and control the international defence trade.

Conclusion

This chapter has provided an overview of the global weapons trade today. What emerges is a rather complicated story involving the long-term history of weapons production, transfer, and control and their contemporary trends. The global trade in weapons has changed considerably over the centuries. The numbers and types of producers and exporters have shifted and the numbers and kinds of recipients have also changed. The motivations for engaging in the arms trade and the ability to control arms transfers have also changed with time. What remains constant is the existence of weapons as an important commodity. Whether produced and traded legally or whether acquired and trafficked illicitly, the world is certainly awash with military items that regularly transcend and travel through and within borders on a daily basis. Therefore, no one actor and no one solution will ever be able to address the global weapons trade alone. Multiple actors and multiple programmes will always be required to successfully manage the very complex nature of international arms transfers. Ultimately, with greater awareness, better research, dedicated leadership, and good policy and practice, the international community may appropriately manage, minimize, and prevent the potential negative consequences, while simultaneously ensuring the necessary and legitimate outcomes, of the global weapons trade.

QUESTIONS

1. Why is the global weapons trade so complex and complicated?
2. Why is it difficult to study and analyse the international arms trade?
3. How has the weapons trade changed over the years?
4. What are the most recent trends in the international arms trade?
5. How do we distinguish between legal, grey, and black arms trade markets?
6. How and why do both weapons supply and demand matter?
7. How are legally produced weapons sometimes diverted into illicit arms markets?
8. What are some of the potential negative consequences associated with unregulated and uncontrolled flows of weapons?
9. What kinds of national, regional, and international arms control measures and agreements have emerged to prevent destabilizing arms transfers?
10. How and why have non-governmental organizations emerged as important arms control actors?

FURTHER READING

- Grimmett, R. F. and Kerr, P. (2012), *Conventional Arms Transfers to Developing Nations, 2004–2011*, Washington, DC: Congressional Research Service, Library of Congress. The annual Grimmett reports offer the most reliable and up-to-date information about arms transfers to the developing world.
- Krause, K. (1995), *Arms and the State: Patterns of Military Production and Trade*, Cambridge: Cambridge University Press. This book provides in-depth coverage of the history of the arms trade, including the various motivations for producing, exporting, and acquiring weapons.
- Lumpe, L. (ed.) (2000), *Running Guns: The Global Black Market in Small Arms*, London: Zed Books. This book focuses on why there is a black market in small arms, how light weapons are illicitly transferred, who engages in illicit arms transaction, and ultimately what can and should be done about it.
- Morrow, J. D. (1993), 'Arms Versus Allies: Trade-offs in the Search for Security,' *International Organization* 47, 2 (Spring). This article outlines some of the important theories regarding state behaviour, alliance formation, and the transfer of weaponry.
- Pearson, F. S. (1994), *The Global Spread of Arms: Political Economy of International Security*, Boulder, CO: Westview Press. This book discusses the political and economic motivations for engaging in the arms trade by detailing who produces weapons, who buys them, for what purposes, and the potential security dilemmas that result.
- Pierre, A. J. (1982), *The Global Politics of Arms Sales*, Princeton, NJ: Princeton University Press. This volume examines the international political causes and consequences of weapons transfers.
- Small Arms Survey (2001–14), *Small Arms Survey 2001–2014*, Cambridge: Cambridge University Press. The annual Small Arms Survey reports are the best source of information regarding small arms and light weapons production, circulation, and control, as well as relevant case study material for examples of specific small arms activities and experiences.
- Stohl, R. and Grillot, S. (2009) *The International Arms Trade*, London: Polity Press. This book provides a history of the arms trade, details how and by whom arms are legally produced and transferred, discusses the evolution and operation of the illicit arms market, outlines the consequences of an unchecked defence trade, and sketches the various ways in which the international arms trade is controlled.

- Stockholm International Peace Research Institute (SIPRI) Yearbook 2013, *Armaments, Disarmament and International Security*, Stockholm, SIPRI. The annual SIPRI Yearbooks provide data on military expenditures, weapons production, and arms transfers around the world, as well as highlighting armed conflict zones and efforts to control weapons flows.
- Stohl, R. , Schroeder, M. , and Smith D. (2006), *The Small Arms Trade*, Oxford: Oneworld. This book discusses the ways in which small arms and light weapons have proliferated around the world, the consequences of such proliferation, and what can be done to address potential concerns.
- Stoker, D. J. and Grant, J. A. (eds) (2003), *Girding for Battle: The Arms Trade in Global Perspective, 1815–1940*, London: Praeger. This volume concentrates on the global defence trade prior to the Second World War by examining all of the relevant factors—political, economic, military, and diplomatic—that influenced the transnational transfer of weapons.

IMPORTANT WEBSITES

- **http://www.sipri.org** The Stockholm International Peace Research Institute (SIPRI) compiles the most reliable information concerning conventional arms transfers.
- **http://www.smallarmssurvey.org** The Small Arms Survey website provides the latest research on the global small arms trade.
- **http://www.un.org/disarmament** The United Nations Office for Disarmament Affairs offers information regarding international efforts to discuss, manage, and solve global arms trade problems.
- **http://www.un.org/disarmament/convarms/Register** The United Nations Register of Conventional Arms catalogues information regarding the transfer of defence and military items as reported by individual countries.
- **http://www.controlarms.org** The Control Arms Campaign is a network of non-governmental organizations focused on the adoption of a global Arms Trade Treaty.

Visit the Online Resource Centre that accompanies this book for lots of interesting additional material: www.oxfordtextbooks.co.uk/orc/collins4e/

25

Health and Security

Stefan Elbe

Chapter Contents

Reader's Guide

Which diseases pose threats to security? Scholars and policy makers now acknowledge at least three links between health and security. First, some diseases have been identified as threats to *human* security. The human security framework draws particular attention to diseases—such as **HIV/AIDS**, malaria, and tuberculosis—that are endemic in many low-income countries. Such diseases continue to cause millions of deaths annually and pose substantial challenges to the survival and well-being of individuals and communities. Second, some recently emerging infectious diseases, such as SARS, avian flu (H5N1), 'swine' flu (H1N1) and Ebola, have also been identified as threats to national security because their rapid spread could cause high death tolls and trigger significant economic disruption. Given the contemporary speed and rate of international travel, even states with more elaborate public health infrastructures feel vulnerable to new infectious diseases that may initially emerge outside their borders. Finally, some diseases have also been identified as narrower threats to bio-security within the context of international efforts to combat terrorism. Here concerns have focused on the spectre of a terrorist attack using a disease-causing biological agent such as anthrax, smallpox, or plague. The chapter concludes by contrasting two different ways in which this health–security nexus can be understood.

Introduction

Health issues are back on the international agenda—and not just as a matter of low politics. They are 'back' in the sense that they had already become the subject of international diplomacy as early as 1851, when delegates of the first International Sanitary Conference gathered in Paris to consider joint responses to the cholera epidemics that had overrun the European continent in the first half of the nineteenth century. Yet during the twentieth century the pertinence of controlling potentially pandemic microbes was gradually overshadowed by the more pressing concerns of avoiding the spectre of renewed wars, and the ever-present potential for a nuclear confrontation. The twentieth century's deep addiction to war, coupled with its important advances in medicine, reinforced the view in the West that the world was moving in a direction in which infectious diseases would eventually be controlled—exemplified so quintessentially by the confident declaration made in 1948 by US Secretary of State George Marshall that the conquest of all infectious diseases was imminent. This confidence has been profoundly shaken.

At the outset of the twenty-first century, there is once again considerable international anxiety about a host of potentially lethal 'rogue' viruses circulating the planet—including relatively new ones such as H1N1 'swine' flu, the highly pathogenic strand of avian influenza (H5N1), and the corona viruses responsible for Severe Acute Respiratory Syndrome (SARS) and Middle East Respiratory Syndrome (MERS). Other infectious diseases such as HIV/AIDS, tuberculosis, and malaria remain endemic in many developing countries and have made devastating comebacks—often in drug-resistant forms. At the same time, states in the West and elsewhere remain apprehensive about the consequences of a potential terrorist attack using biological weapons. Collectively, these concerns have begun to displace the optimism of the twentieth century, giving way to a renewed sense of unease. Nothing reflects this more poignantly than the fact that the responses to these health issues are increasingly articulated in the language of security—giving rise to the notion of health security.

Health and human security

The links between health and security were identified with the push towards strengthening human security—a framework pioneered by the United Nations Development Program (UNDP) in its 1994 *Human Development Report*. The human security framework seeks to redress the perceived imbalance in security thinking that has predominated during past decades. By developing a 'people-centric' account of security revolving around the needs and welfare of ordinary individuals, rather than predominantly around the protection of sovereign states, human security activists wish to challenge the narrow twentieth-century equation of security with the absence of armed conflict between states. Specifically, the *Human Development Report* outlined seven areas or components of human security that policy makers should devote greater attention and political capital to: economic security (poverty, homelessness); food security (famine, hunger); health security (disease, inadequate health care); environmental security (ecological degradation, pollution, natural disasters); personal security (physical violence, crime, traffic accidents); community security (oppression, discrimination); and political security (repression, torture, disappearance, human rights violations) (UNDP 1994: 24–5). As part of this broader approach to security, the report also highlighted the considerable burden that infectious diseases continue to pose in the developing world—including **HIV/AIDS**, **tuberculosis**, and **malaria**. It is estimated that these three diseases alone cause between four and five million people to die every year.

Whilst the initial *Human Development Report* did not define the notion of 'health security' in greater detail, the subsequent 2003 report of the Commission on Human Security—*Human Security Now*—filled this gap by devoting an entire chapter to 'health security'. 'Good health', the report (Commission on Human Security 2003: 96) argued, 'is both essential and instrumental to achieving human security'. It is essential in the sense that human security is ultimately about protecting lives, and this is not possible to achieve without also reducing the scale of a range of lethal diseases. The report argued further that health is also 'instrumental' for human security because it allows sick adults to resume work, helps secure the material well-being of families, allows children to stay in school, and so on. Endemic diseases are thus simultaneously *direct* threats to human security because they can cause death, and also broader, *indirect* threats to human security because, where the burden of disease is significant, this has knock-on ramifications for several other dimensions of human security.

Perhaps no disease illustrates those links between health and human security more poignantly than the

Table 25.1 Regional HIV and AIDS statistics, 2012

Region	Adults and children living with HIV/AIDS	Adults and children newly infected with HIV	Adult and child deaths due to AIDS
Sub-Saharan Africa	25 million	1.6 million	1.2 million
Middle East and North Africa	260,000	32,000	17,000
South and South-East Asia	3.9 million	270,000	220,000
East Asia	880,000	81,000	41,000
Oceania	48,000	2,100,500	1,200
Latin America	1.5 million	86,000	52,000
Caribbean	250,000	12,000	11,000
Eastern Europe and Central Asia	1.3 million	130,000	91,000
Western and Central Europe	860,000	29,000	7,600
North America	1.3 million	48,000	20,000
Total	35.3 million	2.3 million	1.6 million
	[32.2 million–38.8 million]	[1.9 million–2.7 million]	[1.4 million–1.9 million]

Source: UNAIDS (2013: A4).

global AIDS **pandemic**. As rates of HIV/AIDS increased dramatically in the course of the 1990s, the disease began to pose immense human security challenges for many developing countries—so much so that the former director of the Joint United Nations Program on HIV/AIDS (UNAIDS) argued: 'As a global issue . . . we must pay attention to AIDS as a threat to human security, and redouble our efforts against the **epidemic** and its impact' (Piot 2001). UNAIDS is the specialized United Nations agency tasked with addressing the international spread of HIV/AIDS. Established in 1995, UNAIDS is located at the centre of a complex network of various United Nations programmes and affiliated organizations, including the World Health Organization and the World Bank. Its political objectives are to mobilize leadership for effective action against the spread of HIV/AIDS, to monitor and evaluate its spread, and to support an effective response. As such, UNAIDS also collates international statistics about the extent of the AIDS pandemic. It is actually very difficult to determine exactly how many people are living with HIV/AIDS in the world and how many are dying from **AIDS-related illnesses**. Generating such data would not only be impossible in the light of immense financial and logistical constraints, but would also necessitate testing virtually every member of the human population for HIV—raising difficult ethical questions around compulsory testing. Nevertheless it is estimated by UNAIDS (2013) that around 1.6 million[1] people die annually of AIDS-related illnesses, while a further 2.3 million people[2] continue to become newly infected with the virus every year (see Table 25.1). Contrary to widespread belief, HIV/AIDS is not at all confined to sub-Saharan Africa. Every region of the world currently has a significant number of people living with HIV/AIDS.

[1] 1.6 million in 2012, stated in UNAIDs 2013 Global Report—http://www.unaids.org/en/media/unaids/contentassets/documents/epidemiology/2013/gr2013/UNAIDS_Global_Report_2013_en.pdf.

[2] 2.5 million in 2012, stated in 2013 UNAIDs Global Report—http://www.unaids.org/en/media/unaids/contentassets/documents/epidemiology/2013/gr2013/UNAIDS_Global_Report_2013_en.pdf.

Health security

Although access to life-prolonging medicines has recently become more widely available in many low-income countries, the experiences with HIV/AIDS prior to the international roll-out of medicines were formative in showing how, beyond their direct mortality, infectious diseases can also have further ramifications for a range of other dimensions of human security. For example, amidst rapidly rising rates of HIV/AIDS at the outset of the twenty-first century, analysts observed that the disease was also beginning to affect health security more generally by placing additional stresses on health-care facilities, which are frequently already stretched in the first place. An early study of the impact of HIV/AIDS on the health sector in South Africa conducted in 2003 found that the AIDS epidemic was having several negative impacts, such as causing the loss of health-care workers and generating increased levels of absenteeism, with just under 16 per cent of the health-care workforce in the Free State, Mpumalanga, KwaZulu-Natal, and North West provinces being HIV-positive. It also found that the rise in the number of HIV/AIDS patients seeking clinical care had led to an increased workload for health-care staff, as well as lowering staff morale. With some 46.2 per cent of patients in public hospitals being HIV-positive at the time, the study concluded that at times non-AIDS patients had even been 'crowded out' of the system in order to accommodate patients living with HIV/AIDS (Shisana et al. 2003). A study from Kenya conducted around the same time, and based on a sample of hospitals, detected similar trends—with an increase in AIDS-related admissions and 50 per cent of patients on medical wards living with HIV/AIDS. Focus-group discussions conducted in the context of that study also revealed that one of the reasons why the Kenyan health-care systems had such high levels of attrition, with scores of personnel leaving the sector, was a fear of becoming infected with HIV (in addition to high workloads, poor remuneration, and poor working conditions) (Cheluget et al. 2003). Another study of the impact in Swaziland in turn subsequently estimated that up to 80 per cent of bed occupancy in the medical and paediatric wards was related to HIV/AIDS (Kober and van Damme 2006). Those studies showed that the human security ramifications of infectious diseases like HIV/AIDS are not confined to the direct mortality caused by the illness, but also result from the ripple effects of the disease through much wider social structures—including health-care systems.

Economic security

Defined as 'an assured basic income—usually from productive and remunerative work, or in the last resort from some publicly financed safety net' (UNDP 1994: 25)—economic security is another important component of human security affected by widespread infectious diseases such as HIV/AIDS. Over the past decade, household studies have suggested that impact to be twofold. Households affected by HIV/AIDS were likely to experience a reduced earning capacity, as persons are unable to work, or are tied down to caring for the affected family member. For example, a 2002 comparative study of rural and urban households in South Africa conducted by Booysen and Bachman (2002) showed that those households affected by HIV/AIDS had on average only 50–60 per cent of per-capita income of non-affected households. HIV/AIDS additionally generated new costs for treatment and, in the case of death, additional funeral expenditures, legal costs, medical bills, and so forth (Drimie 2003). Other studies carried out by the World Bank amidst escalating rates of HIV infection at the time similarly suggested increased expenditure by these households on medical care and funerals, as well as a reduction in spending on non-food items (see Barnett and Whiteside 2006: 203–5). The early and difficult experiences of HIV/AIDS over the past decade thus showed how infectious diseases can have an additional impact on human security in that it can undermine the ability of individuals and households to ensure their economic security.

Food security

The experience with HIV/AIDS even showed that the spread of new infectious diseases could affect food security, defined as requiring 'that all people at all times have both physical and economic access to basic food. This requires not just enough food to go round. It requires that people have ready access to food' (UNDP 1994: 27). The crucial point here is that the physical availability of food is only part of the equation when it comes to food insecurity. Even when such food is physically available, people may still hunger and starve if they do not have access or entitlement to this food. During many famines, the problem is the lack of purchasing power and the poor distribution of food, rather than the absence of food itself. This distinction is crucial, because HIV/AIDS can generate food insecurities by skewing the access of certain individuals and groups to food. At the height of the AIDS epidemic in sub-Saharan Africa, the negative impact of HIV/AIDS on food security prompted the famine researcher Alex de Waal to advance a 'new-variant famine' thesis, which argues that 'AIDS attacks exactly those capacities that enable people to resist famine. AIDS kills young adults, especially women—the people whose labor is most needed' (de Waal 2002). A study carried out by the Food and Agriculture Organization (FAO) of 1,889 rural households in northern Namibia, southern Zambia, and around Lake Victoria in Uganda later found that households affected by HIV/AIDS, particularly if they are headed by women, were finding it increasingly difficult to ensure their food security (FAO 2003). Another study of fifteen villages in three districts of Malawi carried out by Shah et al. (2002) found that many households affected by HIV/AIDS experienced loss of labour (70 per cent), reported delays of agricultural work (45 per cent), leaving fields unattended (23 per cent), changing crop composition (26 per cent), but much of the impact depends on when the disease arrived (that is, pre- or post-harvest), the existence of other stress factors, and the relative economic status of households. Although HIV/AIDS is, therefore, unlikely to create a 'supply-shock' in terms of food production in and of itself, HIV/AIDS can nevertheless have negative implications for households by interacting in complex ways with their ability to secure access to food (de Waal 2006: 89–92; Gillespie 2006).

In all these ways the challenging experiences with the AIDS pandemic over the past decade illustrate very clearly how widespread, lethal diseases not only represent direct threats to human security, but can also shape additional dimensions of human security—including health security, economic security, and food security. Taken in conjunction with the large number of lives the disease claims annually, many in fact still consider HIV/AIDS to represent one of the world's most pressing contemporary human security threats. It is precisely one of those crucial contemporary issues that the human security framework wishes to highlight and where its advocates would like to see increased international coordination in terms of scaling up the prevention, treatment, and care for people living with HIV/AIDS, as well as for people affected by other endemic diseases such as malaria and tuberculosis. This emphasis on health issues within the framework of human security renders the latter one of the principal sites in contemporary world politics where health issues are increasingly being discussed, deliberated, and responded to in the language of security—albeit in a context in which the meaning of security is itself significantly expanded and redefined. Considering health issues as threats to human security is, in the end, just as much a matter of definitional fiat, and of redefining security, as it is of making substantially novel empirical claims about the impact of these diseases in developing countries.

KEY POINTS

- A range of health issues have been given renewed prominence within the framework of human security.
- The AIDS pandemic is widely perceived as one of the most serious and on-going human security threats, with more than thirty million people currently estimated to be living with HIV/AIDS. Malaria and tuberculosis also remain endemic in several developing countries and continue to claim many lives every year.
- In addition to posing a direct security threat to peoples' lives, diseases also represent indirect threats to their security.

Health and national security

Further links have been identified between health and national security. Here, too, the AIDS pandemic has been instructive in showing how infectious diseases can simultaneously bear upon both human security *and* national security concerns. Within the state-centric perspective of national security, HIV/AIDS has received further attention by policy makers over the past decade, because it was feared that the disease could have a detrimental impact on the armed forces of the worst affected countries. Evidence about the impact of HIV/AIDS in the armed forces is very patchy, subject to considerable controversy and continuously evolving. Yet there is some evidence that the rapid spread of HIV/AIDS initially posed considerable challenges to the operational efficiency of several armed forces in sub-Saharan Africa (see Case Study 25.1).

Although HIV/AIDS was the first infectious disease to be identified as a threat to national security in the twenty-first century, it is not the only one.

CASE STUDY 25.1 The South African National Defence Force (SANDF)

Information about the impact of HIV/AIDS on Africa's armed forces has been extremely difficult to obtain because of its sensitive nature. Even in those militaries that test soldiers for HIV/AIDS, officials have been extremely reluctant to make such information public, as it may well point to potential weaknesses in the armed forces. Over the past years, some information has nevertheless begun to emerge about the ways in which HIV/AIDS was initially perceived as a serious threat to the operational efficiency of the South African National Defence Force (SANDF).

South Africa is already home to the largest number of persons living with HIV/AIDS in Africa. When asked several years ago specifically about the impact of HIV/AIDS on its armed forces, the South African National Defence Force (SANDF) claimed that HIV prevalence in the armed forces was around 23 per cent, which was slightly higher than the civilian population and amounted to roughly 16,000 soldiers. Many analysts suspected at the time that in reality this figure could be much higher, perhaps as high as 40 per cent, which would put the number closer to 28,000 (Heinecken 2001; Meyer 2004). Even the official figure was high enough, however, to prompt the United States and SANDF to set up a programme aimed at establishing the rate of HIV infection in the armed forces more conclusively and evaluating the effects of anti-retroviral treatments on SANDF. Because of human rights considerations, SANDF could not force its soldiers to be tested, but SANDF did set up a programme where soldiers can come forward voluntarily to be tested. Initially 1,089 soldiers came forward to be tested, of whom 947 (89 per cent) tested positive. The average age of those who tested positive was 34 years, and 60 per cent of them were married. Although this figure was not representative of SANDF as a whole (most of those who came forward to be tested probably suspected that they were HIV-positive already), it left no doubt that the issue of HIV/AIDS has been a very serious one for many armed forces in Africa over the past two decades.

In the light of these figures, senior officials in SANDF expressed serious concerns about the impact of HIV/AIDS on the military's combat readiness because of the high levels of absenteeism the illness induces. They estimated that a soldier in the early stages of illness would be absent on average 20 days a year, rising to 45 days for soldiers displaying symptoms. Soldiers who had developed full-blown AIDS were estimated to be absent on average for a minimum of 120 days per year. SANDF therefore believed that it would lose between 338,000 and 560,000 working days annually because of the illness. SANDF was further concerned with the fact that many of those most affected by HIV/AIDS in SANDF are in the age group of 23–32, which is the age group from which most of the operationally deployable soldiers, officers, non-commissioned officers, and highly skilled members of the armed forces are drawn. The perceived danger here was that over the course of several years, HIV/AIDS could hollow out this middle rank, creating gaps and shortfalls within the armed forces. This impact on SANDF was all the more significant because of South Africa's leadership role on the African continent and because the country wishes to play an expanding role in African peacekeeping operations, which it can only do with a healthy military. Although many AIDS-related medicines are now more readily available, the initial experiences of the SANDF with HIV/AIDS illustrate very well that newly emerging infectious diseases can also have important ramifications within the realist conception of security by creating new challenges for the armed forces in particular.

High-income countries have also expressed considerable unease about how new infectious diseases threaten their populations and economies within the context of increased globalization and rapid international travel. An influential report issued in 1992 by the Institute of Medicine in the United States entitled *Emerging Infections: Microbial Threats to Health in the United States* already warned that the emergence of the AIDS pandemic illustrated how 'some infectious diseases that now affect people in other parts of the world represent potential threats to the United States because of global interdependence, modern transportation, trade, and changing social and cultural patterns' (Lederberg et al. 1992: v). By the end of the decade, these anxieties had reached a sufficient level for parts of the US government to officially designate such infectious diseases as threats to national security. The United States National Intelligence Council, for example, produced an influential and widely cited National Intelligence Estimate entitled *The Global Infectious Disease Threat and its Implications for the United States*. The findings of the report, declassified in January 2000, confirmed many of these fears by pointing out that, since 1973, at least thirty previously unknown disease agents have been identified (including some for which there is no cure such as HIV, Ebola, Hepatitis C, and the Nipah virus). It also found that in this same period at least twenty older infectious diseases have re-emerged, frequently in drug-resistant form—most notably amongst them tuberculosis, malaria, and cholera. The report concluded: 'New and re-emerging infectious diseases will pose a rising global health threat and will complicate US and global security over the next 20 years. These diseases will endanger US citizens at home and abroad, threaten US armed forces deployed overseas, and exacerbate social and political instability in key countries and regions in which the United States has significant interests' (National Intelligence Council 2000).

By their very nature, infectious diseases lend themselves particularly well to such securitizations. They are usually caused by microbes that are imperceptible to the human eye. Consisting, in the case of viruses, merely of a piece of nucleic acid (DNA or RNA) wrapped in a thin coat of protein, they exist at the very margins of our conceptions of life. Human beings could be exposed to them at any time without knowing it, and yet suffer a quick and violent death not long thereafter. They are, in this respect, 'silent' and 'invisible' killers. Perhaps nothing is more frightful to many people than a lethal danger they have no way of detecting. Even the famous microbiologist Louis Pasteur, who explored the germ theory of disease, eventually developed an obsessive fear of microbes, refusing to shake hands with people, carefully wiping his plates before eating, and on more than one occasion even examining food served as dinner parties with his portable microscope. As in other areas of life, uncertainty tends to breed anxiety. It is this innate and all too human fear of microbes that makes them particularly amenable to being portrayed not just as important health issues, but as national security threats as well. Over the past decade, three infectious diseases in particular have been portrayed as such national security threats, each discussed in the following sub-sections.

SARS

Widely regarded as the first infectious disease epidemic of the twenty-first century, SARS is thought to have emerged in the Guangdong Province of China in November 2002—a region known for its lively markets where humans and livestock mingle in close proximity. Symptoms of the new disease included a high fever, a dry cough, and shortness of breath or breathing difficulties. However, it was not until 11 February 2003 that the Chinese Ministry of Health forwarded reports of 305 cases of acute respiratory syndrome to the World Health Organization, by which time at least five deaths had been reported in Guangdong Province. The new disease appeared to confirm all the earlier fears about how a newly emerging infectious disease could rapidly spread across the globe through modern transport infrastructure. Perhaps nothing exemplified this more clearly than the fate of Dr Liu Jianlun, a local Chinese doctor who initially treated patients infected with the new disease. He subsequently travelled from Guangdong Province to Hong Kong in order to attend a wedding. He stayed on the ninth floor of the four-star Metropole hotel (in Room 911), where the disease quickly began to spread to other guests staying on that floor of the hotel. In epidemiological terms he is now referred to a 'superspreader'; the World Health Organization ultimately attributes more than 4,000 worldwide cases of SARS to this doctor alone (National Intelligence Council 2003: 10). Those who became infected by him subsequently travelled as far as Singapore, Hong Kong, Vietnam, Ireland, Canada, and the United States, where they, in turn, infected more than 350 people directly or indirectly. Another doctor who had treated the first cases of SARS in Singapore also reported symptoms before boarding a flight from New York back to Singapore on 14 March, and had to disembark prematurely in Frankfurt, Germany, for immediate hospitalization and isolation.

Wide-ranging international cooperation amongst scientists and laboratories revealed that SARS is caused by a new coronavirus, which is believed to have crossed over from the animal to the human population. This is because evidence of infection with the coronavirus could also be found in several animal groups, including Himalayan masked palm civets, Chinese ferret badgers, raccoon dogs, and domestic cats.

By the time the last human chain of transmission was broken in July 2003, there had been 8,098 reported SARS cases, causing 774 deaths in 26 different countries. SARS killed about 10 per cent of those infected, although the chances of survival in the event of an infection were heavily dependent upon the age of the victim. Less than 1 per cent of persons aged 24 years or younger died from the disease, up to 6 per cent of those aged 25–44 years old died, and up to 15 per cent of persons aged 44–64 years old died. The great risk was for persons aged 65 or older, of which 55 per cent succumbed (National Intelligence Council 2003: 16). Geographically, SARS left its deepest mark in Asia, with China, Taiwan, and Singapore accounting for more than 90 per cent of cases, although notable outbreaks also occurred in Toronto. Moreover, the effects of the SARS outbreak were not confined to these deaths alone.

The disease also caused widespread fear amongst populations around the world, especially as there was no cure readily available, and its transmission patterns remained unclear for a considerable period of time. People thus began to wear masks covering their noses and mouths, began to avoid public places such as restaurants and cinemas, and ceased to travel. In conjunction with the decision of many investors to put investment plans in the region on hold, the SARS outbreak also had considerable economic consequences for the region. The travel and tourism sectors were particularly badly hit, with room bookings and airline seat bookings in several cases being down by more than 50 per cent on previous years. In countries such as China, Singapore, and Canada public-health agencies also implemented quarantine and isolation procedures, restricting the movements of those perceived to be at risk of being infected with the virus. Some countries even introduced thermal scanners at airports in order to detect people with symptoms of fever. Although it ultimately proved possible to contain SARS through quarantine and other public-health measures, many policy makers felt that the writing was now clearly on the wall and that things could have been much worse, especially if the coronavirus had achieved more efficient human-to-human transmission. For many, the SARS episode thus represented a warning of what could happen if a renewed flu pandemic ravaged the human population in the twenty-first century.

Influenza pandemic

There were three such human flu pandemics in the twentieth century alone—in 1918, 1957, and 1968. The first of these was particularly severe, breaking out within the harsh conditions of the First World War and leading to the deaths of tens of millions of people around the world. Policy makers at the World Health Organizations and in several national governments remain concerned today that the H5N1 strand of avian flu has the potential to evolve eventually into such a renewed pandemic, and are framing avian flu as a threat to national security. Writing in the *New York Times* in 2005, Senators Barack Obama and Richard Lugar argued:

> When we think of the major threats to our national security, the first to come to mind are nuclear proliferation, rogue states and global terrorism. But another kind of threat lurks beyond our shores, one from nature, not humans—an avian flu pandemic. An outbreak could cause millions of deaths, destabilize Southeast Asia (its likely place of origin), and threaten the security of governments around the world.
>
> Obama and Lugar (2005)

The US *National Security Strategy* (2006) further pointed to the dangers posed by 'public health challenges like pandemics (HIV/AIDS, avian influenza) that recognize no borders', arguing that 'the risks to social order are so great that traditional public health approaches may be inadequate, necessitating new strategies and responses' (White House 2006: 47). *The National Security Strategy of the United Kingdom* (Cabinet Office 2008) similarly cited pandemics alongside terrorism and weapons of mass destruction as part of a 'diverse but interconnected set of threats and risks, which affect the United Kingdom directly and also have the potential to undermine wider international stability' (Cabinet Office 2008: 3). Pandemic threats also continue to reside at the top of the UK national risk register and are identified as a (top) Tier 1 threat in the latest National Security Strategy (Cabinet Office 2010: 27). Most recently, pandemic threats were similarly flagged up in France's 2013 Whitepaper setting out French national security policy for the period 2014–19 (Kittelsen 2013: 7; Livre Blanc 2013).

The scenario that policy makers are particularly concerned about is that of a zoonic (animal-to-human) transmission of an influenza virus that subsequently recombines or mutates to achieve efficient human-to-human transmission. If such a virus emerges, it will in all likelihood be spread through coughing and sneezing, and people will probably be infectious before they actually become aware of any symptoms. This latter fact is crucial and would make a future flu pandemic much more difficult to contain than SARS, where people mostly became infectious only after developing symptoms. The first step in this chain—the zoonic 'leap' from the animal to human populations—was already documented in 1997 in Hong Kong. Officials sought to deal with this danger quickly and at great cost to the animal population by ordering virtually the entire poultry population of Hong Kong (some 1.5 million birds) to be destroyed. Although these measures appeared successful, there was a further outbreak in February of 2003, again in Hong Kong. By June 2008, there had been 385 confirmed cases of bird flu (H5N1) according to the World Health Organization, of which 243 died. The fatality rate for human cases of avian influenza is thus much higher than in the case of SARS, with more than 60 per cent of infected persons dying. Again the region most seriously affected is Asia, with China, Indonesia, Thailand, and Vietnam (but also Egypt) accounting for the majority of cases. On rare occasions, it has also been possible for H5N1 to become transmitted between people, but usually only in situations of very close contact with this person during the acute phase of the illness, and even when this spread has occurred, it has not gone beyond one generation of close contacts.

Despite the anxieties that these developments generate, it is worth bearing in mind that, given the wide geographic spread of the virus in birds, as well as the high number of cases of infection in poultry, the numbers of human infections are at the moment comparatively 'low', which indicates that the virus does not 'jump' the species barrier that easily. If it does, the estimates used by the World Health Organization and the Centers for Disease Control and Prevention (CDC) in the United States indicate that there could be between 2 million and 7.4 million deaths worldwide, with many more becoming ill and requiring hospitalization. Vaccines need to be virus specific, and therefore it is very difficult to create effective vaccines in advance of a pandemic; we simply do not yet know exactly what such a virus might look like. Policy makers have therefore focused their efforts on stockpiling antiviral medicines, and drawing up lists of who should receive priority access to such medicines in the case of a renewed pandemic. Many questions still remain, however, about the efficacy of these drugs, and governments are therefore also trying to increase the worldwide capacity for producing vaccines so that, once the latter are developed, more doses can be manufactured and distributed more quickly.

Ebola virus disease

During 2014, renewed international alarm was triggered by a novel outbreak of Ebola virus disease in West Africa. At the time of writing, the World Health Organizations (WHO 2015) reports 27,049 cumulative cases of Ebola infections since the beginning of the outbreak in Guinea, Liberia, and Sierra Leone—the three West African countries most heavily affected by the outbreak. WHO further reports 11,149 deaths from the disease so far—a figure likely to further increase as the epidemic is not yet contained. Already, this makes it both the largest and deadliest Ebola outbreak in history.

The scale of the 2014 Ebola outbreak in West Africa caught many experts by surprise. Earlier outbreaks of Ebola had mostly occurred in other parts of Africa, had been very sporadic, had mostly occurred in rural settings, and had led to comparatively low numbers of deaths. Therefore national and international institutions did not immediately recognize the significance of the new outbreak in West Africa. Non-governmental organizations like Médicins Sans Frontières (MSF) initially provided the majority of international assistance on the ground, but such organizations alone could not prevent the spread of Ebola into major urban areas, and thus a much larger proportion of the population also becoming effected.

As the scale of the outbreak continued to grow in the second half of 2014, and the magnitude of the challenge became more widely appreciated, several leaders of influential institutions began to describe the outbreak in terms of a crisis and security threat. The director of the US CDC referred to the situation in West Africa as 'spiraling out of control'. The Senior UN System Coordinator for Ebola Disease echoed that 'the outbreak is moving beyond our grasp'. Organizations on the ground concurred, with the International President of Doctors Without Borders arguing that 'the world is losing the battle to contain it [Ebola]. Leaders are failing to come to grips with the transnational threat' and the Director General of the World Health Organization simply but plainly describing Ebola as 'a global threat' (Morrison 2014). By October 2014, the international concern about Ebola had reached such heights that the influential *Economist* magazine could lead with the daunting headline of 'The War on Ebola'.

Recasting the Ebola crisis as a transnational and global security threat also enabled the issue to be discussed by the United Nations Security Council. When the Security Council convened on 9 September 2014 to discuss the crisis, Ebola became only the second disease in its history to be discussed by the Council—with HIV/AIDS having set the precedent in 2000. The Liberian Defence Minister briefed the Security Council that his country lacked 'infrastructure, logistical capacity, professional expertise and financial resources to effectively address this disease'. He also said that 'the deadly Ebola virus has caused a disruption in the normal functioning of our state' (BBC News 2014). This echoed earlier warnings issued by leaders of other heavily affected countries like Sierra Leone, whose president had similarly claimed that 'The very essence of our nation is at stake' (Gostin et al 2014). On 18 September 2014, the UNSC formally declared the Ebola outbreak in Africa as a 'threat to international peace and security' as part of Resolution 2177.

Reframing the Ebola outbreak as a security threat also paved the way for a much stronger military involvement in the international response. Humanitarian organizations working on the ground, which were historically quite reluctant to call for outside military intervention, began to see no other way of getting on top of the outbreak than to involve the armed forces. MSF and Oxfam thus began to call for troops to be sent to West Africa. Peter Piot, who had earlier been involved in drawing links between HIV/AIDS and security whilst Executive Director of UNAIDS, and who had helped identify the Ebola virus in 1976, similarly called for a 'quasi-military' intervention.

The rationale behind these calls was that humanitarian aid alone would not suffice to control the spread of the disease, and that humanitarian organizations were simply overwhelmed with what was unfolding on the ground. In the absence of an available medical treatment for Ebola, the response had to rely predominantly on traditional public health measures like isolation, quarantine, and so forth. Here it was hoped that military capabilities in terms of logistics, biohazard response, and so forth could help to meet the challenge. Their call was eventually heeded when the governments of the United States, the United Kingdom, France, and China announced that they would soon be making military deployments to the region to assist with the response.

Although the links between health and security helped to mobilize these resources, drawbacks of this approach also became visible. Framing Ebola as a security threat risked facilitating the disproportionate use of force and privileging short-termism. Guinea, Liberia, and Sierra Leone all declared states of emergency, including curfews and executive orders that allowed for arrests without court orders. The UK, the USA, and other countries issued airport screening and quarantines, whilst vital international flights to the region were suspended and dramatic media coverage fuelled popular fears far beyond West Africa. Moreover, the militarized response has raised difficult challenges for already stretched armed forces, whilst at the same time jarring with much longer and often painful legacies of outside military intervention in the region. All the while, and as with previous infectious disease outbreaks, the sustainability of this emergency response remains uncertain. Although linking Ebola to security concerns was powerful in mobilizing resources in the short term, experience has shown that they are difficult to maintain in the long run (Elbe 2006).

KEY POINTS

- Since the turn of the century many policy makers have also come to view newly emerging infectious diseases as threats to their national security.
- The SARS outbreak of 2002–3 confirmed many of these fears, showing how a new infectious disease can rapidly spread across the globe, causing widespread fear amongst populations and generating serious economic consequences.
- Although the SARS outbreak was contained, strong concerns remain about the spectre of a more lethal and infectious flu pandemic emerging in the future.
- The slow international response to the Ebola outbreak in West Africa shows that significant gaps in global health security remain.

Health and bio-security

Some diseases have also acquired a greater security salience because terrorists or other political groups might attempt a mass casualty attack by deliberately releasing a disease-inducing biological agent. Such agents could enter the bodies of civilians through inhalation if the agent is successfully transformed into an aerosol form. Alternatively, they could enter the human body by means of ingestion if, for example, food or water supplies are contaminated with such an agent. Two events have raised the concern of governments about such a scenario. First, the attacks of 9/11 showed that terrorists—if capable—might not shy away from using such weapons. Indeed, from the perspective of a terrorist group, many characteristics of a biological agent may be deemed advantageous. First, several of these agents are naturally occurring and can thus be more readily acquired. Second, they would require only small quantities to have substantial effects. Third, these agents are not perceptible to the human eye; once released, they would initially evade the human senses of smell, taste, and so on, and would therefore allow a potential terrorist time to escape undetected. Finally, the very same quality that has long made biological weapons of dubious military use—namely, their inability to differentiate between civilians and combatants—are unlikely to deter would-be terrorists. However, these advantages also need to be balanced with some disadvantages associated with the use of biological agents, including the risk that the terrorist might become infected as well, the technical difficulty involved in successfully stabilizing and weaponizing these agents, and the fact that attacks with biological agents are heavily susceptible to weather conditions such as wind, levels of cloud cover, and so on (Ryan and Glarum 2008: 35). Expert opinion thus remains divided as to how probable such an attack actually is.

One event that substantially increased anxieties about the possibility of such a scenario materializing was the discovery that anthrax letters were being sent in the United States in 2001—a time when the country was still reeling from the attacks of 9/11. There were probably two separate batches of anthrax letters sent from mail boxes in Princeton, New Jersey. The first batch, thought to consist of approximately five letters, was sent around 18 September 2001 to media offices, including American Media Incorporated, broadcasters and editors in New York City, and to a tabloid publisher in Boca Raton, Florida. These letters were initially dismissed as hate mail and/or left unopened. A second batch of letters was then mailed on 8 October 2001, two of which went to Democratic senators in Washington, DC. The first of these was opened on the morning of 15 October in the Hart office building of the Senate majority leader Tom Daschle. It would take a week before it was established that these second round of infections had come from letters, by which time many more had become exposed. It was later also discovered that the anthrax used was of the Ames strain, which had been used for several years in the US biological weapons programme (Guillemin 2005: 173–6). Although the attacks of 9/11 and the letters laced with anthrax were a crucial catalyst in terms of placing the combat of terrorism at the heart of the international security agenda, anxieties about such a biological attack actually pre-date 2001. In 1995, the Aum Shinrikyo cult in Japan had already released Sarin nerve gas in the Tokyo subway (see Case Study 25.2).

All these events contributed to a climate in which it was felt that more concerted efforts needed to be undertaken to protect populations in the event of such an attack. In the United States, the Centre for Disease Control and Prevention (CDC) were charged with drawing up a list of the biological agents that might be used in such an attack. Its list consists of Category A agents, which are highly infectious, have high mortality rates, can be easily disseminated, and are difficult to treat medically. They would thus have a highly disruptive effect if used in a biological attack. Examples of such agents are anthrax, botulism, plague, smallpox, tularemia, and viral hemorrhagic fevers (for example, Ebola, Marburg, Lassa, Machupo). Category B agents, in turn, comprise those agents that cause lower mortality rates, have moderate **morbidity** rates, and can be treated more readily. They include brucellosis, epsilon toxin of Clostridium perfringens, food-safety threats (for example, salmonella species, Escherichia coli O157:H7, Shigella), glanders, melioidosis, psittacosis, Q fever, Ricin toxin, Staphylococcal enterotoxin B, typhus fever, and viral encephalitis (for example, Venezuelan equine encephalitis, eastern equine encephalitis, western equine encephalitis), and water-safety threats (for example, Vibrio cholerae, Cryptosporidium parvum). Finally, Category C agents refer to emerging pathogens with potential for future weaponization, such as Nipah virus and hantavirus.

In the United States, two new initiatives were also launched to respond to potential attacks with these agents: projects BioWatch and BioShield. BioWatch consists of a network of sensors (or stations) in thirty-one cities that analyse particles in the air through a filter system. These filters are collected daily and analysed at the CDC for traces of six agents: anthrax, brucellosis, glanders, meliodosis, plague, smallpox, and turlremia. This process has a turnaround time of at least thirty-six hours (Ryan and Glarum 2008: 262). Project BioShield, in turn, was designed to increase the 'medical defences' of the United States against a range of possible pathogens. At a cost of around US$5.6 billion over a ten-year period, Project BioShield included the purchasing and storing of significant stockpiles of medicines as well as vaccines. It also seeks to fund research into developing new medicines and vaccines to protect populations against such agents. Both programmes have ultimately proved controversial and have encountered significant difficulties in meeting their objectives.

CASE STUDY 25.2 Aum Shinrikyo attacks in Tokyo

In 1995, the Aum Shinrikyo cult in Japan received widespread media attention when it released Sarin nerve gas into the Tokyo subway system. The attack was carried out with a chemical rather than a biological substance. It was also not a very sophisticated operation, effectively relying on the use of an umbrella to poke holes into plastic bags. Nevertheless, the release killed twelve people, and hospitalized around 1,000, with thousands more needing to seek medical care. The 1995 operation was also not the first time the cult had struck. A similar attack had occurred in the town of Matsumoto eight months earlier, killing seven people (Guillemin 2005: 158).

The Aum Shinrikyo cult was first established in 1984 by Shoko Asahara as a countermovement to the perceived decadence of modern societies. The cult ultimately hoped to create a new type of society and eventually grew in size to between 10,000 and 60,000 members (Rosenau 2001: 291). The cult was operating internationally, with various contacts in post-Soviet Russia, Australia, Germany, Taiwan, and the former Yugoslavia. It even had an office in New York City. It was also well financed, with funding in the range of an estimated US$20 million (Guillemin 2005: 159).

The cult had intended to use biological weapons such as anthrax, Q fever, Ebola, and botulinum toxin on ten separate occasions (Ryan and Glarum 2008: 16). After being arrested, the head of their germ development, Seiichi Endo, later revealed that from 1990 to 1993, the cult had released aerosolized anthrax and botulinum toxin on several occasions at Japan's legislature (the Diet), the Imperial Palace, as well as several other places in Tokyo and even at the US military base of Yokusaka (Zubay et al. 2005: 134–5). Fortunately for those involved nobody became infected, most probably because the strain used was similar to that used in animal vaccination, which is of little danger to humans and has low virulence (Zubay et al. 2005: 135).

The precedents set by Aum Shinrikyo prompted a growing climate of fear in which it was felt that more concerted efforts needed to be undertaken to protect populations in the event of such an attack. Long before the tumultuous events of the autumn of 2001, those incidents showed that a bioterrorist attack is more than just a hypothetical possibility—even if the attempt to place a more precise probability on such an attack occurring is fraught with difficulties.

Others, however, have also taken heart from the fact that the Aum Shinrikyo group ultimately failed to procure biological weapons—despite its clear intentions of doing so. In many ways, the group fulfilled most of the ideal conditions that ought to have led to success in terms of producing such weapons, including a network of front companies, possessing key staff, funding, sufficient time, and so forth. Although it is difficult to come to firm conclusions given the classified nature of much of the information surrounding the cult's activities, the group encountered at least three significant difficulties: (1) acquiring sufficiently lethal strands of key biological agents such as anthrax bacilli; (2) challenges in terms of finding efficient ways of delivering and dispersing the agent; and (3) internal organizational difficulties (Rosenau 2001: 293). Even a well-funded non-state group like Aum Shinrikyo thus encountered considerable obstacles in developing viable biological weapons, showing that—in practice—developing and procuring biological weapons remains a complicated process, which requires selection of the desired biological agent, obtaining this agent, then working upon this agent in such a manner that it can become weaponized, before also creating a method for disseminating it.

KEY POINTS

- Since the late 1990s, many policy makers have focused on disease-causing biological agents within the context of their efforts to combat domestic and international terrorism.
- The activities of Aum Shinrikyo in Japan, as well as the person(s) responsible for sending letters laced with anthrax in the United States, highlighted a perceived lack of preparedness amongst many countries to deal with the effects of a terrorist attack using such an agent.
- Some governments have launched substantial programmes to increase the speed with which such an outbreak could be detected, and ways to respond to such an attack.

Conclusion

This chapter outlined the ways in which health issues have acquired a greater security salience in the context of three competing security frameworks: human security, national security, and bio-security. How, then, is this merging of health and security to be understood? Many analysts have followed the broad tenets of securitization theory (see Buzan et al. 1998) and have identified this emerging health–security nexus as the 'securitization' of health. In this view, health issues have now become the latest in a long line of wider social issues—such as drugs, migration, the environment, and so on—to become securitized—that is, framed as existential threats requiring the adoption of emergency measures. This, however, is not the only way in which the emerging health–security nexus can be conceptualized. It can also be understood from the opposite perspective.

For years scholars outside the discipline of security studies, most notably in sociology, have also been tracing the progressive 'medicalization' of societies, whereby more and more social problems are considered and responded to as medical problems, and where the medical professions (along with pharmaceutical companies) have seen substantial material benefits as well as enjoying an enhanced social position (Conrad 2007). Viewed from this perspective, the recent merging of health and security could be understood not just as the securitization of health, but also as a wider manifestation of the medicalization of security. Put differently, these three debates on health and security are also sites in contemporary world politics where security itself becomes partially redefined in medical terms, requiring the greater involvement of the medical professions. The deeper question that the emerging health–security interface gives rise to, therefore, is whether it is best understood as the securitization of health, or as the medicalization of security.

QUESTIONS

1. What is the relationship between health and human security?
2. What are the implications of HIV/AIDS for human security?
3. To what extent are infectious diseases also a threat to national security?
4. What can be done to reduce the spread of infectious diseases in the context of rapid international travel?
5. What, if anything, is gained by referring to diseases as security issues, rather than as health or medical issues?
6. What lessons can be learned from the securitization of health for securitization theory?
7. What lessons can be learned from the SARS outbreak of 2002–3?
8. Are the threats of bioterrorism and an influenza pandemic exaggerated?
9. Do non-infectious diseases have security implications as well?
10. Is the health–security nexus a manifestation of the securitization of health, or of the medicalization of security?

FURTHER READING

- Rushton, Simon and Jeremy Youde (eds) (2014). *Routledge Handbook of Global Health Security*, Oxford: Routledge. This is an edited collection containing a wide range of detailed articles and perspective on the links between health and security.
- Chen, Lincoln, Leaning, Jennifer, and Narasimhan, Vasant (eds) (2003), *Global Health Challenges for Human Security*, Cambridge, MA: Harvard University Press. This volume contains a range of chapters covering the concept of human security and how it relates to several contemporary global health issues.

- de Waal, Alex (2006), *AIDS and Power: Why There is No Political Crisis—Yet*, London: Zed Books. This book presents a useful overview of what is known about the links between AIDS and security, and also questions many widespread assumptions about the security implications of HIV/AIDS.
- Elbe, Stefan (2010), *Security and Global Health: Towards the Medicalization of Insecurity*, Cambridge: Polity Press. This book provides a comprehensive overview of the links between health and security and advances a new way of conceptualizing the health security interface as the 'medicalization' of security.
- Fidler, David (2004), *SARS: Governance and the Globalization of Disease*, New York: Palgrave. This book analyses the implications of the SARS crisis for the global governance of health and contemporary world politics. Many of the insights are also relevant to the governance of infectious diseases more generally.
- Fidler, David and Gostin, Lawrence (2008), *Biosecurity in the Global Age: Biological Weapons, Public Health and the Rule of Law*, Stanford. CA: Stanford University Press. A book analysing the security threat posed jointly by the spread of infectious diseases and biological weapons.
- Guillemin, Jeanne (2005), *Biological Weapons: From the Invention of State-Sponsored Programs to Contemporary Bioterrorism*, New York: Columbia University Press. This book offers a comprehensive account of the historical evolution of biological weapons, including the challenges involved in responding to the threat of bioterrorism.
- Price-Smith, Andrew (2001), *The Health of Nations: Infectious Disease, Environmental Change, and their Effects on National Security and Development*, Cambridge, MA: MIT Press. One of the first books systematically to set out the relationships between health issues and national security.

IMPORTANT WEBSITES

- **http://www.sussex.ac.uk/globalhealthpolicy/** The website of the Centre for Global Health Policy at the University of Sussex.
- **http://www.chathamhouse.org/research/global-health** The website of the Centre on Global Health Security at Chatham House.
- **http://www.who.int** The website of the World Health Organization, which has information on most of the diseases discussed in this chapter.
- **http://www.upmchealthsecurity.org** The website of the Center for Health Security at the University of Pittsburgh Medical Center (UPMC).
- **http://ec.europa.eu/health/preparedness_response/hsc/index_en.htm** The website of the Health Security Committee of the European Commission.
- **http://www.ghd-net.org/** The website of the network on Global Health Diplomacy.

Visit the Online Resource Centre that accompanies this book for lots of interesting additional material: www.oxfordtextbooks.co.uk/orc/collins4e/

26

Transnational Crime

Jeanne Giraldo and Harold Trinkunas

Chapter Contents

Reader's Guide

This chapter explains why many governments have increasingly come to consider transnational crime as a threat to national security. It explores both the reasons for and the nature of the increase in transnational crime since the end of the Cold War. It also considers what we know about how transnational crime is organized and finds that our understanding is quite limited. The chapter also explores debates over the strength and nature of the 'nexus' between transnational crime and terrorism. It concludes by discussing how the government response to transnational crime has evolved over time.

Introduction

The growth of **transnational crime** during recent decades is indisputable, but its impact varies considerably across the globe. While **organized crime** has always been with us, new trends in the international system, particularly globalization, have made it increasingly possible for criminal enterprises to cross both physical and virtual borders. As the rate of globalization of trade, finances, and travel accelerates, we should expect crime to become even more transnational in the future and to increasingly adopt flexible network forms of organization. This means that more countries will be exposed to the effect of transnational crime on individual security, societies, and the rule of law at a time when the phenomenon is becoming more difficult to address and contain. The persistence of poorly governed or essentially ungoverned spaces around the globe, which provide fertile home bases for transnational crime, means that even states with strong law enforcement are vulnerable to spill-over effects (Clunan and Trinkunas 2010). It is on these occasions that transnational crime may become a threat to global order.

Thinking about transnational crime is difficult from a traditional international security perspective, which typically focuses on questions of war and peace, conflict and cooperation, often with a state-centric perspective. The threat posed by transnational crime has both international and sub-national dimensions, and, as we will see in this chapter, it has implications for national security, public safety, and even the stability of regimes. Its ability to transcend borders and commit crimes far from its origins, its covert nature, and its ability to corrupt and subvert government agents makes it challenging for states to anticipate threats and prepare their defences. It is even more difficult for governments to think about whether this type of threat can be countered with traditional security instruments, although there have been controversial calls for a greater use of military and intelligence assets to counter transnational crime. For this reason, the theoretical lenses used in this chapter to understand the problem have less to do with our traditional interpretations of international relations and draw more heavily on theories about organizational forms and domestic politics.

This chapter examines the emergence of transnational crime as an international security threat. We provide an overview of how transnational crime changed with increasing globalization and the weakening of state authority in the aftermath of the Cold War. We discuss the debates over how transnational crime is organized, which range from those who view it as highly hierarchical to those who argue it is closer to a decentralized market, and the implications of each model for our understanding of the severity of the threat and how to counter it. This includes an assessment of the arguments concerning the potential links that may develop between transnational crime and terrorism. We conclude by analysing government responses to transnational crime.

KEY POINTS

- Transnational crime is perceived as a major international security threat by some governments and scholars, but traditional theories of international relations are less useful for understanding the threat.
- International trends such as globalization may have the unintended consequence of opening new spaces for the development of transnational crime.
- The threat posed by transnational crime is growing in scope and severity in some parts of the world, and it affects even states with strong law-enforcement agencies.
- Using theories about organizational forms and domestic politics provides us with insights about the nature of the threat and how to address it.

Definitions and key concepts

Transnational crime

Traditionally, transnational crime has referred to criminal activities extending into and violating the laws of two or more countries. In 2000, the United Nations in its Convention against Transnational Organized Crime defined transnational crime even more broadly to encompass any criminal activity that is conducted in more than one state, planned in one state but perpetrated in another, or committed in one state where there are spill-over effects into neighbouring jurisdictions (United Nations 2000). Efforts to typify the nature of the activities labelled as transnational crime are similarly encompassing, as is suggested in Background 26.1.

The increasing globalization of economic activity has provided a wider range of activities and opportunities for crime to cross national boundaries than in the past. Criminals, like businesses in the licit economy, seek to match supply and demand and to take advantage of differences in profits, regulations, and risk levels between markets. These differences may emerge from the availability of supply in certain regions that can be matched to demand in others, such as the flow of narcotics from Afghanistan and South America into Europe and the United States. In other cases, criminals may exploit differences in the regulation of activities, as is often the case in **money laundering** transactions that take advantage of variations in banking secrecy between offshore financial havens and conventional banks. Variations in risk in performing activities may also shape the geographical presence of transnational crime, with criminal enterprises

BACKGROUND 26.1 Categories of transnational crime

1. Money laundering
2. Illicit drug trafficking
3. Corruption of public officials
4. Infiltration of legal businesses
5. Fraudulent bankruptcy
6. Insurance fraud
7. Cybercrime
8. Theft of intellectual property
9. Illicit traffic in arms
10. Terrorism
11. Aircraft hijacking
12. Piracy
13. Hijacking on land
14. Trafficking in persons
15. Trade in human body parts
16. Theft of art and cultural objects
17. Environmental crime
18. Other illicit smuggling

Fourth United Nations Survey of Crime Trends and Operations of Criminal Justice Systems (1994), cited in Mueller (2001). Updated with information from 2010 report Globalization of Crime (UNODC 2010).

developing their **home bases** in low-risk, poorly governed states, such as Nigeria, or in under-governed areas within otherwise strong states, such as the *favelas* (shantytowns) of Rio de Janeiro in Brazil. Criminal activities are likely to take place in **host nations**, where higher risks are compensated for by the lure of higher profits. Other countries are less important as markets (or hosts) for transnational crime groups, but contribute to the illicit economy as trans-shipment states, through which illicit goods pass, or as **service states** (as in the case of money-laundering havens).

Organized crime

When governments and international organizations refer to transnational crime, they most often mean transnational *organized* crime. For example, the Europol Convention on the European Law Enforcement Organization noted that its objective was to target 'terrorism, unlawful drug trafficking and other serious forms of international crime *where there are factual indications that an organized criminal structure is involved*' (EU 1995; emphasis added); and in 2000 the United Nations issued the Convention against Transnational Organized Crime. This raises the question of what the qualifier 'organized' adds to our understanding of transnational crime.

As the UN definition in Key Quotes 26.1 indicates, organized crime is differentiated from other crime in that it is *profit-driven* and *on-going* (that is, a one-time offence would not be included).[1] While everyone can agree on these two dimensions, a more encompassing definition of organized crime has proved elusive. Originally, the term 'organized crime' was used to refer to hierarchical crime groups that were believed to monopolize the criminal market in a given area; to deploy violence and corruption systematically in pursuit of their illicit activities; and to perceive abnormally high profit levels that allowed them to threaten political and economic structures. When applied to transnational crime, this view lent itself to notions of a centrally orchestrated conspiracy by leaders of organized crime groups to carve up the world into their own individual fiefdoms. While most analysts no longer believe in notions of monopolistic control, many still see systemic violence and corruption as the essence of organized crime. Transnational organized crime is often (mistakenly) thought to refer to complex and sophisticated organizations with a centralized leadership directing cross-border operations.

KEY QUOTES 26.1 United Nations' definition of organized crime

'Organized crime is defined as any "structured group of three or more persons existing for a period of time and acting in concert with the aim of committing one or more serious crimes or offenses . . . in order to obtain, directly, or indirectly, a financial or other material benefit".'

'A structured group is one that is not randomly formed for the immediate commission of an offence and that does not need to have formally defined roles for its members, continuity of its membership or a developed structure.'

Article 2, UN Convention against Transnational Organized Crime (United Nations 2000).

[1] Note that hijacking and terrorism from the original UN list of transnational crime (see Background 26.1) would be excluded by this definition.

Other analysts put a great deal of emphasis on the network form of organization as the defining characteristic of transnational crime since the 1990s, highlighting the entrepreneurial flair, scale, sophistication, flexibility, efficiency, and resilience of this form of organization.[2] **Networks** (defined simply by their parts—the component entities or '**nodes**'—and the relationships or 'links' between them) are a decentralized, 'flat' organizational form said to enable criminals to maximize their profits while minimizing their risk from law enforcement. Collaboration between individuals is often ad hoc and transitory, with the networks being formed and disbanded as circumstances warrant (Williams 2001). Under these conditions, many analysts feel it is more appropriate to talk about criminal 'structures' or 'enterprises' rather than 'groups' (which implies a clearly defined membership, UN definition notwithstanding).

Finally, a key group of scholars argues that it is more important to think of transnational crime as a marketplace rather than a network of groups (Beare 2003; Naylor 2004). The need to minimize risk (that is, to avoid law enforcement) and other limits imposed by the illicit marketplace means criminal organizations will tend to be small, vulnerable, and competitive—a far cry from the monopolies or collusive oligarchies stressed in the traditional, hierarchical vision of organized crime. While network theorists point to the adaptability and sophistication of criminal networks as a key source of their resilience in the face of law-enforcement efforts, the market scholars note that the 'great majority of what is conventionally defined as crime is the province of small-time losers' (Naylor 2004: 10). From this perspective, the resilience of transnational crime can be attributed to the inexorable logic of the marketplace—supply rising to meet demand—rather than the sophistication or entrepreneurial flair of networks.

How can these competing visions be reconciled? Most observers agree that transnational crime groups vary greatly in their size, organization, and modes of operation and that hierarchies, networks, and markets coexist. The challenge for organized crime theorists and law enforcement practitioners is to determine which organizational logics operate in any given situation and determine empirically (rather than assume) whether the logics are correlated with other factors such as types of crime, patterns of cooperation with other groups, linkages to the legal world, different threat levels, and vulnerability to law enforcement or other interventions.

[2] Although it is commonly believed that it is easier for law enforcement to dismantle hierarchical organizations than networks, it is not clear whether this is the case because networks are more flexible and sophisticated or simply because police agencies tend to focus more on hierarchical organizations and have more information about them (Kenney 2007).

KEY POINTS

- Transnational crime involves on-going profit-driven criminal activity that crosses national boundaries.
- Not all organized crime is transnational, but there are growing incentives for criminal enterprises to operate across national borders because of differences in the supply and demand for illegal goods and services among countries.
- Most observers agree that transnational crime groups vary greatly in their size, organization, and modes of operation.
- Proponents of a hierarchical view of organized crime view these groups as wealthy, powerful, violent, and under the control of a small number of individuals.
- Others argue that most transnational crime operates through networks of individuals and small groups who operate on a transitory or ad hoc basis to minimize the risk from law enforcement.
- Critics argue that organized crime is in fact highly disorganized, and resembles more a market for illicit goods and services than an organization. Proponents of this view minimize the threat posed by organized criminals to states and societies.

The increase in transnational crime

Transnational crime is not a new phenomenon. Organized crime groups have operated transnationally for decades, if not centuries. How then can we account for the widespread alarm over transnational crime beginning in the 1990s and intensifying after the terrorist attacks of 9/11? Many observers argue that much of the initial concern was generated by the military, intelligence, and broader national security communities in search of a justification for their relevance (and budgets) in the post-Cold War era (Beare 2003). Although there is some truth to this, there is also a consensus that a very real increase in the scale and scope of transnational crime occurred following the end of the Cold War and continued during the first two decades of the twenty-first century.

Transnational crime has become global in scale and is no longer exclusive to certain geographical areas or ethnic groups. There has been a marked increase in the number and size of illegal markets, the number of groups involved, the number of countries affected, and the overall amount of illicit trade. Whereas illegal markets were small and isolated in the past, today illicit markets tend to be interrelated, mutually supporting, and more embedded in the legal economy than ever. The 'democratization' of crime has been matched by an increasing reliance on decentralized, network forms of organization.

The increased scale and scope of transnational crime and its changing nature can be explained in large part by two developments. First, the increased transnational flow of people, goods, and money in the second half of the twentieth century (a process often referred to as 'globalization') has contributed to the growth of both licit and illicit economies that operate across national boundaries. Second, a wave of 'dual transitions' (away from closed economies and authoritarian political regimes) and an increase in civil unrest with the end of the Cold War undermined state authority in a number of countries, providing a home base for crime groups or otherwise facilitating the operation of transnational criminal networks.

Globalization

The increased transnational flow of people, goods, and money that occurred during the second half of the twentieth century was greatly facilitated by advances in communications and transportation technologies, such as the advent of inexpensive passenger air travel, the personal computer, the Internet, and cellular communications. However, the process of globalization, properly understood, is not just a matter of technological innovation but is even more fundamentally linked to the economic and political reforms that reduced the restrictions on the international movement of goods, people, and money, starting in the 1980s and picking up speed in the twenty-first century. In addition, a wave of market-oriented reforms in the developing and developed world reduced barriers to trade and promoted the development of export-based economies. Politically, a wave of transitions towards democracy, beginning in 1974 in Southern Europe and moving to Latin America in the 1980s and on to Africa, Eastern Europe, and the former Soviet Union following the fall of the Berlin Wall, increased transnational flows. Borders that had been closed shut under authoritarian rule now spilled open.

This largely positive process of economic and political liberalization had a 'dark side'. In an increasingly global marketplace, illicit actors, like their licit counterparts, took advantage of business opportunities wherever they occurred. The growth of global trade and global financial networks provided an infrastructure and cover that illicit actors could exploit. For example, as a result of the creation of the North American Free Trade Area, trade between the United States and Mexico grew from $81.5 billion in 1993 to $247 billion in 2000 and to over $530 billion in 2014. This land border is also one of the main routes for the smuggling of illegal goods and aliens into the United States. Burgeoning cross-border traffic increases the opportunities for criminals to hide their activities within the flow of legal commerce. The globalization of financial markets has accelerated dramatically since the 1980s, making it easier for criminals to move and store their profits quickly and secretly. Legal and regulatory responses to the 2008 global financial crisis in no way reduced the challenge faced by governments, which is to find the criminal 'signal' within the 'noise' generated by the large amount of international trade and financial flows produced by globalization.

At the same time, globalization increased the importance of 'network' forms of organization for both legal and illegal enterprises. Hierarchical organizations no longer had to recruit personnel with the full range of specialized skill sets necessary for various operations; instead these functions could be 'contracted out'. In the criminal world, fluid and readily adaptable networks of individuals and organizations could group together and disband as required by the needs of particular illicit ventures. Operations such as money laundering or the manufacturing of false identities could be outsourced to independent specialized contractors, who might very well be part of multiple criminal networks. The ability to increasingly conduct such operations over the global Internet added to the viability of transnational networks and illicit global marketplaces. In short, innovations in technology and the proliferation of illicit markets had the effect of 'democratizing' the criminal underworld, making it easier for individuals to participate in crime without the need for large, hierarchical organizations to provide the infrastructure and necessary social contacts.

The increased movement of people across borders—and their ability to remain in contact with their homelands long after they had resettled elsewhere—encouraged this phenomenon. The end of the Cold War created new opportunities for economic migrants from the former Soviet states, as did the continuing economic disparities between the developing and developed world. The sharp increase in civil conflicts around the globe also created a new generation of refugees. These diasporas have provided the family and ethnic ties that help facilitate a transnational criminal enterprise. Groups such as the Chinese triads operating in Hong Kong, the United States, and Western Europe or Kosovar drug smuggling networks in Western Europe, depend on the links maintained between individuals of similar cultural backgrounds across borders. Unassimilated ethnic minority populations are often vulnerable to exploitation by criminals even in developed countries, yet they are also fearful of cooperation with law enforcement.

Despite the undeniable importance of family and ethnic ties in facilitating collaboration, this element can be overemphasized—and often is, given law enforcement's tendency to focus on these visibly different groups (see Background 26.2). However, of the forty organized crime groups in sixteen countries studied by UNODC, only thirteen were based on shared ethnic identities (and another ten were based on shared social characteristics; the other half had no strong shared identity). Collaboration *between groups* is even less likely to depend on shared identities, being driven instead by opportunism (UNODC 2002)—as was first emphasized with the widely noted alliance between Colombian cartels and the Sicilian mafia in the late 1980s to facilitate the entry of cocaine into Europe. In some cases, a shared position of marginalization within a society can facilitate cooperation between different ethnic groups, as was the case with Vietnamese vendors of smuggled cigarettes and Polish smugglers in East Germany (von Lampe and Johansen 2003).

The undermining of state authority

Globally, dual transitions toward free-market economies and democracy in the 1980s and 1990s contributed greatly to the increased mobility of people, goods, and money that provided increased opportunities for transnational crime. In many countries these dual transitions have contributed to the spread of transnational crime in another way as well. This section refers to transitions that have gone awry, leaving behind a state that is often unable to assert the rule of law (so-called grey areas) or even to exert control over its territory (creating 'ungoverned areas'). These grey and ungoverned areas have provided the home base for a wide range of groups engaged in transnational criminal activities: from organized criminals to warlords to insurgents. It is worth noting that many criminal organizations prefer poorly governed grey areas rather than completely ungoverned territories in which to base their operations. Grey areas have the advantage of ready access to banks, communications, and transportation, while the cost of physical security in truly ungoverned areas is quite high (Clunan and Trinkunas 2010).

In some cases, such as Russia and many of the post-Soviet states, organized crime took advantage of the dual transitions to enhance their **power** and corrupt the state (Shelley 2008). In Russia, economic 'fixers' that had greased the wheels of the pre-1991 command economy and small organized crime groups that survived the Soviet period joined with some discharged elements of the Soviet intelligence and security apparatus and emerging entrepreneurs to take advantage of the poorly regulated transitional economy. Combining inside knowledge of state enterprises and resources, access to intelligence and surveillance files, experience and contacts in the West, and expertise in violence and intimidation, these new organized crime elements were well positioned to exploit the weaknesses of the emerging Russian state to great personal advantage (Finckenauer and Voronin 2001). The efforts of these emerging organized crime groups did much to undermine investor confidence in the Russian economy, driving up the cost of doing business and aggravating a scarcity of legal capital for legitimate business development. They also delegitimized the subsequent Russian democratic regime by calling into question its ability to maintain the rule of law and provide for public safety. This eventually contributed to broader popular support for a more authoritarian style of government under President Vladimir Putin in the 2000s.

In other cases, such as the Balkans and various countries in Africa, failed transitions to democracy resulted in open warfare, a situation that lends itself to the creation of ties between political elites and criminal elements that persist even when the conflict ends.

BACKGROUND 26.2 Sample of prominent transnational criminal 'clusters'

The following are not 'single and interconnected criminal groups in their own right' but are more appropriately thought of as 'clusters' of groups (UNODC 2002: 8). These broad labels are a convenient (but potentially misleading) shorthand used by the media and law-enforcement agencies to refer to individuals and groups that share ethnic or social characteristics, and may show some similarities in structure and organizations.

Italian Mafia. In Italy, this is a generic term applied to the Sicilian Mafia, the Neapolitan Camorra, the Calabrian 'Ndrangheta, and the Apulian Sacra Corona Unita. It is known for its connections to other organized crime elements, such as the Colombian drug-trafficking cartels.

Russian organized crime. Based on legacy organized crime groupings that exploited the inefficiency of the Soviet centrally planned economy, these groups continue to operate, even in an increasingly authoritarian Russian state under President Putin. They include persons from all the former Soviet states, including prominently Russians, Ukrainians, Chechens, Georgians, and Azeris. They are known to have connections to organized crime in the United States and Western Europe.

Chinese Triads. Working predominantly from Hong Kong and Taiwan rather than the Chinese mainland, these groups are involved with drug trafficking, prostitution, gambling, extortion, and human trafficking. They have developed a global presence throughout the Chinese international diaspora.

Japanese Yakuza (Boryokudan). These Japanese-based gangs engage in some transnational crime, mainly drug trafficking and human smuggling for prostitution. Their activities are concentrated in Japan, South East Asia, and the United States.

Mexican and other Latin American drug cartels. These groups are highly specialized and organized around the various stages of production and transportation of cocaine, heroin, and marijuana from Bolivia, Peru, Colombia, and Mexico into the United States through land, sea, and air routes. Insurgent groups in Colombia and Peru became involved in this type of organized crime as well. Mexican transnational criminal groupings have become especially prominent in the first two decades of the twenty-first century.

Nigerian organized crime. These transnational organizations take advantage of the weak rule of law in their home country and the Nigerian diaspora throughout the world to engage in organized drug trafficking, computer and mail fraud, and various forms of financial fraud.

Williams and Savona (1998). On criminal 'clusters' see UNODC (2002) and White House (2011). For specific cases, see Digest of Organized Crime Cases (UNODC 2012).

In the case of the Balkans, the embargo against the warring states created new asymmetries that could be exploited by organized crime through the trafficking of commodities, gasoline, and arms. With the connivance of local government officials, organized crime groups trafficked women into Western Europe and, in some instances, to the peacekeeping forces attempting to reduce the level of conflict. These groups included the highest levels of society within the former Yugoslavia, including the government leadership of Serbia, which used these networks to enrich themselves and provide the supplies necessary for their forces to continue the war. Similarly, Kosovar drug traffickers in Western Europe generated the funding necessary to support the insurgency of the Kosovo Liberation Army in their home territory. In the wake of the war, these organized crime elements proved to be particularly difficult to control, at one point even participating in the assassination of the Serbian Prime Minister, Zoran Dindic, in 2003. The inclusion of law enforcement, intelligence, and military officials in these transnational crime networks explains their ability to endure beyond the end of the Balkan wars and the advent of democracy in the region (Saponja-Hadzic 2003).

KEY POINTS

- Transnational crime increased in scale and scope by the 1990s, with a jump in the number of groups involved, the range of countries affected, the number and density of illicit markets, and the prevalence of networks.
- The increased globalization of trade, finances, and travel has produced an environment conducive to transnational crime by making it easier for criminals to move illicit profits and illegal goods, provide services, and smuggle persons across state borders.
- Political transitions to democracy and economic transitions to free markets since the 1980s, often simultaneously in the same country, have occasionally gone awry, undermining state capacity to enforce the rule of law and creating new opportunities for organized crime to penetrate societies and governments in transition.

Transnational crime and terrorism

Groups that use terrorist methods have long relied on crime as a means to fund their activities. For example, many Marxist-Leninist terrorist groups of the 1970s and 1980s engaged primarily in domestic crimes—bank robbery, extortion, or kidnapping in the country where they operated—for funds. With the vast increase in opportunities for transnational crime in recent decades, it is not surprising that transnational terrorist groups (as well as those located in a single country) have increasingly engaged in crime as a source of financing. Despite high levels of Iranian and Syrian support for Hezbollah, supporters of the group have engaged in various criminal schemes to raise funds, such as cigarette smuggling and coupon fraud in the United States and smuggling and counterfeiting in the loosely regulated 'Tri-border' frontier area of Argentina, Brazil, and Paraguay. Similarly, Al-Qaeda cells in Western Europe have engaged in credit-card fraud. Warlords in Africa have benefited from illicit trade in diamonds; Boko Haram insurgents in Nigeria rely on extorting local populations and human trafficking; Iraqi insurgents have resold hijacked petroleum and traffic in drugs; and guerrillas and **paramilitary** groups in Colombia (both of whom use terrorist tactics) participated in the cocaine trade during the past two decades.

In short, the same democratizing effects of globalization that increased the opportunities for criminal activity apply to terrorists. The decentralization of transnational crime groups that was evident by the 1990s contributed to the ability of 'terrorists' to increase their involvement in crime. In addition to engaging in criminal activities to fund their activities (and sometimes cooperating with criminals in illicit trading), terrorists also seek the services provided by criminals for operational reasons—for example, buying weapons from illicit arms traffickers or false identity documents from counterfeiters. One of the greatest fears is that terrorists will be able to procure weapons of mass destruction from criminals.

While no one disputes these connections, there has been a great deal of disagreement over their meaning and the future course of events (for a review of the debate and evidence, see Williams 2008). The 'criminal–terrorist nexus' *can* be overstated—governments have incentives to discredit terrorists by labelling them as criminals, concerned only with profits, and law enforcement stands to benefit from more resources and powers by invoking the spectre of a 'strategic alliance' between the two. This view assumes that criminals and terrorists share an interest in both money making and destabilizing the state and that the multiplier effect of cooperating to attain their goals will be devastating.

While there is more contact between criminals and terrorists than ever before, collaboration is by no means automatic, nor—with the exception of the smuggling of nuclear materials—is it likely to have the devastating effects that some predict. As the US State Department emphasizes, the two groups share 'methods but not motives', and this tends to limit their collaboration. Criminals interested in profits may at times engage in tactical collaboration with terrorists, particularly where the latter control essential territory or resources (just as multinational corporations acting in conflict zones sometimes collaborate with insurgents or local warlords). In contrast, when criminal organizations are strong, they are likely to create barriers to entry for terrorists (and other individuals) interested in criminal activities. Even when collaboration brings monetary benefits, criminals may eschew it so as not to attract unwanted attention from law enforcement.

The different motives of the two groups also mean it is incorrect to predict an inevitable convergence of the two in the future. The ideological motives of terrorists usually persist, despite their participation in criminal activities: 'fighters turned felons' are a relatively rare phenomenon. For example, this label had been applied to the Islamic Movement of Uzbekistan but could not explain why a profit-driven group would fight to the death on behalf of the Taliban in Afghanistan in 2002. A more problematic phenomenon is that of 'felons turned zealots'. There is some evidence that criminals and terrorists who share jail cells also develop shared interests in joint criminal and terrorist ventures upon their release. This has been documented not only in South Asia, but also in the 2004 Madrid bombings, in which a radicalized drug dealer played an instrumental role, and in the 2014 Charlie Hebdo attacks in Paris, where prior to the attack, the assailants had come into contact and been mentored by an imprisoned radical affiliated with Al-Qaeda that they had met while serving prison time together.

Despite these caveats, it is important for policy makers and law enforcement to develop strategies to address the link between crime and terrorism. The risk of 'catastrophic criminality' requires particular attention to the smuggling of nuclear material. Targeting the criminal activities of terrorists is unlikely to bankrupt any organization, as most groups have diversified funding streams, but it could hinder their ability to fund and arm themselves on the margins. As importantly, identifying the criminal nexus within terrorism can provide an entry point into otherwise hermetic organizations for counterterrorist and intelligence specialists to exploit.

KEY POINTS

- Terrorist groups often rely on crime to fund and carry out their operations.
- There is increasing concern over the connections between terrorism and transnational criminal groups, but in most cases these are episodic 'marriages of convenience'.
- The radicalization of criminals by terrorists during periods when they are in close proximity, such as when they share prison cells, is one way in which criminal expertise is made available to terrorist groups.

Assessing the threat

Transnational criminal groups cause harm to individuals and societies with the profit-driven crimes they carry out. For example, drug trafficking contributes to levels of substance abuse, petty crime, and the spread of HIV/**AIDS** by intravenous drug-users. Lost productivity, work accidents, and increased expenditures on health care are all economic costs associated with drug use. Coca production in South America has led to the deforestation of increasing areas of the Amazon forest and to the pollution of land and waterways with the chemicals used for growing and processing coca. These costs are often cited to justify viewing drug trafficking as a threat to human security or environmental security (see Think Point 26.1).

Often, however, transnational crime is characterized as a *national* security threat, requiring a quantitatively and qualitatively different response from government. This sometimes occurs when the *level* of harm caused by transnational crime reaches epidemic proportions—for example, the increase in the HIV infection rate unleashed by drug use in Russia. Or, if the crime itself is of a serious enough nature—for example, smuggling of nuclear material—the threat posed would be considered a matter for national security experts. Most often, however, the *perpetrators* of transnational crime—rather than the crimes themselves—are seen as the real threats to national security. According to this view, increasingly wealthy and powerful criminals undermine the state, democracy, and the economy through the use of corruption, violence, and reinvestment of their profits in the licit economy.

On a very basic level, the ability of transnational crime enterprises to evade state border controls and provide new avenues for the illicit transportation of goods and persons challenges the state's ability to exercise its core functions as guarantor of national sovereignty, the holder of the monopoly on the legitimate use of force, and provider of the common good. In the course of their activities, transnational criminal enterprises corrupt and undermine numerous state agencies, providing mechanisms by which transnational criminal enterprises can affect the very nature of government and state policy in the host countries. At the extremes, transnational criminal enterprises become so powerful at certain moments as to challenge and replace the state's monopoly on the use of force, as has occurred in some remote areas of the drug-producing regions of Colombia, Peru, and Bolivia.

Second, transnational crime may become a fundamental threat through its power to corrupt or coerce government officials. In some states, transnational criminal enterprises have taken advantage of the instability that accompanied transitions to democracy to become entrenched, using corruption to extend their influence into the upper reaches of the state and thus shield themselves from law enforcement. This threat becomes more serious in cases where states have limited capacity to protect themselves from such threats, as is the case in small island nations in the Caribbean and South Pacific, or in local or provincial governments within larger federal states. In extreme situations, the power of organized crime relative to governments may lead to hybrid forms of governance in which politicians, law enforcement, and transnational criminal organizations form mutually supporting networks, as has been observed in the slums of Rio de Janeiro, the suburbs of Buenos Aires, and certain cities and towns in Mexico.

Third, governments view transnational crime as a security threat to the extent that it undermines democratic stability by calling the legitimacy of new regimes into question. The perceived fecklessness of law enforcement in new democracies to respond to transnational crime and public insecurity contributes to undermining public confidence and loyalty to the new regime. In the extreme, popular reaction can

THINK POINT 26.1 Human trafficking and transnational crime

Transnational human trafficking has garnered an increasing amount of attention since the end of the Cold War. In 2014, the US State Department estimated that 20 million persons were trafficked across international borders for the purpose of forced labour or involuntary prostitution. Many millions more suffer this fate within national borders. It is also estimated that 80 per cent of the victims are women or girls, many of whom are trafficked for the purpose of sexual servitude. Approximately half the victims are minors. The Terrorism, Transnational Crime and Corruption Center at George Mason University estimates that the industry generates between US$10 billion and US$40 billion per year.

Transnational criminal organizations play a major role in facilitating and profiting from this modern form of slavery. Victims are lured by scams or false promises made by criminal gangs, or sometimes are simply taken by force. Profits may derive from the smuggling process itself, since criminal gangs are often paid by employers at the destination for the delivery of forced labourers. In the case of integrated transnational networks, criminal organizations benefit directly by exploiting victims' labour in prostitution rings or other illegal ventures once they have reached their destination. Trafficking organizations typically move victims from less developed to more developed countries. A good deal of human trafficking takes place in South East Asia, but there are also well-established trafficking networks connecting states of the former Soviet Union to Western Europe, and Latin America to the United States.

Human trafficking is not just another profit centre for transnational criminal organizations, but it is one of the activities these groups undertake that is viewed as a direct and growing threat to human and national security. On an individual level, human trafficking directly attacks a victim's human rights, health, and safety by pressing them into forced labour, exposing them to increased risk of sexually transmitted disease, physical assault, and mental illness, particularly post-traumatic stress disorder. It also degrades communities by breaking up families and lowering levels of trust among community members, particularly because many victims come first into contact with trafficking networks through acquaintances. However, governments also perceive human trafficking as a threat to national security. In part, this is because trafficking networks are facilitated by official corruption, so they have a corrosive effect on the integrity of security forces. However, governments also worry that these dark networks may be used to traffic more than victims, serving as conduits for terrorist organizations, epidemic disease, or other nefarious threats to the state and its citizens.

Governments have reacted with increasing vigour to this threat, particularly in the developed world. Breaking up human trafficking networks is a classic example of a threat that requires a transnational response, since it crosses borders, but also an inter-agency response within states. In 2000, the United Nations adopted two protocols against the trafficking of women and the trafficking of migrants as part of the Convention against Transnational Organized Crime. In 2008, the Council of Europe Convention on Action against Trafficking in Human Beings came into effect. At the national level, countries such as the United Kingdom have explicitly criminalized trafficking in forced labour. Within the United States, there have been federal efforts since 1998 to develop a national response to human trafficking through horizontal integration among different agencies (forty-two were involved at one count), but also vertical integration between national and local officials, typically taking the form of special task forces operating in urban areas hit particularly hard by this form of crime. However, conflicts between US government agencies over funding, jurisdiction, personnel, and information sharing are often cited as obstacles to effective government action against human trafficking. Similar inter-agency conflicts and lack of cooperation is also reported in many national anti-trafficking efforts. This suggests that there is still a long way to go before states develop effective responses to human trafficking.

Langberg (2008).

lead to the replacement of governments or regimes, sometimes producing a restoration of democracy, as occurred during the Orange Revolution in Ukraine in 2004, but at other times leading to a nostalgia for more authoritarian forms of government, as arguably occurred in Russia during the first Putin presidency (2000–8). This aspect of the threat posed by transnational crime is of concern to major powers such as the United States and the European Union that have a vested interest in promoting democracy.

Fourth, transnational crime is seen as a threat to economic development (and therefore national security). The UNODC estimated the cost of transnational crime as 3.6 per cent of global GDP in 2011 (UNODC 2011). Organized crime is perceived as a threat to development in so far as it undermines the rule of law and deters foreign investment by increasing the level of violence and insecurity in host communities. In addition, criminals often reinvest their proceeds in the legal economy as part of its money-laundering efforts, and these criminally affiliated businesses often have an unfair competitive advantage through their access to cheap capital and their ability to intimidate competitors in the market.

While this threat assessment is true for some organized crime structures and countries, it is often incorrectly applied across the board to all instances of 'transnational organized crime'. Recall, however, that the minimalist definition of transnational organized crime used by governments and international organizations means there is a great deal of variation in the size, structure, and activities of these groups. In particular, they vary greatly in the factors that are often considered the 'trademarks' of organized crime; the extent to which they use violence and corruption to facilitate their crimes; and the degree to which they penetrate the legal economy. This variation can help explain the very different threat perceptions of organized crime held by groups of academics that study the topic. In particular, analysts who study criminal markets in advanced industrial democracies are more likely to stress the 'disorganized' nature of criminal networks and downplay the threat posed by these groups. These critics point to misleading and sensationalized media coverage of 'mafia-like' organized crime groups; political rhetoric based on grossly over-inflated official estimates of criminal profits; and undifferentiated threat assessments by law enforcement based on unclear methodological and empirical grounds to argue that the threat is exaggerated (Naylor 2004; van Duyne 2004). In other countries, organized crime lives up to its billing as violent, corrupting, and disruptive of national economies.

The challenge for students of transnational organized crime is to develop empirically grounded theories of the threat transnational crime poses, rather than assuming the threat based on the 'transnational organized crime' label (which tends to be most readily applied to ethnic groups operating at the margins of society). For example, while many observers believe that hierarchical organizations are more wealthy, corrupt, and violent than other criminal structures, there is a lack of empirical information to determine whether this is the case.[3] Others have suggested that organized crime groups be categorized not according to their organizational logic but rather in terms of the different ways they are embedded in society (von Lampe 2004). Groups embedded in high-level social and political structures are likely to pose a greater threat (through corruption and penetration of the licit economy) than those that operate at the margins of society.

[3] Though see UNODC (2002), which surveys forty crime groups in sixteen countries and finds that hierarchical groups are more likely to employ violence and corruption than criminal networks.

KEY POINTS

- The crimes committed by transnational criminal groups often harm individuals and societies, posing a threat to human security.
- Transnational crime often comes to be seen as a national security threat because of the added danger posed by the modus operandi of the perpetrators of transnational crime.
- Policy makers and law-enforcement agencies are particularly concerned with the extent to which wealthy and powerful criminal groups engage in corruption and violence in ways that undermine the state, democracy, and the economy.

Government responses

Transnational criminal organizations are not inherently more sophisticated or dangerous than other crime structures, but they do tend to pose greater challenges for governments, which are much more constrained than illicit actors by borders and traditional norms of sovereignty. In an effort to deal with the increasingly transnational and decentralized nature of criminal networks, governments have globalized their law-enforcement efforts, harmonizing laws to remove loopholes exploited by criminals and creating police networks to facilitate cross-national cooperation. The overwhelming emphasis on transnational crime as a national security threat since the end of the Cold War (and especially after the terrorist attacks of 9/11) has meant increased resources for law enforcement, incursions on civil liberties, as revealed by former US National Security Agency contractor Edward Snowden in 2013, increasingly blurred lines between law-enforcement and national security apparatuses (particularly intelligence agencies), and an emphasis on targeting criminal organizations rather than criminal markets.

Global policing trends: increased coordination and securitization

The 'war on drugs', rather than a concern with transnational crime per se, led the United States to place an increased emphasis on both bilateral and multilateral cooperation on law enforcement in the 1980s. The USA used financial sticks and carrots to promote drug-control efforts in producer and transit nations; pushed hard in multilateral circles for the 1988 UN Convention against Illicit Traffic in Narcotic Drugs and Psychotropic Substances and the G7's establishment of the Financial Action Task Force to promote laws and expertise for countering the money laundering associated with the drug trade; and encouraged sometimes reluctant European law-enforcement agencies to adopt more aggressive and intelligence-based approaches to counter narcotics trafficking.

With the extension of transnational crime to new areas of the globe in recent decades, increasing numbers of nations began to see transnational crime as a serious problem and were willing to take measures to reduce the asymmetries between countries though harmonization of legislation and increasing police capacity and networking. This trend was reinforced by the emphasis placed on it by the United States in the 1990s and by expanded and deepening regional integration in the European Union, which created additional incentives and opportunities for law-enforcement cooperation (Andreas and Nadelmann 2006). One example is the European Police Office (EUROPOL), which was established in 1992 as part of the Maastricht Treaty creating the European Union; its initial focus on fighting drugs soon expanded to other forms of transnational crime, and this broader emphasis was formalized in the 2002 annex to the Europol Convention. Globally, the 2000 UN Convention against Transnational Organized Crime and 2003 UN Convention against Corruption are also indicative of increased international cooperation on transnational crime.

The terrorist attacks of 9/11 in the United States and the subsequent emphasis on fighting terrorism only deepened already unprecedented levels of cross-national cooperation. The blurring of lines between law-enforcement and national security agencies and missions that had already begun with the emphasis of transnational crime as a national security threat only increased with the fear of 'catastrophic criminality', forcing law-enforcement agencies to engage in the worst-case scenario planning usually reserved for the military and national security apparatus. A decade after 9/11, the 2011 US national strategy to combat organized crime still focuses on possible linkages to terrorism to justify more aggressive efforts. Despite significant disagreements on how to address terrorism, there was significant international convergence on the role of law enforcement. Many governments were willing to embrace more drastic responses, devoting additional resources to law enforcement and introducing more draconian legal measures, some of which arguably endangered civil liberties, such as the forfeiture of all assets held by persons participating in organized crime schemes, not just those related to the crime itself. In addition, governments considered how emerging technologies, often derived from military programmes, could be put to use in improving the ability of government to gather information on transnational crime and, in some cases, how the military could be used to attack this threat.

Evaluating government responses

Overwhelmingly, the government response to transnational crime has focused on targeting the individuals and organizations perpetrating the crime rather than the criminal markets in and of themselves. In the case of the drug trade, for instance, leaders or 'critical nodes' of drug-trafficking organizations are targeted (depending upon whether they are hierarchies or networks), as are criminal assets. In decades past, less attention was paid to reducing the demand for drugs or the social conditions that contribute to the attractiveness of illicit crop cultivation in favour of 'tough-on-crime' approaches. This organizational focus has been justified by governments on the grounds that targeted criminal organizations are so powerful, violent, and corrupt that they pose an even greater immediate threat to the state and democracy than the drug trafficking itself—as has been the case in Mexico during the past decade (see Case Study 26.1).

Law-enforcement approaches that target criminal organizations have had some tactical successes. For example, in Colombia, the Cali and Medellin cartels were dismantled and 50 per cent of the transnational organized crime groups identified in a 1999 UNODC survey were defunct by the time of the study's publication in 2002. However, the overall strategic effectiveness of this approach has been called into question. In the short-to-medium run, law-enforcement efforts tend to increase corruption (paying off officials is only necessary if criminals have something to fear from law enforcement) and violence (as criminals compete to fill the organizational vacuums left open by law-enforcement successes). In the medium-to-long run, tactical successes in one country can lead to the spread of illicit markets to other countries and strengthen new sets of actors, who may pose an even graver threat to the state (see Case Study 26.1)—without having much effect on the price and availability of illicit goods.

CASE STUDY 26.1 Targeting criminal organizations: trade-offs, and unintended consequences

Mexico has experienced dramatically high levels of violence due to conflicts among drug trafficking organizations (DTOs) and between DTOs and the state. Over 134,000 Mexicans died due to homicide between 2006 and 2013, which for the same period, exceeds the combined rate of violent deaths in two countries suffering from internal wars, Iraq and Afghanistan. Mexico has had as many as six to ten large drug cartels during this period, but Mexico's strategy of targeting the leadership of DTOs has led to their fragmentation into nearly a hundred smaller groups at war with each other. In addition, there has been a dramatic surge in crime in Central America, where local youth gangs are increasingly involved with DTOs, and criminal violence has produced a surge in internal displacement and transnational migration. The dramatic rise in violence in this region is the unintended consequence of anti-crime policies in South America and unsuccessful security strategies in Mexico (Felbab-Brown 2014).

Efforts by Colombia, with the support of the United States, to destroy the Medellin and Cali cartels shifted power in the illicit narcotics economy away from traffickers in South America. In addition, a policy of targeting the air transportation of narcotics from Peru towards the United States, known as air bridge denial, forced Colombian traffickers to rely more heavily on transnational criminal organizations in Mexico to deliver their products to the US market. Mexico's police forces, which are often poorly trained, underpaid, and corrupt, were unprepared to deal with the surge in smuggling and violence across their jurisdictions.

In 2006, the administration of President Felipe Calderón in Mexico decided to confront the drug cartels by pursuing a strategy of 'high-value targeting'—killing or capturing drug kingpins with the intent of disrupting what were assumed to be hierarchical criminal organizations. This strategy differed from that of previous Mexican governments, which had tended to negotiate informal bargains with DTOs to contain violence and establish predictability in illicit markets. A surge in trafficking displaced from Colombia and accompanying violence led the Calderón administration to conclude that a new approach was needed to contain what was seen as a challenge to the state. The Calderón administration's strategy was influenced by what was perceived as a successful effort in Colombia, where leaders such as Pablo Escobar of the Medellin cartel had been removed from the field, with disastrous consequences for the organizations they led.

In Mexico, this strategy proved to be counter-productive in terms of reducing violence. Given the large number of trafficking organizations in Mexico, the removal of any one set of leaders, such as the Beltran Leyva brothers, simply led to conflict among the remaining cartels for control of illicit markets and trafficking routes into the United States. The Mexican state was simply not powerful enough to go after all the groups at once, and the result was a criminal war that produced stunningly high levels of internal conflict in Mexico. This outcome was somewhat predictable given what Colombia experienced in the 1990s. There, the defeat of the Cali and Medellin cartels led to a fragmentation of drug trafficking organizations and the rise of violent non-state actors, such as the Fuerzas Armadas Revolucionarias de Colombia (FARC) and right-wing paramilitaries. These actors profited from the drug trade, preyed on the local population, and, at times, challenged the state for territorial control.

A further unintended consequence of Colombia and Mexico's policies has been to displace illicit trafficking routes towards Central America. Drug traffickers increasingly began to use Central America's Northern Triangle (El Salvador, Honduras, and Guatemala) as an alternative route to move illicit products into North America, and to fight against each other for control of *plazas* or trafficking routes along the Mexico/Guatemala border. Central America's security forces, already overwhelmed by a rise in youth gang violence (known as the *maras*), were even less well placed to address the growing presence of DTOs on their territory than Mexico or Colombia (UNDP 2013). As a result, the Northern Triangle countries are now three of the five most violent in the world in terms of homicides per capita.

In 2013, President Peña Nieto came into office in Mexico with a campaign platform that promised to reduce the levels of criminal violence by adopting a strategy that purported to address socio-economic root causes. While homicide levels were reduced over the next two years, this occurred because the Peña Nieto administration has adopted a much less confrontational policy towards DTOs. As a result, the DTOs in Mexico continue to have the organizational capacity to wield high levels of violence with impunity, and they have penetrated deeply into the state and society at the local level. This was highlighted by the massacre of forty-three student-teachers in the town of Iguala in 2014 at the hands of a local drug gang, in complicity with the municipal police and at the direction of the town's mayor. Mexico's civil society reacted with outrage and mass protests at the news of this massacre, dramatically impacting President Peña Nieto's popular standing.

Mexico and Colombia serve as a cautionary tale about the unintended consequences that national-level anti-crime strategies can have on transnational criminal enterprises operating on a regional scale. In each case, governments reacted to the threat of DTOs when they began to use levels of violence that threatened society and the state. Their strategy of High-Value Targeting (HVT) led to the disorganization of trafficking markets, but it actually increased violent competition among a larger number of smaller criminal organizations. In addition, the DTOs reacted by seeking out alternative territories and routes that allowed them to (temporarily) evade the impact of state law enforcement efforts, which had the effect of spreading violent competition into new countries. This suggests the need for a more comprehensive evidence-based approach that asks what regional strategies would really lead to reduced violence and DTO penetration of state and society.

While these 'unintended consequences' are commonplace and well documented, governments continue to fail to anticipate them when devising enforcement strategies.

Although law enforcement is an important part of any strategy to combat transnational crime, the shortcomings previously identified have rightly led to calls for a more comprehensive approach that relies on all elements of national power to address crime. To the extent that transnational crime harms individuals and society, public health ministries, non-governmental organizations (NGOs), and other groups should be involved. For example, devising measures protecting the victim (as in the case of trafficking in persons) and minimizing the harm to society should be given more importance than targeting organizations. Given the harm posed to the integrity of public institutions by corruption, collaborators of organized crime groups in the licit sector should be targeted with as much vigour as the 'career' criminals themselves.

Approaches that focus on the general underlying conditions that facilitate illicit markets, such as state failure or corruption, are important, particularly to the extent that they bring into play actors and approaches often neglected in the traditional law enforcement approach. The World Bank has emphasized building up the capacity of judicial systems as a mechanism to ensure good governance and the rule of law and in addressing corruption. The private sector and NGOs have also contributed, both by setting industry-wide standards designed to combat organized crime, as has been done by the international banking industry, and through civic education designed to help citizens resist the influence of these groups in their lives. NGOs such as Transparency International (founded in 1993) can also play an important role in targeting corruption and in linking transnational crime and a wide range of other important issues on the international agenda such as responses to conflict situations, peacekeeping, promotion of the rule of law, and protection of human rights (Godson and Williams 1998). This brings a new set of groups and agencies to bear on the problem, checks the penetration of government and the private sector by transnational crime, and provides new avenues by which citizens can hold states accountable for this problem.

KEY POINTS

- The US war on drugs largely drove initial state and international responses to transnational crime in the 1980s.
- With the spread of transnational crime that began in the 1990s, nations around the globe increasingly coordinated regional and international responses to crime.
- Governments have come to perceive transnational crime as a national security threat, leading to the temptation to use intelligence assets and the military to supplement law enforcement.
- At the same time, the concern of international financial institutions and non-governmental organizations with corruption and state failure—two issues closely related to transnational crime—holds the promise of more comprehensive national responses to supplement law enforcement.

Conclusion

Transnational crime has expanded aggressively since the late 1980s, particularly since the end of the Cold War opened up new possibilities for criminal enterprises. Continuing globalization during the twenty-first century has facilitated not only the development of new criminal markets but also new forms of organization. The available evidence suggests that organized crime is becoming more difficult to fight because it has become more adaptable and resistant to available law-enforcement strategies. Even if organized crime networks turn out to be more vulnerable than many analysts believe, the ability for organized crime to form tactical or strategic alliances more easily today should give governments cause for concern.

Ironically, the global trends most welcomed by leaders in developed countries—globalization, democratization, and economic liberalization—also have a dark side: the capacity to create new spaces for the spread of transnational crime. Just as these trends promote greater political, economic, and personal freedom, they also facilitate the ability of criminals to transcend national jurisdictions. Even if countries were to decide that the costs of globalization outweighed the benefits, these are trends that are largely beyond the control of any single government. The question becomes one of how to contain this phenomenon and reduce the harm it causes.

This is particularly true if we consider that organized crime not only targets individuals but also undermines societies, particularly those in transition to democracy and free markets. The threat that transnational crime poses to whole regions, be it the Horn of Africa or the Balkans, means that even governments with relatively robust law-enforcement capabilities and a well-established rule of law are faced with the spill-over effects of transnational crime based in poorly governed areas of the globe.

Does this level of a national security threat justify the use of intelligence and military assets, and, perhaps, even a certain level of expediency in the pursuit of justice? Not all governments or societies will concur. Those countries where law enforcement and judiciaries are highly capable and adapt sufficiently quickly to contain transnational crime are unlikely to face such a choice. However, in countries where voters believe that the rule of law and personal safety is disappearing, pressure will develop for politicians to seek more draconian solutions. This is particularly true where a link is established, correctly or not, between transnational crime and terrorism. In extreme cases, it can lead to support for more authoritarian forms of government and restrictions on free markets, as has arguably occurred in Putin's Russia.

The question is therefore what can government, the private sector, and civil society do to reduce the harm caused by transnational crime before they are driven to extreme measures? Clearly, there is room for solutions short of militarization. One approach suggests greater cooperation between law-enforcement and national intelligence assets to address threats that cross borders. Others have suggested greater attention to preventive measures, particularly by those developed states with the greatest stake in the success of the emerging international system. To the extent that the United States, the European Union, Japan, and other leading democracies value free elections and free markets, then it makes sense for them to engage in capacity-building processes designed to strengthen the rule of law and law-enforcement agencies, particularly in countries that are experiencing so-called dual transitions. Given what we also know about the consequences of civil war for the proliferation of transnational crime, this also suggests another arena for anticipatory measures.

QUESTIONS

1. What factors enabled the expansion of transnational crime after the Cold War ended?
2. What is new about transnational crime today?
3. Does it matter if transnational crime is organized as hierarchies, as networks, or as markets?
4. Is transnational organized crime a greater threat than other forms of illicit activity?
5. What factors affect the extent to which terrorist groups and transnational criminal groups cooperate?
6. What indicators should we consider in deciding whether transnational crime has become a national security threat?
7. Why are governments tempted to use military and intelligence assets to address transnational crime? What problems might arise from such a response to this threat?

FURTHER READING

- Andreas, Peter and Nadelmann, Ethan (2006), *Policing the Globe: Criminalization and Crime Control in International Relations*, New York: Oxford University Press. Description and analysis of the internationalization of crime control, from the 1800s through 2005.
- Arquilla, J. and Ronfeldt, D. (eds) (2002), *Networks and Netwars: The Future of Terror, Crime and Militancy*, Santa Monica, CA: RAND Corporation, 61-97; http://www.rand.org/publications/MR/MR1382/MR1382.ch3.pdf. This RAND

study uses network theory to explain the organization of transnational crime and argues that networked criminal organizations are more flexible and robust than the governments that target them.

- Naylor, R. T. (2004), *Wages of Crime: Black Markets, Illegal Finances, and the Wages of Crime*, Cornell, NY: Cornell University Press. This book presents a critique of the view of organized crime as a powerful hierarchical organization and a threat to national security.
- Reichel, Philip , and Jay Albanese (eds) (2013), *Handbook of Transnational Crime and Justice*, Thousand Oaks, CA: Sage Publications. An up-to-date review of the theoretical literature on transnational crime.
- United Nations Office on Drugs and Crime (2010), *The Globalization of Crime: A Transnational Organized Crime Threat Assessment*, Vienna, Austria: UNODC, http://www.unodc.org/documents/data-and-analysis/tocta/TOCTA_Report_2010_low_res.pdf. In-depth report of the findings from a 2010 study of transnational organized crime.
- United Nations Office on Drugs and Crime (2012), *Digest of Organized Crime Cases*, Vienna: Austria: UNODC, http://www.unodc.org/documents/organized-crime/EnglishDigest_Final301012_30102012.pdf. Thorough review of the lessons learned by key states in combating organized crime.
- Williams, Phil (2008), 'Terrorist Financing and Organized Crime: Nexus, Appropriation or Transformation?', in Sue Eckert and Thomas Biersteker, *Countering the Financing of Terrorism*, Milton Park, UK: Routledge 2008, 126–49. While focused on the financial dimension, this chapter provides a critical assessment of the argument that terrorism and transnational criminal organizations are converging and may begin to cooperate to a greater extent.

IMPORTANT WEBSITES

- **http://www.organized-crime.de** Klaus von Lampe Organized Crime Research. Although the geographical focus of this website is the USA and Germany, its social-science perspective and collection of organized crime definitions, papers, book reviews, and web links makes it an essential resource.
- **http://nij.gov/publications/Pages/annual-reports.aspx** National Institute of Justice, US Department of Justice. This website provides a comprehensive collection of official reports and commissioned research publications that provide an overview of the US perspective on organized crime.
- **http://policy-traccc.gmu.edu** Transnational Crime and Corruption Center, George Mason University. This centre brings together a large collection of academic and policy research on transnational crime (with a focus on Russia and former Soviet states), as well as providing a comprehensive set of links to other online resources on this subject.
- **http://www.unodc.org** United Nations Office on Drugs and Crime (UNODC). The UNODC is one of the leading international agencies focused on assisting states in developing international efforts to fight drug trafficking, terrorism, and organized crime.

Visit the Online Resource Centre that accompanies this book for lots of interesting additional material: www.oxfordtextbooks.co.uk/orc/collins4e/

27

Cyber-Security

Myriam Dunn Cavelty

Chapter Contents

Reader's Guide

This chapter looks at why cyber-security is considered one of the key national security issues of our times. The first section provides the necessary technical background information. The second section unravels three different, but interrelated ways to look at cyber-security: the first discourse has a technical focus and is about viruses and worms; the second looks at the interrelationship between the phenomenon of **cyber-crime** and **cyber-espionage**; the third turns to a military and civil defence-driven discourse about the double-edged sword of fighting wars in the information domain and the need for critical infrastructure protection. Based on this, the third section looks at selected protection concepts from each of the three discourses. The final section sets the threat into perspective: despite heightened media attention and a general feeling of impending cyber-doom in some government circles, the level of cyber-risk is generally overstated.

Introduction

Information has been considered a significant aspect of **power**, diplomacy, and armed conflict for a very long time. Since the 1990s, however, information's role in international relations and security has diversified and its importance for political matters has increased, mostly due to the proliferation of **information and communication technology (ICT)** into all aspects of life in post-industrialized societies. The ability to master the generation, management, use but also manipulation of information has become a desired power resource since the control over knowledge, beliefs, and ideas is increasingly regarded as a complement to control over tangible resources such as military forces, raw materials, and economic productive capability. Consequently, matters of cyber-(in)-security—although not always under this name—have become a security issue.

In this chapter, the cyber-(in)-security logic is unpacked in four sections as described in the Reader's Guide, with the first providing the necessary technical background information on why the information infrastructure is inherently insecure, how computer vulnerabilities are conceptualized, who can exploit them, and in what ways.

Information security 101

Cyberspace connotes the fusion of all communication networks, databases, and sources of information into a vast, tangled, and diverse blanket of electronic interchange. A 'network ecosystem' is created; it is virtual and it 'exists everywhere there are telephone wires, coaxial cables, fibre-optic lines or electromagnetic waves' (Dyson et al. 1996). Cyberspace, however, is not only virtual, since it is also made up of servers, cables, computers, satellites, etc. In popular usage we tend to use the terms cyberspace and **Internet** almost interchangeably, even though the Internet, albeit the most important one, is just one part of cyberspace.

Cyber-security is both about the insecurity created by and through this new place/space and about the practices or processes to make it (more) secure. It refers to a set of activities and measures, both technical and non-technical, intended to protect the bioelectrical environment and the data it contains and transports from all possible threats.

The inherent insecurity of computer networks

Today's version of the Internet is a dynamic evolution of the Advanced Research Projects Agency Network (ARPANET), which was mainly designed for optimized information exchange between the universities and research laboratories involved in United States Department of Defense (DoD) research. At the time, there was no apparent need for a specific focus on security, because information systems were being hosted on large proprietary machines that were connected to very few other computers. Therefore, the network designers emphasized robustness and survivability over security.

Due to the dynamic evolution of ARPANET, this turned into a legacy problem. What makes systems so vulnerable today is the confluence of the same basic network technology (not built with security in mind), the shift to smaller and far more open systems (not built with security in mind), and the rise of extensive networking at the same time. In addition, the commercialization of the Internet in the 1990s led to an even bigger security deficit. There are significant market-driven obstacles to IT-security: there is no direct return on investment; time-to-market impedes extensive security measures; and security mechanisms have a negative impact on usability so that security is often sacrificed for functionality (Anderson and Moore 2006).

There are additional forces keeping cyberspace insecure: **Big Data** is considered the key IT trend of the future, and companies want to use the masses of data that we produce every day to tailor their marketing strategies through personalized advertising and prediction of future consumer behaviour. Therefore, there is little interest in encrypted (and therefore secure) information exchange. On top of this, the intelligence agencies of this world have the same interest in data that can be easily grabbed and analysed. Furthermore, the **NSA revelations of 2013** have exposed that intelligence services are making cyberspace more insecure directly—in order to be able to have more access to data, and in order to prepare for future cyber-conflict, they buy and exploit so-called **zero-day vulnerabilities** in current operating systems and hardware to inject malware into numerous strategically opportune points of the Internet infrastructure (Dunn Cavelty 2014).

Computer vulnerabilities and threat agents

The terminology in information security is often seemingly congruent with the terminology in national security discourses: it is about threats, agents, vulnerabilities, etc. However, the terms have very specific meanings so that seemingly clear analogies must be used with care. The main focus of the cyber-security discourse are information *attacks* (both passive and active), defined as (potentially) damaging events orchestrated by a human adversary ('threat agents'). The most common label bestowed upon them is **hacker** (Erickson 2003). For members of the computing community, 'hacker' describes a member of a distinct social group (or sub-culture); a particularly skilled programmer or technical expert who knows a programming interface well enough to write novel software. A particular ethic is ascribed to this subculture: a belief in sharing, openness, and free access to computers and information; decentralization of government; and in improvement of the quality of life (Levy 1984). In popular usage and in the media, however, the term hacker generally describes computer intruders or criminals.

In the cyber-security debate, hacking is considered a modus operandi that can be used not only by technologically skilled individuals for minor misdemeanours, but also by organized actor groups with truly bad intent, such as terrorists or foreign states. Some few hackers have the skills to attack those parts of the information infrastructure considered 'critical' for the functioning of society. Although most people would lack the motivation to cause violence or severe economic or social harm, government officials fear that individuals with the capability to cause serious damage could be swayed and corrupted by monetary incentives.

Hacking tools

The term used for the tools of a cyber-attack is **malware** (malicious + software). Well-known examples are *viruses and worms*, computer programs that replicate functional copies of themselves with varying effects ranging from mere annoyance and inconvenience to compromise of the confidentiality or integrity of information. There are also *Trojan horses*, programs that masquerade as benign applications but set up a back door so that the hacker can return later and enter the system. Often system intrusion is the main goal of more advanced attacks: if the intruder gains full system control, or 'root' access, he has unrestricted access to the inner workings of the system (Anonymous 2003). Due to the characteristics of digitally stored information an intruder can delay, disrupt, corrupt, exploit, destroy, steal, and modify information. Depending on the value of the information or the importance of the application for which this information is required, such actions will have different impacts with varying degrees of gravity.

KEY POINTS

- Cyberspace has both virtual and physical elements. We tend to use the terms cyberspace and Internet interchangeably, even though cyberspace encompasses far more than just the Internet.
- Cyber-security is both about the insecurity created through cyberspace and about the technical and non-technical practices of making it (more) secure.
- The Internet started as ARPANET in the 1960s and was never built with security in mind. This legacy, combined with the rapid growth of the network, its commercialization, and several economic and strategic interests make computer networks inherently insecure.
- Information security uses a vocabulary very similar to national security language, but has specific meanings. Cyber-attacks are the main focus of the cyber-security discourse. Attackers are called hackers.
- The umbrella term for all hacker tools is malware. The main goal of advanced attacks is full system control, which allows the intruder to delay, disrupt, corrupt, exploit, destroy, steal, or modify information.

Three interlocking cyber-security discourses

The cyber-security discourse originated in the USA in the 1970s, built momentum in the late 1980s and spread to other countries in the late 1990s. The US government shaped both the threat perception and the envisaged countermeasures with only little variation in other countries. On the one hand, the debate was decisively influenced by the larger post-Cold War strategic context in which the notion of asymmetric vulnerabilities, epitomized by the multiplication of malicious actors (both state and non-state) and their increasing capabilities to do harm, started to play a key role. On the other hand, discussions about cyber-security always were and still are influenced by the ongoing **information revolution**, which the United States is shaping both technologically and intellectually by discussing its implications for international relations and security and acting on these assumptions.

The cyber-security discourse was never static because the technical aspects of the information infrastructure are constantly evolving. Most importantly, changes in the technical sub-structure changed the referent object. In the 1970s and 1980s, cyber-security was about those parts of the private sector that were becoming digitalized and also about government networks and the classified information residing in it. The growth and spread of computer networks into more and more aspects of life changed this limited referent object in crucial ways. In the mid-1990s, it became clear that key sectors of modern society, including those vital to national security and to the essential functioning of (post-)industrialized economies, had come to rely on a spectrum of highly interdependent national and international software-based control systems for their smooth, reliable, and continuous operation. The referent object that emerged was the totality of **critical (information) infrastructures** that provide the way of life that characterizes our societies.

When telling the cyber-security-story we can distinguish between three different, but often closely interrelated and reinforcing discourses, with specific threat imaginaries and security practices, referent objects, and key actors. The first is a technical discourse concerned with malware (viruses, worms, etc.) and system intrusions. The second is concerned with the phenomena cyber-crime and cyber-espionage. The third is a discourse driven initially by the US military, focusing on matters of **cyber-war** initially but increasingly also on **critical infrastructure protection** (see Figure 27.1).

Viruses, worms, and other bugs (technical discourse)

The technical discourse is focused on computer and network disruptions caused by different types of malware. As early as 1988, the ARPANET had its first major network incident: the 'Morris Worm'. The worm used so many system resources that the attacked computers could no longer function and large parts of the early Internet went down. The devastating effects led

Figure 27.1 Three discourses

	Technical	Crime–espionage	Military/civil defence
Main actors	▪ Computer experts ▪ Anti-virus industry	▪ Law enforcement ▪ Intelligence community	▪ National security experts ▪ Military ▪ Civil defence establishment
Main referent object	▪ Computers ▪ Computer networks	▪ Business networks ▪ Classified information (government networks)	▪ Military networks, networked armed forces ▪ Critical (information) infrastructures

to the setup of a centre to coordinate communication among computer experts during IT emergencies: a Computer Emergency Response Team (CERT). This centre, now called the CERT Coordination Center, still plays a considerable role in computer security today and served as a role model for many similar centres all over the world. Around the same time, the anti-virus industry emerged and with it techniques and programs for virus recognition, destruction, and prevention.

The worm also had a substantial psychological impact by making people aware just how insecure and unreliable the Internet was. While it had been acceptable in the 1960s that pioneering computer professionals were hacking and investigating computer systems, the situation had changed by the 1980s. Society had become dependent on computing in general for business practices and other basic functions. Tampering with computers suddenly meant potentially endangering people's careers and property; and some even said their lives (Spafford 1989). Ever since, malware as 'visible' proof of the persuasive insecurity of the information infrastructure has remained in the limelight of the cyber-security discourse; and it also provides the back-story for the other two discourses. Table 27.1 lists some of the most prominent examples.

Most obviously, the history of malware is a mirror of technological development: the type of malware, the type of targets, and the **attack vectors** all changed with the technology and the existing technical countermeasures (and continue to do so). This development goes in sync with the development of the cyber-crime market, which is driven by the huge sums of money available to criminal enterprises at low risk of prosecution. While there was a tongue-in-cheek quality to many of the viruses in the beginning, viruses have long ago lost their innocence. Even though prank-like viruses have not disappeared, computer security professionals are increasingly concerned with the rising level of professionalization coupled with the obvious criminal (or even strategic) intent behind attacks. Advanced malware is targeted: a hacker picks a victim, scopes the defences, and then designs malware to get around them (Symantec 2010). The most prominent example for this kind of malware is Stuxnet (see Case Study 27.2). However, some IT security companies have recently warned against overemphasizing so called **advanced persistent threat** attacks just because we hear more about them (Verizon 2010: 16). Only about 3 per cent of all incidents are considered so sophisticated that they were impossible to stop. The vast majority of attackers go after small-to-medium-sized enterprises with bad defences. These types of incidents tend to remain under the radar of the media and even law enforcement.

KEY POINTS

- In 1988, the Morris Worm downed large parts of the early Internet, proving the theory right and making clear that the Internet was a very insecure technology.
- As a consequence, the CERT Coordination Center was founded. It is still very active today and has served as a model for similar computer emergency response teams in many countries.
- There is a long list of prominent malware which often made headlines. Over the years, malware has become more sophisticated and more clearly linked to criminal intent.
- The most dangerous malware is tailored to a specific target for high effect. However, the large majority of attacks remains fairly unsophisticated and go after small or medium-sized enterprises with little IT security awareness and/or investment.

Cyber-crooks and digital spies (crime-espionage discourse)

The cyber-crime discourse and the technical discourse are very closely related. The development of IT law (and, more specifically, Internet or cyber-law) in different countries plays a crucial role in the second discourse because it allows the definition and prosecution of misdemeanour. Not surprisingly, the development of legal tools to prosecute unauthorized entry into computer systems coincided with the first serious network incidents described here (cf. Mungo and Clough 1993).

Cyber-crime has come to refer to any crime that involves computers and networks, like a release of malware or spam, fraud, and many other things. Until today, notions of computer-related economic crimes determined the discussion about computer misuse. However, a distinct national security dimension was established when computer intrusions (a criminal act) were clustered together with the more traditional and well-established espionage discourse. Prominent hacking incidents—such as the intrusions into high-level computers perpetrated by the Milwaukee-based '414s'—led to a feeling in policy circles that there was

Table 27.1 Prominent malware

Name of malware	Year of discovery	Creator	Infected	Effect
Morris Worm	1988	Robert Morris (computer student), USA	UNIX systems	Slowed down machines in the ARPANET until they became unusable; huge impact on the general awareness of insecurity
Michelangelo	1992	(unknown)	DOS systems	Overwrote the first hundred sectors of the hard disk with nulls; caused first digital mass hysteria
Back Orifice	1998	Cult of the Dead Cow (hacker collective), USA	Windows 98	Tool for remote system administration (Trojan horse)
Melissa	1999	David L. Smith (programmer), USA	Microsoft Word, Outlook	Shut down Internet mail; clogged systems with infected e-mails
I Love You	2000	Reomel Ramores and Onel de Guzman (computer students), Philippines	Windows	Overwrote files with copy of itself; sent itself to the first fifty people in the Windows Address Book
Code Red	2001	(unknown)	Microsoft web servers	Defaced websites; used machines for DDoS-attacks
Nimda	2001	(unknown)	Windows workstations and servers	Allowed external control over infected computers
Blaster	2003	Jeffrey Lee Parson (18-year-old student), USA	Windows XP and 2000	DDos-attacks against 'windowsupdate.com'; side effects: system crash; was suspected to have caused black-out in USA (could not be confirmed)
Slammer	2003	(unknown)	Windows 95–XP	DDoS-attacks; slowed down Internet traffic worldwide
Sasser	2004	Sven Jaschan (computer science student), Germany	Windows XP and Windows 2000	Internet traffic slow down; system crash
Zeus	2007	(unknown), available to buy in underground computer forums	Windows	Steals banking and other information; forms botnets
Conficker (several versions)	2008	(unknown)	Windows	Forms botnets
Stuxnet	2010	Attributed to US and Israeli government (Operation Olympic Games)	SCADA system (Siemens industrial software and equipment)	Spies on and subverts industrial systems
Duqu	2011	(unknown)	Windows	Looks for information useful in attacking industrial control systems; code almost identical to Stuxnet (copy-cat software)
Flame	2012	Attributed to US and Israeli government (Operation Olympic Games)	Windows	Cyber-espionage (mainly in the Middle East)
Regin	2014	Unknown, probably NSA; also used by British intelligence agency GCHQ	Windows	Targeted data collection

a need for action (Ross 1991): if teenagers were able to penetrate computer networks that easily, it was assumed that better organized entities such as states would be even better equipped to do so. Other events, like the Cuckoo's Egg incident, the Rome Lab incident, Solar Sunrise, or Moonlight Maze made apparent that the threat was not just one of criminals or juveniles, but that classified or sensitive information could be acquired relatively easily by foreign nationals through hackers (see Table 27.2).

The so-called **attribution problem**—which refers to the difficulty in clearly determining those initially responsible for a cyber-attack plus identifying their motivating factors—is the big challenge in the cyber-domain. Due to the architecture of cyberspace, online identities can be optimally hidden. Blame on the basis of the 'cui bono'-logic (which translates into 'to whose benefit?') is not sufficient proof for political action. Attacks and exploits that seemingly benefit states might well be the work of third-party actors operating under a variety of motivations. At the same time, the challenges of clearly identifying perpetrators also gives state actors convenient 'plausible deniability and the ability to officially distance themselves from attacks' (Deibert and Rohozinski 2009: 12).

There are three trends worth mentioning. First, tech-savvy individuals (often juveniles) with the goal of mischief or personal enrichment shaped the early history of cyber-crime. Today, professionals dominate the field. The Internet is a near-ideal playground for semi- and organized crime in activities such as theft (like looting online banks, intellectual property, or identities) or for fraud, forgery, extortion, and **money laundering**. Actors in the 'cyber-crime black market' are highly organized regarding strategic and operational vision, logistics, and deployment. Like many real companies, they operate across the globe.

Second, the cyber-espionage story has changed. For many years, there has been an increase in allegations that China is responsible for high-level penetrations of government and business computer systems in Europe, North America, and Asia. Because Chinese authorities have stated repeatedly that they consider cyberspace a strategic domain and that they hope that mastering it will equalize the existing military imbalance between China and the USA more quickly, many officials readily accuse the Chinese government of deliberate and targeted attacks or intelligence gathering operations. However, these allegations almost exclusively rely on anecdotal and circumstantial evidence. Furthermore, the NSA revelations in 2013 by Edward Snowden have made clear how massive the data collection by Western governments through cyberspace for strategic information gathering is and have given the cyber-espionage discourse a new direction.

The third trend is the increased attention that **hacktivism**—the combination of hacking and activism—has gained in recent years. WikiLeaks, for example, has added yet another twist to the cyber-espionage discourse. Acting under the hacker-maxim 'all information should be free', this type of activism deliberately challenges the self-proclaimed power of states to keep information, which they think could endanger or damage national security, secret. It emerges as a cyber-security issue in government discourse because of the way a lot of the data has been stolen (in digital form) but also how it is made available to the whole world through multiple mirrors (Internet sites). Somewhat related are the multifaceted activities of hacker collectives such as Anonymous or LulzSec. They creatively play with anonymity in a time obsessed with control and surveillance and humiliate high-visibility targets by **DDoS-attacks**, break-ins, and the release of sensitive information. Furthermore, it seems more and more governments are accepting, if not sponsoring, hacktivist activities.

KEY POINTS

- The notion of computer crime and the development of cyber law coincided with the first network attacks. Although this discourse is mainly driven by economic considerations until today, political cyber-espionage, as a specific type of criminal computer activity, started worrying officials around the same time.
- Over the years, cyber-criminals have become well-organized professionals, operating in a consolidated cyber-crime black market.
- China is often blamed for high-level cyber-espionage, both political and economic. However, there is little hard evidence for this.
- As there is no way to clearly identify perpetrators that want to stay hidden in cyberspace (attribution problem), anyone could be behind actions that seemingly benefit certain states. States can also plausibly deny being involved.
- Politically motivated or activist break-ins by hacker collectives that go after high-level targets, with the aim to steal and publish sensitive information or just ridiculing them by targeting their websites, have recently added to the feeling of insecurity in government circles.

Table 27.2 Cyber-crime and cyber-espionage

Name of incident	Year of occurrence	Description	Perpetrators
414s break-ins	1982	Break-ins into high-profile computer systems in the United States	Six teenage hackers from Milwaukee
Hanover Hackers (Cuckoo's Egg)	1986–1988	Break-ins into high-profile computer systems in the United States	German hacker recruited by the KGB
Rome Lab incident	1994	Break-ins into high-profile computer systems in the United States	British teenage hackers
Citibank incident	1994	$10 million siphoned from Citibank and transferred the money to bank accounts around the world	Russian hacker(s)
Solar Sunrise	1998	Series of attacks on DoD computer networks	Two teenage hackers from California plus one Israeli
Moonlight Maze	1998	Pattern of probing of high-profile computer systems	Attributed to Russia
Titan Rain	2003–	Access to high-profile computer systems in the United States	Attributed to China
Zeus Botnet	2007	Trojan horse 'Zeus'; controlled millions of machines in 196 countries	International cyber-crime network; over 90 people arrested in US alone
GhostNet	2009	Cyber-spying operation; infiltration of high-value political, economic, and media locations in 103 countries	Attributed to China
Operation Aurora	2009	Attacks against Google and other companies to gain access to and potentially modify source code repositories at these high tech, security, and defence contractor companies	Attributed to China
Wikileaks Cablegate	2010	251,287 leaked confidential diplomatic cables from 274 US embassies around the world, dated from 28 December 1966 to 28 February 2010	Wikileaks, not-for-profit activist organization
Operations Payback and Avenge Assange	2010	Coordinated, decentralized attacks on opponents of Internet piracy and companies with perceived anti-WikiLeaks behaviour	Anonymous, hacker collective
Sony and other corporate as well as government attacks	2011	Highly publicized hacktivist operations	LulzSec, hacker collective
Theft of CO2-Emmission Papers	2011	Theft of 475,000 carbon dioxide emissions allowances worth €6.9 million, or $9.3 million	Attributed to organized cyber-crime (purpose probably money laundering)
NSA revelations	2013	Leaking of classified information that showed the extent of (US government) surveillance programs through cyber-means	United States National Security Agency (NSA)
Sony Pictures Hack	2014	Series of hacks and data release about Sony international, cumulating in cancellation of movie 'The Interview' (which shows violent death of North Korean leader Kim Jong Un)	Attributed to North Korea

Cyber(ed) conflicts and vital system security (military–civil defence discourse)

The Gulf War of 1991 created a watershed in US military thinking about cyber-war. Military strategists saw the conflict as the first of a new generation of **information age** conflicts in which physical force alone was not sufficient, but was complemented by the ability to win the information war and to secure 'information dominance'. As a result, American military thinkers began to publish scores of books on the topic and developed doctrines that emphasized the ability to degrade or even paralyse an opponent's communications systems (cf. Campen 1992; Arquilla and Ronfeldt 1993).

In the mid-1990s, the advantages of the use and dissemination of ICT that had fuelled the revolution in military affairs were no longer seen only as a great opportunity providing the country with an 'information edge' (Nye and Owens 1996), but were also perceived as constituting an over-proportional vulnerability vis-à-vis a plethora of malicious actors. Global information networks seemed to make it much easier to attack the US asymmetrically and, as such, an attack no longer required big, specialized weapons systems or an army: borders, already porous in many ways in the real world, were non-existent in cyberspace. There was widespread fear that those likely to fail against the American military would instead plan to bring the USA to its knees by striking vital points fundamental to the national security and the essential functioning of industrialized societies at home. Apart from break-ins into computer networks that contained sensitive information (see previous section), exercises designed to assess the plausibility of information warfare scenarios and to help define key issues to be addressed in this area demonstrated that US critical infrastructure presented a set of attractive strategic targets for opponents possessing information warfare capabilities, be it terrorist groups or states.

At the same time, the development of military doctrine involving the information domain continued. For a while, **information warfare** remained essentially limited to military measures in times of crisis or war. This began to change around the mid-1990s, when the activities began to be understood as actions targeting the entire information infrastructure of an adversary—political, economic, and military, throughout the continuum of operations from peace to war. NATO's 1999 intervention against Yugoslavia marked the first sustained use of the full spectrum of information warfare components in combat. Much of this involved the use of propaganda and disinformation via the media (an important aspect of information warfare), but there were also website defacements, a number of DDoS-attacks, and (unsubstantiated) rumours that Slobodan Milosevic's bank accounts had been hacked by the US armed forces.

The increasing use of the Internet during the conflict gave it the distinction of being the 'first war fought in cyberspace' or the 'first war on the Internet'. Thereafter, the term cyber-war came to be widely used to refer to basically any phenomenon involving a deliberate disruptive or destructive use of computers. For example, the cyber-confrontations between Chinese and US hackers plus many other nationalities in 2001 have been labelled the 'first Cyber World War'. The cause was a US reconnaissance and surveillance plane that was forced to land on Chinese territory after a collision with a Chinese jet fighter. In 2007, DDoS-attacks on Estonian websites were readily attributed to the Russian government, and various government officials claimed that this was the first known case of one state targeting another using cyber-warfare (see Case Study 27.1).

CASE STUDY 27.1 Estonian 'cyber-war'

When the Estonian authorities removed a bronze statue of a Second World War-era Soviet soldier from a park a cyberspace-'battle' ensued, lasting over three weeks, in which a wave of so-called Distributed Denial of Service attacks (DDoS) swamped various websites—among them the websites of the Estonian parliament, banks, ministries, newspapers, and broadcasters—disabling them by overcrowding the bandwidths for the servers running the sites.

Even though it will likely never be possible to provide sufficient evidence for who was behind the attacks, various officials readily and publicly blamed the Russian government. Also, despite the fact that the attacks bore no truly serious consequences for Estonia other than (minor) economic losses, some officials even openly toyed with the idea of a counter-attack in the spirit of Article 5 of the North Atlantic Treaty, which states that 'an armed attack' against one or more NATO countries 'shall be considered an attack against them all'. The Estonian case is one of the cases most often referred to in government circles to prove that there is a rising level of urgency and need for action.

Table 27.3 Instances of cyber(ed)-conflict

Name of incident	Year of occurrence	Description	Actors/perpetrators
Gulf War	1991	First of a new generation of conflicts where victory is no longer dependent only on physical force, but also on the ability to win the information war and to secure 'information dominance'	US military
Dutch hacker incident	1991	Intrusions into Pentagon computers during Gulf War; access to unclassified, sensitive information	Dutch teenagers
Operation 'Allied Force'	1999	'The first Internet War'; sustained use of the full-spectrum of information warfare components in combat; numerous hacktivism incidents	US military, hacktivists from many countries
'Cyber-Intifada'	2000–2005	E-mail flooding and Denial-of-Service (DoS) attacks against government and partisan websites during second Intifada	Palestinian and Israeli hacktivists
'Cyber World-War I'	2001	Defacement of Chinese and US websites and waves of DDoS-attacks after US reconnaissance and surveillance plane was forced to land on Chinese territory	Hacktivists from many nations (Saudi Arabia, Pakistan, India, Brazil, Argentina, Malaysia, Korea, Indonesia, Japan)
Iraq	2007	Cyber-attack on cell phones, computers, and other communication devices that terrorists were using to plan and carry out roadside bombs	US military
Estonia DDoS-attacks	2007	DDoS-attacks against websites of the Estonian parliament, banks, ministries, newspapers, and broadcasters	Attributed to Russian government
Georgia DDoS-attacks	2008	DDoS-attacks against numerous Georgian websites	Attributed to Russian government
GhostNet infiltrations	2009	GhostNet related infiltrations of computers belonging to Tibetan exile groups	Attributed to Chinese government
Stuxnet	2010	Computer worm that might have been deliberately released to slow down Iranian nuclear programme	US government (+ Israel)
Korean network intrusions	2011	Botnets and DDos-attacks against government websites; experts suspected North Korean 'cyber-weapons' test	Attributed to North Korean government

Similar claims were made in the confrontation between Russia and Georgia of 2008. In other cases, China is said to be the culprit (see previous section and Table 27.3).

The discovery of Stuxnet in 2010 changed the overall tone and intensity of the debate (see Case Study 27.2).

Due to the attribution problem, it was impossible to know for certain who was behind this piece of code, though many suspected one or several state actors (Farwell and Rohozinski 2011). In June 2012, an investigative journalist suggested that Stuxnet is part of a US and Israeli intelligence operation and that it was indeed programmed and released to sabotage the

CASE STUDY 27.2 Stuxnet

Stuxnet is a computer worm that was discovered in June 2010 and has been called '[O]ne of the great technical blockbusters in malware history' (Gross 2011). It is a complex program. It is likely that writing it took a substantial amount of time, advanced-level programming skills, and insider knowledge of industrial processes. Therefore, Stuxnet was the most expensive malware ever found at that time. In addition, it behaves differently from malware released for criminal intent: it does not steal information and it does not herd infected computers into so-called **botnets** from which to launch further attacks. Rather, it looks for a very specific target: Stuxnet was written to attack Siemens' *Supervisory Control And Data Acquisition* (SCADA) systems that are used to control and monitor industrial processes. In August 2010, the security company Symantec noted that 60 per cent of the infected computers worldwide were in Iran. It was also reported that Stuxnet damaged centrifuges in the Iran nuclear programme. This evidence led several experts to the conclusion that one or several nation states—most often named are the USA and/or Israel–were behind the attack. No official statement has ever been issued, but the involvement of the US government seems quite certain by now.

On another note, Stuxnet provided a platform for an ever-growing host of cyber-war experts to speculate about the future of cyber-aggression. Internationally, Stuxnet has had two main effects: first, governments all over the world are currently releasing or updating cyber-security strategies and are setting up new organizational units for cyber-defence (and -offence). Second, Stuxnet can be considered a 'wake-up' call: ever since its discovery, increasingly serious attempts to come to some type of agreement on the non-aggressive use of cyberspace between states are undertaken.

Iranian nuclear programme. For many observers, Stuxnet as a 'digital first strike' marks the beginning of the unchecked use of **cyber-weapons** in military-like aggressions (Gross 2011). However, other reports think this unlikely (cf. Sommer and Brown 2011), mainly due to the uncertain results a cyber-war would bring, the lack of motivation on the part of the possible combatants, and their shared inability to defend against counterattacks.

Future conflicts between nations will most certainly have a cyberspace component but they will be just a part of the battle. It is therefore more sensible to speak about cyber(ed) conflicts, conflicts 'in which success or failure for major participants is critically dependent on computerized key activities along the path of events' (Demchak 2010). Dubbing occurrences as 'cyber-war' too carelessly bears the inherent danger of creating an atmosphere of insecurity and tension and fuelling a cyber-security dilemma: many countries are currently said to have functional cyber-commands or be in the process of building one. Because cyber-capabilities cannot be divulged by normal intelligence-gathering activities, uncertainty and mistrust are on the rise.

KEY POINTS

- The Gulf War of 1991 is considered to be the first of a new generation of conflicts in which mastering the information domain becomes a deciding factor. Afterwards, the information warfare doctrine was developed in the US military.
- Increasing dependence of the military, but also of society in general, on information infrastructures made clear that information warfare was a double-edged sword. Cyberspace seemed the perfect place to launch an asymmetrical attack against civilian or military critical infrastructures.
- The US military tested its information warfare doctrine for the first time during a NATO operation 'Allied Force' in 1999. It was the first armed conflict in which all sides, including actors not directly involved, had an active online presence, and in which the Internet was actively used for the exchange and publication of conflict-relevant information. Thereafter, the term 'cyber-war' came to be used for almost any type of conflict with a cyber-component.
- The recent discovery of a computer worm that sabotages industrial processes and was programmed by order of a state actor has alarmed the international community. Some experts believe that this marks the beginning of unrestrained cyber-war among states.
- Others think that highly unlikely and warn against an excessive use of the term cyber-war. Future conflicts between states will also be fought in cyberspace, but not exclusively. One useful term for them is cyber(ed) conflicts.

KEY IDEAS 27.1 Presidential Commission on Critical Infrastructure Protection

Following the Oklahoma City Bombing, President Bill Clinton set up the Presidential Commission on Critical Infrastructure Protection (PCCIP) to look into the security of vital systems such as gas, oil, transportation, water, telecommunications, etc. The PCCIP presented its report in the fall of 1997 (President's Commission on Critical Infrastructure Protection 1997). It concluded that the security, economy, way of life, and perhaps even the survival of the industrialized world were dependent on the interrelated trio of electrical energy, communications, and computers. Further, it stressed that advanced societies rely heavily upon critical infrastructures, which are susceptible to classical physical disruptions and new virtual threats. While the study assessed a list of critical infrastructures or 'sectors'—for example the financial sector, energy supply, transportation, and the emergency services—the main focus was on cyber-risks. There were two reasons for this decision: first, these were the least known because they were basically new, and second, many of the other infrastructures were seen to depend on data and communication networks. The PCCIP linked the cyber-security discourse firmly to the topic of critical infrastructures. Thereafter, CIP became a key topic in many other countries.

Reducing cyber-in-security

The three different discourses have produced specific types of concepts and countermeasures in accordance with their focus and main referent objects (see Figure 27.2), some of which are discussed later.

Despite fancy concepts such as **cyber-deterrence**, the common issue in all discourses is information assurance, which is the basic security of information and information systems. It is common practice that the entities that own a computer network are also responsible for protecting it (governments protect government networks, militaries only military ones, and companies protect their own, etc.). However, there are some assets considered so crucial to the functioning of society in the private sector that governments take additional measures to ensure an adequate level of protection. These efforts are usually subsumed under the label of **critical (information) infrastructure protection**.

In the 1990s, critical infrastructures became the main referent object in the cyber-security debate. Whereas critical infrastructure protection (CIP) encompasses more than just cyber-security, cyber-aspects have always been the main driver (see Key Ideas 27.1). The key challenge for CIP efforts arise from the privatization and deregulation of large parts of the public sector since the 1980s and the globalization processes of the 1990s, which have put many critical infrastructures in the hands of private (transnational) enterprises. This creates a situation in which market forces alone are not sufficient to provide the aspired-for level of security in designated critical infrastructure sectors,[1] but state actors are also incapable of providing the necessary level of security on their own (unless they heavily regulate, which they are usually reluctant to do).

Public–Private Partnerships (PPP), a form of cooperation between the state and the private sector, are widely seen as a panacea for this problem in the **policy community**—and cooperation programmes that follow the PPP idea are part of all existing initiatives in the field of CIP today, though with varying success. A large number of them are geared towards facilitating information exchange between companies and between companies and government on security, disruptions, and best practices. Mutual win–win situations are to be created by exchanging information that the other party does not have: the government offers classified information acquired by its intelligence services about potentially hostile groups and nation states in exchange for technological knowledge from the private sector that the public sector does not have (President's Commission on Critical Infrastructure Protection 1997: 20).

Information assurance is guided by the management of risk, which is essentially about accepting that one is (or remains) insecure: the level of risk can never be reduced to zero. This means that minor and probably also major cyber-incidents are bound to happen

[1] The most frequently listed examples are banking and finance, government services, telecommunication and information and communication technologies, emergency and rescue services, energy and electricity, health services, transportation, logistics and distribution, and water supply.

Figure 27.2 Countermeasures

	Technical	Crime–espionage	Military/civil defence
Main actors	▪ Computer experts ▪ Anti-virus industry	▪ Law enforcement ▪ Intelligence community	▪ Security professionals, military, civil defence establishment
Main referent object	▪ Computers ▪ Computer networks	▪ Business sector ▪ Classified information	▪ Military networks, networked forces ▪ Critical infrastructures
Protection concept		**Information assurance**	
National level	▪ **CERTs (specific for different domain, milCert, govCert, etc.)**	▪ **Computer law**	▪ **Critical (information) infrastructure protection** ▪ **Resilience** ▪ **Cyber-offence; cyber-defence; cyber-deterrence**
International level	▪ **International CERTs** ▪ **International information security standards**	▪ **Harmonization of law (Convention on Cybercrime)** ▪ **Mutual judicial assistance procedures**	▪ **Arms control** ▪ **International behavioural norms**

because they simply cannot be avoided, even with perfect risk management. This is one of the main reasons why the concept of resilience has gained so much weight in recent debates (Perelman 2007). Resilience is commonly defined as the ability of a system to recover from a shock, either returning back to its original state or to a new adjusted state. Resilience accepts that disruptions are inevitable and can be considered a 'Plan B' in case something goes wrong.

In the military discourse, the terms cyber-offence, cyber-defence, and cyber-deterrence are often used as countermeasures. Under closer scrutiny, cyber-defence (and to some degree -offence) are not much more than fancy words for information assurance practices. Cyber-deterrence, on the other hand, deserves some attention. Cyberspace clearly poses considerable limitations for classical deterrence. Deterrence works if one party is able to successfully convey to another that it is both capable and willing to use a set of available (often military) instruments against him if the other steps over the line. This requires an opponent that is clearly identifiable as an attacker and has to fear retaliation—which is not the case in cyber-security because of the attribution problem. However, this is not stopping US government officials from threatening to use kinetic response in case of a cyber-attack on their critical infrastructures (Gorman and Barnes 2011).

Naturally, the military discourse falls back on well-known concepts such as deterrence, which means that the concept of cyber-deterrence, including its limits, will remain a much discussed issue in the future. In theory, effective cyber-deterrence would require a wide-ranging scheme of offensive and defensive cyber-capabilities supported by a robust international legal framework as well as the ability to attribute an attack to an attacker without any doubt. The design of defensive cyber-capabilities and the design of better legal tools are relatively uncontested. Many international organizations and international bodies have taken steps to raise awareness, establish international partnerships, and agree on common rules and practices. One key issue is the harmonization of law to facilitate the prosecution of perpetrators of cyber-crime.

While there is wide agreement on what steps are necessary to tackle international cyber-crime, states are unwilling to completely forgo offensive and aggressive use of cyberspace. Due to this, and increasingly so since the discovery of Stuxnet, efforts are underway to control the military use of computer exploitation through arms control or multilateral behavioural **norms**, agreements that might pertain to the development, distribution, and deployment of cyber-weapons, or to their use. However, traditional capability-based arms control will clearly not be of much use, mainly due to the impossibility of verifying limitations on the technical capabilities of actors, especially non-state ones. The avenues available for arms control in this arena are primarily information exchange and norm-building, whereas structural approaches and attempts to prohibit the means of cyber-war altogether or restricting their availability are largely impossible due to the ubiquity and dual-use nature of information technology.

KEY POINTS

- There are a variety of approaches and concepts to secure information and critical information infrastructures. The key concept is a risk management practice known as information assurance, which aims to protect the confidentiality, integrity, and availability of information and the systems and processes used for the storage, processing, and transmission of information.
- Critical (information) infrastructure protection (C(I)IP) has become a key concept in the 1990s. Because a very large part of critical infrastructures are no longer in the hands of government, CIP practices mainly build on public–private partnerships. At the core of them lies information sharing between the private and the public sector.
- Because the information infrastructure is persuasively insecure, risk management strategies are complemented by the concept of resilience. Resilience is about having systems rebound from shocks in an optimal way. The concept accepts that absolute security cannot be obtained and that minor or even major disturbances are bound to happen.
- The military concepts of cyber-defence and cyber-offence are militarized words for information assurance practices. Cyber-deterrence, on the other hand, is a concept that moves deterrence into the new domain of cyberspace.
- If cyber-deterrence were to work, functioning offensive and defensive cyber-capabilities, plus the fear of retaliation, both militarily and legally, would be needed. This would also include the ability to clearly attribute attacks.
- Internationally, efforts are underway to further harmonize cyber-law. In addition, because future use of cyberspace for strategic military purposes remains one of the biggest fears in the debate, there are attempts to curtail the military use of computer exploitation through arms control or multilateral behavioural norms.

The level of cyber-risk

Different political, economic, and military conflicts clearly have had cyber(ed)-components for a number of years now. Furthermore, criminal and espionage activities with the help of computers happen every day. Cyber-incidents are causing minor and occasionally major inconveniences. These may be in the form of lost intellectual property or other proprietary data, maintenance and repair, lost revenue, and increased security costs. Beyond the direct impact, badly handled cyber-attacks have also damaged corporate (and government) reputations and have, theoretically at least, the potential to reduce public confidence in the security of Internet transactions and e-commerce if they become more frequent.

However, in the entire history of computer networks, there have been only very few examples of attacks or other type of incidents that had the potential to rattle an entire nation or cause a global shock. There are even fewer examples of cyber-attacks that resulted in actual physical violence against persons or property (Stuxnet being the most prominent). The huge majority of cyber-incidents have caused minor losses rather than serious or long-term disruptions. They are risks that can be dealt with by individual entities using standard information security measures and their overall costs remain low in comparison to other risk categories like financial risks.

This fact tends to be disregarded in policy circles, because the level of cyber-fears is high and the military discourse has a strong mobilizing power. This has important political effects. A large part of the discourse evolves around 'cyber-doom' (worst-case) scenarios in the form of major, systemic, catastrophic incidents involving critical infrastructures caused by attacks. Since the potentially devastating effects of cyber-attacks are so scary, the temptation to not only think about worst-case scenarios but also give them a lot of (often too much) weight despite their very low probability is high.

There are additional reasons why the threat is overrated. First, as combating cyber-threats has become a highly politicized issue, official statements about the level of threat must also be seen in the context of different bureaucratic entities that compete against each other for resources and influence. This is usually done by stating an urgent need for action (which they should take) and describing the overall threat as big and rising. Second, psychological research has shown that risk perception is highly dependent on intuition and emotions, as well as the perceptions of experts (Gregory and Mendelsohn 1993). Cyber-risks, especially in their more extreme form, fit the risk profile of so-called 'dread risks', which appear uncontrollable, catastrophic, fatal, and unknown. There is a propensity to be disproportionally afraid of these risks despite their low probability, which translates into pressure for regulatory action of all sorts and a willingness to bear high costs of uncertain benefit.

The danger of overly dramatizing the threat manifests itself in reactions that call for military retaliation (as happened in the Estonian case and in other instances) or other exceptional measures. Though the last section has shown that there are many different types of countermeasures in place, and that most of them are in fact not exceptional, this kind of threat rhetoric invokes enemy images even if there is no identifiable enemy, favours national solutions instead of international ones, and centres too strongly on national security measures instead of economic and business solutions. Only computer attacks whose effects are sufficiently destructive or disruptive need the attention of the traditional national security apparatus. Attacks that disrupt non-essential services, or that are mainly a costly nuisance, should not.

KEY POINTS

- The majority of cyber-incidents so far have caused minor inconveniences and their cost remains low in comparison to other risk categories. Only very few attacks had the potential for grave consequences and even fewer actually had any impact on property. None have ever caused loss of life.
- Despite this, the feeling persists in policy circles that a large-scale cyber-attack is just around the corner. The potential for catastrophic cyber-attacks against critical infrastructures, though very unlikely, remains the main concern and the main reason for seeing cyber-security as a national security issue.
- The level of cyber-risk is overstated. Reasons are to be found in bureaucratic turf battles due to scarce resources and in the fact that cyber-risks are so called 'dread risks', of which human beings are disproportionally afraid. Overstating the risk comes with the danger of prioritizing the wrong answers.

Conclusion

Despite the increasing attention cyber-security is getting in security politics and despite the possibility of a major, systemic, catastrophic incident involving critical infrastructures, computer network vulnerabilities are mainly a business and espionage problem. Depending on their (potential) severity, however, disruptive incidents in the future will continue to fuel the military discourse, and with it fears of strategic cyber-war. Certainly, thinking about (and planning for) worst-case scenarios is a legitimate task of the national security apparatus. However, they should not receive too much attention in favour of more plausible and more likely problems.

In seeking a prudent policy, the difficulty for decision makers is to navigate the rocky shoals between hysterical doomsday scenarios and uninformed complacency. Threat representation must remain well informed and well balanced not to allow over-reactions with costs that are too high and benefits that are uncertain. For example, an 'arms race' in cyberspace, based on the fear of other states' cyber-capabilities, would most likely have hugely detrimental effects on the way humankind uses the Internet. Also, solving the attribution problem would come at a very high cost for privacy. Even though we must expect disturbances in the cyber-domain in the future we must not expect outright disasters. Some of the cyber-disturbances may well turn into crises, but a crisis can also be seen as a turning point rather than an end state where the aversion of disaster or catastrophe is always possible. If societies become more fault tolerant psychologically and more resilient overall, the likelihood for catastrophe in general and catastrophic system failure in particular can be substantially reduced.

Cyber-security issues are also challenging for students and academics more generally. Experts of all sorts widely disagree how likely future cyber-doom scenarios are—and all of their claims are based on (educated) guesses. While there is at least proof and experience of cyber-crime, cyber-espionage, or other lesser forms of cyber-incidents on a daily basis, cyber-incidents of bigger proportions (**cyber-terror** or cyber-war) exist solely in the form of stories or narratives. The way we imagine them influences our judgement of their likelihood; and there are an infinite number of ways in how we could imagine them. Therefore, there is no way to study the 'actual' level of cyber-risk in any sound way because it only exists in and through the representations of various actors in the political domain. As a consequence, the focus of research necessarily shifts to contexts and conditions that determine the process by which key actors subjectively arrive at a shared understanding of how to conceptualize and ultimately respond to a security threat.

? QUESTIONS

1. Who benefits in what ways from calling malware cyber-weapons?
2. What are the pros and cons of abolishing anonymity (and therefore partially solving the attribution problem) on the Internet in the name of security?
3. What side effects does the indiscriminate use of the terms cyber-terror and cyber-war have?
4. Are hacktivism activities a legitimate way to express political or economic grievances?
5. What are the limits of traditional arms control mechanisms applied to cyber-weapons?
6. Why does the intelligence community not have more information on the cyber-capabilities of other states?
7. What are the similarities and what the differences between information security and national security?
8. Which aspects of cyber-security should be considered a part of national security, and which aspects should not? Why?
9. What might be the next referent object in the cyber-security discourse?

FURTHER READING

- Arquilla, J. and Ronfeldt, D. F. (eds) (1997), *In Athena's Camp: Preparing for Conflict in the Information Age*, Santa Monica: RAND. This is one of the key texts about information warfare.
- Brown, K. A. (2006), *Critical Path: A Brief History of Critical Infrastructure Protection in the United States*, Arlington, VA: George Mason University Press. Provides a comprehensive overview of the evolution of critical infrastructure protection in the United States.
- Deibert, R. and Rohozinski, R. (2010) 'Risking Security: Policies and Paradoxes of Cyberspace Security', *International Political Sociology* 4 / 1: 15–32. An intelligent account of the threat discourse that differentiates between risks to cyberspace and risks through cyberspace.
- Dunn Cavelty, M. (2008), *Cyber-Security and Threat Politics: US Efforts to Secure the Information Age*, London: Routledge. Examines how, under what conditions, by whom, for what reasons, and with what impact cyber-threats have been moved on to the political agenda in the USA.
- Libicki, M. (2009), *Cyberdeterrence and Cyberwar*, Santa Monica: RAND. Explores the specific laws of cyberspace and uses the results to address the pros and cons of counterattack, the value of deterrence and vigilance, and other defensive actions in the face of deliberate cyber-attack.
- National Research Council (2009), *Technology, Policy, Law, and Ethics Regarding U.S. Acquisition and Use of Cyberattack Capabilities*, Washington, DC: The National Academies Press. Focuses on the use of cyber-attack as an instrument of US policy and explores important characteristics of cyber-attack.
- Sommer, P. and Sommer, I. (2011), Reducing Systemic Cybersecurity Risk, OECD Research Report, http://www.oecd.org/dataoecd/3/42/46894657.pdf. A down-to-earth report that concludes that it is extremely unlikely that cyber-attacks could create problems like those caused by a global pandemic or the recent financial crisis, let alone an actual war.

IMPORTANT WEBSITES

- **http://cipp.gmu.edu** George Mason University (GMU), Critical Infrastructure Protection (CIP) Program Website: the GMU CIP program is a valuable source of information for both US and international CIP-related issues and developments.
- **http://www.schneier.com** Schneier on Security: Bruce Schneier is a refreshingly candid and lucid computer security critic and commentator. In his blog, he covers computer security issues of all sorts.
- **http://www.iwar.org.uk** The Information Warfare Site: an online resource that aims to stimulate debate on a variety of issues involving information security, information operations, computer network operations, homeland security, and more.
- **http://www.infowar.com** Infowar Site: a site dedicated to tracking open source stories relating to the full spectrum of information warfare, information security, and critical infrastructure protection.

Visit the Online Resource Centre that accompanies this book for lots of interesting additional material: www.oxfordtextbooks.co.uk/orc/collins4e/

28

After the Return to Theory: The Past, Present, and Future of Security Studies

Ole Wæver and Barry Buzan

Chapter Contents

Reader's Guide

This chapter presents an interpretation of the past and present of security studies with an emphasis on the changing periods of theory production and practical problem solving. The field started out as a distinct US specialty much shaped by the new conditions of the 1940s set by nuclear weapons and a long-term mobilization against the Soviet Union, two factors that created a need for a new kind of civilian expert in defence and strategy. From an American, think-tank based, interdisciplinary field, security studies became institutionalized as a part of one discipline, International Relations (IR), increasingly international and with theory anchored in the universities. Since the 1990s, the field has been in a new period of high theory productivity, but largely in two separate clusters with the USA and Europe as centres of each. This analysis is used as a basis for raising some central questions and predictions about the future of the field.

Introduction

The fact that a book like the present one can be made, indeed had to be made, to present an existing field to people entering it testifies to major change in security studies. Had a similar book been produced in previous decades, it would have looked very different. A 1950s version would have been very short. In the 1960s, it would have been structured with chapters on different kinds of policy questions—strategy, economy of defence, decision making—and in some of these (notably the chapter on strategy) there would have been a lot of theory (deterrence theory), but the theories would not have competed for dealing with the same questions; a division of labour would have kept them in different chapters. The 1970s edition would probably have been thinner on theory and more comprehensive in the thematic chapters—and it would have come with a companion volume (in German) denouncing the whole field as part of the repressive, militarized, Cold War system. The 1980s textbook would have been a reader of texts arguing for and against the continued relevance of the field, its possible widening or even dissolution and merger into wider fields. With developments in the 1990s, the field has come to take a shape as reflected in the structure of this volume: the wideners have succeeded enough for chapters on different sectors of security to be necessary, and a number of theories now compete for tackling the whole field of security. In the first decades of the twenty-first century, this reshaped discipline seems to gain increased attention, generate more undergraduate courses and not least more—often theoretically inclined—PhD projects. This augmented attraction is supported both by the prominence of 'security' in the era of the 'global war on terror' and 'climate security', and by the availability of the family of theories that sprang up during the 1990s.

Our focus in this chapter is on *security theory*, which we define as theory that aims at the understanding and/or management of security issues. Such theory at different points in time resembles developments within general IR theory, while at other points there is less contact. For instance, some major developments in IR theory, such as 1970s interdependence and regime theory, had minimal impact on security studies (at the time, at least), and some security theories were (originally) specific to security studies, such as deterrence theory or the **Copenhagen School**, not general theories of IR. Other cases of security theory are simultaneously IR and security theory, such as **constructivism**, feminism, or democratic peace. While distinct from IR theory, security theory is also different from security studies at large, because much work in security studies does not deal explicitly with theory. Thus, security theory is a specific subset of security studies and one whose development has gone through distinctive phases. (See Key Ideas 28.1.)

One peculiarity of this field is that it is divided more strongly than comparable fields into subsets without mutual recognition, often without even mutual awareness. Especially in European journals, conferences, departments, and research centres, one finds a lively discussion of a number of relatively recent approaches: Critical Security Studies, feminism, the Copenhagen School, the **Paris School**, and the merits of all these compared to 'the traditional approach'. Go to most departments in the USA or the leading journals, such as *International Security* and *Security Studies*, and most scholars there would say 'who?' and 'what?' about authors intensely discussed by a large number of scholars especially in Europe and parts of the

KEY IDEAS 28.1 Terminology

The names 'strategic studies' and 'security studies' (or 'international security studies') are used by some authors interchangeably, while others use them systematically on different objects. It is possible to give distinct definitions, typically with security studies being broader, and strategic studies the narrower subset oriented towards military issues (e.g. Buzan 1991a; Betts 1997). However, in a historical overview like the present, it would be anachronistic to use such terminology for the whole period. 'Strategic studies' was the established term from the 1940s into the 1980s, and we use it accordingly, retaining the construction of the time with most often military affairs as the self-evident core of the field and circles around this drawn more or less narrowly. From the 1980s and onwards, this field was in most contexts relabelled as security studies, and only in some places but far from all was the hard-core military part of this field assigned the specific name 'strategic studies'. Therefore, we do not use here a systematic distinction between the two terms, but let them cover the whole area and use mostly strategic studies in the early period and security studies in the later. Today, the name 'strategic studies' seems mostly to linger on because it is institutionalized in outfits like the 'International Institute for Strategic Studies', *Journal of Strategic Studies* and *Journal of Military and Strategic Studies*. The dominance of the term 'strategic studies' during the Cold War was in any case more pervasive in the UK than in the USA.

developing world (Wæver 2012a). In turn, the mostly American main scene has had theoretical debates centred on offensive versus defensive realism, the relative importance of ideational variables, and the role of power and institutions in orders (and empires). These debates did not structure the universe for most scholars in the rest of the world.

Therefore, when this concluding chapter attempts an assessment of where we are, where we came from, and not least where we might be going, it needs to follow an asymmetrical structure, where the first part treats the field as homogeneous—a kind of unified centre–periphery structure with the US definition of security studies unrivalled—while the later part splits into two parallel tracks. In the very last part of the chapter this evolves further into a global constellation, where theory emerges from many parts of the world, not least beyond the West. The chapter is structured chronologically. The first section looks at the origins and institutional structure of security studies—what and where is it? The second covers the so-called Golden Age, the formative period of strategic studies when most notably deterrence theory was developed and game theory applied to it (and in turn given much original impetus at the level of abstract theory), to assist in the handling of novel challenges from nuclear weapons. The third section is about the immediate post-Golden Age, when strategic studies was consolidated as an integral part of the security establishment, and theory often lost out to 'hectic empiricism' (Buzan 1981, 2000), which might in turn have contributed to the decline of strategic studies as a field. A fourth section deals with the soul-searching debates on widening and (sub)disciplinary identity during the 1980s and 1990s, culminating in various theoretical innovations. The final section looks from the current situation of theoretical wealth into a future where these theories have begun to change their mutual relationships while also developing new ways to be involved with the main issues on the policy agenda.

The first and second sections deal overwhelmingly with the USA, because this is where modern strategic studies emerged and found its characteristic shape. When modern-style strategic studies grew elsewhere, even where independent traditions existed, this happened to such a large extent by attempts to copy or import the American experience, that the formative period of American strategic studies became the referent point for the field everywhere. A systematic comparison of American and European strategic studies is therefore presented towards the end of the second section (referring to the status in the early 1970s), and only in the latest phases do distinct trajectories become self-reliant enough that a story of two parallel tracks can explain the peculiarity of debates unrecognizable to each other. The World beyond the West is for similar reasons only dealt with quite marginally, and mostly towards the end of this chapter.

The origins and institutional structure of security studies

War and peace, threats and strategy, as well as demographics and epidemics: issues like these have been on the agenda of thinkers and writers for centuries. However, anything resembling security studies as we now know it did not become a distinct field of study until around the end of the Second World War. As always, *when* a field is established, it is easy to see predecessors and preparatory work done in previous phases, and thus security studies can be projected back into the inter-war period with reference to work done on the causes and prevention of wars (Baldwin 1995).

The novelty in the 1940s, however, was the emergence of a distinct category of work at the intersection of military expertise and university-based social science aimed at delivering policy-relevant knowledge supported by a broad, interdisciplinary academic knowledge base. In large part because of the unprecedented implications of nuclear weapons for war fighting, but also because of the broad-spectrum challenge to the USA posed by the Soviet Union (ideological and economic, as well as military) and the general prestige gained during the Second World War by both natural scientists (new weapons, code breaking) and social scientists (for example, in advising on strategic bombing priorities), civilian experts would now also specialize in military issues under the heading of security. That the leading strategic thinkers should be mainly civilians was what distinguished post-1945 security studies both from what had been done before, and from what continued to be done outside the West.

This institutional innovation happened at the same time as the concept of security moved centre stage, becoming the guiding idea over previously supreme slogans such as defence and national interest (Yergin 1977; Wæver 2012b).

General enabling conditions in the USA were: optimism about the usefulness of science; the possibility of rational solutions to societal problems; novel security issues that seemed not only urgent and primary but very much so (nuclear weapons and the Soviet, communist threat); generous funding for research; and exponential expansion of higher education.

The main key to the emergence of strategic studies around the time of the end of the Second World War and the beginning of the Cold War was the need for civilian experts to balance the military leadership, a need driven certainly by technological developments (nuclear weapons and the rapid rise of war avoidance as the key strategic imperative), but also by broader political considerations about the potentially problematic political implications of long-term mobilization.

The military driver is straightforward: gradually, it became clear how radically nuclear weapons would transform the security equations, and the kind of expertise needed differed from the classical military one. At some risk of oversimplification (actual planning was quite a bit more mixed), the problem was that wars should no longer be fought but avoided, and ways should be found so that the possibility/impossibility of war generated by nuclear deployments could be manipulated for political gain. The centre of gravity shifted from the tactical and operational level to true long-term strategy (Brodie 1949), and from the deployment of a given technology to the targeted development of fast-changing technologies for the future. Although at first it seemed that even the games of deterrence could be seen as controlled by the bottom line of what would happen in an actual fight, it gradually became necessary to treat nuclear strategy as a partly independent universe to be analysed in its own right. This demanded a completely different form of knowledge from the one delivered by military experts. As succinctly put by Richard Betts (1997: 13): 'Nuclear war spurred theorizing because it was inherently more theoretical than empirical: none had ever occurred.' Or, in the words of Richard Smoke (1976: 275), the first precondition for the emergence of security studies was a 'complexity dissectible by abstract analysis'.

While this is probably a relatively uncontroversial interpretation of the emergence of security studies, it should also be noticed that the combination of nuclear weapons and the Cold War meant a need to coordinate more closely military and non-military considerations. Already wartime experiences had shown, especially in the USA, how challenging it was to coordinate economic, political, and military planning (Etzold 1978: 1–2; Hogan 1998: 25). As it began to be clear that the Cold War could become a drawn-out, all-encompassing, and existential struggle, the idea took hold that one needed a form of integrated understanding, where these different forms of knowledge could become combined, and this was a major part of the reasoning behind the National Security Act of 1947—in addition to closer coordination of the services plus intelligence reform (Stuart 2008).

The specific challenge of the USA, with its 'no-standing-armies' tradition having to organize for long-term mobilization, shaped the emerging civil–military interface in strategic studies. It was a deep-seated argument within American political thought that a permanent military institution would be a threat to democracy because it could be misused by 'a tyrant', an anti-democratic executive (Publius 1787–8; Bailyn 1992; Deudney 1995). Also, it was only during the Second World War that 'the uniformed heads of the US armed services assumed a pivotal and unprecedented role in the formulation of the nation's foreign policies' (Stoler 2000: ix). Therefore, when the USA moved towards institutionalizing an unprecedented level of military mobilization, this could not be done purely in terms of 'war' or 'defence'. This is a central part of the explanation for the rise of the term 'security' to cover the mobilization in more inclusive and 'civilian' terms (Wæver 2008, 2012b). And it conditioned a particular space for civilian expertise in a military-centred universe. The Cold War mobilization inevitably entailed a tension between American liberalism and military professionalism, and the field of strategic studies emerged as part of the institutional responses to this tension (Lasswell 1950; Huntington 1957).

KEY POINTS

- Security studies as a distinct field of study was born in the 1940s in the USA.
- Nuclear weapons created a strategic challenge not governable by traditional military expertise.
- Long-term, broad-based mobilization collided with an American wariness of 'standing armies'. Where the USA had traditionally kept war and peace more distinct than other states, the new situation called for a new cover term (security) and new experts (security studies) in order not to end up in permanent war and at the mercy of the military—or the enemy.

The Golden Age of security studies

The period of the 1950s and 1960s is widely celebrated as one where the field was simultaneously productive, influential, and relatively coherent. Although the field contained a wide variety of other kinds of work (to which we return shortly), the central and defining area was game theory and nuclear strategy. We pay particular attention to this period for two reasons. First, it was the formative period of the new discipline, and therefore developments in the so-called Golden Age are not just episodes equal to many others; they defined how security studies was perceived: for good and bad these developments were the quintessential work of security studies. Second, this marked a (first) high point of theorization, and we want to point to the pattern of ebb and flow of theory making within security studies.

The work on game theory and deterrence theory was a rare instance of an intellectual development that scores high in terms of theoretical creativity and sophistication, and simultaneously policy relevance. Very often this is seen as a trade-off—policy relevance/utility versus theoretical abstraction/sophistication (cf. Hill 1994; Lepgold and Nincic 2001)—but when nuclear weapons created a novel challenge of understanding a situation that was hypothetical and speculative through-and-through and open to swift and dramatic developments, a very sophisticated theoretical boom gained centrality politically. At the same time, this development became highly influential within the academic world, because the nature of the object allowed for a high degree of abstraction and formalization that scored well on the criteria of the day for a new, more 'scientific' form of International Relations. Under a Cold War situation with a booming US economy, a mood of technological optimism and a willingness to support social science as part of the solution to social challenges (including not only the Cold War struggle but social problems of all kinds), the reward was high for new approaches that seemed to move IR in the direction of the use of scientific methods and tools, ranging from coding of events data allowing for computerized data processing, through cybernetic models and experimental psychology, to game theory. Deterrence theory became a success story in this context for two reasons. On the one hand, it produced a seemingly productive ('progressive') research programme where theoretical work produced ever new and more complex problems that could in turn be dealt with by new theoretical moves. On the other hand, all this seemed highly useful because the theories actually produced their own reality of abstractions, the world of 'secure second-strike capability', 'extended deterrence', and 'escalation dominance'.

This was reflected in the critique from peace research and critical theory that the whole 'Golden Age' idea is a self-glorifying construction of academics whose real accomplishment was to make morally corrupt government policies (MAD, Vietnam) look respectable and/or inevitable. Some critics said that this whole literature produced validating smoke-screens for what the politicians and the military wanted to do anyway: build up a huge nuclear force and promote military Keynesianism (Green 1966, 1968; Senghaas 1969). Although it is undoubtedly true that these theories legitimized deterrence and nuclear weapons as such, it is not fair to conclude that their 'influence' on policy was illusory. Theories of deterrence shaped the whole way of making sense of nuclear weapons, and thereby influenced the shape, if not necessarily the size of investments. The relative merits and roles of bombers, missiles, submarines, the uses and non-uses of tactical nuclear weapons, and how to avoid vulnerability of systems (the famous basing study by Wohlstetter et al. in 1954)—for all such policies, there was a clear link from theorists to policy makers. But, in relation to targeting, there was a major slippage where Strategic Air Command largely continued with its own roughly 'first-strike'-oriented policy (Rosenberg 1983). If one counter-factually imagined that the civilian experts had not existed at all, it seems much more probable that the whole nuclear build-up would have been shaped by an old-fashioned military logic of maximizing 'fire power' without much concern for overall stability and the political possibilities for signalling and manoeuvring. Nuclear *quantity* was probably a product of semi-independent dynamics having to do with the military industrial complex and the overall politics of sizing the defence budget, but it should be beyond doubt that Golden Age theorizing produced a different mix of nuclear weapons with different qualities and locations, and a different role in policy, from what would otherwise have happened. For better or worse, this story of the Golden Age and deterrence theory became the heart of the discipline—its founding myth somewhat similar to the way the first great debate operates in IR theory.

What is most unique about this particular episode is, however, the degree to which policy-oriented work made significant contributions to general theory. This was not just application of work done elsewhere to policy questions or transfer of knowledge to the political world, as we have come to expect of **think tanks**. Neither was it, as with the most recent think tanks, primarily about lobbying for specific policies, although the work of **RAND** clearly served the general interests of the air force and had built-in biases towards a distrustful policy vis-à-vis the Soviet Union (Green 1968). This did not prevent lasting contributions to game theory. Even a mathematician prefacing the sixtieth anniversary edition of von Neumann and Morgenstern's foundational *Theory of Games and Economic Behavior* (Kuhn 2004: x) posits that 'many observers agree' that RAND was one of two centres in which game theory flourished in the first post-war decade (see also Dimand and Dimand 1996: 142–3). One need just mention the 1950 invention at RAND of the prisoner's dilemma (Poundstone 1992: 103) and the late 1950s bargaining twist given to game theory by Thomas Schelling (1960b). It is quite easy to see how these developments grew out of specific challenges relating especially to the nuclear situation. Noticeably, these were also major contributions to basic science at the same time (Dodge 2006).

The second biggest example from the Golden Age of policy-relevant work that simultaneously constituted general theory was systems analysis, a method for solving problems of force structure and resource allocation that drew on economic theory as well as operations research developed by natural scientists, engineers, and economists during the Second World War (Stern 1967; Smoke 1976: 290–3). Several pioneering RAND studies were implemented into policy, notably the famous 'air-bases' study by Wohlstetter et al. (1954). Several of the leading representatives entered the Kennedy administration—McNamara's 'whiz kids' (Brodie 1965; Kaplan 1983). From there, this method and related RAND techniques like the 'Planning-Programming-Budgeting-System' 'spread through most of the federal government' (Smoke 1976: 292). It is generally underestimated today how much of early strategic studies was not only inspired by the *discipline* of economics (Hitch 1960; Schelling 1960a) but was actually *about* economics. A typical early course or 1960s–1970s textbook in strategic studies had strategy and deterrence as the biggest sub-field, but the second biggest would usually be 'the economics of defence'—not so puzzling given the size of the American defence budget! (See Knorr and Trager 1977 for a broader treatment of 'economic issues and national security'.) The image nowadays is often that Cold War strategic studies was obsessed with military questions, and this is partly true—it was mostly the economics of *defence* planning—but strategy was closely followed by economics as a key concern. Most of these textbooks had either no definition of security studies or just a vacuous or circular definition of security (something like securing the state or essential values against threats; cf surveys in Buzan 1983; Buzan and Hansen 2009). What, de facto, held the field together was a focus on defence as a peculiar effort by society and an attention to all the related dimensions necessary for this; that is, selection, funding, management, and politico-strategic utilisation of military force, and the support thereof by various non-military instruments. Strikingly, clear definitions of this kind of security studies were only articulated much later, in the context of the 1980s–1990s debate on widening. That is, their appearance testified to the opposite of what they stated: that the field by then encapsulated a broader agenda within which this narrow definition was a possible bastion of resistance (see Key Quote 28.1). During the Golden Age where a definition like Walt's corresponded well to actual practice, it had rarely if ever been spelled out—this was not necessary, but implied.

Many other things happened in strategic studies around this nexus, but the identity and nature of the field were shaped by the Golden Age episode. Beyond nuclear strategy, important areas within strategic studies were systems analysis (planning, organization), arms control, alliance politics, counter-insurgency, and organization of government institutions and decision making (Smoke 1976). In the late 1960s and early 1970s, were added area studies and internal developments (bureaucratic politics; decision making). Later in the 1970s came perceptions, arms race theory, proliferation of nuclear weapons, proliferation of advanced military technology, utility of force, strategic intelligence, conventional strategy, and self-reflections of the field (Bull 1968; Gray 1977; Howard 1979).

Many of the new developments (notably perceptions and decision making) were reactions to the difficulties that the classical form of security studies ran into. The overly rational game theory became complemented by theories of 'irrationality' like bureaucratic politics, and this, along with the **Vietnam War**, became a turning point towards the next phase. The USA entered the war with all the instruments of strategic studies in high esteem. The Kennedy administration and McNamara's time as Secretary of Defense marked a high point in the belief in the social-scientific vision of security knowledge (Morgenthau 1962). But, in the words of Colin Gray (1982: 90), the strategists knew 'next to nothing' about 'peasant nationalism in Southeast Asia or about the mechanics of a counter-revolutionary war'.

KEY POINTS

- The defining moment—or founding myth—for security studies was the development of deterrence theory, which both spurred general theory of a 'basic science' nature (game theory) and simultaneously fed directly into policy.
- The economics of defence was the second biggest field in early security studies.

Institutionalization and stagnation

The crisis for security studies—or what Baldwin (1995) dubs the move into a phase of 'decline'—was, however, not only about external challenges to an otherwise perfect theoretical construction. The previous period had already witnessed some 'internal weakening' of the mainstream strategy scholarship. Even in the core area of nuclear (and other forms of military) strategy, the highly theoretical and academic scholarship of the earlier period had succumbed to 'hectic empiricism' (Buzan 2000). The task of security scholarship was to keep up with fast-changing technologies and the twists and turns of political developments. Increasing amounts of effort therefore went into ever-more detailed work on technical specificities and narrow perfection of isolated bits of knowledge.

The corrupting influence of policy was, however, not the only explanation. During the 1970s and 1980s, the very abstraction of deterrence logic more or less broke down under the weight of its own complexity (ex post/ex ante, limited nuclear war, rationality debates), causing an exhausted drift towards general or existential deterrence (Morgan 1983; Freedman 1988). The Golden Age lost its lustre also because the internal logic of its key contribution atrophied.

A further complication of the policy–academe interaction has to do with an aspect that is very often ignored in the debates these days, especially within the more critical and/or European forms of security studies: in the post-Golden Age period, the field was marked by a gradual IR-ification of security studies. It moved from interdisciplinarity into becoming one of IR's two pillars, paralleling International Political Economy (IPE). Not only did this mean that IR became almost formalized as consisting of these two components (in the USA symbolized by two lead journals, *International Security* and *International Organization*); more importantly in the present context—seen from the angle of security studies itself—it meant that IR became the main disciplinary context for security studies theorizing, in striking contrast to the early Golden Age situation. Previously, the leading scholars came from a variety of backgrounds—sociology, mathematics, psychology, natural sciences, political science, and quite a lot of economists. Increasingly, one discipline came to dominate: political science (Wæver 2010). In the retrospective construction of mainstream security thinking, (neo)realism and strategic studies came to be seen as almost synonymous, whereas, in actual history, they emerged as part of separate communities, shaped by different dynamics and only with limited personal overlaps (Hagemann 2011; Wæver 2015: 85).

Since the late 1960s, 'strategic studies' has become the subject for specific courses as part of general IR/political science departments (Smoke 1976: 292; Gray 1982: 86) and not least in specific, specialized institutes, often with government support, such as SAIS at Johns Hopkins, the Saltzman Institute at Columbia, and Harvard's 'John M. Olin Institute'. The military academies and (especially in the USA) the 'war schools' of each service became another arena for systematic teaching of courses in security studies. Particularly in the USA, scholars—with military or civilian background—in these latter institutions have been natural participants in the 'international security studies'/'international security and arms control' sections of ISA (International Studies Association) and APSA (American Political Science Association) that were set up in the 1980s. 'Security *theory*' almost only develops within the civilian, university-based part—no longer in the think tanks. It is important for understanding the current situation regarding security theory, that the field is now closely intertwined with the (sub)discipline of IR in universities.

The potential problem for policy in this academicized development has been compensated by a gradual modification of the role of think tanks in the USA. In the early period, the leading think tanks—notably the pioneering RAND Corporation—housed (within their social science sections) heavy theory work and large innovative projects. Today theory has moved to the universities, and think tanks have come under strong competitive pressure for delivering fast, usable policy guidance. Some think tanks have been politicized and operate not only from a political perspective but as a key element in political strategies for conservatives or liberals; others are still loosely tied to the services, but follow the policy agenda closely (Rich 2004; Buzan and Hansen 2009). It has become much rarer to find theory even explicitly discussed in think tank work, but it is clearly drawn upon. The result is a chain construct, where academe, think tanks, and policy makers are distinct and each purifies its role. Persons might travel between the categories—move from think tank to university or to policy, or vice versa—but, as institutions, they are distinct. This is, as we will return to in the next section, much less clearly the case outside the USA (probably because of weaker competitive pressures on the intellectual market).

Structural observation about the different kinds of intellectual institutions in strategic studies is also the ideal context for characterizing the difference between the USA and Western Europe during the early decades, a comparison that should be introduced here because the contrast will carry increasing weight as our story unfolds. In Europe, even in the UK, think tanks from the beginning mostly had the roles with which they are associated today: to influence policy in a specific direction, to mobilize the public behind policy, and at best to digest, popularize, and apply academic work done elsewhere into a more useful format for policy makers (Abelson 2002; Haas 2002; Parmar 2004). In the area of foreign and security affairs, most policy-oriented work took place in 'foreign-policy institutes', which rarely engaged in more theoretical efforts. One partial exception was in the early decades of the International Institute for Strategic Studies (IISS), in London, where the series of *Adelphi Papers* especially included serious research, often by scholars from around the world who were resident at the Institute for a period. But generally, during the Cold War Europeans characteristically conducted their political arguments over political and military strategy—often against the USA—on the basis of theories made in the United States.

The most important non-American contributions to strategic studies were probably Hedley Bull's (1961) foundational work on arms control and the continuous interaction of American social science scholarship with a tradition of British work steeped in classical military strategy (Basil Liddell Hart, Michael Howard, Lawrence Freedman, and P. M. S. Blackett). The US–European contrast is clearly expressed in the way France's leading IR scholar, Raymond Aron, wrote repeatedly about Clausewitz, and France's main entries in the history of post-war strategic thought are two generals involved with the argument behind France's independent nuclear force. This is in contrast to the centrality in the USA of a kind of strategy rooted in modern social science and relatively independent of classical military strategy. In hindsight, it can be seen that Pierre Hassner (1997), throughout the Cold War and after, produced a unique series of analyses of the political dimension of security anchored in political theory, but this did not take off as a style or approach establishing itself as a distinct presence in security studies, and most of his work during the Cold War appeared in policy-oriented anthologies on current challenges as 'the French chapter', rarely recognized for the theory work it constituted (Gloannec and Smolar 2003).

The distinct phenomenon of strategic studies emerged in Europe clearly as an imported American speciality. A most revealing testimony to the asymmetrical relationship is the incredibly condescending tone in Wohlstetter and Wohlstetter's 1963 report on the state of strategic studies in Europe. They give marks to the different national research communities (good to Sweden, not so good England, hope for Germany, and so on). Security studies was not born simultaneously in two places, and developments cannot be compared as independent phenomena. It emerged in the USA and was exported to Europe. Since European security studies mostly took shape in the late 1960s and early 1970s, it became the post-Golden, institutionalized, theory-has-already-been-done kind of work that struggled to keep up with the newest technological developments to assess optimal Western military policy vis-à-vis the Soviet Union.

Strategic studies beyond the NATO area (Japan, third world, Israel, and so on) has been almost solely of the kind resembling political argumentation with a bit of factual, technical expertise—never 'basic conceptual analysis' (Wohlstetter and Wohlstetter 1966). An interesting parallel to the US case was the Soviet one, where think-tank-like 'institutes' gained a distinct niche producing research with a different theoretical orientation than the (Marxist-Leninist) one in the dominant academic institutions. It is far beyond the remit of this chapter to include a detailed and nuanced coverage of this development, but, in striking parallel to the USA, real-world challenges formed the basis for innovative work in an institutional setting with a creative tension between two creative tensions: combining a bond with a distance to high academe and a similar duality in relation to policy itself. Comparable developments were not found to the same extent in Europe.

Nowhere beyond the USA did anything occur, within an independent field of strategic studies, similar to 'RAND's ability to produce systematic, long-range, 'creative' research rather than to engage in mere short-range tinkering with other peoples' ideas' (Green 1968: 304). If one chooses anachronistically to project the history of security studies back into the inter-war period, it can be noted that the think tanks of the day (the first such) produced policy-oriented work that simultaneously was theoretically innovative and entered the annals of IR-theory history. This happened in think tanks such as the 'Institute for Government Research' (later Brookings), Carnegie, the Council on Foreign Relations, and the Hoover Institution, plus Chatham House in Britain. They contributed to the formulation of plans for the international order in the inter-war period, and much of the thinking recorded in IR theory's history as 'idealism' was produced in connection to these.

Thus, the simultaneity of policy and theory work in universities and especially in separate institutions characterized both the inter-war and the first post-war periods in the USA, but this changed towards the end of the 1960s. 'Having played a central role in the development of deterrence theory, economists were by [the 1970s] found hardly anywhere in the academic study of military affairs. RAND had also evolved into a bureaucratized contract research organization as much as a think tank and was no longer the hothouse of theoretical ferment it had been in the 1950s' (Betts 1997: 16).

A final element to cover regarding this phase is the parallel track constituted by peace research in relation to security studies. These two tracks merge only during the 1980s and 1990s, and, despite some overlaps of subject matter (arms racing, arms control, war), generally treated each other as political rivals divided by the acceptability, or not, of the whole structure of nuclear deterrence specifically, and the role of war in human relations generally (Buzan and Hansen 2009). Sometimes peace research would be treated as 'left-wing' security studies, and on other occasions as something (very much) other than security studies. Most often, peace research repaid the latter favour by seeing itself as certainly not 'security studies'. Early peace research ironically emerged in forms reminiscent of strategic studies—as a scientific alternative to mainstream IR. Much inter-war IR had been programmatically constructed as aiming for the production of peace, and thus the history of peace research can quite easily be anchored in inter-war (and immediate post-war) classics such as Quincy Wright's *A Study of War* (1942) and Lewis Fry Richardson's books, *Generalized Foreign Politics* (1939), *Arms and Insecurity* (1949), and *Statistics of Deadly Quarrels* (1960). After 1945, the UNESCO-sponsored attempt to form a social-science-based study of war was dismissed by the emerging discipline of International Relations (Aron 1957; Waltz 1959), and consequently peace research formed with roots mostly in the 'softer' or more humanistic social sciences such as sociology and psychology, with pioneers like Herbert Kelman and Johan Galtung. An irony of this is that the same impulse towards 'scientific' approaches spurred the development of strategic studies mostly anchored in game theory and thus economics. Some of the most 'scientific' work, such as quantitative events data and psychological experiments managed to count as both peace research, security studies, and IR (cf. the Correlates of War project and the *Journal of Conflict Resolution*). Especially in Europe, peace research went through a radicalization in the late 1960s and early 1970s, and so-called critical peace research with strongholds in Germany, the Netherlands, and Scandinavia, came to see strategic studies as part of the problem.

Especially in analyses like Dieter Senghaas's critique of deterrence theory (Senghaas 1969) and Johan Galtung's work on violence (Galtung 1969), mainstream theories were understood as part of the balance of terror, bipolar, Cold War system of militarization, superpower dominance, and exploitation of the third world. Critical peace research was usually not seen as part of strategic studies or even security studies, either by the mainstream or by the critics themselves. The critics did not write in the name of security, but more often in the name of *peace* depicting 'security' as a destructive pursuit (Jahn et al. 1987; Wæver 2008). Peace and security were symbols of the opposing sides during the Cold War (Buzan 1984; Wæver 2008).

The period 1965–80 has been seen by many observers as less successful, and by Baldwin (1995) it was even labelled 'decline'. Already in the 1970s, however, some new developments had begun that came into clearer focus in the 1980s. Critics of the traditional approach had started to make the case for the inclusion of security challenges in, for example, the economic and environmental sectors (Brandt et al. 1980; Palme et al. 1982; Buzan 1983; Ullmann 1983; Nye and Lynn-Jones 1988; Mathews 1989).

KEY POINTS

- 1965–80 marked a period both of stagnation for security studies in terms of theory development, and of institutionalization in textbooks, courses, and organizations.
- Security studies went from being interdisciplinary to being mostly understood as political science, often as one of International Relations' two pillars (IPE being the other).
- Security studies, invented in the USA, was copied—often with direct American assistance—in Western Europe and in the rest of the world, especially among allies.
- The think tanks gradually stopped being innovative, interdisciplinary places for thinking and became increasingly routinized producers of more narrow, technical problem solving.
- Peace research developed on a parallel but so far separate track, and especially its most distinct, critical branch was seen neither by its representatives nor by security studies as part of the latter.

Disciplinary questioning and theoretical relaunch

There is no need here to rehash the familiar story of the wide/narrow debate of the 1970s and especially 1980s. The debate as such is covered well elsewhere—within and beyond (Buzan and Hansen 2009: 156–225) the present volume—but for the present purpose of this chapter it is necessary to understand the way the field developed theoretically in the 1980s and 1990s, not so much the debate as such, but the theoretical approaches that emerged out of this debate.

KEY QUOTE 28.1 Narrow definition of security studies

'[S]ecurity studies may be defined as *the study of the threat, use and control of military force*'
Walt (1991: 212).

Of particular interest is the parallel turn to increasingly abstract and ambitious theorizing on both sides of the Atlantic—on separate tracks. The US mainstream of security studies focused on debates over offensive and defensive realism, some discussion of constructivism, democratic peace, and a debate on power versus institutions in empire/order building—all shaped by a quest for empirically validated generalizations about cause–effect relationships. A specific form of knowledge is hegemonic: cause–effect statements backed up either by statistical data or more often by historical case studies (Walt 1999; Wæver 2012a). In Europe, a debate emerged between a number of more or less critical theories: Critical Security Studies, feminism, Copenhagen School, Paris School, and poststructuralism.

The different form of knowledge in Europe relates to a conflicting conception of the relationship to policy: less inclined to search for cause–effect generalizations to assist policy makers in calculating policy, more partaking in political reflections—that is, more the role of public 'intellectual' than 'expert'. It is striking, however, that, parallel to both these theoretical clusters, lots of specific 'technical expertise' developed on both sides, and they were often less different than the theories: knowledge about **AIDS** as a security problem, health security, or missile defence. On top of this practical, empirical knowledge, two *different* clusters of theorization have developed. This general split partly reflects a more 'problem-solving' tradition in US social science versus a more critical one in Europe, but recent developments are more extreme than the usual pattern, and security studies was largely coherent across the Atlantic during the Cold War, with the deep split developing only during the 1980s and especially after the end of the Cold War (see Think Point 28.1).

While it would probably be wrong to *explain* this difference by policy needs (that is, an externalist sociology of science), the pattern is clearly reinforced by the pattern of world power at the beginning of the twenty-first century. In a world that might be described as consisting of one superpower and four great powers ('1 + 4' according to Buzan and Wæver 2003; Buzan 2004b) or uni-multipolar (Huntington 1999) with the USA seeing and handling it as **unipolar** and the other great powers acting according to multipolar logic, the different angles of watching the world point to different *forms* of knowledge (Wæver 2012a, 2015): US decision makers and academics see the USA as the actor that shapes

THINK POINT 28.1 Places, persons, and paradigms

When we talk in broad terms about 'European' and 'US' theories, this should not be taken as statements generalizing about scholars in Europe and the USA respectively, but as a reference to distinct arenas of theoretical discussions. Some scholars located in the USA draw from and contribute to debates that mostly take place in Europe and—more obviously—many scholars in Europe work from theories made in the USA and aim their publications at American colleagues. In the discipline of International Relations, there is a US-centred, global discipline that overlaps and intersects with weaker independent traditions like the English School, French IR, and non-Western contributions. We do not want to deny the importance of 'American-style' work done by Europeans and vice versa, but we want to point out how disconnected different sets of theoretical debate are, and these tend to have their main institutional anchorage (journals, research institutions, organizations) in different continents.

the world and accordingly they need knowledge about cause–effect relationships in order to understand how to work the material they act upon (the world).

From a European perspective, in contrast, it is more common to see the main voice of security as an external factor to deal with (the USA) and therefore to be in a tension-ridden relationship to security as such. Calls for action in the name of security can be seen as part of US attempts to organize the world—for example under the slogan of a global war on terror (Buzan and Wæver 2003: 297, 300, 303, 2009; Buzan 2006), and therefore 'Europe' takes a position vis-à-vis security where it is possible to problematize pronouncements about what is a security issue (that is, de-securitize) and insist on a wider concept of security—for example, an interpretation of terror and terror fighting that emphasizes economic and political mechanisms. Therefore, the whole question of what should and should not count as security issues and how to conceptualize security is much closer to the European policy agenda than to the US one.

The difference also expresses a general meta-theoretical divide—with the USA the more rationalist, Europe the more reflectivist (Tickner and Wæver 2009)—but this is far from the whole story. At least two other elements need to be taken into account (Wæver 2012a): one is the different relationship to the *concept of security*. In Europe, the debate on this has stayed part of the field. It is seen as part of the ongoing practice of being a security analyst, to reflect on and problematize the concept—in order to understand and unveil the actions by practitioners in the name of security, but also as the politico-ethical self-reflection of a scholar who inevitably 'does security' when working in the name of security. In the USA, the question of the concept of security is seen as at most a necessary 'define your terms' operation in order to delineate what is counted in and out. When done with, one knows what is security or not, and the concept is not interesting in itself any more (Key Quote 28.1).

The other element is the exact form of knowledge that is valued. In contrast to the situation in general IR, where the USA was dominated especially in the 1990s by **rational choice** and in later years by large-N quantitative studies, the US security studies field is absolutely *not* hard-core rational choice or number-crunching. The leading security theory journals, *International Security* and *Security Studies*, publish rather little formalized rational choice, and even soft rational choice that draws on economic theory or organizational theory is far from valued in the way it is in journals such as *International Organization* or *International Studies Quarterly* (Wæver 1998, 2013; Brown 2000). The typical article in *International Security* uses historical case studies—maybe one in-depth historical case study—to examine a hypothesis framed as a cause–effect relationship and very often tied into general debates that are, on the one hand, of sweeping magnitude, and, on the other hand, boiled down to the measurement of one or a few variables, such as offensive versus defensive motivations (do states maximize power or security?), the importance of ideational variables, or whether international order builds on pure power or also on institutions and legitimacy. Although each of these debates could easily be phrased as broad philosophical issues (as predecessors of each were in previous decades) or as ethical dilemmas, the American security literature constructs these questions as part of a tight, causal machinery, where a single, crucial question of how the logic unfolds is to be settled by empirical knowledge.

The most focused and sustained debate has probably been offensive versus defensive realism (plus neoclassical realism), where a number of monographs (some major ones reviewed in Rose 1998) tried to use historical case studies to settle big, causal questions (see also Mearsheimer 2001). Similarly, the challenge from constructivism, which in Europe turned into major self-reflective debates on the conditions and responsibility of scholarship, became in US security studies mostly a question of testing the influence of ideational variables in the big causal picture (Desch 1998; Tannenwald and Wohlforth 2005).

The top-level policy debate on American grand strategy under presumed unipolarity was academically addressed mainly in terms of the proper expectations regarding the balancing behaviour of others (Brooks and Wohlforth 2005), which again hinges mostly on the general questions from the offensive–defensive realism debate, and second on the power of institutions. The latter question generated a very focused debate easily stylized (and taught) as Ikenberry versus Wohlforth (Ikenberry 2002). Realism traditionally took unipolarity to be impossible, and the strictest of neorealists—Waltz himself—actually predicted that it *would* not last long. Those who wanted to argue that some kind of preponderance could endure faced the challenge of *explaining* its relative stability. The major competing explanations emphasized, on the one hand, the United States' uniquely reassuring liberal form of hegemony partly derived from attributes of the US state, partly built into US policy of institution building and self-binding, and, on the other hand, the purely power-based stability of a situation where the USA is *so* superior that balancing becomes impossible. (The debate is collected in Ikenberry 2002; see also Mearsheimer 2001; Buzan and Wæver 2003; Buzan 2004b; Brooks and Wohlforth 2005; Deudney 2006; Ikenberry et al. 2011.) The debate clearly had immediate implications for optimizing American grand strategy. But it was conducted less in terms of a future-oriented, purposive, and partly ethical debate about what future to aim for, and almost solely as (if it was) a theoretical-empirical debate over what theory can explain the past record. During the presidency of Bill Clinton, the debate on democratic peace had much the same status: the seemingly most relevant knowledge for security studies to supply to policy makers is whether there is or is not a reliable causal connection between democracy and peace (Lepgold and Nincic 2001: ch. 5). After the collapse of Bush Era global can-do-ism, US scholarship has come to include more work on terrorist movements and their internal dynamics, as well as a predictable rehashing of the debate for and against US decline.

The common denominator tying together these Euro-American differences is diverging understandings of the *role* of security studies, their function vis-à-vis policy. In the USA, this is most clearly understood as theory uncovering causal laws about the workings of world politics, which enables policy makers to make the right choices when facing situations where these relationships are relevant. This in turn reflects a situation of an *acting* power, one that has to decide about how to shape world affairs, and it reflects a clear division of labour between politics, policy advice, and academic research.

In circles more clearly anchored on the European side, the trend was towards critical theories of various kinds that reflected on the practices of policy and problematized the nature of security making. This goes for Aberystwyth-style Critical Security Studies, the Bourdieu-inspired work around Didier Bigo as well as the Copenhagen School, feminists and radical postmodernists such as Dillon, Constantinou, and Der Derian. Here, the concept of security has stayed part of the ongoing debate, and the form of knowledge differs from the one in the American mainstream, and is closer to that of a critical intellectual reflecting openly about one's own political responsibility—who argues about one's analytical and theoretical choices in terms of their political implications (Booth 1997, 2007; Wyn Jones 1999; Bigo 1996, 2002a, 2002b; Huysmans 2002, 2006; Buzan et al. 1998; Buzan and Hansen 2009).

A part of this story is the role of peace research and its change during the 1980s. With the new peace movement, peace research suddenly gained a new practical relevance. What Håkan Wiberg (1988) has called 'the peace research movement' had to fulfil its function as the natural intellectual adviser (more or less asked for) to the peace movement (Jahn 1984). This led in much of North European peace research to a new 'realism'. Peace research became pro-security and pro-Europe (where previously it had been anti-security in the name of peace and anti-Europe in the name of the third world). Even defence was reappropriated as alternative defence (non-offensive defence) (Møller 1991).

Security became, during this period, a meeting ground for strategic studies, which had until then operated more with *power* as the guiding concept and peace research having obviously *peace* as the key concept. In the 1980s, *security* emerged as a more constructive analytical concept (Buzan 1984; Jahn et al. 1987). Power thinking is a national concern and sees anarchy as inescapable and the end of the story—peace is cosmopolitan and claims that anarchy has to go before anything good can be achieved. In contrast, security is a relational concept (that is, in-between national and cosmopolitan), and sees anarchy as a spectrum, where conditions can be improved in the direction of a mature anarchy (Buzan 1984). In this sense, security became the middle ground and increasingly explicit as the basis for much IR work from the 1980s and onwards.

Peace research institutes, especially in the 1980s, were often in a position somewhat parallel to that of think tanks during Golden Age strategic studies. The link to policy was very different—not official advisers to policy makers—but European security studies gained political relevance (in a broader sense) because of the politicization of security issues during the period defined by the peace movement, Reagan, and Gorbachev. The setting was—as in the 1950s—simultaneously interdisciplinary and connected to current developments in theory in the different disciplines. Peace research in contrast to university IR was under pressure to deal with relevant issues, but there was no expectation of immediate delivery of policy answers. At RAND in the 1950s, the theorists were given extraordinary leeway to pursue highly abstract, idiosyncratic theoretical tracks, which clearly could not be justified in terms of a guaranteed pay-off vis-à-vis products to be delivered to policy makers (Stern 1967). Precisely, therefore, publications often ended up being innovative solutions to policy questions. Similarly peace research was interdisciplinary, politically oriented, but with a distance both to immediate policy responsibility and to the major powers of the academic system. It is less clear whether there were policy effects, but our main point here is the impact of political involvement on theory. As rightly noted by Betts (1997: 32) in relation to traditional strategic studies: 'Ironically, in the past quarter century, policy experience has enriched academic research more than the reverse.' The same might be said about the 1980s and the birth of critical, European theories. A volatile political situation, a sense of importance and relevance, and engagement in heated political debates clearly contributed to the birth of these theories, and, in a few cases, theorists probably had some role as intellectuals of or for social movements such as the peace movements and Pugwash as well as some, mostly oppositional, political parties, but in general the effect of practice on theory was probably larger than vice versa.

Several observers (and observer participants) have noted that the debates among the new critical schools of security studies—to some extent seen as a 'European' development—have become surprisingly productive and generated theory of broader relevance and inspiration to the field of IR in general (Huysmans 1998b; Eriksson 1999; Williams 2003). Security studies in the USA largely works with theories that are developed within IR and then tested and refined within security studies on security cases—neorealism, soft constructivism, and so on (Wæver 2012a). The most monumental illustration of this is the nature of constructivism in American security studies. The main work here is the big Katzenstein volume on *The Culture of National Security* (Katzenstein 1996b). This was mainly manned by scholars who did not have a long-term involvement with security affairs. They were IR scholars who had taken part in the theory wars on the constructivist side, and it seemed the right move at the time to prove constructivism on the home ground of materialist approaches: security. Quite visibly this is a foray by general IR theorists into security studies for the sake of making a point within IR theory debates. The new 'European' schools, in contrast, did not develop deductively from the guiding symbolic positions within the theory debates (and therefore they are often hard to pin down—is the Copenhagen School constructivist, neorealist, postmodernist, or all of these?); they emerged as part of the engagements on a distinct security scene, and the theoretical innovations *have become* part of the theory landscape in IR theory. For instance, one can find discussions of securitization theory in general IR journals (Williams 2003; Balzacq 2005; Vuori 2008) in ways that constitute the main investigations of the potential for IR of drawing on **speech-act theory** in general. Similarly, debates within the discipline (at least in Europe) of the political role of researchers have been conducted with security theory as the platform (Eriksson 1999; Huysmans 2002). The fate of Frankfurt-style 'Critical Theory' in IR has also been decisively influenced by security studies. The attempts in the 'fourth debate' in the 1980s to launch Critical Theory were largely abortive, and postmodern approaches came to structure the metatheoretical scene to a much larger extent. But gradually Critical Theory gained a position in the general IR landscape mainly because of the success of Ken Booth and others in showing its value within the area of security (Wyn Jones 1999; Booth 2005b, 2007).

One might ask now whether these lively debates in and among the new schools still qualify as 'security studies'. Have they simply become IR and lost the in-between position that defines security studies? Where the first-generation representatives of the different schools—Booth, Bigo, Buzan, Wæver—had developed their arguments in engagements with policy questions and in direct interaction with policy makers and think tanks, the next generation would be more clearly academically defined and develop these arguments in a more isolated academic setting. However, the set-up continues to be one where security theory is located between the IR discipline as such and technical experts and practitioners, only with the arrows somewhat different from the North American ones (see Figure 28.1).

The place of security experts here underlines the point that much work in European and North American research institutes is quite similar: detailed technical work on AIDS as an epidemic; on the proliferation of missile technology; on the efficiency of various counterterrorist strategies. Most of what goes on in foreign-policy institutes as well as the IISS in Europe and in American think tanks is of this nature, delivering on the demand of politicians for factual knowledge here-and-now on a question that came up yesterday and needs an answer tomorrow (maybe with the main difference that in the USA this is often structured more as a partisan advocacy for a specific policy, and in Europe as seemingly neutral, technical background knowledge). The point here is that, as soon as this is reflected on in terms of theory—when an interaction emerges between, on the one hand, technical experts in say European foreign-policy institutes or Washington think tanks, and, on the other, in university circles, for instance through PhD students who do work that is simultaneously part of their university-based PhD and part of the research institute—the theoretical context differs. In the USA, this will usually be the discussions reflected in *International Security*, whereas in parts of Europe, the young scholars will relate to and draw inspiration from the new theories that emerged in European research institutes and now mainly thrive in European universities.

On both sides, it is essential to the particular nature of security theory that there is a distinct category of 'policy knowledge' that functions as expertise supporting policy—a form of knowledge that security theory in the USA wants to assist, while security theory in Europe (to draw the contrast sharply) treats it as a main empirical source for critical analysis. Critics of current policy in the USA will aim to obtain a policy change by presenting theoretical generalizations based on empirical data that give scientific credentials to a different policy as more likely to achieve the aims aspired to. Critics working with the theories here associated with European security studies are more likely to criticize politically and ethically the current policy for its aims and effects and to expose the involved 'policy knowledge' as a part of policy-making, structurally complicit and produced from the policy maker's perspective, rather than criticizing it for being scientifically wrong and up for revision.

Beyond the West, security theory throughout the 1980s meant the frames of reference used in think tanks dealing with military matters, most strongly articulated in countries like Argentina, Brazil, Chile, Egypt, Iran, Turkey, India, and Pakistan (Tickner and Wæver 2009). These frames were usually vague general common-sense realism, or (especially in Latin America) if they were more distinct theories then they were of a more geopolitical ilk. Increasingly, a new security studies has emerged in most parts of the world, most often affiliated with universities, and often engaging more with European than American traditions, for example, South African scholars have contributed important reflections on the concept of emancipation in Critical Security Studies, not wrestled with offensive versus defensive realism (Tickner and Blaney 2012). Human Security resonated where

Figure 28.1 The position of security theory in North America and Europe

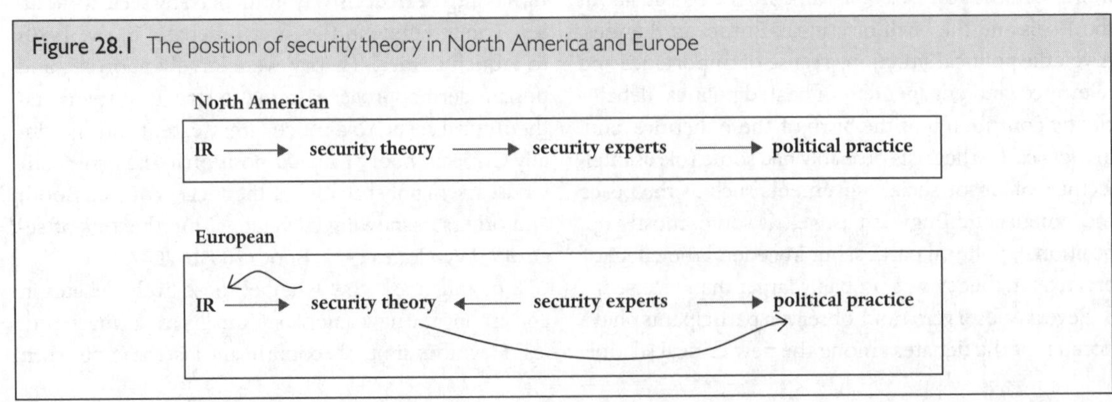

security and development were most closely linked (see Chapter 10), while Africa was often presented as exhibit A for the case against IR approaches being relevant at all to real-world concerns. East Asian schools paid much attention to securitization theory as an element in an original literature on 'non-traditional security', often anchored in Singapore and Hong Kong (see Chapter 12 and Curley and Siu-Lun 2008). Another project that also places itself between, and bridges, the dominant approaches in the USA and Europe was an impressive edited volume by Muthiah Alagappa (1998). Empirically, it is a comprehensive investigation of 'Asian Security Practices', and as the subtitle 'material and ideational influences' indicates, it follows a US 'soft mainstream' approach in including constructivist elements as a causal question about ideational factors. It is representative of much work done by scholars in, especially, South Korea, Singapore, and India.

The most thought-provoking developments in relation to foreshadowing a future global landscape of security theory are taking place in China. The most determined project at producing a non-Western theory, the Chinese School, aspires to build general theory based on Chinese traditions, Chinese history and political theory (Qin 2010; Yan 2010; Nielsen & Kristensen 2013; Wang & Buzan 2014). However, this has evolved during a period where the overriding substantial IR question for Chinese scholars to address has been a policy question from the security field: Various versions of 'peaceful rise' thinking were meant to counter a US 'China threat' story (Buzan 2010). Given that the principal conceptions of 'theory' in China places it closer to practice than in the West, it is not hard to see how each attempt to construct a general IR theory from China, at the same time offered an explanation why and how China's rise can be peaceful. However, it is a remarkable development that this takes place not only or primarily through direct writings on 'peaceful rise', but as part of a broader, general theory building effort. And as Chinese policy makers and think tankers possibly shift towards a more ambitious 'China Dream', it will be interesting to see whether the more IR discipline centred construction of general theory continues with its own momentum.

As the general global trend is towards a wider distribution of power and a general strengthening of South and East, more security theory is likely to emerge in new locales around the world. As witnessed by the account of the USA and Europe, the link is far from automatic between power, policy, and theorizing, but given the great variety of academic, institutional structures in different rising powers, and the different attitudes towards the importance of theory, it is likely that at least some will yield new security theory applicable beyond its parochial point of origin. Emerging powers are likely to emerge in the field of security theory as well. The next era in security studies is likely to become driven increasingly by interactions along axes other than the previous transatlantic one.

KEY POINTS

- After the debates in the 1980s over wide versus narrow concepts of security and the continuation or not of security studies, the 1990s saw a new turn to ambitious theorizing.
- The Europe-anchored debates continued the reflection on the concept of security and the role of security experts, with the politics of security as the overarching theme.
- The US kind of security studies worked on general IR theories to produce empirically validated cause–effect understandings of the relationships most important to contemporary security.
- The contrast corresponds both to differences in the policy perspective from the only superpower and a regional, great power respectively, to different meta-theoretical traditions, and to contrasting conceptions of the role of a security expert.
- With the global power structure shifting towards rising powers in the East and South, new theories are likely to play an increasing role, with Chinese theories of peaceful rise the strongest case so far.

Conclusion: the powers of theory and the challenges of the future

Security studies in the second decade of the twenty-first century is in a strong position. It has been through a prolonged period of theoretical productivity. Strangely, this has happened to roughly parallel degrees in Europe and the USA, despite the very minimal connections between these two sets of theoretical developments; and increasingly the general strengthening of non-Western theory delivers security theory as well. Now the field is well equipped with a battery of theories and since it is simultaneously seen as generally important, it attracts bright students, and, increasingly, funding. What kind of development will this lead to?

Increasingly, the new 'European' security studies does not remain structured by separate 'schools' (Wæver 2012a). There is a tendency in the fast-growing and very active trans-European community of PhD students to move among and across these schools. Thereby they become treated more as *theories*, where one has to understand their distinct character—they do not blend into one synthesized European security theory—but they can be drawn upon in individual projects as inspiration and instruments. While it is still possible to find contributions (e.g. Booth 2005b) that try to cultivate a situation of competition and theory construction through caricaturing others, it is clearly more common among the emerging generation of scholars to see the combined field of 'New European Security Theories' (NEST) as a joint debate where the different theories are developed and applied through their interaction (Büger and Stritzel 2005; Huysmans 2006). For instance, an expanding debate on the relationship between risk and security is largely conducted in terms set by the theories of the 1990s mixed up with the main social theories of risk (Aradau and van Münster 2007; Rasmussen 2010; Petersen 2012). Important recent work on 'the politics of possibility' and 'speculative security' (de Goede 2012; Amoore 2013) use securitization theory's focus on exceptional measures as a foil to develop a more Paris-School-like argument about the procedures that have evolved, where the mere possibility of something, the imagination of scenarios, become the centre of preparations irrespective of classical calculations of risk. Analyses like these provide a new generation of analytical models.

The future of security theory in the USA should be assessed in a different manner, because the theories there are less security specific than the European theories and more closely integrated into the main constellation of IR theories. The future of these security theories is therefore inseparable from the general prospects for IR theory. As often noticed (e.g. Goldmann 1988), US theory debates within IR tend to be about general theories—frameworks potentially explaining everything or at least a major part of every important question. The main theories in the security field are expressed in such general terms that, if valid, they would be overarching frameworks for our general understanding of international relations. Therefore, their fate as security theories hinges on their ability to prevail in the general debates in the discipline of IR, and these are at the moment quite inconclusive and somewhat unfocused (Wæver 2013; Wight et al. 2013). The only strong candidate for a kind of hegemony is rational choice as meta-theory, and this is exactly the theory that is comparatively weak within security studies even in the USA. Therefore, it is unlikely that the internal dynamics of the theory debate will be decided by a general prevalence of one of the current candidates.

More important for the future development of each theory in both Europe and the USA is probably how it handles some of the current issues on the political agenda. The two sets of theories will be working on partly overlapping sets of questions, as indicated in many chapters of this book. Probably, it will mostly be the European theories that try to make sense out of environmental security, health security, identity issues, and gender, while the US theories will be most active in areas such as proliferation of weapons of mass destruction and global military stability. Both will work on terror and anti-terror practices (with Europeans comparatively more attentive to domestic practices, the USA to international operations). Also, both will work on migration and the tension between security and liberty, including the logic of exceptionalism, although at least at present the theoretical side of this is far more developed in the debate among the European schools, while in the USA this is mostly policy work disconnected from the main theories but with some notable exceptions (like Andreas and Biersteker 2003). Both will be working on the role and nature of technology, globalization, risk society, and international economic order. This quick picture shows that there will actually be many points of contact between the currently disconnected fields of theory. A major question is, therefore: will they merge again—not in agreement but in debate? Will there be more exchange between the different research environments? Some signs in this direction can be found in the acceptance of a somewhat widened security agenda in American textbooks, while—as always—all major American theories are read in Europe. The particularly heavy-handed usage of security justifications under the administration of George W. Bush (2001–8), spurred an increased interest among American scholars in the European theories, not least securitization theory. As the polarization of IR's '4th debate' (**rationalism**-versus-**reflectivism**) wears off, there are also signs of European critical scholars reintegrating arguments about **power** and polarity; maybe they too were motivated by the Bush administration.

What will happen when the theories meet first trans-Atlantically and later globally on issues of common concern? Will they try to learn from contrasting insights from different kinds of theories? The academic world is usually quite slow, so if we look at the cumulative effect of 15 years of reaction to 9/11 there were, on the one hand, some overlapping concerns about the question of to what extent the US-initiated war on terror could and would become a globally structuring political programme (Buzan 2006; Ikenberry et al. 2011; de Goede 2012).

On the other hand, the more general attempt to develop cumulative research agendas for a world where the fight against terror topped the policy agenda happened very much on separate tracks. Here, it is striking that the European approaches have refined their analysis of *Anti*-Terror, that is sophisticated analyses of the emerging rationalities of Western societies in the post-9/11 period (Bigo 2002a, 2002b; de Goede 2012; Petersen 2012; Amoore 2013), while the spearhead of mainstream security studies in the USA has been an increased understanding of *Terrorism*. The leading journal *International Security* compiled a collection of recent articles where the two focal points clearly are to understand the inner dynamics of terrorist groups and the efficiency of different strategies against them, notably decapitation (Cronin et al. 2014). In terms of more short-term reactions to new surprising events, it was thought-provoking to see how the quickest, strong, and theory-driven intervention in the Ukraine crisis came from neither novel US theorizing, nor critical European approaches, but John Mearsheimer (2014) writing almost as a classical realist, exposing hubris and self-righteousness in a Western policy unwilling to understand the security needs of another major power. The almost total silence from critical theorists on an issue so close to home for most European scholars points to a worrying division of labour that has emerged. The 'new security theories' do 'new security issues', like environment and disease, and they do the dark side of dominant policies; but (with notable exceptions: Peoples 2010; Pouliot 2010), they do not engage with military security, so 'traditional security' is accepted by all parties to be the domain of 'traditional theories'.

Fast-rising concerns over environmental/climate security could easily provide another big linking issue. It seems less likely, however, that the rise of China will work in this way because the rise of China threatens US unipolar status, and is therefore becoming a more central concern of US security studies than its European counterpart. The broader coming to terms with a post-Western world is unlikely to become a fruitful theoretical challenge, even in their separate universes. Americans insist on repeating the debate on decline (i.e. about themselves, not listening to new voices), while European security studies is mostly about Europe. That challenge might have to wait for non-Western scholars to lift it.

Beyond the West, theorizing is in most cases running parallel to the main definition of policy issues. Therefore, some of it will remain local and be ignored by scholars elsewhere. However, some important meeting points can be discerned. Human security debates in the West are likely to be increasingly impacted by scholarship from especially Africa and the Middle East. The Asian approach to non-traditional security should find a voice within the European debates. Work on Islamic approaches to IR might become listened to in the West as policy becomes more and more serious about not transforming the region top-down but acting strategically in relation to a region dominated by regional actors. Most importantly, however, will be the question of how debates within rising powers about power transition are mediated with debates from declining powers on the same issue.

With or without such a meeting, this will be a time when theory is central to security studies. What can be envisaged here is not a 'new great debate' between coalitions of security theories—rather a new encounter between different debates in which the theories to some extent represent a division of labour brought to bear on common problems. The grand theories of the 1990s as well as the more recent innovations will have to prove themselves in a dual challenge. The first question to each is does it have the inner vitality to become a dynamic research programme that continues to evolve? This depends largely on the constellation of key concepts—is this at once tight enough to be operational and open enough to generate puzzles and research problems? So far the signs here are quite promising. The second challenge is to be able to take up in interesting ways the political challenges of the day. In that regard, security studies will continue to grapple with the problem noted long ago by Waltz (1979: 112): 'States, like people, are insecure in proportion to the extent of their freedom. If freedom is wanted, insecurity must be accepted.'

KEY POINTS

- Security studies is in the advantageous position of housing much theoretical productivity and issues high on the public agenda, attracting therefore both funding and talent. Whether this opportunity will be used to produce better theories is yet to be seen.
- The different new 'schools' in Europe increasingly intersect and form a field with opportunities for a new generation to combine and innovate across the theories.
- In the United States, the development of security theory is tied up with the general trends of the IR discipline.
- Both families of theories as well as their interaction will be much influenced by their ability to engage in relevant ways with the main issues on the policy agenda.

? QUESTIONS

1. Why was it primarily in the USA that strategic studies formed as a separate field?
2. Why did the Vietnam War not become the generator of new waves of theorization to deliver on this new policy challenge?
3. On the basis of the previous chapters in this book as well as this chapter, to what extent does 'security studies' appear to be one integrated field, or is it more appropriately seen as two or more arenas sharing a name but separated by either geographical or meta-theoretical distance?
4. Would you explain the increasing distance between security theorizing in Europe and the USA mainly by differences in foreign policy, general philosophical orientations, institutional differences within the academic world, or other factors?
5. Why does constructivism lead to such different kinds of work in the USA and Europe?
6. What is difference between the form of knowledge in US and European work?
7. What institutional reforms regarding universities, think tanks, policy institutes, or policy-making would be most conducive to better security theory and better security policy?
8. What are the most important questions on the policy agenda to get a better understanding of, and why do these not become the most active areas of research?
9. Do the current policy challenges point to a need for new interdisciplinary configurations?
10. Is a close connection between theory and policy conducive or disruptive for good theory?
11. If the distribution of power in the global system becomes less unbalanced, and security theory starts to emanate from many quarters, will this result in a thoroughly fragmented field, or will it become more integrated as policy makers and scholars get a real need to understand powerful others – for security reasons?

FURTHER READING

- Brown , Michael E. (ed.) (2000), *Rational Choice and Security Studies: Stephen Walt and his Critics, Cambridge*, MA: MIT Press. Stephen Walt's attack on rational choice approaches to security is both interesting as an exploration of the pros and cons of this approach, and as a clarification of how security studies, *International Security* style, defines itself methodologically and meta-theoretically.

- Buzan, Barry (1983), *People, States and Fear: The National Security Problem in International Relations*, Brighton: Wheatsheaf (2nd edn subtitled *An Agenda for International Security Studies in the Post Cold War Era*), Boulder CO: Lynne Rienner 2001; re-issued with a new introduction as ECPR classic (2007). A defining work from the second productive period, which both summarizes the preceding reflections on the concept of security and puts forward an original synthesis that made one of the first coherent cases for widening.

- Buzan, Barry and Hansen, Lene (2009), *The Evolution of International Security Studies*, Cambridge: Cambridge University Press. Surveys the history of security studies, traditional as well as critical forms, and offers an explanation in terms of driving forces that shaped debates in ISS.

- Buzan , Barry , Wæver, Ole , and de Wilde, Jaap (1998), *Security: A New Framework for Analysis*, Boulder, CO: Lynne Rienner (Chinese translation 2004). The main theoretical statement from the Copenhagen School. While its world analysis is more fully elaborated in a 2003 book, the defining categories of the theory are put forward here: securitization and sectors.

- Gray, Colin (1982), *Strategic Studies and Public Policy: The American Experience*, Lexington, KY: University Press of Kentucky. A critical history of early strategic studies, which combines observations about institutions, politics, and theory.

- Guzzini , Stefano and Jung , Dietrich (eds) (2004), *Contemporary Security Analysis and Copenhagen Peace Research*, London: Routledge. Explores the role of peace research (especially in Northern Europe) in furthering the emergence of the new European security theories.

- Huysmans, Jef (2006) *The Politics of Insecurity: Security, Migration and Assylum in the EU*, London: Routledge. State-of-the-art discussion—and partial synthesis—of some of the main theories from Europe: Copenhagen School, Paris School, and post-structuralist political theory.

- Ikenberry, G. John (ed.) (2002), *America Unrivaled: The Future of the Balance of Power*, Ithaca, NY: Cornell. Includes a number of powerful contributions that represent the main American debates over both offensive/defensive realism and international orders built on power/institutions.

- Jervis, Robert (1976), *Perception and Misperception in International Politics*, Princeton, NJ: Princeton University Press. One of the main books (together with Allison's (1971) *Essence of Decision*) to open up the psychological and decision-making approaches to strategic thinking in opposition to rational actor models.

- Krause , Keith and Williams , Michael C. (eds) (1997), *Critical Security Studies: Concepts and Cases*, Minneapolis: University of Minnesota Press. The defining work from Critical Security Studies, which includes sufficient diversity to represent much of the new work in general, not only one narrowly defined school, and paradoxically thereby produces the ideal manifesto for CSS.

- Schelling, Thomas C. (1960), *The Strategy of Conflict*, Cambridge, MA: Harvard University Press. One of the most original works from the (first) Golden Age, produced at RAND, eventually earning the author a 2005 Nobel Prize in economy (or in security studies, if one reads closely the justification from The Royal Swedish Academy of Sciences). Even fun to read.

IMPORTANT WEBSITES

- **http://www.isn.ethz.ch** International Relations and Security Network, Center for Security Studies, ETH, Zurich, Switzerland. A good collection of links to both current security issues and centres of research. From here one can get to the institutes, journals, and organizations, of which there are too many to list individually here.

- **http://www.mitpressjournals.org/is** *International Security*, the leading mainstream journal.

- **http://www.tandf.co.uk/journals/titles/09636412.asp** *Security Studies*, another high-ranking journal mostly publishing American mainstream research, but often more open to deep theoretical debate than *International Security*.

- **http://ejt.sagepub.com** *European Journal of International Relations*. Much of the debate over the new European theories has taken place in general IR journals such as *EJIR*, *International Political Sociology*, *Review of International Studies*, and *Millennium*.

- **http://sdi.sagepub.com** *Security Dialogue* has recently developed into one of the leading places for discussion on 'human security', 'risk/security', 'gender and security', and the new European theories, while it is also relatively strong on critical policy articles.

Visit the Online Resource Centre that accompanies this book for lots of interesting additional material: www.oxfordtextbooks.co.uk/orc/collins4e/

Glossary

There is no single correct or agreed-upon definition of any of these terms, as you will no doubt have noticed already. This can be unsettling if you are used to the idea that there is a 'right answer' or the 'right definition'. The definitions offered indicate how they have been used in this book. The important thing is for you to be clear about how your sources use these terms and be clear about how you are using them yourself.

1925 Geneva Protocol for the Prohibition of the Use in War of Asphyxiating, Poisonous, or Other Gases, and of Bacteriological Methods of Warfare Outlawed the use in war of asphyxiating poisonous gases and liquids.

1972 Anti-Ballistic Missile Treaty The treaty banned the United States and the Soviet Union from constructing national missile defences. After giving the six months' notice called for by the Treaty, the United States withdrew from the agreement in June 2002, citing the Treaty's fundamental obsolescence. Critics decried the move, but the deployment of extremely modest US missile defences have failed to generate an appreciable international response.

1972 Biological and Toxin Weapons Convention (BWC) Opened for signature on April 1972. Parties agreed not to stockpile biological weapons and toxins. In 1996, the fourth review conference failed to reach an agreement on verification procedures to strengthen the 1972 agreement. Although signatories continue to abide by the agreement, the treaty has not entered into force.

2002 Moscow Treaty Agreement between the United States and Russia to cut deployed offensive strategic nuclear warheads to between 1,700 and 2,200 by 31 December 2012. Unlike previous arms control treaties between the superpowers, this treaty leaves it up to the parties to determine the pace of reductions and exact composition of its forces on New Year's Eve 2012.

9/11 A widely accepted shorthand way of referring to the 11 September 2001 al-Qaeda attack on the two towers of the World Trade Center in New York City, the Pentagon in Washington DC, and the failed attempt to crash a fourth aircraft into the White House.

Advanced persistent threats A cyber-attack category, which connotes an attack with a high degree of sophistication and stealithiness over a prolonged duration of time. The attack objectives typically extend beyond immediate financial gain.

Agency–structure debate This refers to whether the structure of the international system directs the behaviour and actions of its parts. A neorealist view of this debate is that the structure of anarchy conditions the behaviour of states. The opposite view would be that actors construct the structure. Constructivists argue that both structures and actors influence each other.

Agenda for Peace A report to the UN Secretary-General in January 1992 advocating peacekeeping, peacemaking, and conflict prevention as priorities for avoiding military confrontations.

AIDS Acquired Immunodeficiency Syndrome or Acquired Immune Deficiency Syndrome; it refers to a host of symptoms and illnesses caused by the weakening of the human immune system due to infection with the human immunodeficiency virus.

AIDS-related illnesses Illnesses such as pneumocystis pneumonia (a lung infection) and Kaposi's sarcoma (a skin cancer) that accompany the onset of AIDS; strictly speaking people do not die of AIDS, but of AIDS-related illnesses.

Alienation In historical materialist thought: the lack of control by most people of their labour in a context in which this is represented as natural and inevitable, with people often feeling this alienation emotionally, as they spend most of their lives doing work they do not believe in just to survive.

Alliance The coming-together of a group of states with a formal agreement to work together to accomplish a particular military security objective.

Al-Qaeda (The Base) A network of extremist Muslim groups, initially organized by Osama bin Laden, which seeks to drive Western ideas and influence out of Muslim countries.

Al-Qaeda in the Arabian Peninsula (AQIM) Local global jihadists operating in Yemen who have affiliated with Al-Qaeda.

Al-Qaeda in the Islamic Maghreb Local dissident groups in the region have reformed and connected themselves into the global jihad as a local franchise of Al-Qaeda.

Anarchy In the field of international politics, a term for the absence of any ultimate power and authority over states. In short, the absence of a world or regional government, or binding international law, that is superior to states; it does not mean that international relations are chaotic.

Anthrax Disease caused by the *Bacillus anthracis* bacterium that forms in spores. The infection in humans can occur in the skin, lungs, and digestive tract and is often contracted from infected animals (e.g. sheep). It is not contagious, but, because humans can be infected by coming into contact with anthrax spores, it is considered to be a good candidate for weaponization.

Arms control Represents 'restraint internationally exercised upon armaments policy, whether in respect of the level of armaments, their character, deployment or use'.

Attack vectors A path or means by which unauthorized access to a computer or network can be gained.

Attribution problem Refers to the difficulty to clearly determine who is initially responsible for a cyber-attack due to the fact that online identities can be hidden.

Audience It consists of a group (public opinion, politicians, military officers, or other elites) that needs to be convinced that a referent object is existentially threatened.

Aum Shinriyko A Japanese religious cult that released Sarin gas in the Tokyo subway system in an effort to kill thousands.

Autocrat A political ruler wielding strong centralized powers of governance and little popular legitimacy for that power.

Autonomy Being free from any higher power or authority, or, inside a state, being free within a specified geographical area or sphere of activity from such authority. In international politics states claim autonomy on a scale unmatched by, accorded to, or exercised by any other political actor.

Balance of power In international politics, a term used primarily in three ways; first, to refer to an existing distribution of power among members of an international system; second, to refer to a distribution of power in which—among the major members—power is distributed so that the members balance each other's power and therefore constrain each other; third, to label a strategy for state security that is preoccupied with creating or maintaining a distribution of power in the system that is considered beneficial in terms of maintaining security and stability.

Balancing The options available to a state for increasing its military capabilities and ability to defend. There are two key types of balancing. External balancing refers to forming alliances with other states, thereby enabling the state to draw on other states' resources. When people think about balancing, this is the type they usually imagine. There is, however, a second key type of balancing—internal balancing: a state's internal efforts to increase its own economic capability and to build larger and/or better military forces.

Bandwagoning When the response by a government to the rise of an increasingly powerful state is to associate or ally itself with it. This is in contrast to a strategy of opposing or balancing—trying to offset the power of—such a powerful state.

Big Data Refers to datasets whose size is beyond the ability of typical database software tools to capture, store, manage, and analyse. Analysis of Big Data is both a process and framework that refers to tools and methodologies that aim to transform massive quantities of raw data into 'data about data'—for analytical purposes.

Biopolitics In his later writings, Michel Foucault turned to the analysis of contemporary political life, and argued that since the middle of the nineteenth century the state has been basing claims to legitimacy on its capacity to make populations live. That is, the state has increasingly come into the business of providing for the health, education, and well-being of its people, which has in turn underpinned the state's claim to the right to continue. This notion of the biopolitical states is in contrast to the traditional sovereign state, which based its legitimacy on the basis of its ability to kill.

Bipolar The label for a power distribution in an international system in which two states are roughly equal in power and are each much more powerful than any of the other members. As a result, the power of each balances that of the other, and each has a number of states associated or allied with it. The relations between the two giants and between the two blocs dominate the politics of the system.

Black market Commercial activity where goods are bought and sold in violation of laws or regulations.

Blackmail Pro-active use of threats and limited force to initiate target action.

Botnets (or bots) A collection of compromised computers connected to the Internet. They run hidden and can be exploited for further use by the person controlling them remotely.

Bretton Woods system The institutional arrangements created by the USA and the UK for managing the post-Second World War international economic system, including the International Monetary Fund, the International Bank for Reconstruction and Development (now the World Bank), and the General Agreements on Tariffs and Trade as the primary institutions.

Brute/full-scale force Use of force to impose compliance on the adversary or settle the dispute at hand.

Bugs Term used to describe an error, flaw, mistake, failure, or fault in a computer program that produces an incorrect or unexpected result, or causes it to behave in unintended ways.

Capitalism A mode of production characterized by private property, the profit motive, competition, and freedom of contract with this system guaranteed by the state and norms that are embedded in the habits and practices of states and international organizations. Historical materialists disagree with the liberal position that this is a free, just, mutually beneficial system in tune with human nature. The representation of aspects of economics by realism and liberalism as somehow non-political and private is regarded by historical materialists as serving the interests of capitalists (by allowing them to retain unelected and for the most part unaccountable control).

Capitalists (capitalist ruling class) Those who own and control the means of production of goods and services in capitalism.

Causality The relationship between cause and effect.

Chemical Weapons Convention An agreement by which state parties agree never, under any circumstances, to acquire, stockpile, or transfer chemical weapons, to use chemical weapons, to prepare to use chemical weapons, or to induce others to engage in activity prohibited by the Convention. The Convention entered into force on 29 April 1997. The Organization for the Prohibition of Chemical Weapons in The Hague, Netherlands, is responsible for implementing the Chemical Weapons Convention.

Civil society (1) The totality of all individuals and groups in a society who are not acting as participants in any government institutions; or (2) all individuals and groups who are neither participants in government nor acting in the interests of commercial companies. The two meanings are incompatible and contested. There is a third meaning: the network of social institutions and practices (economic relationships, family and kinship groups, religious, and other social affiliations) that underlie strictly political institutions.

Class In historical materialist terms class refers to one's position in relation to ownership or control of the physical and financial assets necessary for production (at this stage in history mostly capitalist production). Hence there are in capitalist society two basic classes—a ruling class of capitalists, which retains as profit some of the value produced by labour, and a ruled class of workers compelled to sell their labour to capitalists in order to survive—but also managers, etc. In contrast, social class refers to perceived and objective stratifications of society, whereas elites are composed of those with concentrations of power of any kind. Classes and elites may overlap, may be united on some things and divided on others, and their unity or division may be perceptual or objective.

Coercive diplomacy Use of threats and limited force to influence the adversary to stop or undo something it has already embarked upon.

Cold War The global competition from 1945 to 1989 (when the wall dividing West and East Germany came down) between capitalist and communist states in which the United States and Soviet Union did not fight each other directly but backed local rivals in armed conflicts. At its peak in the early 1980s, the two alliances (NATO and the Warsaw Pact) deployed over 60,000 nuclear weapons and spent $1,000 billion a year (2006 prices) on the military.

Commodification Turning previously non-monetary social relations into monetary relations.

Commodity Commodities are a class of goods for which there is demand, but are qualitatively the same, whoever supplies them. For example, the price of copper is universal, not dependent on the supplier, and is determined as a function of the market as a whole. Contrast this with other types of goods, such as a computer, where price is influenced by brand and perceived quality, among other factors.

Common security Joint action by a number of states to address shared problems that cannot be solved by the actions of any single state.

Comprehensive Test Ban Treaty (CTBT) A disarmament measure, this treaty bans nuclear testing, thereby disrupting the development of human capital and technology needed to create and maintain a nuclear arsenal. Over 148 countries have signed the CTBT. The United States Senate failed to ratify the treaty in December 1999. The United States and the rest of the world, however, have maintained a nuclear-test moratorium so far in the twenty-first century.

Conflict management Concerns the amelioration of conflict between one or more parties.

Constructivism General 'school' within IR theory that rose during the late 1980s–early 1990s to become the leading alternative to the dominant rationalist theories of neorealism and neoliberalism. Constructivists emphasize the importance of ideational factors such as culture, beliefs, norms, ideas, and identity. Constructivism covers a wide spectrum from the borderland to poststructuralism/postmodernism to 'soft constructivists', who share the postivism and state-centrism of mainstream approaches.

Copenhagen School Emerged at the Conflict and Peace Research Institute (COPRI) of Copenhagen and represented by the writings of Barry Buzan, Ole Wæver, Jaap de Wilde, and others. It is partly about widening the threats and referent objects, especially societal/identity, partly about paying more attention to the regional level, but mainly about focusing on securitization—the social processes by which groups of people construct something as a threat—thus offering a constructivist counterpoint to the materialist threat analysis of traditional strategic studies.

Crime syndicates Loosely tied gangs that engage in organized criminal activity.

Critical (information) infrastructures Critical infrastructure includes all systems and assets whose incapacity or destruction would have a debilitating impact on the national security and the economic and social well-being of a nation. Critical information infrastructures are components such as telecommunications, computers/software, Internet, satellites, fibre optics, etc.

Critical infrastructure protection Measures to secure all systems and assets whose incapacity or destruction would have a debilitating impact on the national security, and the economic and social well-being of a nation.

Critical realism The philosophical position that there are social structures independent of discourses about them, which have the capacity to have particular effects and which have more potential to change in some ways than in others.

Critical Security Studies Based partly on a critique of the state-centric paradigm and partly on the prescription for emancipatory action. See Chapters 7 and 8 in this volume.

Cuban Missile Crisis One of the most dangerous crises of the Cold War, when in October 1962 the United States blocked the Soviet installation of medium-range nuclear-armed missiles in Cuba.

Cultural autonomy The granting of rights in relation to the means of cultural reproduction, such as autonomy over educational and religious institutions.

Cultural cleansing The deliberate destruction of symbols, signs, and institutions, such as schools, museums, and places of worship of one ethnic group by another.

Cultural nationalism A movement/project designed to generate strong feelings of self-identification, emphasizing various commonalities such as language, religion, and history.

Cyber-crime A criminal activity done using computers and the Internet.

Cyber-deterrence Influencing an actor, either by denying the potential gains of the actor or by threatening punishment through the use of retaliation, in order to prevent the actor from utilizing cyberspace as a means to degrade, disrupt, manipulate, deny, or destroy any portion of the critical national infrastructure.

Cyber-espionage The unauthorized probing to test a target computer's configuration or evaluate its system defences, or the unauthorized viewing and copying of data files.

Cyberspace The electronic medium of computer networks, in which online communication takes place.

Cyber-terror Unlawful attacks against computers, networks, and the information stored therein, to intimidate or coerce a government or its people in furtherance of political or social objectives. Such an attack should result in violence against persons or property, or at least cause enough harm to generate the requisite fear level to be considered 'cyber-terrorism'. The term is also used loosely for cyber-incidents of a political nature.

Cyber-war The use of computers to disrupt the activities of an enemy country, especially deliberate attacks on communication systems. The term is also used loosely for cyber-incidents of a political nature.

Cyber-weapon Malware used for cyber-war activities.

DDoS-attack Attempt to make a computer or network resource unavailable to its intended users, mostly by saturating the target machine with external communications requests so that it cannot respond to legitimate traffic, or responds so slowly as to be rendered effectively unavailable.

Democratic peace A theory claiming that democratic states do not go to war with each other, with variants of the theory differing as to what it is about democracies—as democracies—that produces this behaviour.

Desecuritization Refers to a process that reintroduces a securitized matter into the standard political domain.

Deterrence Use of threats and specific actions to discourage the adversary from doing something in the first place.

Development Extensive enhancement of a society's basic capabilities and resources. This is of great interest to many governments because they can tap the additional capabilities and resources for their own purposes and can cite them to build political popularity and legitimacy with citizens.

Dialogical Relating to and in the form of dialogue.

Discourse In its most loose usage of the term by adherents of objectivism, a discourse is simply a way of describing or labelling a real phenomenon. In contrast, for constructivists, discourses are practices (words and other actions) that play an active role by giving phenomena meaning, by being inherently normative (that is, having inbuilt ideas of right and wrong), and by silencing (that is, making it more difficult to understand the phenomenon in other ways).

Dismal science An early version of economics claimed that population growth would always match or exceed economic growth so that poverty was inevitable, which led to economics being labelled a dismal science.

Dutch disease A phenomenon that marks many of those economies heavily reliant upon the exploitation of natural resources (such as oil and gas). Vast quantities of revenue and foreign direct investment into an economy work to drive up the exchange rate. In turn, this higher rate reduces the competitive nature of other domestic sectors (primarily industrial), thus 'hollowing out' the economy and increasing reliance on resource 'rents'. This has consequences for the responsiveness of governments, as those dependent on income generated from rents rather than taxes are not driven to ensure political legitimacy to the same extent.

Economic Community of West African States (ECOWAS) A regional group of fifteen West African countries founded in 1975 to promote economic integration.

ECOWAS monitoring group (ECOMOG) A multinational armed force that was established in West Africa by the Economic Community of West African States (ECOWAS); it is not a standing army, but rather an agreement for cooperation between several militaries in the region to work together when necessary.

Elite accommodation The process of managing or accommodating the threat by powerful elites, including strongmen, to the security of the regime, usually through various forms of power sharing, patronage, or graft.

Emancipation Emancipation refers to the freeing of people from the structures of oppression or domination in which they find themselves. Various forms of critical theory are driven by a political commitment to emancipation from different structures of oppression and domination. Generally, post-Marxist Critical Theory will speak of emancipation in the singular, emphasizing its belief that the political economy is the root of all oppression; poststructural critical theories are more likely to speak of emancipations in the plural, emphasizing the multiple forms of domination, or the multiple means of subjection.

Empirical Relating to facts as opposed to abstractions such as theories or values.

'End of history' The German philosopher Hegel saw history as an evolution through repeated struggles towards a perfect society. Francis Fukuyama, in 1992, suggested that, with the collapse of communism and the triumph of democracy and capitalism, this evolution was now coming to an end.

Endogenous Having internal origin; associated with a referent such as 'inside the state'.

Energy diversification High levels of energy security depend upon ensuring a diversified set of energy sources. In this context, diversification can refer to meeting needs through a range of energy *types* (such as oil, solar, nuclear), or to meeting needs through a range of sources of one particular energy type. By diversifying oil production away from the Persian Gulf, the USA and other key consumers hope to improve their energy security, by making their economies less reliant on the unstable Middle East.

Environment That part of the Earth's surface that includes living organisms, the remains of living organisms, and the physical and chemical components of the total system necessary for, or involved in the process of, life (Boyden et al. 1990: 314).

Environmental change Short- and long-term changes in biological, physical, and chemical components and systems resulting from both human activities and natural processes.

Environmental security The assurance that individuals and groups have that they can avoid or adapt to environmental change without critical adverse effects.

Epidemic An usually large or rapid outbreak of a contagious disease that exceeds the normal level in a particular population at a given time.

Epistemic violence The imposition of one knowledge system onto other peoples, practices, and places in ways that actively deny, discredit, and destroy other knowledge systems, including local ones, which are treated as inferior.

Epistemology Epistemology is the *study* of the way we know. Within a theory or approach, the epistemology refers to the set of assumptions about how knowledge is generated that inform that theory or approach. All forms of scholarship must make assumptions about knowledge; therefore they must have an epistemology.

Ethnic cleansing The deliberate killing, use of violence, or deportation of members of one ethnic group by another.

Eurocentrism The assumption of European exceptionalism in analysis of world history. The practice of seeing the world from a European perspective—whether conceptually, theoretically, empirically, or normatively—and the implied belief in the superiority of European culture, civilization, institutions, and ways of knowing.

Euzkadi ta Askatasuna (ETA) The Basque dissident group that has used terrorism for over twenty-five years in an effort to achieve independence for the region.

Excess production capacity The amount of spare production potential that is not currently being used. Acts as a cushion for international energy markets, where in times of crisis additional capacity can be brought online to stabilize prices. Saudi excess capacity is vast, and has been used at many points in history (such as during the 1991 Gulf War) to stabilize markets.

Existential threat Threats to the continued existence of a referent object. Individuals face an existential threat when they are threatened with death; states face an existential threat when, among other things, they are threatened with external invasion and conquest. Existential threats are the most serious threats a referent object can face, and thus are seen to justify the most extensive measures to secure against them.

Exogenous Having external origin; often associated with a referent such as 'outside the state'.

Exploitation In historical materialism this refers to the fact that workers are paid less than the value of their labour: this surplus value, as it is called by historical materialists, goes to the capitalist as profit. Hence the concept of exploitation is used here both to describe something and also to make a negative value judgement on it.

Export control A legal and regulatory measure to monitor the shipment of sensitive, particularly military-related, items out of one country and to another country or customer that may be a security concern.

Extraordinary measures Such measures go beyond rules ordinarily abided by and are thus located outside the bounds of political procedures and practices. Their adoption involves the identification and classification of some issue as an existential threat.

Failed state A state that is incapable of and/or unwilling to meet the basic needs of its population, provide domestic order, and represent national interests externally. This term is often used in the context of assumptions that the lack of performance is mainly due to factors internal to that state and that external intervention or occupation is therefore legitimate and necessary. Hence it can have ideological functions, with the role of global capitalism or the actions of external actors in undermining that state capacity or preventing its establishment obscured.

Fascists (Italy) The right-wing party that used violence and terrorism to help Benito Mussolini take power in Italy in 1922.

Fatah The major faction in the Palestinian Liberation Organization when it was opposed to Israel has reappeared in the West Bank and Gaza in opposition to Hamas.

Femininity/feminism The advocacy of women's rights based upon ideas of equality between men and women. Note, though, that there are many variations of feminism. These include liberal, radical, and Marxist categories.

Fiat currency A currency backed by the good faith of the governing authorities, but containing no intrinsic value. A gold coin, for example, requires no government to hold value; melt down the images, and the value remains. A US dollar bill, however, when ripped into pieces, becomes worthless.

Foreign direct investment (FDI) Investment carried out with the aim of acquiring a lasting interest in an enterprise operating in an economy other than that of the investor, the investor's purpose being to have an effective voice in the management of the enterprise.

Free ride Obtaining something valuable by relying on the efforts of others to supply it while doing little oneself to obtain it. For example, a country in a strategically vital location may remain safe while doing little to protect itself if it has a powerful ally (a good example is Japan).

Free-trade agreement An agreement among a limited number of states to remove all or nearly all the barriers between them on trade, flows of money, and other economic activities—in contrast to an arrangement to do this that is open to all members of the international system who wish to join.

Gamma radiation Also known as penetrating radiation because dense shielding is needed to protect individuals from its effects. Gamma radiation is high-energy ionizing radiation, which is one of the first effects produced by a nuclear detonation. Because it can penetrate the body, it is usually the primary cause of radiation sickness.

Gender Refers not just to the biological differences between men and women but to a set of culturally shaped and defined characteristics, which underpin the notion of what it is to be a man or a woman.

Geneva Conventions There are four Geneva Conventions, signed 12 August 1949, and the two additional Protocols of 8 June 1977. In addition, there are many other international treaties that govern the conduct of war or establish human rights standards.

Genocide Usually refers to the deliberate killing of civilians with the intention of destroying an ethnic, national, religious, or other group in whole or in part.

Global jihad The term for a loose network of Muslim extremist groups seeking to fight Western influence in Muslim countries and in some cases to establish a new caliphate for all Muslims.

Global North The section of humanity that is deeply integrated into advanced capitalism, is wealthy, and on behalf of which the global South is contained and securitized. The global North has a major presence in Southern states via those elites that are part of the global North.

Global South The section of humanity that consumes minimally and that is marginalized, uninsured, policed, and repressed. Northern states have substantial parts of their population that are part of the global South.

Global War on Terror A general term used by President George W. Bush of the United States to cover the vigorous US response to the 9/11 attacks in New York and Washington.

Globalization A term for the process, and the effects, of a sharp increase in the interactions among societies in recent decades in economic matters, population shifts, cultural interactions, information flows, and other areas. Often seen as revolutionizing international politics and the world; often criticized as grievously harmful.

Greenham Common Site of a US airbase. From 1981 until 1999 tens of thousands of women either lived at or visited the Greenham Common airbase in the UK. The women protested against the decision made by NATO to site cruise missiles at the base. It was the site of a number of high-profile protests. In December 1982, for example, 30,000 women joined hands to 'embrace the base'. In March 1991, the United States removed the cruise missiles under the terms of the 1987 INF (Intermediate Nuclear Forces) agreement.

Guantanamo Naval Base US naval base in Cuba that has served as a prison for detaining suspected terrorists.

Guerrilla Someone fighting for primarily political purposes, usually against a state, as part of a group that is not as rigidly hierarchically organized as a regular army. Literally someone fighting a small war.

Gunrunner A person who smuggles weapons and military equipment from one destination to another, typically in violation of the law.

Hacker Term used in two main ways, one positive and one negative. Can mean a person particularly skilled with computers (positive) or be used as a general term for a computer criminal (negative).

Hacktivism The combination of hacking and activism, including operations that use hacking techniques against a target's Internet site with the intention of disrupting normal operations.

Hamas (acronym in Arabic for Islamic Resistance Movement) Islamic group in the Gaza Strip and West Bank that seeks to create an Islamic Palestinian state encompassing both the Occupied Territories and Israel and that has relied on suicide attacks.

Hegemon/hegemony A state or coalition much more powerful than any other state or likely coalition and thus able to dominate an international system.

Historical materialism Human history, politics, and subjectivity are influenced by particular forms of the ownership and control of the production of goods and services and associated class conflict. At its most useful, HM sees the economic and the political as inseparable, does not assert that economics determines everything else, considers the possibility that human subjectivity (thoughts and feelings) play a significant role, produces historically specific analyses rather than supposedly universal generalizations, and draws on the insights of other theoretical perspectives.

HIV The human immunodeficiency virus that causes AIDS. It is transmitted through sexual contact with an infected person, by sharing needles with someone who is infected, from mother to child during or after birth, and through transfusions with infected blood.

Home bases Used to designate countries where organized crime groups originate, often because the rule of law is weak and law enforcement is ineffective.

Horizontal competition Where groups must change their ways because of the overriding linguistic and cultural influences of others.

Host nations Term used to designate countries that are the main targets of transnational crime organizations.

Human security Emphasizes the safety and well-being of individuals, groups, and communities as opposed to prioritizing the state and its interests.

Humanitarian intervention Article 24(1) Chapter VII of the UN Charter gives the Security Council the power to 'restore international peace and stability' if a threat, including a humanitarian disaster, is imminent and if there is consensus in the Council. The intervention in the Kosovo crisis, however, was undertaken without the Security Council's approval.

Ideology Ideology can be described as a world-view, made up of a comprehensive and internally consistent set of ideas about the world, particularly on what the social world consists of and how it operates. It will include, implicitly or explicitly, a set of attitudes, moral beliefs, and empirical beliefs. An ideology should provide some explanation of how the world has come to be as it is and an opinion on how the world should be, in order to provide a guide to action.

IGOs Intergovernmental organizations; organizations with governments as the members.

Illicit An act that is not only illegal, but is contrary to accepted practice or custom. Illicit actions are often considered immoral actions.

Imperialism Relations of domination and subordination across societies. In historical materialist thought, imperialism connects the global order to particular forms of state–society relations in class terms that are themselves expressions of particular modes of production.

Indigenous peoples A term that refers to groups protected in international or national legislation as having a set of specific rights based on their historical ties to a particular territory, and their cultural or historical distinctiveness from other populations.

Information age Signifies the current era that is characterized by information, especially the ability of individuals to transfer information freely, and to have instant access to knowledge previously unavailable.

Information and communications technology An umbrella term that includes any communication device or application, encompassing: radio, television, cellular phones, computer and network hardware and software, satellite systems, etc., as well as the various services and applications associated with them, such as videoconferencing and distance learning.

Information revolution The dynamic evolution and propagation of information and communication technologies into all aspects of life.

Information warfare A form of modern warfare, in which information takes centre stage.

Insecurity The risk of something bad happening to a thing that is valued.

Insecurity dilemma The unique situation in which a state's primary threats originate from the internal rather than external sphere, and where efforts by the ruling elite to increase regime security creates further insecurity for the regime, the state, and society.

Insurgent A guerrilla seeking to overthrow a state. This term has fewer connotations of legitimacy than guerrilla, and even fewer than the term 'resistance' member.

International Atomic Energy Agency (IAEA) An agency of the United Nations, the IAEA was created as part of the Eisenhower administration's 'Atoms for Peace' initiative to allow the civilian application of nuclear power to generate electricity. The IAEA is charged with monitoring the civilian application of nuclear technology to guarantee that nuclear materials and know-how are not diverted into clandestine programmes to develop nuclear weapons.

International civil society The label for the efforts of myriads of non-governmental organizations active in international politics in pressuring and lobbying governments, in calling attention to issues, problems, and developments, and in taking direct action to deal with them. These efforts are seen by some analysts as evidence of, and a major contribution to, the development of a global community.

International Criminal Court The first ever permanent, treaty-based, international criminal court established to promote the rule of law and to ensure that the gravest international crimes do not go unpunished. The Court is complementary to national criminal jurisdictions. The jurisdiction and functioning of the Court are governed by the provisions of the Rome Statute. The Rome Statute of the International Criminal Court was established on 17 July 1998 and entered into force on 1 July 2002.

International regimes Clusters of norms and patterns of behaviour, sometimes codified in international agreements and managed through international organizations, that have been developed to manage the interactions among states and other entities in specific areas of activity. Examples include the regimes on the conduct and treatment of diplomatic personnel, on nuclear non-proliferation, and on proper reactions to the outbreak of highly contagious and lethal diseases.

International relations An interdisciplinary area of study, also called international politics, which at its core examines interactions between states but, with the inclusion of world politics, now canvasses a broader array of interactions, issues, and actors.

Internet A worldwide system of computer networks in which users at any one computer can, if they have permission, get information from any other computer.

Intersubjectivity Refers to the fact that ideas and concepts are held in common by a group.

Intra-state war The primary form of international conflict today, in which organized and sustained political violence takes place between armed groups representing the state and one or more non-state groups. It takes place primarily within the borders of a single state, but usually has significant international dimensions and a tendency to spill over into bordering states.

IRA (Irish Republican Army) Group that has used terrorism and violence in its efforts to achieve the union of Northern Ireland with the Republic of Ireland.

Irish National Liberation Army (INLA) Dissident group in Northern Ireland that has combined nationalist with a Marxist-Leninist leftist ideology to justify its attacks.

Islamic Jihad Small group in the Gaza Strip and West Bank that has sought to create an Islamic Palestinian state and which has frequently relied on suicide attacks.

Islamic State in Iraq and Syria (ISIS) ISIS draws upon Islamic extremists in Syria who are fighting the government in that region and who have invaded northern Iraq in an effort to create a fundamentalist Islamic state.

Just War Theory An ancient notion drawn principally from the Christian tradition but with some contribution from Islamic thought that assumes that states occasionally need to go to war with one another but that attempts to minimize war's dire consequences by spelling out both the conditions that must exist before the war is initiated (*jus ad bellum*) and what states can and cannot do during the conflict (*jus in bello*).

Korean War One of the worst East–West confrontations of the Cold War era, the Korean War (1950–3) initially involved a North Korean invasion of South Korea in June 1953 but was fought principally between the Chinese and a UN force headed by the United States.

Ku Klux Klan (KKK) American racist and right-wing group that first appeared in the nineteenth century after the Civil War and that was active again in the 1920s, 1960s, and 1970s.

Kurds Ethnic group in Turkey (and Iraq and Iran) that has been involved in terrorist campaigns directed towards creating an independent state.

Launder The process of 'washing' dirty money in that funds earned from illegal or illicit activities are routed through various legitimate businesses or financial markets.

Leaderless resistance Term used to describe loose organizations where the leadership suggests courses of action or identifies possible targets but avoids issuing direct orders to avoid arrest or prosecution.

Liberal/liberalism A school of thought in the study of international politics emphasizing the existence of an international society with common habits and practices that enable growing cooperation and collective management of international politics. Liberals tend to believe that world politics is basically evolving towards tolerance and peace because these cooperative developments lead to reducing conflict, insecurity, and warfare without sacrificing national sovereignty.

Licence Legal permission to engage in a particular, authorized action.

Limited force Use of force to influence the adversary to comply that leaves the adversary with a capacity for continued resistance.

Malaria A life-threatening parasitic disease transmitted by mosquitoes; it is characterized by fever and influenza-like symptoms, including chills, headache, and malaise.

Malware A collective term for all types of malicious code and software.

Manhattan Project Codename given to the British–American effort to build a fission bomb during the Second World War.

Marxism An influential school of thought in international politics derived from the ideas of Karl Marx, Lenin, and others. It stresses the role of dominant classes and the dynamics of international capitalism in shaping the behaviour of governments, and of dominant states and societies in maintaining a very unequal, and exploitative, international system.

Masculinity Those qualities that are considered appropriate to a man, usually associated with strength and bravery.

Mass atrocities Usually used as shorthand for the widespread and systematic use of war crimes, ethnic cleansing, and crimes against humanity. Such crimes include the deliberate killing of civilians without genocidal intent and the forced displacement of populations.

Material violence The application of physical force, particularly to human beings in ways that cause pain, distress, fear, suffering, or death and the destruction of built environments.

Middlemen People who act as 'go-betweens' and connect buyers and sellers in a particular area of trade.

Migration The movement of people from one place to settle in another, especially a foreign country. The host society, through a shift in the composition of the population, might be changed by the influx of those from outside.

Militarism The prevalence of military sentiments among people and the idea that military efficiency or military preparedness is the highest duty of the state.

Militarization The process by which some aspect of social relations is integrated into the organization of physical violence and threats of violence for political purposes (cf. militarism).

Millennium Development Goals (MDGs) Eight international development goals that were established following the Millennium Summit of the United Nations in 2000.

Misogyny A dislike, perhaps even a deep-seated dislike, for women or characteristics traditionally associated with women.

Mode of production A way of producing, distributing, and exchanging goods and services, including the wider social relations associated with that, such as ideas about the meaning of freedom, individuality, and so on.

Money laundering Process by which money derived from illegal activities is made to appear as if proceeding from legitimate business enterprises.

Morbidity The number of people in a given population afflicted with a disease.

Multipolar A power distribution in an international system in which three or more major states are much more powerful than any others and roughly equivalent in power among themselves. Shifting patterns of collusion and rivalry among these states, reflecting their preoccupation with the distribution of power among them, dominate the politics of the system.

Narco-trafficking The transport and distribution of illegal drugs.

Neoliberalism A set of market-liberal economic policies with its roots in the classical economic theory of Adam Smith (1723–90) and others. In the developing world, neoliberalism emerged in opposition to the development strategies based on import-substitution industrialization that had dominated the period 1945 to the early 1980s. Development grounded in neoliberal theory is often linked to the Washington Consensus (reducing the role of the state, privatization, deregulation, trade and financial liberation, promoting foreign direct investment) and is a key feature of the structural adjustment programmes promoted by the IMF and World Bank. More recently, attention has been drawn to neoliberalism as the economic ideology behind capitalist globalization.

Neorealism–structural realism A variant of the realist theoretical perspective that emphasizes anarchy and the distribution of power among the major states (the system structure) as the key factors shaping the behaviour of governments, as opposed to the domestic characteristics of states—leadership, nature of political system, national culture, etc. This was the dominant approach in the field in the 1970s and 1980s.

Networks A series of nodes that are connected.

Neutrality The adoption by a state of a particular legal stance, recognized by the other states in the international community, that forbids it from being a member of a military alliance, or of pursuing policies that clearly identify it with such an alliance.

NGOs Non-governmental organizations of individuals or groups, across or above national boundaries, that do not include governments.

Nodes The elements that make up a network. These may be individuals or organizations. Law enforcement attempts to identify the nodes that are most critical to the functioning of the network and strike at these.

Non-interference An important principle of international society that holds that states should not interfere in the domestic affairs of other states. This principle is enshrined in Article 2(7) of the UN Charter.

Non-politicized issue An issue is said to be non-politicized when it is not a matter for state action and is not included in public debate.

Non-Proliferation Treaty (NPT) One of the key arms-control treaties of the Cold War era, the NPT was open for signature in 1968 and allows countries to develop civil nuclear power under international inspection, but not nuclear weapons. By 2006, 187 countries had signed.

Non-state actor A term widely used to mean any actor that is not a government. Ambiguity is best avoided by referring separately to categories, transnational actors, and international organizations.

Non-traditional security This category of security studies focuses on non-military challenges to security. It incorporates the state but also includes other referent objects.

Norms Concern the moral and ethical dimensions of international affairs, such as rules, beliefs, and ideas.

NSA revelations of 2013 Refers to the leaking of top secret documents about a global surveillance program of the United States National Security Agency (NSA) and its international partners by ex-NSA contractor Edward Snowden.

Objective/objectivism The view that we can know what is real and what has been distorted by misrepresentation in ideology, propaganda, or, in its loosest sense, discourse.

Ontology Ontology is the *study* of being. Within a theory or approach, the ontology refers to the set of assumptions about the nature of being in the world that inform that theory or approach. All forms of social investigation must make assumptions about the nature of the world they investigate (what kinds of thing populate that world, what sorts of relationship exist among those things); therefore they must have an ontology.

Organized crime Profit-driven crime committed by any 'structured group of three or more persons existing for a period of time and acting in concert'.

Oslo Accords Agreement in 1993 between Israel and the PLO that provided for increasing degrees of self-governance for the Palestinians in parts of the West Bank and the Gaza Strip but that collapsed in the face of attacks by extremists on both sides.

Pandemic The outbreak of infectious disease across a geographically extensive area; a regional or global epidemic.

Paramilitary Someone fighting for primarily political purposes, usually on behalf of a state, as part of a group that is not as rigidly hierarchically organized as a regular army.

Paris School Draws especially on the theories of Pierre Bourdieu and Michel Foucault to establish an approach that studies the discursive and non-discursive practices through which especially bureaucratic agencies construct insecurity and unease in their competition for tasks and control. Technologies of surveillance and control are much emphasized, especially in the study of issues such as migration and terrorism.

Patriot Act (United States) Legislation passed after 9/11 providing the government with greater surveillance opportunities and greater freedom to deal with suspected terrorists.

Peace building Actions that support political, economic, social, and military measures and structures, aiming to strengthen and solidify political settlements in order to redress the causes of conflict.

PLO (Palestinian Liberation Organization) Umbrella liberation organization representing a variety of secular and nationalist Palestinian groups.

Pluralistic security community A concept developed by Karl Deutsch of a group of independent and sovereign states so harmonious in their relations that they have no inclination to go to war with each other and thus do not fear each other. It was first applied to the states in the North Atlantic region associated with NATO and the West in the 1950s.

Policy community All the actors that inform and participate in the process of formulating policy, which can include politicians, members of the judiciary, public servants, academics, members of the private sector, think tanks, civil society groups, and policy analysts.

Political entrepreneur Someone who makes resource allocation decisions and takes risks. This person sees an opportunity to profit politically and takes the action necessary to seize this opportunity.

Political (ethnic) nationalism As with cultural nationalism, a movement/project designed to generate feelings of self-identification, but where this carries with it an explicit territorial element.

Politicized issue An issue becomes politicized when it is part of public policy and managed within the standard political system.

Popular Front for the Liberation of Palestine (PFLP) Palestinian group that combined nationalism with Marxist-Leninist views and that was frequently at odds with the PLO leadership.

Postcolonial critique Analysis of world politics—whether in epistemological, theoretical, empirical, or normative terms—from the point of view of those subject to European imperialism and its consequences across the past five centuries. Postcolonial critique seeks to open space for transformation of the world in anti-imperial ways.

Post-Marxism Claims to draw on but also to have transcended Marxism, mainly by having Marxist ideas playing a secondary and adapted role within an approach mainly drawing on other theorizing. Post-Marxism can be so 'post' that it is for all practical purposes non-Marxist.

Post-positivism Post-positivism is a generic term to refer to those theories and approaches that reject positivism as an adequate epistemology for the investigation of social life. Most forms of critical social theory are post-positivist in their epistemologies.

Poststructuralism This is the most thoroughgoing version of constructivism and places even more emphasis on the analysis of discourse.

Power The resources available to a state for building military forces. Key elements of power include a state's wealth, population, and technological sophistication. In this context, power does not refer to the ability to influence other states; instead, it refers narrowly to a state's potential to build military forces and the assets required effectively to command them.

Prevalence rate An epidemiological term referring to the proportion of those suffering from a disease in a particular population; it is usually cited in percentages.

Prevention of Terrorism Acts (United Kingdom) A series of acts giving the British government increased powers and discretion to deal first with suspected IRA terrorists and then with terrorists in general.

Prisoners of War (POW) Prisoners of War are combatants captured by the opposing side in war. They are imprisoned, usually until the end of conflict, but may be traded. Historically, few rules have governed the treatment of POWs until the Geneva and Hague Conference and the conventions of 1864, 1899, and 1907, which declared that POWs should be treated humanely.

Private military companies (PMCs) Corporate bodies that specialize in the provision of services associated with security and the use of force. There exist a huge number of such companies, providing a wide range of services, from static security of infrastructure to logistical support for state militaries, and from bodyguards to high-end military training and operations. States such as the USA have become increasingly reliant on these firms, which make up a rising proportion of personnel in any military campaign.

Prospect theory A theory of human perception that seeks to explain how an individual's actions might be influenced by perceived values of gains and losses as opposed to actual objective values.

Pugwash The Pugwash Conferences on Science and World Affairs is an international organization facilitating international dialogue among scholars and political practitioners to handle global security threats. A manifesto by Bertrand Russell and Albert Einstein in 1955 called for scientists to face the dangers of nuclear weapons, and a conference was held in Pugwash, Nova Scotia, in 1957. During the Cold War, the organization was often an important back channel between US and Soviet experts and intellectuals. Pugwash and its co-founder, Joseph Rotblat, received the Nobel Peace Prize in 1995 for their work for nuclear disarmament.

Punjab Indian province where Sikh dissidents used guerrilla warfare and terrorism in an effort to gain autonomy or independence for their religious group.

Q-fever Fever caused by the bacterium *Coxiella burneti*. Only about half of the people infected by the bacteria show symptoms. Because the bacterium is resistant to heat and drying, it would make a suitable agent for aerosol delivery. Although it is lethal in only about 2 per cent of cases, people who suffer Q-Fever can remain sick for months and require intensive medical treatment to counteract secondary infections (pneumonia and hepatitis).

RAND RAND Corporation was set up in 1946 by the US Air Force under contract to the Douglas Aircraft Company. In 1948 it became an independent non-profit organization and during the 1950s it formed the model for the modern think tank, famous enough for it to feature in the film *Dr Strangelove* as 'the BLAND Corporation'. In addition to research in engineering, health policy, and many other fields, inter-disciplinary work between especially mathematics, economics, and political science pioneered game theory and deterrence theory.

Rape/genocidal rape The forcing of women to have sex without their consent. Genocidal rape refers to the use of sex as an instrument of war used deliberately to humiliate women of a certain ethnicity or identity.

Rational choice Theories that focus on strategic, instrumental calculation and draw on economics in establishing models, where actors and their incentives are given, while often sophisticated calculations drawn from game theory explain behaviour, outcomes, and the effects of institutions and other conditions.

Rationalism One side of the main theoretical debate in IR theory during the 1980s and 1990s—the position, which adopts from rational-choice theory the general premise that theory should start from actors with given identities and interests, is that a specified rationality assumption explains behaviour (without necessarily including the more technical instruments of rational-choice theory). Neorealism and neoliberal institutionalism have been the main representatives of rationalist IR theory. (The terminology of rationalism versus reflectionism was introduced by Robert Keohane in 1988.)

Realist/realism The view that world politics is anarchic (in the sense of there being no overall authority, not chaos), the key actors are states, the key element of power is military power, and the moral duty of the decision maker is to serve the national interest. Realists assert that they see world politics as it really is, that world politics changes but does not progress, and it is the inherent sense of state insecurity that is critical in understanding the dynamics of international politics.

Red Army Faction (also often referred to as the Baader-Meinhof Gang) Small group of West German terrorists that mounted attacks against the state, and capitalism in general, in the 1970s and 1980s.

Red Brigades Large Italian leftist group that launched a major terrorist campaign that at times disrupted the Italian state and that took years for the state to defeat.

Referent object (of security) Common to most notions of security is the *protection* of some thing from a threat of some kind. The thing to be protected is the referent object. In conventional security studies, the referent object is generally considered to be the state. Other approaches to security consider other referent objects: for example, individuals, societies, economies, or the environment.

Reflectivism The counter-position to rationalism, where constructivists, feminists, poststructuralists, critical theorists, and moral theorists, among others, argue that state identities and interests are not given or stable but produced and reproduced continuously. Norms and identity shape policy as much as material interests. Often reflectivist theories will posit understanding rather than science-like explanation as the aim of research. (The terminology of rationalism versus reflectionism was introduced by Robert Keohane in 1988.)

Regime security A condition where the governing elite is secure from the threat of forced removal from office and can generally rule without major challenges to its authority.

Regimes The most widely used definition is formal or informal institutional arrangements consisting of 'sets of implicit or explicit principles, norms, rules, and decision-making procedures around which actors' expectations converge in a given area of international relations' (Krasner 1983: 2) The idea is that the participants in a regime understand and accept the proper ways of behaving on the matters to which a regime pertains, much like the way a code of etiquette in a culture works.

Regional trade arrangement An agreement among states in a specified geographic region making it easier for them to trade with each other and harder for outside states to trade with them, giving the members special trade advantages. This contradicts having a free trade international economic system.

Responsibility to Protect (R2P) A commitment made by all UN Member States in 2005 that they have a responsibility to protect their populations from genocide, war crimes, ethnic cleansing, and crimes against humanity and that the international community has a duty to take timely and decisive action in situations where the state manifestly fails in its responsibility.

Revolutionary Armed Forces of Colombia (FARC) Leftist group that has joined with Colombian drug cartels to prevent government control of significant areas of the country and has threatened the stability of the government.

Rule Effective control over a specified territory and the people who reside there by exercising the powers of a government.

Sarin A chemical weapon, originally developed in Germany as a pesticide in the 1930s, Sarin is a colourless, odourless, and tasteless liquid at room temperature. It interferes with the nervous system by impeding the proper function of the neurotransmitter acetylcholine. Exposure to Sarin causes neurons to be continuously stimulated by acetylcholine, leading to convulsions, coma, and suffocation.

Securitization Refers to the accepted classification of certain and not other phenomena, persons, or entities as existential threats requiring emergency measures. Through an act of securitization, a concern is framed as a security issue and moved from the politicized to the securitized.

Securitize A so-called speech act that elevates an issue with the objective of making it critically important.

Securitized issue An issue is securitized when it requires emergency actions beyond the state's standard political procedures.

Securitizing actor Refers to an actor who initiates a move of securitization through a speech act. Securitizing actors can be policy makers or bureaucracies but also transnational actors and individuals.

Security The assurance people have that they will continue to enjoy those things that are most important to their survival and well-being.

Security dilemma The situation that arises when one state, in seeking to be more secure, expands its military capabilities but, in doing so, increases fears in other states about their security so that they also build up their military capabilities. The dilemma is that states end up no more secure, perhaps even less, in spite of and because of their individual efforts to make themselves safe.

Service states Used to designate countries where transnational criminal organizations can easily access services designed to provide cover for their activities, such as false identities, or launder the proceeds of their activities.

Shadow of the future When the expectation of future benefits from cooperation makes it easier in the present to get that cooperation. Cooperation is easier when it, and the benefits it can provide, are not a one-shot deal.

Sikhs Religious group in India that includes extremists who attempt to achieve autonomy or independence to maintain the group vis-à-vis the majority Hindu population.

Small arms Firearms that are relatively small and light and can be easily managed and used by an individual. Small arms typically include weapons such as handguns, rifles, machine guns, and rocket-propelled grenades.

Smart bombs A colloquial term for a precision-guided munition designed to achieve a high rate of accuracy in targeting.

Social science This approach assumes that fact and value can be separated sufficiently to generate theoretically grounded hypotheses that can be tested against evidence. In other words, description (what is), explanation (why it is), and prescription (what should be) are treated as separable.

Societal identity The self-identification by members of the community as constituting 'us'; that is to say, a shared sense of belonging to the same collectivity, most often ethno-national and religious groups.

Societal security dilemma Where the actions of one society, in trying to increase its security (strengthen its identity), causes a reaction in a second, which, in the end, causes a decrease in its own security (weakens its identity).

Soft security Emphasizes mechanisms other than military ones that enhance the safety and well-being of states or other actors.

Southern African Development Community (SADC) An international organization promoting regional cooperation in economic development in southern Africa.

Sovereignty The legal status of having effective control over a specified territory and the people who reside there, and recognized by other sovereign states as having such control and being entitled to be regarded as sovereign. Being sovereign entitles a state, and its government, to be free, under most circumstances, of responsibility to any higher authority and of interference from outside in its internal affairs.

Speech act Consists of a discursive representation of a certain issue as an existential threat to security.

Speech-act theory Speech is commonly considered to refer to objects and actions outside itself; speech-act theory examines those instances in which actions are performed *by virtue* of their being spoken. Naming, marrying, and promising are notable examples of speech acts. Securitization treats security as a speech act.

State collapse A condition where the main state institutions and governing processes completely fail and cease to function in any meaningful sense, through either internal processes of mismanagement or overwhelming challenges to state authority. The most visible signal of state collapse is the total breakdown of law and order. State collapse creates a power vacuum that is then filled by alternative forms of power and governance.

State security A condition where the institutions, processes, and structures of the state are able to continue functioning without the threat of collapse or significant opposition, despite threats to the current regime or changes to the make-up of the ruling elite.

State-centric/state-centricity A term that is used loosely, often to describe the realist paradigm that is said to give priority to protection of the state above all else. See Chapter 2.

Strategic culture Those 'beliefs and assumptions that frame . . . choices about international military behaviour, particularly those concerning decisions to go to war, preferences for offensive, expansionist, or defensive modes of warfare, and levels of wartime casualties that would be acceptable' (Rosen 1995: 12).

Strongmen A term used to describe individuals or groups who possess a degree of coercive power in their own right and who pose a challenge to weak state rulers. Typically, they include local politicians or tribal leaders with private armies, warlords, and criminal gangs, well-armed and organized ethnic or religious groups, and various private militia.

Structural adjustment programmes Structural Adjustment Programmes (SAPs) are economic policies for developing countries that have been promoted by the World Bank and International Monetary Fund (IMF) since the early 1980s by the provision of loans conditional on the adoption of such policies. SAPs policies reflect the neoliberal ideology that drives globalization. They aim to achieve long-term or accelerated economic growth in poorer countries by restructuring the economy and reducing government intervention. SAPs policies include reduction of government services through public spending cuts/budget deficit cuts, reducing tax on high earners, wage suppression, privatization, and business deregulation, among others. Governments are also encouraged or forced to reduce their role in the economy by privatizing state-owned industries, including the health sector, and opening up their economies to foreign competition. One important criticism of SAPs, which emerged shortly after they were first adopted and has continued since, concerns their impact on the social sector, and this is reflected in the post-Washington consensus and similar thinking that promotes economic reform while protecting and possibly increasing social expenditure.

Structural realism See neorealism.

Structural violence Deaths and suffering caused by the way society is organized so that huge numbers of people lack the means necessary to avoid starvation, preventable illness, and so on.

Taliban Extreme Islamic religious group that established itself as the ruling government in most of Afghanistan and supported Al-Qaeda prior to 9/11. It was overthrown by US supported forces.

Tamil Tigers (Liberation Front of Tamil Eelam) Group in Sri Lanka that has used guerrilla warfare and terrorist attacks (including many suicide attacks) in an effort to achieve an independent Tamil state on the island.

Teleology The notion that history inevitably involves overall progress in a single direction.

Terrorism The use of force or the threat of force by organized groups too weak to use other methods in an effort to achieve political goals with attacks directed towards a target audience beyond the victims and where either the terrorists or the targets are non-governmental actors.

Think tank A research institute or other organization providing advice and ideas for policy makers or business leaders. Around 1960 the term came to be used primarily to describe RAND and other institutions assisting the armed forces and defence planners. The number and partisan affiliation of think tanks in the USA accelerated during the 1980s and 1990s, leading to a decline in their status as independent advisers and an increase in their role as producers of ideological munition. Foreign-policy institutes and to some extent peace research institutes have fulfilled parallel functions in Europe and elsewhere, where, however, American-style think tanks have begun to expand as well.

Traditional security Security is defined in geopolitical terms, encompassing aspects such as deterrence, power balancing, and military strategy. The state, and especially its defence from external military attacks, is the exclusive focus of study.

Transaction costs The concept that putting together a serious, complicated agreement, particularly between governments, is not free. Time, effort, compromises, political capital concessions, and so on are all costly, so if there is a way significantly to ease these costs, cooperation becomes much easier to undertake.

Transnational crime Criminal activity that is conducted in more than one state, planned in one state but perpetrated in another, or committed in one state where there are spillover effects into neighbouring jurisdictions. The phrase is often used more specifically to refer to transnational *organized* crime—crimes that cross national borders, are profit driven, and are committed by a group organized for that purpose.

Tuberculosis A bacterial disease that usually attacks the lungs, but can also affect the kidney, spine, or brain. Like the common cold, it is contagious and spreads through the air from person to person. If left untreated, tuberculosis is fatal. More recently, some strains of tuberculosis resistant to all medicines have also emerged.

Tularemia Disease caused by bacterium *Francisella tularensis* often found in animals (e.g. rodents). The vector (means of transmission) to humans in naturally occurring disease is the flea. As a weapon, the bacterium is highly infectious and would probably be distributed as an aerosol that would produce a severe respiratory illness.

UN Conference on the Human Environment (UNCHE) Also known as the Stockholm Environment Conference, this was held in May 1972 and was the first major international meeting on global environmental issues.

UN Conference on Trade and Development (UNCTAD) A UN agency set up specifically to improve the trading position of developing world states. It met for the first time in Geneva in 1964.

Unipolar The term for the structure of an international system that has a hegemon—one dominant state that provides a single pole of concentrated power—and this structure dominates the politics of the system.

United Nations Charter The Charter is the legal regime that created the United Nations as the world's only 'supranational' organization. It is the key legal document limiting the use of force to instances of self-defence and collective peace enforcement endorsed by the United Nations Security Council.

Uranium-235 A key ingredient of a nuclear weapon. It is called a 'fissile' material because an atom of uranium-235 can be split into roughly two equal-mass pieces when struck by a neutron. If a large enough mass of uranium-235 is brought together, a self-sustaining chain reaction results after the first fission occurs. If large amounts of U-235 are brought together quickly, a supercritical reaction occurs, which is the basis of both fission and fusion nuclear weapons.

Venezuelan equine encephalitis A mosquito-borne viral illness that causes flu-like symptoms, which can progress to encephalitis in a relatively small number of cases. Because it is a virus, observers fear that it could be subject to genetic manipulation to infect and incapacitate thousands of people quickly.

Vertical competition Where groups are pushed towards either narrower or wider societal identities because of integration or disintegration.

Veteran A term used to describe people who have served in national armed forces. This term is usually associated with those who have served in the US military.

Vietnam War Fought between the Viet Cong guerrillas and the North Vietnamese Army, on the one hand, and the South Vietnam Army and the United States, on the other. US involvement was principally between 1965 and its final withdrawal in 1973. North and South Vietnam were ultimately unified under the control of the North.

Warlord A military leader who exercises civil power in a region, such as collecting taxes, providing a semblance of law and order and engaging in commerce, either in alliance with or in defiance of the central state. The warlord commands the personal loyalty of a private army and rules by virtue of his war-making ability.

Weak states States possessing one or more of the following characteristics: infrastructural incapacity, evidenced by weak institutions and the inability to penetrate and control society effectively or enforce state policies; lack of coercive power and a failure to achieve or maintain a monopoly on the instruments of violence; and the lack of national identity and social and political consensus on the idea of the state.

Weathermen Radical leftist group in the United States that used terrorist tactics in their opposition to the government and the war in Vietnam but never achieved the notoriety or gained the support that some West European leftist groups did.

Westphalia A general settlement in 1648 that ended the Thirty Years War and in doing so laid the basis for the European state system, particularly with respect to the sovereignty and autonomy of the states. Hence the international system, with sovereign states as the members, is still referred to as the Westphalian system.

Wilsonian internationalism A powerful component of American thinking and preferences in foreign policy since early in the twentieth century, which received its initial elaboration in President Woodrow Wilson's efforts after the First World War to use American leadership to reorder the international system along liberalist lines so as to eliminate major wars.

Xenophobic Term used to describe those who are violently opposed to foreigners or foreign ideas and cultures.

Zero-day vulnerabilities A zero-day vulnerability refers to a hole in software that is unknown to the vendor. This hole can be exploited by hackers before the vendor becomes aware and fixes it (a zero-day attack). Depending on what can be done with them, some zero-day vulnerabilities have high strategic value.

References

Abelson, D. E. (2002), *Do Think Tanks Matter? Assessing the Impact of Public Policy Institutes*, Kingston, Ontario: McGill-Queen's University Press.

Abernethy, D. (2000), *The Dynamics of Global Governance: European Overseas Empires, 1415–1980*, New Haven: Yale University Press.

Acharya, A. (2001), 'Human Security: East versus West', *International Journal*, 56 / 3: 442–60.

Adams, G. (1982), *The Politics of Defence Contracting: The Iron Triangle*, New Brunswick, NJ: Transaction Books.

Adger, N., Pulhin, J., Barnett, J., Dabelko, G., Hovelsrud, G., Levy, M., Oswald Spring, Ú., and Vogel, C. (2014), 'Human Security', in C. Field, V. Barros, D. Dokken, K. Mach, M. Mastrandrea, T. Bilir, M. Chatterjee, K. Ebi, Y. Estrada, R. Genova, B. Girma, E. Kissel, A. Levy, S. MacCracken, P. Mastrandrea, and White (eds), *Climate Change 2014: Impacts, Adaptation, and Vulnerability. Part A: Global and Sectoral Aspects. Contribution of Working Group II to the Fifth Assessment Report of the Intergovernmental Panel on Climate Change*, Cambridge: Cambridge University Press, 755–91.

Adler, E. (1992), 'The Emergence of Cooperation: National Epistemic Communities and the International Evolution of the Idea of Nuclear Arms Control', *International Organization*, 46 / 1: 101–45.

Adler, E. (1997), 'Seizing the Middle Ground: Constructivism in World Politics', *European Journal of International Relations*, 3 / 3: 319–59.

Adler, E. (2008), 'The Spread of Security Communities: Communities of Practice, Self-Restraint, and NATO's Post-Cold War Transformation', *European Journal of International Relations*, 14 / 2: 195–230.

Adler, E. and Barnett, M. (1998), 'Security Communities in Theoretical Perspective', in E. Adler and M. Barnett (eds), *Security Communities*, Cambridge: Cambridge University Press, 3–28.

Agence France Presse (2003), 'Thailand set to declare victory in drugs war', 2 December.

Aggestan, L. and Hyde-Price, A. (eds) (2000), *Security and Identity in Europe*, London: Macmillan.

Agius, C. (2006), *The Social Construction of Swedish Neutrality: Challenges to Swedish Identity and Sovereignty*, Manchester: Manchester University Press.

Agius, C. and Devine, K. (eds) (2011), Special Issue on Neutrality and 'Military Non-Alignment': Exploring Norms, Discourses and Practices, *Cooperation and Conflict*, 46 / 3.

Ahmed, A. (2013), *The Thistle and the Drone*, Washington, DC: Brookings Institution Press.

Akaha, T. (1991), 'Japan's Comprehensive Security Policy: A New East Asian Environment', *Asian Survey*, 31 / 4: 324–40.

Akerlof, G. A. (1970), "The Market for "Lemons": Quality Uncertainty and the Market Mechanism", *Quarterly Journal of Economics*, 84 / 3: 488–500.

Alagappa, M. (1998), *Asian Security Practice: Material and Ideational Influence*, Stanford, CA: Stanford University Press.

Alavi, H. (1972), 'The State in Post-Colonial Societies: Pakistan and Bangladesh', *New Left Review*, 1 / 74: 59–81.

Albright, D. and Hinderstein, C. (2005), 'Unraveling the A. Q. Khan and Future Proliferation Networks', *Washington Quarterly*, 28 / 2: 111–28.

Alibek, K. (2000), *Biohazard*, New York: Random House.

Aljazeera (2014), 'Did austerity cause a humanitarian crisis in Greece?', 7 January, http://www.aljazeera.com/indepth/opinion/2014/01/did-austerity-cause-humanitarian-crisis-greece-2014165152464538.html.

Alkiri, S. (2004), 'A Vital Core that must be Treated with the Same Gravitas as Traditional Security Threats', *Security Dialogue*, 35 / 3: 359–60.

Allan, J. (2002), *The Middle East Water Question: Hydropolitics and the Global Economy*, London: I. B. Taurus Publishers.

Allen, J. and Hammett, Chris (1998), *A Shrinking World?: Global Unevenness and Inequality*, Oxford: Oxford University Press.

Allison, G. (1971), *Essence of Decision: Explaining the Cuban Missile Crisis*, Boston: Little, Brown and Co.

Alonso, Harriet Hyman (1993), *Peace as a Woman's Issue: History of the US Movement for World Peace and Women's Rights*, New York: Syracuse University Press.

Alpern Engel, B. (1992), 'Engendering Russia's History: Women in Post-Emancipation Russia and the Soviet Union', *Slavic Review*, 51/2: 309–21.

Amoore, L. (2013), *The Politics of Possibility: Risk and Security Beyond Probability*, Durham: Duke University Press Books.

Anand, S. and Segal, P. (2014), *The Global Distribution of Income*, International Development Institute Working Paper 2014–01. King's International Development Institute, London.

Anderson R. and Moore, T. (2006), 'The Economics of Information Security', *Science*, 314: 610–23.

Andreas, P. and Biersteker, T. J. (2003), *The Rebordering of North America; Integration and Exclusion in a New Security Context*, London: Routledge.

Andreas, P. and Nadelmann, E. (2006), *Policing the Globe: Criminalization and Crime Control in International Relations*, New York: Oxford University Press.

Anghie, A. (2005), *Imperialism, Sovereignty and the Making of International Law*, Cambridge: Cambridge University Press.

Anievas, A. and Manchanda, N. (2015), *Race and Racism in International Relations: Confronting the Global Colour Line*, London: Routledge.

Annan, K. (1998), 'Secretary-General Reflects on "Intervention" in Thirty-Fifth Annual Ditchley Foundation Lecture', *Press Release* SG/SM/6613, 26 June.

Annan, K. (1999), 'Annual Report of the Secretary-General to the United Nations General Assembly', 20 September, http://www.un.org/press/en/1999/19990920.sgsm7136.html.

Anonymous (2003), *Maximum Security: A Hacker's Guide to Protecting your Internet Site and Network*, Indiana: Sams Publishing.

Anthony, M., Emmers, R., and Acharya, A. (eds) (2006), *Non-Traditional Security in Asia: Dilemmas in Securitization*, London: Ashgate Publishing.

Aradau C. and van Münster R. V. (2007), 'Governing Terrorism through Risk: Taking Precautions, (Unknowing the Future', *European Journal of International Relations*, 30/1: 89–115.

Aras, B. and Polat, R. K. (2008), 'From Conflict to Cooperation: Desecuritization of Turkey's Relations with Syria and Iran', *Security Dialogue*, 39/5: 495–535.

Arend, A. C. and Beck, R. J. (1993), *International Law and the Use of Force: Beyond the UN Charter Paradigm*, London: Routledge.

Armbrust, Walter (2011), 'The revolution against neoliberalism', *Jadaliyya*, updated 23 February, http://www.jadaliyya.com/pages/index/717/the-revolution-against-neoliberalism-.

Arms Control Association (2007), *Convention on Certain Conventional Weapons (CCW) at a Glance*, Washington, DC: Arms Control Association.

Aron, R. (1957), 'Conflict and War from the Viewpoint of Historical Sociology', in R. Aron, J. S. Bernard, and T. H. Pear (eds), *The Nature of Conflict*, Paris: UNESCO, 177–203.

Arquilla, J. and Ronfeldt, D. F. (1993), 'Cyberwar is Coming!', *Comparative Strategy*, 12/2: 141–65.

Arquilla, J. and Ronfeldt, D. F. (eds) (1997), *In Athena's Camp: Preparing for Conflict in the Information Age*, Santa Monica: RAND.

Arquilla, J. and Ronfeldt, D. F. (eds) (2002), *Networks and Netwars: The Future of Terror, Crime and Militancy*, Santa Monica, CA: Rand Corporation, 61–97; http://www.rand.org/publications/MR/MR1382/MR1382.ch3.pdf.

Art, R. J. (1980), 'To What Ends Military Power?', *International Security*, 4/Spring: 3–35.

Art, R. J. (2003), 'Introduction', in R. J. Art and P. M. Cronin (eds), *The United States and Coercive Diplomacy*, Washington, DC: United States Institute of Peace, 3–20.

Art, R. J. and P. M. Cronin (eds) (2003), *The United States and Coercive Diplomacy*, Washington: United States Institute of Peace, 3–20.

Ash, T. G. (2003), 'Is There a Good Terrorist?', in Charles W. Kegley, Jr (ed.), *The New Global Terrorism: Characteristics, Causes, Controls*, Upper Saddle River, NJ: Prentice Hall, 60–70.

Asia Foundation (2007), *Afghanistan in 2007: A Survey of the Afghan People*, Kabul Office, http://asiafoundation.org/publications/pdf/20.

Asia Foundation (2008), *Afghanistan in 2008: A Survey of the Afghan People*, Kabul Office, http://asiafoundation.org/country/afghanistan/2008-poll.php.

Asia Foundation (2011), *Afghanistan in 2011: A Survey of the Afghan People*, Kabul Office, http://asiafoundation.org/publications/pdf/989.

Asia-Pacific Centre for the Responsibility to Protect (2008), 'Cyclone Nargis and the Responsibility to Protect', 16 May www.r2pasiapacific.org/images/stories/food/cyclone%20nargis%20and%20the%20responsibility%20to%20protect.pdf.

Atwood, D., Glatz, A., and Muggah, R. (2006), *Demanding Attention: Addressing the Dynamics of Small Arms Demand*, Geneva: Small Arms Survey.

Austin, J. and Bruch, C. (eds) (2000), *The Environmental Consequences of War: Legal, Economic and Scientific Perspectives*, Cambridge: Cambridge University Press.

Ayoob, M. (1995), *The Third World Security Predicament: State Making, Regional Conflict, and the International System*, Boulder, CO: Lynne Rienner.

Ayoob, M. (1997), 'Defining Security: A Subaltern Realist Perspective', in K. Krause and M. C. Williams (eds), *Critical Security Studies: Concepts and Cases*, Minneapolis: University of Minnesota Press, 121–46.

Ayoob, M. (2002), 'Humanitarian Intervention and State Sovereignty', *The International Journal of Human Rights*, 16/1: 81–102.

Baaz, M. E. and Stern, M. (2009), 'Why Do Soldiers Rape? Masculinity, Violence, and Sexuality in the Armed Forces in the Congo (DRC)', *International Studies Quarterly*, 53/4: 495–518.

Bacevich, A. J. (2006), *The New American Militarism: How Americans Are Seduced by War*, Oxford: Oxford University Press.

Baechler, G. (1999), *Violence through Environmental Discrimination: Causes, Rwanda Arena, and Conflict Model*, Dordrecht: Kluwer.

Bailyn, B. (1992), *The Ideological Origins of the American Revolution*, Cambridge, MA, and London: Belknap Press and Harvard University Press.

Bain, W. (2001), 'The Tyranny of Benevolence: National Security, Human Security and the Practice of Statecraft', *Global Society*, 15/3: 277–94.

Bal, I. and Laciner, S. (2001), 'The Challenge of Revolutionary Terrorism to Turkish Democracy, 1960–1980', *Terrorism and Political Violence*, 14/4: 90–115.

Baldwin, D. (1995), 'Security Studies and the End of the Cold War', *World Politics*, 48/1: 117–41.

Balzacq, T. (2005), 'The Three Faces of Securitization: Political Agency, Audience and Context', *European Journal of International Relations*, 11/2: 171–201.

Balzacq, T. (2010), 'Constructivism and Securitization Studies', in M. D. Cavelty and V. Mauer (eds), *The Routledge Handbook of Security Studies*, Abingdon: Routledge, 56–72.

Balzacq, T. (ed.) (2011), *Securitization Theory: How Security Problems Emerge and Dissolve*, New Security Studies Series, London: Routledge.

Ban Ki-moon (2008), 'Responsible Sovereigns', address of the UN Secretary-General, SG/SM/11701, 15 July.

Baran, P. A. and Sweezy, P. M. (1966), *Monopoly Capital*, New York: Monthly Review Press.

Barkawi, T. (2006), *Globalization and War*, London: Rowman & Littlefield.

Barkawi, T. (2010), 'Empire and Order in International Relations and Security Studies', in R. Denemark (ed.), *The International Studies Encyclopedia*, Chichester: Wiley-Blackwell, Vol. III, 1360–79.

Barkawi, T. and Brighton, S. (2013), 'Brown Britain: Postcolonial Politics and Grand Strategy', *International Affairs*, 89/5: 1109–23.

Barkawi, T. and Laffey, M. (eds) (2001), *Democracy, Liberalism and War: Rethinking the Democratic Peace Debates*, Boulder, CO: Lynne Rienner.

Barkawi, T. and Laffey, M. (2002), 'Retrieving the Imperial: *Empire* and International Relations', Millennium, 31/1: 109–27.

Barkawi, T. and Laffey, M. (2006), 'The Postcolonial Moment in Security Studies', *Review of International Studies*, 32/4: 329–52.

Barker, C., Cox, L., Krinsky, J., and Nilsen, A. G. (eds) (2013), *Marxism and Social Movements*, Leiden: Brill.

Barnett, J. (2001), *The Meaning of Environmental Security: Ecological Politics and Policy in the New Security Era*, London: Zed Books.

Barnett, J. (2010), *Climate Change in Small Island States*, London: Earthscan.

Barnett, J. and Adger, N. (2003), 'Climate Dangers and Atoll Countries', *Climatic Change*, 61/3: 321–37.

Barnett, M. (2002), *Eyewitness to a Genocide: The United Nations and Rwanda*, Ithaca, NY: Cornell University Press.

Barnett, T. and Whiteside, A. (2006), *AIDS in the Twenty-First Century: Disease and Globalization*, 2nd edn, Basingstoke: Palgrave.

Basham, V. (2011), 'Kids with Guns: Militarization, Masculinities, Moral Panic, and (Dis)Organized Violence', in J. Marshall Beier (ed.), *The Militarization of Childhood: Thinking Beyond the Global South*, New York: Palgrave Macmillan, 175–93.

Basham, V. (2013), *War, Identity and the Liberal State: Everyday Experiences of the Geopolitical in the Armed Forces*, Abingdon: Routledge.

Baudrillard, J. (1994), *Simulacra and Simulation*, trans. Sheila Faria Glaser, Ann Arbor: University of Michigan Press.

Baudrillard, J. (1995), *The Gulf War Did Not Take Place*, trans. Paul Patton, Bloomington: Indiana University Press.

Bayley, M. (2014), 'The "Re-turn" to Empire in IR: Colonial Knowledge Communities and the Construction of the Idea of the Afghan Polity, 1809–38', *Review of International Studies*, 40/3: 443–64.

Baylis, J. and Wirtz, J. J. (2012), *Strategy in the Contemporary World*, Oxford: Oxford University Press.

Baylis, J., Wirtz, J., and Gray, C. S. (eds) (2015), *Strategy in the Contemporary World*, 5th edn, Oxford: Oxford University Press.

Bazergan, R. (2002), *HIV/AIDS & Peacekeeping: A Field Study of the Policies of the United Nations Mission in Sierra Leone*, London: International Policy Institute.

BBC News (2003), 'Thais swear to stay drug-free', 1 April, http://news.bbc.co.uk/1/hi/world/asia-pacific/2895383.stm.

BBC News (2004), Michael Howard's speech on immigration and asylum, http://news.bbc.co.uk/1/hi/uk_politics/3679618.stm.

BBC News (2006a), 'Saudis 'foil oil facility attack', 24 February, http://news.bbc.co.uk/1/hi/world/middle_east/4747488.stm.

BBC News (2006b), 'Shell evacuates Nigeria workers', 16 January, http://news.bbc.co.uk/1/hi/world/africa/4615890.stm.

BBC News (2014), 'Ebola outbreak "threatens Liberia's national existence"', 9 September, http://www.bbc.co.uk/news/world-africa-29136594.

Beare, M. E. (ed.) (2003), *Critical Reflections on Transnational Organized Crime, Money Laundering, and Corruption*, Toronto: University of Toronto Press.

Becker, G. S. (1969), 'Crime and Punishment: An Economic Approach', *Journal of Political Economy*, 76/2: 169–217.

Bedford, D. and Workman, T. (1997), 'The Great Law of Peace: Alternative Inter-Nation(al) Practices and the Iroquoian Confederacy', *Alternatives*, 22/1: 87–111.

Beevor, A. (2002), *Berlin: The Downfall 1945*, London: Penguin.

Behnke, A. (2007), 'Presence and Creation: A Few (Meta-)Critical Comments on the C.A.S.E. Manifesto', *Security Dialogue*, 38/1: 105–11.

Beier, J. M. (2005), *International Relations in Uncommon Places: Indigeneity, Cosmology, and the Limits of International Theory*, New York: Palgrave Macmillan.

Beier, J. M. (ed.) (2009), *Indigenous Diplomacies*, Basingstoke: Palgrave Macmillan.

Beier, J. M. (2014), *The Militarization of Childhood: Thinking Beyond the Global South*, 2nd edn, Basingstoke: Palgrave Macmillan.

Beier, J. M. and Arnold, S. L. (2005), 'Becoming Undisciplined: Toward the Supradisciplinary Study of Security', *International Studies Review*, 7/1: 41–62.

Beier, M. (2001), 'Postcards from the Outskirts of Security: Defence Professionals, Semiotics, and the NMD Initiative', *Canadian Foreign Policy*, 8/2: 39–49.

Bellamy, A. J. (2004), 'Ethics and Intervention: The "Humanitarian Exception" and the Problem of Abuse in the Case of Iraq', *Journal of Peace Research*, 41/2: 131–47.

Bellamy, A. J. (2006), 'Whither the Responsibility to Protect? Humanitarian Intervention and the 2005 World Summit', *Ethics and International Affairs*, 20/2: 143–69.

Bellamy, A. J. (2009), *Responsibility to Protect: The Global Effort to End Genocide and Mass Atrocities*, Cambridge: Polity Press.

Bellamy, A. J. (2012), *Massacres and Morality: Mass Killing in an Age of Civilian Immunity*, Oxford: Oxford University Press.

Bellamy, A. J. (2014), *Responsibility to Protect: A Defense*, Oxford: Oxford University Press.

Bellamy, A. J. and McDonald, M. (2002), 'The Utility of Human Security: Which Humans? What Security? A Reply to Thomas & Tow'. *Security Dialogue*, 33/3, 373–7.

Bellamy, Ian (1981), 'Towards a Theory of International Security', *Political Studies*, 29 / 1: 100–5.

Berger, P. and Luckmann, T. (1991), *The Social Construction of Reality: A Treatise in the Sociology of Knowledge*, London: Penguin.

Berger, T. U. (1996), 'Norms, Identity, and National Security in Germany and Japan', in P. J. Katzenstein (ed.), *The Culture of National Security. Norms and Identity in World Politics*, New York: Columbia University Press, 317–56.

Berman, E. (2009), *Radical, Religious, and Violent: The New Economics of Terrorism*. Cambridge, MA: MIT Press.

Berman, E. and Laitin, D. D. (2008), 'Religion, Terrorism and Public Goods: Testing the Club Model', *Journal of Public Economics*, 92 / 10–11: 1942–67.

Bernstein, J. (2008), *Nuclear Weapons: What you Need To Know*, New York: Cambridge University Press.

Berube, Alan (2011), 'A Metro Lens on the New National Poverty Data', The New Republic, updated 14 September 2011, http: / / www.tnr.com / blog / the-avenue / 94934 / metro-lens-the-new-national-poverty-data.

Betts, R. (1997), 'Should Strategic Studies Survive', *World Politics*, 50 / 1: 7–33.

Betts, R. K. (2012), *Conflict After the Cold War*, 4th edn, Upper Saddle River, NJ: Prentice Hall.

Beverley, J. (1999), *Subalternity and Representation: Arguments in Cultural Theory*, Durham: Duke University Press.

Bezhan, F. (2012), 'Karzai backs Afghan clerics over stronger restrictions on women', 8 March, *Radio Free Europe / Radio Liberty*.

Bhambra, G. (2007), *Rethinking Modernity: Postcolonialism and the Sociological Imagination*, New York: Palgrave Macmillan.

Biddle, S. (2004), *Military Power: Explaining Victory and Defeat in Modern Battle*, Princeton, NJ: Princeton University Press.

Biersteker, T. J. and Weber, C. (eds) (1996), *State Sovereignty as Social Construct*, Cambridge: Cambridge University Press.

Bigo, D. (1996), *Polices en résaux, l'expérience européenne*, Paris: Presses de Sciences Po.

Bigo, D. (2002a), 'To Reassure and Protect, after September 11', in Social Science Research Council, 'After September 11', www.ssrc.org / sept11 / essays / bigo.htm.

Bigo, D. (2002b), 'Security and Immigration: Toward a Critique of the Governmentality of Unease', *Alternatives*, 27 / Feb suppl.: 63–92.

Bilgin, P. (2010), 'The "Western-Centrism" of Security Studies: "Blind Spot" or Constitutive Practice?', *Security Dialogue*, 41 / 6: 615–22.

Bilgin, P. and Morton, A. D. (2002), 'Historicizing Representations of "Failed States": Beyond the Cold War Annexation of the Social Sciences?', *Third World Quarterly*, 23 / 1: 55–80.

Bill, J. (1988), *The Eagle and the Lion: The Tragedy of American–Iranian Relations*, London: Yale University Press.

Birnbaum, M. (2011), 'France sent arms to Libyan rebels', *The Washington Post*, 29 June.

Biswas, S. (2014), *Nuclear Desire: Power and the Postcolonial Nuclear Order*, Minneapolis: University of Minnesota Press.

Bitzinger, R. A. (2003), *Towards a Brave New Arms Industry?'*, Adelphi Paper 356, London: International Institute for Strategic Studies.

Bjorgo, T. (ed.) (2005), *Root Causes of Terrorism: Myths, Reality, and Ways Forward*, London: Routledge.

Black, J. (2005), *Why Wars Happen*, London and New York: Routledge.

Blair, T. (1999), 'Doctrine of the International Community', speech to the Economic Club of Chicago, Hilton Hotel, Chicago, 22 April.

Blair, T. (2000), 'Speech by the Prime Minister at Warwick University', 14 December, www2.warwick.ac.uk / services / communications / archive / clinton / blairsspeech.

Blakeley, R. (2009), *State Terrorism and Neoliberalism: The North in the South*, London: Routledge.

Blakeley, R. (2013), 'Human Rights, State Wrongs, and Social Change: The Theory and Practice of Emancipation', *Review of International Studies*, 39 / 3: 599–619.

Blaut, J. M. (1993), *The Colonizer's Model of the World: Geographical Diffusionism and Eurocentric History*, New York: The Guilford Press.

Blechman, B. and Wittes, T. C. (1999), 'Defining Moment: The Threat and Use of Force in American Foreign Policy', *Political Science Quarterly*, 114 / 1: 1–30.

Bleiker, R. (1997), 'Forget IR Theory', *Alternatives: Global, Local, Political*, 22 / 1: 57–85.

Bloom, M. (2007), 'Female Suicide Bombers: A Global Trend', *Daedalus*, 136 / 1, 94–102.

Boeles, Jan (1990), 'EU monitor mission to the Former Yugoslavia', quoted in Robert Fisk, 'Waging war on history', *Independent*, 20 June 1994.

Bogaert, Koenraad (2011), 'Global dimensions of the Arab Spring and the potential for anti-hegemonic politics', *Jadaliyya,* updated 21 December 2011, http: / / www.jadaliyya.com / pages / index / 3638 / global-dimensions-of-the-arab-spring-and-the-poten.

Böge, V. (1999), 'Mining, Environmental Degradation and War: The Bougainville Case', in M. Suliman (ed.), *Ecology, Politics and Violent Conflict*, London: Zed Books, 211–27.

Boix, Carles (2011), 'Democracy, Development, and the International System', *American Political Science Review*, 105 / 4: 809–28.

Bolton, J. (2007), *Surrender is Not an Option: Defending America at the United Nations and Abroad*, New York: Threshold Editions.

Booth, K. (1975), 'Disarmament and Arms Control', in John Baylis, Ken Booth, John Garnett, and Phil Williams, *Contemporary Strategy: Theories and Policies*, London: Croom Helm.

Booth, K. (1991), 'Security and Emancipation', *Review of International Studies*, 17 / 4: 313–26.

Booth, K. (1997), 'Security and Self: Reflections of a Fallen Realist', in Keith Krause and Michael C. Williams (eds), *Critical Security Studies: Concepts and Cases*, Minneapolis: University of Minnesota Press, 83–119.

Booth, K. (2005a), 'Beyond Critical Security Studies', in Booth (ed.), *Critical Security Studies and World Politics*, Boulder, CO: Lynne Rienner, 259–78.

Booth, K. (ed.) (2005b), *Critical Security Studies and World Politics*, Boulder, CO: Lynne Rienner.

Booth, K. (2007), *Theory of World Security*, Cambridge: Cambridge University Press.

Booysen, F. and Bachmann, M. (2002), 'HIV / AIDS, Poverty and Growth: Evidence from a Household Impact Study Conducted in the Free State Province, South Africa', paper presented at the Annual Conference of the Centre for the Study of African Economies, Oxford, March.

Bormann, N. (2008), *National Missile Defence and the Politics of US Identity: A Poststructural Critique*, Manchester: University of Manchester Press.

Boureston, J. (2002), 'Assessing Al Qaeda's WMD Capabilities', 2 September, http: / / www.isn.ethz.ch / Digital-Library / Publications / Detail / ?ots591=0c54e3b3-1e9c-be1e-2c24-a6a8c7060233&Ing=en&id=34612.

Boyden, S., Dovers, S., and Shirlow, M. (1990), *Our Biosphere under Threat: Ecological Realities and Australia's Opportunities*, Melbourne: Oxford University Press.

Branch, J. (2014), *The Cartographic State: Maps, Territory, and the Origins of Sovereignty*, Cambridge: Cambridge University Press.

Brandt, W., et al. (1980), *North-South: A Programme for Survival: Report of the Independent Commission on International Development Issues* ('Brandt Report'), Cambridge, MA: MIT Press.

Braun C. and Chyba, C. F. (2004), 'Proliferation Rings: New Challenges to the Nuclear Nonproliferation Regime', *International Security*, 29 / 2: 5–49.

Brenner, N., Peck, J. and Theodore, N. (2010), 'Variegated Neoliberalization: Geographies, Modalities, Pathways', *Global Networks*, 10 / 2: 182–222.

Broad, R. and Cavanagh, J. (2009), *Development Redefined: How the Market Met its Match*, Boulder, CO: Paradigm.

Brocklehurst, H. (2006), *Who's Afraid of Children? Children, Conflict and International Relations*, Aldershot: Ashgate.

Brockway, F. (1933), *The Bloody Traffic*, London: Victor Gollanez.

Brodie, B. (ed.) (1946), *The Absolute Weapon: Atomic Power and World Order*, New York: Harcourt, Brace & Co.

Brodie, B. (1949), 'Strategy as a Science', *World Politics*, 1 / 4: 467–88.

Brodie, B. (1959), *Strategy in the Missile Age*, Princeton, NJ: Princeton University Press.

Brodie, B. (1965), 'The McNamara Phenomenon', *World Politics*, 17 / 4: 672–86.

Brooks, E. (1974), 'The Implications of Ecological Limits to Development in Terms of Expectations and Aspirations in Developed and Less Developed Countries', in Anthony Vann and Paul Rogers (eds), *Human Ecology and World Development*, London and New York: Plenum Press.

Brooks, S. G. and Wohlforth, W. C. (2005), 'Hard Times for Soft Balancing', *International Security*, 30 / 1: 72–108.

Brown, K. A. (2006), *Critical Path: A Brief History of Critical Infrastructure Protection in the United States*, Arlington, VA: George Mason University Press.

Brown, L. (1977), 'Redefining National Security', Worldwatch Paper No. 14, Washington: Worldwatch Institute.

Brown, M. E. (ed.) (2000), *Rational Choice and Security Studies: Stephen Walt and his Critics*, Cambridge, MA: MIT Press.

Brown, M., Lynn-Jones, S., and Miller, S. (eds) (1996), *Debating the Democratic Peace*, Cambridge, MA: MIT Press, 301–34.

Brownlie, I. (1974), 'Humanitarian Intervention', in John N. Moore (ed.), *Law and Civil War in the Modern World*, Baltimore: Johns Hopkins University Press, 217–21.

Brzezinski, Z. (2003–4), 'Hegemonic Quicksand', *National Interest*, 74: 5–16.

Brzoska, M. and Ohlson, T. (eds) (1986), *Arms Production in the Third World*, London: Taylor and Francis.

Buckley, Mary (1989), *Women and Ideology in the Soviet Union*, London: Harvester Wheatsheaf.

Büger, C. and Stritzel, H. (2005), 'New European Security Theory: Zur Emergenz eines neuen europäischen Forschungsprogramms—Tagungsbericht: Critical Approaches to Security in Europe, Rencontres doctorales Européennes sur le thème de la Sécurité, Paris 2004', in *Zeitschrift für Internationale Beziehungen*, 12/2: 437–46.

Bukovansky, M. (1997), 'American Identity and Neutral Rights from Independence to the War of 1812', *International Organization*, 51/2: 209–43.

Bull, H. (1961), *The Control of the Arms Race*, London: Weidenfeld and Nicolson.

Bull, H. (1968), 'Strategic Studies and its Critics', *World Politics*, 20/4: 599–600.

Burbank, J. and Cooper, F. (2010), *Empires in World History: Power and the Politics of Difference*, Princeton, NJ: Princeton University Press.

Burchill, S. (2001), 'Liberalism', in S. Burchill, L. Linklater, R. Devetak, et al. (eds), *Theories of International Relations*, 2nd edn, Basingstoke: Palgrave Macmillan.

Burke, A. (2013), 'Security Cosmopolitanism', *Critical Studies on Security*, 1/1: 13–28.

Burr, W. (2008), 'Prevent the Re-emergence of a New Rival', The Making of the Cheney Regional Defense Strategy, 1991–1992, National Security Archive, Electronic Briefing Book 255, 26 February.

Bush, G. W. (2001), 'Address to a Joint Session of Congress and the American People', 20 September, www.whitehouse.gov/news/releases/2001/09/20010920-8.html.

Bush, G. W. (2007), *State of the Union Address 2007*, 23 January.

Buzan, B. (1981), 'Change and Insecurity: A Critique of Security Studies', in Barry Buzan and R. J. Barry Jones (eds), *Change and the Study of International Relations: The Evaded Dimension*, London: Pinter, 155–72.

Buzan, B. (1983), *People, States and Fear: The National Security Problem in International Relations*, Brighton: Wheatsheaf Books.

Buzan, B. (1984), 'Peace, Power, and Security: Contending Concepts in the Study of International Relations', *Journal of Peace Research*, 21/2: 109–25.

Buzan, B. (1991a), *People, States and Fear: An Agenda for International Security in the Post-Cold War Era*, 2nd edn, London: Harvester Wheatsheaf.

Buzan, B. (1991b) 'Is International Security Possible?', in K. Booth, *New Thinking about Strategy and International Security*, London: Harper Collins, 31–55.

Buzan, B. (1993), 'Societal Security, State Security, and Internationalisation', in O. Wæver, B. Buzan, M. Kelstrup, and P. Lemaitre (eds), *Identity, Migration and the New Security Agenda in Europe*, London: Pinter, 41–58.

Buzan, B. (2000), '"Change and Insecurity" Reconsidered', in Stuart Croft and Terry Terriff (eds), *Critical Reflections on Security and Change*, London: Frank Cass, 1–17.

Buzan, B. (2001), 'Human Security in International Perspective', in Mely C. Anthony and Mohamed Jawar Hassan (eds), *The Asia Pacific in the New Millennium: Political and Security Challenges*, Kuala Lumpur: Institute of Strategic and International Studies, 583–96.

Buzan, B. (2004a), 'What is Human Security? A Reductionist Idealistic Notion that Adds Little Analytical Value', *Security Dialogue*, 35/3: 369–70.

Buzan, B. (2004b), *The United States and the Great Powers: Word Politics in the Twenty-First Century*, Cambridge: Polity.

Buzan, B. (2006), 'Will the "Global War on Terrorism" be the New Cold War?', *International Affairs*, 82/6: 1101–18.

Buzan, B. (2010), 'China in International Society: Is "Peaceful Rise" Possible?', *The Chinese Journal of International Politics*, 3/1: 5–36.

Buzan, B. and Hansen, L. (2009), *The Evolution of International Security Studies*, Cambridge: Cambridge University Press.

Buzan, B. and Sen, G. (1990), 'The Impact of Military Research and Development Priorities on the Evolution of the Civil Economy in Capitalist States', *Review of International Studies*, 16/4: 321–39.

Buzan, B. and Wæver, O. (1997), 'Slippery? Contradictory? Sociologically Untenable? The Copenhagen School Replies', *Review of International Studies*, 23: 241–50.

Buzan, B. and Wæver, O. (2003), *Regions and Powers: The Structure of International Security*, Cambridge: Cambridge University Press.

Buzan, B. and Wæver, O. (2009), 'Macrosecuritization and Security Constellations: Reconsidering Scale in Securitization Theory', *Review of International Studies*, 35/2: 253–76.

Buzan, B., Kelstrup, M., Lemaitre, P., Tromer, E., and Wæver, O. (1990), *The European Security Order Recast: Scenarios for the Post-Cold War Era*, London: Pinter.

Buzan, B., Wæver, O., and de Wilde, J. (1998), *Security: A New Framework for Analysis*, Boulder, CO: Lynne Rienner.

Byers, M. (2005), 'High Ground Lost', Winnipeg Free Press, 18 September, p. B3.

Byman, D. L. and Waxman, M. C. (2002), *The Dynamics of Coercion: American Foreign Policy and the Limits of Military Might*, Cambridge: Cambridge University Press.

Byman, D., Waxman, M., and Larson, E. (1999), *Air Power as a Coercive Instrument*, Santa Monica, CA: RAND, MR-1061-AF.

CAAT (Campaign Against the Arms Trade) (2005), *Who Calls The Shots? How Corporate-Government Collusion Drives Arms Exports*, London: CAAT.

Caballero-Anthony, M., Emmers R., and Acharya, A. (2006), *Non-Traditional Security in Asia: Dilemmas of Securitization*, Aldershot: Ashgate.

Cabinet Office (2008), *The National Security Strategy of the United Kingdom: Security in an Interdependent World*, London: The Stationery Office.

Cabinet Office (2010), *A Strong Britain in an Age of Uncertainty: The National Security Strategy*, London: Cabinet Office.

Cammack, P. (2006), 'The Politics of Global Competitiveness', Papers in the Politics of Global Competitiveness, No. 1, Institute for Global Studies, Manchester Metropolitan University, e-space Open Repository.

Cammack, P. (2007), 'RIP IPE', Papers in the Politics of Global Competitiveness, No. 7, Institute for Global Studies, Manchester Metropolitan University, e-space Open Repository.

Campbell, D. (1992), *Writing Security: United States Foreign Policy and the Politics of Identity*, Manchester: Manchester University Press.

Campbell, D. (1998a), *Writing Security: United States Foreign Policy and the Politics of Identity*, rev. edn, Minneapolis: University of Minnesota Press.

Campbell, D. (1998b), *National Deconstruction: Violence, Identity, and Justice in Bosnia*, Minneapolis: University of Minnesota Press.

Campbell, H. (2013), *Global Nato and the Catastrophic Failure in Libya: Lessons for Africa in the Forging of African Unity*, New York: Monthly Review Press.

Campbell, K. M. (2004), 'The End of Alliances? Not So Fast', *The Washington Quarterly*, 27/2: 151–63.

Campen, A. D. (ed.) (1992), *The First Information War: The Story of Communications, Computers and Intelligence Systems in the Persian Gulf War*, Fairfax: AFCEA International Press.

CAN Corporation (2007), *National Security and the Threat of Climate Change*, Virginia: CAN Corporation.

Caney, S. (1997), 'Human Rights and the Rights of States: Terry Nardin on Non-Intervention', *International Political Science Review*, 18/1: 27–37.

Carnegie Commission (1997), *Preventing Deadly Conflict—Final Report*, Washington: Carnegie Commission on Preventing Deadly Conflict.

Carpenter, R. C. (2006), *'Innocent Women and Children': Gender, Norms and the Protection of Civilians*, Aldershot: Ashgate.

Carr, Edward Hallett (1945), *Nationalism and After*, New York: Macmillan.

Carr, E. H. (1981), *The Twenty Years' Crisis 1919–1939: An Introduction to the Study of International Relations*, Houndmills: Macmillan.

Carson, R. (1962), *Silent Spring*, Boston: Houghton Mifflin.

Carter, A., Clark, H., and Randle, M. (2013), *A Guide to Civil Resistance, London*: Green Print, Merlin Press.

CASE Collective (2006), 'Critical Approaches to Security in Europe: A Networked Manifesto', *Security Dialogue*, 37/4: 443–87.

CASE Collective (2007), 'Europe, Knowledge, Politics: Engaging the Limits: The CASE Collective Responds', *Security Dialogue*, 38/4: 559–76.

Cavanagh, John, Cheru, Fantu, Collins, Carole, Duncan, Cameron, and Ntube, Dominic (1985), *From Debt to Development: Alternatives to the International Debt Crisis*, Washington, DC: Institute for Policy Studies.

CCM (2008), *The Convention on Cluster Munitions—CCM*, http://www.clusterconvention.org/.

CDIAC (Carbon Dioxide Information Analysis (2014), 'Recent Greenhouse Gas Concentrations', updated February 2014, DOI: 10.3334/CDIAC/atg.032:

Central Intelligence Agency (2012), 'East and South Korea', *CIA World Fact Book*, 27 March, https://www.cia.gov/library/publications/the-world-factbook/geos/kn.html.

Césaire, A. (2000), *Discourse on Colonialism*, New York: Monthly Review Press.

Ceyhan, A. and Tsoukala, A. (2002), 'The Securitization of Migration in Western Societies: Ambivalent Discourses and Policies', *Alternatives*, 27/February suppl.: 21–40.

Chalk, P. (1996), *West European Terrorism and Counterterrorism: The Evolving Dynamic*, Houndmills: Macmillan.

Chalmers, D. M. (1965), *Hooded Americanism: The History of the Ku Klux Klan*, New York: Quadrangle Books.

Chamayou, G. (2015), *Drone Theory*, London: Penguin Books.

Chandler, D. (2005), 'The Responsibility to Protect: Imposing the Liberal Peace', in Alex J. Bellamy and Paul D. Williams (eds), *Peace Operations and Global Order*, London: Routledge, 59–82.

Chatterjee, P. (2004), *The Politics of the Governed: Reflections on Popular Politics in Most of the World*, New York: Columbia University Press.

Chaturvedi, V. (ed.) (2000), *Mapping Postcolonial Studies and the Postcolonial*, London: Verso.

Cheluget, B. K., Ngare, C., Wahiu, J., Mwikya, L., Kinoti, S., and Ndyanabangi. B. (2003), 'Impact of HIV/AIDS on Public Health Sector Personnel in Kenya', Presentation to the ECSA Regional Health Ministers' Conference in Livingstone, Zambia, 17–21 November.

Chen, S. and Ravallion, M. (2012), *An Update to the World Bank's Estimates of Consumption Poverty in the Developing World*, Briefing note, World Bank, Washington.

Chen, L. Leaning, J., and Narasimhan, V. (eds) (2003), *Global Health Challenges for Human Security*, Cambridge, MA: Harvard University Press.

Chesterman, S. (2001), *Just War or Just Peace? Humanitarian Intervention and International Law*, Oxford: Oxford University Press.

Chivers, C. J. (2011), 'Experts Fear Looted Libyan Arms May Find Way to Terrorists', *New York Times*, http://www.nytimes.com/2011/03/04/world/africa/04weapons.html?_r=1

Chomsky, N. (1973), *For Reasons of State*, London: Fontana Collins.

Chomsky, N. and Herman, E. S. (1979), *The Washington Connection and Third World Fascism: The Political Economy of Human Rights*, Boston: South End Press.

Christie, R. (2010), 'Critical Voices and Human Security: To Endure, to Engage or to Critique', *Security Dialogue*, 41/2: 169–90.

Clary, C. (2004), 'A. Q. Khan and the Limits of the Non-Proliferation Regime', *Disarmament Forum*, 4: 33–42.

Claude, I. (1964), *Swords into Ploughshares: The Problems and Progress of International Organization*, New York: Random House.

Clunan, A. and Trinkunas, H. (2010), *Ungoverned Spaces: Alternatives to State Authority in an Era of Softened Sovereignty*, Stanford, CA: Stanford University Press.

CNA Corporation (2007), *National Security and the Threat of Climate Change*, Alexandria, VI: CNA Corporation.

CNN (2008), 'Iraq Signs $3 Billion Oil Deal with China', 30 August, http://edition.cnn.com/2008/BUSINESS/08/30/iraq.china.oil.deal/index.html.

Cochrane, J. (2003), 'Blood in Bangkok Streets', *Newsweek*, 10 March.

Coebergh, J. (2005), 'Sudan: The Genocide has Killed More than the Tsunami', *Parliamentary Brief*, 7/9: 5–7.

Cohen, G. A. (2009), *Why Not Socialism?*, Princeton, NJ: Princeton University Press.

Cohen, R. (2008), 'How Kofi Annan Rescued Kenya', *New York Review of Books*, 55/13: 14 August.

Coker, C. (2002), *Globalization and Insecurity in the Twenty-First Century: NATO and the Management of Risk*, Adelphi Paper No. 345, Oxford: Oxford University Press.

Collier, P. (2000), *Economic Causes of Civil Conflict and their Implications for Policy*, Washington, DC: World Bank, http://reliefweb.int/sites/reliefweb.int/files/resources/B7598814338CA6DEC1256C1E0042BE82-civilconflict.pdf.

Collier, Paul and Institute of Economic Affairs (Great Britain) (1998), *Living Down the Past: How Europe can Help Africa Grow*, Studies in Trade and Development (Institute of Economic Affairs (Great Britain)), London: Institute of Economic Affairs.

Collins, A. (2003), *Security and Southeast Asia: Domestic, Regional and Global Issues*, Boulder, CO: Lynne Rienner.

Collins, A. (2005), 'Securitization, Frankenstein's Monster and Malaysian Education', *Pacific Review*, 18/4: 565–86.

Collins, J. (2011), *Global Palestine*, London: Hurst and Company.

Collins, J. (2012), *Building a People-Oriented Security Community the ASEAN Way*, Abingdon: Routledge.

Commission on Human Security (2003), *Human Security Now*, www.humansecurity-chs.org/finalreport/FinalReport.pdf.

Conca, K. (1997), *Manufacturing Insecurity: The Rise and Fall of Brazil's Military-Industrial Complex*, London: Lynne Rienner.

Conca, K. (2002), 'The Case for Environmental Peacemaking', in K. Conca and G. Dabelko (eds), *Environmental Peacemaking*, Baltimore: Johns Hopkins University Press, 1–22.

Conca, K. and Dabelko, G. (eds) (2002), *Environmental Peacemaking*, Baltimore: John Hopkins University Press.

Concise Oxford Dictionary (2006), Oxford: Oxford University Press.

Connell, R. W. and Messerschmidt, J. W. (2005), 'Hegemonic Masculinity: Rethinking the Concept', *Gender & Society*, 19/6: 829–59.

Conrad, P. (2007), *The Medicalization of Society: On the Transformation of Human Conditions into Treatable Disorders*, Baltimore: Johns Hopkins University Press.

Cook, Sarah and Jolly, Susan (2001), *Gender and Poverty in Urban China*, Brighton: Institute for Development Studies.

Cooper, J. M., Jr, (2009), *Woodrow Wilson: A Biography*, New York: Alfred A. Knopf.

Cooper, N. (2000), 'The Pariah Agenda and New Labour's Ethical Arms Sales Policy', in Richard Little and Mark Wickham-Jones (eds), *New Labour's Foreign Policy: A New Moral Crusade?*, Manchester: Manchester University Press, 147–67.

Cooper, N. and Mutimer, D. M. (eds) (2012), *Reconceptualizing Arms Control*, Oxford: Routledge.

Cooper, N. and Turner, M. (2013), 'The Iron Fist of Liberal Intervention inside the Velvet Glove of Kantian Idealism: A Response to Burke', *Critical Studies on Security*, 1/1: 35–41.

Copeland, D. (2000), *The Origins of Major War*, Ithaca, NY: Cornell University Press.

Copeland, D. C. (2006), 'The Constructivist Challenge to Structural Realism: A Review Essay', in S. Guzzini and A. Leander (eds), *Constructivism and International Relations: Alexander Wendt and his Critics*, Abingdon and New York: Routledge, 1–20.

Corcoran-Nantes, Y. (2005), *Lost Voices: Central Asian Women Confronting Transition*, London and New York: Zed Books.

Cordesman, A. and Al-Rodhan, K. (2005), *The Changing Risks in Global Oil Supply and Demand: Crisis or Evolving Solutions?*, Washington, DC: Center for Strategic and International Studies.

Coronil, F. (1997), *The Magical State: Nature, Money, and Modernity in Venezuela*, Chicago: University of Chicago Press.

Cox, M. and Stokes, D. (2012), *US Foreign Policy*, Oxford: Oxford University Press.

Cox, R. (1981), 'Social Forces, States and World Orders: Beyond International Relations Theory', *Millennium*, 10/2: 126–55.

Cox, R. (1985), 'Social Forces, States and World Orders: Beyond International Relations Theory', in Robert O. Keohane (ed.), *Neorealism and its Critics*, New York: Columbia University Press, 204–54.

Crawford, N. (1994), 'A Security Regime among Democracies: Cooperation among Iroquois Nations', *International Organization*, 48/3: 345–85.

Credit Suisse (2012), *Global Wealth Report*, Zurich: Credit Suisse AG Research Institute.

Crenshaw, M. (1998), 'Questions to be Answered, Research to be Done, Knowledge to be Applied', in Walter Reich (ed.), *Origins of Terrorism: Psychologies, Ideologies, Theologies, States of Mind*, Washington, DC: Woodrow Wilson Center Press, 247–60.

Crenshaw, M. (2003), 'Coercive Diplomacy and the Response to Terrorism', in R. J. Art and P. M. Cronin (eds), *The United States and Coercive Diplomacy*, Washington, DC: United States Institute of Peace, 305–57.

Croddy, E. A. and Wirtz, J. (eds) (2005), *Weapons of Mass Destruction: An Encyclopedia of Worldwide Policy, Technology, and History*, 2 vols, Santa Barbara, CA: ABC-Clio.

Cronin, A. K. (2009), *How Terrorism Ends: Understanding the Decline and Demise of Terrorist Campaigns*, Princeton, NJ: Princeton University Press.

Cronin, A. K. et al. (2014), *Responding to Terrorism: A Batch from International Security*, The MIT Press digital publication.

Cronin, P. M., Ratner, E., Colby, E., Hosford, Z. M., and Sullivan, A. (2014), *Tailored Coercion Competition and Risk in Maritime Asia*, Washington, DC: Center for a New American Century.

Crouch. D. (2014), 'The Rise of Anti-Immigrant Sweden Democrats: We Don't Feel at Home Any More and it's Their Fault', *Observer*, 14 December.

Cruickshank, J. W. (ed.) (2007), *Critical Realism: The Difference It Makes*, London: Routledge.

Curley, M. G. and Siu-lun, W. (eds.) (2008), *Security and Migration in Asia: The Dynamics of Securitisation*, Milton Park: Routledge.

Daalder, I. H. (ed.) (1993), *Rethinking the Unthinkable: New Directions for Nuclear Arms Control*, London: Routledge.

Dabelko, G. (2009), 'Planning for Climate Change: The Security Community's Precautionary Principle', *Climatic Change*, 96/1–2: 13–21.

Dalby, S. (1990), *Creating the Second Cold War: The Discourse of Politics*, New York: Guilford Press.

Dalby, S. (1992a), 'Ecopolitical Discourse: "Environmental Security" and Political Geography', *Progress in Human Geography*, 16/4: 503–22.

Dalby, S. (1992b), 'Security, Modernity, Ecology: The Dilemmas of Post-Cold War Security Discourse', *Alternatives*, 17: 95–134.

Dalby, S. (2002), *Environmental Security*, Minneapolis: University of Minnesota Press.

Dalby, S. (2009), *Security and Environmental Change*, Cambridge: Polity Press.

Dalby, S. and Ó Tuathail, G. (1998), *Rethinking Geopolitics*, London: Routledge.

Dam, K. (2001), *The Rules of the Global Game*, University of Chicago Press: Chicago.

Danielsson. B. and Danielsson, M. (1986), *Poisoned Reign: French Nuclear Colonialism in the Pacific*, London: Penguin.

Dauphinée, E. (2008), *The Ethics of Researching War: Looking for Bosnia*, Manchester: University of Manchester Press.

Dauvergne, P. (1998), 'Weak States, Strong States: A State-in-Society Perspective', in P. Dauvergne (ed.), *Weak and Strong States in Asia-Pacific Societies*, Australia: Allen and Unwin, 1–10.

Davis, M. (2001), *Late Victorian Holocausts: El Niño Famines and the Making of the Third World*, London: Verso.

Davis, M. (2006), *Planet of Slums*, London: Verso.

de Costa, R., (2009), 'Indigenous Diplomacies before the Nation-State', in J. Marshall Beier, ed., *Indigenous Diplomacies*, New York: Palgrave Macmillan, 61–77.

de Goede, M. (2012), *Speculative Security: The Politics of Pursuing Terrorist Monies*, Minneapolis and London: University of Minnesota Press.

de Soysa, I. (2000), 'The Resource Curse: Are Civil Wars Driven by Rapacity or Paucity?', in M. Berdal and D. Malone (eds), *Greed and Grievance: Economic Agendas and Civil Wars*, Boulder, CO: Lynne Rienner, 113–36.

de Waal, A. (2002), *'New-Variant' Famine: How Aids Has Changed the Hunger Equation*, 20 November, http://allafrica.com/stories/200211200471.html.

de Waal, A. (2006), *AIDS and Power: Why There is No Political Crisis—Yet*, London: Zed Books.

de Waal, A. (2007), 'No Such Thing as Humanitarian Intervention: Why We Need to Rethink How to Realize the "Responsibility to Protect" in Wartime', *Harvard International Review*, 21: 1–7.

Defense Security Cooperation Agency (2005), 'Saudi Arabia: Continued Assistance in the Modernization of the SANG', news release, transmittal no. 06–05, 3 October.

Deibert, R. and Rohozinski, R. (2009), 'Tracking GhostNet: Investigating a Cyber Espionage Network', *Information Warfare Monitor*, Toronto: The Munk School of Global Affairs.

Deibert, R. and Rohozinski, R. (2010), 'Risking Security: Policies and Paradoxes of Cyberspace Security', *International Political Sociology*, 4/1: 15–32.

Demchak, C. (2010), 'Cybered Conflict as a New Frontier', *New Atlanticist*, http://www.acus.org/new_atlanticist/cybered-conflict-new-frontier.

Deng, F. M., Kimaro, S., Lyons, T., Rothchild, D., and Zartman, W. (1996), *Sovereignty as Responsibility: Conflict Management in Africa*, Washington, DC: Brookings Institution.

Department of Defense (2007), *Transforming the Way DoD Looks at Energy: An Approach to Establishing an Energy Strategy*, Report FT602T1, April.

Der Derian, James (1995), 'The Value of Security: Hobbes, Marx, Nietzsche, and Baudrillard', in Ronnie D. Lipschutz (ed.), *On Security*, New York: Columbia University Press, 24–45.

Desch, M. C. (1998), 'Culture Clash: Assessing the Importance of Ideas in Security Studies', *International Security*, 23/1: 141–70.

Deudney, D. (1990), 'The Case against Linking Environmental Degradation and National Security', *Millennium: Journal of International Studies*, 19/3: 461–76.

Deudney, D. (2006), *Bounding Power: Republican Security Theory from the Polis to the Global Village*, Princeton, NJ: Princeton University Press.

Deudney, D. H. (1995), 'The Philadelphian System: Sovereignty, Arms Control, and Balance of Power in the American States-Union, circa 1787–1861', *International Organization*, 49/2: 191–228.

Deutsch, K. (1957), *Political Community and the North Atlantic Area*, New York: Greenwood Press.

Devine, K. M. (2006), 'The Myth of "The Myth of Irish Neutrality": Deconstructing Concepts of Irish Neutrality Using International Relations Theories', *Irish Studies in International Affairs*, 17: 115–39.

Dicken, Peter (1992), *Global Shifts: The Internationalization of Economic Activity*, 2nd edn, London: Paul Chapman Publisher.

Diken, B. and Laustsen, C. B. (2005), 'Becoming Abject: Rape as a Weapon of War', *Body & Society*, 11/1: 11–28.

Dillon, M. (1996), *Politics of Security: Towards a Political Philosophy of Continental Thought*, London: Routledge.

Dillon, M. (2006), *Governing Terror*, London: Palgrave Macmillan.

Dillon, M. and Lobo-Guerrero, L. (2008), 'Biopolitics of Security in the 21st Century: An Introduction', *Review of International Studies*, 34/2: 265–92.

Dillon, M. and Neal, A. W. (eds) (2008), *Foucault on Politics, Security and War*, Basingstoke: Palgrave Macmillan.

Dimand, M. A. and Dimand, R. W. (1996), *The History of Game Theory, Volume I: From the Beginnings to 1945*, London: Routledge.

Dingley, J. and Kirk-Smith, M. (2002), 'Symbolism and Sacrifice in Terrorism', *Small Wars and Insurgencies*, 13/1: 102–28.

Dixon, N. (1976), *On the Psychology of Military Incompetence*, London: Basic Books.

Dodge, R. (2006), *The Strategist: The Life and Times of Thomas Schelling*, New Hampshire: Hollis Pub Co.

Donnelly, J. (1998), *International Human Rights*, 2nd edn, Boulder, CO: Westview.

Doty, R. L. (1996), *Imperial Encounters: The Politics of Representation in North–South Relations*, Minneapolis: University of Minnesota Press.

Doty, R. L. (1999), 'Immigration and the Politics of Security', *Security Studies*, 8/2–3: 71–93.

Douzinas, Costas (2011), 'The IMF must realise that, in Greece, the treatment is worse than the disease', *The Guardian*, updated 15 December 2011, http://www.guardian.co.uk/commentisfree/2011/dec/15/imf-greece-treatment-worse-disease.

Doyle, M. (1997), *Ways of War and Peace*, London: Norton.

Drayton, R. (2002), 'The Collaboration of Labour: Slaves, Empires and Globalizations in the Atlantic World, c.1600–1860', in A. G. Hopkins (ed.), *Globalization in World History*, London: Pimlico, 98–114.

Dreyer, I. and Popescu, N. (2014), 'Do Sanctions against Russia Work?', *European Union Institute for Security Studies Issue Brief* 35 (December).

Drezner, D. W. (1998), 'Conflict Expectations and the Paradox of Economic Coercion', *International Studies Quarterly*, 42 / December: 709–31.

Drimie, S. (2003), 'HIV / AIDS and Land: Case Studies from Kenya, Lesotho and South Africa', *Development Southern Africa*, 20 / 5: 647–58.

Dubois, W. E. B. (1925), 'Worlds of Colour', *Foreign Affairs*, 3 / 3: 423–44.

Duffield, M. (2001), *Global Governance and the New Wars: The Merging of Development and Security*, London: Zed Books.

Duffield, M. (2007), *Development, Security and Unending War: Governing the World of Peoples*, Cambridge: Polity.

Dunn Cavelty, M. (2008), *Cyber-Security and Threat Politics: US Efforts to Secure the Information Age*, Abingdon: Routledge.

Dunn Cavelty, M. (2014), 'Breaking the Cyber-Security Dilemma: Aligning Security Needs and Removing Vulnerabilities', *Science and Engineering Ethics*, 20 / 3: 701–15.

Dutton, P. A. (2014), *China's Maritime Disputes in the East and South China Seas*, Testimony before a Hearing of the House Foreign Affairs Committee, 14 January.

Dycus, S. (1996), *National Defense and the Environment*, Hanover, NH: University Press of New England.

Dyson, E., Gilder, G., Keyworth, G., and Toffler, A. (1996), 'Cyberspace and the American Dream: A Magna Carta for the Knowledge Age', *The Information Society*, 12 / 3: 295–308.

Easterly, W. (2001), *The Elusive Quest for Growth: Economists' Adventures and Misadventures in the Tropics*, Cambridge, MA: MIT Press.

Edkins, J. (2003), *Trauma and the Memory of Politics*, Cambridge: Cambridge University Press.

Edmonds, M. (ed.) (1981), *International Arms Procurement: New Directions*, New York: Pergamon Press.

Elbe, S. (2006), 'Should HIV / AIDS be Securitized?', *International Studies Quarterly*, 50 / 1: 119–44.

Elbe, S. (2009), *Virus Alert: Seurity, Governmentality and the AIDS Pandemic*, New York: Columbia University Press.

Elbe, Stefan (2010), *Security and Global Health: Towards the Medicalization of Insecurity*, Cambridge: Polity Press.

Elkins, C. and Pederson, S. (eds) (2005), *Settler Colonialism in the Twentieth Century*, New York: Routledge.

Elliott, K. A., Hufbauer, G. C., and Oegg, B. (2008), 'Sanctions', *The Concise Encyclopedia of Economics*. Library of Economics and Liberty, http: / / www.econlib.org / library / Enc / Sanctions.html.

Ellison, Jesse (2011), 'The Military's Secret Shame', *Newsweek*, 4 March, http: / / www.newsweek.com / militarys-secret-shame-66459.

Elman, C. (1996), 'Horses for Courses: Why Not Neorealist Theories of Foreign Policy?', *Security Studies*, 6 / 1: 7–53.

Elshtain, J. B. (1987), *Women and War*, New York: Basic Books.

Elshtain, J. B. (ed.) (1992), *Just War Theory*, Oxford: Basil Blackwell.

Emmers, R. (2003), 'ASEAN and the Securitization of Transnational Crime in Southeast Asia', *The Pacific Review*, 16 / 3: 419–38.

Emmers, R. (2003), *Cooperative Security and the Balance of Power in ASEAN and the ARF*, London: RoutledgeCurzon.

Emmers, R. (2004), *Non-Traditional Security in the Asia-Pacific: The Dynamics of Securitisation*, Singapore: Eastern Universities Press.

Emmers, R. (2010), *Geopolitics and Maritime Territorial Disputes in East Asia*, Abingdon: Routledge.

Emmers, R. (2013), *Resource Management and Contested Territories in East Asia*, Basingstoke: Palgrave Macmillan.

Emmers, R., Greener, B. K., and Thomas, N. (2008), 'Securitising Human Trafficking in the Asia-Pacific: Regional Organisations and Response Strategies', in M. G. Curley and S. L. Wong (eds), *Security and Migration in Asia: The Dynamics of Securitisation*, Abingdon: Routledge, 59–82.

Enders, W. and Sandler, T. (2006), *The Political Economy of Terrorism*, Cambridge: Cambridge University Press.

Energy Information Administration (EIA) (2011), 'International Energy Outlook 2011', September, www.eia.doe.gov.

Energy Information Administration (EIA) (2014), 'International Energy Outlook 2014', September, www.eia.doe.gov.

Enloe, Cynthia (1989), *Bananas, Bases and Beaches: Making Feminist Sense of International Politics*, London: Pinter.

Enloe, C. (1993), *The Morning After: Sexual Politics at the End of the Cold War*, London: University of California Press.

Enloe, C. (2004), *Maneuvers*, Berkeley and Los Angeles, University of California Press.

Enloe, Cynthia (2004), *The Curious Feminist*, London: University of California Press.

Enloe, C. (2007), *Globalization and Militarism: Feminists Make the Link*, Lanham: Rowman & Littlefield.

Enloe, C. (2010), *Nimo's War, Emma's War: Making Feminist Sense of the Iraq War*, Berkeley: University of California Press.

Enloe, C. (2015), 'The Recruiter and the Sceptic: A Critical Feminist Approach to Military Studies', *Critical Military Studies*, 1/1: 3–10.

Epstein, Charlotte (2011), 'Who Speaks? Discourse, the Subject and the Study of Identity in International Politics', *European Journal of International Relations*, 17/2: 327–50.

Ericksen, P. (2008), 'What is the Vulnerability of a Food System to Global Environmental Change?', *Ecology and Society*, 13/2: 14.

Erickson, J. (2003), *Hacking: The Art of Exploitation*, San Francisco: No Starch Press.

Eriksson, J. (1999), 'Observers or Advocates? On the Political Role of Security Analysts', *Cooperation and Conflict*, 34/3: 311–30.

Escobar, A. (1995), *Encountering Development: The Making and Unmaking of the Third World*, Princeton, NJ: Princeton University Press.

Escobar, A. (2010), 'Worlds and Knowledges Otherwise: The Latin American Modernity/Coloniality Research Program', in W. Mignolo and A. Escobar (eds), *Globalization and the Decolonial Option*, London: Routledge, 33–64.

Esty, D., Goldstone, J., Gurr, T., Harff, B., Levy, M., Dabelko, G., Surko, P., and Unger, A. (1999), 'State Failure Task Force Report: Phase II Findings', *Environmental Change and Security Project Report*, 5: 49–72.

Etzold, T. H. (1978), 'American Organization for National Security 1945–50', in Thomas H. Etzold and John Lewis Gaddis (eds), *Containment: Documents on American Policy and Strategy, 1945–50*, New York: Columbia University Press, 1–23.

EU (1995), European Union, The Europol Convention, Article 2, www.europol.europa.eu/index.asp?page=legalconv.

Evangelista, Matthew (2011), *Gender, Nationalism and War: Conflict on the Movie Screen*, Cambridge: Cambridge University Press.

Evans, G. (2008), *The Responsibility to Protect: Ending Mass Atrocity Crimes Once and for All*, Washington: Brookings Institution.

Evans, P. (2004), 'Human Security and East Asia: In the Beginning', *Journal of East Asian Studies*, 4: 263–84.

Ewan, P. (2007), 'Deepening the Human Security Debate: Beyond the Politics of Conceptual Clarification', *Politics*, 27/3: 182–9.

Fabian, J. (2002), *Time and the Other: How Anthropology Makes its Object*, New York: Columbia University Press.

Falk, R. (1971), *This Endangered Planet: Prospects and Proposals for Human Survival*, New York: Random House.

Fanon, F. (1990), *The Wretched of the Earth*, London: Penguin Books.

Fanon, F. (2008), *Black Skin, White Masks*, London: Pluto Press.

FAO (Food and Agriculture Organization of the United Nations) (2003), *HIV/AIDS and Agriculture: Impacts and Responses—Case Studies from Namibia, Uganda and Zambia*, Rome: Food and Agricultural Organization, December.

FAO (2010), *Global Forest Resources Assessment 2010*. FAO Forestry Paper 163, FAO, Rome.

FAO (2011), *The State of Food Insecurity in the World 2011*, Rome: Food and Agriculture Organization.

Farah, D. and Braun, S. (2007), *Merchant of Death: Money, Guns, Planes and the Man Who Makes War Possible*, Hoboken, NJ: Wiley.

Farrell, T. (2002), 'Constructivist Security Studies: Portrait of a Research Program', *International Studies Review*, 4/1: 49–72.

Farwell, J. P. and Rohozinski, R. (2011), 'Stuxnet and the Future of Cyber War', *Survival: Global Politics and Strategy*, 53/1: 23–40.

Fazal, T. M. (2004), 'State Death in the International System', *International Organisation*, 58/2: 311–44.

Fehl, C. (2004), 'Explaining the International Criminal Court: A "Practice Test" for Rationalist and

Constructivist Approaches', *European Journal of International Relations*, 10/3: 357–94.

Felbab-Brown, V. (2014), 'Changing the Game or Dropping the Ball? Mexico's Security and Anti-Crime Strategy on President Enrique Peña Nieto', The Brookings Institution, Washington DC, November.

Fidler, D. (2004), SARS: *Governance and the Globalization of Disease*, New York: Palgrave.

Fidler, D. and Gostin, L. (2008), *Biosecurity in the Global Age: Biological Weapons, Public Health and the Rule of Law*, Stanford, CA: Stanford University Press.

Fierke, K. M. (2001), 'Critical Methodology and Constructivism', in K. M. Fierke and K. E. Jørgensen (eds), *Constructing International Relations: The Next Generation*, New York: M. E. Sharpe, 115–35.

Fierke, K. M. (2002), 'Links across the Abyss: Language and Logic in International Relations', *International Studies Quarterly*, 46/3: 331–54.

Fierke, K. M. (2007), *Critical Approaches to International Security*, Cambridge: Polity.

Fierke, K. M. and Jørgensen, K. E. (eds) (2001), *Constructing International Relations: The Next Generation*, New York: M. E. Sharpe.

Fierke, K. M. and Wiener, A. (1999), 'Constructing Institutional Interests: EU and NATO Enlargement', *Journal of European Public Policy*, 6/5: 721–42.

Finckenauer, O. and Voronin, Y. A. (2001), 'The Threat of Russian Organized Crime', *National Institute of Justice*, NCJ 187085, June.

Findlay, T. (2002), *The Use of Force in UN Peace Operations*, Oxford: Oxford University Press for SIPRI.

Finnemore, M. (1996), 'Constructing Norms of Humanitarian Intervention', in P. J. Katzenstein (ed.), *The Culture of National Security: Norms and Identity in World Politics*, New York: Columbia University Press, 153–85.

Finnemore, M. (2003), *The Purpose of Intervention: Changing Beliefs about the Use of Force*, Ithaca, NY: Cornell University Press.

Finnemore, M. (2008), 'Paradoxes in Humanitarian Intervention', in Richard M. Price (ed.), *Moral Limit and Possibility in World Politics*, Cambridge: Cambridge University Press, 197–224.

Finnemore, M. and Sikkink, K. (1998), 'International Norm Dynamics and Political Change', *International Organization*, 52/4: 887–917.

Finnemore, M. and Sikkink, K. (2001), 'Taking Stock: The Constructivist Research Program in International Relations and Comparative Politics', *Annual Review of Political Science*, 4: 371–416.

Flint, J. and de Waal, A. (2008), *Darfur: A New History of a Long War*, rev. and updated edn, London: Zed Books.

Floyd, R. (2010), *Security and the Environment: Securitisation Theory and US Environmental Security Policy*, Cambridge: Cambridge University Press.

Fortna, V. P. (2008), *Does Peacekeeping Work? Shaping Belligerents' Choices after Civil Wars*, Princeton, NJ: Princeton University Press.

Fox, M. (2004), 'Girl Soldiers: Human Security and Gendered Insecurity', *Security Dialogue*, 35/4: 465–79.

Franck, T. and Rodley, N. (1973), 'After Bangladesh: The Law of Humanitarian Intervention by Military Force', *American Journal of International Law*, 67/2: 275–305.

Frederking, B. (2003), 'Constructing Post-Cold War Collective Security', *American Political Science Review*, 97/3: 363–78.

Freedman, L. (1988), 'I Exist; Therefore I Deter', *International Security*, 13/1: 177–95.

Freedman, L. (1992), 'The Concept of Security', in Mary Hawksworth and Maurice Kogan (eds), *Encyclopaedia of Government and Politics*, 2nd edn, London: Routledge, II, 752–61.

Freedman, L. (ed.) (1998), *Strategic Coercion: Concepts and Cases*, Oxford: Oxford University Press.

Freedman, L. (2004), *Deterrence*, Cambridge: Polity Press.

Fukuyama, F. (1992), *The End of History and the Last Man*, New York: Free Press.

Gaddis, J. (1986), 'The Long Peace: Elements of Stability in the Postwar International System', *International Security*, 10/4: 99–142.

Galtung, J. (1969), 'Violence, Peace and Peace Research', *Journal of Peace Research*, 6/3: 167–91.

Galtung, J. (1990), 'Cultural Violence', *Journal of Peace Research*, 27/3: 291–305.

Ganguly, S. and Kraig, M. R. (2005), 'The 2001–2002 Indo-Pakistani Crisis: Exposing the Limits of Coercive Diplomacy', *Security Studies*, 14/2: 290–324.

GCR2P (2008), Global Centre for the Responsibility to Protect, 'The Georgia–Russia Crisis and the

Responsibility to Protect: A Background Note', http://www.globalr2p.org/publications/132.

Geertz, C. (1973), *The Interpretation of Cultures*, New York: Basic Books.

George, A. L. and Simons, W. E. (eds) (1994), *The Limits of Coercive Diplomacy*, 2nd rev. edn, Boulder, CO: Westview.

George, A. L., Hall, D., and Simons, W. E. (1971), *The Limits of Coercive Diplomacy: Laos, Cuba, Vietnam*, Boston: Little, Brown.

George, S. (1976), *How the Other Half Dies*, New York: Penguin Books.

Gettleman, J. (2007), 'Rape epidemic raises trauma of Congo War', *The New York Times*, 7 October.

Gheciu, A. (2005a), 'Security Institutions as Agents of Socialization? NATO and the "New Europe"', *International Organization*, 59/4: 970–1012.

Gheciu, A. (2005b), *NATO in the New Europe: The Politics of Socialization after the Cold War*, Stanford, CA: Stanford University Press.

Gheciu, A. (2008), *Securing Civilization: The EU, NATO, and the OSCE in the Post-9/11 World*, Oxford: Oxford University Press.

Gillespie, S. (ed.) (2006), *AIDS, Poverty, and Hunger: Challenges and Responses*, Washington, DC: International Food Policy Research Institute.

Gilligan, C. (2009), '"Highly Vulnerable?" Political Violence and the Social Construction of Traumatized Children', *Journal of Peace Research*, 46/1: 119–34.

Gilpin, R. (1981), *War and Change in World Politics*, Cambridge: Cambridge University Press.

Giraldo, J. and Trinkunas, H. A. (eds) (2007), *Terrorism Finance and State Responses: A Comparative Perspective*, Palo Alto, CA: Stanford University Press.

Glaser, C. (1991), *Analyzing Strategic Nuclear Policy*, Princeton, NJ: Princeton University Press.

Glaser, C. (1994–5), 'Realists as Optimists: Cooperation as Self-Help', *International Security*, 19/3: 50–90.

Glaser, C. (1997), 'The Security Dilemma Revisited', *World Politics*, 50/1: 171–201.

Glaser, C. (2010), *Rational Theory of International Politics: The Logic of Competition and Cooperation*, Princeton, NJ: Princeton University Press.

Gleick, P. (1991), 'Environment and Security: The Clear Connections', *Bulletin of the Atomic Scientists*, 47/3: 17–21.

Glenn, J. (2008), *Globalisation: North–South Perspectives*, Oxford: Routledge.

Gloannec, A.-M. Le, and Smolar, A. (eds) (2003), *Entre Kant et Kosovo: Études offertes à Pierre Hassner*, Paris: Presses de Sciences Po.

Godson, R. and Williams, P. (1998), 'Strengthening Cooperation against Transnational Crime', *Survival*, 40/3 (Autumn).

Goetschel, L. (1999), 'Neutrality: A Really Dead Concept?', *Cooperation and Conflict*, 34/2: 115–39.

Goldmann, K. (1988), *Change and Stability in Foreign Policy: The Problems and Possibilities of Detente*, Princeton, NJ: Princeton University Press.

Goodale, M. and Postero, N. (eds) (2013), *Neoloberalism Interrupted: Social Change and Contested Governance in Contemporary Latin America*, Stanford, CA: Stanford University Press.

Gorman, S. and Barnes, J. E. (2011), 'Cyber combat: Act of war Pentagon sets stage for U.S. to respond to computer sabotage with military force', *The Wall Street Journal*, 31 May.

Gostin, L. O., Lucey, D., and Phelan, A. (2014), 'The Ebola Epidemic: A Global Health Emergency', *The Journal of the American Medical Association*, 312/11: 1095–6.

Graham, D. T. (2000), 'The People Paradox: Human Movements and Human Security in a Globalising World', in D. T. Graham and N. K. Poku (eds), *Migration, Globalisation and Human Security*, London: Routledge, 192–9.

Graham, G. (1997), *Ethics and International Relations*, Oxford: Blackwell.

Gray, C. (1982), *Strategic Studies and Public Policy: The American Experience*, Lexington, KY: University Press of Kentucky.

Gray, C. S. (1977), 'Across the Nuclear Divide: Strategic Studies Past and Present', *International Security*, 2/1: 24–46.

Gray, C. S. (1999), *The Second Nuclear Age*, Boulder, CO: Lynne Rienner.

Grayson, K. (2003), 'Securitization and the Boomerang Debate: A Rejoinder to Liotta and Smith-Windsor', *Security Dialogue*, 34/3.

Grayson, K. (2008), *Chasing Dragons: Security, Identity, and Illicit Drugs in Canada*, Toronto: University of Toronto Press.

Green, P. (1966), *Deadly Logic: The Theory of Nuclear Deterrence*, Columbus, OH: Ohio State University Press.

Green, P. (1968), 'Science, Government, and the Case of RAND: A Singular Pluralism', *World Politics*, 20/2: 301–26.

Gregory, D. (2010), 'War and Peace', *Transactions of the Institute of British Geographers*, 35/2: 154–85.

Gregory, D. (2011), 'From a View to a Kill: Drones and Late Modern War', *Theory, Culture & Society*, 28/7–8: 188–215.

Gregory, R. and Mendelsohn, R. (1993), 'Perceived Risk, Dread, and Benefits', *Risk Analysis*, 13/3: 259–64.

Grillot, S. J. and Cruise, R. (2010), *Protecting Our Ports*, Farnham: Ashgate.

Grillot, S. J. and Messitte, Z. (2013), *Understanding the Global Community*, Norman: University of Oklahoma Press.

Grimmett, R. F. and Kerr P. (2012), *Conventional Arms Transfers to Developing Nations, 2004–2011*, Washington, DC: Congressional Research Service, Library of Congress.

Gross, M. J. (2011), 'Stuxnet Worm: A declaration of cyber-war', *Vanity Fair*, April.

Grovogui, S. (2002), 'Postcolonial Criticism: International reality and modes of inquiry', in G. Chowdhery and S. Nair (eds), *Power, Postcolonialism and International Relations*, London: Routledge, 33–55.

Grovogui, S. (2006), 'Mind, Body and Gut! Elements of a Postcolonial Human Rights Discourse', in B. G. Jones (ed.), *Decolonizing International Relations*, Lanham: Rowman & Littlefield, 179–96.

Gruffydd Jones, B. (2008), 'The Global Political Economy of Social Crisis: Towards a Critique of the "Failed State" Ideology', *Review of International Political Economy*, 15/2: 18–205.

The Guardian (2014), 'Hamid Karzai', *The Guardian*, http://www.theguardian.com/world/hamid-karzai.

Guha, R. (1988), 'On Some Aspects of the Historiography of Colonial India', in R. Guha and G. C. Spivak (eds), *Selected Subaltern Studies*, New York: Oxford University Press, 37–44.

Guillemin, J. (2005), *Biological Weapons: From the Invention of State-Sponsored Programs to Contemporary Bioterrorism*, New York: Columbia University Press.

Gurr, T. R. (1993), *Minorities at Risk*, Washington, DC: United States Institute of Peace Press.

Gurr, T. (2000), *People versus States: Minorities at Risk in the New Century*, Washington, DC: United States Institute of Peace Press.

Gusterson, H. (1998), *Nuclear Rites: A Weapons Laboratory at the End of the Cold War*, Berkeley and Los Angeles: University of California Press.

Gusterson, H. (1999), 'Nuclear Weapons and the Other in the Western Imagination', *Cultural Anthropology*, 14/1: 111–43.

Guzzini, S. and Jung, D (eds) (2004), *Contemporary Security Analysis and Copenhagen Peace Research*, London: Routledge.

Guzzini, S. and Leander, A. (eds) (2006), *Constructivism and International Relations. Alexander Wendt and his Critics*, Abingdon and New York: Routledge.

Haacke, J. and Williams, P. D. (2008), 'Regional Arrangements, Securitization and Transnational Security Challenges: The African Union and the Association of Southeast Asian Nations Compared', *Security Studies*, 17/4: 775–809.

Haas, R. N. (2002), 'Think Tanks and US Foreign Policy: A Policy-Maker's Perspective', *US Foreign Policy Agenda*, 7/3 (November), http://2001-2009.state.gov/s/p/rem/15506.htm.

Haass, R. (ed.) (1998), *Economic Sanctions and American Diplomacy*, New York: Council on Foreign Relations.

Hagemann, A. M. B. (2011), *Security as a Vocation: Realists and Strategists in the Halls of Wisdom and the Corridors of Power*, Copenhagen: MA Thesis.

Halikiopoulou, D. and Vasilopoulou, S. (2014), 'Support for the Far Right in the 2014 European Parliament Elections: A Comparative Perspective', *The Political Quarterly*, 85/3: 285–8.

Halperin, S. (2006), 'International Relations Theory and the Hegemony of Western Conceptions of Modernity', in B. G. Jones (ed.), *Decolonizing International Relations*, Lanham: Rowman & Littlefield, 43–63.

Hanieh, Adam (2011), 'Egypt's orderly transition? International aid and the rush to structural adjustment', *Jadaliyya*, updated 29 May 2011, http://www.jadaliyya.com/pages/index/1711/egypts-%E2%80%98orderly-transition%E2%80%99-international-aid-and.

Hansen, B. (2000), *Unipolarity and the Middle East*, Richmond, Curzon Press.

Hansen, C. (1988), *US Nuclear Weapons: The Secret History*, New York: Orion Books.

Hansen, L. (2000), 'The Little Mermaid's Silent Security Dilemma and the Absence of Gender in the Copenhagen School', *Millennium: Journal of International Studies*, 29/2: 285–306.

Hansen, L. (2006), *Security as Practice: Discourse Analysis and the Bosnian War*, London: Routledge.

Harbom, L. and Wallensteen, P. (2007), 'Armed Conflict, 1989–2006', *Journal of Peace Research*, 44/5: 623–34.

Harkavy, R. E. (1975), *The Arms Trade and International Systems*, Cambridge: Ballinger Publishing Company.

Harvey, D. (2007), *A Brief History of Neoliberalism*, Oxford: Oxford University Press.

Harvey, D. (2014), *Seventeen Contradictions and the End of Capitalism*, London: Profile Books.

Hassner, P. (1993), 'Beyond Nationalism and Internationalism: Ethnicity and World Order', *Survival*, 35/2: 49–65.

Hassner, P. (1997), *Violence and Peace: From the Atomic Bomb to Ethnic Cleansing*, trans. Jane Brenton, Budapest: Central European University Press.

Haubrick, D. (2003), 'September 11, Anti-Terror Laws and Civil Liberties: Britain, France and Germany Compared', *Government and Opposition*, 38/1: 3–28.

Hayden, R. (1996), 'Imagined Communities and Real Victims: Self-Determination and Ethnic Cleansing in Yugoslavia', *American Ethnologist*, 23/4: 273–96.

Hayes, J. (2011), 'Britain at War: Securitization, Identity, and the War in Iraq', *Social Science Research Network (SSRN)*, APSA 2011 Annual Meeting Paper, 1–21.

Heinecken, Lindy (2001), 'Living in Terror: The Looming Security Threat to Southern Africa', *African Security Review*, 10/4: 6–17.

Heininen, L. (1994), 'The Military and the Environment: An Arctic Case', in J. Kakonen (ed.), *Green Security or Militarized Environment*, Aldershot: Dartmouth, 155–67.

Heisler, M. and Layton-Henry, Z. (1993), 'Migration and the Links between Social and Societal Security', in O. Wæver, B. Buzan, M. Kelstrup, and P. Lemaitre (eds), *Identity, Migraton and the New Security Agenda in Europe*, London: Pinter, 148–66.

Herd, G. P. and Lofgren J. (2001), '"Societal Security" in the Baltic States and EU Integration', *Cooperation and Conflict*, 36/3: 273–96.

Herring, E. (2011), 'Variegated Neoliberalization, Human Development and Resistance: Iraq in Global Context', *International Journal of Contemporary Iraqi Studies*, 5/3: 337–45.

Herring, E. and Buzan, B. (1998), *The Arms Dynamic in World Politics*, Boulder, CO: Lynee Rienner.

Herring, E. and Rangwala, G. (2006), *Iraq in Fragments: The Occupation and its Legacy*, London: Hurst and Cornell University Press.

Herring, E. and Stokes, D. (2011a), 'Critical Realism and Historical Materialism as Resources for Critical Terrorism Studies', *Critical Studies on Terrorism*, 4/1: 5–21.

Herring, E. and Stokes, D. (eds) (2011b), 'Special Issue: Bringing Critical Realism and Historical Materialism into Critical Terrorism Studies', *Critical Studies on Terrorism*, 4/1.

Herz, J. H. (1950), 'Idealist Internationalism and the Security Dilemma', *World Politics*, 2/2: 157–80.

Heyward, Andrew (2003), *Political Ideologies: An introduction*, 3rd edn, Basingstoke: Palgrave Macmillan.

Hicks Stiehm, J. (ed.) (1983), *Women and Men's Wars*, Oxford: Pergamon Press.

Hicks Stiehm, J. (1989), *Arms and the Enlisted Woman*, Philadelphia: Temple.

Hill, C. (1994), 'Academic International Relations: The Siren Song of Policy Relevance', in Christopher Hill and Pamela Beshoff (eds), *Two Worlds of International Relations: Academics, Practitioners and the Trade in Ideas*, London: Routledge, 3–25.

Hirschkind, C. and Mahmood, S. (2002), 'Feminism, The Taliban and the Politics of Counterinsurgency', *Fathom Archive*, fathom.lib.uchicago.edu/1/777777190136

Hitch, C. J. (1960), *The Uses of Economics*, P-2179-RC, Santa Monica, CA: Rand Corporation.

Hobson, J. (2004), *The Eastern Origins of Western Civilization*, Cambridge: Cambridge University Press.

Hoffman, B. (2006), *Inside Terrorism*, rev. and expanded edn, New York: Columbia University Press.

Hoffmann, S. (1977), 'An American Social Science: International Relations', *Daedalus*, 106/3: 41–60.

Hofstader, R. (1970), 'Reflections on Violence in the United States', in R. Hofstader and M. Wallace (eds), *American Violence: A Documentary History*, New York: Alfred A. Knopf, 3–43.

Hogan, M. J. (1998), *A Cross of Iron: Harry S. Truman and the Origins of the National Security State, 1945–1954*, Cambridge: Cambridge University Press.

Holsti, K. (1996), *The State, War, and the State of War*, Cambridge: Cambridge University Press.

Holt, V. K. and Berkman, T. C. (2006), *The Impossible Mandate? Military Preparedness, The Responsibility to Protect and Modern Peace Operations*, Washington, DC: Henry L. Stimson Center.

Homer-Dixon, T. (1999), *Environment, Scarcity, and Violence*, Princeton, NJ: Princeton University Press.

Hooks, B. (1995), 'Feminism and Militarism: A Comment', *Woman's Studies Quarterly*, 3–4: 58–64.

Hopf, T. (1998), 'The Promise of Constructivism in International Relations Theory', *International Security*, 23/1: 171–200.

Hough, Peter (2008), *Understanding Global Security*, 2nd edn, London: Routledge.

Howard, Michael (1979), 'The Forgotten Dimensions of Strategy', *Foreign Affairs*, 57/5: 975–86.

Hülsse, R. (2008), 'The Metaphor of Terror: Terrorism Studies and the Constructivist Turn', *Security Dialogue*, 39/6: 571–92.

Human Rights Watch (1999), 'World Report, Violence against Women', http://www.hrw.org/legacyworldreport99/women/women2.html.

Human Rights Watch (2007), 'Saudi Arabia: Events of 2006', *World Report 2007*, New York: Human Rights Watch.

Human Security Report Project (2013), *Human Security Report 2013: The Decline in Global Violence: Evidence, Explanation, and Contestation*, Vancouver: Human Security Press.

Huntington, S. (1999), 'The Lonely Superpower', *Foreign Affairs*, 78/2: 35–49.

Huntington, S. P. (1957), *The Soldier and the State: The Theory and Politics of Civil–Military Relations*, Cambridge, MA: Harvard University Press.

Hutchinson, J. (1994), 'Cultural Nationalism and Moral Regeneration', in J. Hutchinson and A. D. Smith (eds), *Nationalism*, Oxford: Oxford University Press, 122–31.

Huysmans, J. (1995), 'Migrants as a Security Issue: The Dangers of "Securitizing" Societal Issues', in R. Miles and D. Thranhardt (eds), *Migration and European Security: The Dynamics of Inclusion and Exclusion*, London: Pinter, 53–72.

Huysmans, J. (1998a), 'Security! What Do You Mean? From Concept to Thick Signifier', *European Journal of International Relations*, 4/2: 226–55.

Huysmans, J. (1998b), 'Revisiting Copenhagen: Or, On the Creative Development of a Security Studies Agenda in Europe', *European Journal of International Relations*, 4/4: 479–506.

Huysmans, J. (2000), 'The European Union and the Securitization of Migration', *Journal of Common Market Studies*, 38/5: 751–77.

Huysmans, J. (2002), 'Defining Social Constructivism in Security Studies: The Normative Dilemma of Writing Security', *Alternatives*, 27/suppl.: 41–62.

Huysmans, J. (2006), *The Politics of Insecurity: Security, Migration and Asylum in the EU*, London: Routledge.

Huysmans, J. and Bounfino, A. (2008), 'Politics of Exception and Unease: Immigration, Asylum, and Terrorism in Parliamentary Debates in the UK', *Political Studies*, 56/4: 766–88.

ICISS (2001), International Commission on Intervention and State Sovereignty, *The Responsibility to Protect*, Ottawa: IDRC.

Ignatieff, M. (1993), *Blood and Belonging: Journeys into the New Nationalism*, London: Vintage.

Ignatieff, M. (2001), *Virtual War*, London: Vintage.

Ijaw Youth Council (1998), *Kaiama Declaration*, 11 December, http://www.unitedijaw.com/kaiama.htm.

Ikenberry, G. J. (2000), *After Victory*, Princeton, NJ: Princeton University Press.

Ikenberry, G. J. (ed.) (2002), *American Unrivaled: The Future of the Balance of Power*, Ithaca, NY: Cornell University Press.

Ikenberry, J. G., Mastanduno. M., and Wohlforth, W. C. (eds) (2011), *International Relations Theory and the Consequences of Unipolarity*, Cambridge: Cambridge University Press.

ILO (2012), *Global Employment Trends*, Geneva: International Labour Organisation.

Inayatullah, N. and Blainey, D. (2004), *International Relations and the Problems of Difference*, London: Routledge.

International Crisis Group (2006a), 'The Swamps of Insurgency: Nigeria's Delta Unrest', Africa Report No. 115, August.

International Crisis Group (2006b), 'Fuelling the Niger Delta Crisis', Africa Report No. 118, 28 September.

Isaksson E. (ed.) (1988), *Women and the Military System*, Basingstoke: Palgrave Macmillan.

Jackson, N. J. (2006), 'International Organizations, Security Dichotomies and the Trafficking of Persons and Narcotics in Post-Soviet Central Asia: A Critique of the Securitization Framework', *Security Dialogue*, 37 / 3: 299–317.

Jackson, R. (2005), *Writing the War on Terrorism: Language, Politics and Counter-Terrorism*, Manchester: Manchester University Press.

Jackson, R. (2014), *Confessions of a Terrorist*, London: Zed Books.

Jackson, R. and Sinclair, S. J. (eds) (2012), *Contemporary Debates on Terrorism*, Abingdon: Routledge.

Jackson, R. H. (1990), *Quasi-States: Sovereignty, International Relations, and the Third World*, New York: Cambridge University Press.

Jackson, R. H. (2002), *The Global Covenant: Human Conduct in a World of States*, Oxford: Oxford University Press.

Jackson, T. (2009), *Prosperity Without Growth: Economics for a Finite Market*, London and Sterling VA: Earthscan.

Jacob, C. (2015), '"Children and Armed Conflict" and the Field of Security Studies', *Critical Studies on Security*, 3 / 1: 14–28.

Jahn, B. (2000), *The Cultural Construction of International Relations*, London: Palgrave Macmillan.

Jahn, E. (1984), 'Zum Verhältnis von Friedensforschung, Friedenspolitik und Friedensbewegung', *Dialog*, 1 / 1: 21–31.

Jahn, E., Lemaitre, P., and Wæver, O. (1987), *European Security: Problems of Research on Non-Military Aspects*, Copenhagen Papers 1, Copenhagen: Copenhagen Peace Research Institute.

Jakobsen, P. V. (1998), *Western Use of Coercive Diplomacy after the Cold War: A Challenge for Theory and Practice*, London: Macmillan Press.

Jakobsen, P. V. (2009), *Nordic Approaches to Peace Operations: A New Model in the Making?*, London: Routledge.

Jakobsen, P. V. (2010), 'Coercive Diplomacy', in A. Collins (ed.), *Contemporary Security Studies*, 2nd edn, Oxford: Oxford University Press, 277–98.

Jakobsen, P. V. (2011), 'Pushing the Limits of Military Coercion Theory', *International Studies Perspectives*, 12 / 2: 153–70.

Jakobsen, P. V. (2012), 'Reinterpreting Libya's WMD Turnaround—Bridging the Carrot–Coercion Divide', *The Journal of Strategic Studies*, 35 / 4: 489–512.

Jensen, D. and Lonergan, S. (eds) (2012), *Assessing and Restoring Natural Resources in Post-Conflict Peacebuilding*, Abingdon: Routledge.

Jentleson, B. W. and Whytock, C. A. (2005–6), 'Who "Won" Libya? The Force-Diplomacy Debate and its Implications for Theory and Policy', *International Security*, 30 / 3: 47–86.

Jervis, R. (1976), *Perception and Misperception in International Politics*, Princeton, NJ: Princeton University Press.

Jervis, R. (1978), 'Cooperation under the Security Dilemma', *World Politics*, 30 / 1: 167–214.

Jervis, R. (1989), *The Meaning of the Nuclear Revolution*, Ithaca, NY: Cornell University Press.

Jervis, R. (1991), 'The Spiral of International Security', in Richard Little and Michael Smith (eds), *Perspectives on World Politics*, 2nd edn, London: Routledge, 91–101.

Jim Yong Kim (2014), 'Jim Yong Kim: The high costs of institutional discrimination', *Washington Post*, 27 February.

Jin, J. Y. (2010), 'The Securitization of Infectious Diseases', *Contemporary International Relations*, 20 / 4: 139–59.

Job, B. A. (ed.) (1992), *The Insecurity Dilemma: National Security of Third World States*, Boulder, CO: Lynne Rienner.

Joenniemi, P. (1988), 'Models of Neutrality: The Traditional and the Modern', *Cooperation and Conflict*, 23 / 1: 53–67.

Johansson-Nogués, E. (2013), 'Gendering the Arab Spring? Rights and (In)Security of Tunisian, Egyptian and Libyan Women', *Security Dialogue*, 44 / 5–6: 393–409.

Johnson, C. (2006), *Nemesis: The Last Days of the American Republic*, New York: Metropolitan Books.

Jones, B. G. (ed.) (2006), *Decolonizing International Relations*, Lanham: Rowman & Littlefield.

Jones, L. (2011), 'Beyond Securitization: Explaining the Scope of Security Policy in Southeast Asia', *International Relations of the Asia-Pacific*, 11/3: 403–32.

Jones, N. (2011), 'Heating up Tensions', *Nature Climate Change*, 1: 327–9.

Joosse, P. (2007), 'Leaderless Resistance and Ideological Inclusion: The Case of the Earth Liberation Front', *Terrorism and Political Violence*, 19/3: 351–68.

Joseph, J. (2011), 'Terrorism as a Social Relation within Capitalism: Theoretical and Emancipatory Implications', *Critical Studies on Terrorism*, 4/1: 23–37.

Joya, A. (2011), 'The Egyptian Revolution: Crisis of Neoliberalism and the Potential for Democratic Politics', *Review of African Political Economy*, 38/129: 367–86.

Kahl, C. (2006), *States, Scarcity, and Civil Strife in the Developing World*, Princeton, NJ: Princeton University Press.

Kahneman, D. (2002), 'Maps of Bounded Rationality: A Perspective on Intuitive Judgment and Choice', Nobel Memorial Prize in Economics Lecture, 8 December.

Kaldor, M. (1999), *New and Old Wars: Organised Violence in a Global Era*, Cambridge: Polity Press.

Kaldor, M. (2011), 'Human Security', *Society and Economy*, 33/3: 441–8.

Kaldor, M. (2013), 'Comment on Security Cosmopolitanism' *Critical Studies on Security*, 1/1: 42–5.

Kaplan, F. (1983), *Wizards of Armageddon*, Stanford, CA: Stanford University Press.

Kapstein, E. B. (1992), *The Political Economy of National Security*, New York: McGraw-Hill.

Karl, R. (2002), *Staging the World: Chinese Nationalism at the Turn of the Twentieth Century*, Durham: Duke University Press.

Katt, M. (2014), 'Blurred Lines: Cultural Support Teams in Afghanistan' National Defense University Press, 30 September, http://ndupress.ndu.edu/Media/News/NewsArticleView/tabid/7849/Article/577569/jfq-75-blurred-lines-cultural-support-teams-in-afghanistan.aspx.

Katz, D. (2011), 'Hydro-Political Hyperbole: Examining Incentives for Overemphasizing the Risks of Water Wars', *Global Environmental Politics*, 11/1: 12–35.

Katzenstein, P. J. (1996a), 'Introduction: Alternative Perspectives on National Security', in P. J. Katzenstein (ed.), *The Culture of National Security: Norms and Identity in World Politics*, New York: Columbia University Press, 1–32.

Katzenstein, P. J. (ed.) (1996b), *The Culture of National Security: Norms and Identity in World Politics*, New York: Columbia University Press.

Kegley, C., Jr, (1995), 'The Neorealist Challenge to Realist Theories of World Politics: An Introduction', in C. Kegley, (ed.), *Controversies in International Relations Theory*, New York: St Martins Press, 1–24.

Kegley, C. W. Jr (ed.) (2003), *The New Global Terrorism: Characteristics, Causes, Controls*, Upper Saddle River, NJ: Prentice Hall.

Kegley, C. W. and Blanton, S. L. (2009), *World Politics: Trends and Transfiormations, 2009–2010 Update Edition*, New York: St Martin's Press.

Kegley, C. W. and Raymond, G. A. (1982), 'Alliance Norms and War: A New Piece in an Old Puzzle', *International Studies Quarterly*, 26: 572–95.

Kelle, A. (2007), 'Securitization of International Public Health: Implications for Global Health Governance and the Biological Prohibitation Regime', *Global Governance*, 13/2: 217–35.

Kennedy, C. (2007), *The Origins of the Cold War*, Basingstoke: Palgrave Macmillan.

Kennedy, P. (1988), *The Rise and Fall of the Great Powers*, London, Random House.

Kennedy, R. F. (1969), *Thirteen Days*, New York: Norton.

Kennedy-Pipe, Caroline (2004), 'Whose Security? State-Building and the "Emancipation" of Women in Central Asia', *International Relations*, 18/1: 91–107.

Kenney, M. (2007), *From Pablo to Osama: Trafficking and Terrorist Networks, Government Bureaucracies, and Competitive Advantage*, University Park, PA: Pennsylvania State University Press.

Keohane, R. O. (1984), *Cooperation and Discord in the World Political Economy*, Princeton, NJ: Princeton University Press.

Keohane, R. (1988), 'International Institutions: Two Approaches', *International Studies Quarterly*, 32/4: 379–96.

Keohane, R. O. (2000), 'Ideas Part-Way Down', *Review of International Studies*, 26/1: 125–30.

Khalili, L. (2011), 'Gendered Practices of Counterinsurgency', *Review of Interview Studies*, 37/4: 1471–91.

Khalili, L. (2013), *Time in the Shadows: Confinement in Counterinsurgencies*, Stanford, CA: Stanford University Press.

King, G. and Murray, C. J. L. (2001–02), 'Rethinking Human Security', *Political Science Quarterly*, 116/4: 585–610.

Kissinger, H. (1956), 'Force and Diplomacy in the Nuclear Age', *Foreign Affairs*, 34: 349–66.

Kissinger, H. (2014), *World Order*, New York: Penguin Press.

Kittelsen, Sonja (2013), *The EU and the Securitization of Pandemic Influenza*, Doctoral Thesis, Aberystwyth University.

Klare, M. (2004), *Blood and Oil: How America's Thirst for Petrol is Killing Us*, London: Penguin.

Klare, M. (2008), *Rising Powers Shrinking Planet: The New Geopolitics of Energy*, New York: Metropolitan Books.

Klein, B. (1994), *Strategic Studies and World Order*, Cambridge: Cambridge University Press.

Klein, Naomi (2008), *The Shock Doctrine: The Rise of Disaster Capitalism*, London: Penguin.

Klotz, A. (1995), 'Norms Reconstituting Interests: Global Racial Equality and US Sanctions against South Africa', *International Organization*, 49/5: 451–78.

Knorr, K, (1970), 'The International Purposes of Military Power', in J. Garnet, (ed.), *Theories of Peace and Security*, London: Macmillan.

Knorr, K. and Trager, F. N. (1977), *Economic Issues and National Security*, Lawrence, KA: Regents Press.

Kober, K. and van Damme, W. (2006), 'Public Sector Nurses in Swaziland: Can the Downturn be Reversed?', *Human Resources for Health*, 4/13: 1–11.

Kolodziej, Edward A. (2005), *Security and International Relations*, Cambridge: Cambridge University Press.

Kowert, P. (2001), 'The Peril and Promise of Constructivist Theory', *Ritsumeikan Kokusai Kenkyu (Ritsumeikan Journal of International Studies)*, 13/3: 157–70.

Krasner, S. D. (ed.) (1983), *International Regimes*, Ithaca, NY: Cornell University Press.

Krasner, S. D. (ed.) (1999), *Sovereignty: Organized Hypocrisy*, Princeton, NJ: Princeton University Press.

Krasner, S. D. (2000), 'Wars, Hotel Fires, and Plane Crashes', *Review of International Studies*, 26: 131–6.

Kratochwil, F. (1991), *Rules, Norms, and Decisions: On the Conditions of Practical and Legal Reasoning in International Relations and Domestic Affairs*, Cambridge: Cambridge University Press.

Kratochwil, F. V. (2001), 'Constructivism as an Approach to Interdisciplinary Study', in K. M. Fierke and K. E. Jørgensen (eds), *Constructing International Relations: The Next Generation*, New York: M. E. Sharpe, 13–35.

Krause, K. (1995), *Arms and the State: Patterns of Military Production and Trade*, Cambridge: Cambridge University Press.

Krause, K. (1998), "Critical Theory and Security Studies: The Research Programme of 'Critical Security Studies'", *Cooperation and Conflict*, 33/3: 298–333.

Krause, K. and Williams, M. C. (1997a), 'From Strategy to Security: Foundations of Critical Security Studies', in K. Krause and M. C. Williams (eds), *Critical Security Studies: Concepts and Cases*, Minneapolis: University of Minnesota Press, 33–59.

Krause, K. and Williams, M. C. (eds) (1997b), *Critical Security Studies: Concepts and Cases*, Minneapolis: University of Minnesota Press.

Krepon, M. (1984), *Strategic Stalemate: Nuclear Weapons and Arms Control in American Politics*, London: Macmillan.

Krishna, S. (1993), 'The Importance of being Ironic: A Postcolonial View on Critical International Relations Theory', *Alternatives*, 18: 385–417.

Krishna, S. (1999), *Postcolonial Insecurities: India, Sri Lanka, and the Question of Nationhood*, Minneapolis: University of Minnesota Press.

Krishna, S. (2001), 'Race, Amnesia and the Education of International Relations', *Alternatives: Global, Local, Political*, 26/4: 401–24.

Krishna, S. (2009), *Globalization and Postcolonialism: Hegemony and Resistance in the Twenty-First Century*, Lanham: Rowman & Littlefield.

Kubálková, V. (ed.) (2001), *Foreign Policy in a Constructed World*, New York: M. E. Sharpe.

Kuhn, H. W. (2004), 'Introduction', in John von Neumann and Oskar Morgenstern, *Theory of Games and Economic Behavior, Sixtieth Anniversary*

Edition, Princeton, NJ: Princeton University Press, vii–xiv.

Kunreuther, H. and Slovic, P. (1978), 'Economics, Psychology, and Protective Behavior', *American Economic Review*, 68/2: 64–9.

Kupchan, C. A. (2014), 'The Normative Foundations of Hegemony and the Coming Challenge to Pax Americana', *Security Studies*, 23/2: 219–57.

Kuperman, A. J. (2008), 'The Moral Hazard of Humanitarian Intervention: Lessons from the Balkans', *International Studies Quarterly*, 52/1: 49–80.

Kydd, A. (2005), *Trust and Mistrust in International Relations*, Princeton, NJ: Princeton University Press.

Kymlicka, W. (2001), 'Justice and Security in the Accommodation of Minority Nationalism: Comparing East and West', Working Paper, Central European University.

Laffey, M. and Weldes, J. (2004), 'Representing the International: Sovereignty after Modernity?', in P. Passavant and J. Dean (eds), *Empire's New Clothes: Reading Hardt and Negri*, New York: Routledge, 121–42.

Laffey, M. and Weldes, J. (2008), 'Decolonizing the Cuban Missile Crisis', *International Studies Quarterly*, 52: 555–77.

Laffey, M., Guterson, H., and Duvall, r. (eds) (1999), *Cultures of Insecurity: States, Communities and the Production of Danger*, Minneapolis: University of Minnesota Press.

Lagarde, Christine (2011), 'Briefing from Director of IMF to World Bank Working Group', Geneva: unpublished.

Langberg, D. R. (2008), 'US Government Response to Human Trafficking in the Twenty-First Century', in Richard Weitz, (ed.), *Project on National Security Reform: Case Studies (Volume I)*, Washington, DC: Center for the Study of the Presidency.

Lapid, J. and Kratochwil, F. (eds) (1999), *The Return of Culture and Identity in IR Theory*, Boulder, CO: Lynne Reiner.

Larsen, J. (ed.) (2002), *Arms Control: Cooperative Security in a Changing Environment*, Boulder, CO: Lynne Rienner.

Larsen, J. A. (2009), 'An Introduction to Arms Control and Cooperative Security', in Jeffrey A. Larsen and James J. Wirtz (eds), *Arms Control and Cooperative Security*, Boulder, CO: Lynne Rienner, 1–15.

Larsen, J. A. and Wirtz, J. J. (eds) (2009), *Arms Control and Cooperative Security*, Boulder, CO: Lynne Reiner.

Lasswell, H. D. (1950), *National Security and Individual Freedom*, New York, Toronto, and London: McGraw-Hill.

Lavoy, P. R., Sagan, S. D., and Wirtz, J. J. (eds) (2000), *Planning the Unthinkable: How New Powers will Use Nuclear, Chemical and Biological Weapons*, Ithaca, NY: Cornell University Press.

Lawler, P (1995), *A Question of Values: Johan Galtung's Peace Research*, Boulder, CO: Lynne Rienner Publishers.

Layne, C. (2006), *The Peace of Illusions: American Grand Strategy from 1940 to the Present*, Ithaca, NY: Cornell University Press.

Lederberg, J., Shope, R. S., and Oaks, S. C., Jr, (eds) (1992), *Emerging Infections: Microbial Threats to Health in the United States*, Committee on Emerging Microbial Threats to Health, Institute of Medicine, Washington: National Academy Press.

Leech, G. (2006), *Crude Interventions: The United States Oil and the New World (Dis)Order*, London: Zed Books.

Lefever, E. W. (ed.) (1962), *Arms and Arms Control*, New York: Praeger.

Lekic, Slobodan (2011), 'Terrorists Seeking Missing Libyan Missiles', *The Associated Press*, http://news.yahoo.com/us-says-terrorists-seeking-missing-libyan-missiles-151821492.html.

Lemkin, R. (1944), *Axis Rule in Occupied Europe*, Washington: Carnegie Endowment.

Lepard, B. (2002), *Rethinking Humanitarian Intervention: A Fresh Legal Approach Based on Fundamental Ethical Principles in International Law and World Religions*, University Park, PA: Pennsylvania State University Press.

Lepgold, J. and Nincic, M. (2001), *Beyond the Ivory Tower: International Relations Theory and the Issue of Policy Relevance*, New York: Columbia University Press.

Levitt, M. (2009), 'Disrupting Iran's Weapons Smuggling', *Middle East Strategy at Harvard*, https://blogs.law.harvard.edu/mesh/2009/11/disrupting-irans-weapons-smuggling/.

Levy, S. (1984), *Hackers: Heroes of the Computer Revolution*, New York: Anchor Press.

Libicki, M. (2009), *Cyberdeterrence and Cyberwar*, Santa Monica: RAND.

Lindholm, Helena (1993), 'Introduction: A Conceptual Discussion', in H. Lindholm, (ed.), *Ethnicity and Nationalism: Foundation of Identity and Dynamics of Conflict in the 1990s*, Gothenburg: Nordnes.

Lindqvist, S. (1998), *Exterminate All the Brutes*, London: Granta Books.

Liotta, P. H. (2002), 'Boomerang Effect: The Convergence of National and Human Security', *Security Dialogue*, 33 / 4: 473–88.

Lippmann, W. (1943), *US Foreign Policy: Shield of the Republic*, Boston: Little, Brown.

Lipumba, N. (1994), *Africa beyond Adjustment*, Washington, DC: Overseas Development Council.

Livre Blanc (2013), *Le Livre blanc sur la défense et la sécurité nationale*, Paris: Direction de linformation légale et administrative.

Locke, E. (2010), 'Refining Strategic Culture: Return of the Second Generation', *Review of International Studies*, 36 / 1: 685–708.

Losurdo, D. (2015), *War and Revolution: Rethinking the 20th Century*, London: Verso.

Lucht, Hans (2011), 'Greece must not leave asylum seekers at the mercy of extremists', *The Guardian*, updated 29 December 2011, http: / / www.theguardian.com / commentisfree / 2011 / dec / 29 / greece-asylum-seekers-extremists.

Luciani, Giacomo (1989), 'The Economic Content of Security', *Journal of Public Policy*, 8 / 2: 151–73.

Luck, E. (2008), 'The United Nations and the Responsibility to Protect', *Policy Analysis Brief* (August), The Stanley Foundation, 1–11.

Luckhman, R. and Kirk, T. (2013), 'The Two Faces of Security in Hybrid Political Orders: A Framework for Analysis and Research', *Stability: International Journal of Security & Development*, 2 / 2: 1–130.

Lumpe, L. (ed.) (2000), *Running Guns: The Global Black Market in Small Arms*, London: Zed Books.

Luttwak, E. N. (1995), 'Toward Post Heroic Warfare', *Foreign Affairs*, May–June: 109–22.

Luttwak, E. N. (1999), 'Give War a Chance', *Foreign Affairs*, 78 / 4: 36–44.

Lutz, J. M. and Lutz, B. J. (2007), *Terrorism in America*, New York: Palgrave.

Lutz, J. M. and Lutz, B. J. (2010), 'Democracy and Terrorism', *Perspectives on Terrorism*, 4 / 1, 63–74.

Lutz, J. M. and Lutz, B. J. (2011), *Terrorism: The Basics*, London: Routledge.

Lutz, J. M. and Lutz, B. J. (2013), *Global Terrorism*, 3rd edn, London: Routledge.

Lutz, B. J., Lutz, J. M., and Ulmschneider, G. W. (2002), 'British Trials of Irish Nationalist Defendants: The Quality of Justice Strained', *Studies in Conflict and Terrorism*, 25 / 4: 227–44.

Lynch, C. (2011), 'Arms dealer Victor Bout convicted', *The Washington Post*, http: / / www.washingtonpost.com / world / national-security / arms-dealer-viktor-bout-convicted / 2011 / 11 / 02 / gIQAHglsgM_story.html.

McCoy, A. (2009), *Policing America's Empire: The United States, The Philippines, and the Rise of the Surveillance State*, Madison: The University of Wisconsin Press.

MacFarlane, S. N. and Yuen Foong Khong (2006), *Human Security and the UN: A Critical History*, United Nations Intellectual History Project, Bloomington: Indiana Univeristy Press.

Macqueen, N. (2011), *Humanitarian Intervention and the United Nations*, Edinburgh: Edinburgh University Press.

McGrew, Anthony G. and Poku, Nana (2007), *Globalization, Development and Human Security*, Cambridge, UK; Malden, MA: Polity.

McGuire, M. (1986), 'The Insidious Dogma of Deterrence', *Bulletin of the Atomic Scientists*, 42 / 10: 24–9.

Macmillan, L. (2009), 'The Child Soldier in North–South Relation', *International Political Sociology*, 3 / 1: 36–52.

McSweeney, B. (1996), 'Identity and Security: Buzan and the Copenhagen School', *Review of International Studies*, 22 / 1: 81–93.

McSweeney, B. (1999), *Security, Identity and Interests: A Sociology of International Relations*, Cambridge: Cambridge University Press.

Makinda, S. (2005), 'Security in International Society: A Comment on Alex J. Bellamy and Matt McDonald', *Australian Journal of Political Science*, 40 / 2: 275–88.

Malek, A. (1963), 'Orientalism in Crisis', *Diogenes*, 44: 103–40.

Mandel, R. (2011), *Dark Logic: Transnational Criminal Tactics and Global Security*, Stanford: Stanford University Press.

Mansfield, E. D. and Snyder, J. (1989), 'Democratization and the Danger of War', in J. Mueller, (ed.), *Retreat from Doomsday: The Growing Obsolescence of Major War*, New York: Basic Books.

Martin, M. and Owen, T. (eds) (2013), *Routledge Handbook of Human Security*, New York: Routledge.

Marx, K. (1859), *A Contribution to the Critique of Political Economy*, www.marxists.org/archive/marx/works/1859/critique-pol-economy.

Marx, K. (1875), *Critique of the Gotha Program*, www.marxists.org/archive/marx/works/1875/gotha.

Masco, J. (1999), 'States of Insecurity: Plutonium and Post-Cold War Anxiety in New Mexico, 1992–1996', in J. Weldes, M. Laffey, H. Gusterson, and R. Duvall (eds), *Cultures of Insecurity: States, Communities and the Production of Danger*, Minneapolis: University of Minnesota Press, 203–31.

Masco, J. (2006), *The Nuclear Borderlands: The Manhattan Project in Post-Cold War New Mexico*, Princeton, NJ: Princeton University Press.

Mathews, J. T. (1989), 'Redefining Security', *Foreign Affairs*, 68/2: 162–77.

Matthew, R., Barnett, J., McDonald, B., and O'Brien, K. (eds) (2009), *Global Environmental Change and Human Security*, Cambridge, MA: MIT Press.

Mayhew, E. (2005), 'A Dead Giveaway: A Critical Analysis of New Labour's Rationale for Supporting Military Exports', *Contemporary Security Policy*, 26/1: 62–83.

Maynes, C. (1995), 'Relearning Intervention', *Foreign Policy*, 98/Spring: 96–113.

Mbembe, A. (2001), *On the Postcolony*, Berkeley: University of California Press.

Mearsherimer, J. (1994), 'The False Promise of International Institutions', *International Security*, 19/3: 5–49.

Mearsheimer, J. (2001), *The Tragedy of Great Power Politics*, New York: Norton.

Mearsheimer, J. (2005), 'Hans Morgenthau and the Iraq War: Realism versus NeoConservatism', https://www.opendemocracy.net/democracy-americanpower/morgenthau_2522.jsp.

Mearsheimer, J. (2014), 'Why the Ukraine Crisis is the West's Fault: The Liberal Delusions that Provoked Putin', *Foreign Affairs*, 93/5: 77–89.

Melman, S. (2003), 'In the Grip of a Permanent War Economy', *CounterPunch*, 15 March.

Menon, R. (2003), 'The End of Alliance', *World Policy Journal*, 20/2: 1–20.

Mertus, J. (2000), 'The Legality of Humanitarian Intervention: Lessons from Kosovo', *William and Mary Law Review*, 41/4: 1743–87.

Meyer, Jani (2004), 'SANDF unveils shock Aids data'. *IOL News*, 1 August 2004, http://www.iol.co.za/news/south-africa/sandf-unveils-shock-aids-data-1.218577#.VW17KYd7Cag.

Mgbeoji, I. (2006), 'The Civilised Self and the Barbaric Other: Imperial Delusions of Order and the Challenges of Human Security', *Third World Quarterly*, 27/5: 855–69.

Migdal, J. (1988), *Strong Societies and Weak States: State–Society Relations and State Capabilities in the Third World*, Princeton, NJ: Princeton University Press.

Mignolo, W. (2000), *Local Histories/Global Designs: Coloniality, Subaltern Knowledges, and Border Thinking*, Princeton, NJ: Princeton University Press.

Mignolo, W. (2010), 'Introduction: Coloniality of Power and De-Colonial Thinking', in W. Mignolo and A. Escobar (eds), *Globalization and the Decolonial Option*, London: Routledge, 1–21.

Mignolo, W. and Escobar, A. (eds) (2010), *Globalization and the Decolonial Option*, London: Routledge.

Mikdashi, Maya (2011), 'Neoliberalism's forked tongue', *Jadaliyya*, updated 17 May 2011, http://www.jadaliyya.com/pages/index/1606/neoliberalisms-forked-tongue.

Milanovic, Branko (2002), *Can We Discern the Effect of Globalization on Income Distribution? Evidence from Household Budget Surveys*, Washington, DC: World Bank.

Miller, E. A. and Toritsyn, A. (2004/5), 'Bringing the Leader Back In: Internal Threats and Alignment Theory in the Commonwealth of Independent States', *Security Studies*, 14/2: 325–63.

Milliken, J. (1999), 'The Study of Discourse in International Relations: A Critique of Research and Methods', *European Journal of International Relations*, 5/2: 225–54.

Milliken, J. (2001), *The Social Construction of the Korean War: Conflict and its Possibilities*, Manchester: Manchester University Press.

Minear, L. and Weiss, T. G. (1995), *Mercy under Fire: War and the Global Humanitarian Community*, Boulder, CO: Westview Press.

Ministry of Foreign Affairs of Japan (2014), 'Comprehensive Economic Partnership Agreement Between the Republic of India and Japan', http://www.mofa.go.jp/region/asia-paci/india/epa201102/.

Mittelman, J. (2010), *Hyperconflict: Globalization and Insecurity*, Stanford, CA: Stanford University Press.

Møller, B. (1991), *Resolving the Security Dilemma in Europe: The German Debate on Non-Offensive Defence*, London: Brassey's Defence Publishers.

Moran, D. and Russell, D. (2008), 'The Militarization of Energy Security', *Strategic Insights*, 7/1 (February).

Moravcsik, A. (1997), 'Taking Preferences Seriously: A Liberal Theory of International Politics', *International Organization*, 51/4: 513–53.

Moravcsik, A. (2001), 'Constructivism and European Integrations: A Critique', in T. Christiansen, K. E. Jørgensen, and A. Wiener (eds), *The Social Construction of Europe*, London: Sage, 176–88.

Morgan, P. M. (1983), *Deterrence: A Conceptual Analysis*, 2nd edn, Beverley Hills, CA: Sage.

Morgan, P. M. (2003), *Deterrence Now*, Cambridge: Cambridge University Press.

Morgan, P. M. (2006), *International Security: Problems and Solutions*, Washington, DC: CQ Press.

Morgenthau, H. J. (1962), 'The Trouble with Kennedy', *Commentary*, 33/1: 51–5.

Morris, J. (1995), 'Force and Democracy: The US/UN Intervention in Haiti', *International Peacekeeping*, 2/3: 391–412.

Morris, J. and Wheeler, N. J. (2006), 'Justifying Iraq as a Humanitarian Intervention: The Cure Is Worse than the Disease', in W. P. S. Sidhu and Ramesh Thakur (eds), *The Iraq Crisis and World Order: Structural and Normative Challenges*, Tokyo: United Nations University Press, 444–63.

Morrison, S. J. (2014), *Ebola's Hard Lessons*, Washington, DC: Center for Strategic and International Studies. 5 September, http://www.smartglobalhealth.org/blog/entry/Ebolas-Hard-Lessons/.

Morrow, J. D. (1993), 'Arms Versus Allies: Trade-Offs in the Search for Security', *International Organization*, 47/2: 207–33.

MOSOP (1990), 'Ogoni Bill of Rights', October, http://www.mosop.org/ogoni_bill_of_rights.html.

Mueller, G. O. W. (2001), 'Transnational Crime: Definitions and Concepts', in Phil Williams and Dimitri Vlassos (eds), *Combating Transnational Crime: Concepts, Activities and Responses*, London: Frank Cass Publishers, 13–21.

Mueller, J. (1989), *Retreat from Doomsday: The Growing Obsolescence of Major War*, New York: Basic Books.

Muller, B. (2010), *Security, Risk and the Biometric State: Governing Borders and Bodies. New Security Studies Series*, London: Routledge.

Mungo, P. and Clough, B. (1993), *Approaching Zero: The Extraordinary Underworld of Hackers, Phreakers, Virus Writers, and Keyboard Criminals*, New York: Random House.

Münkler, H. (2005), *The New Wars*, Cambridge: Polity Press.

Muppidi, H. (2012), *The Colonial Signs of International Relations*, London: Hurst & Company.

Murphy, C. N. (2000), 'Global Governance: Poorly Done and Poorly Understood', *International Affairs*, 76/4: 789–03.

Musah, A.-F. and Kayode, Fayemi, J. (2000), *Mercenaries: An African Security Dilemma*, London: Pluto.

Mutimer, David (2000), *The Weapons State: Proliferation and the Framing of Security*, Boulder, CO: Lynne Rienner.

Myers, N. (1986), 'The Environmental Dimension to Security Issues', *Environmentalist*, 6/4: 251–7.

Myers, N. (1987), 'Population, Environment, and Conflict', *Environmental Conservation*, 14/1: 15–22.

Myrdal, A. (1980), *The Game of Disarmament: How the United States and Russia Run the Arms Race*, Nottingham: Spokesman Books.

Nadarajah, S. and Rampton, D. (2015), 'The Limits of Hybridity and the Crisis of Liberal Peace', *Review of International Studies*, 41/1: 49–72.

Naff, T. (1992), 'Water Scarcity, Resource Management, and Conflict in the Middle East', in E. Kirk, (ed.), *Environmental Dimensions of Security: Proceedings from an AAAS Annual Meeting Symposium*, Washington, DC: American Association for the Advancement of Science, 25–30.

Naim, M. (2006), *Illicit: How Smugglers, Traffickers and Copycats are Hijacking the Global Economy*, New York: Anchor Books.

Nantais, C. and Lee, M. F. (1999), 'Women in the United States Military: Protectors or Protected? The Case of Prisoner of War, Melissa Rathburn-Nealy', *Journal of Gender Studies*, 8/2: 181–90.

Nation (2004), 'Thaksin issues warning to Police', *Nation* (Thailand), 5 October.

National Intelligence Council (2000), 'The Global Infectious Disease Threat and its Implications for the US', Washington, DC: National Intelligence Council, www.cia.gov/cia/reports/nie/report/nie99-17d.html.

National Intelligence Council (2003), 'SARS: Down but Still a Threat', Washington, DC: National Intelligence Council, www.dni.gov/nic/PDF_GIF_otherprod/sarsthreat/56797book.pdf.

National Research Council (2009), *Technology, Policy, Law, and Ethics Regarding U.S. Acquisition and Use of Cyberattack Capabilities*, Washington, DC: The National Academies Press.

NATO (2007), 'The Protection of Critical Infrastructures', *Committee Report*, 162 CDS 07 E rev 1, NATO Parliamentary Assembly.

Naylor, R. T. (2004), *Wages of Crime: Black Markets, Illegal Finance, and the Underworld Economy*, Cornell, NY: Cornell University Press.

Neocleous, M. (2008), *Critique of Security*, Montreal: McGill-Queen's University Press.

Newman, E. (2001), 'Human Security and Constructivism', *International Studies Perspectives*, 2/3: 239–51.

Newman, E. (2010), 'Critical Human Security Studies', *Review of International Studies*, 36/1: 77–94.

Nielsen, R. T. and Kristensen, P. M. (2013), '"You Need to do Something that the Westerners cannot Understand": The Innovation of a Chinese School of IR', in N. Horsburgh, A. Nordin, and S. Breslin (eds), *Chinese Politics and International Relations: Innovation and Invention*, Abingdon: Routledge, 97–118.

Nikitin, M. B., Feickert, A., and Kerr, P. K. (2013), *Syria's Chemical Weapons: Issues for Congress*, CRS Report for Congress 7-5700.

Niva, S. (1999), 'Contested Sovereignties and Postcolonial Insecurities in the Middle East', in J. Weldes, M. Laffey, H. Gusterson, and R. Duvall (eds), *Cultures of Insecurity: States, Communities and the Production of Danger*, Minneapolis: University of Minnesota Press, 147–72.

North, D. C. (1994), 'Economic Performance through Time', *American Economic Review*, 84/3: 359–68. First presented in Stockholm on 9 December 1993 as the Sveriges Riksbank Prize Lecture in Economic Sciences in Memory of Alfred Nobel, http://www.nobelprize.org/nobel_prizes/economics/laureates/1993/north-lecture.html.

NRDC (2001), *The US Nuclear War Plan: A Time For Change*, New York: Natural Resources Defense Council.

Nun, J. (2000), 'The End of Work and the "Marginal Mass" Thesis', *Latin American Perspectives*, 27/1: 6–32.

Nye, J. and Lynn-Jones, S. (1988), 'International Security Studies: A Report of a Conference on the State of the Field', *International Security*, 12/4: 5–27.

Nye, J. S., Jr and Owens, W.A. (1996), 'America's Information Edge', *Foreign Affairs*, March/April: 20–36.

O'Brien, R., Goetz, A., Scholte, J., and Williams, M. (2000), *Contesting Global Governance: Multilateral Institutions and Global Social Movements*, Cambridge: Cambridge University Press.

O'Connor, P. (2002), 'Australia to ask neighbors to join struggle against people smuggling', *Associated Press*, 23 February.

O'Tuathail, G. (1996), *Critical Geopolitics*, London: Routledge.

Obama, B. and Lugar, R. (2005), 'Grounding a pandemic', *New York Times*, 6 June.

Oberleitner, G. (2005), 'Human Security: A Challenge to International Law?', *Global Governance*, 11: 185–203.

OECD (2009), *Economic Globalisation: Foreign Direct Investment*, Paris: Organisation for Economic Co-operation and Development.

Office of US Trade Representative (2012), 'U.S.–Korea Free Trade Agreement'. Office of the United States Trade Representative, http://www.ustr.gov/trade-agreements/free-trade-agreements/korus-fta/.

Ogata, S. and Cels, J. (2003), 'Human Security—Protecting and Empowering the People', *Global Governance*, 9: 273–82.

Onuf, N. (1989), *World of our Making: Rules and Rule in Social Theory and International Relations*, Columbia, SC: University of South Carolina Press.

Onuf, N. (1998), 'Constructivism: A User's Manual', in V. Kubláková, N. Onuf, and P. Kowert (eds), *International Relations in a Constructed World*, New York: M. E. Sharpe, 58–78.

Onuf, N. (2002), 'Worlds of our Making: The Strange Career of Constructivism in International Relations', in D. J. Puchala, (ed.), *Visions of International Relations: Assessing an Academic Field*, Columbia, SC: University of South Carolina Press, 119–41.

Ortiz, I. and Cummins, M. (2011), *Global Inequality: Beyond the Bottom Billion—A Rapid Review of Income Distribution in 141 Countries*, United Nations Children's Fund (UNICEF), New York.

Osgood, R. E. (1968), *Alliances and American Foreign Policy*, Baltimore: Johns Hopkins University Press.

Owen, T. (2004), 'Human Security—Conflict, Critique and Consensus: Colloquium Remarks and a Proposal for a Threshold-Based Definition', *Security Dialogue*, 35/3: 373–87.

Owens, P. (2012), 'Human Security and the Rise of the Social', *Review of International Studies*, 38: 547–67.

Oye, K. A. (ed.) (1986), *Cooperation under Anarchy*, Princeton, NJ: Princeton University Press.

Palan, R. (2000), 'A World of their Making: An Evaluation of the Constructivist Critique in International Relations', *Review of International Studies*, 26/4: 575–98.

Palme, O. et al. (1982), *Common Security: A Blueprint for Survival: Report of the Independent Commission on Disarmament and Security Issues [Palme Report]*, New York: Simon and Schuster.

Pant, H. V. (2012), *Handbook of Nuclear Proliferation*, New York: Routledge.

Parekh, B. (1997), 'Rethinking Humanitarian Intervention', *International Political Science Review*, 18/1: 49–69.

Paris, R. (2001), 'Human Security: Paradigm Shift or Hot Air?', *International Security*, 26/2: 87–102.

Paris, R. (2004), 'Still an Inscrutable Concept', *Security Dialogue*, 35/3: 370–1.

Parisi, L. and Corntassel, J. (2009), 'A "Revolution within a Revolution": Indigenous Women's Diplomacies', in J. Marshall Beier (ed.), *Indigenous Diplomacies*, New York: Palgrave Macmillan, 79–95.

Parmar, I. (2004), 'Institutes of International Affairs: Their Roles in Foreign Policy-Making, Opinion Mobilization and Unofficial Diplomacy', in Diane Stone and Andrew Denham (eds), *Think Tank Traditions: Policy Research and the Politics of Ideas*, Manchester: Manchester University Press, 19–33.

Paul, D. (1999), 'Sovereignty, Survival and the Westphalian Blind Alley', *Review of International Studies* 25: 217–31.

Paul, T. V., Harknett, R. J., and Wirtz, J. J. (eds) (1998), *The Absolute Weapon Revisited: Nuclear Arms and the Emerging International Order*, Ann Arbor: University of Michigan Press.

Paul, T. V., Morgan, P. M., and Wirtz, J. (eds) (2009), *Complex Deterrence: Strategy in the Global Age*, Chicago, University of Chicago Press.

Pearson, F. S. (1994), *The Global Spread of Arms: Political Economy of International Security*, Boulder, CO: Westview Press.

Peluso, N. and Harwell, E. (2001), 'Territory, Custom, and the Cultural Politics of Ethnic War in West Kalimantan, Indonesia', in N. Peluso and M. Watts (eds), *Violent Environments*, Ithaca, NY: Cornell University Press, 83–116.

Peluso, N. and Watts, M. (eds) (2001), *Violent Environments*, Ithaca, NY: Cornell University Press.

Peoples, C. (2010), *Justifying Ballistic Missile Defence: Technology, Security and Culture*, Cambridge Studies in International Relations 112, Cambridge: Cambridge University Press.

Peoples, C. and Vaughan-Williams, N. (2010), *Critical Security Studies: An Introduction*, London: Routledge.

Peou, Sorpong (2015), *Human Security Studies: Theories, Methods and Themes*, London: World Scientific Publishing.

Perelman, L. J. (2007), 'Shifting Security Paradigms: Toward Resilience', in J. A. McCarthy (ed.), 'Critical Thinking: Moving from Infrastructure Protection to Infrastructure Resilience', *CIP Program Discussion Paper Series* (Washington: George Mason University), 23–48.

Perkovich, G. (1999), *India's Nuclear Bomb: The Impact on Global Proliferation*, Berkeley: University of California Press.

Persaud, R. B. (2001), *Counter-Hegemony and Foreign Policy: The Dialectics of Marginalized Global Forces in Jamaica*, Albany: State University of New York Press.

Petersen, K. L. (2012), 'Risk Analysis—A Field within Security Studies?' *European Journal of International Relations*, 18/4: 693–717.

Peterson, V. S. (1992), 'Security and Sovereign States: What is at Stake in Taking Feminism Seriously?', in V. S. Peterson (ed,.), *Gendered States: Feminist (Re) Visions of International Relations Theory*, Boulder, CO: Westview, 31–64.

Pick, Daniel (1993), *War Machine: The Rationalisation of Slaughter in the Modern Age*, New Haven and London: Yale University Press.

Pierre, A. J. (1982), *The Global Politics of Arms Sales*, Princeton, NJ: Princeton University Press.

Pillar, P. R. (2001), *Terrorism and US Foreign Policy*, Washington, DC: Brookings Institution.

Piot, P. (2001), 'AIDS and Human Security', speech delivered at the United Nations University, Tokyo, 2 October, http://www.data.unaids.org/media/speeches01/piot_tokyo_02oct01_en.doc.

Pirages, D. and DeGeest, T. (2004), *Ecological Security: An Evolutionary Perspective on Globalization*, Lanham: Rowman and Littlefield.

Pletsch, C. (1981), 'The Three Worlds, or the Division of Social Scientific Labor, circa 1950–1975', *Comparative Studies in Society and History*, 23/4: 565–90.

Poetry Foundation (2013), *LANDAYS: Introduction*. Cited from, http://www.poetryfoundation.org/media/landays.html.

Poges, T. (2010), *Politics as Usual*, Cambridge and Malden: Polity Press.

Poku, N. K. (2006), *AIDS in Africa: How the Poor are Dying*, London: Polity Press.

Poku, N. K. and Mdee, A. (2011), *Politics in Africa: A* New Introduction, London: Zed Books.

Poku, N. K. and Whitman, J. (eds) (2011), *Third World Quarterly Special Issue: The Millennium Development Goals: Challenges, Prospects and Opportunities*, January.

Pouliot, V. (2010), *International Security in Practice: The Politics of NATO–Russia Diplomacy*, Cambridge: Cambridge University Press.

Poundstone, W. (1992), *Prisoner's Dilemma*, New York: Doubleday.

Powell R. (1999), *In the Shadow of Power: States and Strategies in International Politics*, Princeton, NJ: Princeton University Press.

Prashad, V. (2012), *The Poorer Nations: A Possible History of the Global South*, London: Verso.

President's Commission on Critical Infrastructure Protection (1997), *Critical Foundations: Protecting America's Infrastructures*, Washington, DC: US Government Printing Office.

Price-Smith, A. (2001), *The Health of Nations; Infectious Disease, Environmental Change, and their Effects on National Security and Development*, Cambridge, MA: MIT Press.

Prins, G. (ed.) (1993), *Threats without Enemies: Facing Environmental Insecurity*, London: Earthscan.

Priscoli, J. and Wolf, A., (2009), *Managing and Trsnforming Water Conflicts*, Cambridge: Cambridge University Press.

Publius (1787–8), Alexander Hamilton, James Madison, and John Jay, *The Federalist*, www.constitution.org/fed/federa00.htm.

Qin, Y. (2010), 'International Society as a Process: Institutions, Identities, and China's Peaceful Rise', *Chinese Journal of International Politics*, 3 (2): 129–153.

Radu, M. (2002), 'Terrorism after the Cold War', *Orbis*, 46/2: 363–79.

Ramakrishna, K. and Tan, A. (2003), 'The New Terrorism: Diagnosis and Prescriptions', in Andrew Tan (ed.), *The New Terrorism: Anatomy, Trends and Counter-Strategies*, Singapore: Eastern Universities Press, 3–29.

Ramsbotham, O., Woodhouse, T., and Miall, H. (2011), *Contemporary Conflict Resolution*, 3rd edn, Cambridge and Malden, MA: Polity.

Ramsey, P. (2002), *The Just War: Force and Political Responsibility*, Lanham, MD: Rowman & Littlefield.

Rasmussen, M. V. (2010), 'Risk and Security', *International Studies Compendium*, Oxford: Blackwell Publishing, www.isacompendium.com.

Rengger, Nicholas (1999), *International Relations, Political Theory and the Problem of Order: Beyond International Relations Theory?* London: Routledge.

Renner, M. (1991), 'Assessing the Military's War on the Environment', in L. Brown (ed.), *State of the World1991*, New York: W. W. Norton, 132–52.

Reno, W. (1998), *Warlord Politics and African States*, Boulder, CO: Lynne Rienner.

Reus-Smit, C. (1992), 'Realist and Resistance Utopias: Community, Security and Political Action in the New Europe', *Millennium: Journal of International Studies*, 21: 1–28.

Reus-Smit, C. (1996), 'The Constructivist Turn: Critical Theory after the Cold War', Research School of Pacific and Asian Studies, Australian National University, Department of International Relations, Canberra, Working Paper No. 4.

Reuters (2010), 'Anti-austerity protesters clash with police in Athens', *The Guardian*, updated 15 December 2010, http://wobblygoblin.wordpress.com/tag/riots/page/4/

Reichel, P. and Albanese, J. (eds) (2013), *Handbook of Transnational Crime and Justice*, Thousand Oaks, CA: Sage Publications.

Rice, S. Graff, C., and Pascual, C. (eds) (2010), *Confronting Poverty: Weak States and U.S. National Security*, Washington, DC: Brookings Institution Press.

Rich, A. (2004), *Think Tanks, Public Policy, and the Politics of Expertise*, Cambridge: Cambridge University Press.

Rich, P. B. (ed.) (1999), *Warlords in International Relations*, London: Macmillan.

Richardson, E. (2013), 'Hidden in Plain Sight: Racism in International Relations Theory', *Cambridge Review of International Studies*, 26/1: 71–92.

Richardson, L. F. (1960), *Statistics of Deadly Quarrels*, Pittsburgh: Boxwood Press.

Rind, David (1995), 'Drying Out the Tropics', *New Scientist*, 6 May.

Risse-Kappen, T. (1994), 'Ideas do Not Float Freely: Transnational Coalitions, Domestic Structures, and the End of the Cold War', *International Organization*, 48/2: 185–214.

Roberts, A. (1993), 'Humanitarian War: Military Intervention and Human Rights', *International Affairs*, 69/3: 429–9.

Rodríguez-Garavito, C., Barrett, P., and Chavez, D. (2008), *The New Latin American Left: Utopia Reborn*, London: Pluto.

Roe, P. (2001), 'Misperception and Minority Rights: Romania's Security Dilemma', European Centre for Minority Issue (ed.), *European Yearbook of Minority Issues, Volume 1, 2001/2*, Bozen/Bolzano: Brill, The European Academy, 1: 349–71.

Roe, P. (2002), 'Misperception and Ethnic Conflict: Transylvania's Societal Security Dilemma', *Review of International Studies*, 28/1: 57–74.

Roe, P. (2004), 'Securitization and Minority Rights: Conditions of Desecuritization', *Security Dialogue*, 35/3: 279–94.

Roe, P. (2005), *Ethnic Violence and the Societal Security Dilemma*, London: Routledge.

Roe, P. (2008), 'Securitizing Saddam: Actor, Audience(s) and Emergency Measures in the UK's Decision to Invade Iraq', *Security Dialogue*, 39/6: 615–35.

Rogers, P. (2008), *Global Security and the War on Terror: Elite Power and the Illusion of Control*, London and New York: Routledge.

Rogers, P. (2010), *Losing Control: Global Security in the 21st Century*, 3rd edn, London: Pluto Press.

Rogers, P. and Ramsbotham, O. (1999), 'Then and Now: Peace Research—Past and Future', *Political Studies*, XLVII: 740–54.

Rosato, S. (2003), 'The Flawed Logic of Democratic Peace Theory', *American Political Science Review*, 94/4: 585–602.

Rose, G. (1998), 'Neoclassical Realism and Theories of Foreign Policy', *World Politics*, 51/1: 144–72.

Rosen, S. P. (1995), 'Military Effectiveness: Why Society Matters', *International Security*, 19/4: 5–31.

Rosenau, W. (2001), 'Aum Shinrikyo's Biological Weapons Program: Why Did it Fail?' *Studies in Conflict and Terrorism*, 24/4: 289–301.

Rosenberg, D. A. (1983), 'The Origins of Overkill', *International Security*, 7/4: 3–71.

Ross, A. (1991), 'Hacking Away at the Counterculture', in C. Penley and A. Ross (eds), *Technoculture*, Minneapolis: University of Minnesotta Press, 107–34.

Rudolph, S. (2005), 'The Imperialism of Categories: Situating Knowledge in a Globalizing World', *Perspectives on Politics*, 3/1: 5–14.

Ruggie, J. G. (1998), 'What Makes the World Hang Together? Neo-Utilitarianism and the Social Constructivist Challenge', *International Organization*, 52/4: 855–85.

Ruggie, J. G. (2006), 'Interim Report of the Special Representative of the Secretary-General on the Issue of Human Rights and Transnational Corporations and Other Business Enterprises', UN Doc. E/CN.4/2006/97, February.

Rummel, R. J. (1994), *Death by Government*, London: Transaction Press.

Rupert, M. and Smith, H. (eds) (2002), *Historical Materialism and Globalization*, London: Routledge.

Rupert, M. and Solomon, S. (2006), *Globalization and International Political Economy*, Lanham, MD: Rowman & Littlefield.

Rushton, S. and Youde, J. (eds) (2014), *Routledge Handbook of Global Health Security*, Oxford: Routledge.

Russett, B. (1971), 'An Empirical Typology of International Military Alliances', *Midwest Journal of Political Science*, 15: 262–89.

Rutherford, K. (2010), *Disarming States: The International Movement to Ban Landmines*, Westport, CT: Praeger.

Rutledge, I. (2006), *Addicted to Oil: America's Relentless Drive for Energy Security*, London: I. B. Tauris.

Ryan, J. and Glarum, J. (2008), *Biosecurity and Bioterrorism: Containing and Preventing Biological Threats*, New York: Elsevier.

Saad Filho, Alfredo and Johnston, D. (2005), 'Introduction', in Alfredo Saad Filho and D. Johnston (eds), *Neoliberalism: A Critical Reader*, London: Pluto Press, 1–6.

Sabaratnam, M. (2013), 'IR in Dialogue . . . But Can We Change the Subjects? A Typology of Decolonising Strategies for the Study of World Politics', *Millennium: Journal of International Studies* 39/3: 781–03.

Sabaratnam, M. (2016), *Decolonising Intervention: International Statebuilding in Mozambique*, London: Rowman and Littlefield International.

Saferworld (2005), *Turning the Page: Small Arms and Light Weapons in Albania*, London: Saferworld.

Saferworld (2007), *The Good, the Bad and the Ugly: A Decade of Labour's Arms Exports*, London: Saferworld.

Sagan, S. and Waltz, K. (2003), *The Spread of Nuclear Weapons: A Debate Renewed*, 2nd edn, New York: Norton.

Sageman, M. (2008), *Leaderless Jihad: Terrorist Networks in the Twenty-First Century*, Philadelphia: University of Pennsylvania Press.

Said, E. (1978), *Orientalism*, New York: Pantheon Books.

Said, E. (1993), *Culture and Imperialism*, New York: Alfred A. Knopf.

Said, E. (1995), 'East isn't East', *Times Literary Supplement*, 4792: 3–5.

Said, E. (2004), '*Orientalism* and After', in G. Viswanathan (ed.), *Power, Politics and Culture: Interviews with Edward W. Said*, London: Bloomsbury, 262–79.

Sakai, H. (2003), 'The End of Comprehensive Security? The Evolution of Japanese Security Policy in the Post-September 11-Terrorism World', *Indian Journal of Asian Affairs*, 16: 71–98.

Salehi, R. and Ali, S. H. (2006), 'The Social and Political Context of Disease Outbreaks: The Case of SARS in Toronto', *Canadian Public Policy*, 32/4: 373–85.

Salter, M. (2007), 'On Exactitude in Disciplinary Science: A Response to the Network Manifesto', *Security Dialogue*, 38/1: 113–22.

Salter, M. and de Larrinaga, M. (2014), 'Cold CASE: A Manifesto for Canadian Critical Security Studies', *Critical Studies on Security* 2/1: 1–19.

Saponja-Hadzic, M. (2003), 'Serbia after Djindjic: The Maelstrom of its Own Crimes', *World Press Review*, 50/6, www.worldpress.org/Europe/1082.cfm#down.

Sarkar, S. (2002), 'The Decline of the Subaltern in *Subaltern Studies*', in D. Ludden (ed.), *Reading Subaltern Studies: Critical History, Contested Meaning and the Globalization of South Asia*, London: Anthem Press, 400–29.

Sasse, G. (2005), 'Securitization or Securing Rights? Exploring the Conceptual Foundations of Policies towards Minorities and Migrants in Europe', *Journal of Common Market Studies*, 43/4: 673–93.

Saurin, J. (2006), 'International Relations as the Imperial Illusion; or, the Need to Decolonize IR', in B.G. Jones (ed.), *Decolonizing International Relations*, Lanham: Rowman & Littlefield, 23–42.

Scheffer, D. J. (1992), 'Towards a Modern Doctrine of Humanitarian Intervention', *University of Toledo Law Review*, 23/2: 253–93.

Schell, J. (1982), *The Fate of the Earth*, New York: Knopf.

Schelling, T. C. (1960a), 'The Role of Theory in the Study of Conflict', RAND Research Memorandum 2515 (abridged version published in *Midwest Journal of Political Science*, May 1960 and as Schelling 1960b: ch. 1).

Schelling, T. C. (1960b), *The Strategy of Conflict*, Cambridge, MA: Harvard University Press.

Schelling, T. C. (1966), *Arms and Influence*, New Haven: Yale University Press.

Schelling, T. C. (1985–6), 'What went Wrong with Arms Control?', *Foreign Affairs*, 64/2: 219–33.

Schelling, T. C. and Halperin, M. H. (1961), *Strategy and Arms Control*, New York: Twentieth Century Fund.

Schimmelfennig, F. (1998), 'NATO Enlargement: A Constructivist Explanation', *Security Studies*, 8/2–3: 198–234.

Scholte, J. A. (2005), *Globalization: A Critical Introduction*, 2nd edn, Basingstoke: Palgrave Macmillan.

Schlosser, E. (2014), *Command and Control: Nuclear Weapons, the Damascus Accident and the Illusion of Safety*, New York: The Penguin Press.

Schnurr, M. and Swatuk, L. (eds) (2012), *Natural Resources and Social Conflict*, Basingstoke: Palgrave Macmillan.

Scholte, Jan Aart (2005), *Globalization: A Critical Introduction*, 2nd edn, Basingstoke: Palgrave Macmillan.

Schweller, R. (1998), *Deadly Imbalances: Tripolarity and Hitler's Strategy of World Conquest*, New York: Columbia University Press.

Seager, J. (1993), *Earth Follies*, New York: Routledge.

Seckinelgin, H., Bigirumwami, J., and Morris, J. (2010), 'Securitization of HIV/AIDS in Context: Gendered Vulnerability in Burundi', *Security Dialogue*, 41/5: 515–35.

Secretariat of the Convention on Biological Diversity (2010), *Global Biodiversity Outlook 3*, Secretariat of the Convention on Biological Diversity, Montreal.

Sederberg, P. C. (2003), 'Global Terrorism: Problems of Challenge and Response', in Charles W. Kegley Jr (ed.), *The New Global Terrorism: Characteristics, Causes, Controls*, Upper Saddle River, NJ: Prentice Hall, 267–84.

Sen, A. (1999), *Development as Freedom*, New York: Anchor Books.

Senghaas, D. (1969), *Abschreckung und Frieden: Studien zur Kritik organisierter Friedlosigkeit*, Frankfurt/M.: Suhrkamp.

Seth, S. (2011), 'Postcolonial Theory and the Critique of International Relations', *Millennium*, 40/1: 167–83.

Seth, S.(ed.) (2011), *Postcolonial Theory and International Relations: A Critical Introduction*, London: Routledge.

Shah, M. K., Osborne, N., Mbilizi, T., and Vilili, G. (2002), *Impact of HIV/AIDS on Agriculture Productivity and Rural Livelihoods in the Central Region of Malawi*, Lilongwe, Malawi: Care International.

Shapiro, J. (2013), *The Terrorist's Dilemma: Managing Violent Covert Organizations*, Princeton, NJ: Princeton University Press.

Shaw, K. (2002), 'Indigeneity and the International', *Millennium: Journal of International Studies*, 31/1: 55–81.

Sheehan, Michael (2005), *International Security: An Analytical Survey*, Boulder, CO: Lynne Rienner.

Sheehan, Michael (2005), *The International Politics of Space*, London and New York: Routledge.

Shelley, L. (2008), 'The Divergent Organized Crime of Eastern Europe and the Soviet Successor States', *HEUNI Papers*, 28: 51–70.

Sherman, Nancy (2010), *The Untold War: Inside the Hearts, Minds and Souls of our Soldiers*, New York: W. W. Norton & Company.

Sherry, M. S. (1995), *In the Shadow of War: The United States since the 1930s*, New Haven: Yale University Press.

Shiffman, G. M. and Jochum, J. J. (2011), *Economic Instruments of Security Policy: Influencing the Choices of Leaders*, 2nd edn, London: Palgrave Macmillan.

Shinawatra, T. (2003), 'Keynote Address', Willard Hotel, Washington, 10 June, www.us-asean.org/Thailand/thaksinvisit03/speech.asp.

Shisana, O., Hall, E., Maluleke, K. R., Stoker, D. J., Shwabe, C., Colvin, M., Chauveau, J., Botha, C., Gumede, T., Fomundam, H., Shaikh, N., Rehle, T., Udjo, E., and Grisselquist, D. (2003), *The Impact of HIV/AIDS on the Health Sector: National Survey of Health Personnel, Ambulatory and Hospitalized Patients and Health Facilities*, Pretoria: Human Sciences Research Council and the Medical Research Council.

Singer, P. (2003), *Corporate Warriors: The Rise of the Privatized Military Industry*, Ithaca, NY: Cornell University Press.

Singh, J. (1998), 'Against Nuclear Apartheid', *Foreign Affairs*, 77/5: 411–52.

SIPRI (2012), *Stockholm International Peace Research Institute Database*, http://www.sipri.org/databases/armstransfers.

Sjostedt, R. (2008), 'Exploring the Construction of Threats: The Securitization of HIV/AIDS in Russia', *Security Dialogue*, 39/1: 7–29.

Skjelsbaek, I. (2001), 'Sexual Violence and War: Mapping out a Complex Relationship', *European Journal of International Relations*, 7/2: 211–37.

Slim, H. (2008), *Killing Civilians: Method, Madness and Morality in War*, New York: Columbia University Press.

Sloan, E. (2002), *The Revolution in Military Affairs*, Montreal: McGill-Queens Press.

Small Arms Survey (2001), 'Crime, Conflict, Corruption: Global Illicit Small Arms Transfers', Graduate Insitute of International Studies, Geneva (ed.), *Small Arms Survey 2001: Profiling the Problem*, Oxford: Oxford University Press, 165–95.

Small Arms Survey (2007), 'Completing the Count: Civilian Firearms', Graduate Insitute of International Studies, Geneva (ed.), *Small Arms Survey 2007: Guns and the City*, Cambridge: Cambridge University Press, 39–71.

Small Arms Survey (2011), 'Man-Portable Air Defense Systems, Research Notes: Weapons and Markets', Graduate Insitute of International Studies, Geneva (ed.), *Small Arms Survey 2011*. Cambridge: Cambridge University Press, 1–34.

Smith, A. (1776/1904), *An Inquiry into the Nature and Causes of the Wealth of Nations*, ed. Edwin Cannan, Library of Economics and Liberty, http://www.econlib.org/library/Smith/smWN.html.

Smith, A. (1790), *The Theory of Moral Sentiments*, Library of Economics and Liberty, http://www.econlib.org/library/Smith/smMS.html.

Smith, A. D. (1993), 'The Ethnic Sources of Nationalism', *Survival*, 35/1: 48–62.

Smith, Helena (2011), 'Rise of the Greek far right raises fears of further turmoil', *The Guardian*, updated 16 December 2011, http://www.theguardian.com/world/2011/dec/16/rise-greek-far-right-turmoil.

Smith, M. (1986), *Realist Thought from Weber to Kissinger*, Baton Rouge, LA: Louisiana State University Press.

Smith, M. E. (2010), *International Security: Politics, Policy, Prospects*, Basingstoke: Palgrave Macmillan.

Smith, S. (1996), 'Positivism and Beyond', in K. Booth, S. Smith, and M. Zalewski (eds), *International Theory: Positivism and Beyond*, Cambridge: Cambridge University Press, 11–44.

Smith, S. (2005), 'The Contested Concept of Security', in K. Booth (ed.), *Critical Security Studies and World Politics*, Boulder, CO: Lynne Rienner, 27–62.

Smith, T. (1994), *America's Mission: The United States and the Worldwide Struggle for Democracy in the Twentieth Century*, Princeton, NJ: Princeton University Press.

Smith, V. L. (2003), 'Constructivist and Ecological Rationality in Economics', *American Economic Review*, 93/3: 465–508.

Smoke, R. (1976), 'National Security Affairs', in F. I. Greenstein and N. W. Polsby (eds), *Handbook of Political Science*, 8, Reading, MA: Addison-Wesley, 247–361.

Snow, D. M. (1991), *National Security*, 2nd edn, New York: St Martins Press.

Snyder, G. H. (1997), *Alliance Politics*, Ithaca, NY: Cornell University Press.

Snyder, J. (1977), *The Soviet Strategic Culture: Implications for Limited Nuclear Operations*, Santa Monica: Rand Corporation, http://www.rand.org/pubs/reports/R2154.

Snyder, J. (1991), *Myths of Empire: Domestic Politics and International Ambition*, Ithaca, NY: Cornell University Press.

Snyder, J. (1998), *The Myths of Empire: Domestic Politics and International Ambition*, Ithaca, NY: Cornell University Press.

Soederberg, S. (2005), 'Recasting Neoliberal Dominance in the Global South: A Critique of the Monterrey Consensus', *Alternatives*, 30: 325–64.

Soeya, Y. (2005), 'Japanese Security Policy in Transition: The Rise of International and Human Security', *Asia-Pacific Review*, 12/1: 103–16.

Solingen, E. (1998), *Regional Orders at Century's Dawn: Global and Domestic Influences on Grand Strategy*, Princeton, NJ: Princeton University Press.

Solingen, E. (2007), *Nuclear Logics: Contrasting Paths in East Asia and the Middle East*, Princeton, NJ: Princeton University Press.

Sommaruga, C. (2004), 'The Global Challenge of Human Security', *Foresight: The Journal of Futures Studies, Strategic Thinking and Policy*, 6/4: 208–11.

Sommer, P. and Brown, I. (2011), 'Reducing Systemic Cyber Security Risk', Report of the International Futures Project, IFP/WKP/FGS (2011) 3, Paris: OECD.

Sommer, P. and Sommer, I. (2011), Reducing Systemic Cybersecurity Risk, OECD Research Report, http://www.oecd.org/dataoecd/3/42/46894657.pdf

Sorokin, P. (1937), *Social and Cultural Dynamics*, New York: American Books.

Soroos, M. (1994), 'Global Change, Environmental Security, and the Prisoner's Dilemma', *Journal of Peace Research*, 39/3: 317–2.

Soroos, M. (1997), *The Endangered Atmosphere: Preserving a Global Commons*, Columbia: University of South Carolina Press.

Spafford, E. H. (1989), 'The Internet Worm: Crisis and Aftermath', *Communications of the ACM*, 32/6: 678–87.

Sprout, H. and Sprout, M. (1971), *Toward a Politics of Planet Earth*, New York: Von Nostrand Reinhold.

Stachowitsch, S. (2012), 'Military Gender Integration and Foreign Policy in the United States: A Feminist International Relations Perspective', *Security Dialogue*, 43/4: 305–21.

Stachowitsch, S. (2013), 'Military Privatization and the Remasculinization of the State: Making the Link between the Outsourcing of Military Security and Gendered State Transformations', *International Relations*, 27/1: 74–94.

Stanley, J. and Pearton, M. (1972), *The International Trade in Arms*, New York: Praeger.

START (2014), Global Terrorism Database, National Consortium for the Study of Terrorism and Responses to Terrorism, University of Maryland, http://www.start.umd.edu/gtd

Stavrianakis, A. (2010), *Taking Aim at the Arms Trade: NGOs, Global Civil Society and the World Military Order*, London: Zed Books.

Stavrianakis, A., Selby, J., and Oikonomou, I. (eds) (2012), *Militarism and International Relations: Political Economy, Security and Theory*, London: Routledge.

Stavrianos, L. S. (1981), *Global Rift: The Third World Comes of Age*, New York: William Morrowand Company.

Steans, J. (1998), *Gender and International Relations. An Introduction*, Cambridge: Polity Press.

Stern, J. (2000), *The Ultimate Terrorists*, Cambridge, MA: Harvard University Press.

Stern, S. (1967), 'Who Thinks in a Think Tank', *New York Times Magazine*, 16 Apr.

Stiglitz, J. (2003), 'Foreword', in Svetlana Tsalik, *Caspian Oil Windfalls: Who Will Benefit?*, New York: Caspian Revenue Watch, Open Society Institute.

Stiglmayer, Alexandra (ed.) (1994), *The War against Women in Bosnia-Herzegovina*, London: University of Nebraska.

Stoett, P. (1999), *Human and Global Security*, Toronto: University of Toronto Press.

Stohl, R. and Grillot, S. (2009), *The International Arms Trade*, London: Polity Press.

Stohl, R., Schroeder, M., and Smith D. (2006), *The Small Arms Trade*, Oxford: Oneworld.

Stoker, D. J. and Grant, J. A. (eds) (2003), *Girding for Battle: The Arms Trade in Global Perspective, 1815–1940*, London: Praeger.

Stokes, D. (2005), *America's Other War: Terrorizing Colombia*, London: Zed Books.

Stokes, D. and Raphael, S. (2010), *Global Energy Security and American Hegemony*, Baltimore, MD: Johns Hopkins University Press.

Stoler, M. A. (2000), *Allies and Adversaries: The Joint Chiefs of Staff, the Grand Alliance, and US Strategy in World War II*, Chapel Hill, NC: University of North Carolina Press.

Strange, Susan (1986), *Casino Capitalism*, Oxford and New York: Basil Blackwell.

Stuart, D. T. (2008), *Creating the National Security State: A History of the Law that Transformed America*, Princeton, NJ: Princeton University Press.

Suhrke, A. (1999), 'Human Security and the Interests of States', *Security Dialogue*, 30/3: 265–76.

Sylvester, C. (1996), 'The Contributions of Feminist Theory to International Relations', in Steve Smith, Ken Booth, and Maryisa Zalewski (eds), *International Theory: Positivism and Beyond*, Cambridge: Cambridge University Press.

Sylvester, C. (2007), 'Anatomy of a Footnote', *Security Dialogue*, 38/4: 547–8.

Symantec (2010), *Internet Security Threat Report*, vol. 16 (Mountain View).

Tadjbakhsh, S. and Chenoy, A. M. (2009), *Human Security: Concepts and Implications*, London: Routledge.

Tann, A. H. T. (2006), *The Politics of Terrorism: A Survey*, London: Routledge.

Tannenwald, N. (1999), 'The Nuclear Taboo: The United States and the Normative Basis of Nuclear Non-Use', *International Organization*, 53/3: 433–68.

Tannenwald, N. and Wohlforth, W. C. (eds) (2005), Special issue on 'The Role of Ideas and the End of the Cold War', *Journal of Cold War Studies*, 7/2: 3–12.

Tesón, F. R. (1997), *Humanitarian Intervention: An Inquiry into Law and Morality*, 2nd edn, New York: Transnational Publishers.

Tesón, F. R. (1998), *A Philosophy of International Law*, Boulder, CO: Westview Press.

Tesón, F. R. (2003), 'The Liberal Case for Humanitarian Intervention', in J. L. Holzgrefe and Robert O. Keohane (eds), *Humanitarian Intervention: Ethical, Legal and Political Dilemmas*, Cambridge: Cambridge University Press.

Thakur, R. (2004), 'Iraq and the Responsibility to Protect', *Behind the Headlines*, 62/1: 1–16.

Theiler, T. (2003), 'Societal Security and Social Psychology', *Review of International Studies*, 29/2: 249–68.

Themnér, L. and Wallensteen, P. (2014), 'Armed Conflicts, 1946–2013', *Journal of Peace Research*, 51/4: 541–54.

Therborn, G. (2008), *From Marxism to Post-Marxism?*, London: Verso.

Thomas, C. (1987), *In Search of Security: The Third World in International Relations*, Boulder, CO: Lynne Rienner.

Thomas, C. (2000), *Global Governance, Development, and Human Security*, London: Pluto Press.

Thomas, N. and Tow, W. (2002), 'The Utility of Human Security: Sovereignty and Humanitarian Intervention', *Security Dialogue*, 33/2: 177–92.

Tickner, A. B. and Blaney, D. (eds) (2012), *Thinking the International Differently*, London: Routledge.

Tickner, A. B. and Wæver, O. (eds) (2009), *International Relations Scholarship Around the World*, Book series: Worlding Beyond the West, vol. 1, London: Routledge.

Tickner, J. A. (1992), *Gender in International Relations: Feminist Perspectives on Achieving Global Security*, New York: Columbia University Press.

Tilly, C. (1975), 'Reflections on the History of European State-Making', in C. Tilly, (ed.), *The Formation of National States in Western Europe*, Princeton, NJ: Princeton University Press, 3–83.

Tilly, C. (1990), *Big Structures, Large Processes, Huge Comparisons*, New York: Russell Sage Foundation.

Time (1975), 'The executive mercenaries', 24 February.

Tir, J. and Ackerman, J. (2009), 'Politics of Formalized River Cooperation', *Journal of Peace Research*, 46/5: 623–40.

Tow, W. T. (2001), 'Alternative Security Models: Implications for ASEAN', in A. Tan and K. Boutin (eds), *Non-Traditional Security Issues in Southeast Asia*, Singapore: Institute of Defence and Strategic Studies, 257–85.

True, Jacqui (2012), *The Political Economy of Violence Against Women*, Oxford: Oxford University Press.

Tuchman Mathews, J. (1989), 'Redefining Security', *Foreign Affairs*, 68/2: 162–77.

Tucker, J. B. (ed.) (2000), *Toxic Terror: Assessing Terrorist Use of Chemical and Biological Weapons*, Cambridge, MA: MIT Press.

Tucker, R. K. (1991), *The Dragon and the Cross: The Rise and Fall of the Ku Klux Klan in Middle America*, Hamden, CT: Archon Books.

Tunyasiri, Y. (2003), 'War on drugs—seize more assets, Thakshin urges Police', *Bangkok Post*, 23 March.

Turco, R. P., Toon, O. B., Ackerman, T. P., Pollack, J. B., and Sagan, C. (1990), 'Climate and Smoke: An Appraisal of Nuclear Winter', *Science*, 247: 166–76.

Turner, M. (2005), 'UN "must never again be found wanting on genocide"', *Financial Times*, 16 September.

Tyler, Patrick E. (1992), 'Pentagon drops goal of blocking new superpowers', *New York Times*, 23 May: A1.

Ullman, R. (1983), 'Redefining Security', *International Security*, 8/1: 129–53.

UNAIDS (2013), GLOBAL REPORT: UNAIDS Report on the Global AIDS Epidemic 2013, Geneva: Joint United Nations Programme on HIV/AIDS (UNAIDS), http://www.unaids.org/sites/default/files/en/media/unaids/contentassets/documents/epidemiology/2013/gr2013/UNAIDS_Global_Report_2013_en.pdf.

UNCTAD (2011a) 'Working Paper submitted to OECD closed meeting, 11–12 June 2011', New York:

United Nations Conference on Trade and Development.

UNCTAD (2011b) *Policy Actions to Mitigate the Impact of Highly Volatile Prices and Incomes on Commodity Dependent Countries, and to Facilitate Value Addition and Greater Participation in Commodity Value Chains by Commodity-Producing Countries*, Geneva: United Nations Conference on Trade and Development.

UNDP (1994), United Nations Development Program, *Human Development Report1994*, New York: Oxford University Press.

UNDP (2004), United Nations Development Programme, *UNDP Statement for UNCTAD XI* (São Paulo, Brazil, 14–18 June 2004), New York: United Nations Development Programme.

UNDP (2006), United Nations Development Programme, *UNDP Human Development Report 2006*, New York: Palgrave Macmillan.

UNDP (2013), United National Development Programme, *Citizen Security with a Human Face: Evidence and Proposals for Latin America*, Regional Human Development Report 2013–2014.

UNEP (2002), United Nations Environment Program, *Vital Water Graphics: An Overview of the State of the World's Fresh and Marine Waters*, Nairobi: UNEP.

UNEP (2005), United Nations Environment Program, *One Planet, Many People: Atlas of Our Changing Environment*, Nairobi: UNEP.

UNICEF (2012), 'Water, Sanitation and Hygiene', updated 9 February 2012, http://www.unicef.org/wash/.

United Nations (2000), 'United Nations Convention against Transnational Crime', www.unodc.org/unodc/en/crime_cicp_convention.html.

United Nations (2004), *A More Secure World: Our Shared Responsibility*, Report of the Secretary's General's High-Level Panel on Threats, Challenges and Change, New York: United Nations, www.un.org/secureworld.

United Nations (2005c), World Summit Outcome, A/RES/60/1, 24 Oct.

United Nations Department for Disarmament Affairs (2007), *United Nations Register of Conventional Arms: Information Booklet*, New York: United Nations.

United Nations General Assembly (1970), Declaration on Principles of International Law Concerning Friendly Relation, http://www.un-documents.net/925r2625.htm.

United Nations Office on Drugs and Crime (2010), *The Globalization of Crime: A Transnational Organized Crime Threat Assessment*, Vienna, Austria: UNODC, http://www.unodc.org/documents/data-and-analysis/tocta/TOCTA_Report_2010_law_rev.pdf.

United Nations Office on Drugs and Crime (2012), *Digest of Organized Crime Cases, Vienna*, Austria: UNODC, http://www.unodc.org/documents/organized-crime/English Digest_Final 301012_30102012.pdf.

United States Agency for International Development (2002), *Foreign Aid in the National Interest: Promoting Freedom, Security, and Opportunity*, http://www.au.af.mil/au/awc/awcgate/usaid/foreign_aid_in_the_national_interest-full.pdf.

United States Congress (1979), *The Effects of Nuclear War*, Washington: Congress of the US, Office of Technology Assessment, US Government Printing Office.

United States Department of Homeland Security (2005), *Securing the Nation Against Man-Portable Air Defense Systems*, Washington, DC: United States Department of Homeland Security, http://www.fas.org/asmp/campaigns/MANPADS/2007/securing_the_nation_against_MANPADS.pdf.

UNODC (2002), United Nations Office on Drugs and Crime, Global Programme against Transnational Organized Crime, Results of a Pilot Survey of Forty Selected Organized Criminal Groups in Sixteen Countries, September, www.unodc.org/pdf/crime/publications/Pilot_survey.pdf.

UNODC (2010), *The Globalization of Crime: A Transnational Organized Crime Threat Assessment*, United Nations Office on Drugs and Crime, Vienna: United Nations.

UNODC (2011), *Estimating Illicit Financial Flows Resulting from Drug Trafficking and Other Transnational Organized Crimes*, United Nations Office on Drugs and Crime, Vienna: United Nations.

UNODC (2012), *Digest of Organized Crime Cases*, United Nations Office on Drugs and Crime, Vienna, http://www.unodc.org/documents/organized-crime/EnglishDigest_Final301012_30102012.pdf.

Unruh, J. and Williams, R. (eds) (2013), *Land and Post-Conflict Peacebuilding*, Abingdon: Routledge.

Van Crevald, M. (2001), *Men, Women and War: Do Women Belong in the Front Line?* London: Cassell.

van Duyne, P. C. (2004), 'The Creation of a Threat Image: Media, Policy Making and Organized Crime', in P. C. van Duyne, M. Jager, K. von Lampe, and J. L. Newell (eds), *Threats and Phantoms of Organised Crime, Corruption and Terrorism: Critical European Perspectives*, papers presented at the Fourth Colloquium on Cross-Border Crime, The Netherlands: Wolf Legal Publishers.

Van Evera, S. (1999), *Causes of War: Power and the Roots of Conflict*, Ithaca, NY: Cornell University Press.

Van Niekerk, P. (2002), 'Making a Killing: The Business of War', *The Center for Public Integrity*, 28 October, http://www.icij.org/project/making-killing/business-war.

Vandemoortele, Jan (2003), 'Are the MDGs Feasible?', *Development Policy Journal*, 3: 1–21.

Verizon (2010), *2010 Data Breach Investigations Report: A Study Conducted by the Verizon RISK Team in Cooperation with the United States Secret Service*, New York: Verizon.

von Lampe, K. (2004), 'Measuring Organised Crime: A Critique of Current Approaches', in P. C. van Duyne, M. Jager, K. von Lampe, and J. L. Newell (eds), *Threats and Phantoms of Organised Crime, Corruption and Terrorism: Critical European Perspectives*, papers presented at the Fourth Colloquium on Cross-Border Crime, The Netherlands: Wolf Legal Publishers.

von Lampe, K. and Johansen, P. O. (2003), 'Criminal Networks and Trust', paper presented at the 3rd Annual Meeting of the European Society of Criminology. Helsinki, Finland, 29 August.

von Mises, L. (1949), *Human Action: A Treatise on Economics*. New Haven, CN: Yale University Press.

Vuori, J. A. (2008), 'Illocutionary Logic and Strands of Securitization: Applying the Theory of Securitization to the Study of non-democratic Political Orders', *European Journal of International Relations*, 14/1: 65–99.

Wæver, O. (1993), 'Societal Security: The Concept', in O. Wæver, B. Buzan, M. Kelstrup, and P. Lemaitre (eds), *Identity, Migration and the New Security Agenda in Europe*, London: Pinter, 17–40.

Wæver, O. (1994), 'Insecurity and Identity Unlimited', Working Paper No. XI, Copenhagen: Copenhagen Peace Research Institute.

Wæver, O. (1995), 'Securitization and Desecuritization', in R. Lipschutz (ed.), *On Security*, New York: Columbia University Press, 46–86.

Wæver, O. (1999), 'Securitizing Sectors: Reply to Eriksson', *Cooperation and Conflict*, 34/3: 334–40.

Wæver, O. (2008), 'Peace and Security: Two Evolving Concepts and their Changing Relationship', in H. G. Brauch, U. O. Spring, C. Mesjasz, J. Grin, P. Dunay, N. C. Behera, B. Chourou, P. Kameri-Mbote, and P. H. Liotta (eds), *Globalisation and Environmental Challenges: Reconceptualising Security in the 21st Century*, Heidelberg: Springer Verlag, 99–112.

Wæver, O. (2010), '*Towards a Political Sociology of* Security Studies', *Security Dialogue*, 41/6: 649–58.

Wæver, O. (2012a). 'Aberystwyth, Paris, Copenhagen: New "Schools" in Security Theory and Origins between Core and Periphery', in Arlene B. Tickner and David Blaney (eds), *Thinking the International Differently*, Book Series: Worlding Beyond the West. London: Routledge, 48–71.

Wæver, O. (2012b), 'Security: A Conceptual History for International Relations', paper presented at conference, 'The History of the Concept of Security', arranged by Centre for Advanced Security Theory (CAST) at the University of Copenhagen and the Royal Danish Academy of Sciences and Letters, 26–28 November.

Wæver, O. (2013), 'Still a Discipline after all these Debates?', in T. Dunne, M. Kurki, and S. Smith (eds), *International Relations Theories: Discipline and Diversity*, 3rd edn, Oxford: Oxford University Press, 306–27.

Wæver, O. (2015), 'The History and Social Structure of Security Studies as a Practico-Academic Field', in Trine Villumsen Berling and Christian Bueger (eds), *Security Expertise: Practices, Power, and Responsibility*, London: Routledge, 76–106.

Wæver, O., Buzan, B., Kelstrup, M., and Lemaitre, P. (eds) (1993), *Identity, Migration and the New Security Agenda in Europe*, London: Pinter.

Wagnsson, C., Hellman, M., and Holmberg, A. (2010), 'The Centrality of Non-Traditional Groups for Security in the Globalized Era: The Case of Children', *International Political Sociology*, 4/1: 1–14.

Waisová, Š. (2003), 'Human Security—the Contemporary Paradigm?', *Perspectives*, 20: 58–72.

Walker, R. B. J. (1993), *Inside/Outside*, Cambridge: Cambridge University Press.

Walker, R. B. J. (1997), 'The Subject of Security', in K. Krause and M. C. Williams (eds), *Critical Security*

Studies: Concepts and Cases, Minneapolis: University of Minnesota Press, 61–81.

Wall, D. (2005), *Babylon and Beyond: The Economics of Anti-Capitalist, Anti-Globalist and Radical Green Movements*, London: Pluto Press.

Wallace, L. (ed.) (1999), *Africa: Adjusting to the Challenge of Globalisation*, Washington, DC: International Monetary Fund Publication Service.

Wallerstein, I. (2004), *World-Systems Analysis: An Introduction*, Durham, NC: Duke University Press.

Walt, S. (1987), *The Origin of Alliances*, Ithaca, NY: Cornell University Press.

Walt, S. (1991), 'The Renaissance of Security Studies', *International Studies Quarterly*, 35/ 2.

Walt, S. (1999), 'Rigor or Rigor Mortis? Rational Choice and Security Studies', *International Security*, 23/4: 5–48.

Walton, C. D. (2013), 'The Second Nuclear Age: Nuclear Weapons in the Twenty-First Century', in John Baylis, James Wirtz, and Colin S Gray (eds), *Strategy in the Contemporary World*, Oxford: Oxford University Press, 195–212.

Waltz, K. (1989), 'The Origins of War in Neorealist Theory', in R. I. Rotberg and T. K. Robb (eds), *The Origin and Prevention of Major Wars*, Cambridge: Cambridge University Press.

Waltz, K. (1996), 'International Politics is Not Foreign Policy', *Security Studies*, 6/1: 54–7.

Waltz, K. N. (1959), *Man, the State, and War*, New York: Columbia University Press.

Waltz, K. N. (1979), *Theory of International Politics*, New York: McGraw-Hill.

Wang, J. and Buzan, B. (2014) 'The English and Chinese schools of international relations: comparisons and lessons', *The Chinese Journal of International Politics*, 7 (1), 1–46.

Warren, B. (1980), *Imperialism: Pioneer of Capitalism*, London: Verso.

Watts, M. (2001), 'Petro-Violence: Community, Extraction, and Political Ecology of a Mythic Commodity', in N. Peluso and M. Watts (eds), *Violent Environments*, Ithaca, NY: Cornell University Press, 189–212.

Way, Debra and Polglaze, Karen (2001), 'Fed: strip search powers for guards severe but justified', *AAP Newsfeed*, 6 April.

Wayne, M. I. (2008), *China's War on Terrorism: Counter-Insurgency, Politics and Internal Security*, London: Routledge.

WCED (World Commission on Environment and Development) (1987), *Our Common Future*, Oxford: Oxford University Press.

Weber, C. (1999), 'IR: The Resurrection or New Frontiers of Incorporation', *European Journal of International Relations*, 5/4: 435–50.

Weiss, T. G. (2004), 'The Sunset of Humanitarian Intervention? The Responsibility to Protect in a Unipolar Era', *Security Dialogue*, 35/2: 135–53.

Weiss, T. G. (2007), *Humanitarian Intervention: ideas into Action*, Cambridge: Polity Press.

Weldes, J. (1999a), 'The Cultural Production of Crises: US Identity and Missiles in Cuba', in J. Weldes, M. Laffey, H. Gusterson, and R. Duvall (eds), *Cultures of Insecurity: States, Communities, and the Production of Danger*, Minneapolis: University of Minnesota Press, 35–62.

Weldes, J. (1999b), *Constructing National Interests: The United States and the Cuban Missile Crisis*, Minneapolis: University of Minnesota Press.

Weldes, J., Laffey, M., Gusterson, H., and Duvall, R. (eds) (1999), *Cultures of Insecurity: States, Communities and the Production of Danger*, Minneapolis: University of Minneapolis Press.

Wells, J., Meyers J., and Mulvihill, M. (2001), 'US ties to Saudi elite may be hurting War on Terrorism', *Boston Herald*, 10 December.

Welsh, J. (2004), 'Conclusion: Humanitarian Intervention after 11 September', in J. Welsh (ed.), *Humanitarian Intervention and International Relations*, Oxford: Oxford University Press, 176–88.

Wendt, A. (1992), 'Anarchy is what States Make of It: The Social Construction of Power Politics', *International Organization*, 46/2: 391–425.

Wendt, A. (1994), 'Collective Identity Formation and the International State', *American Political Science Review*, 88: 384–96.

Wendt, A. (1996), 'Identity and Structural Change in International Politics', in Y. Lapid and F. Kratochwil (eds), *The Return of Culture and Identity in IR Theory*, Boulder, CO: Lynne Rienner, 47–64.

Wendt, A. (1999), *Social Theory of International Politics*, Cambridge: Cambridge University Press.

Westing, A. (1986), 'An Expanded Concept of International Security', in A. Westing (ed.), *Global Resources and International Conflict: Environmental Factors in Strategic Policy and Action*, Oxford: Oxford University Press, 183–200.

WFP World Food Programme (2012a), 'Hunger', http://www.wfp.org/hunger.

WFP World Food Programme (2012b), 'Who are the Hungry?', http://www.wfp.org/hunger/who-are.

Wheeler, N. J. (2000), *Saving Strangers: Humanitarian Intervention in International Society*, Oxford: Oxford University Press.

White House (1998), *The National Security Strategy of the United States of America*, Washington, DC: White House, www.au.af.mil/au/awc/awcgate/nss/nssr-1098.pdf.

White House (2002), *The National Security Strategy of the United States of America*, Washington, DC: White House, http://georgewbush-whitehouse.archives.gov/nsc/nss/2002/nss.pdf.

White House (2006), *The National Security Strategy of the United States of America*, Washington, DC: White House, www.strategicstudiesinstitute.army.mil/pdffiles/nss.pdf.

White House (2011), *Strategy to Combat Transnational Organized Crime*, Washington, DC: White House.

WHO (2012), 'Micronutrient Deficiencies', http://www.who.int/nutrition/topics/ida/en/index.html.

WHO (2013), *Global* and Regional Estimates of Violence against Women, http://apps.who.int/iris/bitstream/10665/85239/1/9789241564625_eng.pdf.

World Health Organization (2015), 'Ebola Situation Report 27 May 2015', http://apps.who.int/ebola/en/current-situation/ebola-situation-report-27-may-2015.

Wiberg, H. (1988), 'The Peace Research Movement', in Peter Wallensteen (ed.), *Peace Research: Achievements and Challenges*, Boulder, CO, and London: Westview Press, 30–53.

Wight, C., Hansen, L., and Dunne, T. (eds) (2013), Special Issue: The End of International Relations Theory?, *European Journal of International Relations*, September 19/3.

Wight, C., Hansen, L. and Dunne, T (eds) (2013), 'The End of International Relations Theory?', special issue of *European Journal of International Relations*, vol. 19(3), pp. 405–665.

Wilkin, P. (2002), 'Global Poverty and Orthodox Security', *Third World Quarterly*, 23/4: 633–45.

Wilkinson, C. (2007), 'The Copenhagen School on Tour in Kyrgystan: Is Securitization Theory Useable Outside Europe? ', *Security Dialogue*, 38/1: 5–25.

Wilkinson, P. (2006), *Terrorism versus Democracy: The Liberal State Response*, 2nd edn, London: Routledge.

Williams, M. C. (1998), 'Modernity, Identity and Security: A Comment on the "Copenhagen Controversy"', *Review of International Studies*, 24/3: 435–9.

Williams, M. C. (2003), 'Words, Images, Enemies: Securitization and International Politics', *International Studies Quarterly*, 47/4: 511–31.

Williams, M. C. and Krause, K. (1997), 'Preface: Toward Critical Security Studies', in K. Krause and M. C. Williams (eds), *Critical Security Studies: Concepts and Cases*, Minneapolis: University of Minnesota Press, vii–xxi.

Williams, M. C. and Neumann, I. B. (2000), 'From Alliance to Security Community: NATO, Russia, and the Power of Identity', *Millennium*, 29/2: 357–87.

Williams, P. (2001), 'Transnational Criminal Networks', in J. Arquilla and D. Ronfeldt (eds), *Networks and Netwars: The Future of Terror, Crime and Militancy*, Santa Monica, CA: RAND Corporation, 61–97; www.rand.org/publications/MR/MR1382/MR1382.ch3.pdf.

Williams, P. (2008), 'Terrorist Financing and Organized Crime: Nexus, Appropriation or Transformation', in Thomas J. Biersteker and Sue E. Eckert (eds), *Countering the Financing of Terrorism*, New York: Routledge, 126–49.

Williams, P. and Savona, E. U. (eds) (1998), *The United Nations and Transnational Organized Crime*, London: Frank Cass.

Williams, P. D. (2006), 'Military Responses to Mass Killing: The African Union Mission in Sudan', *International Peacekeeping*, 13/2: 168–83.

Williams, P. D. and Bellamy, A. J. (2005), 'The Responsibility to Protect and the Crisis in Darfur', *Security Dialogue*, 36/1: 27–47.

Wilmer, F. (1993), *The Indigenous Voice in World Politics: Since Time Immemorial*, Newbury Park: Sage.

Wintour, P. (2014), 'UKIP's Manifesto: Immigration, Europe—and that's it', *The Guardian*, 20 May.

Wintrobe, R. (1990), 'The Tinpot and the Totalitarian: An Economic Theory of Dictatorship', *American Political Science Review*, 84:3: 849–72.

Wirtz, J. J. (1994), *The Tet Offensive: Intelligence Failure in War*, 2nd edn, Ithaca, NY: Cornell University Press.

Wirtz, J. J. and Lavoy, P. (2012), *Over the Horizon Proliferation Threats*, Stanford, CA: Stanford University Press.

Wohlstetter, A. J. and Wohlstetter, R. (1963),'The State of Strategic Studies in Europe', report prepared for the Ford Foundation.

Wohlstetter, Albert J. and Wohlstetter, R. (1966), 'The State of Strategic Studies in Japan, India, Israel', report prepared for the Carnegie Endowment for International Peace.

Wohlstetter, A. J., Hoffman, F. S., Lutz, R. J., and Rowen, H. S. (1954), *Selection and Use of Strategic Air Bases*, R-266, Santa Monica, CA: RAND Corporation.

Wolf, E. (1997), *Europe and the People without History*, Berkeley: University of California Press.

Wolfers, A. (1962), *Discord and Collaboration: Essays on International Politics*, Baltimore and London: Johns Hopkins University Press.

Wood, E. M. (1995), *Democracy against Capitalism: Renewing Historical Materialism*, Cambridge: Cambridge University Press.

Wood, E. M. (2005), *Empire of Capital*, London: Verso.

Woodward, B. (2001), 'Bin Laden said to "own" the Taliban: Bush is told he gave regime $100 million', *Washington Post*, 11 October, A01.

Woodward, B. (2007), 'Greenspan: Ouster of Hussein crucial for oil security', *Washington Post*, 17 Sept.

World Bank (2005), *World Development Report 2006: Equity and Development*, Washington, DC: World Bank.

World Bank (2008), *World Development Indicators: Viewing the World at Purchasing Power Parity*, Washington: World Bank, http://siteresources.worldbank.org/DATASTATISTICS/Resources/WDI08_section1_intro.pdf.

World Bank (2009a), *Reshaping Economic Geography*, Washington, DC: World Bank.

World Bank (2009b), *World Development Report 2009: Reshaping Economic Geography*. Washington, DC: World Bank.

World Bank (2011), *World Development Report 2011: Conflict, Security and Development*, Washington, DC: World Bank.

World Bank, Instituto Italo-Africano, and Economic Development Institute (1989), *Strengthening Local Governments in Sub-Saharan Africa: Proceedings of Two Workshops held in Poretta Terme, Italy, March 5–17, 1989*, an EDI policy seminar report; Washington, DC: World Bank.

World Commission on Environment and Development (1987), *Our Common Future*, Oxford: Oxford University Press.

World Social Forum (2002), 'Note from the Organizing Committee on the Principles that Guide the WSF', http://memoriafsm.org/page/carta?locale-attribute=en.

WRI (World Resources Institute) (2011), *Reefs at Risk Revisited*, WRI, Washington, DC.

Wright, Q. (1942), *A Study of War*, Chicago: University of Chicago Press.

Wright, Q. (1965), *A Study of War*, 2nd edn, Chicago: University of Chicago Press.

Wyn Jones, R. (1996), 'Travel without Maps: Thinking about Security after the Cold War', in M. J. Davis, (ed.), *Security Issues in the Post-Cold War World*, Cheltenham: Edward Elgar, 196–218.

Wyn Jones, R. (1999), *Security, Strategy, and Critical Theory*, Boulder, CO: Lynne Rienner.

Yan, X. (2010), *Ancient Chinese Thought, Modern Chinese Power*, Princeton, NJ: Princeton University Press.

Yergin, D. (1977), *Shattered Peace: The Origins of the Cold War and the National Security State*, Boston: Houghton Mifflin Company.

Young, M. (1991), *The Vietnam Wars: 1945–1990*, New York: HarperCollins.

Zacher, M. W. and Matthew, R. A. (1995), 'Liberal International Theory: Common Threads, Divergent Strands', in Charles Kegley, Jr (ed.), *Controversies in International Relations Theory*, New York: St Martins Press, 107–50.

Zartman, I. W. (ed.) (1995), *Collapsed States: The Disintegration and Restoration of Legitimate Authority*, Boulder, CO: Lynne Reiner.

Zehfuss, M. (2002), *Constructivism in International Relations: The Politics of Reality*, Cambridge: Cambridge University Press.

Zehfuss, M. (2011), 'Targeting: Precision and the Production of Ethics', *European Journal of International Relations*, 17/3: 543–66.

Zeldin, T. (1998), *An Intimate History of Humanity*, London: Vintage.

Zinni, Anthony (1998), 'Avoid a Military Showdown with Iraq', *Middle East Quarterly*, September, www.meforum.org/408/anthony-zinni-avoid-a-military-showdown-with-iraq.

Zubay, G., Touma, S., Balfour, R., Hudspeth, J., Puskoor, R., Shah, P., Metha, A., Ward, J., Garrido, M., Chubak, B., Morser, K., Edstrom, W., and Kehoe, K. (2005), *Agents of Bioterrorism: Pathogens and their Weaponization*, New York: Columbia University Press.

Index

A

D

E

F

J

K

L

M

N

O

P

Q

R

S